GRAND PRIX!

by Mike Lang

Acknowledgements

I offer my sincere thanks to all of those people who have provided assistance during the compilation of this book.

I am particularly indebted to my wife, Janet, for typing the manuscript and for her patience; to Colin J. Edgecombe and Robert Zaple who so skilfully originated the circuit diagrams; to all of those photographers who supplied the contemporary photographs which add so much to this book.

Mike Lang

ISBN 0 85429 733 2
Library of Congress catalog card number 92-64084

A FOULIS Motoring Book

First published 1992

© **Mike S. Lang 1992**

Published by:
Haynes Publishing Group
Sparkford, Yeovil, Somerset BA22 7JJ

Distributed in USA by:
Haynes Publications Inc.
861 Lawrence Drive, Newbury Park, California 91320, USA

Printed in England by: J.H. Haynes & Co. Ltd.

Classic Motorbooks
T.M.

729 PROSPECT AVENUE
OSCEOLA, WI 54020, U.S.A. · 1-800-826-6600

ORDER NUMBER	719864-000
CUSTOMER NUMBER	442074
DATE	12/26/95

SOLD TO   JAMES A WALKER

17231 BLACK HAWK 0912
FRIENDSWOOD   TX   77546-0000

LOCATION	ITEM NUMBER	QUANTITY	DESCRIPTION	PRICE	STATUS
03-P3	117607	1	GP V4 1981-84 ✓	12.48	
				11.48	

DEDUCT $1.00 FOR DUST JACKET

MERCHANDISE	SHIPPING/HANDLING	STATE TAX	TOTAL AMOUNT	AMOUNT PAID	BALANCE DUE	CREDIT
12.48	.00	.00	12.48	12.48		

SHIP VIA:
    BP

762323001

HT

THANK YOU FOR YOUR ORDER.   WE LOOK FORWARD TO
SERVING YOU AGAIN IN THE FUTURE.   IF WE CAN BE OF
SERVICE TO YOU, PLEASE CALL US ON OUR TOLL FREE
HOT LINE - 1-800-826-6600.

VISA

762323001

SEE REVERSE SIDE FOR RETURN AND REORDER INFORMATION AND **STATUS** OF UNSHIPPED MERCHANDISE

HT 3

Classic Motorbooks
T.M.

729 PROSPECT AVENUE • OSCEOLA, WI 54020, U.S.A.

FORWARDING AND RETURN POSTAGE GUARANTEED

DATE
    12/26/95
ORDER #
    719864-000
SHIP VIA
    BP   BAG 001

PRESORT SPEC 4TH CLASS
U.S. POSTAGE PAID
OSCEOLA, WISCONSIN
PERMIT NO. 32

PKGID   762323003

TO ▶   JAMES A WALKER
       17231 BLACK HAWK 0912
       FRIENDSWOOD   TX 77546-0000

762323003

Classic Motorbooks
T.M.

729 PROSPECT AVENUE • OSCEOLA, WI 54020, U.S.A.

FORWARDING AND RETURN POSTAGE GUARANTEED

DATE
    12/26/95
ORDER #
    719864-000
SHIP VIA
    BP   BAG 001

PRESORT SPEC 4TH CLASS
U.S. POSTAGE PAID
OSCEOLA, WISCONSIN
PERMIT NO. 32

PKGID   762323004

TO ▶   JAMES A WALKER
       17231 BLACK HAWK 0912
       FRIENDSWOOD   TX 77546-0000

**S
T
A
T
U
S**

STATUS OF UNSHIPPED MERCHANDISE

TOS — Temporarily Out of Stock-expect
to ship within 30 days

NPO — New Publication on Order-will
ship when initial stock is received

OP — Out of Print-no longer being printed
NA — No longer Available from us
OSI — Out of Stock Indefinitely-may be
available in 6-12 months-Please reorder

CREDIT CARD CUSTOMERS — You have been charged only for items shipped plus postage & handling
and sales tax where applicable.

**R
E
T
U
R
N
S**

If for any reason you are not completely satisfied with your purchase, return it **within 14 days**
of receipt for replacement, exchange or refund.

1. Complete information below and return with package.
2. Address your package with return label provided below.
3. For your protection we suggest you return items via UPS or Insured Parcel Post.

Qty	Item #	Description	Desired Action	Reason Code	Unit Price	Total Credit

DESIRED ACTION

1. Please replace
2. Reorder different and/or additional merchandise
3. Please refund by original method of payment

REASON CODE — Please Explain Below

1. Received damaged/defective
2. Received incorrect merchandise
3. Merchandise on back-order too long
4. Unsatisfactory service
5. Other

**R
E
O
R
D
E
R**

If Desired Action is option 1 or 2 above please complete below:

Qty	Item #	Description	Price	Total

Ship to: If Different

Name

Address

City

State   Zip Code

☐ Check or Money order enclosed
☐ Visa   ☐ American Express
☐ Mastercard   ☐ Discover
Card # _____
Expiration date _____
Signature _____

Please indicate form of payment for any amount due.

*Residents of CA, CT, D.C., HI, IL, KS, MA, MN, NE, NM, NV & WI please add your state sales tax.

Return explanation and customer
concerns suggestions or comments.

_____
_____
_____
_____
_____

Use this label to return merchandise. Fasten with cellophane tape.

FROM

_____
_____

TO

Classic Motorbooks ™.

729 PROSPECT AVENUE
OSCEOLA, WI 54020, U.S.A.

Contents

Foreword by Nigel Mansell, OBE

Being invited to write a foreword for one of the volumes in this superbly researched and documented *Grand Prix!* series by Mike Lang is both a privilege and a pleasure.

The period covered by this latest volume is of particular interest to me. It not only coincides with my first four full seasons in Grand Prix racing, as a driver, but also serves to remind me of the great changes which took place within the sport over a very short space of time. These, of course, were brought about mainly by the teams — one by one — making the gradual transition from normally-aspirated to turbo-charged cars, and the considerable differences in technique required of the drivers in order to cope with the enormous increase in the power suddenly at their disposal.

This era evokes for me many memories of the late, great Colin Chapman and the thrill of driving for him at Lotus and 'trying out' the ill-fated double chassis Type 88 which he so cleverly designed, only to see it outlawed amidst the intense political differences which gripped the sport in 1981 and threatened its whole integrity for a while.

Then there was Monaco 1984. Here I was just beginning to savour the reality of leading a Grand Prix for the first time in my career — albeit in atrociously wet conditions — when, climbing the hill to Casino Square flat in fifth gear, I put a rear wheel on to one of the white carriageway markings. Ordinarily, this would have made no difference whatsoever, but in the wet my car was flicked sideways

into the Armco with almost inevitable consequences — broken suspension and retirement. The fact that World Champion designate, Niki Lauda, later suffered the same fate, along with several others who were caught out on the slippery track, did nothing to diminish my disappointment! Happily for me, I was finally to achieve that first, seemingly elusive victory just over a year later, on home territory at Brands Hatch in the Grand Prix of Europe.

There are numerous other memories brought to life within the pages of this book: the silence of Zolder in 1982 following the tragic accident befalling Gilles Villeneuve during the closing moments of qualifying is particularly poignant. But there are lots of happy memories as well, all of which have served to heighten the joy of being able to compete at the very highest level in motor sport.

Finally, I am pleased to say that Mike Lang's attention to detail has once again been admirably portrayed in the following pages and, with a wealth of supporting photographs and statistics, he has succeeded in producing another volume which collectively — with the three previous volumes — chronicles the history of the World Championship in the best possible manner.

Nigel Mansell, OBE
March, 1992

Introduction

The World Championship of Drivers was conceived at the 1949 General Assembly of the FIA (*Fédération Internationale de L'Automobile*), the international controlling body for motor sport. Until then there had been several national Grand Prix races held throughout Europe each year, all direct descendants of the first Grand Prix held in France in 1906. The proposal made by the Italian delegate, Count Antonio Brivio, was that these should be run as a series and a World Championship Trophy awarded to the driver who was most successful. After consideration, the Assembly agreed the proposal, which must have delighted the Automobile Club d'Italia immensely as there seemed little doubt that for the first few years at least the Championship would be won by an Italian driver at the wheel of an Italian car.

It was decided that for the first year, 1950, the national Grand Prix races of Britain, Monaco, Switzerland, Belgium, France and Italy would be qualifying rounds of the Championship. Claims by Argentina, Holland and Spain were also considered but it was decided that the six events named would be sufficient for the first trial year. The United States delegate contended, however, that as the Championship was going to be called the World Championship an event from North America should be included and that this should be the annual Memorial Day 500-mile Sweepstakes at Indianapolis, there being no Grand Prix race as such. It was pointed out that European drivers could enter the race providing they qualified and that it was possible that some American drivers might enter Grand Prix events. The argument was accepted and the World Championship was born the following May when the first event took place at Silverstone.

Each year since then the Championship has been awarded on a points system based on the results of the 'qualifying' races for each particular year. The scoring system has been as follows:

1950–1959: 8, 6, 4, 3 and 2 points, respectively, were awarded for the first five places, with 1 point for fastest lap.

Up to 1957: where more than one driver shared a car they shared any points scored, but from 1958 onwards points were awarded only to a driver who handled the car throughout the race.

In 1960: the point for fastest lap was dropped and 1 point given for sixth place.

In 1961: the winner's points were increased from 8 to 9.

(A driver can only count a specified number of Championship rounds towards his personal total each year and details of this are as shown in the annual World Championship tables.)

This book, the fourth in the series, is the continuing story of the World Championship from 1981 to 1984 and is intended to give an accurate race-by-race account of each event held in that period. Whilst the emphasis is on the drivers' endeavours, the text has been written to show the continual technological advances during the years, changes in teams and, indeed, in conjunction with the text of the first three volumes, the general change in the pattern of motor racing since World War II.

Finally, a detailed record of facts and figures of all drivers scoring even a fraction of a point in World Championship events during the years 1981 to 1984 has been included as an appendix – it should settle a few arguments!

Mike Lang

1981 Politics and more politics

Above all else, the winter of 1980/81 will be remembered in Grand Prix circles for the bitter conflict that raged between Jean-Marie Balestre and Bernie Ecclestone on behalf, respectively, of FISA (La Fédération Internationale du Sport Automobile) and FOCA (the Formula One Constructors' Association). Indeed, it was nothing short of all-out war with FISA unwilling to backtrack on its revised regulations scheduled to take effect from 1 January 1981 – primarily a ban on skirts to reduce cornering speeds – and FOCA simply refusing to comply on the grounds that the two-year notice rule for major changes had not been applied.

To put the matter into perspective it is necessary to go back to 1979 when, following his election as President of the CSI (Commission Sportive Internationale), later to become FISA, Balestre had made it clear from the outset that he was determined to ensure that the governing body would henceforth play a much larger role in the running of Grand Prix racing. Prior to then, over a period of some considerable time, control of the sport had gradually been passing over to FOCA and no more so than in the financial field. Not that there seemed to have been much wrong with this. On the contrary, FOCA had been doing an admirable job of maintaining continuity within the sport; of promoting it to unprecedented levels, in particular by bringing it to the attention of a virtually world-wide audience through selling off rights to numerous television companies; and of completing contractual and financial arrangements with race organizers to the benefit of everyone. However, Balestre had thought otherwise and had deliberately set out on a dictatorial campaign to change things round.

The first real signs of trouble had come the following February (1980) when a newly-formed FISA Executive Committee announced the decision to ban skirts with effect from 1 January 1981 – under the proviso that allowed the usual two-year notice rule to be waived on the grounds of 'safety' – for this had immediately brought howls of protest from the FOCA-aligned teams. Their reaction had not been surprising either. Sliding skirts were by then an integral part of the current-day ground-effect Grand Prix cars and it was only through greater chassis expertise, especially in the field of aerodynamics, that the Ford-Cosworth-engined brigade could hope to make up for power deficiency over the expensive turbo-charged engines already being raced by Renault and being tested by Ferrari and Alfa Romeo. The protests, though, together with a revised package of proposals put forward by FOCA, appeared to fall on deaf ears. This caused even greater antagonism, as was illustrated only too well at the South African Grand Prix when Balestre was systematically prevented from joining in the post-race celebrations on the rostrum.

After that the power struggle had continued to gain momentum rapidly, with Balestre resorting to all kinds of measures to harass FOCA. As a result it became increasingly evident that the skirt ban was only the thin end of the wedge and that he was intent on seeing that financial control should come under the auspices of FISA. Certainly one of the prime examples of these efforts came with the introduction of compulsory drivers' briefings on the morning of each Grand Prix. When several drivers failed to attend the first two briefings at Belgium and Monaco fines were imposed. Then, because most of these went unpaid, the drivers concerned had their licences suspended prior to the next race, the Spanish Grand Prix, which led to a major confrontation and, moreover, to the race being denuded of World Championship status as it was considered illegal! In the meantime, other people and organizations with vested interests in the sport had been growing increasingly concerned about the disharmony and, shortly after the dabacle in Spain, a group of sponsors took the initiative by convening a meeting between representatives of FISA and FOCA to try to thrash out an agreement. Nothing was achieved, for although the FISA representatives accepted compromise proposals put forward by FOCA these were rejected when referred back to Balestre. Consequently the deadlock continued. More meetings – many more – had followed but every suggestion made by FOCA was ultimately turned down and shortly after the end of the 1980 season they finally threw in the towel and announced that they were going their own way with 'The World Federation of Motor Sport' to run 'The World Professional Drivers' Championship'. So now there would be two World Championships?

Throughout the close season several more meetings and discussions took place to try to heal the rift but still there

1981

was no sign of any agreement. Instead, the future of the sport seemed to be in even greater jeopardy by December when the major tyre supplier, Goodyear, suddenly dropped a bombshell and announced its intention to pull out of all racing involvement in Europe forthwith. Now this was really serious; so much so that later that same month the plight of Grand Prix racing became the subject of debate in the House of Commons with a view to taking up the issue at Ministerial level. Quite what came of that is uncertain but, whatever, in mid-January the first real glimmer of hope materialized when, at a meeting arranged for representatives of all of the teams at Ferrari's headquarters in Maranello, an agreement in principle was reached known as the Maranello or Modena Agreement. Essentially this provided for FOCA to retain its financial control of the sport and for a stability in the rules for the next four years, with the constructors having proper representation within FISA. At the same time, however, the skirt ban would remain and it was proposed that no part of a car's bodywork should be less than 6 centimetres above the ground.

But now there was yet another stumbling block – FOCA's contract with the organizers of the South African Grand Prix scheduled for 7 February. This not only specified the date of the race but also gave FOCA the freedom to decide on the regulations governing it which were, of course, in direct conflict to those of FISA. Furthermore, because the organizers refused to accept a revised date offered by FISA, FOCA was left with little choice other than to honour the contract and support the race. Consequently it went ahead and was won by Carlos Reutemann driving a Williams FW07B (complete with sliding skirts!) in wet conditions and, significantly, in the absence of the FISA-aligned teams, Ferrari, Renault, Alfa Romeo, Talbot-Ligier and Osella. Meanwhile, a response was still being awaited from FISA to the Modena Agreement but as a result of the South African Grand Prix going ahead Balestre was refusing even to discuss it. The reason? FOCA had been granted an injunction by the English High Court to prevent anyone from interfering with its contracts for the 1981 races and was now threatening members of the FISA Executive Committee with legal action unless they reversed their decision to deprive the South African Grand Prix of World Championship status – this being considered as 'interference'.

Fortunately, commonsense prevailed at long last. FOCA arranged for the injunction to be temporarily lifted, FISA discussed the Modena Agreement and towards the end of February finally voiced its approval subject to various minor changes which were subsequently written into a new document known as the Concorde Agreement. It seemed that peace had been achieved at last! All legal action was dropped, including libel action both by and against M. Balestre, and a new World Championship calendar was drawn up incorporating a revised date for the Argentinian Grand Prix which should

have taken place back in January. It was too late to do anything about the South African Grand Prix, though, so FOCA reluctantly accepted that it had to be regarded as a non-Championship event.

The Concorde Agreement was a massive document to incorporate every rule and regulation apertaining to the sport. Several of these rules and regulations, of course, had gone unchanged so were merely reprinted but the rest were new and embraced the points agreed at Maranello and other subsequent changes. Primarily, in addition to those already mentioned, these were an increase in the minimum weight limit to 585 kg; a limit of 8 tyres per car per timed practice session; FOCA being committed to provide at least 18 cars for each Grand Prix with a proviso that should less than 15 entered cars be available for the event the promoters should cancel it; a maximum number of 30 cars being accepted for qualifying; drivers who failed to qualify in practice not being allowed to start as reserve drivers; race distances being reduced to a maximum length of 320 kilometres with a proviso for a minimum distance to be covered of 250 kilometres, both subject to a maximum race duration of 2 hours; the drivers finishing in the first three places of a Grand Prix being obliged to attend on the podium at the prize-giving ceremony, failing which the driver in default, except in a case of force majeure, would be liable to pay a fine of $5000; the drivers in the first three places of the FIA F1 World Championship being obliged to be present at the annual FIA Prize-giving ceremony, failing which any absence, except in a case of force majeure, would be punished by a fine of $10,000; and the World Championship scoring system being changed, for instead of splitting the season into two parts it was now going to be taken as a whole with drivers permitted to count their results from one half of the number of events plus three, rounded upwards to the nearest whole number.

Despite the continuation of the political unrest throughout the winter months the various teams carried on preparing for the new season more or less as normal, which meant that there was an awful lot of activity going

The 'twin-chassis' Lotus 88, which was the source of considerable controversy before eventually being banned. (L.A.T. Photographic)

Colin Chapman and his two drivers, Elio de Angelis and Nigel Mansell, pose beside the rather more acceptable Type 87. *(Autosport)*

on behind the scenes. Certainly one of the most exciting projects to emerge was the new Lotus 88, the brainchild of the ever-innovative Colin Chapman, for this had two separate chassis, each with its own springing system. The 'primary chassis', which was a ladder-type construction formed by two longitudinal members of carbon-fibre/Kevlar linked by three titanium crossmembers, comprised the bodywork, side pods, aerofoils and radiators, suspended on small coil-spring/damper units attached to the four wheel uprights by short links; the 'secondary chassis' comprised a carbon-fibre/Kevlar monocoque (this was made up by two skins bonded to Nomex honeycomb in the form of a sandwich), the fuel cell, the engine and gearbox, and the main suspension units, these being of a conventional upper rocker arm/lower wishbone arrangement. Overall the aim was to maximize the benefits of ground-effect by the 'primary chassis' absorbing the aerodynamic loads through a stiff suspension but, at the same time, minimize the effect on the driver and mechanical components by the 'secondary chassis' being allowed a reasonable degree of suspension movement. Sadly for Chapman, though, the car was destined never to take part in a Grand Prix. From its first appearance at Long Beach other teams protested its legality (mainly on the grounds that it infringed the rules that said any specific part of the car having an aerodynamic influence must remain immobile relative to the entirely sprung part of the car) and eventually it was banned by the FIA International Court of Appeal. A slightly revised version of the car, the 88B, which Chapman hoped to run at the British Grand Prix, was also thrown out, so the entire project was put to one side. In the meantime, Lotus fell back on their 1980 cars (the 81s), which were suitably modified to conform to the new regulations, until they were in a position to race their other newly-designed car for 1981 at the Monaco Grand Prix. This was the Lotus 87 which featured an identical carbon-fibre/Kevlar monocoque to that of the 88 but immediately differed by having a conventional single sprung structure (not surprisingly!) and an outward

appearance more akin to the 81. As in 1980, the cars carried the blue, red and silver colours of the Monaco-based Essex Petroleum Company, the team's main sponsor, when they first appeared. Later in the season, however, at the Spanish Grand Prix, this was changed to the black and gold livery of John Player Special cigarettes following a new co-sponsorship deal with John Player and Son who had previously supported the team over a number of years up until the end of 1978. There was also a change of driving strength within the team as Italian Elio de Angelis was promoted to the No. 1 seat to replace Mario Andretti, who had left at the end of the 1980 season, while the No. 2 seat passed to Chapman's hitherto test driver, Nigel Mansell.

Like Lotus, the Parmalat Brabham team also came up with a major technical innovation for the start of the new season. This took the form of a cleverly conceived hydropneumatic suspension system designed by Gordon Murray to enable a car to drop virtually to a ground-effect position at speed, yet rise again as it slowed or became stationary

The 1981 Ford-Cosworth-powered BT49C Parmalat Brabham being driven to victory by Nelson Piquet in the Argentine Grand Prix. *(Phipps Photographic)*

so as to comply with the mandatory 6 centimetre gap between the bodywork and the ground, the logic behind it being that the gap could only be measured when the car

The BMW-powered BT50 Parmalat Brabham shown on its first – brief – public outing during practice for the British Grand Prix at Silverstone, again with Nelson Piquet behind the wheel. *(Autosport)*

1981

was at rest. In other words it was a means of circumnavigating the rules even though it could be considered little less than blatant cheating. Essentially the system worked through two stages. The first, far softer than the second to enable the car's ride height to fall under aerodynamic downforce as the car built up speed, was hydraulic and the second was steel sprung. The only drawback with it, though, was that suspension movement had to be minimized so that the car could maintain constant, minimum clearance with the ground in order to avoid the possibility of pitching and porpoising as a result of which astronomical spring rates were necessary. This, in turn, not only subjected the driver to an exceptionally hard and neck-jarring ride, but also made the car extremely nervous and, indeed, dangerous. Any contact with the slightest bump or kerbing could throw it off line with alarming ferocity, or even lead to a total loss of adhesion causing an accident. Nevertheless, it was considered that the advantage of obtaining superior down-force more than outweighed the disadvantages of the system, as events were quickly to prove. In no time at all it became apparent that Brabham had put one over on their rivals. Indeed, the car's staggering performance soon led to protests being brandished about over its legality. These were over-ruled, however, and for once FISA seemed unwilling to be drawn into the controversy, merely stating that hydraulic suspension systems were acceptable provided that they did not allow a car to break the 6 centimetre ground clearance rule – totally inconclusive! Consequently other teams took the view that if they couldn't beat Brabham they must join them. So very soon similar ideas emerged on adjusting ride height control which led to a new generation of Grand Prix cars commonly referred to as high-powered Go-Karts. Moreover, cars even started appearing with driver-controlled systems and flexible skirts with rubbing strips, albeit fixed, which only served to make an even greater farce of the rules. Once again, though, FISA did not appear to be unduly bothered, and about the only positive action taken was to place a limit on the dimensions of skirts and to stress that they were to consist of a solid material rigidly secured to the side pods.

Apart from being the first car to appear with this rather ingenious suspension system the BT49C, as the 1981 Brabham was designated, differed only in detail from the team's 1980 car, mainly through featuring greater use of carbon-fibre composite panels in the interests of weight reduction, and being fitted with nose fins with turned down ends to help compensate for the loss of sliding skirts. At the same time, however, an entirely new project was under way as Brabham were now looking towards the turbo-charged alternative, and were actively involved with BMW to run cars powered by the German firm's new 4 cylinder engine. Nevertheless, despite extensive testing both during the winter and throughout the new season little became of it during 1981 as the purpose-built BT50 did not take part in any of the races, and only appeared

briefly in practice for the British Grand Prix. Instead, both Nelson Piquet and Hector Rebaque, the same team drivers as in 1980, relied exclusively on the normally-aspirated BT49Cs with which experiments were carried out from time to time using carbon-fibre brake discs in place of the more normal steel discs and also the Weismann transverse-shaft gearbox/final-drive unit that the team had already used occasionally during the previous year.

A third team to introduce something 'special' for 1981 were Marlboro McLaren who had undergone a complete reorganization towards the end of 1980 and became known as McLaren International: a downward spiral of results over the previous two or three years had led to Teddy Mayer being prompted by his team's sponsors to merge with Ron Dennis' successful Project Four Formula 2 outfit. The result of this new partnership was the emergence of a revolutionary chassis with a monocoque of carbon-fibre, costly and time-consuming in its manufacture, but simple in terms of the number of parts, light and immensely strong. Designed by Project Four's chief designer John Barnard (Gordon Cuppock had been elbowed out in the shake-up), the strikingly elegant Marlboro MP4, as it was dubbed, also had an underbody and side panels made of carbon-fibre honeycomb, and the radiators were mounted in carbon-fibre boxes which doubled as ductings and mountings in place of conventional framework and fibreglass. In other respects, though, the

The Marlboro McLaren team show off the new MP4, with its revolutionary carbon-fibre monocoque, at Long Beach. *(Phipps Photographic)*

Reigning World Champion Alan Jones captured at speed in the Saudia-Leyland Williams FWO7C. *(Autosport)*

Renault new-boy, Alain Prost, putting the RE30 through its paces during practice for the British Grand Prix at Silverstone. *(Dave Webb)*

car's general design followed established principles and had conventional suspension of top rocker arms activating inboard-mounted coil-spring/damper units and lower wishbones both front and rear. As an interim measure, until they were ready to race the new MP4, McLaren International also produced refurbished versions of the M29 which, in F-specification, had new bodywork, improved aerodynamics and revised suspension. To drive the cars, the team retained the very capable services of John Watson and recruited the rather inexperienced Italian Andrea de Cesaris to take over the second seat vacated amidst a certain amount of legal acrimony by Alain Prost.

Without doubt the most successful team of 1980 had been Williams, for they had won the Constructors' Championship at a canter and Alan Jones had convincingly carried off the Drivers' title. Consequently it was of little surprise to find the team retaining the same basic design of the FWO7 for their 1981 cars, the FWO7Cs, albeit with fairly substantial modifications. Primarily these involved the front of the monocoque being redesigned so as to provide greater stiffness as well as a much stronger footwell in the interests of protecting the driver's legs and a number of aerodynamic changes to help compensate for the loss of sliding skirts. Among the latter changes to be made were the side pods being reprofiled, the adoption of a full-width front wing, with large end plates, mounted atop the nose cone using sheet steel and a larger rear aerofoil. Other detail modifications were also carried out as the season progressed, not least to a hydro-pneumatic suspension system after the team became among the first to follow the lead set by Brabham. Team drivers, as in 1980, were reigning World Champion Alan Jones and Argentinian Carlos Reutemann.

Apart from Williams and Brabham the only other teams to have actually won any Grand Prix races in 1980 were Renault and Ligier, with honours, just about evenly divided. Of the two, Renault Elf more or less carried on from where they had left off, except for a change in driving strength, and for the start of the new season relied on their turbo-charged RE20 series of cars suitably modified to 'B' specification so as to comply with the ban on sliding skirts. By the time of the Belgian Grand Prix, however, Renault had produced the first two examples of the new RE30 series of cars which were of a much lighter construction than their predecessors, albeit still on the heavy side, more compact and squatter, and they had the turbo-charger units located as low as practically possible on either side of the engine. Even so it was not until Monaco that the new cars actually made their race debuts. This was due to acute handling problems which were only improved with further testing and subtle aerodynamic refinements; a major difficulty being that the cars had been specifically designed to run without skirts of any description. In the meantime, considerable development work continued on the already very powerful 1.5 litre V6 twin turbo-charged engine, with particular emphasis being placed on trying to reduce turbo lag: by mid-season various detail modifications were to lead to the problem being virtually eliminated. As regards the change in driving strength, this came about as a result of the rather sudden departure of Jean-Pierre Jabouille who had raced the turbo-charged Renaults from the outset in 1977, and who had also done very nearly all of the test driving. To replace him, the team enticed Alain Prost away from McLaren after lengthy and difficult negotiations to break an existing contract, while at the same time retaining the services of René Arnoux.

In contrast to Renault, the Gitanes Ligier team underwent a major change of direction during the winter, as in late 1980 Guy Ligier had sold off a large proportion of his interests to the Talbot company (the French conglomerate of Simca, Chrysler and Rootes) which had decided to enter the Grand Prix arena with support from the French Aero-Space firm Engins Matra. Naturally this meant discarding the Ford-Cosworth DFV engine used over the past couple of years and bringing out the Matra V12 unit again, nominally as a stand-in until a 1.5 litre Matra turbo was prepared. Although this had not been used since the end of 1978 further development work had been carried out and it was now capable of producing around 510 bhp at 12,200 rpm. To accommodate the 'old' engine the newly-constituted Talbot-Ligier team produced the JS17 which was a logical development of the Ford-Cosworth-

13

1981

The newly-unveiled Gitanes Ligier JS17, which ran under the Talbot banner and heralded the return of the Matra V12 engine. *(Autosport)*

powered JS11/15. Out of necessity, however, the cockpit was slightly further forward, the car was bigger, was fitted with a large tray-shaped full-width front wing, and also had an aluminium monocoque reinforced with honeycomb material. The suspension, meanwhile, followed the same principles of the 1980 car with top rocker arms activating inboard coil-spring/damper units and lower wishbones all round. Known as Talbots, these blue and white JS17s were driven by Jacques Laffite and, initially, by the ex-Tyrrell driver Jean-Pierre Jarier, for although Jean-Pierre Jabouille had joined the team from Renault as a replacement for Didier Pironi he was still not fully recovered from the leg injuries sustained in the accident at the previous year's Canadian Grand Prix.

So far as Ferrari was concerned, 1980 had been a year best forgotten. For the first time since 1973 the great Italian marque had failed to achieve even one Grand Prix victory owing largely to their hitherto successful flat-12 engine proving uncharacteristically unreliable. But now all that was history. The 3-litre engine was being abandoned and, instead, the team was embarking on a new era of running turbo-charged cars, one of which had already made its first public appearance, albeit briefly, during

Ferrari entered a new era in 1981 by forsaking their familiar 3-litre flat-12 engine and introducing their new 120-degree, 1½-litre V6 turbo-charged engine in the purpose-built 126C, pictured below in the hands of Gilles Villeneuve. *(Autosport)*

practice for the Italian Grand Prix at Imola. Designated the 126C or 126CK, the new power unit was a 120-degree, four camshaft, V6 of 1496cc (81 × 48.4 mm) initially capable of producing around 540 bhp at 11,500 rpm using either a mechanically-driven Comprex pressure wave supercharger system made by Brown Boveri in Switzerland, or twin exhaust-driven turbine/compressor units made by the German firm Kuhnle-Kopp and Kausch (KKK). Because of problems with the Comprex system, however, the team was to rely almost entirely on the KKK turbo-chargers throughout 1981. Originally these were mounted above and ahead of the engine with an inter-cooler in each of the car's sidepods. Later, though, this arrangement was abandoned in favour of a revised layout in which both the twin turbo units and a single large inter-cooler were placed in the vee of the engine to permit the entire system to be piped to a single waste-gate with an adjusting screw to reduce or increase boost pressure as required. To accommodate this new engine, which was used as a fully stressed chassis member, Ferrari produced a car totally traditional by their standards for it had a monocoque of stressed alloy sheeting with a strong internal tubular frame structure and conventional suspension of rocker arms activating inboard coil-spring/damper units and lower wishbones all round. The transmission, too, followed the same principles as the 312T series of cars, for the gearbox was still mounted transversely ahead of the final-drive unit, although it was both stronger and more compact than previously. To drive his new turbo-charged contenders, the Commendatore managed to lure Didier Pironi away from Ligier as a replacement for the now-retired Jody Scheckter, and was more than happy to retain the services of the brilliant French-Canadian Gilles Villeneuve who was promoted to team-leader.

In common with Ferrari the other major Italian team Autodelta Alfa Romeo had also been looking at the turbo-charged alternative throughout 1980 and had, in fact, already carried out extensive work on developing and testing their own 90-degree, 1.5 litre V8 engine. Contrary to expectations, however, they were to continue relying exclusively on their V12 normally-aspirated engine in 1981. These were installed in uprated versions of the Tipo 179s with new riveted aluminium monocoques and with slots in the side-pods to form an air curtain between them and the ground to help compensate for the loss of sliding skirts. Unfortunately, even in the hands of former World Champion Mario Andretti, who had been signed up from Lotus to partner Bruno Giacomelli, the 179Cs were rarely to display any degree of competitiveness. Every attempt to overcome the various problems, mainly in the handling department, seemed to have little or no effect. As a result the team were to have another generally disappointing year, which was something that more or less applied to all of the other remaining established teams, Arrows, ATS, Ensign, Fittipaldi, Osella and Tyrrell.

In brief, Arrows ran modified versions of their 1980 A3s

The Marlboro Alfa Romeo Tipo 179C. *(C.R. Foxworthy)*

The ATS HGS 1. *(Phipps Photographic)*

(now carrying an orange and white livery in deference to their new sponsors Ragno Tiles and Beta Tools) for Riccardo Patrese and their new driver Italian Siegfried Stohr; ATS started the season with their 1980 D4 for Jan Lammers, before introducing their new HGS1(D5);

in 1981 were Theodore and March. Of these, the name Theodore returned as a result of Theodore (Teddy) Yip simply deciding to race a car under his own name again for the first time since 1978. More recently, of course, in 1980, he had taken over control of the now-defunct Shadow

The Ragno-Beta Arrows A3. *(Dave Webb)*

The Ensign N180B. *(Dave Webb)*

Ensign, now unsponsored, produced their N180B for Marc Surer; Fittipaldi, now also unsponsored, entered revised versions of their 1980 F8s (now F8Cs) in an all-white livery for Keke Rosberg and Brazilian Francesco (Chico) Serra who had been recruited by the team as a replacement for the now-retired Emerson Fittipaldi; Denim Osella produced new FA1Bs, which were basically a development of their 1980 cars and initially driven by Miguel-Angel Guerra and Giuseppe (Beppe) Gabbiani, before introducing their George Valentini-designed FA1C at the Italian Grand Prix; finally Tyrrell, yet another team to start the new season without sponsorship, continued to campaign their 1980 010s, under a 'rent-a-drive' arrangement with Eddie Cheever and, initially, Kevin Cogan, prior to being in a position to race their new 011 which was broadly similar to its predecessors but featuring a far stiffer monocoque and improved aerodynamics.

Two names to be reintroduced to the Grand Prix arena

team but, as well as resurrecting an old DN12 (re-christened the Theodore TR2) during the winter for Geoff Lees to drive in the non-Championship South African Grand Prix, he had commissioned the ex-Arrows designer Tony Southgate to come up with a brand new car. The result was the TY01, a conventional British 'kit-car' built around the standard Ford-Cosworth engine/Hewland gearbox arrangement, but distinguished somewhat by having a rather high full-width front wing mounted on a centre pylon atop the nose cone. This new Theodore made its debut at Long Beach and was driven, initially, by Patrick Tambay who had been without a Grand Prix ride ever since losing his place in the Marlboro McLaren team at the end of 1979. The name March, on the other hand, returned as a result of a new partnership formed between John MacDonald's RAM Racing team and March Engineering. However, here again the cars designed by Robin Herd, with assistance from Gordon Coppuck, were totally 15

The Fittipaldi F8C. (*L.A.T. Photographic*)

conventional and destined to be equally as unsuccessful. Painted black and white with sponsorship from Guinness and Rizla, the RAM March 811s were entered for the ex-Tyrrell driver Derek Daly and, until the team reduced their onslaught to a one-car affair, for Chilean Eliseo Salazar.

The only one completely new name to appear in 1981 was Toleman who, in 1980, had convincingly won the European Formula 2 Championship and was now taking the big step forward into Grand Prix racing with a new Formula 1 challenger designed by South African Rory Byrne, the designer of Ted Toleman's successful Formula

The Denim Osella FA1B. (*Dave Webb*)

The Tyrrell 011. *(Phipps Photographic)*

2 cars. Not only did this represent the arrival of an entirely new British Formula 1 team but it also marked the return to Grand Prix racing of the Italian Pirelli tyre company for the first time in 25 years, as well as resulting in the first Formula 1 car to be powered by the new Hart 415T turbo-charged engine. The TG181, as this all-new car was designated, had a monocoque constructed of aluminium alloy bonded around a honeycomb structure with box-section extensions projecting rearwards to transmit torsional and beam loads from the rear suspension to the main monocoque, the Hart engine, like its Formula 2 counterpart, not being a stressed chassis member. Suspen-

sion was fairly conventional with top rocker arms activating inboard-mounted coil-spring/damper units and lower wishbones all round but the brakes, large by any standards, were mounted outboard at both the front and the rear. The new Brian Hart-developed engine, meanwhile, was a twin ohc, 4 cylinder in-line unit of 1494cc (88 × 61.5 mm) which, using either two small Garrett AiResearch turbo units or a single large one, was initially capable of producing a rather modest 490 bhp at 9500 rpm driven through a Toleman/Hewland gearbox. Finished off in a predominantly blue colour scheme, with red and white trim, the TG181s were sponsored primarily by the Italian

The Theodore TY01. *(Autosport)*

The RAM March 811. *(C.R. Foxworthy)*

1981

Candy Domestic Appliances firm and SAIMA, the Italian freight forwarding company, and entrusted to the team's 1980 drivers, Brian Henton and Derek Warwick. Fortunately the team had the foresight to lay out the new cars in such a way as to facilitate different types of turbo engine operation and experimentation, as from their first public appearance in practice at Imola, in deference to their Italian sponsors, progress was severely hampered by overheating and other teething problems. Indeed, all sorts of revisions were to be progressively carried out to try to bring the cars up to a competitive level, but it was to prove a long hard struggle, taking until the Italian Grand Prix before even one of them finally graduated beyond qualifying and actually took part in a race.

Finally, Goodyear's sudden withdrawal only served to put another shadow on the future of Grand Prix racing, as it seemed as if no-one would have any tyres except for Ferrari, Renault and Talbot-Ligier, who were all contracted to Michelin, and Toleman who had an exclusive contract with Pirelli. Indeed, it had been partly due to serving so many teams, and the associated financial burden, that had influenced Goodyear's decision in the first place. Fortunately, though, Michelin stepped in to temporarily bridge the gap by announcing that they were prepared to supply everyone with standardized tyres for the first three races. In addition, the Bernie Ecclestone-owned/Jean Mosnier-managed International Race Tire Service Ltd (IRTS), which had been formed in 1975 to service and sell Goodyear racing tyres throughout Europe, entered into a joint venture with Avon Tyres Ltd and said that they intended filling the void left by Goodyear. It was stressed, however, that their tyres would have to be purchased. The outcome of this was that Avon tyres returned to Grand Prix racing, after an absence of 20 years, at Imola when Fittipaldi became the first team to take up the offer. In the meantime, Michelin extended their original, much appreciated gesture until the French Grand Prix when Goodyear did a partial U-turn and returned to the scene to supply, initially, just the Williams and Brabham teams. At the same time RAM March, Theodore and Ensign switched to the IRTS-supplied Avon tyres, while Michelin immediately changed their policy by concentrating on their contracted teams (these now included Alfa Romeo) and inviting the remaining teams to purchase standardized tyres if they so wished. A new tyre war was under way!

The car that brought the only completely new name to the sport in 1981, the Hart-engined Toleman TG181. *(Phipps Photographic)*

VIth United States Grand Prix (West)

Long Beach: March 15
Weather: Warm and sunny
Distance: 80.5 laps of 3.251km
circuit = 261.70km (162.62 miles)

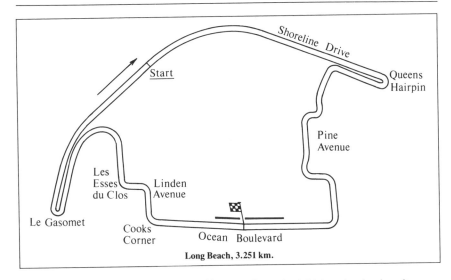

Long Beach, 3.251 km.

At long last the 1981 World Championship season was under way. FISA and FOCA had finally sorted out their differences, the long-awaited agreement having been concluded just a few days earlier, and no less than 16 teams, fielding a total of 29 drivers, were now ready to embark on a new, hopefully peaceful campaign.

The action actually started on Friday with an untimed practice session in the morning followed by the first hour of qualifying in the afternoon. Not surprisingly, with no pre-race testing having been possible due to Long Beach being a street circuit, the overall scene was soon one of frantic activity, for not only were drivers having to become accustomed to their surroundings but also to their skirt-less cars, several of which were new and, in the main, fitted with larger wings, softer springs and revised side-pod profiles. In addition, a number of drivers were also having to become acquainted with standardized radial Michelin tyres for the first time following the withdrawal of Goodyear. So, one way and another, there was a lot to learn, but while the drivers were all hard at work there was already another dark cloud looming on the horizon as a row was now brewing over the legality of the new Lotus 88, even though it had been accepted and passed by the race scrutineers on the previous day. Eventually, matters took a turn for the worse from the point of view of the Lotus team when the majority of the other team managers protested to the race organizers. At first there was not much response but then, after activities had ended for the day, came the announcement that the protest was being upheld. By then the car had already run into various teething problems, including the failure of the fuel pump drive which had brought it to an abrupt halt

early on its initial outing in the afternoon leaving de Angelis spending most of the day in his Lotus 81 back-up car. In the meantime, the early pace-setter had turned out to be the new Williams FWO7C of Alan Jones, the reigning World Champion being alone in having lapped in the 1 min 20 sec bracket at 1 min 20.911 sec. Indeed, the Williams team seemed to be carrying on from where they had left off in 1980, for Reutemann was well up the time sheets, as well, with fourth fastest time of 1 min 21.739 sec. Another team ending the first day with smiles was Ferrari. Villeneuve was third fastest at 1 min 21.723 sec, a time achieved in the spare Ferrari fitted with the twin KKK turbo-charger unit after the Brown Boveri Comprex supercharger system had failed on his intended race chassis, and Pironi fifth fastest at 1 min 21.828 sec. Also well satisfied with the results at the end of the first day were an inspired Jarier, who had clinched second best time of 1 min 21.722 sec in the new blue and white Talbot-Matra, and Patrese, who rounded off those in the 1 min 21 sec bracket after a fine effort in the orange and white Arrows.

The smiles of the previous day in the Ferrari camp rapidly started disappearing on Saturday morning when, during the untimed session, Villeneuve's race car, fitted with the KKK turbo-charger unit from the spare car overnight, developed serious engine trouble. To make matters worse for the Italian marque, the gearbox on Pironi's sister car started leaking oil from its gearbox, and then the spare care, that Villeneuve took over, was found to be running with a persistent misfire. Problems of varying degrees were also keeping other teams busy, but once again it was the Lotus 88 that stole most of the headlines when, without warning or any

reason, it was suddenly black-flagged and deemed to be illegal, an occurrence that was totally bewildering to an incensed Colin Chapman, as after having lodged an appeal against the Stewards' decision of the previous evening he had been told that the car would be permitted to run after all!

Attention now became focused on the final hour of qualifying. De Angelis was back in the Lotus 81 once more, the Ferrari team had reorganized themselves, a new engine having been fitted to Villeneuve's car. Elsewhere everything seemed to be running much according to plan except for McLaren as Watson, after having made little progress with the new MP4 chassis, had now switched to the older and spare M29F. For the second day running it was Jones who was setting the pace, and this remained the pattern until

Starting Grid	
	R. Patrese Arrows-Ford (1 min 19.399 sec)
A. Jones Williams-Ford (1 min 19.408 sec)	C. Reutemann Williams-Ford (1 min 20.149 sec)
N. Piquet Brabham-Ford (1 min 20.289 sec)	G. Villeneuve Ferrari (1 min 20.462 sec)
M. Andretti Alfa Romeo (1 min 20.476 sec)	N. Mansell Lotus-Ford (1 min 20.573 sec)
E. Cheever Tyrrell-Ford (1 min 20.643 sec)	B. Giacomelli Alfa Romeo (1 min 20.664 sec)
J.P. Jarier Talbot-Matra (1 min 20.787 sec)	D. Pironi Ferrari (1 min 20.909 sec)
J. Laffite Talbot-Matra (1 min 20.925 sec)	E. de Angelis Lotus-Ford (1 min 20.928 sec)
A. Prost Renault (1 min 20.980 sec)	H. Rebaque Brabham-Ford (1 min 21.000 sec)
K. Rosberg Fittipaldi-Ford (1 min 21.001 sec)	P. Tambay Theodore-Ford (1 min 21.298 sec)
F. Serra Fittipaldi-Ford (1 min 21.409 sec)	M. Surer Ensign-Ford (1 min 21.522 sec)
R. Arnoux Renault (1 min 21.540 sec)	J. Lammers ATS-Ford (1 min 21.758 sec)
A. de Cesaris McLaren-Ford (1 min 22.028 sec)	J. Watson McLaren-Ford (1 min 22.183 sec)
G. Gabbiani Osella-Ford (1 min 22.213 sec)	

Did not qualify:
K. Cogan (Tyrrell-Ford) 1 min 22.284 sec
D. Daly (March-Ford) 1 min 22.356 sec
M. Guerra (Osella-Ford) 1 min 22.673 sec
S. Stohr (Arrows-Ford) 1 min 23.504 sec
E. Salazar (March-Ford) 1 min 24.383 sec

about half-way through the session when the Australian, with an improved time of 1 min 19.408 sec to his credit, brought the left rear wheel of his car into contact with the wall at the last corner before the pits and bent the suspension. Undaunted, Jones immediately switched cars but, despite trying as hard as ever, he found the spare FWO7B less to his liking and eventually had to settle for second place on the grid immediately ahead of team-mate Reutemann who collected third spot with a time of 1 min 20.149 sec. Ahead of the Williams pair, meanwhile, was none other than Patrese with the much-modified Arrows A3, the Italian claiming a thoroughly well deserved first-ever pole position at 1 min 19.399 sec. Behind these first three, Piquet had moved up to a fine fourth spot with a much-improved time of 1 min 20.289 sec, the Brazilian altogether happier now that the hydro-pneumatic system of ride height control on his car had been abandoned in favour of a conventional suspension following troubles throughout Friday, and then came Villeneuve in the quicker of the two Ferraris at 1 min 20.462 sec. Andretti was next, obviously enjoying his first outing for Alfa Romeo and posting sixth fastest time of 1 min 20.476 sec. He, in turn, was followed by Mansell, Cheever in the unsponsored Tyrrell, and team-mate Giacomelli, while Jarier, disappointed to end up only tenth fastest overall after the promising start on Friday, Pironi and Laffite were all quick enough to join them in the top half of the grid. Of the rest, one of the main disappointments was the position of the two Renault drivers. Prost had wound up only 14th fastest after having spent a lot of his time in the team's spare car due to a wall-banging incident on Friday followed by gearbox trouble on Saturday, and Arnoux was an even more despondent 20th, both men complaining of lack of grip and understeer. The McLaren

duo of Watson (driving with a sprained wrist thanks to a game of squash earlier in the week) and de Cesaris were also well down the time sheets in their M29Fs. However, they had at least managed to scrape onto the 24-car grid which was more than could be said of Cogan, Guerra, Stohr and the two March drivers, Daly and Salazar, who had all failed to find enough speed for one reason or another, the Italian Arrows recruit having had his hopes dashed first by damaging the suspension of his race car during the morning and then by suffering an engine failure in the spare car right at the start of the final session.

The fine weather enjoyed throughout the two practice days continued into Sunday with clear blue skies and a warm sun. During the morning, amidst a variety of supporting events, there was a 30 minute warm-up session which saw both Ferraris fitted with the KKK turbo-chargers, the Comprex system having been temporarily put to one side, and Rebaque's Brabham with a Hewland gearbox in place of the Weismann unit that the Mexican had been using throughout practice until a component failure late on Saturday afternoon. About the only real drama to occur was Mansell clipping the wall at the Queen's hairpin and damaging the rear right-hand corner of his Lotus 81, although there were worried faces at Renault when Prost's car was found to have developed an in-curable misfire. Eventually, this led to the French team having to commission their spare care into use for the race, while the Lotus mechanics carried out hasty repair work for their English driver.

The start and finish lines at Long Beach were on opposite sides of the circuit, so after having formed up on a dummy grid in front of the pits and patiently waited for 2 p.m. to

approach, the 24 cars, led by Patrese's Arrows, eventually set off for their starting positions on Shoreline Drive. Now the adrenalin was really flowing, and within moments of everyone taking up their places on went the starting lights. Red quickly gave way to green with Patrese, intent on making full use of his hard-earned pole position, roaring away into an immediate lead. The rest followed, Reutemann getting the jump over his somewhat hesitant team-mate, to head the pursuit, but then down the outside on the approach to the Queen's hairpin came rushing the red Ferrari of Villeneuve. On went the brakes but in a determined, briefly successful, attempt to wrest the lead Ville-neuve had overcooked it! A split second later he was sliding wide and fighting armfuls of opposite lock to keep the wayward Ferrari under control as Patrese, Reutemann and Jones all nipped through on the inside. Behind them there was an even greater commotion. De Cesaris somehow managed to run into the backs of both Rebaque and Prost which had the net result of momen-tarily launching the Brabham into the air and sending the Renault slithering sideways across the track into retirement. The young Italian also had to retire on the spot, while a somewhat shaken Rebaque carried on apparently none the worse.

It soon became evident that Patrese's practice performance had been no flash in the pan for he quickly started putting day-light between himself and the two Williams of Reutemann and Jones. As this continued, with the three of them gradually easing away from the rest of the field, there was a tremen-dous tussle going on behind, with a whole queue of the cars forming up behind Vill-eneuve. Not that this was to last long as on

Riccardo Patrese roars off into the lead at the start. *(Phipps Photographic)*

1981

The early battle for fourth place with Nelson Piquet's Brabham currently sandwiched between the new Ferrari 126Cs of Didier Pironi and Gilles Villeneuve, and with Eddie Cheever keeping up remarkably well in his Tyrrell. *(Autosport)*

lap 4 the Ferrari driver slid wide exiting the hairpin before the main straight and, before he had realized it, both team-mate Pironi and Piquet had squeezed past to leave him at the mercy of Cheever, the American going really well in his Tyrrell which had been decked out in Cogan's Michelob Beer sponsorship colours overnight. Lower down the order, meanwhile, it was not long before more trouble was brewing. At the end of lap 5 Lammers was seen heading for the pits to have the front aerofoil removed from his ATS after coming into contact with the rear of Serra's Fittipaldi. Three laps later Watson followed him in with a sick engine that was ultimately to result in retirement on lap 16, while on the very next lap Rebaque called in to complain of handling problems, unaware that his rear anti-roll bar had been broken in the first corner contretemps, only to be sent out again on a fresh set of rubber! Arnoux was yet another early pit visitor, complaining of front-end vibrations with his Renault which after the race was diagnosed to have been caused by a faulty shock-absorber, and while he was there de Angelis was seen climbing out of his Lotus opposite the pits having just clouted the car's rear end against the wall on the way out of the preceding corner. Minutes later there was an even more significant occurrence when, on lap 18, Villeneuve suddenly slowed dramatically in sixth place and coasted to rest out on the circuit with a broken drive-shaft.

At twenty laps, quarter-distance, Patrese was still controlling the race beautifully out in front. Nevertheless, Reutemann was far from making it easy for him, constantly keeping the orange and white car firmly in his sights, while Jones was still steadily pounding along behind the pair of them seemingly content with third place, for the time being at least. Then, after an ever-increasing gap, came Piquet and Pironi having just swopped places and they, in turn, were well clear of the rest being led by Cheever, Andretti and Laffite. Certainly at this stage it seemed as if not even Reutemann's sustained pressure was going to rob the Italian of his first Grand Prix victory, but sadly for him the situation was to change dramatically over the next few minutes with the first warning coming on lap 24 when the Arrows' engine momentarily spluttered. On this occasion the Arrows recovered sufficiently to enable Patrese to block Reutemann's attempt to overtake, but a lap later the problem became even more apparent with the Arrows' engine developing a misfire. As a result, the unlucky Patrese could hold off his adversary no longer, and when Jones also went by the next time round he headed for the pits where well over a lap was lost whilst the spark box was being replaced. That was bad enough, but as if to rub salt in the wound, the problem was still there once Patrese rejoined the fray and after a second pit stop still failed to cure matters the unlucky driver finally retired on lap 33, the cause of his downfall later being traced to a blocked fuel filter caused by fibre-glass resin on the inside of his fuel tank being affected by petrol. In the meantime, other changes were also taking place. Mansell and Gabbiani had both disappeared from the lap charts in quick succession after bringing their

cars into contact with the wall, Jarier was now having to drive his Talbot with a bent steering arm following a slight coming-together with Tambay's Theodore at the Queen's hairpin on lap 27 and, even more significantly, the race now had yet another new leader, as on his 32nd lap Reutemann had locked his front brakes whilst in the process of lapping Surer's Ensign, gone kerb-hopping and given Jones the simplest of opportunities to nip past. On this same lap Laffite had also found a way by Andretti and so, with half-distance rapidly approaching, the leader-board now read Jones, Reutemann, Piquet, Pironi, Cheever and Laffite.

Just past the half-way mark there was yet more drama which began when Laffite tried to slip through on the inside of Cheever under braking for the right-hander after the pits and finished up ramming the Tyrrell as it turned into the corner. The Tyrrell appeared to emerge unscathed (it later transpired that the gear mechanism had been damaged with the loss of second gear) but the Talbot was now effectively out of the race with its nose twisted and gaping skywards. But that was to be by no means the end of the episode. As Laffite was limping slowly back to the pits, Lammers and Giacomelli, caught up in a dispute of their own, had a complete misunderstanding as they came up to pass the stricken car and proceeded to run over one another to such good effect that both were obliged to follow the Frenchman into the pits and retirement, Giacomelli hurting his hand into the bargain. Rosberg was also forced out of the race at about the same time due to engine problems with his Fittipaldi, and so the streets of Long Beach were rapidly becoming decidedly empty with only twelve cars still in the running. Of these, there was now little doubt about the order of the first three as Jones was steadily pulling away from Reutemann and he, in turn, was now around half a minute clear of Piquet who was nursing a sore hand from a stiff gear change. At this stage Pironi also looked reasonably settled in fourth place but after only a few more laps the Ferrari developed fuel-feed trouble and quickly started losing ground to Andretti's Alfa Romeo, the American now in fifth place after having caught and passed Cheever's Tyrrell on lap 44. As the problem worsened, being particularly pronounced through the long left hander before the hairpin onto the main straight, so the gap decreased with Andretti finally being able to take full advantage of the situation to move ahead on lap 54. Just a lap later Cheever also forged past the ailing Ferrari, and eventually, after losing yet another place to Tambay's impressive-looking Theodore, Pironi was forced to give up the unequal struggle, pulling off into the pits to retire on lap 67 with the fuel-feed problem causing the turbocharger to overheat. Now only nine cars were left as Jarier had just parked his Talbot 21 out on the circuit with an apparent electrical failure, while earlier Rebaque had spun off after trailing around at the back of the field following a second pit stop. Surer's race was nearly over as well as on lap 71 the Ensign's electrics died and with it went seventh place. After that, though, there were no further changes and eventually the race ran out with Jones cruising home to a comfortable victory ahead of team-mate Reutemann to make it a resounding Williams 1-2.

Results		
1	A. Jones (Williams-Ford)	1 hr 50 min 41.33 sec (140.979 kph/ 87.600 mph)
2	C. Reutemann (Williams-Ford)	1 hr 50 min 50.52 sec
3	N. Piquet (Brabham-Ford)	1 hr 51 min 16.25 sec
4	M. Andretti (Alfa Romeo)	1 hr 51 min 30.64 sec
5	E. Cheever (Tyrrell-Ford)	1 hr 51 min 48.03 sec
6	P. Tambay (Theodore-Ford)	1 lap behind.
7	F. Serra (Fittipaldi-Ford)	2 laps behind
8	R. Arnoux (Renault)	3 laps behind

Fastest lap: A. Jones (Williams-Ford) on lap 31 in 1 min 20.901 sec (144.659 kph/89.887 mph)

Retirements

A. de Cesaris (McLaren-Ford) accident on lap 1, A. Prost (Renault) accident on lap 1, E. de Angelis (Lotus-Ford) accident on lap 13, J. Watson (McLaren-Ford) engine on lap 16, G. Villeneuve (Ferrari) drive-shaft on lap 18, N. Mansell (Lotus-Ford) accident on lap 26, G. Gabbiani (Osella-Ford) accident on lap 27, R. Patrese (Arrows-Ford) fuel feed on lap 33, J. Lammers (ATS-Ford) accident on lap 41, B. Giacomelli (Alfa Romeo) accident on lap 42, J. Laffite (Talbot-Matra) accident on lap 42, K. Rosberg (Fittipaldi-Ford) engine on lap 42, H. Rebaque (Brabham-Ford) spun off on lap 50, J.P. Jarier (Talbot-Matra) electrics on lap 65, D. Pironi (Ferrari) fuel feed on lap 67, M. Surer (Ensign-Ford) electrics on lap 71.

X° Grande Prêmio do Brasil

Rio de Janeiro: March 29
Weather: Wet
Duration: 2 hours (62 laps of 5.031 km circuit = 311.92 km (193.82 miles))

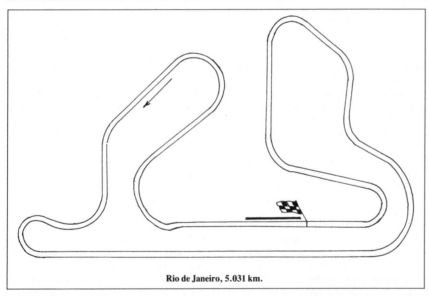

Rio de Janeiro, 5.031 km.

From Long Beach the Grand Prix 'circus' now headed south to the Autodromo Internacional do Rio de Janeiro which, for the first time in three years, was to be the venue for the Brazilian round of the World Championship. Since then, of course, a number of new drivers had arrived on the scene. So to them, in particular, the provision of an unofficial test session on the Wednesday afternoon before the race was most welcome, as indeed it was for Jean-Pierre Jabouille hoping at long last to prove fit enough to take up his place in the Talbot-Matra team. The Frenchman's return, in fact, marked only one of three changes in the line-up from the previous race as former Brabham driver Ricardo Zunino had taken over the rent-a-drive Tyrrell that Kevin Cogan had failed to qualify at Long Beach, while a complete newcomer to Formula 1, Ricardo Londono-

Bridge, had recently bought his way into Mo Nunn's Ensign team. Unfortunately, for this young Colombian driver, though, nothing was to go according to plan. First, after Surer had given the Ensign a brief shake-down to check everything out, he managed only a few slow laps before inadvertently tangling with Rosberg's Fittipaldi. Then, even worse, he subsequently found himself being barred from taking part in official practice when it was discovered that he had failed to obtain the required competition iicence. End of story, except that Surer now had a drive after all! In the meantime, the afternoon was presenting other teams with an ideal opportunity of trying out their latest modifications and, in some quarters, attempting to overcome handling problems caused by the circuit's numerous constant-radius corners. Of particular interest, but surrounded by a lot of controversy, was the reappearance of Piquet's Brabham BT49C fitted with the hydro-pneumatic suspension system, for at speed it was quite obvious to everyone that the gap between the bodywork of the car and the track was considerably less than the mandatory 6 centimetres demanded when it was at a standstill or leaving and arriving in the pits. Even so it was the return of the twin-chassis Lotus 88 that once again attracted most of the attention. However, after the events that had occurred over the past few days during which ACCUS (the United States national motorsporting authority) had upheld Colin Chapman's appeal at Long Beach and stated that the car should not have been excluded from the race there, no-one was saying too much at this stage in spite of FISA having subsequently announced that such a decision only applied in the USA. As a result de Angelis was able to concentrate on trying to iron out an understeer problem with the new car in relative peace and in the hopes of being able to use it for the race.

After a day off for the drivers on Thursday it was back to work in earnest on Friday for the start of official practice. Although lap times had not counted for anything, Reutemann had been quickest during Wednesday's test session and, once qualifying got under way preceded by the usual 90 minutes of untimed practice, it was the Argentinian Williams driver who again established himself as the pace-setter. Even Jones was unable to match his team-mate's times, being consistently around a second slower and complaining of difficulty in balancing his car. The rest were getting nowhere by comparison, with one exception. That was Piquet who, in spite of having to rely on the spare Brabham because of trouble with the fuel system on his regular car, was making really splendid progress for his home Grand Prix. This continued, and eventually the Brazilian stopped the clocks at 1 min 35.786 sec which, although not quick enough to oust

Starting Grid

	N. Piquet (Brabham-Ford) (1 min 35.079 sec)
C. Reutemann Williams-Ford (1 min 35.390 sec)	
	A. Jones Williams-Ford (1 min 36.337 sec)
R. Patrese Arrows-Ford (1 min 36.667 sec)	
	A. Prost Renault (1 min 36.670 sec)
B. Giacomelli Alfa Romeo (1 min 37.283 sec)	
	G. Villeneuve Ferrari (1 min 37.497 sec)
R. Arnoux Renault (1 min 37.561 sec)	
	M. Andretti Alfa Romeo (1 min 37.597 sec)
E. de Angelis Lotus-Ford (1 min 37.734 sec)	
	H. Rebaque Brabham-Ford (1 min 37.777 sec)
K. Rosberg Fittipaldi-Ford (1 min 37.981 sec)	
	N. Mansell Lotus-Ford (1 min 38.003 sec)
E. Cheever Tyrrell-Ford (1 min 38.160 sec)	
	J. Watson McLaren-Ford (1 min 38.263 sec)
J. Laffite Talbot-Matra (1 min 38.273 sec)	
	D. Pironi Ferrari (1 min 38.565 sec)
M. Surer Ensign-Ford (1 min 38.570 sec)	
	P. Tambay Theodore-Ford (1 min 38.726 sec)
A. de Cesaris McLaren-Ford (1 min 38.780 sec)	
	S. Stohr Arrows-Ford (1 min 39.190 sec)
F. Serra Fittipaldi-Ford (1 min 39.326 sec)	
	J.P. Jarier Talbot-Matra (1 min 39.398 sec)
R. Zunino Tyrrell-Ford (1 min 39.798 sec)	

Did not qualify:
J. Lammers (ATS-Ford) 1 min 39.844 sec
J.P. Jabouille (Talbot-Matra) 1 min 40.306 sec
G. Gabbiani (Osella-Ford) 1 min 40.709 sec
M. Guerra (Osella-Ford) 1 min 40.984 sec
E. Salazar (March-Ford) 1 min 43.267 sec
D. Daly (March-Ford) No time.

Reutemann from top spot at 1 min 35.390 sec, was nevertheless more than enough to beat Jones' best time of 1 min 36.337 sec. Predictions that the turbo-charged cars would blow away the opposition on the long straights, meanwhile, were proving to be ill-founded, for neither the Renaults nor the Ferraris were featuring at all strongly. Indeed they would have been completely overshadowed had it not been for Prost squeezing in a lap of 1 min 37.147 sec (fourth fastest time) during the afternoon, a particularly creditable performance as the Frenchman was having an otherwise frustrating day with gearbox and brake problems. Frustrating was also a word that summed up the feelings in the Essex-Lotus camp. Having had the Lotus 88 accepted by the scrutineers

on the previous day, some of their 'colleagues' had since lodged another protest against the legality of the car, and in similar circumstances to those at Long Beach de Angelis had been black-flagged again. Furthermore, having undergone a second examination by the scrutineers during the morning, the car had now had a ban slapped on it for the rest of the weekend on the basis that the bodywork touched the ground, and so for a despairing Colin Chapman the day ended on a particularly unhappy note.

On Saturday Reutemann's hopes of retaining pole position quickly evaporated. Piquet saw to that. Back in his regular Brabham BT49C fitted with the hydro-pneumatic suspension and displaying all the characteristics of a good ground-effect chassis, the Brazilian absolutely delighted the partisan crowd during final qualifying by going on to lap the 5.031 km circuit in an unchallenged 1 min 35.079 sec before light rain started to dampen the track. Reutemann and Jones, meanwhile, both failed to improve on their Friday times for no obvious reason. Even so they were still comfortably second and third fastest as the best anyone else could manage was a lap in 1 min 36.667 sec thanks to another polished performance from Patrese (he had ended the first day fifth fastest despite damaging his car over the kerbs) in the Arrows. Where were the turbo runners? Well once again they were languishing with only Prost, showing a preference to the spare Renault, being able to lap to within even 2 seconds of Piquet's pole-winning time and ultimately winding up with fifth place on the grid at 1 min 36.670 sec. Not that this was altogether surprising as team-mate Arnoux spoiled his chances somewhat by under-steering off into the catch-fences and doing sufficient damage to bring Prost's abandoned race car back into service for the remainder of the weekend. Meanwhile the two Ferrari drivers, both using the KKK turbo-chargers, were suffering from incurable handling problems. To compound their troubles Villeneuve also had the on-board fire extinguisher trigger itself at one point, and Pironi was finding it difficult to acclimatize to the spare chassis that he had been obliged to take over following a similar incident to that of Arnoux during the morning untimed session. The end result was that Pironi qualified a disappointing 17th, while Villeneuve and Arnoux were in seventh and eighth places respectively, sandwiched between the reliable running Alfa Romeos of Giacomelli and Andretti. Among the others, headed by de Angelis' Lotus 81, there had been a late change in the line-up as Jabouille, obviously still in considerable pain from his right leg, had looked unlikely to qualify and stood down in favour of Jarier. Even then, though, there was a danger that only one Talbot-Matra might make the race, as after less than a handful of laps Jarier stopped just beyond

the start/finish line with a broken throttle cable. Then, when he took over Laffite's intended race car which had undergone an engine change following a failure during the morning (this had led to Laffite switching to the team's spare chassis), the fresh unit refused to run properly. However, in the final reckoning it transpired that Jarier had just made it, his best lap of 1 min 39.398 sec being 23rd fastest and having come on the very lap during which the throttle cable had snapped! Right behind the Frenchman, although under somewhat less dramatic circumstances, Zunino had also qualified the second Tyrrell, but less successful were Lammers with the ATS, Gabbiani and Guerra with their Osellas and the two RAM March drivers, Salazar and Daly, the Irishman never having had an opportunity to qualify as his practice had ended on Friday morning when a front wishbone pulled out from the monocoque and caused an accident from which he had been fortunate to escape injury.

After having shown signs of gradually deteriorating throughout practice, the weather took a turn for the worse on race morning with grey skies and rain. As a result the customary 30 minute warm-up session was more hectic than usual, with drivers busy adjusting their cars to suit the changed conditions. In spite of all the activity, though, the only incident to occur was Mansell hitting the barriers, when a rear suspension pick-up point broke away from his gearbox, and doing sufficient damage to the car for him to be left pondering over his prospects of even being in the race. Fortunately, for the young Englishman, the Lotus mechanics were up to the task and completed repairs just in time for their driver to join the other 23 starters on the grid. Piquet, along with Pironi and Stohr, now surprised everyone by opting her slick tyres in the seemingly vain hope that the skies would soon clear.

When the green starting lights went on Piquet was left desperately trying to find traction on the soaking wet track, so it was Reutemann who surged off into the lead with Jones and Patrese vying for second place. Giacomelli also got away well but the two Renaults were both slow off the mark and, worse, were struck from behind causing absolute mayhem as a chain reaction set in. Amazingly no-one was hurt in the ensuing collisions and the majority of the field was able to continue, some drivers taking to the grass verge to avoid trouble. Nevertheless, Andretti, Arnoux and Serra all had to retire their badly bent cars on the spot, and Cheever was left driving his Tyrrell slowly round to the pits where he was to lose several laps having damaged rear suspension components replaced. The marshals, meanwhile, carried out a commendably quick clearing-up exercise so when the leaders eventually came round to complete their opening lap, 23

1981

With final preparations complete, Nelson Piquet (one of just three drivers not to opt for wet-weather tyres) is about to lead the field away on the parade lap prior to the start of the race. *(L.A.T. Photographic)*

unaware of all the drama that had just taken place, it was almost as if nothing had happened. As for the order of the race, it was still Reutemann out in front with Jones having outbraked Patrese half way round the circuit to take up second place. Then, after these first three, it was Giacomelli from de Angelis, Rosberg, Villeneuve, Prost, Surer, Watson, Lafite, de Cesaris, Rebaque and Jarier before Piquet, visibly struggling to keep his Brabham pointing in the right direc-

tion, finally appeared in 15th place ahead of the others.

Reutemann and Jones quickly started to assert themselves at the head of the race, pulling away from Patrese at the rate of around a second per lap. Giacomelli, on the other hand, was dropping away even further. Moreover, the Italian was soon in trouble, for not long after being edged out of fourth place by de Angelis at the end of the long back straight on lap 4 the sole surviving Alfa

Romeo developed a misfire and within another three laps was heading for the first of no less than five pit stops before the cause could finally be traced to a faulty coil. In the meantime, Rosberg gratefully accepted fifth place, and he was now being followed by a monumental scrap involving Villeneuve, Watson, Surer, Prost, Jarier and Laffite. They were really going at it and, although Villeneuve was forced to drop out of the battle on lap 10 for a new nose cone follow-

Even a badly contorted nose cone, resulting from a start-line collision with Alain Prost's Renault, failed to dampen the enthusiasm of Gilles Villeneuve during the early stages of the race. Here he is shown early on the tenth lap, at which point he had just been forced to concede to the Renault and was about to make an inevitable pit stop. *(Autosport)*

ing the start-line shunt in which he'd clobbered Prost's Renault, the remaining five carried on unabashed, Jarier now ahead of Prost and up into an excellent eighth place from the back row of the grid! To add to the excitement they were now also gaining on Rosberg, for the rain had temporarily eased off and the slightly drier track was causing the Fittipaldi to develop understeer tendencies. In fact, by lap 14 Watson was not only right up with the Finn but forcing his way past, while just two laps later Jarier also made it through having already gained yet another place on the previous lap at the expense of Surer. Still Rosberg continued to lose places, Surer going past on lap 18 followed by Prost on lap 20, although for the Frenchman it all became academic on the next lap when, in the process of lapping Pironi, the Ferrari driver suddenly spun as he moved over, slid off into the catch-fences and took the Renault with him. Only minutes later Stohr's Grand Prix debut was ended equally as abruptly by Tambay half spinning his Theodore whilst lapping the Italian and punting the Arrows off the track, this bringing the retirement tally up to seven, as earlier in the race de Cesaris' McLaren had rolled to a halt with dead electrics.

With thirty laps completed the two Williams drivers were still going round as serenely as ever, about 2 seconds apart and enjoying a good half-minute advantage over Patrese running in a lonely third place. A further 20 seconds in arrears, de Angelis was likewise confidently holding down fourth place, but behind him Watson was really

having his work cut out to stay ahead of Surer, Laffite and Jarier, all four remaining tightly bunched up, only with Jarier now at the back of the quartet after having slid wide going into the hairpin on the 29th lap. Exciting though this was, the crowd's attention had now become firmly fixed on Piquet. Aided by the drying track, their local hero was not only still on the same lap as the leaders but making real progress at long last. He'd already overtaken Mansell's Lotus, which was not handling at all well, and was now homing in on Tambay and Rosberg. Soon the tension could be felt all around the circuit, and when he finally caught and passed them both in rapid succession on lap 38 to move up into ninth place the crowd went absolutely wild with delight. Unfortunately for Piquet (and the crowd), though, that was to be the end of his charge as within minutes the rain came on harder with the result that he was struggling for grip all over again, even spinning in full view of the main grandstand at one point, dropping back and cursing himself for the bad choice of tyres. In the meantime, the battle for fifth place had virtually come to an end as on lap 35 Watson had spun onto the grass at the end of the long back straight and dropped to a somewhat distant eighth place, while Surer had finally shaken off the close attention of the two Talbot-Matra drivers. Furthermore, the Swiss now had his sights firmly fixed on de Angelis and, with the Italian beginning to struggle with a collapsed rear shock-absorber, as well as a slow puncture, closed up remorselessly over the next few laps

before eventually taking over fourth spot during lap 49.

On lap 56, with seven more to go, attention became increasingly centred around the Williams pit for a signal 'JONES-REUT' was hung over the pit wall. Eventually, or so everyone thought, Reutemann would slow momentarily and wave his team-leader by – only he didn't. Three more times the signal went out but still Reutmann failed to respond, and as he completed the 62nd lap out came the chequered flat - the two-hour rule had come into effect. It was all over. Another Williams 1–2, but this time in the wrong order! Almost exactly a minute later, Patrese appeared in third place, Surer was fourth with fastest lap to his credit, as well as giving Mo Nunn his best-ever result, and also in the points were de Angelis and an appreciative Laffite. Appreciative because on lap 47, with the damp conditions causing his engine to misfire, he had been repassed by Jarier but unlike Reutemann, who later insisted that he had intended waving Jones past on what he thought was going to be the last lap, his team-mate had responded to a pit signal in the closing stages and dropped back again to finish seventh. Behind Jarier and a lap down, Watson came home in a rather unhappy eighth place, pondering what might have been had he not spun, and he was followed at varying intervals by the remaining seven runners, Rebaque, because of rear suspension trouble, and Villeneuve, because of a turbo failure, having both joined the retirement list at around the half-way mark.

Results						
1	C. Reutemann (Williams-Ford)	2 hr 00 min 23.66 sec (155.450 kph/ 96.592 mph)	7	J.P. Jarier (Talbot-Matra)	2 hr 01 min 53.91 sec	Also running at finish: E. Cheever (Tyrreil-Ford) 13 laps behind, B. Giacomelli (Alfa Romeo) 22 laps behind
2	A. Jones (Williams-Ford)	2 hr 00 min 28.10 sec	8	J. Watson (McLaren-Ford)	1 lap behind	Fastest lap: M. Surer (Ensign-Ford) on lap 36 in 1 min 54.302 sec. (158.453 kph/98.458 mph)
3	R. Patrese (Arrows-Ford)	2 hr 01 min 26.74 sec	9	K. Rosberg (Fittipaldi-Ford)	1 lap behind	
4	M. Surer (Ensign-Ford)	2 hr 01 min 40.69 sec	10	P. Tambay (Theodore-Ford)	1 lap behind	**Retirements** M. Andretti (Alfa Romeo) accident on lap 1, R. Arnoux (Renault) accident on lap 1, F. Serra (Fittipaldi-Ford) accident on lap 1, A. de Cesaris (McLaren-Ford) electrics on lap 10, D. Pironi (Ferrari) accident onlap 20, A. Prost (Renault) accident on lap 21, S. Stohr (Arrows-Ford) accident on lap 21, H. Rebaque (Brabham-Ford) rear suspension on lap 23, G. Villeneuve (Ferrari) turbo-charger on lap 26.
5	E. de Angelis (Lotus-Ford)	2 hr 01 min 50.08 sec	11	N. Mansell (Lotus-Ford)	1 lap behind	
6	J. Laffite (Talbot-Matra)	2 hr 01 min 50.49 sec	12	N. Piquet (Brabham-Ford)	2 laps behind	
			13	R. Zunino (Tyrrell-Ford)	4 laps behind	

XVII° Gran Premio de la Republica Argentina

Buenos Aires: April 12
Weather: Hot
Distance: 53 laps of 5.9682 km
circuit = 316.31 km (196.55 miles)

Pre-race scrutineering – the Lotus 88 is banned again! Nothing new, only on this occasion Colin Chapman had had enough. On the following morning, Friday, he issued a strongly worded statement clearly expressing

his feelings on the matter and, in particular, his view 'what used to be fair competition between sportsmen had degenerated into power struggles and political manoeuvrings between manipulators and money men

attempting to take more out of the sport than they put into it', adding that 'I am now on my way home to watch the progress of the US Space Shuttle to refresh my mind'. Chapman did indeed return home before the race, for the first time in his 22-year-long involvement in Grand Prix racing, but that was to be by no means the end of the saga. On the following day FISA president Jean-Marie Balestre, in spite of being at the race as a

1981

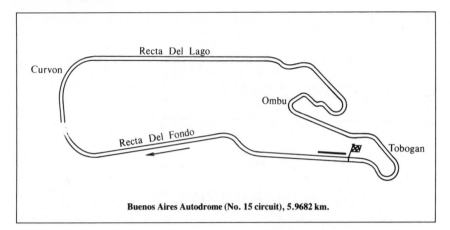

Buenos Aires Autodrome (No. 15 circuit), 5.9682 km.

so-called impartial observer, called a Press conference and announced that the statement amounted to a breach of the Concorde agreement, as well as bringing the World Championship into disrepute, and added that FISA was imposing upon the Essex Team Lotus a fine of US$100,000. He then elaborated on this by referring to a forthcoming FIA court hearing which had been convened to decide the fate of the controversial Lotus 88 following appeals received from the RAC (on behalf of Brabham, Williams and McLaren), FFSA, its French equivalent, (on behalf of Renault and Talbot-Ligier) and the Italian Automobile Club (on behalf of Ferrari, Alfa Romeo and Osella) against the decision of the USA National Court concerning the conformity of the Lotus 88 and he said: 'As and when a high court is convened to examine a case, the parties involved must abstain from any inopportune public intervention and submit themselves with discretion to the authority of the judges. When signing the Concorde agreement, Mr Chapman undertook to respect this. He has just breached this undertaking in a scandalous manner'. End of the episode? No! First there were mutterings from other teams of a race boycott (this, thankfully, never materialized) unless the fine was withdrawn. Then followed a further statement, prepared jointly, from very nearly all of them indicating their concern at the manner in which Balestre had dealt with Chapman's Press Release and the imposition of such a hefty fine – at the time it produced no response, but ten days later the fine was to be revoked!

Incredibly, the presence of M. Balestre also triggered off another row, as on the Friday evening he appeared on local television and said that the Arrows chassis was illegal because its bodywork had failed a 6 centimetre ground clearance test earlier in the day. True, Patrese's Arrows had, as had de Angelis' Lotus 81 and Pironi's Ferrari for that matter, but a protest from Jack Oliver that the 6 centimetre block of wood used in random checks had not been level had since been upheld and the original claim that all three cars were illegal withdrawn by the

organizers. Out went another statement – 'Team Ragno Arrows reserves the right to request the executive committee of FISA for its authorization to take legal proceedings against the president of FISA, Jean-Marie Balestre, in response to his false and slanderous accusations'. Yes, the entire situation was becoming ludicrous, and just to add to the discontent Frank Williams managed to upset Gordon Murray by lodging an unsuccessful protest about the legality of the Brabham with its hydro-pneumatic suspension, even though he had more or less admitted in Brazil that the car was legal!

With so much off-track activity the real purpose of the weekend almost seemed to be superfluous. To Colin Chapman, and possibly one or two others, it probably was, but for all that it was business as usual out on the track. Since Brazil, Gordon Murray had been busy perfecting the Brabham hydropneumatic suspension system as excessive wheel movement had been causing the underneath of the car's side-pods to scrape the ground, while one or two other shortcomings had also shown up. All these problems had now been rectified, or so it was hoped, and certainly once the official timekeepers took up duty on Friday afternoon there was obviously little wrong with the car for Piquet was soon out setting a blistering pace on the recently resurfaced track and in a class of his own. In fact, there seemed little doubt that it was this that eventually led to the protest from Frank Williams later in the day as neither of his drivers could approach the Brazilian's ultimate time of 1 min 42.665 sec, let alone beat it, Reutemann turning in 1 min 43.935 sec before an engine failure put paid to his activities towards the end of the session and Jones, complaining of a down-on-power engine, managing no better than 1 min 44.662 sec. Not that it was either of the two Williams drivers who came closest to Piquet. That honour went to Prost who made a few people sit up and take note by pushing his Renault around in 1 min 42.981 sec. Arnoux, in the same chassis that he had used in Rio, only now rebuilt around a new mono-

coque, was also well up the time sheets with fourth fastest time of 1 min 43.997 sec which suggested that the French turbo-charged cars were ideally suited to this fast circuit. On paper, at least, the same should have applied to the Ferraris, running with KKK turbo-chargers again following drive-belt problems with the Comprex system during unofficial testing on Thursday. But whilst there was definitely no question of any power deficiency, both Villeneuve and Pironi were experiencing severe handling problems through the turns. Consequently, this was being reflected in their lap times and, although the French-Canadian ended up a very respectable fifth fastest (1 min 44.236 sec), he looked to be on the brink of disaster more often than not in his gallant efforts to be up amongst the front-runners. Pironi, on the other hand, failed to break the 1 min 45 sec barrier and was five places lower behind Jones, Rebaque's Brabham (now also fitted with hydro-pneumatic suspension and with a Hewland gearbox rather than the Weismann unit), Patrese's Arrows and Watson's new McLaren MP4 which, despite having just arrived back from extensive testing in England, was plagued by poor handling – it was subsequently found that the car had been fitted with a faulty shock-absorber!

Although conditions for final qualifying were still dry, heavy overnight rain, which had persisted throughout much of the morning, had washed away the rubber resulting in the track being slower. Certainly there was no hint of anyone approaching Piquet's Friday time and, indeed, while he spent the afternoon running on full tanks, only two of the first six drivers on Friday managed to make any improvement at all. They were Jones, who went on to head the day's time sheets by achieving a lap in 1 min 43.638 sec during the closing minutes of practice, moving up to third spot on the grid in the process, and Villeneuve, who turned in a 1 min 44.132 sec lap after more heroics in the Ferrari that included several trips onto the grass as well as blowing up two V6 engines in successive days! However, in spite of the French-Canadian's efforts, he still failed even to hold his grid position, for apart from being overtaken by Jones he also lost a place to Rebaque, emphasizing the effectiveness of the Brabham hydro-pneumatic suspension by posting the afternoon's fifth fastest time (Prost, Arnoux and Reutemann were the others to lap quicker than the Mexican) of 1 min 44.100 sec – sixth fastest overall. Rosberg only just failed to 'jump' the Ferrari driver as well, for despite being hampered by brake problems and indifferent handling with the unsponsored Fittipaldi, the Finn came out a mere 0.059 sec slower at 1 min 44.191 sec. The rest, meanwhile, were nowhere by comparison. Even Patrese, who had qualified so well for the first two races, was out of the picture, troubled by an engine that refused to pull at peak revs and, like so many others, unable to find any extra speed. The Alfa Romeos of Andretti and Giacomelli were not showing anywhere near their recent form either, with both drivers finishing well down in the slower half of the grid complaining of down-on-power engines, later to be blamed on a duff batch of ignition coils, and inferior handling. Meanwhile the situation within the Talbot-Ligier team was little short of desperate. For a start, a new set of variable rate double springing tested by Guy Ligier in France had turned out to be too soft and caused a row between him and team manager Gerard Ducarouge, and then it had proved impossible to persuade the Matra engines to run on twelve cylinders for

Jean-Pierre Jabouille, who failed in his quest to qualify the second Talbot-Matra. (*Autosport*)

any length of time. Consequently, with the handling of the Talbots also leaving much to be desired, it was little surprise to find Laffite qualifying in only 21st place, and the second car, entrusted solely to Jabouille for there was no sign of Jarier, not even qualifying, the lanky Frenchman (still not 100% fit) joining the two Osella and the two RAM March drivers who also failed to go quick enough to join the 24-car grid.

Throughout practice, and even before, the motor racing fraternity in Argentina had been giving vent to their feelings about the politics within the Williams team following Brazil and, in particular, showing antagonism towards Jones – their hero, after all, was Reutemann, and for them this was to be HIS weekend! The Australian, though, was taking it all in his stride, and when someone

from the grandstand opposite the pits had produced a home-made pit board on Saturday showing 'REUT-JONES' he and Frank Williams had immediately responded by holding up their own pit boards showing 'JONES-REUT'. Naturally, this had nearly caused a riot and probably would have done had Reutemann not held up another board indicating 'REUT-JONES', for this had quickly turned the jeers into cheers and chants of 'Lole – Lole – Lole'. As it was, this little incident led to scores of more 'REUT-JONES' boards appearing from the massive crowd on race day, and at one point during the morning Frank Williams persuaded several of the teams to simultaneously hold up 'JONES-REUT' boards in response. Again there was a near riot but, at the same time, the crowd seemed to be really enjoying it all,

The start of the race with Alan Jones already drawing alongside the Brabham of pole-sitter and eventual winner Nelson Piquet. (*Autosport*)

especially when some of the teams subsequently changed their boards to read 'REUT-JONES'. Meanwhile, amidst all the joviality, the Williams team ran into a late problem. During an otherwise uneventful warm-up session, except for Villeneuve and Mansell both having harmless spins, Jones returned to the pits perturbed that his engine wasn't as it should be. There wasn't time to even consider an engine change, so when Jones later took up his place on the starting grid, amidst more jeers from the crowd, he could only hope that a cure had been effected by his mechanics who had gone over the fuel-injection system.

When the start came all the indications were that the Williams' problems had been cured, for Jones got off the line brilliantly and was away into the lead. Nevertheless Piquet, not faced with a tyre choice for this race as conditions were hot and dry, quickly restored the status-quo by driving around the outside of the green and white car on the way out of the long right-hander at the end of the straight, and from there went on to complete the first lap unchallenged. Behind Jones, Reutemann ('Lole') had slotted into third place, while Patrese had charged through to an excellent fourth ahead of Arnoux and Prost in their Renaults and also Rebaque in the number 2 Brabham. Villeneuve, on the other hand, had already thrown away his hard-earned grid position by overdoing things half-way round the lap and dropping virtually to the back of the field in company with de Cesaris, who had been forced onto the grass in his efforts to avoid the Ferrari, and spun. Further back still, Cheever had gone one better. He had 'cooked' his clutch on the line and was now destined to become the first retirement, although this went largely unnoticed as by the time that he had pulled off the track after completing one slow lap Reutemann had sent the crowd wild by overtaking Jones for second place, the Australian discovering to his dismay that his engine was still not reaching peak revs. To add to the excitement a number of other places throughout the field were also changing hands and up amongst the leaders, on the same lap, Prost and Rebaque both elbowed

their way past Arnoux. Only a lap later they were at it again, dishing out the same treatment to Patrese, and immediately setting their sights on Jones' Williams. This was all fast and furious stuff, and more than some engines could obviously cope with, for both Pironi and Mansell ended their third laps by turning off into the pits trailing ominous-looking clouds of blue smoke, while next time round they were joined by Rosberg when the fuel pump belt broke on the Fittipaldi.

By lap 10 Piquet had pulled out an almost incredible 15 second advantage over Reutemann and was looking totally invincible. Prost was now third with Rebaque barking at his heels, the pair of them having quickly dispensed with Jones who, in turn, was now having to keep a watchful eye on Arnoux, and also Watson going particularly well in the new McLaren. Patrese, meanwhile, had slipped back to eighth place with a front-end vibration but, nevertheless, was staying clear of a good scrap raging between Andretti and Tambay in spite of the Alfa Romeo misfiring at the top end of the rev band, as well as handling poorly, and the Theodore frequently belching out puffs of blue smoke from its engine. For all that, the crowd's attention was staying firmly fixed on Reutemann's progress. With Piquet running away at nearly 2 seconds per lap the situation was already auguring none too well for them, but when Rebaque went past Prost under braking on the eleventh lap and immediately started visibly gaining on their beloved 'Lole' it was looking decidedly worse. Indeed, within just four more laps, the few remaining cheers turned to groans for the Mexican, underlining the supremacy of the Brabham's ingenious suspension system, had not only moved right up onto the tail of their hero but was pulling out of the Williams' slipstream along the straight and blasting past. Moreover, Rebaque quickly established himself in second place and so, with Piquet now leading the race by some 25 seconds, the two blue and white cars were soon totally dominating proceedings. For the time being, at least, the other leading positions also looked settled at this stage for Prost was making no noticeable

impression on Reutemann but, equally, was still lapping quickly enough to remain clear of Jones and Arnoux even though he was being bothered by a front tyre vibration and a gearbox problem. Further back, meanwhile, de Angelis was carving his way up through the field following a spin on the third lap, making even better progress than Villeneuve, but for Surer the race had turned sour, as on lap 15 the Ensign had gone out with a major engine failure. Laffite was now about to retire the lone Talbot-Matra as well, due to chronic understeer and front-end vibrations, while a pit stop at the end of lap 13 to change his rear aerofoil in an attempt to improve the handling of the ATS had left Lammers bringing up the rear and caused another frown from team owner Gunther Schmidt – at one point during practice Lammers had wanted to swop to a smaller front wing and in a heated argument Schmidt had bent it completely out of shape!

Although Serra disappeared from the fray with a seized gearbox on lap 28, the next really significant occurrence came on lap 33. By then a Brabham 1-2 victory seemed a certainty, but suddenly Rebaque slowed dramatically and pulled onto the grass verge – the rotor arm in his distributor had broken and he was out of the race. Not surprisingly, the crowd responded by going wild again, for Reutemann was now automatically promoted to second place and, of course, if one Brabham could fail so could another! But their hopes were to be in vain as Piquet continued to circulate with almost monotonous regularity to comfortably lead a race that had degenerated into little more than a high-speed procession, the Brazilian eventually easing right off in the closing stages yet still winning by a margin of very nearly half a minute to round off a near-perfect weekend. Only 'near perfect' because during Friday's practice he had had the fright of his life when some carbon-fibre brakes fitted to the spare Brabham had failed at the hairpin and brought him to within inches of running over a photographer! Meanwhile, behind the jubilant Piquet, Reutemann's second place still produced a rapturous reception from the crowd, and they at least had the consolation

Results					
1	N. Piquet (Brabham-Ford)	1 hr 34 min 32.74 sec (200.737 kph/ 124.732 mph)	7	R. Patrese (Arrows-Ford)	1 lap behind
2	C. Reutemann (Williams-Ford)	1 hr 34 min 59.35 sec	8	M. Andretti (Alfa Romeo)	1 lap behind
3	A. Prost (Renault)	1 hr 35 min 22.72 sec	9	S. Stohr (Arrows-Ford)	1 lap behind
4	A. Jones (Williams-Ford)	1 hr 35 min 40.62 sec	*10	B. Giacomelli (Alfa Romeo)	2 laps behind
5	R. Arnoux (Renault)	1 hr 36 min 04.59 sec	11	A. de Cesaris (McLaren-Ford)	2 laps behind
6	E. de Angelis (Lotus-Ford)	1 lap behind	12	J. Lammers (ATS-Ford)	2 laps behind
			13	R. Zunino (Tyrrell-Ford)	2 laps behind
			*Not running at finish		

Fastest lap: N. Piquet (Brabham Ford) on lap 6 in 1 min 45.287 sec (204.066 kph/126.800 mph)

Retirements
E. Cheever (Tyrrell-Ford) clutch on lap 2, D. Pironi (Ferrari) engine on lap 3, N. Mansell (Lotus-Ford) engine on lap 3, K. Rosberg (Fittipaldi-Ford) fuel pump belt on lap 4, M. Surer (Ensign-Ford) engine on lap 15, J. Laffite (Talbot-Matra) front-end vibration/handling on lap 19, F. Serra (Fittipaldi-Ford) gearbox on lap 28, H. Rebaque (Brabham-Ford) ignition on lap 33, J. Watson (McLaren-Ford) crownwheel and pinion on lap 36, P. Tambay (Theodore-Ford) engine on lap 37, G. Villeneuve (Ferrari) drive-shaft on lap 41.

of knowing that he now led the World Championship; Prost was third, while Jones and Arnoux completed the short list of finishers to cover the full distance, the diminutive Frenchman crossing the line with a flat-spotted front tyre after a vain attempt to overtake the Williams earlier in the race, and also a bent front wing, causing understeer, after later having been hit by a bird! Only seven others were still there at the finish as Watson, looking all set for a finish in the points, had been forced to retire at the end of lap 36 with a broken crown-wheel and pinion, a lap later Tambay had pulled off the track with no oil left in his engine, on lap 41 Villeneuve had spun a second time and been forced out with a broken drive-shaft, and, just over a lap from home, Giacomelli had run out of fuel. Andretti, ending his race with a broken exhaust to add to his other troubles, only just made it as well, for his Alfa Romeo ran out of fuel as it crossed the line. As it was, the American finished in a somewhat frustrating eighth place behind de Angelis and Patrese who had swopped places in the closing stages after the Arrows driver had been forced to ease up with a sticking throttle.

That should have been the end of it. However, after the race it was announced that Zunino had been penalized one minute because of having taken a short cut back onto the track following a spin which meant that the Argentinian automatically lost two places in the final classification. Then, wait for it, there was yet another protest about the legality of the Brabhams, this time from the Renault team. Again it was rejected and so the final results stood.

1° Gran Premio di San Marino

Imola: May 3
Weather: Showery
Distance: 60 laps of 5.040 km
circuit = 302.40 km (187.90 miles)

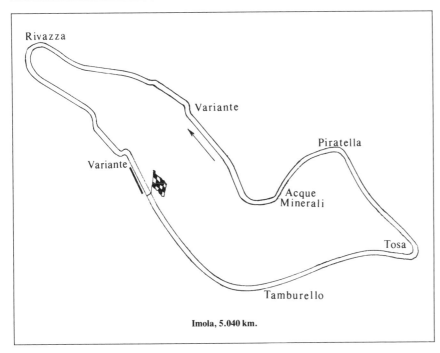

Imola, 5.040 km.

Although this was to be the first San Marino Grand Prix, the Imola circuit had already been used the previous year to host the Italian Grand Prix as a one-off affair. Indeed, it had been the success of that race that had spurred the Italians into obtaining permission to hold this event, cleverly circumnavigating the International rules about distances between circuits in the same country by involving the Automobile Club of San Marino and naming the race after the nearby Principality which had no racing circuit of its own.

Unfortunately, the weekend got off to just about the worst possible start. Already the Essex-Lotus team had withdrawn their entries following a decision from the FIA International Court of Appeal to uphold the appeals lodged by the RAC, FFSA and ACI, as this had effectively banned the Lotus 88 and Colin Chapman no longer considered the 81s to be competitive. Then, on Friday morning, there was talk of other teams also boycotting the race following some quite remarkable scenes in pre-race scrutineering on the day before – every car had been disqualified except the Renaults, Talbots and the new Tolemans! Basically, the scrutineers had applied the letter of the Law as regards moveable aerodynamic devices, and had thrown out flexible skirts attached to the lower edges of side-pods, plastic or rubber 'seals' used between the bodywork and rear wheels, and also any flexible extensions attached to the bottom of end-plates on nose fins. They had also expressed concern over the Brabham's hydro-pneumatic suspension system as well as similar systems which had now been adopted by Williams, Tyrrell, Arrows, Fittipaldi and Osella, and declared that they would only be considered legal provided that the 6 centimetre ground clearance was maintained. The result of all of this was that only half a dozen team owners allowed their drivers to participate in Friday's opening practice session, after having complied with the scrutineers' demands, as the rest went off to attend a hastily-convened FOCA meeting to discuss the situation even though some of them, notably Williams, had also brought their cars into line and were more interested in getting on with the job in hand. Eventually, a compromise was reached whereby the 'trick' suspensions could remain provided that the 6 centimetre ground clearance was met, but flexible skirts had to be discarded or replaced by a rigid variety. By that time, however, the opening practice session had ended and so, to accommodate everyone, an extra session was arranged for the early afternoon and the start of the first period of qualifying delayed until 4.30 p.m.

During the extra practice session five judges were positioned at various vantage points around the circuit to check that cars were not touching the track with their bodywork. This proved to be a futile exercise as it was soon discovered that they all were at one point or another and so the idea was scuppered. In its place, the organizers then announced that ground clearance checks would be made on every car as they left the pits to begin the first hour of qualifying and again on each occasion that they returned to the pits, using level pads at each end of the pit lane and 6 centimetre blocks. Of course, that didn't work out too well either! It took so long to check each car in turn before they were allowed out onto the circuit that drivers near the back of the queue that had formed had to wait around for the best part of 15 minutes, causing frustration and a detrimental effect on engine temperatures. To add to the problem, one or two other drivers who had been near the front of the queue then returned to the pit lane after completing a few laps and found the entrance to their pit blocked by the still-uncleared queue. Consequently, tempers became even more frayed and the entire episode not only reached farcical proportions, but made a complete mockery of Grand Prix racing being what was supposed to be the very pinnacle of motor sport. Meanwhile, for the long-suffering spectators, who were far from keeping their feelings to themselves, there was at least something to cheer about eventually – one of their beloved Ferraris, that of Villeneuve, was logging the fastest times. The French-Canadian was actually out in a brand new chassis with a 15 centimetre aluminium spacer inserted between its engine and gearbox to increase the length of the wheelbase, thereby moving the centre of gravity further forward, and using it to such good effect that within less than a handful of laps he had gone around the slightly modified circuit – the Acqua Minerali 'chicane' had been eased since the previous year – in just 1 min 35.576 sec (189.838 kph). Even so, he

was not entirely having things all his own way for Prost and Arnoux were also lapping very impressively in their turbo-charged Renaults, as was Reutemann showing best among the normally-aspirated brigade in his Williams. Furthermore, Villeneuve's efforts were to be curtailed shortly after recording his best time for his engine let go and, although he quickly reverted to the spare Ferrari, in normal wheelbase configuration, any hopes of going even faster were quickly dashed by a broken turbo, something that seemed to confirm the view that the Italian team were turning up the boost pressure too high as during the morning Pironi had suffered a similar failure. Whatever, it proved critical, as by the end of the afternoon Villeneuve had been bumped off the provisional pole by Arnoux who had gone on to record a superior time of 1 min 35.281 sec. Prost had nearly squeezed ahead as well, achieving 1 min 35.579 sec, while Reutemann had peaked at 1 min 35.844 sec to end up fourth fastest ahead of Pironi (1 min 36.168 sec) in the second Ferrari. Apart from Jones, no-one else had even lapped below 1 min 37 sec, not even Piquet who had been plagued with poor handling with his Brabham following the ban on flexible skirts, and was down in eighth place on the time sheets behind Patrese.

Thankfully, Saturday's practice was allowed to proceed largely unimpeded by officialdom, and everything ran to schedule, a 90 minute untimed session taking place in the morning followed by the final hour of qualifying in the afternoon. Of course, it was the afternoon session that really mattered and it was now that Villeneuve, showing a preference for the spare Ferrari, set the place alight by reeling off a succession of laps that no-one else could even approach let alone beat, his best coming out at 1 min 34.523 sec. After that the French-Canadian casually sat out the remainder of practice to watch the others, and was later joined by Reutemann after another outstanding performance in the Williams had netted the Argentinian second fastest time of 1 min 35.229 sec, a spectacular, yet harmless, spin at the pits chicane underlining just how hard he had been trying. The two Renault drivers, meanwhile, had both run into trouble and were in no position to improve on their Friday times which, in the event, left them sharing the second row of the grid. Arnoux was unable to persuade the engine in his car to run on more than five cylinders, while Prost was in an even worse plight and reduced to the involuntary role of spectator for nearly the entire afternoon when the engines in both his race car and the team's spare chassis lost their boost pressure. Jones, too, was unable to improve on his Friday time due to gearbox trouble and later, when this had been put right, by being held up in traffic. As a result, the Australian found

himself being elbowed back from a provisional sixth place on the grid to an unfamiliar eighth, as by the end of the afternoon Piquet had come to terms with his Brabham and brought his lap times down to 1 min 35.733 sec, pipping Pironi for fifth place on the grid in the process, and Watson had taken the earlier of two new McLaren MP4s on hand around in a very creditable seventh fastest time overall of 1 min 36.241 sec. Patrese was next and somewhat disappointed not to have finished higher as his Arrows had been rebuilt around a new monocoque, and modified to accommodate one of the latest Ford-Cosworth engines, as well as a hydropneumatic suspension system. However, like other teams trying the 'trick' suspension, the furore in scrutineering and subsequent events on Friday had caused confusion as to whether it would be allowed, and just to add to his problems he had been forced to sit out the first half of final qualifying waiting for further changes to be made to his car – the officials had not been satisfied with the revised skirt material being used and demanded something more rigid again! After Patrese, only three other drivers had still managed to lap the 5.040 km circuit in under 1 min 37 sec. These were Laffite, who had hoisted the quicker of the two Talbot-Matras up to tenth place, and both Giacomelli and Andretti in their Alfa Romeos. In the meantime, there were one or two surprises among the rest. For a start, Italian Michele Alboreto, having secured a drive in the second Tyrrell with one-off sponsorship from Imola Co-op Ceramica, had not only qualified for a Grand Prix at his first attempt in a very respectable seventeenth place but he had also out-qualified his rather more experienced team-mate, Cheever. In the ATS team, too, much the same applied for having obtained financial backing from a group of businessmen associated with the Swedish pop group ABBA, Slim Borgudd had been entered in a second car and he had also qualified at his first attempt, albeit in last place on the 24-car grid. A somewhat dejected and embarrassed Lammers, on the other hand, had failed to make the cut and found himself in the company of Stohr, Daly, Serra and the two Toleman drivers, Henton and Warwick, both of whom were way off the pace all weekend thanks mainly to installation problems with their turbo-charged Hart engines.

After warm and sunny conditions throughout practice, the weather took a dramatic turn on Saturday night, with violent thunderstorms, and on Sunday morning everything was still thoroughly wet and miserable. Consequently, with the rain continuing, the morning warm-up session saw some really feverish activity with cars being adjusted to wet settings and the like, but even so everything seemed to be going well, with the only detrimental incident to occur being de Cesa-

A cheerful sight for the dampened spectators at Imola as the Ferrari 126Cs of Gilles Villeneuve and Didier Pironi lead the field on the opening lap. *(Phipps Photographic)*

ris spinning off and bending the nose cone of his McLaren M29F. Overnight the Ferrari team had been busy converting their cars back to standard wheelbase form (Pironi's car had also appeared in long wheelbase configuration on Saturday), as well as installing new engines with the boost pressure significantly turned down, and it was noticeable that only Brabham, Fittipaldi and Talbot-Ligier were still using their 'trick' suspensions.

The rain had stopped by the time that the cars were leaving the pits in readiness for the start of the race in the afternoon and it seemed possible that the weather would continue to improve. Not unnaturally, this caused a certain amount of indecision over choice of tyres even though the track was still very wet. After his mistake in Brazil, however, Piquet was certainly not prepared to take another gamble, and nor were many others, come to that, as when they all set off on the pace lap only Rosberg, Tambay and Surer had discarded their wet-weather covers for slicks. Round they went, with Villeneuve being given a rapturous reception in the leading Ferrari, and then all attention became fixed on the starting lights. Seconds later red had quickly (very quickly!) given way to green and the first Grand Prix of San Marino was on. Up front, Reutemann was first to show, but as the field streamed into the first long left-hander Villeneuve took over control, while Pironi, who had still been rolling into his grid position when the green lights went on, took only until the next corner to elbow the Williams back to third place. Jones, after a meteoric start from the fourth row, also tried to overtake Reutemann by diving through on the inside at the same corner but, with his team-mate holding

the racing line, failed to make it and instead finished up with a bent nose fin as the two cars made contact! Further down the field there was an even greater commotion there moments later when Guerra's Osella suddenly slid wide and was promptly shoved off the track and into the guard-rail by Salazar's March. The March driver was able to continue, albeit with a bent nose fin, but the Argentinian's Grand Prix debut was over already and, worse, he was soon to be on his way to hospital with a broken ankle. The rest, meanwhile, went on to complete the opening lap unhindered, the grandstands erupting as the Ferraris of Villeneuve and Pironi roared past in first and second places. Reutemann was still third and then came Jones, Patrese, Arnoux, Watson, Laffite and the two Brabhams of Piquet and Rebaque followed by the rest, Prost bringing up the rear after gearbox trouble had forced him to start the race in second gear.

There was no change in the order of the first three at the end of the second lap with Villeneuve and Pironi still confidently holding off Reutemann and, if anything, easing away a little. In fourth place, however, it was now Patrese as Jones was in all kinds of trouble with his ill-handling Williams following the contretemps with his team-mate, and after persevering for one more lap, losing yet more places, he dived into the pits for a new nose cone. Whilst there, the World Champion also changed to slick tyres as the track was already becoming drier, but when he subsequently charged back out into the race he had lost over a lap on the leaders and was even further back than Prost who was about to retire in any case with the loss of more gears. By this time the second Williams was also giving trouble – it had developed a

severe vibration, later believed to have been caused by the wet-weather Michelins moving on their rims. Whatever, on lap 6 Reutemann went straight on across the grass at the last chicane, and although he quickly regained the track it was still too late to prevent Patrese from going through and taking over the pursuit of the two Ferraris. Back in fifth place, meanwhile, Arnoux had also had a busy moment on the previous lap at exactly the same spot when Watson had tried to dive through on his inside under braking and ended up running into the back of him. It was the McLaren, though, that had come off worst, having had its front wing torn off, and this was now about to bring Watson into the pits for a replacement. The incident had also promoted Laffite to sixth place and now he, too, was looking for a way round the Renault. On lap 7 he thought that he had found one but, like Watson, failed to make it and, instead, put himself out of the race with bent front suspension and extensive front bodywork damage. Arnoux was not so fortunate on this occasion either, for quite apart from losing his place to Piquet, the Renault now had a bent front wheel and a broken exhaust pipe with the result that two laps later he was forced to give way to Rebaque in the second Brabham.

The Ferrari demonstration run finally came to an end after fourteen laps when Villeneuve suddenly peeled off into the pits and changed his wet-weather tyres for slicks. Unfortunately this was to prove a tactical error for no sooner had the French-Canadian rejoined the race than down came the rain. Consequently, he was obliged to stop again two laps later, this time screaming for wet-weather covers, but by then he had lost the best part of a lap and was way down in 14th place. The rain also brought Watson (he had changed to slicks during his pit stop), Jones, Tambay and Surer into the pits for wet-weather tyres over the next few minutes, but Rosberg didn't need any as on lap 15 the engine in the Finn's Avon-shod Fittipaldi had blown up and he was already out of the race. In the meantime, more and more attention was being paid to Piquet's progress as he had caught and passed Reutemann on lap 15 and was now in third place hammering after Patrese's Arrows. It wasn't to take him long to catch the Italian either, whistling past on lap 22 and, much to the consternation of the crowd, immediately setting about wiping out the 10 second deficit to Pironi. As this continued, with the gap gradually diminishing, Andretti quietly disappeared from mid-field on lap 27 with gearbox trouble with his Alfa Romeo, and this was followed, only moments later, by a somewhat controversial incident involving his team-mate, Giacomelli. The Italian, in fact, had already just had a brush with de Cesaris in a desperate, though unsuccessful, attempt to keep him at bay and now, on lap 29, he adopted much the same ploy on Cheever when he pulled his Tyrrell alongside. However, this time round Giacomelli appeared to deliberately move right over on his adversary, made quite violent contact, and in the next instant both cars were careering off the track into retirement. More trouble quickly followed. On lap

32 Gabbiani decided that he had been following Alboreto long enough and tried to run through on the inside of the Tyrrell at Tosa. But there just wasn't the room and there was another collision and yet two more retirements! Naturally, with all this drama occurring in front of him, Villeneuve was rapidly climbing up the lap charts once more. In fact, the French-Canadian now took over the eighth spot from which Alboreto had just been forcibly ejected, and was obviously determined to improve still further, flinging his Ferrari around with all of his usual bravado, and setting one fastest lap after another as he gave chase to Arnoux and de Cesaris who had just swopped places. His team-mate, in the other Ferrari, meanwhile, was not enjoying the same benefit of comparatively fresh rubber and was beginning to struggle for grip, which was not being helped at all by a broken skirt. Of course, only Pironi knew of his problems but what was noticeable was that even Tambay, whom Pironi had earlier lapped, was staying right up with the leading Ferrari and, more to the point, Piquet was now in a position to start mounting a serious challenge.

On lap 45 Villeneuve's stirring drive was rewarded with another place when he caught and passed Arnoux. However, the joy that this brought to the crowd was eradicated only two laps later when Pironi's gallant efforts to stay out in front, making the most

of the turbo power to compensate for the deteriorating handling of the Ferrari, were finally ended by Piquet squeezing past under braking for the last chicane. That settled it, for once in the lead Piquet quickly pulled away and from there went on to score his second Grand Prix victory on the trot unchallenged. For the Ferrari team (and the crowd), meanwhile, things went from bad to worse in the closing stages. First Pironi had to virtually sit and watch as Patrese, Reutemann and Rebaque all took turns to relegate him to an eventual fifth place as his car's handling worsened along with its worn rear tyres. Then Villeneuve, after moving up into a points-winning position by overtaking de Cesaris on lap 49, suddenly slowed dramatically on the penultimate lap with a slipping clutch and had to undergo the frustrating experience of being repassed by the Italian McLaren driver to finish out of the points in seventh place. Behind the French-Canadian, Arnoux soldiered on to come home in eighth place, gearbox trouble adding to his other problems. Surer was ninth and Watson was tenth after managing to scramble past Tambay's Theodore on the very last lap. Jones, Borgudd and Jabouille were also still there at the finish, although the Frenchman was too far behind to be classified after a race punctuated by numerous pit stops because of fuel-feed and handling problems with his Talbot-Matra.

Results

1	N. Piquet (Brabham-Ford)	1 hr 51 min 23.97 sec (162.873 kph/ 101.204 mph)	7	G. Villeneuve (Ferrari)	1 hr 53 min 05.94 sec		
2	R. Patrese (Arrows-Ford)	1 hr 51 min 28.55 sec	8	R. Arnoux (Renault)	1 lap behind		
			9	M. Surer (Ensign-Ford)	1 lap behind		
3	C. Reutemann (Williams-Ford)	1 hr 51 min 30.31 sec	10	J. Watson (McLaren-Ford)	2 laps behind		
4	H. Rebaque (Brabham-Ford)	1 hr 51 min 46.86 sec	11	P. Tambay (Theodore-Ford)	2 laps behind		
5	D. Pironi (Ferrari)	1 hr 51 min 49.84 sec	12	A. Jones (Williams-Ford)	2 laps behind		
6	A. de Cesaris (McLaren-Ford)	1 hr 52 min 30.58 sec	13	S. Borgudd (ATS-Ford)	3 laps behind		

Also running at finish: J.P. Jabouille (Talbot-Matra) 15 laps behind.

Fastest lap: G. Villeneuve (Ferrari) on lap 46 in 1 min 48.064 sec (167.900 kph/104.328 mph)

Retirements
M. Guerra (Osella-Ford) accident on lap 1, A. Prost (Renault) gearbox on lap 4, J. Laffite (Talbot-Matra) front suspension on lap 7, K. Rosberg (Fittipaldi-Ford) engine on lap 15, M. Andretti (Alfa Romeo) gearbox on lap 27, E. Cheever (Tyrrell-Ford) accident onlap 29, B. Giacomelli (Alfa Romeo) accident on lap 29, G. Gabbiani (Osella-Ford) accident on lap 32, M. Alboreto (Tyrrell-Ford) accident on lap 32, E. Salazar (March-Ford) engine on lap 39.

XXXIX Grote Prijs van Belgie

Zolder: May 17
Weather: Changeable
Distance: 54 laps of 4.262 km
circuit = 230.15 km (143.01 miles)

After the excellent race at Imola it was now time to move on to Zolder for the Belgian Grand Prix. Here there was to be an immediate problem as under the terms of the Concorde Agreement only thirty cars could be accepted for qualifying (two each from Ferrari, Renault, Talbot-Ligier, Alfa Romeo, Osella and Toleman and a further eighteen from FOCA), whereas there were thirty-two drivers entered for the race, the

same thirty as at Imola except for Italian Piercarlo Ghinzani standing in for the injured Miguel Angel Guerra, plus Elio de Angelis and Nigel Mansell marking the return of the Essex Lotus team to the fold. To reduce the number, ATS were pressurized into withdrawing one of their two entries, which led to Jan Lammers being asked to stand down by team owner Gunther Schmidt, and also 'opted out' was Theodore

on the grounds of being the last team to enter the Championship. Naturally, this meant that Patrick Tambay also had no role to play which seemed particularly unfair after his recent performances, and any hopes of a reprieve when other teams indicated their willingness for him to take part in practice were dashed by Ferrari's Marco Piccinini insisting that the Concorde Agreement should be properly implemented.

In many ways Piccinini's actions were ironic as Ferrari, in common with very nearly every team, were now paying a blatant disregard to the regulations in another respect. Only days earlier FISA had issued a state-

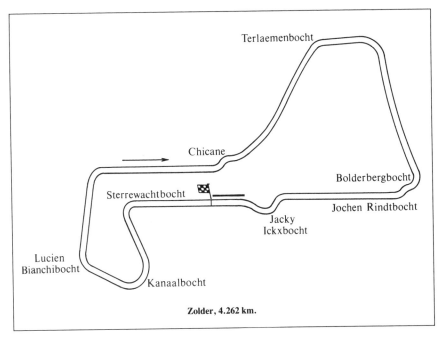

Zolder, 4.262 km.

ment indicating its acceptance of hydraulic, pneumatic and similar springing systems, and also skirts provided that they were of a solid nature but, at the same time, it had included the words: 'No ride height adjusting device should allow the car in its lowest position to have a ground clearance of less than 6 centimetres.' In other words it meant that the 6 centimetre ground clearance was an absolute minimum that had to be maintained at all times. The vast majority of the teams, though, were ignoring this part of the statement and instead were using all manner of means to operate their cars at much lower levels of ground clearance once they were out on the track, some even using locking devices to achieve this. Meanwhile, another aspect of the rules being abused, although not actually being broken, was the use of rubber skirts in some quarters. Rubber, it was argued, was a solid material even though it was quite obvious to everyone that FISA had made an unfortunate choice of words and really meant rigid!

When the business of qualifying commenced on Friday afternoon the race officials set aside an area at the entrance to the pit lane in which to carry out ground clearance checks. They were seemingly prepared to turn a blind eye to how suspension systems behaved out on the track, but were at least determined to enforce some sort of standard, stating beforehand that lap times recorded by any driver whose car subsequently failed the test would be discounted for the period immediately prior to such an occurrence. This was to prove significant for two drivers, in particular. Jones was one of them, for after going out and showing everyone the quickest way round the tight little circuit by posting a best time of 1 min 22.20 sec he turned off the track only to find one of his

Williams' side-pods sticking in the 'down' position. As a result the car failed the test and his efforts had proved a complete waste of time for he now had to start all over again. But after that nothing really went right for him. First, after repairs had been effected to cure the problem, it was only a matter of minutes before he suffered an engine failure. Then, after switching to the spare Williams, not fitted with the team's hydro-mechanical suspension, the session was drawing to a close and the best that he could manage in the short amount of time available was a 1 min 23.82 sec lap which was only sixth fastest. Even so, this was a whole lot better when compared to Daly's plight. No-one had told the Irishman that the rear of the right-hand side-pod of his RAM March, not even enjoying the benefit of a 'trick' suspension, had snagged the checking device at one point, so he had carried on practising normally only to find at the end of the afternoon that he was being credited with no time at all! This really did make a mockery of the situation for here was one of the few cars that was otherwise perfectly legal in the true sense of the word.

Apart from the trouble involving Jones and Daly, the qualifying session had proceeded more or less as normal for very nearly everyone else, and when their lap times were announced it was seen that Reutemann had upheld honours admirably for the Williams team by being at the top of the time sheets at 1 min 22.28 sec. Furthermore, this was the best part of a full second quicker than even Piquet had managed in the runner-up spot, the Brazilian having lapped in 1 min 23.13 sec, and obviously none the worse for a spectacular off-course excursion during the afternoon whilst giving the spare Brabham an airing. The incident had, however, put

paid to Rebaque's chances of pulling up his lap times following an early engine failure and, instead, the Mexican was left way down the order in 21st place. Like Piquet, Watson, had also dented his pride during the course of the afternoon after spinning off in the latest McLaren MP4 at the first left-hander beyond the pits. Fortunately, for the Ulster-man, this had occurred almost at the end of the session by which time he had already achieved a very respectable lap in 1 min 23.73 sec to finish up being fifth fastest immediately behind the Arrows of Patrese (1 min 23.67 sec) and Pironi who was quickest of the turbo runners at 1 min 23.47 sec in his Ferrari. Villeneuve was also well up the list, seventh fastest, with the other Ferrari in spite of having been obliged to use the team's spare car in the closing minutes after he had earlier had to abandon his race car out on the circuit with not one, but two broken drive-shafts! Right behind the enthusiastic French-Canadian, a pleasant surprise was to see Cheever's Tyrrell up in eighth place, notwithstanding complaints from the American of poor handling, and then came Laffite, whose Talbot was obviously benefiting from a hydro-pneumatic suspension system operated by an engine-driven pump, followed by Mansell rounding off the first ten after having used one of a trio of Lotus 81s, on hand for himself and de Angelis, to good effect. Where were the Renaults? Well, perhaps the least said the better. As it was, neither Prost nor Arnoux had been able to come to terms with the handling of a pair of brand new RE30s that the French team had brought along, added to which Arnoux's car had later stopped with a broken distributor drive belt. Then, after having reverted to one of two earlier RE20Bs on hand, which Prost had already done by then, Arnoux had subsequently spun off twice after completing less than a handful of laps, and on the second occasion his car had become stuck in the sand at the first left-hander beyond the pits. As a result, Arnoux was near the bottom of the time sheets, actually 25th fastest, while Prost, who had come to within inches of hitting his team-mate's abandoned car shortly afterwards when he had almost lost it at the same corner, had struggled on to finish up a rather lowly twelfth in the standings, sandwiched between Rosberg's Avon-shod Fittipaldi and Stohr's Arrows, the young Italian having easily put up his best performance to date.

That should have been the end of the story for the day, but sadly it wasn't as during the final minutes of qualifying there had been a nasty accident in the pit lane. One of the Osella mechanics, Giovanni Amadeo, had slipped off the platform by the pit wall and been struck by Reutemann's Williams just as the Argentinian had been setting off for a final run. There was certainly no question of Reutemann having been at fault as due to the narrowness of the pit lane and general congestion in the immediate vicinity there had just been no way in which he could have taken evasive action; besides which he had not been going particularly fast at the time. Even so, he had been left deeply distressed by the affair and the fact that he was holding the provisional pole position had paled into insignificance. The poor Italian, meanwhile, had been rushed off to hospital with serious head injuries which, tragically, were to claim his life just three days later.

The weather decided to play its part in proceedings on Saturday with persistent rain falling throughout most of the final hour of qualifying. For Tambay, this change in conditions was particularly ironic as at the end of the morning untimed session the Candy Toleman team had withdrawn Warwick's car following the onset of serious engine problems and the Frenchman had finally been given the opportunity of trying to qualify. But now, of course, it was a lost cause and although Tambay tried everything he knew with the Theodore he still failed by some 5 seconds to bump even Ghinzani off the grid. After his troubled practice of the day before, Arnoux also failed to hoist himself on to the grid for similar reasons, but he, too, gave it all he had got and actually recorded the afternoon's third fastest time for what it was worth, finishing up behind Villeneuve and Jones who proved themselves by far the quickest drivers in the wet. However, for Arnoux there was still more trouble to come as later he found himself being held in police custody overnight after incurring the wrath of a gate marshal by queue-jumping on his way home from the circuit. The marshal had sat on the bonnet of his car so as to impede his progress and Arnoux had responded by giving the poor chap an unwanted, and uncomfortable, lift for the 3 mile trip to his hotel!

On race day the weather was still not very settled, with the odd shower or two of rain falling, but by early afternoon when the 24 starters were leaving the pits for the warm-up lap the track was dry and it seemed reasonable to assume that it would stay that way. It also seemed reasonable to assume that the starting procedure would follow its accepted format but, instead, soon after all of the cars had formed up on the grid several of the drivers started unhitching their safety harnesses, climbing out of their cars and assembling at the front of the grid. Now this was not at all what was supposed to happen, and it was to cost each of the drivers concerned a fine of $5000. However, at a meeting of the Grand Prix Drivers' Association in the morning, chaired by former World Champion Jody Scheckter, it had been decided to stage a protest against the lack of attention being paid to drivers' views and, in particular, against the organizers' failure to accede to a request for a pre-qualifying session, both to accommodate Tambay and to reduce the number of cars taking part in official practice to twenty-six. To complete the 'happy' scene the mechanics, incensed by Friday's pit lane accident and the generally cramped working conditions, had also decided to air their discontent by staging a similar protest with the result that for several minutes the grid area was in a state of chaos with people everywhere. Meanwhile, the organizers were determined that the start of the race should not be delayed, especially with television coverage to consider, and although drivers began returning to their cars there were still people standing around the grid area when the signal was suddenly given for what everyone thought was to be a second warm-up lap. Anyhow, off they went with Piquet, not Reutemann as it should have been, leading the way and the rest gradually joining in but completely out of order relative to their grid positions, as drivers who had remained in their cars were obviously able to set off quicker than their protesting colleagues. To add to the confusion Piquet then overshot his grid position when he returned and so was waved off for another lap which, by the time that he eventually took up his correct grid position, led to engine temperatures of some of the other cars starting to rise alarmingly due to the delay. At this stage it still seemed likely that there would be a proper pace lap but the organizers had decided otherwise and although Patrese was now frantically waving his arms above his head – his engine had stalled – on went the red starting lights. Almost simultaneously Patrese's chief mechanic, Dave Luckett, leapt over the barriers with an air-line, on sheer impulse as it was certainly against the rules, and as he crouched down behind the stricken Arrows so the red lights changed to green, the starter no doubt encouraged by Reutemann clearly indicating that his water temperature was becoming critical. Jones, of course, could see only too well what was happening and promptly moved over to his left, as did Cheever and Mansell, but drivers further down the grid had no idea of what was going on, nor was there a yellow flag out to indicate the potential danger. As a result Stohr, after quite innocently pulling over to the right of Rosberg's Fittipaldi, suddenly found himself confronted by his team-leader's stationary car and, despite hitting the brakes, ran straight into the back of him, trapping the unfortunate mechanic at the same time. Fortunately, Patrese's gearbox took the brunt of the impact and Luckett miraculously survived the ordeal, although he had sustained a broken leg, fractured hand and facial lacerations. In the meantime, the race was still in progress with Piquet leading from Reutemann and Pironi, but apart from black flags starting to appear there seemed to be no attempt being made to bring things to a halt. Twice the leaders roared past the pits looking for a red flag only to find there was none and in the end it was Pironi who took the initiative by slowing right down and stopping in front of the pits after having made quite clear his intentions to the drivers behind him.

Well over half an hour later, with Dave Luckett having been rushed off to a nearby hospital and the Arrows team understandably taking no further part in the day's activities, the grid reformed in readiness for the re-start. This time there was a proper pace lap and this time they all got away cleanly, Reutemann leading until the first left-hander where Pironi squeezed his Ferrari through on the inside of the Williams to take over up front. At the end of the lap he was still there with Reutemann holding on gamely in second place ahead of Piquet, Watson, Jones, Villeneuve, Laffite, Rosberg, Mansell, Cheever, de Angelis and the others all giving chase except for Prost who was already heading for the pits with a slipping clutch. A second start had obviously proved too much for the turbo-charged Renault and although Prost subsequently rejoined the race he was in the pits again at the end of the next lap, this time to retire and round off a thoroughly disappointing weekend for the French team. By then there was a distinct pattern beginning to emerge at the front of the race, for Jones had got the better of Watson at the first left-hander on the second lap and, along with Pironi, Reutemann and Piquet, was now pulling clear of the rest of the pack to become embroiled in a fascinating leadership scrap. This continued with all four drivers pushing one another all the way, but through it all Pironi was stubbornly holding on to the lead, his Ferrari's sheer power compensating for any handling deficiencies through the turns. Only on the tenth lap was there a change in the order when Reutemann found himself coming uncomfortably close to the Ferrari at the right-hander leading on to the back straight, and had to momentarily lift off, for this was all that was needed for both Piquet and Jones to get alongside and out-drag him in the run up to the chicane. A lap later there was more excitement. Not content with third place, Jones now made a run up on the inside of Piquet's Brabham at the chicane before the pits but, with neither driver prepared to concede, wheels touched and the Brazilian's two-in-a-row victory run ended with the Brabham's nose tangled in the catch-fencing. Jones, on the other hand, got away with it and, moreover, within just two more laps was leading his team-mate past Pironi's Ferrari which was now suffering from fading brakes. Later on the same lap the hard-charging Laffite – he'd forged ahead of Villeneuve on the second lap and more recently scrambled past Watson under braking for the last chicane – also moved ahead of the Ferrari which then started dropping away. In fact, for the Italian team prospects were no longer looking good at all as Villeneuve was also in trouble with chronic handling problems caused by his hydro-pneumatic suspension not functioning properly. Only the rear half was doing its job! As it was, the French-Canadian was now in sixth place struggling to keep Mansell's Lotus 81 at bay. Further back still, Rosberg had disappeared from ninth place soon after being overtaken by de Angelis when the Fittipaldi's gear lever had come off in his hand, de Cesaris had retired the McLaren M29F with gearbox trouble and Jabouille had slipped to the back of the field after a pit stop to complain of poor handling with his Talbot. The rest, though, were still charging around and still on the same lap as

Carlos Reutemann on his way to another victory for Williams. *(Phipps Photographic)*

the leaders.

On lap 20 Jones, coming like a sling-shot out of the fast right-hander leading on to the back straight, suddenly found fourth gear becoming neutral and was powerless to prevent the leading Williams from sliding straight on across the grass into the barriers. Mere second-degree burns from the extremely hot radiator water could be considered a lucky escape! So now Reutemann took over up front from Laffite and an inspired Mansell who had just moved from seventh to third in less than two laps, the young Birmingham lad having disposed of both Villeneuve and Watson in rapid succession on lap 18 and now Pironi's near-brakeless Ferrari. Watson, Villeneuve and de Angelis also moved ahead of Pironi before the lap was out, and on lap 29 Cheever and Rebaque, engaged in a private duel of their own, elbowed the Ferrari even further down the field. But for all that the race had now developed into something of a procession, for Reutemann was steadily increasing his lead over Laffite who, in turn, was keeping well out of Mansell's reach. Watson, too, was coming under no threat from Villeneuve and although the French-Canadian had de Angelis constantly biting at his heels any hopes that the Lotus driver might have had of getting past were thwarted by the Ferrari's superior straight-line speed.

Even the little battle for seventh place fizzled out on lap 40 when Rebaque, now in front of the Tyrrell, missed his braking point for one òf the fast left-handers and promptly spun off into the catch-fences, creating yet more work for the Brabham mechanics. Indeed, it was almost a relief when rain developed shortly afterwards for this ultimately brought out the chequered flag fifteen laps early and at long last the whole sorry episode of the 1981 Belgian Grand Prix was over.

In accordance with the regulations, the finishing order was determined by the order at the end of the previous lap. This was rather fortuitous for Cheever as on the final race lap his Tyrrell had rolled to a halt with a blown-up engine. As it was he was now in the points by being classified sixth behind Reutemann, Laffite, Mansell (taking his first Championship points), Villeneuve and de Angelis. Watson, meanwhile, had dropped right away in the closing stages with fourth gear playing up on his McLaren MP4 and was classified in a frustrating seventh place ahead of Pironi, Giacomelli and Andretti in their ill-handling Alfa Romeos, Surer, Alboreto and finally Ghinzani who had completed a Grand Prix at his first attempt in spite of having had a terrifying moment on the 18th lap when the rear aerofoil had parted company with his Osella!

Results			
1	C. Reutemann (Williams-Ford)	1 hr 16 min 31.61 sec (180.445 kph/ 112.123 mph)	
2	J. Laffite (Talbot-Matra)	1 hr 17 min 07.67 sec	
3	N. Mansell (Lotus-Ford)	1 hr 17 min 15.30 sec	
4	G. Villeneuve (Ferrari)	1 hr 17 min 19.25 sec	
5	E. de Angelis (Lotus-Ford)	1 hr 17 min 20.81 sec	
6	E. Cheever (Tyrrell-Ford)	1 hr 17 min 24.12 sec	
7	J. Watson (McLaren-Ford)	1 hr 17 min 33.27 sec	
8	D. Pironi (Ferrari)	1 hr 18 min 03.65 sec	
9	B. Giacomelli (Alfa Romeo)	1 hr 18 min 07.19 sec	
10	M. Andretti (Alfa Romeo)	1 lap behind	
11	M. Surer (Ensign-Ford)	2 laps behind	
12	M. Alboreto (Tyrrell-Ford)	2 laps behind	
13	P. Ghinzani (Osella-Ford)	4 laps behind	

Fastest lap: C. Reutemann (Williams-Ford) on lap 37 in 1 min 23.30 sec (184.192 kph/ 114.451 mph)

Retirements
A Prost (Renault) clutch on lap 3, K. Rosberg (Fittipaldi-Ford) gearbox on lap 11, N. Piquet (Brabham-Ford) accident on lap 11, A. de Cesaris (McLaren-Ford) gearbox on lap 12, A. Jones (Williams-Ford) accident on lap 20, G. Gabbiani (Osella-Ford) engine on lap 23, F. Serra (Fittipaldi-Ford) engine on lap 30, J.P. Jabouille (Talbot-Matra) transmission on lap 36, H. Rebaque (Brabham-Ford) spun off on lap 40.

XXXIXᵉ Grand Prix de Monaco

Monte Carlo: May 31
Weather: Warm and sunny
Distance: 76 laps of 3.312 km
circuit = 251.71 km (156.41 miles)

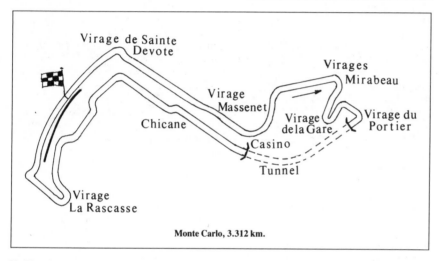

Monte Carlo, 3.312 km.

Unlike the situation at Zolder a fortnight earlier, there was no question of not having pre-qualifying at Monaco as only 26 cars were being allowed to take part in official practice and there were again 32 drivers entered for the race. To sort things out it was decided that the 22 drivers of the eleven teams to have scored Championship points in 1980 would have an automatic right to take part and that the remainder – Gabbiani and Ghinzani (Osella), Lammers and Borgudd (ATS) Daly and Salazar (RAM March), Henton and Warwick (Toleman), Tambay (Theodore) and Surer (Ensign) – would have to earn that right by achieving the four fastest times during a 60 minute pre-qualifying session starting at 8 a.m. on the Thursday preceding race day. As a prelude to the weekend's activities this hour-long thrash proved to be quite exciting, although there were no real surprises. Tambay's Theodore, a brand new chassis, came out fastest at 1 min 30.492 sec, followed by Surer's Ensign and the two Osellas', Daly's hopes of progressing further being ended by a broken drive-shaft and Lammers' by hav-

ing his entry withdrawn by Gunther Schmidt before even being given a chance!

Once the initial 'weeding-out' had been completed it was not long before the opening 90 minute session of official practice began and now, with the 'aces' out on the track, the pace was soon around 2 seconds quicker, Piquet going particularly well. The Williams duo of Jones, another driver using a brand new chassis, and Reutemann were right up there, too, but this was to be expected. What was surprising, in view of the fact that the turbo-charged cars were considered by many not to be very suitable for street circuits, was that Villeneuve was also lapping consistently quickly in his Ferrari. However, the Italian team had come well prepared with revised camshafts and valve gear to achieve better torque characteristics from their V6 engine and this, combined with the French-Canadian's usual forceful driving, was obviously having the desired effect. Pironi, on the other hand, made the headlines for the wrong reasons by bringing his sister car into contact with the barriers at La Rascasse and doing sufficient damage to bring the spare

Ferrari into service. All was not well within the Renault camp, either. Quite apart from more handling problems with the new RE30 series of cars on which the French team were now concentrating, Arnoux first ran into trouble with his gear linkage malfunctioning and then, during the closing minutes of the session, his engine started losing power which meant that he was going to be relegated to the spare RE20B for the first period of qualifying, there being insufficient time for an engine change. During the morning Jabouille also ran into engine trouble with his Talbot-Matra, but elsewhere things were running relatively smoothly and the Essex Lotus team went away particularly pleased with the way the pair of new 87s that they had brought along had performed, even though both cars were understeering more than their drivers would have liked.

Pironi continued his 'rock-ape antics' in the afternoon by crashing the spare Ferrari into the barriers after overdoing things quite early on going into Massenet. Fortunately, the Frenchman emerged from the wreckage unscathed but, of course, that was the end of his practice for the day. There were no more Ferraris left! With Arnoux having already commandeered the spare Renault, Prost was in a similar situation when the gear linkage broke on his new car. Moreover, Prost had to subsequently undergo the frustrating experience of watching helplessly as his best lap of 1 min 27.623 sec slipped from being second fastest at that point to an eventual eighth, as by the end of the hour-long session Villeneuve (1 min 26.891 sec), Jones (1 min 26.938 sec), Mansell (1 min 27.174 sec), Patrese (1 min 27.447 sec), Laffite (1 min 27.468 sec) and Andretti (1 min 27.512 sec) had all lapped quicker, Mansell's performance being particularly outstanding and completely overshadowing his rather more experienced team-mate who was well over a second slower. Reutemann also beat Prost's time during the afternoon but he was only credited with ninth fastest time of 1 min 27.643 sec after his best time had been disallowed. The Williams' suspension had stayed in the 'down' position and this had led to the car being amongst a few others to fail a ground clearance check – these checks were being carried out at the entrance to the pit lane using a laser beam set up on a purpose-made flat area of concrete. In the meantime, the one driver that no-one had beaten, or even approached, was Piquet. The Brazilian, openly blaming Jones for the Zolder incident and threatening retaliation if he ever did anything similar again, had really set the place alight and lapped in a quite incredible 1 min 25.710 sec (139.111 kph) using the spare Brabham BT49C. Indeed, such was his superiority that suggestions were being made in some quarters that the car was underweight. Laffite, in particular, was so incensed about it that he went away and freely expressed his opinions for publication in the French sporting newspaper L'Equipe, suggesting that Piquet had two cars, his race car and an ultra-light qualifying car, and that no-one would do anything about it because

the Brabham team was owned by Bernie Ecclestone and everyone was frightened of him! In the event nothing did come of it, with Brabham designer Gordon Murray emphatically denying the allegations.

On Friday the circuit was set aside for participants of various supporting events scheduled to take place over the weekend, but on Saturday it was business as usual for the Grand Prix teams. Since Thursday, Ferrari had transported a fourth 126CK over from Italy which was to prove a wise move as during the morning untimed session Pironi ran into yet more problems when the engine in his repaired race chassis blew up. However, this was to be just the start of another troubled day for the Frenchman as no sooner had he started concentrating on lowering his lap times in the final hour of qualifying with the new spare car than he spun off into the barriers again at Massenet. It seemed almost unbelievable and, moreover, there was now a distinct possibility that the 1980 pole-man might not even make the grid, for as he limped back to the pits with a flat rear tyre and bent suspension it was quite obvious that his qualifying run was over for the day. Villeneuve, meanwhile, had the other Ferrari well and truly wound up and, while Piquet was concentrating on setting up his Brabham for the race, went on to record the afternoon's fastest time in a particularly dramatic lap in which he only just about held everything together scrambling past a slower car going into Tabac. His reward, 1 min 25.788 sec – less than eight-hundredths of a second away from grabbing Piquet's 'safe' pole position! Mansell, as well, continued to astound everyone with his quick and skilful driving in the new Lotus 87, finishing up by being the only other driver to lap in under 1 min 26 sec with a time of 1 min 25.815 sec for a splendid third place on the grid. Reutemann and Patrese were next, both just failing to join the elite at 1 26.010 sec and 1 min 26.040 sec respectively, and then up into sixth place came de Angelis who had improved by well over 2 seconds on the first day, to 1 min 26.259 sec, after having had the gear ratios and ride height of his Lotus 87 converted to the same settings as those of his impressive young team-mate. Jones, on the other hand, had slipped back to seventh place on the grid thanks mainly to the fuel system of his new Williams going on the blink. Even so he had still managed to bring his lap times down to 1 min 26.538 sec which was a most creditable performance, especially when bearing in mind that his left thigh was causing discomfort following the Zolder shunt. Laffite and Prost, before losing fourth gear, also produced laps in the 1 min 26 sec bracket to occupy the next two places, while Watson rounded off the front half of the grid by coming nearest not to join them after taking his McLaren MP4 around in 1 min 27.058 sec, interestingly enough running the

car with conventional suspension after having used the team's hydro-pneumatic system throughout Thursday. In contrast, de Cesaris, using a McLaren MP4 for the first time, seemed quite happy with the 'trick' suspension and, despite bending a rocker arm at the chicane during the course of the afternoon, finished up just 0.064 sec slower than his team-leader. As a result the young Italian had earned his best grid position of the season so far, being in eleventh place immediately ahead of Andretti and a somewhat disgruntled Arnoux – the Frenchman once again had been forced to rely on the spare Renault for qualifying after crashing his race car into the barriers by the swimming pool right at the start of the afternoon session!

With the size of the grid being limited to twenty cars instead of the more usual 24 at other circuits several of the remaining drivers had been scrambling around trying to qualify. In fact, Pironi must have been sweating somewhat during the closing stages of practice as by then even the slowest drivers were lapping well under 1 min 30 sec, and his best time was only 1 min 28.266 sec. However, in the final reckoning Pironi had made it, albeit by less than two-tenths of a second, and the six unlucky ones were Rosberg and Serra with their Fittipaldis, after trying both Avon and Michelin tyres; Gabbiani and Ghinzani with their Osellas; Jabouille, after more engine problems with his Talbot-Matra and, causing the biggest surprise of all, Rebaque after his efforts to hoist himself on to the grid had ended with a broken drive-shaft.

Clear blue skies and a warm sun were in evidence on race day, and by early afternoon, with the 30 minute warm-up session having produced no late problems of any consequence, everything augured well for the 39th running of the Monaco Grand Prix, even though the crowd attendance was well down on past years – perhaps people were becoming sickened with all the politics that were plaguing the sport! Traditionally the track was officially opened by Prince Rainier and Princess Grace but they were away in the United States attending their son's graduation from college. So, instead, the honour was delegated to twice-winner of the race and local resident Maurice Trintignant who toured the circuit in a Grand Prix Bugatti prior to final preparations being commenced for the 3.30 p.m. start. But then, shortly afterwards, and with everyone awaiting the final count-down, came unexpected drama – a kitchen fire had broken out at the Loews Hotel situated on the outside of the old Station hairpin and above the tunnel. Naturally, with a lot of the access roads closed off for the race, this caused quite a panic among the emergency services and, although they eventually got through and the fire was extinguished, the start of the race had to be delayed. To make matters worse much of the

1981

water used to douse the flames then began pouring out through the basement of the hotel and into the tunnel, and for a while it looked as if the race might even have to be cancelled. However, after consultations between the race organizers, Bernie Ecclestone and GPDA president Jody Scheckter, during which time the flow of water gradually reduced to a trickle, it was finally decided to allow the drivers two warm-up laps and to declare the area of track between Portier and the exit of the tunnel to be a 'no-overtaking' zone.

When at long last the race did get under way, almost exactly one hour late, Piquet took off like a scalded cat to lead the charge through Ste. Devote and up the hill to the Casino. The rest of the field also got away well but, as the mid-field runners started the ascent from Ste. Devote, de Cesaris and Prost suddenly banged wheels and in the next instant, after becoming momentarily airborne, the McLaren was crashing down across the front of Andretti's Alfa Romeo, putting both cars out of the race on the spot. Fortunately, Prost managed to keep everything under control and continued apparently none the worse, but lower down the order Surer ran over a piece of debris and was left driving around to the pits to have a punctured front tyre replaced. In the meantime, Piquet was still leading the race and as he roared past the pits for the first time was already looking in complete command, being several car lengths clear of Villeneuve who had slotted into second place. Tucked right in behind the Ferrari, Mansell was third and then came Reutemann, Jones, Patrese, de

Angelis, Laffite, Prost, Arnoux, Watson, Tambay, Cheever, Stohr, Giacomelli, Pironi and Alboreto, all still fairly well bunched up.

The order remained settled for the first nine laps, the only change coming on lap 10 when Stohr made the first of a string of pit stops before retiring his Arrows with an incurable misfire. Nevertheless, there was no lack of interest, for while Piquet had by now opened up a near 3 second advantage, Villeneuve still had Mansell and the two Williams drivers pressing him all the way. Patrese and de Angelis were also keeping up well and when the Ferrari driver had trouble in lapping Surer's Ensign on lap 12 this brought all six cars even closer together. Indeed, they were so close that two laps later when the rear of Mansell's Lotus snapped slightly out of line in the tunnel Reutemann promptly clipped the back of the car and was subsequently obliged to go into the pits to have a bent nose wing replaced, dropping to seventeenth place and over a lap behind the leaders in the process. On the following lap Mansell also dived into the pits complaining that his Lotus had become unstable and although he, too, rejoined the race after a rear wheel had been changed it was only another lap before he stopped for good with what was later diagnosed to be a broken rear suspension rocker arm. Up front, meanwhile, Piquet had extended his lead to over 6 seconds and Jones, having automatically assumed third place, was obviously determined to do something about it for he was now all but climbing on the back of Villeneuve's Ferrari. Sure enough, on lap 20, the Williams was pulling alongside the Ferrari

down the short squirt to Mirabeau and diving past on the inside under braking. That settled it, for Villeneuve was in no position to retaliate as his brakes were beginning to fade and, in fact, while Jones set to work on catching the leading Brabham, it was only another five laps before the French-Canadian had to give best to Patrese. Sadly for the Italian, though, his third place lasted barely five laps as on its 30th tour the Arrows came to rest at Casino Square with a broken gearbox pinion. Only three laps later de Angelis, after briefly taking over fourth place following his compatriot's demise, also lost all interest in the race when his Lotus 87 crawled to a halt along the harbour front with a blown-up engine. Moreover, this incident took Arnoux out as well, for as the Frenchman arrived at the old Station hairpin his Renault ran into a large patch of oil deposited by the Lotus and skated off into the barriers. Still the dramas continued. On the very next lap Cheever spun at the Mirabeau following a slight coming-together with Pironi's Ferrari, the American gathering it all up but only after Pironi, Giacomelli and Alboreto had scrambled past, and then, just minutes later, Reutemann's climb back up through the field was brought to a stop by a broken gearbox, the Argentinian retiring at the pits to end an unprecedented run of no less than 15 successive race finishes in the points.

By half-distance (38 laps) the situation between Piquet and Jones were becoming decidedly interesting, for the Australian had tigerishly reduced the gap to a mere 2 seconds. On the next lap it was even less, and when Piquet was slightly held up whilst lapping Surer's Ensign for the second time shortly afterwards this was all that was needed to bring the two leading cars together. Now the tension could be felt all around the tortuous circuit and it seemed only a matter of time before the race had a new leader. However, Piquet obviously felt otherwise and, although his driving started looking a little ragged on the odd occasion, he continued to keep the Brabham in front by throwing off every challenge from his adversary over the next six laps. After that he even pulled away again by a small margin as on the 46th tour the Williams slid wide coming out of Portier, and for a while the pressure eased slightly for him, with Jones apparently content to hold the gap to around 2 seconds. In the meantime, Prost quietly retired his Renault from sixth place at Casino Square with a broken valve, and on lap 51 there was a commotion at Ste. Devote when Alboreto spun on his way out of the chicane and was promptly collected by Giacomelli's Alfa Romeo, this putting an end to a good scrap over what had become seventh place. Watson, looking all set to relieve Laffite of his inherited fourth place after a spirited drive in the McLaren, also had to retire a few

Gilles Villeneuve's Ferrari leads Nigel Mansell's Lotus 87 and the two Williams FW07Cs of Carlos Reutemann and Alan Jones down to the old Station Hairpin during the opening stages of the race whilst lying in second place. *(L.A.T. Photographic)*

minutes later with a blown-up engine but this went largely unnoticed as all attention had suddenly been diverted to the Tabac corner. Piquet, still having to keep a very watchful eye on Jones' Williams, had been coming up to lap Tambay's Theodore which was going slower than usual as it was running short of gears. But in a fit of over-anxiety the Brazilian had made a rare error of judgement by trying to squeeze through on the inside of the slower car when there just wasn't the room, locked up a front wheel and had gone skating straight across the track into the barriers. Fortunately only his pride had been damaged, but as a race it was now all over, or so it appeared, as Jones was left leading with a good half-minute advantage over Villeneuve. Furthermore, there were only another five cars left after that, well spread out and running in the order Laffite, Pironi, Cheever, Tambay and Surer.

Even before Piquet's abrupt departure from the race, Jones had become aware that his engine had started spluttering very occasionally, and over the course of the next few minutes this gradually became more noticeable. The red fuel pressure light in the Williams' cockpit was now also showing, and on lap 67, with still plenty of time in hand over Villeneuve, he decided to stop and take on more fuel, thinking that maybe the tanks were running dry or else the fuel system was failing to pick up the last few remaining litres. However, to his dismay, Jones quickly discovered that the problem was still there after he had charged back out into the race and, worse, his lead had dwindled to only 6

A tired, but well satisfied, Gilles Villeneuve pictured at the post-race presentation ceremony after scoring his first victory of the season, a result that also marked the first-ever victory for a turbo-charged Ferrari. *(L.A.T. Photographic)*

seconds. To the spectators, of course, and to the fanatical Italian supporters, in particular, this really brought the race back to life, and with Villeneuve responding to pit signals like a bull being shown a red cloth the excitement reached fever pitch. In the end just four quick laps were enough for by then, regardless of fading brakes, Villeneuve was not only right on the ailing Williams' tail but streaking past in front of the pits. After that it really was all over and, to the accompaniment of ships' hooters and sirens from the

harbour and hysterical reactions from the spectator enclosures, Villeneuve drove on to give the 1½ litre turbo-charged Ferrari its first Grand Prix victory. Meanwhile, a bitterly disappointed Jones managed to coax his spluttering Williams home to second place after very nearly coming to a stop at one point, finishing 39.91 sec behind the jubilant winner. Then came Laffite followed by Pironi, Cheever, Surer and, finally, Tambay who had completed most of the second half of the race with a seized third gear.

Results

1	G. Villeneuve (Ferrari)	1 hr 54 min 23.38 sec (132.029 kph/ 82.039 mph)	5	E. Cheever (Tyrrell-Ford)	2 laps behind
2	A. Jones (Williams-Ford)	1 hr 55 min 03.29 sec	6	M. Surer (Ensign-Ford)	2 laps behind
3	J. Laffite (Talbot-Matra)	1 hr 55 min 52.62 sec	7	P. Tambay (Theodore-Ford)	4 laps behind
4	D. Pironi (Ferrari)	1 lap behind			

Fastest lap: A. Jones (Williams-Ford) on lap 48 in 1 min 27.470 sec (136.311 kph/84.700 mph)

Retirements

A. de Cesaris (McLaren-Ford) accident on lap 1, M. Andretti (Alfa Romeo) accident on lap 1, S. Stohr (Arrows-Ford) electrics on lap 15, N. Mansell (Lotus-Ford) rear suspension on lap 16, R. Patrese (Arrows-Ford) gearbox on lap 30, E. de Angelis (Lotus-Ford) engine on lap 33, R. Arnoux (Renault) accident on lap 33, C. Reutemann (Williams-Ford) gearbox on lap 34, A. Prost (Renault) engine on lap 46, M. Alboreto (Tyrrell-Ford) accident on lap 51, B. Giacomelli (Alfa Romeo) accident on lap 51, J. Watson (McLaren-Ford) engine on lap 53, N. Piquet (Brabham-Ford) accident on lap 54.

XXVII° Gran Premio de España

Jarama: June 21
Weather: Very hot
Distance: 80 laps of 3.312 km
circuit = 264.96 km (164.64 miles)

Preparations for the Spanish Grand Prix had presented FOCA with a problem for they had 20 potential runners again, whereas under the terms of the Concorde Agreement they were only allowed 18 and, unlike Monaco, there was to be no pre-qualifying. However, to rectify matters they had once more exerted pressure on the ATS team to enter

only one car, which resulted in the unfortunate Jan Lammers being left out in the cold for the third successive race, and had similarly persuaded John MacDonald to reduce his campaign to running just the one car. Moreover, MacDonald had agreed to do this for the remainder of the season and had now released Eliseo Salazar (and his sponsorship

money) to the under-financed Ensign team as a replacement for Marc Surer, the Swiss having failed to raise the necessary sponsorship to keep himself in Mo Nunn's outfit. Changes were also to be found elsewhere in the line-up. Osella had installed another young Italian, Giorgio Francia, in their second car and Spaniard Emilio de Villota had entered himself in his old Aurora Williams FW07. Of course, this latter entry now meant that there were 31 cars when only a maximum of 30 were permitted to take part in official practice, but because the ATS

1981

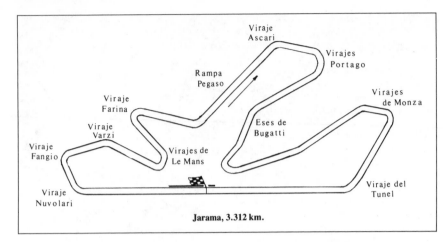

Jarama, 3.312 km.

team were late in arriving at the circuit and unable to present their car for scrutineering on time, the organizers overcame this by vetoeing Borgudd's entry. After the end of Friday morning's opening practice session, though, FISA issued a Press Release stating that if de Villota was allowed to participate the race would be discounted for the World Championship. As a result the organizers quickly changed their minds – de Villota was out and Borgudd was in!

During the morning untimed session, which had started late after a bout of brink-manship with the 'medical' helicopter, and had been highlighted by de Cesaris slithering off the track when a steering arm broke on his McLaren MP4, it had been noticeable that of all the cars out practising the Talbot-Ligier of Laffite was looking particularly well suited to the twisty little Jarama circuit. The Frenchman, in fact, was using a brand new JS17 incorporating detailed aerodynamic revisions following recent testing at Dijon, and he was absolutely delighted with the car's handling. He was no longer complaining about the performance of the V12 Matra engine either for, although there was still a deficiency in straight-line speed, further development had improved matters considerably and, with different camshafts, it was now capable of running some 500/600 rpm higher than previously. Indeed, Laffite was altogether happier than of late, and once the official time-keepers took up duty for the first period of qualifying this was instantly reflected in his lap times for he was up there amongst the best of them. Even when he became one of a number of drivers to fall foul of the ground-clearance checks (being carried out at the entrance to the pit lane) at one point during the afternoon and had his lap times scrubbed, it appeared to do little to upset him for he simply carried on more determined than ever. To some drivers, on the other hand, these checks were causing increasing irritation which was not being helped at all by the organizers' insistence on suspending activities on every occasion that someone spun off or broke down so

that the afflicted car or cars could be retrieved, as this led to the qualifying session being a somewhat prolonged and disjointed affair. Among those to blame for the inter-ruptions were Stohr and Borgudd who ran into one another at the end of the main straight, and also Serra who later went off at exactly the same spot after banging wheels with Salazar's Ensign. In spite of all of the delays, though, some pretty respectable lap times were recorded with Jones (1 min 14.424 sec), Reutemann (1 min 14.808 sec), Laffite (1 min 14.822 sec) and Prost (1 min 14.980 sec) all breaking the 1 min 15 sec barrier and Watson very nearly joining them after taking his McLaren MP4 around in 1 min 15.094 sec. De Angelis was also well in the hunt after achieving sixth fastest time of 1 min 15.399 sec in his Lotus 87, now painted black and gold following his team's new sponsorship tie-up with John Player & Son, but team-mate Mansell was down in eleventh place on the time-sheets, behind Andretti, Patrese, Rosberg and de Cesaris, after having been obliged to stop practising early when he felt his engine start to tighten. Even lower in the order, and causing a major upset in the Brabham camp, was Piquet who had come out only 17th fastest after com-plaining of inconsistent handling and lack of grip through the numerous corners. This was a real surprise, and another was to find Pironi and Villeneuve only 12th and 13th fastest respectively in their Ferraris. But they, too, were complaining of diabolical handling, added to which Pironi's car, run-ning with higher boost pressure, had been trailing thick grey smoke towards the end of the session following the failure of a bearing seal in his turbo.

Friday had been hot, but on Saturday the weather was almost unbearable and not at all conducive to fast motoring. Nevertheless, the morning untimed session saw everyone hard at work preparing for the final hour of qualifying, and there was certainly no lack of drama with cars seemingly spinning off in all directions as well as various mechanical frail-ties showing up. Among those to strike

trouble were Jones and Watson, who both suffered engine failures; Pironi, who had another bearing seal fail in his turbo; de Angelis, who damaged the nose and one of the side-pods of his Lotus 87 after a spin; and Gabbiani who crashed heavily in his Osella when a wheel flew off. Furthermore, this last incident put paid to any hopes that Francia might have had of making the grid as the young Italian was now obliged to hand his car over to his team-leader.

Because of all the problems in the morn-ing, it was just as well that the final qualifying session started nearly half an hour late due to the organizers having constantly interrupted proceedings again so that stranded cars could be retrieved for this, at least, had allowed extra time for the overworked mechanics to put everything right once more. Even then Jones and Watson had to wait around for their engine changes to be completed. However, once they did finally get under way both very quickly joined Laffite, Reutemann and Prost in what was developing into an exciting battle for pole position. Pironi, also late in going out due to the amount of time necessary to replace the turbo-chargers on his Ferrari, no doubt wished that he could have been involved as well but before he had really got going his clutch packed up! Arnoux was another destined to have a particularly frustrating afternoon, managing a grand total of only four laps following turbo-compressor trouble on both his race chassis and the spare Renault, while de Cesaris spoiled his chances by spinning off into the sand at the end of the main straight after covering a mere three laps. Meanwhile, numerous other drivers were complaining of indifferent handling and lack of grip for the second day running but, in spite of this, and the extremely hot conditions, very nearly all of them were making progress in the right direction so far as lap times were concerned, one of the few exceptions being de Angelis following his off-course excursion in the morning as this had seemingly upset his car's handling. Naturally, most of the attention was fixed on the absorbing pole position battle and this finally ended with Laffite clinching the coveted spot for the third year in a row in this particular race after setting an entirely new standard by breaking the 1 min 14 sec barrier at 1 min 13.754 sec (161.662 kph). Even Jones had been unable to reply to that but, with an improved time of 1 min 14.024 sec, was comfortably ensconced in second place on the grid ahead of team-mate Reutemann (1 min 14.342 sec), Watson (1 min 14.657 sec), Prost (1 min 14.669 sec), Giacomelli (1 min 14.897 sec) and Villeneuve (1 min 14.987 sec) who had also produced sub-1 min 15 sec laps. Piquet, surprisingly, had remained out of the picture and, despite improving by over 1½ seconds on the first day, had to be satisfied with an eventual ninth place on the grid, one place lower than Andretti who, like Giacomelli, was finding his Alfa Romeo a somewhat better proposition than recently now that it had been converted back to near-1980 specification. In addition to Piquet, there were also a few other surprises in the final grid order as Patrese had been suffering from lack of traction out of the slow corners with his Arrows and was down in 12th place behind the black and gold Lotus 87s of de Angelis and Mansell; Prioni and Arnoux, because of their problems, were 13th and 17th respectively; and Jabouille was an even more despondent 19th after having lapped very nearly

3 seconds slower than his pole-winning team-mate and brother-in-law. In contrast, a pleasant surprise was to see Daly qualify for his first Grand Prix of the season, the Irishman winding up on 22nd spot and obviously benefiting from bodywork revisions carried out to his RAM March 811. Salazar had also qualified on his first outing in the Ensign after having just pipped Alboreto for 24th and last place on the grid.

There was still no let-up in the scorching hot weather on Sunday and as pre-race formalities began with some of the drivers being presented, to the King of Spain, following his arrival by royal helicopter in mid-afternoon, the temperature was over 100°F (38°C). In fact, it was so hot that this seemed to be at least one of the reasons why the spectator attendance was noticeably down on past years, although it was almost certain that disenchantment over both the sport's recent political troubles and de Villota's exclusion from the event was also having a detrimental effect. Whatever, the comparatively small size of the crowd was the source of a major disappointment as the twenty-four cars started leaving the pits for the warm-up lap prior to forming up on the grid. For a change, after the various delays throughout practice, everything was now running nicely on time for the Talbot-sponsored race and, with just a few minutes remaining to the 4 p.m. start, the field was flagged off for the pace lap. On completing the lap and slotting into pole position, however, Laffite felt his Talbot creeping forward due to the clutch dragging and was forced to hold the car in check by dabbing the brakes. As a result, the Frenchman was quite literally caught out on the wrong foot when the green lights appeared and so, instead of a blue and white car, it was a green and white car, that of Jones, which surged forward into the lead. Behind the two front-row men, Reutemann swerved around the back of the slow-moving Talbot to take up second place, while a typically brilliant start from Villeneuve saw the French-Canadian catapult through from seventh spot on the grid to third place in the race, bending the front wing of Prost's Renault with the Ferrari's right rear wheel as the two cars turned into the first right-hander in the process! Amidst more bumping and boring lower down the order, Pironi also bent the front wing of his Ferrari out of shape against the back of Patrese's Arrows, which then suffered a similar fate after being brought into contact with someone else, and de Cesaris was involved in a slight contretemps with Rebaque. Somehow, though, they all kept everything together and went on to complete a fast and furious opening lap with Jones leading the way and pulling out a small advantage over team-mate Reutemann. Villeneuve was still in third place but already he was looking for better things and, as the leading trio flashed past the pits for the first

time, the Ferrari driver jinked out of Reutemann's slip-stream and proceeded to scramble past on the outside of the Argentinian under braking for the first right-hander. Meanwhile, Andretti was up to an excellent fourth place and after that came Prost, Watson, Giacomelli, Piquet, Patrese and Pironi with the unfortunate Laffite down in eleventh place ahead of the rest.

During the next 12 laps it seemed as if nothing could prevent Jones from scoring a runaway victory for he continued to increase his advantage at the rate of very nearly a full second per lap. Towards the end of lap 14, however, the reigning World Champion suddenly made an uncharacteristic error of judgement going into the double right-hander leading on to the main straight, locked up his front brakes and understeered off the track into the sandy run-off area. Fortunately, as had been the case during an otherwise uneventful lunch-time warm-up session when the Williams' throttle linkage had become deranged and sent Jones momentarily off the track then, the car appeared to be undamaged by the incident. Nevertheless, by the time that Jones had been push-started back into the race more than half the field had gone past and first place had become 16th. So now, somewhat to his surprise, Villeneuve took over up front, the French-Canadian still running ahead of Reutemann but never being allowed more than a few car length's leeway even though the second Williams was starting to jump out of third gear. Not far behind them, Prost had just found a way round Andretti's Alfa Romeo in spite of the Renault's damaged front wing, Piquet had come through to a fighting fifth place and, only a little further back again, Watson was busy fending off the close attentions of the fast-rising Laffite. Pironi, having quickly disposed of Patrese and Giacomelli back on the second lap, was also staying in reasonably close contact with the leaders at this stage. But on lap 20 hopes of a decent finish disappeared when he understeered off the track and subsequently ended the lap by diving into the pits for new front tyres and to have the Ferrari's damaged front wing replaced, joining Cheever who was already there having a broken throttle pedal repaired on his Tyrrell. Earlier in the race pit stops had also delayed Tambay (to have a damaged nose cone replaced), Daly (to free sticking throttle slides) and Jabouille (to have his brakes adjusted), but the only retirement so far had been de Cesaris who had notched up his third accident of the weekend by spinning off into the catch-fences half-way round his tenth lap.

As the race progressed it was becoming increasingly clear that Villeneuve was holding sway out in front simply by making full use of the Ferrari's superior straight-line speed to compensate for its poor handling, as 41

1981

for lap after lap Reutemann would close right up to him through the corners only to have to undergo the frustrating experience of watching helplessly as the red car pulled away again along the straight. While this continued Patrese retired his Arrows in the pits with a cooked engine, the overheating possibly caused by the bent front wing restricting the flow of air to the radiator, and on lap 25 Piquet stirred up the dust at the first right-hander by attempting to squeeze through on the inside of Andretti's Alfa Romeo, locking up his brakes and promptly hitting the Italian car amidships as it turned into the corner, for that immediately led to both cars careering off the track. Even so, only Watson and Laffite were able to take advantage of the situation as Piquet gathered it all up quickly enough to resume in sixth place, while Andretti managed to drag his Alfa Romeo out of the sand just before de Angelis arrived, the Italian Lotus driver now in eighth place after having moved ahead of Patrese on lap 7 and, more recently, Giacomelli. To his dismay, however, Andretti soon discovered that the accident had upset his car's handling and within three more laps was not only behind de Angelis but slipping back into the clutches of Mansell, next up in the second black and gold Lotus even though he, too, was far from happy with his car's handling. But before anything came of that there was an even more significant change on lap 29 when Prost, after a race fraught with inconsistent handling, thanks to his bent nose wing, suddenly spun out of third place and was forced to retire on the spot with a stalled engine.

At half-distance the tense situation between Villeneuve and Reutemann was still the same as ever with the Argentinian quite simply unable to do a thing about it in spite of trying everything he knew. Only a few seconds behind them Watson was similarly doing an excellent job of keeping Laffite out and, at the same time, staying well clear of Piquet who was now running in a comparatively lonely fifth place ahead of de Angelis and Mansell in their spaced out Lotus 87s, the young Englishman having overtaken Andretti back on the 32nd lap. Since then Jones had also passed the ill-handling Alfa Romeo in his continuing efforts to claw his way back up through the field but, like his team-mate, he was now being bothered by gearbox trouble and was no longer able to use second gear. Consequently, hopes of making much further progress were looking slim for the World Champion. Indeed, at this stage, all of the leading positions seemed reasonably settled apart from the fact that the slightest mistake from either Villeneuve or Watson would immediately change things round. However, Piquet obviously had other ideas about the situation (unintentionally!) as on lap 44 his Brabham suddenly flew straight off the track, at the same spot as Jones had earlier, for no obvious reason other than driver error and remained firmly stuck in the sand. The third retirement in successive races! And just to make matters worse for the Brabham team it was only minutes later that Rebaque retired the second car with a broken gearbox. Stohr, already delayed by a pit stop, also retired the second Arrows with engine problems at about the same time, but of far greater consequence, so far as the race was concerned, was Laffite finally out-manoeuvering Watson as they came up to lap Jabouille on lap 49 and almost immediately pulling away to give chase to the pair up front.

By lap 60 an already exciting race was turning into a real thriller. Villeneuve was still preserving a precarious-looking lead, Laffite had now not only moved right in behind Reutemann but was already feinting to overtake him, and Watson was no more than a second or so away in fourth place. De Angelis, too, was fast coming into the reckoning due to the comparatively slow pace of the race as Villeneuve struggled more and more for grip around the corners as his tyres deteriorated. In spite of the lack of grip and the enormous pressure, though, Villeneuve remained unflustered. Even when Laffite took over the gauntlet after a disastrous lap 62 for Reutemann in which he was outbraked by the Frenchman at the end of the straight and then boxed in behind Salazar's Ensign, losing another place to Watson, it made no difference, for the Ferrari driver continued to throw off every challenge, not so much by blocking the track but by holding his line. Into the final lap, after some 20 minutes of the first five cars running in absolute tandem and the tension almost unbearable, it was still the same and, although Villeneuve slid wide for the umpteenth time coming out of the last right-hander, the Ferrari's sheer horsepower advantage kept it in front. Across the line it was Ferrari, Talbot, McLaren, Williams and Lotus, covered by little more than a second to round off what surely must have been the best Grand Prix in years. Nearly half a minute behind them, but almost unnoticed in the excitement surrounding Villeneuve's remarkable victory, Mansell came home in sixth place and he was followed, at varying intervals, by the remaining 11 runners as the only other retirement during the latter stages of the race had been Jabouille with brake problems.

Just one sequence of the thrilling leadership tussle as Gilles Villeneuve fends off a determined Carlos Reutemann, watched here by the closely-following Jacques Laffite. (Autosport)

Results

1	G. Villeneuve (Ferrari)	1 hr 46 min 35.01 sec (149.156 kph/ 92.681 mph)	
2	J. Laffite (Talbot-Matra)	1 hr 46 min 35.23 sec	
3	J. Watson (McLaren-Ford)	1 hr 46 min 35.59 sec	
4	C. Reutemann (Williams-Ford)	1 hr 46 min 36.02 sec	
5	E. de Angelis (Lotus-Ford)	1 hr 46 min 36.25 sec	
6	N. Mansell (Lotus-Ford)	1 hr 47 min 03.59 sec	
7	A. Jones (Williams-Ford)	1 hr 47 min 31.59 sec	
8	M. Andretti (Alfa Romeo)	1 hr 47 min 35.81 sec	
9	R. Arnoux (Renault)	1 hr 47 min 42.09 sec	
10	B. Giacomelli (Alfa Romeo)	1 hr 47 min 48.66 sec	
11	F. Serra (Fittipaldi-Ford)	1 lap behind	
12	K. Rosberg (Fittipaldi-Ford)	2 laps behind	
13	P. Tambay (Theodore-Ford)	2 laps behind	
14	E. Salazar (Ensign-Ford)	3 laps behind	
15	D. Pironi (Ferrari)	4 laps behind	
16	D. Daly (March-Ford)	5 laps behind	

Also running at finish: E. Cheever (Tyrrell-Ford) 19 laps behind.

Fastest lap: A. Jones (Williams-Ford) on lap 5 in 1 min 17.818 sec (153.219 kph/95.206 mph)

Retirements

A. de Cesaris (McLaren-Ford) accident on lap 10, R. Patrese (Arrows-Ford) engine on lap 22, A. Prost (Renault) accident on lap 29, N. Piquet (Brabham-Ford) accident on lap 44, S. Stohr (Arrows-Ford) engine on lap 44, H. Rebaque (Brabham-Ford) gearbox on lap 47, J.P. Jabouille (Talbot-Matra) brakes on lap 53.

LXVIIᵉ Grand Prix de France

Dijon-Prenois: July 5
Weather: Cool and changeable
Distance: 80 laps of 3.800 km
circuit = 304.00 km (188.90 miles)

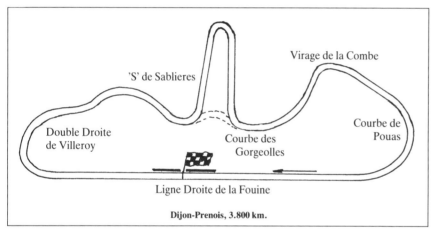

Dijon-Prenois, 3.800 km.

After having been held at Paul Ricard in 1980, this year's French Grand Prix returned to the 3.8 kilometre Dijon-Prenois autodrome in Eastern France. Here the main talking point of the weekend was to be tyres, as immediately following the epic Spanish race the Goodyear Tyre Company had announced its decision to return to the sport, although support was to be limited, initially at least, to the Williams and Brabham teams. Nevertheless, this had now effectively triggered off a new tyre war as Michelin had responded by stating that from now on their development programme would be restricted to only their contracted teams, Renault, Talbot-Ligier, Ferrari and Alfa Romeo, adding that standardized tyres would remain available to other teams provided that they were prepared to pay for them. Prior to the start of practice, though, Michelin were persuaded to continue supplying McLaren, Lotus and Tyrrell for the time being and so, in the end, only Arrows, Fittipaldi, Osella, ATS, RAM March and Theodore had to cough up money, the last two opting to buy

new Avon tyres along with, eventually, Mo Nunn's little Ensign outfit which started out with some old Goodyear covers left over from 1980. Apart from this business over tyres, there were few changes from Jarama and only then mainly due to a not unexpected announcement from Jean-Pierre Jabouille of his decision to retire after never really having fully recovered from the leg injuries sustained during the 1980 Canadian Grand Prix. As a result Talbot-Ligier, who were retaining Jabouille as a test driver and engineer, had brought Patrick Tambay (free of any contractual obligations to Teddy Yip) into their line-up and, in turn, Marc Surer had taken over the Theodore. Meanwhile, the only other change as regards driving strength was to be found at Osella who were running just the one car for 'Beppe' Gabbiani this weekend as Miguel Angel Guerra was still not fit enough to make a come-back, and Giorgio Francia was unavailable due to other commitments. On the technical front, too, everything was reasonably stable, with the only new car on hand being yet another of

the McLaren MP4s to have been built, although among various modifications to have been carried out between races was Patrese's Arrows being given a new rear suspension and a slim-line gearbox casing in the interests of improved air-flow around the back-end of the car, and also the Renault RE30s being fitted with new double-deck rear wings as well as extended side-pods.

Heavy rain on Friday morning led to the opening practice session being a virtual waste of time, for although it eventually stopped the track remained wet throughout. Fortunately, though, by early afternoon a keen wind had just about dried everything up and, apart from a further brief shower of rain, the first period of qualifying was able to proceed somewhat more like normal. Even so, to the Williams and Brabham teams the loss of valuable testing time was of particular significance in the quest to adapt their cars to the Goodyear crossply tyres, something that was soon being reflected in the lap times, for neither the Williams duo of Jones and Reutemann nor Piquet were anywhere near the pace being set by the quickest among the favoured Michelin-shod runners. To make matters more difficult for the two British teams, Jones had been forced into the spare Williams after another bout of gearbox trouble with his intended race chassis, and Piquet hadn't gone far when he, too, had to switch cars due to the onset of a brake fluid leak. Although it applied to everyone, 6 centimetre ground clearance checks being carried out at both the exit and the entrance to the pit lane were not exactly helping matters either, as this merely added to the frustrations. Consequently, when it was all over, it was no real surprise to find that even the fastest among this somewhat unhappy trio, Reutemann, was down in eighth place on the time-sheets at 1 min 08.83 sec (a time which had later been equalled by de Cesaris), while Piquet and Jones were only eleventh and twelfth respectively behind Mansell. Ahead of them, meanwhile, were Watson, who was absolutely delighted with

1981

Starting Grid

	R. Arnoux (5)
	Renault
J. Watson (3)	(1 min 05.95 sec)
McLaren-Ford	
(1 min 06.36 sec)	A. Prost (2)
	Renault
N. Piquet (1)	(1 min 06.36 sec)
Brabham-Ford	
(1 min 06.91 sec)	A. de Cesaris (14)
	McLaren-Ford
J. Laffite (7)	(1 min 07.03 sec)
Talbot-Matra	
(1 min 07.09 sec)	C. Reutemann (4)
	Williams-Ford
E. de Angelis (8)	(1 min 07.42 sec)
Lotus-Ford	
(1 min 07.52 sec)	A. Jones (18)
	Williams-Ford
M. Andretti (11)	(1 min 07.53 sec)
Alfa Romeo	
(1 min 07.56 sec)	G. Villeneuve (–)
	Ferrari
B. Giacomelli (13)	(1 min 07.60 sec)
Alfa Romeo	
(1 min 07.63 sec)	N. Mansell (10)
	Lotus-Ford
D. Pironi (9)	(1 min 07.72 sec)
Ferrari	
(1 min 08.09 sec)	H. Rebaque (6)
	Brabham-Ford
P. Tambay (–)	(1 min 08.21 sec)
Talbot-Matra	
(1 min 08.47 sec)	K. Rosberg (–)
	Fittipaldi-Ford
R. Patrese (15)	(1 min 09.35 sec)
Arrows-Ford	
(1 min 09.37 sec)	E. Cheever (16)
	Tyrrell-Ford
D. Daly (19)	(1 min 09.88 sec)
March-Ford	
(1 min 09.94 sec)	M. Surer (12)
	Theodore-Ford
E. Salazar (–)	(1 min 10.21 sec)
Ensign-Ford	
(1 min 10.50 sec)	M. Alboreto (17)
	Tyrrell-Ford
*F. Serra	(1 min 10.64 sec)
Fittipaldi-Ford	
(1 min 10.86 sec)	

*Non-starter: F. Serra (Fittipaldi-Ford)
1 min 10.86 sec

Did not qualify:
S. Stohr (Arrows-Ford) 1 min 11.24 sec
B. Henton (Toleman-Hart) 1 min 11.28 sec
S. Borgudd (ATS-Ford) 1 min 12.20 sec
G. Gabbiani (Osella-Ford) 1 min 12.24 sec
D. Warwick (Toleman-Hart) 1 min 13.65 sec

Numbers in brackets denote grid positions for restart.

his ever-improving McLaren MP4, and had responded by turning in the afternoon's fastest time of 1 min 07.05 sec, Arnoux (1 min 07.09 sec) and Prost (1 min 07.57 sec) in their Renaults, Villeneuve (1 min 07.60 sec) and Pironi (1 min 08.09 sec) in their Ferraris and, finally, de Angelis (1 min 08.40 sec) and Laffite (1 min 08.71 sec). All seven drivers had made the most of the soft qualifying rubber that Michelin had supplied to their respective teams.

The weather was still indifferent on Saturday with overcast skies and the same cold wind. Nevertheless, above all else it was dry,

thereby enabling everyone to make the most of the 90 minute untimed session to prepare for the final hour of qualifying – or so it seemed. As it happened things didn't exactly work out as planned for some of them, with Mansell being the first to hit trouble when he pulled up at a marshals' post with his Lotus 87 merrily on fire. A fuel pipe had become detached. But the marshals then proceeded to turn a comparatively minor problem into a near disaster by over-reacting and covering the entire car from top to bottom with extinguisher foam which, subsequently, was to take an age for the Lotus mechanics to clean up. It also left Mansell with no alternative other than to revert to the older and spare Lotus 81, although not before Villeneuve had gone one better and brought activities to a temporary halt by simply overdoing things and crashing at the fast downhill right-hander leading on to the main straight. Luckily the French-Canadian walked away from the scene unharmed apart from a scratch on his cheek caused by a catch fencing pole having clouted the side of his helmet and, after the damaged Ferrari had been retrieved, was ready to go out again in the team's spare car when practice resumed some 20 minutes later. However, for the Ferrari mechanics there was to be no respite, for no sooner had they knuckled down to the task of straightening out Villeneuve's car than Pironi suffered a spectacular engine failure. Other teams were also having their share of problems, albeit under somewhat less dramatic circumstances. That is until just as the flag was about to come out to signify the end of the session when Warwick caused a major headache in the Toleman camp by inexplicably sliding off into the barriers at the hairpin in his TG181B and badly damaging the monocoque.

Come the start of the final hour both Mansell and Villeneuve's cars had been made ready for their respective drivers but because the engine change on Pironi's car was still in the process of being completed the Frenchman took over the spare Ferrari as an interim measure. The Toleman team, on the other hand, had no spare car for Warwick and, although repairs were in hand, they were to take so long that the Englishman was destined to remain a spectator, not only for the afternoon but for the rest of the weekend after having ended the first day in the non-qualifying zone yet again. In the meantime, the pace out on the track was soon warming up nicely with the battle for pole position developing into a three-cornered contest between Watson, in the impressively stable-looking McLaren MP4, and the two Renault drivers, Arnoux and Prost, who were finding the cool conditions ideal for their turbo-charged V6 engines. The conditions, of course, equally suited the turbo-charged Ferraris, but both Villeneuve and Pironi were struggling against the now

usual problem of poor handling, and making nowhere near the same impression. Indeed, neither driver could better his Friday time despite some truly gallant efforts that included Villeneuve nearly – very nearly – going off again at the same spot as in the morning, his Ferrari sideways more often than not throughout most of the afternoon. Furthermore, amidst an almost universal lowering of lap times, they found themselves rapidly sliding down the grid order and, in fact, by the end of practice Villeneuve had been elbowed back to a disappointing eleventh place, and Pironi to an even more lowly fourteenth, behind Giacomelli and Mansell. In complete contrast, Arnoux had celebrated what was his 33rd birthday in fine style by going faster and faster before finally wrapping up pole position with a real flier in 1 min 05.95 sec (207.430 kph), pipping Watson and Prost, who had turned in identical times of 1 min 06.36 sec, by very nearly half a second. Immediately behind these first three, the Brabham team had obviously made good progress in adapting to the Goodyear crossplies, as Piquet had netted fourth fastest time of 1 min 06.91 sec – a splendid performance when considering that he was using race rubber unlike his Michelin-shod rivals – and then came de Cesaris, underlining the suitability of the McLaren MP4 to the circuit with a pleasantly surprising fifth fastest time of 1 min 07.03 sec. Laffite was next at 1 min 07.09 sec and then followed a closely matched quartet comprising Reutemann and Jones in their Williams, de Angelis and Andretti, all four covered by a mere 0.14 sec. Among the rest, Tambay had qualified for his first race in the Talbot-Ligier reasonably comfortably, as had Surer in the Avon-shod Theodore in spite of quite severe handling problems, but the Arrows team was particularly unhappy with the outcome of practice. An openly disenchanted Patrese had qualified in only 18th spot on his standardized Michelin tyres and Stohr had failed altogether, having been bumped off the grid in the closing minutes by Serra after the Brazilian had taken over the spare Fittipaldi following an engine failure on his usual car.

Serra's efforts in scrambling on to the back of the grid were to go unrewarded, as during Sunday morning's warm-up session he damaged his Fittipaldi beyond immediate repair after sliding off into the catch-fences at Pouas and had to be posted a non-starter. Hopes of using the team's spare car had been dashed by an engine that refused to run properly. Consequently, with reserve drivers no longer permitted under the Concorde Agreement, only twenty-three cars eventually lined up on the grid for the 1 p.m. start in conditions that were cool and mainly overcast. The start, itself, could well have had disastrous consequences as, due to an electrical fault, the starting lights caused all kinds of confusion with their erratic behaviour – red and green appearing almost simultaneously, then red on its own, then green! As it was most drivers managed to keep out of each other's way, even though some of them took off sooner than others, and about the only casualty was Jones' Williams which finished up with a bent steering tie-rod after being brought into contact with Andretti's Alfa Romeo. Nevertheless, the fiasco had completely thrown Arnoux in pole position and it was Piquet who led the field through the first right-hander, the Brazilian having swerved around the back of Watson's McLaren and outdragged the Ulsterman and Prost in the run up to the braking area. Villeneuve was another not to have wasted a moment in getting under way and was quickly up into a splendid fifth place from 11th on the grid, worrying de Cesaris just ahead of him. Arnoux, meanwhile, went on to complete the opening lap in a disgruntled ninth place behind Laffite, Andretti and Reutemann, while Jones, who was to last only two more laps before stopping to have the bent steering tie-rod replaced, was a further two places lower in the order behind Pironi.

Piquet immediately started to assert himself out in front which suggested that Goodyear might well have come up with a better race tyre than Michelin especially after Prost, losing little time in dealing with Watson on the third lap, seemed powerless to prevent the Brabham from continuing to draw away. Meanwhile, there was some really exciting wheel-to-wheel stuff taking place just behind the leading trio with positions changing hands one after the other. Initially, after he'd barged past de Cesaris, also on the third lap, it was Villeneuve in fourth place. But then, on lap 6, Reutemann took over after having systematically worked his way past Andretti and Laffite on the second lap and de Cesaris on the fourth. Arnoux, too, was obviously out to make amends for his tardy start for he had followed Reutemann up through the field and on lap 8 was up into a somewhat more respectable fifth place with Villeneuve now sixth. After that, though, the leading positions began to settle down with the next change of any significance not occurring until the start of lap 16. At that point Laffite then decided that he had had enough of watching de Cesaris following Villeneuve around the circuit and forced his way by the Italian McLaren driver under braking for the first right-hander past the pits to see what he could do about the Ferrari. To his dismay, however, Laffite soon discovered that he was becoming involved in another cat-and-mouse game just as at Jarama and, despite making a number of determined efforts to displace the red car, repeatedly failed to make it past.

After twenty laps Piquet's lead had grown to more than 10 seconds, helped to some extent by Prost now having difficulty selecting fourth gear in his Renault. Despite his

problems, however, the Frenchman was still maintaining a useful advantage over Watson who, in turn, was running alone in third place after Reutemann had earlier closed up to him only to have dropped back again with a blistering left front tyre. In fifth place, too, Arnoux was doing little more than holding his ground with the result that most of the attention was remaining fixed on Villeneuve's attempts to hold on to sixth place from Laffite and de Cesaris who were staying tightly bunched up behind the Ferrari. To add to the interest, only a short distance away Pironi was coming under attack from Rebaque who had been making noticeable progress in the second Brabham ever since the start of the race. This continued with the Mexican getting the better of Pironi in a somewhat desperate manoeuvre on the very next lap – the Brabham and Ferrari momentarily banging wheels – and then taking only until lap 29 before ousting de Cesaris from eighth place. Not content with that, Rebaque then immediately set about Laffite, and within another lap was pulling out of the Talbot's slipstream along the straight and moving up yet another place. After that, though, Rebaque found his progress being halted by the irrepressible Villeneuve and simply had to sit it out until lap 42 when the French-Canadian finally decided that he had a good enough reason to move over – an electrical failure had cut the Ferrari's engine dead! By this time other changes had occurred as Arnoux had caught and passed Reutemann back on lap 33, and de Angelis, having followed Rebaque past Pironi on the 21st lap, had more recently elbowed his way in between Laffite and de Cesaris to lie eighth. However, even more interesting was the fact that the leaders had now closed up somewhat, for a problem with sticking throttle slides on his Brabham ever since the early stages of the race was making the business of lapping slower cars more difficult than usual for Piquet, and this had enabled Prost, in spite of not being able to select fourth gear at all now, to reduce the deficit to little more than 6 seconds. Meanwhile, Watson, having a trouble-free run, was visibly gaining ground in third place. Furthermore, all three were now in the process of lapping the group battling it out for sixth place and, with Jones starting to shadow Piquet all around the circuit, albeit four laps in arrears after further pit stops for fresh front tyres and to check a suspected loose wheel nut, the next few laps produced a flurry of excitement with cars seemingly all over one another. In the midst of it all Reutemann repassed Arnoux on lap 45 when the second Renault also began giving its driver gearbox problems, and behind them de Cesaris did likewise to de Angelis on the same lap. Once through all the heavy traffic, though, Piquet emerged still holding a good 6 second advantage over Prost and was looking pretty secure until

shortly afterwards, on lap 54, when light rain started to fall on the far side of the circuit. At first it was barely noticeable but within minutes virtually the entire circuit was awash due to a sudden downpour and as Piquet came round to complete his 59th lap he turned off into the pits after being confronted by a red flag. The race was being stopped – just one lap short of 75% of the race distance at which point it could have been considered finished.

The heavy shower of rain disappeared as quickly as it had come and just over half an hour later, with the track almost dry again, the nineteen cars that had still been running at the end of the original race (Salazar, Rosberg and Tambay had been the only retirements apart from Villeneuve) were lining up in front of the pits for the restart of what had now become a two-part event. In accordance with the rules the actual grid order for the restart was determined by the finishing positions in the first part of the race, which was rather unfortunate for de Cesaris as a pit stop at the end of his 56th lap for wet-weather tyres had dropped the Italian way down to fourteenth place. The rules also dictated that the overall result of the Grand Prix would be arrived at by aggregating the times after 58 laps with those of the remaining 22 laps, so from Piquet's point of view even if he was beaten in the second part of the race, provided that it was less than his 6.79 sec advantage in the first part, he would still be the winner.

This time round the starting lights behaved themselves perfectly and when red gave way to green it was Prost who was first off the line with Watson taking up second place from Piquet as the leaders arrived at the first right-hander. The Ulsterman had actually ended the first part of the race a mere 0.49 sec behind Prost and quickly demonstrated his keenness to wipe out the deficit by taking only half a lap before pulling alongside the Renault going into the left-hander after the loop. For a moment, with the McLaren nosing ahead, it looked as if Watson was going to make it, but the still slightly damp track then caused him to slide wide enabling Prost to go ahead once more. Watson, meanwhile, gathered it all up after narrowly avoiding a spin and had to be satisfied to complete the lap still in second place ahead of Arnoux, Piquet, Reutemann, Pironi and the rest except for Laffite who was already out with damaged front suspension after having run into the back of Reutemann's Williams. Rebaque, though, was lucky to be still amongst them as he had also made contact with the Williams early on the lap after spinning wildly in a vain attempt to get past. As it was the Mexican was now bringing up the rear.

It soon became obvious that a decision by Michelin to supply their favoured runners with softer tyres during the interval was

The second part of the rain-interrupted French Grand Prix: John Watson slides wide after attempting to wrest away the lead from Alain Prost, while René Arnoux and Nelson Piquet follow in third and fourth places respectively. *(Phipps Photographic)*

having the desired effect, for in spite of no longer being troubled by sticking throttle slides – these had been freed during prepartions for the restart – Piquet rapidly started losing contact with the leading trio. Moreover, after barely a handful of laps Prost and Watson, circulating around 2 seconds apart, had both eaten away the Brazilian's 6.79 sec advantage and between them were completely dominating proceedings with even

Arnoux unable to sustain the same pace in third place. As this continued Daly retired the RAM March when he felt the engine start to tighten, this putting an end to an eventful afternoon for the Irishman that had included a couple of spins and a lengthy pit stop for a new nose wing, and on lap 17 Piquet's frustrations were not helped at all by Reutemann and Pironi barging past him, even though they were both well in arrears

on aggregate times. Within another lap, however, Reutemann was in trouble and not only behind Piquet again but dropping away dramatically with a misfiring engine which was to take him out of the points and into a thoroughly disappointing tenth place in the final classification. In the meantime, there was no change up front and although Watson keep the pressure on Prost right up until the finish, the Frenchman, with his boost pres-

Alain Prost celebrates his first Grand Prix victory in style, flanked by John Watson, who was classified second, and the third-placed Nelson Piquet. *(Phipps Photographic)*

sure turned up and fourth gear working again, refused to be ruffled and eventually notched up his first Grand Prix victory in front of a near-delirious crowd by the narrow margin of 1.80 seconds, 2.29 seconds on aggregate times. Behind them, Arnoux duly finished on his own in third place, followed some 20 seconds later by Pironi and Piquet who crossed the line virutally together ahead of the other twelve cars still running. In the final classification, though, Piquet had still beaten Arnoux by over 18 seconds and so moved up to third place overall, albeit still pondering at what might have been had the rain held off for just a few more minutes! Completing the list of points finishers was de Angelis after a spirited duel with his teammate, Mansell, in the second part of the race.

Results

1	A. Prost (Renault)	1 hr 35 min 48.13 sec (190.392 kph/ 118.304 mph)	8	M. Andretti (Alfa Romeo)	1 lap behind	17	A. Jones (Williams-Ford)	4 laps behind
2	J. Watson (McLaren-Ford)	1 hr 35 min 50.42 sec	9	H. Rebaque (Brabham-Ford)	2 laps behind			
3	N. Piquet (Brabham-Ford)	1 hr 36 min 12.35 sec	10	C. Reutemann (Williams-Ford)	2 laps behind			
4	R. Arnoux (Renault)	1 hr 36 min 30.43 sec	11	A. de Cesaris (McLaren-Ford)	2 laps behind			
5	D. Pironi (Ferrari)	1 lap behind	12	M. Surer (Theodore-Ford)	2 laps behind			
6	E. de Angelis (Lotus-Ford)	1 lap behind	13	E. Cheever (Tyrrell-Ford)	3 laps behind			
7	N. Mansell (Lotus-Ford)	1 lap behind	14	R. Patrese (Arrows-Ford)	3 laps behind			
			15	B. Giacomelli (Alfa Romeo)	3 laps behind			
			16	M. Alboreto (Tyrrell-Ford)	3 laps behind			

Fastest lap: A. Prost (Renault) on lap 64 in 1 min 09.14 sec (197.859 kph/122.944 mph)

Retirements
E. Salazar (Ensign-Ford) rear suspension on lap 7, K. Rosberg (Fittipaldi-Ford) rear suspension on lap 12, P. Tambay (Talbot-Matra) rear hub bearing on lap 31, G. Villeneuve (Ferrari) electrics on lap 42, D. Daly (March-Ford) engine on lap 56, J. Laffite (Talbot-Matra) front suspension on lap 59. (Results given are the aggregate for the two-part race).

XXXIVth British Grand Prix

Silverstone: July 18
Weather: Warm and sunny
Distance: 68 laps of 4.7185 km
circuit = 320.86 km (199.37 miles)

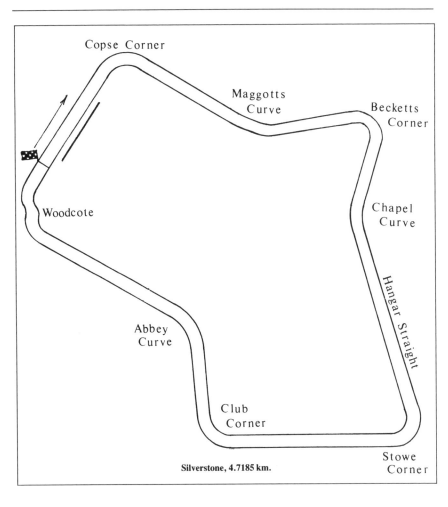

Silverstone, 4.7185 km.

During the period leading up to the Marlboro-sponsored British Grand Prix the Lotus 88 affair had come to the forefront again as Colin Chapman had now produced a 'B' version of his innovative design which, after having been scrutineered, the RAC Motor Sports Association had stated complied with the Formula 1 technical regulations. FISA, on the other hand, disagreed and had responded by referring back to the FIA International Court of Appeal hearing, and by stating that penalties would be imposed if the car was allowed to run, suggesting even that the race might be stripped of World Championship status. The RAC Motor Sports Association had remained firm on the matter, however, and told Chapman that provided the car presented at Silverstone was in all material respects identical to that recently examined it would be passed by the race scrutineers. Naturally, this had delighted the Lotus team chief and, sure enough, when pre-race scrutineering took place on the Wednesday before the race both the originally presented car and two new ones that had been put together were accepted. Then, shortly afterwards, came the first sign of trouble – Ferrari, Talbot-Ligier and Alfa Romeo lodged official protests. Nevertheless, come the start of practice the next day de Angelis and Mansell both went out in the controversial cars and quickly knuckled down to the task of trying to sort them for the first period of qualifying in the afternoon; the now familiar 'John Player Special' legend, incidentally, having been substituted by 'Courage' in deference to the UK Government's restrictions on tobacco advertising. Behind the scenes, though, discussions had already taken place concerning the protests and, soon after the start of

1981

practice, FISA issued a statement to the effect that the Lotus 88B did not comply with the Formula 1 technical regulations and that they were charging the RAC Motor Sports Association, the race officials and Chapman with upholding their decision. This, of course, then led to more discussions and eventually the Stewards, only too well aware that the International Sporting Code gave FISA authority to inflict a penalty, decided that they had no alternative other than to acquiesce. Consequently, with the day's practice sessions having ended in the mean-

time, the lap times set by de Angelis (1 min 16.029 sec) and Mansell (1 min 15.922 sec) had to be scrubbed on the grounds that they had been using illegal cars, and the Lotus team was left in a position of having to completely reorganize themselves. This they subsequently did by converting the two newer 88Bs back to 87 specification overnight and by transporting in the only remaining 87 from their factory at Hethel.

Aside from this latest round of political manoeuverings, the day's activities out on the track had produced problems of another sort for some of the teams. Tyrrell were particularly unhappy as having brought along their brand new 011 for its first public outing, Cheever had contrived to damage it beyond immediate repair during the first qualifying session – he had clipped a kerb at the chicane and not only careered off the track, but gone through three of four layers of catch fencing and head-on into the barriers! Luckily the American had been unharmed in the frightful incident and had subsequently carried on practising in the team's spare 010. Not long afterwards, however, it had been the turn of the Candy Toleman team to be confronted by a major setback when Henton's car also slid off at the chicane with equally disastrous consequences or worse as the Englishman had emerged from the wreckage with a scalded thigh caused by a burst radiator. Talbot-Ligier had had a fraught time of it, too, having seen their cars breaking up rear hub bearings with alarming regularity throughout the day. As a result neither Laffite nor Tambay had been able to get into any sort of rhythm at all and more often than not were forced to take turns behind the wheel of the spare Talbot. Nevertheless, it had not all been gloom and despondency, and for the other French team, Renault, things couldn't have turned out much better as Arnoux (1 min 12.158 sec) and Prost (1 min 12.237 sec) had completely dominated proceedings, their reliably-running RE30s, fitted with new single pillar-mounted rear aerofoils, handling superbly and absolutely flying around the fast Silverstone circuit. Only Piquet, who had given the new BMW-engined Brabham BT50 a brief airing in the morning, had lapped anywhere near as quick for he had taken his more familiar BT49C around in 1 min 12.328 sec whereas everyone else had been at least a full second off the pace apart from Jones in the quicker of the two Williams at 1 min 12.998 sec. Creditable performances from both, especially when bearing in mind that they had been using Goodyear tyres designed to last the race distance, unlike the Michelin qualifying rubber supplied to Renault and the French firm's other favoured runners.

Friday was to be another joy-day for Renault as once again their drivers were uncatchable. Even when Prost was forced to switch cars during the final period of

qualifying, following an engine failure, it made no difference to the overall situation and the front row of the grid was never in doubt, Arnoux clinching his second pole position in a fortnight at 1 min 11.000 sec and Prost coming out a mere 0.046 sec slower in the spare car for second spot. Indeed, such was their margin of superiority that even Piquet, continuing to lead the opposition, was almost a full second behind them this time out, for the best that he could manage on the harder compound Goodyear tyres after using both the Brabham BT49C and the new BT50 was a lap of 1 min 11.952 sec in the Ford-Cosworth-engined car. The Williams team, meanwhile, were all at sixes and sevens as for the second day running both of their drivers were complaining of lack of traction out of the corners, and now they were having engine problems to contend with as well; Jones suffering a broken valve and Reutemann having his progress hampered by an incurable misfire. The result of all of this was that Jones failed to improve on his Thursday time and was elbowed back to seventh place on the grid, while Reutemann, after making only a marginal improvement to 1 min 13.371 sec, was left down in ninth place. Ferrari were not exactly overjoyed at the outcome of practice either as, on paper at least, Silverstone should have been ideally suited to the turbocharged 126CKs. Once again, though, deficiencies in the handling department had kept them out of the picture somewhat, and whilst Pironi, showing no ill-effects from an off-course excursion at Becketts during the morning untimed session, had managed to narrowly pip the impressive-looking McLaren MP4s of Watson and de Cesaris for fourth place on the grid at 1 min 12.644 sec, Villeneuve had come out only eighth fastest. Not that this was entirely surprising, as having opted to use the spare Ferrari, which was running with revised front and rear suspension and seemed to be handling better, the French-Canadian had found the engine down on power!

As far as the rest were concerned the biggest disappointment had to be the plight of the Lotus team drivers as de Angelis had just about scraped on to the grid, in 22nd spot, and Mansell had failed to qualify. Under the circumstances, though, this was fully understandable, as apart from having only the one day in which to sort their hastily-prepared 87s, the pair of them had also had to try to adapt their cars to new tyres as Lotus had now been added to Goodyear's short list of customers. Meanwhile, among other disappointments were Serra being left in the non-qualifying zone after having had his best time squashed due to his Fittipaldi failing a 6 centimetre ground clearance check, and also Henton being bumped off the grid after having ended the first day 19th fastest – the spare Toleman, the team's original chassis, had been much slower and, like Warwick's sister car, had ended practice covered in extinguisher foam after a split exhaust manifold had caused a fire! In contrast to these hard-luck stories, Surer had squeezed the Avon-shod Theodore on to the back of the grid despite a troubled practice with both a brand new, stiffer chassis and the older car; and for the first time since Belgium Osella were in a race, thanks to the efforts of their latest new recruit, Jean-Pierre Jarier. Borgudd, too, had qualified the ATS for the first time since Imola, while Arrows, now using Pirelli tyres after have fallen victim to Michelin's new policy at Dijon, were yet another team to have ended practice in better shape than recently. Patrese had qualified for tenth place on the grid and Stohr 18th, sandwiched between Daly, driving a new and lighter March 811, and Alboreto in fractionally the quicker of the two Tyrrells after having switched from Michelin tyres to some old-stock Goodyears held by his team.

After two days of mainly cool and overcast conditions, Saturday was altogether warmer and brighter and from an early hour the crowds poured into the circuit in their thousands, many of them having camped overnight. The race, itself, was not due to start until 3 p.m. but there was plenty to watch beforehand with supporting events ranging from Formula 3 and saloon car races to a whole variety of displays and demonstrations, including an appearance by the inimitable Red Arrows aerobatic team. In addition, just after mid-day, there was the customary 30 minute warm-up session which passed without any untoward incidents apart from de Cesaris spinning off at Stowe, fortunately doing little more than superficial damage to his McLaren MP4. Andretti, though, felt that his car was lacking in power and so, as a precautionary measure, the Alfa Romeo mechanics subsequently knuckled down to the task of carrying out a hurried engine change. Among the rest the Williams team, after trying both 13 inch and 15 inch front wheels during practice, had opted for the larger ones to avoid any overheating problems, Villeneuve had forsaken the modified spare Ferrari and was back in his more familiar car, Surer was in the new Theodore and Piquet, fastest in the warm-up, was preparing to use carbon-fibre discs for the first time in a race.

A couple of hours or so after the warm-up the waiting was nearly all over. The grid had formed and with the clock ticking away to 3 p.m. Arnoux finally led the field away on the pace lap, the long crocodile of cars snaking their way around the circuit as their drivers sought to bring tyres up to working temperature. Then, with everyone back on the grid once more, on went the starting lights, engines screamed and they were on their way rushing towards Copse Corner and jostling wildly for positions. Out in front the

two Renault drivers had got away superbly but then so had Pironi, and as they turned into the right-hander it was Renault – Ferrari – Renault followed by Brabham and the other Ferrari, Villeneuve having made yet another demon start from the fourth row of the grid. Even so, fifth place was of little interest to the French-Canadian as he clearly demonstrated by storming past Piquet on the approach to Becketts, out-braking Arnoux for Stowe and then moving up to start attacking his team-mate as the cars streamed out of the chicane to complete lap one, led by Prost. Behind them, Arnoux was still holding down fourth place ahead of Piquet, while Jones, Watson, de Cesaris, Reutemann and the two Alfa Romeos of Andretti and Giacomelli completed the front half of an already depleted field – Stohr's Arrows had gone off into the catch-fences at Club Corner and Alboreto was limping slowly round to the pits to retire his Tyrrell with a cooked clutch. This seemed to be of little consequence as far as the crowd was concerned, however, for their eyes were firmly glued on Villeneuve bobbing about all over the place behind Pironi in his attempts to find a way through. Exciting stuff, and even more so at Club Corner for there, momentarily, the two Ferraris were virtually side by side with Villeneuve making a run down the inside of his team-mate. With Pironi holding his line, however, Villeneuve was forced to back off and in the blink of an eye lost his third place to Arnoux. After the next lap, though, having lost another place to Piquet and with Arnoux now ahead of Pironi, it all became academic so far as Villeneuve was concerned for as the leaders filed out of the chicane to complete the fourth tour he suddenly clouted a kerb and in the next instant the Ferrari was spinning wildly amidst plumes of dense tyre smoke. Then, to add to the confusion, he was promptly collected amidships by Jones' closely following Williams, the Australian simply having nowhere else to go. Also tucked up tightly behind, Watson stood on his brakes and just managed to keep out of harm's way as the pair in front of him headed towards the catch-fences, but de Cesaris, in swerving to the left to avoid his team-mate, charged head-on into the catch-fences and out of the race. Bad luck indeed. Jones also retired on the spot, although the amazing Villeneuve, having kept his engine running, pointed his badly damaged Ferrari back in the right direction and rejoined the race, only to make it as far as Stowe before deciding that the car was undriveable! In the meantime, Watson had been passed by Reutemann, Andretti, Giacomelli, Tambay and Laffite before getting properly under way again, but even so considered himself fortunate in coming out of the incident unharmed. Furthermore, he quickly made up lost ground, repassing the two Talbots on successive laps and then moving up behind

Andretti on lap 6 when Giacomelli became the sixth retirement (already!) by stopping at Becketts with a broken gearbox. Ahead of all this drama, meanwhile, Renault appeared to be running away with the race for Prost had already opened up a 6 second advantage while Arnoux was looking more than comfortable in second place ahead of Piquet and Pironi who had just swopped places.

More dust rose on lap 12. This time it was at Becketts when Piquet, having closed to within just a few car lengths of Arnoux's Renault, had the left front tyre suddenly explode on his Brabham. Instantly out of control, the car careered off the track, through the catch-fences and on into the wooden barriers with a sickening thump. Mercifully, though, after having been helped out of the wreckage by marshals, it was found that Piquet had escaped with no more than severe bruising despite initial worries that he might have broken a bone in his left foot. Nevertheless, it had certainly put an end to a gallant chase and left the two Renaults in total command, with Pironi now a distant third. Consequently, with things looking settled up front, the crowd's attention started drifting further down the field and to Watson in particular as while Piquet's drama was being enacted he had overtaken Andretti's Alfa Romeo and was now moving in on Reutemann's Williams. Watson was to waste no time over the matter either, as on the very next lap he caught the Argentinian totally unawares going into the chicane and then immediately followed this up by taking only so far as Becketts before barging past Pironi in another breath-taking manoeuvre, literally seconds prior to the Ferrari turbo expiring in a cloud of smoke! The big question after that, of course, was whether Watson could catch the Renaults. Well, the immediate answer was that it seemed unlikely for they were both over 20 seconds clear, but then on lap 17 came more unexpected drama when Prost suddenly pulled off into the pit lane with a mis-firing engine, and was subsequently forced to retire. Only moments earlier, Tambay had also retired his Talbot somewhat less noticeably with similar trouble after an earlier change of plugs had done nothing to alleviate the problem and so, with barely a quarter of the race run, there had now been no less than ten retirements.

On lap 19 it was the turn of de Angelis to steal the headlines. Ever since the start of the race he had been steadily climbing up through the field from his lowly grid position and, more recently, had moved past Rebaque into sixth place to take up station behind Patrese and Laffite who had themselves swopped places only minutes earlier. Fine progress indeed. But then the Italian blotted his copybook by overtaking the Talbot team-leader at Becketts under the presence of yellow and white flags and with an ambu-

1981

John Watson drives on to an extremely popular victory at Silverstone, shown here being followed, a lap down, by Jacques Laffite's Talbot. (*L.A.T. Photographic*)

his fastest lap, began to slow with the Renault engine no longer sounding so sweet. In fact, it now had a distinct flat note about it, and certainly within a couple more laps it was apparent that the Frenchman was in trouble as for the first time Watson was actually gaining on him. Moreover, it was by two or three seconds on each lap, sending the crowd delirious, and on lap 61 their reactions said it all – Watson had not only wiped out the near half minute deficit but was leading the British Grand Prix! It seemed almost unbelievable, no more so than to Watson himself as he was later to freely admit, but it was real all right, and just over seven laps later the Ulsterman was crossing the line for the final time to score his first Grand Prix victory since Austria 1976 and only the second in his career.

Almost unnoticed in the excitement surrounding the popular winner, things had turned from bad to worse for the unfortunate Arnoux as just under four laps from home he had ground to a halt at Copse Corner with a dead engine. Consequently, it was Reutemann who finished in second place, while in third place, a lap down, was Laffite as Patrese had also gone out with an engine failure in the closing minutes, and Andretti had disappeared on lap 60 with broken throttle linkage caused by no more than a split pin having worked loose! Rosberg and Surer had been yet two more drivers to have retired late in the race and so only five others, Cheever, Rebaque, Borgudd, Daly and Jarier, finished, the last two having been delayed by early pit stops.

lance on the circuit taking Piquet to the medical unit. As a result it was not long before a black flag appeared for car number 11, and on lap 24 de Angelis turned off into the pit lane to be confronted by a stern-faced Steward. Words were exchanged and, believing that he was to be disqualified (incorrectly!), de Angelis unfastened his safety harness, stepped out of his car and walked off in a fit of temper to conclude a thoroughly dismal weekend for the Lotus team. His reactions were also to cost him a £100 fine! In the meantime, the race was fast

degenerating into a procession for, in spite of driving with exceptional fortitude, Watson was making no impression at all on Arnoux, merely holding the gap at around 25 seconds, and most of the other remaining 11 cars were also well spaced out. In fact, apart from Patrese catching Andretti's Alfa Romeo and going past on lap 38, and also Rebaque losing time (and places) with two tyre stops shortly afterwards, there was no significant change at all until just past the 50 lap mark. Then, quite unexpectedly, the race sprang to life again when Arnoux, having just recorded

Results			
1	J. Watson (McLaren-Ford)	1 hr 26 min 54.80 sec (221.509 kph/ 137.639 mph)	
2	C. Reutemann (Williams-Ford)	1 hr 27 min 35.45 sec	
3	J. Laffite (Talbot-Matra)	1 lap behind	
4	E. Cheever (Tyrrell-Ford)	1 lap behind	
5	H. Rebaque (Brabham-Ford)	1 lap behind	
6	S. Borgudd (ATS-Ford)	1 lap behind	
7	D. Daly (March-Ford)	2 laps behind	
8	J. P. Jarier (Osella-Ford)	3 laps behind	
*9	R. Arnoux (Renault)	4 laps behind	
*10	R. Patrese (Arrows-Ford)	4 laps behind	
*11	M. Surer (Theodore-Ford)	7 laps behind	

*Not running at finish.

Fastest lap: R. Arnoux (Renault) on lap 50 in 1 min 15.067 sec. (226.289 kph/140.610 mph)

Retirements
S. Stohr (Arrows-Ford) accident on lap 1, M. Alboreto (Tyrrell-Ford) clutch on lap 1, A. Jones (Williams-Ford) accident on lap 4, A. de Cesaris (McLaren-Ford) accident on lap 4, G. Villeneuve (Ferrari) accident damage on lap 5, B. Giacomelli (Alfa Romeo) gearbox on lap 6, N. Piquet (Brabham-Ford) accident on lap 12, D. Pironi (Ferrari) engine on lap 14, P. Tambay (Talbot-Matra) ignition on lap 15, A. Prost (Renault) engine on lap 17, E. de Angelis (Lotus-Ford) black-flagged on lap 24, K. Rosberg (Fittipaldi-Ford) rear suspension on lap 56, M. Andretti (Alfa-Romeo) throttle linkage on lap 60.

XLIII Grosser Preis von Deutschland

Hockenheim: August 2
Weather: Overcast but mainly dry
Distance: 45 laps of 6.789 km
circuit = 305.50 km (189.83 miles)

Almost immediately following the Silverstone weekend, discussions had taken place between the designers with a view to dispensing with the hydraulic ride height control apparatus and to seek a reduction in

the minimum weight limit by a corresponding amount. However, whilst the designers had been in agreement, Ferrari's Marco Piccinini had objected, and so the virtually solid suspensions, causing cars to be extremely

nervous and subjecting drivers to a severe pounding, were to remain as everyone assembled at the Hockenheim-Ring for round 10 of the World Championship. There were overall few changes in evidence as the driver line-up was identical to the previous race and most of the cars were essentially the same, with the majority of those damaged at Silverstone, including the new Tyrrell 011, having been repaired. Lack of time, though,

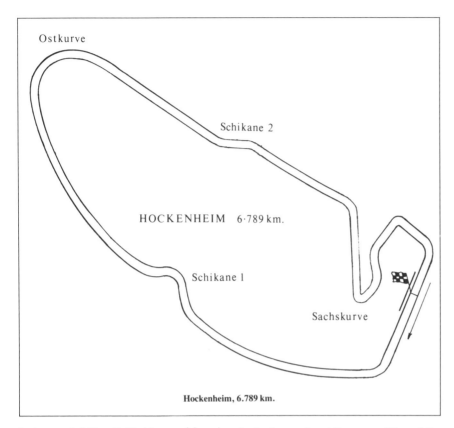

Ostkurve

Schikane 2

HOCKENHEIM 6·789 km.

Schikane 1

Sachskurve

Hockenheim, 6.789 km.

had prevented Piquet's Brabham and Jones' Williams from being straightened out, and instead the two teams had built up new cars for their drivers, both to existing designs. Nevertheless, the new Brabham was generally stiffer than its earlier counterparts and featured carbon-fibre in the side-pods, while the new Williams, like Reutemann's older car, appeared with different-shaped side-pods in an attempt to generate more down-force and also had two small front wings on either side of the nose cone in place of the previously used full-width front wing. In addition, Williams were also preparing to try out new engine covers that incorporated double-intake air-boxes. The Arrows team, meanwhile, had more or less been forced to construct a new car for Stohr as his Silverstone chassis had been a virtual write-off, and for similar reasons Henton was still confined to the original Toleman chassis. Apart from this, about the only other change of note among the remaining teams were Alfa Romeo adopting a revised rear suspension set-up for all of their cars after having tried it briefly on their spare car at Silverstone. Like the McLarens, Lotuses and Talbot-Ligiers, the Italian cars were also devoid of their main sponsor's name to comply with the German ban on cigarette advertising in sport.

Following their engine disasters in the British Grand Prix, Renault had gone away and traced the problem to distorted valve-seats caused by a heat build-up. Consequently minor revisions had since been made

in the hope of avoiding a repetition of the problem, and certainly as far as practice was concerned there seemed to be little wrong with the yellow and black cars. Throughout the two days they proved themselves both very reliable and outstandingly quick around the fast 6.789 km circuit. Indeed, it was nothing short of another complete Renault walk-over just like a fortnight earlier. The only difference on this occasion was that Prost, after finishing up just 0.13 sec slower than Arnoux on the first day at 1 min 48.09 sec, turned the tables on his team-mate on the second day to clinch his first-ever pole position at 1 min 47.50 sec. Moreover, the pole-winning time was achieved in just six laps, for having then used up his permitted two sets of qualifying tyres (super-sticky Michelins) Prost sat back and watched the opposition trying in vain to do something about it. As it was, the nearest anyone got to him, apart from Arnoux turning in 1 min 48.08 sec, was Reutemann clocking up third fastest time of 1 min 48.43 sec – almost exactly a full second slower! However, this was still no mean achievement as quite apart from having spent the whole of Friday's qualifying session in the spare Williams (without the latest aerodynamic modifications) due to a clutch fluid leak and finishing up only tenth fastest, the Argentinian was using what was essentially race rubber. Meanwhile Jones, who had come closest to the Renaults on the first day, had his hopes of improving further dashed by down-on-power engines in both his race car and the

spare Williams, and instead spent most of his time scrubbing in some new race tyres. Even so the World Champion's very respectable Friday time of 1 min 48.49 sec was still comfortably fourth fastest overall as no-one else managed to break the 1 min 49 sec barrier, something which also served to make the Renaults look even more dominant.

Practice, itself, lacked much of the usual excitement due, to a large extent, to the life of the latest Michelin qualifying tyres as this had led to drivers that were using them being out on the circuit for a mere two or three laps at a time, and only twice at that, owing to the limit of eight tyres per driver per timed session. Previously, of course, the tyre limit had been largely academic as two sets of the standardized tyres, or even the less soft rubber available at Dijon and Silverstone, had been more than enough to see each driver through a complete practice session. But now all that had changed, at least as far as the favoured Michelin runners were concerned. In fact, at times the track had seemed almost deserted, what with this, ground clearance checks taking place and cars having worn skirts replaced. But for all that, and a variety of problems affecting a number of the drivers, including Pironi, Villeneuve and Watson all suffering engine failures at different times, the final grid had a familiar look about it apart from the notable absence of Rosberg. The Finn, after two days of failing to come to terms with unpredictable handling from his Fittipaldi, had been left a non-qualifier for a race in which 12 months earlier he had started out in eighth place! For similar reasons Serra had also failed to qualify, while the other four to have missed out were Gabbiani, Alboreto and the two Toleman drivers, Henton having seen his chances slip away with a seized turbo after having ended the first day 24th fastest.

Sunday's mid-day warm-up session produced more than the usual amount of drama, for while Jones proceeded to turn in the quickest time, Villeneuve spun and tore off the rear aerofoil on his Ferrari, Tambay's Talbot suffered its second wheel bearing failure of the weekend, Watson's McLaren and Jarier's Osella both coasted to rest out on the circuit with dead engines, the latter blowing up pretty comprehensively, and Reutemann's Williams developed another of those incurable misfires that had been plaguing the Didcot-based team on and off all season. Consequently there was a lot of extra work to be done prior to the start of the race but, as ever, the overworked mechanics proved equal to the task and by the time that the cars were leaving the pits to form up on the grid all five afflicted drivers were ready

to join in. Interestingly enough, though, Watson had by then opted to race what had started out as being the spare McLaren, and similarly Reutemann had switched to the spare Williams with the older style side-pods despite the fact that his mechanics had completed an engine change on his original car. Like his team-mate, Reutemann had also decided to use the larger diameter, 15 inch, Goodyear front tyres, as indeed had all the other Goodyear runners with the notable exception of Piquet who seemed quite happy with the 13 inch alternatives. At the same time it was also noticeable that the Brazilian had forsaken the carbon-fibre brake discs, used throughout practice, for the more conventional steel counterparts.

Prost had elected to start in pole position from the left-hand side of the track rather than the more usual right-hand side for Hockenheim and when the green lights flashed on, after he had led the field around on the pace lap, it was the Frenchman who charged forward into an immediate lead. Reutemann also got away smartly and managed to squeeze in between the two Renaults as they turned into the first corner while behind them Pironi and Piquet both outdragged Jones in the initial rush to take up fourth and fifth places respectively. The rest of the field was away cleanly as well, but naturally it was all eyes on the leaders as they streamed towards the first chicane whereupon Pironi rushed past Arnoux to take over third place. Then, at the fast Ostkurve, Piquet decided that he would also like to be in front of the Renault, only to bring his front wing into contact with the right rear wheel of the French car as he attempted a run through on the inside and lose his place to Jones and Laffite as he momentarily lifted off. Arnoux, on the other hand, kept going but then started slowing dramatically as the tyre deflated and went on to end the lap limping into the pits with the tyre disintegrating and also with the Renault's right-hand

skirt wearing itself away. By then the rest of the field were already well on their second lap with Prost still leading from Reutemann followed, after a sizeable gap, by Jones, Laffite, Piquet, Villeneuve, Tambay, Andretti and the two McLarens of Watson and de Cesaris who were running ahead of the others strung out behind, Pironi having abruptly departed from a short-lived third place with a blown up Ferrari engine early on the new lap.

It soon became evident that whilst Prost was maintaining his lead he was certainly not running away with the race, for Reutemann was staying right up with him and Jones was catching the pair of them. Not that this was as surprising as it seemed, for quite apart from Prost no longer enjoying any tyre advantage now that he was on race rubber, the Renault's rev limiter was at a much lower setting than in practice, and cutting in fractionally too early at that! In fact, by lap 5 the first three cars were running virtually nose to tail, with Jones wasting little time in taking over the pursuit of the leader by neatly outbraking his team-mate at the second chicane. Piquet was bouncing right back into contention as well after his early fracas with Arnoux, repassing Laffite on lap 4 and taking only another four laps to latch on to Reutemann before elbowing the Argentinian back to fourth place next time round. Further back, meanwhile, Villeneuve had been doing his best to hold down sixth place in his ill-handling Ferrari but was now dropping down the lap charts with deteriorating tyres, somewhat to the relief of his immediate pursuers who had been queuing up behind, and there had also been a considerable amount of drama involving the two McLaren drivers. First Watson, having a difficult weekend due to his car porpoising badly along the fast straights, had gone grass mowing on the third lap and dropped well down the field. Then, just two laps later, and after having previously overtaken both his team-

A defiant Alain Prost narrowly leads Alan Jones and Nelson Piquet through the Hockenheim stadium during the early stages of the German Grand Prix, while Carlos Reutemann is doing his best not to be left behind in fourth place. *(Phipps Photographic)*

leader and Andretti, de Cesaris had banged wheels with Tambay's Talbot at the Sachskurve in another overtaking manoeuvre and spun off into retirement with a stalled engine and bent steering. Salazar, too, had effectively dropped out of the fray as he had ended his fourth lap by going into the pits with smoke billowing from the right front wheel of the Ensign, caused by a leaking brake caliper, and was now some five laps in arrears.

At the end of lap 10 Jones caused a flurry of excitement in the packed stadium by pulling right alongside Prost as they turned into the Sachskurve and sitting it out with him all the way round the corner, the two cars absolutely wheel to wheel. Prost was in a defiant mood, however, and by getting the power down a fraction earlier than Jones arrived at the following right-hander with a sufficient advantage to claim the line and force his assailant to lift off. Nevertheless, it was a close run thing and Jones, far from giving up, continued to harry the French car all around the circuit under the watchful eyes of Piquet who was now closer than ever. As this went on, with Reutemann still holding down fourth place well clear of Laffite, Rebaque continued an impressive climb up through the field by overtaking Tambay for sixth place on lap 12 and at almost the same time Mansell and Daly fell over one another at the first chicane in the midst of their efforts to find a way round Villeneuve's Ferrari. As a result Daly was obliged to go straight into the pits with a bent wheel rim and punctured tyre, after recovering from a quick spin, but Mansell simply charged on after the Ferrari only to run into the back of it on the very next lap and end up in the pits himself with the Lotus's nose cone having been knocked askew. Villeneuve also stopped but, whereas he was soon away again with a fresh set of Michelins, Mansell was out of his car and tearing off his overhauls as ever since the start of the race fuel had been dripping on to his shoulders from a leaking fuel cap! Shortly afterwards, Daly was also out of the race as no sooner had he rejoined

following his pit stop then a rear tie-rod broke on the RAM March.

At twenty laps Prost and Jones were fast coming up to lap Arnoux who was making no impression at all near the back of the field due to the Renault's ruined skirt. Of course, lapping his team-mate should have presented no problem for Prost, but when the moment came on the next lap as they entered the stadium section Arnoux seemed loathe to move over and was still in front, holding the inside line, on the approach to the Sachskurve. Consequently Prost darted to the outside to get past, but then Jones, in a brilliant display of opportunism, made a run up on the inside of both cars, left his braking as late as he dared and emerged from the corner as the new race leader! After that it seemed all over as the World Champion started pulling away at the rate of well over a second per lap. In the meantime, Piquet was giving chase to Reutemann all over again as a few laps earlier the Brabham had run over some metal debris, damaged its left-hand side-pod and skirt and forced the Brazilian to adjust his driving style to meet the changed handling characteristics, dropping behind the Williams in the process. However, in spite of this and the effects of the damaged left front wing ever since the opening lap, Piquet appeared to be coping admirably and proved the point quite emphatically on lap 27 by snatching back third place, just one lap before the engine in the spare Williams suddenly blew up and left a bitterly disappointed Reutemann with a lonely walk back to the pits. Patrese, after having lost seventh place in a quite spectacular spin on the twisty stadium section just a few laps earlier, also retired the Arrows with a blown-up engine about now, while Tambay, having already slowed with his V12 Matra engine misfiring, disappeared into the pits with yet another wheel bearing failure. So now, with seventeen cars left, Laffite was up into fourth place and Rebaque fifth, while Cheever, going well in the new Tyrrell, de Angelis, Andretti, Jarier and Watson completed the short list of runners still on the same lap as the leader.

On lap 30, with light spots of rain starting to make the track a little slippery if not actually wet, Piquet caused a gasp from the crowd when he ran very wide at the same corner where Patrese had earlier spun and ended up putting all four wheels of the Brabham on the verge. By keeping the power down, though, the Brazilian held everything together, eventually regained the track and set off at undiminished speed after Prost once more. Jones, meanwhile, had extended his lead to more than 10 seconds and was showing every sign of romping home to a comfortable victory. That is until lap 33 when he suddenly signalled to his pit that all was not well. Two laps later he did it again, and before another lap was out it was clear to everyone what the problem was – a return of the dreaded Williams' misfire! On the next lap, which saw Piquet forging past Prost into second place, it was even worse and, come lap 39, Jones was forced to watch helplessly as first the Brabham went by him and then the Renault. Finally on lap 42, and out of sheer desperation, Jones made for the pits where the Williams' spark box was replaced, but even this failed to make any difference and merely ended the chance of salvaging any World Championship points for he was now down in a hopeless ninth place. In the meantime, Piquet was marching on to a comfortable, if somewhat lucky victory, the Brazilian eventually completing the 45 laps 11.52 seconds ahead of Prost and reducing Reutemann's lead at the top of the Championship table to just 8 points. Almost exactly a minute later, Laffite duly crossed the line in third place still a long way clear of Rebaque, Cheever was fifth and Watson sixth after having overtaken Jarier, Andretti and de Angelis during the latter stages of the race. The unfortunate Jones, on the other hand, lost two more places to Andretti and Villeneuve in the closing minutes to finish a thoroughly despondent 11th. Although of somewhat less consequence, Surer also ended the race on a rather unhappy note by going off into the tyre barriers in the Theodore just two corners from home!

Results

1	N. Piquet (Brabham-Ford)	1 hr 25 min 55.60 sec (213.294 kph/ 132.534 mph)	
2	A. Prost (Renault)	1 hr 26 min 07.12 sec	
3	J. Laffite (Talbot-Matra)	1 hr 27 min 00.20 sec	
4	H. Rebaque (Brabham-Ford)	1 hr 27 min 35.29 sec	
5	E. Cheever (Tyrrell-Ford)	1 hr 27 min 46.12 sec	
6	J. Watson (McLaren-Ford)	1 lap behind	
7	E. de Angelis (Lotus-Ford)	1 lap behind	
8	J. P. Jarier (Osella-Ford)	1 lap behind	
9	M. Andretti (Alfa Romeo)	1 lap behind	
10	G. Villeneuve (Ferrari)	1 lap behind	
11	A. Jones (Williams-Ford)	1 lap behind	
12	S. Stohr (Arrows-Ford)	1 lap behind	
13	R. Arnoux (Renault)	1 lap behind	
*14	M. Surer (Theodore-Ford)	2 laps behind	
15	B. Giacomelli (Alfa Romeo)	2 laps behind	

Also running at finish: E. Salazar (Ensign-Ford) 6 laps behind

*Not running at finish.

Fastest lap: A. Jones (Williams-Ford) on lap 4 in 1 min 52.42 sec (217.371 kph/135.068 mph)

Retirements
D. Pironi (Ferrari) engine on lap 2, A. de Cesaris (McLaren-Ford) accident on lap 5, N. Mansell (Lotus-Ford) accident damage on lap 12, D. Daly (March-Ford) accident damage on lap 15, P. Tambay (Talbot-Matra) wheel bearing on lap 27, C. Reutemann (Williams-Ford) engine on lap 28, R. Patrese (Arrows-Ford) engine on lap 28, S. Borgudd (ATS-Ford) engine on lap 36.

1981

XIX Grosser Preis von Österreich

Österreichring: August 16
Weather: Overcast but dry
Distance: 53 laps of 5.9424 km
circuit = 314.95 km (195.70 miles)

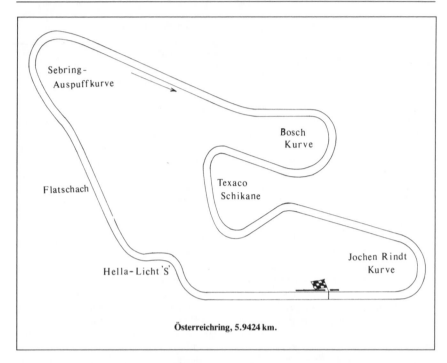

Österreichring, 5.9424 km.

Set in a natural amphitheatre amid pine forests and lush Alpine pastures in the foothills of the Styrian Mountains, the Österreichring was arguably the most scenic circuit of them all. However, this year there was an air of gloom and despondency about the place as it was generally felt that this could well be the last time that the venue would be playing host to a World Championship Grand Prix due to it no longer being a viable financial proposition. For all that, it was down to business as usual come the start of official practice on the Friday morning, and before long the hills, bathed in glorious sunshine, were echoing to the sweet sound of Formula 1 engines. Within minutes, though, there was trouble at the Hella-Licht chicane when Rebaque made contact with Tambay's Talbot, went off the track and badly damaged the left front corner of his Brabham. Uninjured, the Mexican walked back to the pits and was soon out again in his team's spare car. Meanwhile, everyone else, apart from the Fittipaldi team who had withdrawn their entries for Rosberg and Serra due to alleged financial problems, was busy juggling with variables and generally sorting cars for the first period of qualifying. Some teams were also trying out further modifications, among them Ferrari running their two intended race chassis with revised bodywork, reprofiled side-pods and with the rear suspension of both cars held together by a single dural plate in place of the more usual magnesium-alloy casting. During the course

of the morning Pironi's Ferrari also appeared with substantially modified front suspension, but this was purely unintentional and as a result of the Frenchman being responsible for the only other incident of note by going off into the barriers!

With his Ferrari still undergoing repairs at the start of qualifying, Pironi had to sit things out until half-way through the session before finally getting under way again. In the meantime, Rebaque carried on using the spare Brabham but after completing barely a handful of laps he, too, was reduced to the role of spectator when Piquet commandeered the car after the engine in his own car lost its edge. Up to that point the Brazilian had been right in amongst the pacesetters, achieving a personal best time of 1 min 34.871 sec, but unfortunately for him he quickly discovered that the engine in the spare Brabham was showing signs of tiring as well and gave up early without making any further improvement. Nevertheless, Piquet's time still held good for sixth place on the time-sheets as by the end of the afternoon the only drivers to have lapped the 5.9424 km circuit quicker had been Arnoux (1 min 32.682 sec), Prost (1 min 32.978 sec), Villeneuve (1 min 33.334 sec) immediately prior to the Ferrari's engine blowing up, Reutemann (1 min 34.531 sec) and Jones (1 min 34.654 sec), the World Champion having recorded his best time in the spare Williams which seemed to be handling better than his usual car. Apart from Pironi, whose delayed appearance had

produced only ninth fastest time, immediately behind Laffite and de Angelis, the lap times achieved by the rest ran fairly true to form. However, one driver particularly frustrated with the outcome of the first day's practice was Jarier after a leak in the hydraulics of his Osella had led to the car failing a 6 centimetre ground-clearance check and to the loss of his best lap time.

Conditions were again gloriously sunny on Saturday and, if anything, even hotter than the previous day. During the morning untimed session the turbo-charged Renaults were looking as invincible as ever and, as if to demoralize the non-turbo brigade still further, the Ferraris were lapping very quickly as well, or at least whilst they were running, for there were again problems in

Starting Grid

	R. Arnoux
	Renault
A. Prost	(1 min 32.018 sec)
Renault	
(1 min 32.321 sec)	G. Villeneuve
	Ferrari
J. Laffite	(1 min 33.334 sec)
Talbot-Matra	
(1 min 34.398 sec)	C. Reutemann
	Williams-Ford
A. Jones	(1 min 34.531 sec)
Williams-Ford	
(1 min 34.654 sec)	N. Piquet
	Brabham-Ford
D. Pironi	(1 min 34.871 sec)
Ferrari	
(1 min 35.037 sec)	E. de Angelis
	Lotus-Ford
R. Patrese	(1 min 35.294 sec)
Arrows-Ford	
(1 min 35.442 sec)	N. Mansell
	Lotus-Ford
J. Watson	(1 min 35.569 sec)
McLaren-Ford	
(1 min 35.977 sec)	M. Andretti
	Alfa Romeo
J. P. Jarier	(1 min 36.079 sec)
Osella-Ford	
(1 min 36.117 sec)	H. Rebaque
	Brabham-Ford
B. Giacomelli	(1 min 36.150 sec)
Alfa Romeo	
(1 min 36.216 sec)	P. Tambay
	Talbot-Matra
A. de Cesaris	(1 min 36.233 sec)
McLaren-Ford	
(1 min 36.657 sec)	D. Daly
	March-Ford
E. Salazar	(1 min 37.230 sec)
Ensign-Ford	
(1 min 37.631 sec)	S. Borgudd
	ATS-Ford
M. Alboreto	(1 min 37.709 sec)
Tyrrell-Ford	
(1 min 38.084 sec)	M. Surer
	Theodore-Ford
S. Stohr	(1 min 38.522 sec)
Arrows-Ford	
(1 min 38.546 sec)	

Did not qualify:
E. Cheever (Tyrrell-Ford) 1 min 38.583 sec
D. Warwick (Toleman-Hart)
1 min 38.593 sec
B. Henton (Toleman-Hart)
1 min 38.691 sec
G. Gabbiani (Osella-Ford) 1 min 41.198 sec

the engine department with Pironi the one to suffer this time out. Before the 90 minutes had expired Reutemann also had the engine let go on his Williams, although somewhat more spectacularly as a dropped valve led to a con-rod pushing its way through both sides of the crankcase! Other drivers to strike trouble included Alboreto, who coasted to rest out on the circuit with dead electrics in his Tyrrell, and Surer who caused a real flap in the Theodore camp by crashing the team's only car (the chassis raced at Hockenheim had been written off in the last lap incident) and damaging the front suspension. Daly very nearly went off into the barriers as well when a bolt sheared in the RAM March's rear suspension as he was approaching the Boschkurve, but the Irishman recovered brilliantly from the resultant high-speed spin and managed to gather it all up without hitting anything.

By 1 p.m. the start of final qualifying, the morning's carnage had just about been rectified and everyone seemed in reasonable shape to resume the battle for grid positions. However, trouble was still rife as on his very first lap de Cesaris quite literally flew off the track at the Sebring, scattering the grass run-off area with fragments of the McLaren's bodywork before coming to rest; and Pironi, now in the spare Ferrari once more, returned to the pits almost immediately with a turbo unit showing obvious signs of overheating. Then, quite suddenly, came some altogether unexpected drama which brought proceedings to a total standstill – a deer, obviously wanting a closer view of the action, had darted out from the woods at the top part of the circuit and was wandering perilously close to the edge of the track! Some 20 minutes later it was still there but eventually the animal was encouraged back to its more usual habitat, and qualifying was allowed to resume with the notable absence of de Cesaris as the McLaren team had decided not to risk losing their spare car! Even now, though, it was still a pretty fraught affair for some of the drivers. For Surer and Daly, in particular, there was to be no respite, as after covering a mere three laps the repaired Theodore disappeared into the pits with a blown-up engine, and not long afterwards the RAM March had its right rear tyre explode at virtually the same spot that the suspension failure had occurred during the morning. Fortunately, after another superb display of car control, Daly managed to stay on the track, but the flailing rubber did so much damage to the rear end of the March that the team's spare car had to be brought into service for the rest of the weekend. In the meantime, Arnoux and Prost were leaving no-one in any doubt that the front row of the grid was to be another all-Renault affair, for once again they were head and shoulders above the rest, turning in even faster times of 1 min 32.018 sec and 1 min 32.321 sec

respectively. This also meant that Arnoux would be starting the Austrian Grand Prix from pole position for the third year running. In contrast, Villeneuve, Reutemann, Jones and Piquet were among a number of drivers not to improve in the hotter conditions, and, indeed, the only noticeable change affecting the grid order of the other leading runners was brought about by a fine effort from Laffite who moved up to fourth place after recording the afternoon's third fastest time of 1 min 34.398 sec on a new type of Michelin qualifying rubber fitted to his Talbot. Down at the other end of the scale, Daly and Surer had both qualified in spite of their respective troubles, but the final outcome in the Tyrrell camp was surprising to say the least as Alboreto had qualified the old 010 without too much fuss or bother, whereas Cheever, using the newer 011 fitted with Goodyear tyres for the first time, had failed to make the cut, joining Warwick, Henton and Gabbiani.

The weather was hotter than ever by the time of the mid-day warm-up session on Sunday, causing a considerable amount of anxiety over tyre wear in the race, particularly to Renault and Ferrari. Both of these teams were also worried about their turbochargers and, in the case of Ferrari at least, this seemed to be fully justified as after completing only a single lap Villeneuve returned to the pits with a broken turbo unit and had to switch cars. Not that the French-Canadian was alone in running into last-minute problems, as before the half-hour had lapsed the engine in Jarier's Osella had blown up and both those in Tambay's Talbot and Surer's Theodore had developed misfires. So far as the lap times were concerned it was an entirely different story to that of qualifying, as Piquet was fastest, followed by Watson and Jones, the McLaren team-leader enjoying the benefit of a freshly-installed engine and altogether happier with his car in race trim after a practice plagued by excessive down-force and understeer.

As the starting time of 3 p.m. approached, the temperature had dropped considerably with the appearance of grey clouds over the mountains and it seemed that there might even be a possibility of rain. Since the warm-up session the Ferrari mechanics had replaced the turbo unit on Villeneuve's car, and both Jarier's Osella and Tambay's Talbot had undergone engine changes. The Theodore mechanics, meanwhile, had traced Surer's misfire to an electrical problem, but the Swiss was still out of luck as on the warm-up lap his engine cut out completely and he had to be brought back to the starting area on the end of a rope. Furthermore, efforts to restart the engine proved fruitless in the short amount of time available before the start of the race and so, eventually, the car had to be wheeled into the pit lane. The other 23 starters, on the other hand, were

soon being signalled away on the pace lap and just minutes later, after a certain amount of creeping on the grid, the race was under way with Villeneuve timing everything to perfection to lead the pack into the Hella-Licht chicane after squeezing his Ferrari into the gap between Arnoux's Renault and the pit wall. Pironi, in the other Ferrari, also got off the mark exceptionally well from eighth spot on the grid and quickly slotted into fourth place ahead of Laffite, Reutemann, Piquet and Jones on what was a fast and furious opening lap. At the end of the lap the order among the leading cars was still the same but Prost, who had beaten his teammate into second place, was now pulling alongside Villeneuve's Ferrari and, as they headed up the hill towards the Hella-Licht chicane for the second time, managed to scramble past into the lead, helped by the French-Canadian leaving his braking too late and sliding straight through the escape road. Seconds later, with Villeneuve now down to sixth place, Reutemann also arrived at the chicane too quickly and he, too, took to the escape road, dropping behind Piquet and Jones in the process, while at the back of the field Daly went straight into the pits to complain that his engine was running on only seven cylinders.

With a clear track ahead of them, the two Renault drivers proceeded to dominate the early stages of the race by pulling away from the third-placed Ferrari at the almost incredible rate of some 2 seconds per lap. Pironi, on the other hand, was coming under all kinds of pressure from Laffite and staying ahead only through sheer determination and superior straight-line speed as through the corners it was the usual Ferrari story. Moreover, there was soon a whole queue of cars forming behind him for Piquet was having no trouble keeping up in fifth place and, after the third lap, Jones and Reutemann were up there as well, the Williams duo being somewhat more successful in dealing with the other Ferrari. Even when Piquet forged ahead of Laffite on the approach to the Hella-Licht chicane on lap 6 Pironi still remained unimpressed and, in fact, as far as the Brazilian was concerned the overtaking manoeuvre on Laffite had done more harm than good, as having gone over a particularly nasty bump whilst alongside the Talbot he had damaged a skirt. This, in turn, had caused the Brabham to develop understeer tendencies, and within two laps Piquet was down in fifth place once again! By lap 9, however, Pironi's tyres were starting to go off, and at long last the tense situation resolved itself with Laffite, Piquet and Jones going past the Ferrari in rapid succession, and Reutemann following them through next time round. Villeneuve, meanwhile, was in even worse trouble with his Ferrari. Apart from having damaged the skirts in the second lap incident at the chicane his brakes were

1981

Cresting the rise towards the Hella-Licht Schikane during the early stages of the race, Didier Pironi narrowly holds on to third place ahead of Nelson Piquet, eventual winner Jacques Laffite and Alan Jones. *(Autosport)*

playing up. As a result he had already lost another two places to Patrese and Mansell, and now Watson was hard on his heels. Before anything came of that, however, things took a distinct turn for the worse for the French-Canadian as on lap 12 the Ferrari suddenly got away from him at the Bosch-kurve, flew straight off the track and careered on into the barriers with a sickening thump. Mercifully, Villeneuve subsequently walked away from the scene unharmed, but the Ferrari was left in a very sorry state indeed. Earlier in the race Surer had also retired, albeit under somewhat less dramatic circumstances, for although he had eventually joined in after the Theodore mechanics had traced his problem to a broken distributor rotor arm the unfortunate Swiss had not even gone out of sight of the pits before the engine had cut out again. Daly was not much better off either as it had taken no less than three pit stops on successive laps to find out that it was a defective sparking plug causing his engine to run on only seven cylinders and he was now some four laps in arrears. Andretti and Rebaque were two other drivers to have also dropped out of the picture by this time, as the American had been forced to stop for an early fresh set of tyres and the Mexican had stopped briefly to check out a minor engine problem.

With 15 laps completed Laffite had not only steadied the gap between himself and the two Renaults, which at one point had been as much as 18 seconds, but was now reducing it by nearly a second per lap. As in practice, the Talbot was handling superbly, whereas the Renaults were developing increasing understeer through the downhill corners as the fuel load lightened, and this was having an adverse effect on their overall lap times. Piquet, meanwhile, was looking pretty settled in fourth place despite failing to make quite the same impression as Laffite, and then came Jones and Reutemann still running fifth and sixth but not having a particularly happy time of it. The World Champion was struggling against erratic handling caused by a broken spring platform in his rear suspension, while his team-mate was suffering from lack of grip due to having chosen too hard a tyre compound. Further back still, though, Mansell was making noticeably good progress. Since going past Villeneuve he had moved up another place at the expense of Patrese and was now all but climbing over the back of Pironi's Ferrari. In fact, apart from Laffite continuing to chase

the leaders, this seventh place battle became the centre of attention for Patrese and Watson were also right in the thick of it, while de Angelis was looking all set to join the queue. Even when Mansell eventually made it through on lap 17 and immediately began to pull away on his own it was still no less exciting for Patrese, and then Watson, were soon attacking the Ferrari driver just as vigorously. Moreover, this went on for another seven laps at which point Watson finally managed to scramble past Pironi under braking for the Hella-Licht chicane, leaving Patrese and de Angelis faced with the same awkward task. Meanwhile, there was disappointment for Mansell later on this same lap as his fine drive was brought to a premature end when his engine suddenly let go.

On lap 27 the race took on a new dimension when Prost, in the leading Renault, suddenly weaved under braking for the Hella-Licht chicane and then went skating through the escape road before coming to rest with a collapsed left front suspension. Naturally this was a bitter blow to the French team, for although Arnoux automatically took over up front, after a busy moment avoiding his unlucky team-mate, he was now only 5 seconds clear of Laffite and looking more and more vulnerable. The next few minutes did nothing to ease the situation as the Talbot continued to close up remorselessly, and within just five more laps the two cars were running nose to tail with their positions looking all set to be reversed at any moment. However, Arnoux was obviously determined to make a fight of it, in spite of poor brakes to add to his understeer problem, and by hugging the racing line stayed in front right through until lap 39. Then finally, in a moment's hesitation by Arnoux as he came up to lap a group of mid-field runners (de Angelis, Patrese, Pironi and Salazar) at the Texaco Schikane, Laffite snatched the opportunity to squeeze through on the inside for the lead. After that the race was as good as over for, in spite of initially showing signs of retaliating, Arnoux gradually fell away and even a late charge failed to prevent Laffite from going on to score his first Grand

Results		
1	J. Laffite (Talbot-Matra)	1 hr 27 min 36.47 sec (215.698 kph/ 134.028 mph)
2	R. Arnoux (Renault)	1 hr 27 min 41.64 sec
3	N. Piquet (Brabham-Ford)	1 hr 27 min 43.81 sec
4	A. Jones (Williams-Ford)	1 hr 27 min 48.51 sec
5	C. Reutemann (Williams-Ford)	1 hr 28 min 08.32 sec
6	J. Watson (McLaren-Ford)	1 hr 29 min 07.61 sec

7	E. de Angelis (Lotus-Ford)	1 lap behind
8	A. de Cesaris (McLaren-Ford)	1 lap behind
9	D. Pironi (Ferrari)	1 lap behind
10	J. P. Jarier (Osella-Ford)	2 laps behind
11	D. Daly (March-Ford)	6 laps behind

Fastest lap: J. Laffite (Talbot-Matra) on lap 47 in 1 min 37.62 sec (219.142 kph/136.168 mph)

Retirements
M. Surer (Theodore-Ford) ignition on lap 1, G. Villeneuve (Ferrari) accident on lap 12, N. Mansell (Lotus-Ford) engine on lap 24, A. Prost (Renault) front suspension on lap 27, P. Tambay (Talbot-Matra) engine on lap 27, S. Stohr (Arrows-Ford) spun off on lap 28, H. Rebaque (Brabham-Ford) engine on lap 32, B. Giacomelli (Alfa Romeo) engine/fire on lap 35, M. Alboreto (Tyrrell-Ford) engine on lap 41, E. Salazar (Ensign-Ford) engine on lap 44, R. Patrese (Arrows-Ford) engine on lap 44, S. Borgudd (ATS-Ford) brakes on lap 45, M. Andretti (Alfa Romeo) engine on lap 47.

Prix victory of the season just over 5 seconds clear, the jubilant winner openly grateful to his new team-manager, brother-in-law Jean-Pierre Jabouille, who had hand-picked his tyres for the race. Behind the two Frenchmen, Piquet, Jones, Reutemann and Watson crossed the line at varying intervals in unchanged order, the McLaren team leader completing his race with a cracked exhaust manifold pipe, while de Angelis came home seventh after an epic duel with Patrese had ended on lap 44 with the Arrows suffering a major engine failure. After that only de Cesaris, Pironi, Jarier and Daly were still left at the finish as Patrese had been just one of a whole string of retirements in the latter half of the race that had also included a particularly dramatic exit by Giacomelli, the Alfa Romeo having stopped at the entrance to the pit lane on lap 35 with a magnesium fire burning away underneath its engine cover.

XXIX Grote Prijs van Nederland

Zandvoort: August 30
Weather: Warm and sunny
Distance: 72 laps of 4.252 km
circuit = 306.14 km (190.23 miles)

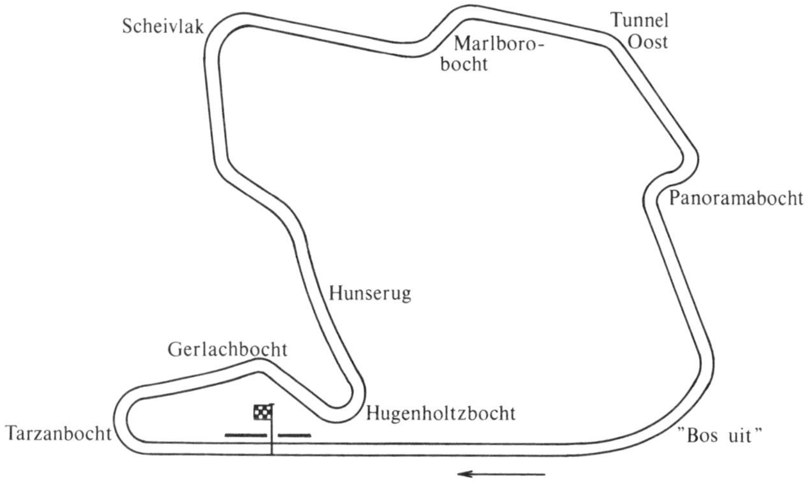

Zandvoort, 4.252 km.

qualifying. And, as usual, things didn't go according to plan for everyone, particularly for Tambay and Warwick as within minutes

Starting Grid	
A. Prost Renault (1 min 18.176 sec)	R. Arnoux Renault (1 min 18.255 sec)
N. Piquet Brabham-Ford (1 min 18.652 sec)	A. Jones Williams-Ford (1 min 18.672 sec)
C. Reutemann Williams-Ford (1 min 18.844 sec)	J. Laffite Talbot-Matra (1 min 19.018 sec)
M. Andretti Alfa Romeo (1 min 19.040 sec)	J. Watson McLaren-Ford (1 min 19.312 sec)
E. de Angelis Lotus-Ford (1 min 19.738 sec)	R. Patrese Arrows-Ford (1 min 19.864 sec)
P. Tambay Talbot-Matra (1 min 19.979 sec)	D. Pironi Ferrari (1 min 20.248 sec)
*A. de Cesaris McLaren-Ford (1 min 20.377 sec)	B. Giacomelli Alfa Romeo (1 min 20.384 sec)
H. Rebaque Brabham-Ford (1 min 20.547 sec)	G. Villeneuve Ferrari (1 min 20.595 sec)
N. Mansell Lotus-Ford (1 min 20.663 sec)	J. P. Jarier Osella-Ford (1 min 21.086 sec)
D. Daly March-Ford (1 min 21.391 sec)	M. Surer Theodore-Ford (1 min 21.454 sec)
S. Stohr Arrows-Ford (1 min 21.568 sec)	E. Cheever Tyrrell-Ford (1 min 21.698 sec)
S. Borgudd ATS-Ford (1 min 21.760 sec)	E. Salazar Ensign-Ford (1 min 22.024 sec)
M. Alboreto Tyrrell-Ford (1 min 22.030 sec)	

*Withdrawn: A. de Cesaris (McLaren-Ford) 1 min 20.377 sec

Did not qualify:
B. Henton (Toleman-Hart) 1 min 22.226 sec
K. Rosberg (Fittipaldi-Ford) 1 min 23.518 sec
F. Serra (Fittipaldi-Ford) 1 min 23.613 sec
G. Gabbiani (Osella-Ford) 1 min 23.898 sec
D. Warwick (Toleman-Hart) 1 min 24.028 sec

From the mountain-side slopes of Austria it was now time to descend to the Dutch coastal resort of Zandvoort where about the only significant change in the entry from the previous race was the Fittipaldi team returning to the fold and preparing to use Pirelli tyres for the first time. Nevertheless, there had been a lot of behind-the-scenes activity between races as Ferrari and Brabham had completely rebuilt the cars damaged by Villeneuve and Rebaque at the Österreich-ring, while no less than five other teams arrived with brand new cars, albeit all to existing designs. These were Renault, who had completed a fifth chassis in their RE30 series, RE34, for Prost which was lighter and built specifically with hydro-pneumatic suspension in mind, unlike its predecessors; Williams, who had assembled another FW07C for Reutemann; Talbot-Ligier, who had similarly put together another JS17 for Tambay; Tyrrell, who now had a second 011 earmarked for Alboreto; finally Toleman, who had another TG181 for Henton to use which was fitted with the latest Hart turbocharged engine nicknamed the 'monobloc' as its cylinder block, cylinder head and crankcase were all contained within a single alloy casting. In addition to this, Theodore had now finished work on rebuilding their original chassis, complete with fins attached to either side of the nose cone, as distinct from the previously used full-width front wing, which meant that Surer once more had the luxury of a spare car, and RAM March had also rebuilt their spare chassis, incorporating a wider track and under-car aerodynamic revisions. Various other teams, meanwhile, had carried out further detail modifications to existing cars, including Lotus who were now about to try out Williams-like twin air-collector boxes over the engines of their 87s (these were to appear only during practice) and Alfa Romeo who had reverted to their older rear suspension configuration as seen prior to the German Grand Prix. The Autodelta team, now having the 'assistance' of ex-Talbot engineer Gerard Ducarouge, had also uprated Andretti's car to 'D' specification in which the front suspension geometry had been altered and a number of changes made in the interests of improved aerodynamics that included the adoption of new and wider side-pods.

As usual the opening practice session on Friday morning was primarily a familiarization exercise and an opportunity for gererally setting up cars for the first period of of taking to the track the new Talbot blew up its Matra engine and the Toleman stopped with turbo trouble caused by sand finding its way into the compressor. Consequently both drivers were soon looking for their teams' spare cars, and not long afterwards they were joined by Arnoux and Mansell whose proposed race cars were running with seemingly incurable misfires. Before the morning was out Pironi also switched to the spare Ferrari after going off into the catch-fences at Scheivlak, but when Gabbiani added his name to the casualty list by crashing his Osella he was less fortunate as the Italian team had no spare car for him to use. Furthermore, there was insufficient time to render the car serviceable for the first period of qualifying, so when the official timekeepers eventually took up duty after lunch Gabbiani was left in the unhappy position of having to spectate. Even then there was still quite a lot of unwanted drama as Warwick's troubles continued when he slid off the track in his Toleman, while Salazar had the throttle jam open on the Ensign which sent him into the sand as well. Then it was Piquet's turn to suffer an engine failure. However, this last incident did not occur until towards the end of the qualifying hour by which time the Brazilian had already lapped the 4.252 km circuit in a pretty respectable 1 min 19.236 sec. In the meantime, it was the familiar story up front as Arnoux, back in his original car once more with the misfire having finally been traced to the ignition system, and Prost had almost effortlessly eased their Renaults to the top of the time-sheets with laps of 1 min 18.255 sec and 1 min 18.279 sec respectively. About the only difference on this occasion was that instead of being whole seconds faster than anyone else it was down to tenths of a second as Jones had his Williams well enough on song to lap in 1 min 18.672 sec, while Reutemann, narrowly pipping Piquet for fourth place in the order, turned in 1 min 19.067 sec despite driving with a stiff neck and being just one of a number of drivers complaining of poor handling and a bumpy ride caused by the 'solid' suspensions.

Causing no surprise to anyone, the Renaults were again quickest during the final period of qualifying. This time out, however, it was Prost who achieved the fastest lap to claim pole position at 1 min 18.176 sec, Arnoux turning in a fractionally slower time than the day before of 1 min 18.301 sec. Jones, meanwhile, was nearly half a second slower than the first day after an engine failure during the morning untimed session had forced him to switch cars, but he was still going to start the race from the second row of the grid as only one driver, apart from the Renault duo, beat his Friday time. That was Piquet who had switched to the spare Brabham, devoid of nose wings, out of choice and responded with a lap in 1 min 18.652 sec.

After the Brazilian came Reutemann, the remaining driver to achieve a sub-1 min 19 sec lap at 1 min 18.844 sec, followed by Laffite and Andretti who both only just failed with very evenly matched times of 1 min 19.018 sec and 1 min 19.040 sec respectively. The American was delighted with his uprated Alfa Romeo, even though one of the new side-pods broke loose early in the session and spoiled his chances of going even quicker. Watson was next but not nearly so happy as, apart from being one of the few others not to improve on his Friday time (he had ended the first day sixth fastest), his McLaren was giving him a particularly bumpy ride and was understeering badly through the slower corners. Even so, the Ulsterman's problems were small compared to those of his Italian team-mate, as once again de Cesaris was up to his usual antics of crashing cars. On this occasion it happened towards the end of practice and, through leaving his braking too late for the Tarzan hairpin, this led to him skating straight off the track and careering head-on into the tyre barrier, damaging the McLaren so badly that there was no hope of repairing the car before the race as the carbon-fibre monocoque had also suffered. Furthermore, Ron Dennis and Teddy Mayer were so incensed about it that they subsequently decided to withdraw de Cesaris' entry rather than allow him to take over Watson's spare car, a move which was rather fortuitous for Alboreto as, having ended up as the fastest non-qualifier after fuel system problems with his new Tyrrell, he was later invited to take part in the race as a substitute for his dejected compatriot. For the remaining five non-qualifiers, on the other hand, there was to be no such reprieve, and once again both Toleman drivers were destined to be spectators on race day, as were Rosberg and Serra in their unimpressive Fittipaldis, and Gabbiani in the second Osella. Of these, Rosberg's hopes had been dashed by an engine failure on his very first lap of the afternoon, while Henton, after having ended the first day 22nd fastest, had seen his chance of defending the position effectively ended during the morning when the new 'monobloc' engine broke and forced him to revert to the team's older and slower spare car. Meanwhile, so far as the rest of those who had qualified were concerned, their final grid positions were much as expected, and although both Ferraris were well down the order this was understandable as a turbo failure on his repaired race car during the morning had left Pironi having to use the spare Ferrari once more for qualifying and both the engine in this and Villeneuve's sister car had been unaccountably down on power.

For a change the race day warm-up session passed without any untoward incidents, but within seconds of the start of the actual race it was a different story altogether. Villeneuve

was first to see to that, for in the midst of attempting another of his quick getaways the French-Canadian suddenly found himself being squeezed out by Patrese's Arrows and Giacomelli's Alfa Romeo. He touched wheels with the two cars, became momentarily airborne and then spun wildly to finish up on the outside of the track with all four wheels of the Ferrari pointing in different directions. Instant retirement! Somehow everyone managed to keep out of the way, but even before Villeneuve had climbed out of his car there was another commotion, this time behind the pits when Andretti gave way to Reutemann only for the Argentinian to thank him by promptly running over the Alfa Romeo's front wing, causing it to gape skywards. Then later, on what was turning out to be an extremely fraught opening lap, Pironi ploughed into the back of Tambay with even more dire consequences as this effectively put both of them out of the race – the Talbot was retired immediately with broken rear suspension while the Ferrari was left limping back to the pits with bent front suspension. After subsequently covering just three more laps, it was also retired. Thankfully the rest of the depleted field actually went on to the complete the lap intact, led by the Renaults of Prost and Arnoux who had both rocketed off the line. Jones, too, had got off to an excellent start to take up third place and he, in turn, was now being pursued by Piquet, Laffite, Reutemann, one highly annoyed Andretti, Watson, de Angelis and Patrese, all forming a continuous blur before a small gap back to Giacomelli and the other survivors.

At the end of the second lap it was much the same, except that there was now no Mansell as after a practice plagued by erratic handling with his Lotus 87, the young Englishman had just coasted to rest with a dead engine. Up front, though, Arnoux was dropping away from his team-mate, which was not as surprising as it seemed for apart from using harder Michelin tyres his engine was lacking its usual punch. Jones, on the other hand, was really charging, and despite an abortive attempt to scramble through on the inside of the Renault under braking for Tarzan soon made up for it by blasting past the turbo-charged car along the main straight of all places later on the same lap. Now Piquet moved in for the kill as well, taking only a further two laps before carrying out a repeat of Jones' overtaking manoeuvre, and by lap 9 the unhappy Frenchman was down in sixth place behind Laffite and Reutemann. By then Andretti had also been sliding down the lap charts and had decided that he had had enough of struggling against inferior handling caused by the Alfa Romeo's bent nose wing and stopped at the pits for a new nose-cone, unfortunately losing almost exactly three laps in the process. Consequently, when the American eventually charged back out into the race he was left well and truly bringing up the rear, which was actually 19th position as a few minutes earlier Daly had become yet another early retirement. The RAM March had broken its rear suspension. At the other end of the race, meanwhile, it was still Prost, but he was by no means having it all his own way for ever since displacing Arnoux, Jones had gradually been reeling him in and was now little more than a second behind the leader. Only a further 3 seconds away, Piquet was seemingly having no problems in holding down third place ahead of Laffite and Reutemann, and then came Watson who had just completed a brilliant overtaking manoeuvre by pulling up on the outside of Arnoux going into the Tarzan hairpin and sitting it out wheel to wheel with the Frenchman all the way round the corner before emerging in front. Further back still, Patrese had also got the better of de Angelis a couple of laps earlier to move up into eighth place. But this was to be a short-lived affair as after 16 laps, apart from having been repassed by his compatriot and dropping behind Rebaque as well, the Arrows team leader was in the pits to retire with damaged suspension, a legacy of the start-line incident with Villeneuve.

As the two leaders completed their 18th lap Jones, having by now moved right in on Prost's tail, made a run up on the outside of the Renault as they approached Tarzan and for a moment seemed to be nosing ahead. Prost, however, was having none of it and merely sat things out under braking before forcing his assailant to back off by moving over fractionally as they went round the corner. It was an exciting moment, nonetheless, and seconds later there was another. This time it was brought about by Reutemann attempting to dive through on the inside of Laffite going into the same corner. But, with the Frenchman hugging the line, as

he was quite entitled to do, there simply wasn't the room. Instead of lifting off, however, Reutemann kept on coming and as the two cars turned into the corner so came the inevitable crunch, the Talbot being struck amidships before spinning backwards off the track and on into the catch-fences and the Williams stopping just beyond the corner with its left front suspension torn apart. Two more retirements, and Championship protagonists at that! Only a lap later they were joined by Giacomelli who had an accident all on his own, going off the track at the right-hander before Scheivlak with dire consequences to the Alfa Romeo but not to himself, and, then, on lap 22, by Arnoux who spun off into the sand, stalled his engine and was unable to restart. After that there were just 14 cars left in the race but still plenty to watch, for there were interesting little scraps going on throughout most of the field. Naturally, though, most of the attention was fixed on the absorbing leadership battle, for Jones, far from giving up, was still attacking Prost as enthusiastically as ever. To make matters even more interesting they were now in the throes of lapping a group of tail-enders, and in a moment's hesitation by Prost as he came up behind Alboreto at Panorambocht on lap 22, Jones seized the opportunity to finally sneak ahead. Not that he was destined to stay there long for after being followed past Alboreto by Prost along the main straight, Jones found the Renault charging through on his inside as they approached Tarzan and almost before realizing it was being elbowed back into second place once more. Undeterred, the World Champion still refused to accept defeat and over the next few laps continued to shadow the yellow and white car all around the circuit waiting for another chance. But it never came and instead, as half-distance approached (36 laps), Jones was having to pay rather more attention to

his tyres as they were starting to go off and showing signs of excessive wear.

At the half-way mark Jones had obviously given up all hope of doing anything more about the leader for Prost was now starting to visibly pull away. Behind them, Piquet was lapping as consistently as ever in third place, albeit some 20 seconds in arrears, while Watson was even further back in fourth place ahead of Rebaque and de Angelis who had long since swopped places. Then, lapped, it was Surer followed by Cheever, Salazar, Alboreto, Stohr, Borgudd and the delayed Andretti; Jarier having disappeared into the pits after 29 laps with the Osella suffering from a broken gearbox. With Prost continuing to edge away from Jones and the rest of the depleted field mainly well spaced out, it now all became rather uninspiring. Indeed, over the next 20 minutes or so the only significant changes to occur came with Cheever suddenly skating off the track in front of Salazar at the Marlborobocht chicane when the Tyrrell's front suspension collapsed without warning, and with Watson coasting to rest with a dead engine after looking all set for his sixth successive finish in the points. Soon after that, however, Salazar woke everyone up by catching and passing Surer to take over sixth spot and, more important still, Jones started noticeably slowing as his tyres deteriorated. Consequently, this brought Piquet closer and closer to him with every lap, and by whole seconds at that, until finally the Brazilian was able to slice through on the inside of the Williams going into Tarzan on the 69th tour. All the while Prost was cruising home to a comfortable and well-deserved victory, and just over three laps later this is how it ended with the French Renault driver joyously acknowledging the chequered flag to notch up his second win of the season. A little over 8 seconds later Piquet duly followed him over the line

---

Prost's Renault and Jones' Williams accelerate out of Tarzan almost side by side during the midst of an absorbing leadership battle . . .

1981

in second place, but it was more than half a minute before Jones finally appeared in third place, one of his rear tyres now down to the canvas! Also in the points were Rebaque, de Angelis and, for the first time, Salazar after a late scrap with Alboreto had ended with the Tyrrell blowing up its engine on the penultimate lap. Andretti had also retired in the latter stages of the race, although under even more spectacular circumstances as a suspension failure on his Alfa Romeo had caused a high-speed shunt from which he had been fortunate to escape uninjured. As a result Stohr, Surer and Borgudd were the only others still there at the finish, the Swiss having completed his race with chronic handling problems, which was not surprising as afterwards it was discovered that the Theodore's bellhousing was coming away from the engine due to the loss of the retaining bolts!

... although ultimately the Frenchman cruised home to a comfortable victory. (Autosport)

Results							Retirements

Results

1	A. Prost (Renault)	1 hr 40 min 22.43 sec (183.002 kph/ 113.712 mph)
2	N. Piquet (Brabham-Ford)	1 hr 40 min 30.67 sec
3	A. Jones (Williams-Ford)	1 hr 40 min 57.93 sec
4	H. Rebaque (Brabham-Ford)	1 lap behind
5	E. de Angelis (Lotus-Ford)	1 lap behind
6	E. Salazar (Ensign-Ford)	2 laps behind
7	S. Stohr (Arrows-Ford)	3 laps behind
8	M. Surer (Theodore-Ford)	3 laps behind
*9	M. Alboreto (Tyrrell-Ford)	4 laps behind
10	S. Borgudd (ATS-Ford)	4 laps behind

* Not running at finish.

Fastest lap: A. Jones (Williams-Ford) on lap 15 in 1 min 21.83 sec (187.061 kph/116.234 mph)

Retirements

G. Villeneuve (Ferrari) accident on lap 1, P. Tambay (Talbot-Matra) accident on lap 1, N. Mansell (Lotus-Ford) electrics on lap 2, D. Pironi (Ferrari) accident damage on lap 5, D. Daly (March-Ford) rear suspension on lap 6, R. Patrese (Arrows-Ford) accident damage on lap 17, J. Laffite (Talbot-Matra) accident on lap 19, C. Reutemann (Williams-Ford) accident on lap 19, B. Giacomelli (Alfa Romeo) accident on lap 20, R. Arnoux (Renault) spun off on lap 22, J. P. Jarier (Osella-Ford) gearbox on lap 30, E. Cheever (Tyrrell-Ford) front suspension on lap 47, J. Watson (McLaren-Ford) electrics on lap 51, M. Andretti (Alfa Romeo) accident on lap 63.

LII° Gran Premio d'Italia

Monza: September 13
Weather: Overcast and showery
Distance: 52 laps of 5.800 km
circuit = 301.60 km (187.40 miles)

After having taken place at Imola in 1980 as a result of the outcry following the first lap accident two years earlier that had claimed the life of Ronnie Peterson, the Italian Grand Prix was now returning to its rightful home of Monza. Here, despite the high attrition rate at Zandvoort, there were few changes in the entry, with the same thirty drivers arriving to do battle for the twenty-four available starting places and most of the teams bringing along the same cars, several of which had necessarily undergone repairs. Once again, though, there were some new cars in evidence come the start of practice as Osella were now ready to race their George Valentini-designed FA1C, which was being entrusted to Jean-Pierre Jarier, while Talbot-Ligier, Alfa Romeo and Lotus had com-pleted further examples of their existing designs for Jacques Laffite, Mario Andretti and Nigel Mansell respectively. Apart from this about the only other change was to be found at Ferrari as they brought along three of their 126CKs to original specification except for having the latest rear suspension first seen in Austria and only one, Pironi's spare chassis, to the 'B' specification.

Only 29 of the 30 drivers present took part in the first hour of qualifying on Friday afternoon, for however hard it was to believe de Cesaris had been up to his usual antics and crashed again midway through the morning untimed session, severely damaging the right rear corner of his McLaren MP4 against the barriers in the vicinity of the first chicane. Quite apart from anything else this had also interrupted everyone else's practice for several minutes and now, with the afternoon session only just about under way, it happened again. This time the interruption was brought about by Pironi who inexplicably understeered off the track on the way out of the second of the Lesmo curves and tore off virtually the entire left-hand side of his Ferrari after he, too, made contact with the barriers. Fortunately, like de Cesaris, he subsequently walked away from the scene unharmed and, after switching to his spare car, soon started lapping even quicker as if to demonstrate as much. In the meantime, there was no need to even guess who were out setting the fastest times, for as usual the Renaults were completely demoralizing the opposition. For a change, though, it was not entirely plain sailing as Prost's hydro-pneumatic suspension was showing a reluctance to operate correctly inasmuch as the front of the car was refusing to settle in its 'down' position, or at least not until after

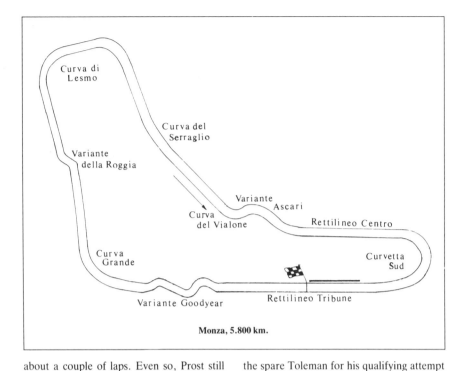

Monza, 5.800 km.

was pandemonium at Ferrari as Pironi had stopped to complain of an engine vibration and been sent out in Villeneuve's spare car, only for the French-Canadian to arrive moments later with smoke belching out from the rear of his race car due to an engine failure. Understandably, Villeneuve was most put out on discovering what had just happened and, moreover, had to subsequently undergo the somewhat galling experience of watching helplessly as other drivers (Pironi included!) elbowed him lower down the grid order. Later in the session Jones' practice also came to an abrupt halt when his engine let go and stranded him out on the far side of the circuit, as did Prost's when, following a misunderstanding whilst attemp-

Starting Grid	
R. Arnoux Renault (1 min 33.467 sec)	C. Reutemann Williams-Ford (1 min 34.140 sec)
A. Prost Renault (1 min 34.374 sec)	J. Laffite Talbot-Matra (1 min 35.062 sec)
A. Jones Williams-Ford (1 min 35.359 sec)	N. Piquet Brabham-Ford (1 min 35.449 sec)
J. Watson McLaren-Ford (1 min 35.557 sec)	D. Pironi Ferrari (1 min 35.596 sec)
G. Villeneuve Ferrari (1 min 35.627 sec)	B. Giacomelli Alfa Romeo (1 min 35.946 sec)
E. de Angelis Lotus-Ford (1 min 36.158 sec)	N. Mansell Lotus-Ford (1 min 36.210 sec)
M. Andretti Alfa Romeo (1 min 36.296 sec)	H. Rebaque Brabham-Ford (1 min 36.472 sec)
P. Tambay Talbot-Matra (1 min 36.515 sec)	A. de Cesaris McLaren-Ford (1 min 37.019 sec)
E. Cheever Tyrrell-Ford (1 min 37.160 sec)	J. P. Jarier Osella-Ford (1 min 37.264 sec)
D. Daly March-Ford (1 min 37.309 sec)	R. Patrese Arrows-Ford (1 min 37.355 sec)
S. Borgudd ATS-Ford (1 min 37.807 sec)	M. Alboreto Tyrrell-Ford (1 min 37.912 sec)
B. Henton Toleman-Hart (1 min 38.012 sec)	E. Salazar Ensign-Ford (1 min 38.053 sec)

Did not qualify:
M. Surer (Theodore-Ford) 1 min 38.114 sec
G. Gabbiani (Osella-Ford) 1 min 38.474 sec
D. Warwick (Toleman-Hart) 1 min 39.279 sec
S. Stohr (Arrows-Ford) 1 min 39.713 sec
K. Rosberg (Fittipaldi-Ford) 1 min 40.345 sec
F. Serra (Fittipaldi-Ford) 1 min 40.437 sec

about a couple of laps. Even so, Prost still managed to achieve comfortably the afternoon's second fastest time of 1 min 34.492 sec while team-mate Arnoux, having no such trouble, stole the show at 1 min 34.042 sec. Such was their superiority that no-one else broke the 1 min 35 sec barrier, but Reutemann came closest at 1 min 35.153 sec followed by Piquet after taking the spare Brabham fitted with the carbon-fibre brake discs around in 1 min 35.449 sec, both drivers somewhat happier now that Goodyear had produced qualifying tyres at long last. Then came Villenueve (1 min 35.627 sec), Watson (1 min 35.795 sec), Pironi (1 min 35.977 sec) and Jones, who finished up eighth fastest at 1 min 35.983 sec despite having to brake early to allow himself time to move his hand between the steering wheel and the gear lever of his Williams owing to a broken finger recently sustained in a brawl following a road-traffic incident in London! The others, meanwhile, were all at least 2 seconds slower than Arnoux, but this was certainly through no lack of effort by any of them. Two drivers, in particular, to have done well were Jarier who had clocked 16th fastest time in spite of some teething problems with the new Osella, and Alboreto who was only one place lower on the time-sheets in the Avon-shod Tyrrell. Rather surprisingly, the Italian had also lapped quicker than team-mate Cheever in the Goodyear-shod Tyrrell but perhaps this had something to do with being on home soil!

When practice resumed the following morning with a further 90 minute untimed session, Pironi was still confined to his spare Ferrari as the Frenchman's original car had proved beyond immediate repair. Henton, on the other hand, who had been forced into

the spare Toleman for his qualifying attempt on Friday as a result of inter-cooler trouble, was back in his original car once more with the Hart 'monobloc' engine. De Cesaris was also at long last back in his McLaren as, unlike the Ferrari, this had been straightened out overnight. Furthermore the Italian actually managed to keep everything under control for a change, and instead it was his team-leader who had a problem on this occasion as before he had gone very far Watson was back in the pits with oil dripping from underneath his car, and he had to revert to the spare McLaren while repairs were being effected. During the morning a few other problems also cropped up. Among them were Surer's Theodore coasting to rest out on the circuit with dead electrics which meant that he, too, had to switch cars after walking back to the pits, while Pironi and Mansell both lost time due to a turbo-charger bearing failure and a stone-pierced water radiator respectively. In the Talbot camp, meanwhile, Laffite had swopped cars with Tambay for no obvious reason other than that he had lapped fractionally slower than his team-mate during the previous afternoon, and so the two Frenchmen were virtually starting all over again from scratch.

Watson's luck deserted him again after lunch, for no sooner had he settled down to the task of trying to improve his lap times than an electrical failure cut the McLaren's engine dead. Consequently, after the Ulsterman had abandoned his car and walked back to the pits, out came the spare McLaren again, although even this was not a straightforward affair as due to an apparent vapour lock several minutes passed before the engine could be encouraged to start. Further along the pit lane, meanwhile, there ting to overtake de Cesaris, the Frenchman ploughed into a line of marker cones which knocked the Renault's front wing back into the right front wheel, damaging both rim and tyre alike. Rather significantly, this latter incident also ended Renault's hopes of having both of their cars on the front row of the grid for the fifth race in succession. Reutemann saw to that, for whilst Arnoux went on to put pole position beyond doubt by pruning his lap times down to 1 min 33.467 sec (223.394 kph), the Argentinian pulled out all the stops in his Williams to turn in a superb second fastest time of 1 min 34.140 sec compared to Prost's marginally improved time of 1 min 34.374 sec. Laffite also excelled in what had started out as Tambay's Talbot by knocking over 1½ seconds off his Friday time to move up to fourth place on the grid at 1 min 35.062 sec, while Jones finished up just one place lower after having got down to 1 min 35.359 sec prior to the engine failure. Piquet, on the other hand, was one of the few drivers apart from the temporarily redundant Villeneuve not to make any improvement during the afternoon, being fractionally slower than the first day at 1 min 35.484 sec. In fact, practice concluded on a somewhat bizarre note for the Brazilian as near the end of qualifying he spun off into the sand at the Ascari chicane when first his brakes failed to respond and then locked up at the rear – it later transpired that a stone had found its way into the right rear brake cooling duct of his Brabham, become jammed between the caliper and wheel and subsequently cut through the rim causing the tyre to deflate! Fortunately little further damage ensued, and Piquet had already gone quick enough to earn a fairly respectable sixth spot on the grid immediately ahead of Watson and Pironi who turned in closely-matched times of 1 min 35.557 sec and 1 min 35.596 sec respectively. Apart from Giacomelli, the fastest Italian and destined to line up on the fifth row of the grid in company with the unhappy Villeneuve, no-one else could even break the 1 min 36 sec barrier, but for all that about the only surprise in the final grid order of the remaining drivers was Patrese finishing up in a disappointing twentieth position in his Arrows after problems in finding a suitable Pirelli tyre compound. However, for the Candy Toleman team there was something to celebrate as at long last one of their cars was in a Grand Prix, Henton having qualified for penultimate position on the grid. The six drivers who failed to qualify, on the other hand, were Surer, Gabbiani, Warwick, Stohr, Rosberg and Serra, and it was almost certainly through Surer's lack of success that prompted the Theodore team to lodge a protest after practice against the legality of the Toleman's skirt system. Whatever, the protest was subsequently over-ruled so it achieved nothing other than to breed con-

tempt, especially when it was remembered that at Zolder the Toleman team had withdrawn one of their cars to make way for none other than the Theodore!

Following two days of rather oppressive weather, race day was no better – indeed, it was worse if anything for it was grey and overcast. During the mid-day warm-up session the atmosphere became even more subdued in the Toleman camp when Henton suddenly went missing but, unlike the weather, this soon changed when it transpired that nothing worse had happened than their driver having spun harmlessly into the sand. Ferrari and ATS, on the other hand, did have something to bother them as both Pironi and Burgudd suffered engine failures, and there were also worried expressions at Alfa Romeo when Andretti's car developed a misfire. Fortunately, with the race not due to start until 3.30 p.m., there was sufficient time to put everything right. Meanwhile, the long wait for the crowd, unimpressive by previous Monza standards, was eased by a variety of supporting events and some energetic demonstration laps by the legendary Juan Manuel Fangio (now 70 years of age) in both a 1951 Tipo 159 Alfa Romeo, similar to that in which he had won his first World Championship title, and a 1954 Lancia D50. Shortly afterwards another famous, even older veteran, Luigi Villoresi, also put in an enthusiastic appearance behind the wheel of the Lancia, a car that unlike Fangio he had raced over 25 years earlier in company with the late Alberto Ascari.

After the reminiscing it was not long before the engines of the current-day Grand Prix cars could be heard being started up in the pits and then, one by one, they were away on the warm-up lap prior to forming on the grid, Reutemann's Williams and Daly's March both devoid of nose fins following successful aerodynamic experiments during practice. Once they were all in their correct starting places final adjustments were made where necessary and eventually, after what seemed an eternity, the field was flagged off on the pace lap led by Arnoux. Unfortunately, on the way round Alboreto's Tyrrell developed an electrical problem which sent the Italian into the pits at the end of the lap and then, as the other twenty-three starters faced the starting lights, the engine in Rebaque's Brabham died. Consequently, only twenty-two cars actually got away, the Brabham subsequently being wheeled into the pit lane for attention. The start, itself, was highlighted by Pironi who charged between Watson and Piquet, past Jones and then outbraked Laffite as they lined up for the first chicane. Not finished yet, the French Ferrari driver then dealt with Reutemann and Arnoux in rapid succession and went on to complete the opening lap in a superb second place with only the fleeing Prost ahead of him. In contrast, Arnoux's opening

lap was little short of a mitigated disaster as apart from being beaten off the line by his team-mate and losing out to the hard-charging Pironi, he also fell victim to a daring overtaking manoeuvre by Reutemann who ran round the outside of him at the Parabolica. As a result, when Arnoux crossed the line for the first time he was down in fourth place with Piquet, Jones, Laffite, Villeneuve, Giacomelli, de Angelis, Watson, Mansell and, strung out closely behind were all the others, except for Alboreto and Rebaque who were still in the pits. Eventually, after everyone else had completed their second lap, both joined the race, but whereas the Tyrrell's problem appeared to have been cured, the Brabham sounded terribly off-colour and within half a lap was coasting to rest with dead electrics.

By the end of the third lap Prost had already opened up a 3 second advantage over Pironi. However, with one of their beloved Ferraris holding down second place and another now in sixth place through Villeneuve having followed Laffite past Jones and Piquet, the partisan crowd were still more than happy with the situation at this early stage of the race. Alas, their joy was to be short-lived as by the end of lap 6 not only had Pironi dropped behind Arnoux and Laffite, who had just overtaken Reutemann on successive laps, but Villeneuve was disappearing into the pits with the rear of his car enshrouded by smoke from a blown turbo. On the following lap there were more groans when Pironi lost another place to Reutemann and started falling back into the clutches of Jones and Piquet, the Frenchman finally succumbing to them both during the tenth lap. In the meantime, Laffite's impressive charge to third place had petered out and instead he was now sliding down the lap charts at an even quicker rate than Pironi due to a deflating left rear tyre. Ordinarily this would have brought him straight into the pits for a tyre change. But, instead, Laffite decided to stay out as rain had developed in the vicinity of the Ascari chicane and the Parabolica and there seemed a distinct possibility that the race would be stopped. Indeed Prost, for one, was gesticulating as much to the officials at the start/finish line area but they failed to respond and at the first chicane on lap 12 Laffite's ploy backfired when the punctured tyre blew, sending the Talbot sliding off into the sand. Moments later, Borgudd disappeared from near the back of the field after being caught out by the slippery surface at the Parabolica, and then on the following lap, with the rain coming down harder, Cheever also spun at the same corner before coming to rest at the edge of the track with a stalled engine thanks to having cooked his clutch at the start. Moreover, this latter incident took out Arnoux as well, for as the Frenchman, first to arrive on the scene, took evasive action he locked up his brakes and

A busy track on lap 16 with Piquet, Pironi, a fast-rising Tambay and Watson having all just followed Bruno Giacomelli's Alfa Romeo (out of the picture) past Reutemann's down-on-grip Williams. *(Autosport)*

went sliding straight off into the sand! As a result Renault were left with their hopes pinned entirely on Prost who was now leading the race by very nearly 15 seconds from Jones, the World Champion automatically assuming second place after having slipped past a troubled Reutemann a couple of laps earlier. Troubled, because unlike his teammate, Reutemann was now suffering from an acute lack of grip on the slippery surface due to running with no nose fin and also by having a harder 'B' compound Goodyear tyre on his left rear wheel as distinct from the four 'C' compound Goodyears fitted to Jones' sister car. Furthermore, the Argentinian was now being caught by his immediate pursuers and on lap 16, in spite of the rain having more or less stopped again, had to sit and watch as first an inspired Giacomelli rushed past and then Piquet, Pironi, a fast-rising Tambay and Watson all quickly following suit to leave him trailing in eighth place.

On lap 20, with Tambay having now promoted himself to fourth place behind Giacomelli, came a very nasty moment indeed when Watson's McLaren ran fractionally wide on the way out of the second of the fast Lesmo curves and hooked its two left-hand wheels onto the kerbing. For a second or so it seemed inconsequential. But then, as if to illustrate once more just how dangerous the current breed of Grand Prix cars were with their rock-hard suspensions, the McLaren suddenly snapped sideways before spinning backwards across the track and hitting the barriers on the opposite side with such force that the left rear wheel and suspension became entangled in the gap between the two layers of Armco. The impact also resul-

ted in the engine and gearbox parting company with the rest of the car and to a fire developing due to the fuel lines being pulled apart. Fortunately the automatic valves quickly cut off the fuel supply and the flames soon vanished. More important still, Watson had survived the ordeal and eventually emerged from the undamaged monocoque, which had come to rest on the grass verge, visibly shaken but otherwise unharmed. A miraculous escape by any standards! Meanwhile, the McLaren's engine and gearbox had careered across the track right in front of the delayed Alboreto and, despite taking evasive action by driving on to the grass verge on the left-hand side of the track, the Italian failed to make it through, and instead made contact with the barriers to become another retirement. Reutemann, next along, also took to the grass and actually managed to get through unscathed, although the excursion cost him a place to Andretti and very nearly another to de Cesaris who both stuck to the track despite having to run over some of the debris. Just three laps later, however, it was almost certain that the debris from Watson's McLaren was responsible for Tambay's promising drive in fourth place being ended abruptly. Whatever, the Talbot's left rear tyre suddenly deflated and, like his teammate earlier, Tambay slid off the track. There had been other retirements by now as well, for Salazar had suffered a tyre failure at the Curva Grande on his fourteenth lap, while Patrese and Mansell had both ended their races in the pits with a broken gearbox and handling problems caused by a broken skirt respectively. Consequently there were now only twelve cars left, with Prost still leading the way and having extended his

advantage over Jones to nearly 20 seconds.

Apart from Giacomelli dropping out of an excellent third place when his Alfa Romeo jammed in fifth gear and forced him to make a pit stop, the next few laps produced little change. But then, with the track almost entirely dry once more and remaining virtually unaffected by another brief shower of rain, Reutemann began to speed up again, and on lap 33 re-passed Andretti to take over fifth spot just as de Angelis was in the process of swopping places with de Cesaris a short distance behind. Five laps later Reutemann also caught and passed Pironi and immediately started giving chase to Piquet who was a fraction over 10 seconds ahead of him at this stage. Meanwhile Pironi, long since plagued by acute understeer caused by the Ferrari having worn its skirts away, was soon coming under attack from Andretti, but just when it looked as if the American was about to pounce on lap 41 the Alfa Romeo's flywheel coupling sheared. As a result, instead of moving up a place, Andretti found himself crawling into the pits to join Daly in retirement, the Irishman having pulled in minutes earlier with the March suffering from a broken gearbox. All the while more and more attention was becoming fixed on Reutemann's progress, for he was catching Piquet by whole seconds with each lap. In fact, by lap 44 the gap was down to a mere 5 seconds, but Piquet then began to speed up himself and appeared to have full control of the situation even when Reutemann produced what was to be the fastest lap of the race on his 48th tour. However, on the final lap, as Prost cruised home to a comfortable victory after having led all the way, and Jones duly crossed the line in second place 63 despite being hampered by a broken valve spring during the closing stages, there came unexpected drama. Piquet's engine suddenly blew up! This, of course, immediately let Reutemann through into third place and, by reason of still being on the same lap as the jubilant Prost, de Angelis and Pironi (they had swopped places on lap 44) also moved ahead of Piquet. De Cesaris, on the other hand, never had the opportunity as he slid off the track on the last lap when a tyre deflated, and finished up being classified seventh, one place lower than the unfortunate Piquet. After that came Giacomelli and Jarier with the new Osella, both two laps in arrears, and finally Henton in the Toleman, three laps behind but delighted to have finished the race non-stop even though he had been troubled by a persistent mis-fire at the top end of the Hart engine's rev band throughout.

Results

1	A. Prost (Renault)	1 hr 26 min 33.897 sec (209.045 kph/ 129.894 mph)
2	A. Jones (Williams-Ford)	1 hr 26 min 56.072 sec
3	C. Reutemann (Williams-Ford)	1 hr 27 min 24.484 sec
4	E. de Angelis (Lotus-Ford)	1 hr 28 min 06.799 sec
5	D. Pironi (Ferrari)	1 hr 28 min 08.419 sec
*6	N. Piquet (Brabham-Ford)	1 lap behind
*7	A. de Cesaris (McLaren-Ford)	1 lap behind
8	B. Giacomelli (Alfa Romeo)	2 laps behind
9	J. P. Jarier (Osella-Ford)	2 laps behind
10	B. Henton (Toleman-Hart)	3 laps behind

* Not running at finish.

Fastest lap: C. Reutemann (Williams-Ford) on lap 48 in 1 min 37.528 sec (214.092 kph/133.030 mph)

Retirements

H. Rebaque (Brabham-Ford) electrics on lap 1, G. Villeneuve (Ferrari) turbo-charger on lap 6, S. Borgudd (ATS-Ford) spun off on lap 11, J. Laffite (Talbot-Matra) tyre failure on lap 12, E. Cheever (Tyrrell-Ford) spun off on lap 12, R. Arnoux (Renault) spun off on lap 13, E. Salazar (Ensign-Ford) tyre failure on lap 14, M. Alboreto (Tyrrell-Ford) accident on lap 17, R. Patrese (Arrows-Ford) gearbox on lap 19, J. Watson (McLaren-Ford) accident on lap 20, N. Mansell (Lotus-Ford) handling on lap 21, P. Tambay (Talbot-Matra) tyre failure on lap 23, D. Daly (March-Ford) gearbox on lap 37, M. Andretti (Alfa Romeo) flywheel coupling on lap 41.

XXth Canadian Grand Prix

Montreal: September 27
Weather: Cold and wet
Duration: 2 hours (63 laps of 4.410 km circuit = 277.83 km (172.63 miles)

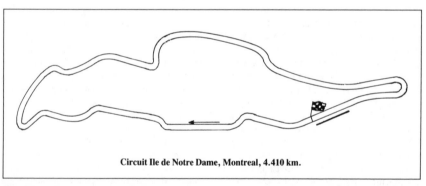

Circuit Ile de Notre Dame, Montreal, 4.410 km.

Within a few days of the curtains coming down on the European season at Monza all of the teams were heading across the Atlantic for the first of the two end of season North American rounds, the Labatt-sponsored Canadian Grand Prix scheduled to take place at Montreal's tight and twisty Ile Notre Dame circuit. As was to be expected, bearing in mind the amount of travel involved, everyone took along sufficient machinery and equipment so as, hopefully, to see them through both events. But for all that, the line-up was essentially familiar, as although there were yet two more brand new cars in evidence, a McLaren MP4 for John Watson to replace the chassis written off in his spectacular accident at Monza and another Brabham BT49C for Nelson Piquet, both had been constructed around the same general design principles as those of their predecessors. However, the Ferrari team had rung the changes with their 126CKs, for this time round Gilles Villeneuve and Didier Pironi had both been entered in the 'B' specification cars and only the spare chassis was to the earlier configuration. In addition, all three were in short wheelbase form, being devoid of the alloy spacers utilized between the engine and the gearbox. Elsewhere most of what few changes were apparent were restricted to some of the cars having larger wings and also larger brakes and brake cooling aids so as to enable them to cope better with the tortuous nature of the circuit. Renault, though, had been particularly busy between races, as apart from having revised the fuel injection system for their cars, designed to improve low-speed pick-up, they had also made strenuous efforts to reduce the overall weight of Prost's RE34 by producing carbon-fibre aerofoils, both front and rear, and also new side-pods of honeycomb material. So far as the drivers were concerned, meanwhile, the only new face was to be found at Arrows as Siegfried Stohr had been dropped in favour of the French-

Canadian Formula Atlantic ace, Jacques Villeneuve.

Due to the unavailability of the circuit for pre-race testing, for the same reasons as those at Long Beach and Monaco, the opening practice session on Friday morning was the scene of some truly frantic activity with all thirty drivers present thrashing around for lap after lap as they sought to acclimatize both themselves and their cars to the surroundings. This, in itself, should have proved a relatively straightforward exercise but, instead, nearly all of them were having a dreadful time, for the cars, with their near-solid suspensions, were finding bumps and undulations that no-one even knew existed before and were being thrown off line with frightening ferocity. Nowhere was worse than the flat-in-fifth kink just beyond the pits, for here cars were quite literally bouncing all over the road; the Ferraris, in particular, looking to be on the brink of disaster every time that Villeneuve and Pironi went through. Somehow – and it was really quite remarkable – the vast majority managed to keep out of trouble, apart from a few of them having the odd harmless spin, and about the only real casualty was Pironi when he finally did let his Ferrari get away from him. Even then, damage was little more than superficial, and the main problem facing his mechanics once the car had been towed back to the pits seemed to be that of cleaning off the mud resulting from several days of virtually non-stop rain leaving the run-off areas sodden.

During the afternoon the sense of urgency was more apparent than ever, for there was no guarantee that the rain might not return on Saturday, and everyone was anxious to make the most of the current warm and dry conditions of what could well be the only realistic chance of qualifying for grid positions. For once the Renaults were off the pace, but this was not entirely surprising for apart from the circuit hardly being of the type to bring out the best from the turbocharged cars the French team, like the other Michelin runners for that matter, were having problems in getting their tyres up to optimum working temperature. Even worse, they were in trouble in the engine department as a result of the revised fuel injection system not functioning properly and allowing the V6s to run on too lean a mixture. Arnoux, in particular, was right out of the picture in both his intended race chassis

(until suffering a major engine disaster) and the team's spare car; and even Prost, who later had a turbo let go, could only muster what was to be the session's eighth fastest time of 1 min 31.629 sec. Life in the Ferrari camp, too, was equally as fraught, for Pironi ran out of road again and had to pack up early, while Villeneuve, after a variety of problems ranging from an oil leak through to a broken turbo gasket had forced him to abandon his race car, found the spare chassis oversteering excessively! Quite a number of various mechanical frailties also affected the progress of some of the other drivers during the course of the afternoon, but not among them were Piquet, Reutemann and Jones. All three, taking over their teams' spare cars out of choice (Williams had brought along four cars) and benefiting from a fresh supply of Goodyear super-sticky qualifying tyres, had really got down to business. Indeed they were the only ones to lap under 1 min 30 sec, with Piquet coming out fastest at 1 min 29.211 sec followed by Reutemann at 1 min 29.601 sec and Jones at 1 min 29.728 sec, the reigning World Champion still driving with a broken finger and showing no signs of easing up even though he had recently announced his decision to retire from the sport at the end of the season. After that there was a gap of very nearly 1½ seconds back to de Angelis who was nonetheless in an excellent fourth place on the time-sheets at 1 min 31.212 sec. Rebaque was surprisingly well up the order as well, having achieved fifth fastest time of 1 min 31.545 sec before the onset of gearbox trouble with his Brabham, while Laffite (1 min 31.593 sec) and Watson (1 min 31.617 sec) were the others to lap quicker than the rather unhappy Prost.

Contrary to expectations, the weather was still warm and dry on Saturday, and after another busy 90 minute untimed session in the morning attention became focused on the final hour of qualifying. As far as the grid was concerned, however, the first three places were to go unchanged, for once again Piquet, Reutemann and Jones were in top form and out recording the fastest times with more sub-1 min 30 sec laps. The only difference on this occasion was that it was Reutemann who went quickest of all but even his best lap of 1 min 29.359 sec was still not enough to oust Piquet from pole position due to the Brazilian's superior Friday time. As an interesting aside, Piquet also made the headlines for another reason before the end of practice through infringing the regulations concerning the limit of eight tyres per car per timed session by 'borrowing' one of Rebaque's rear tyres. It all came about after Arnoux had apparently deliberately moved over on him approaching the first righthander beyond the pits and caused him to stand on his brakes, blistering a rear tyre in the process, for so incensed was Piquet that he had been looking to avenge himself.

However, Reutemann had then spotted that instead of a number 5 scrawled on one of Piquet's rear tyres it was a number 6 and immediately complained to the Stewards which resulted in Piquet's lap times recorded on the odd pair of tyres, slower in any case, being disallowed and a severe reprimand being handed out. The incident also delayed the issue of the official practice times, but when they were eventually released and the grid was drawn up everything was much as expected except that Mansell had hoisted himself up to a splendid fifth spot with a time of 1 min 29.997 sec, nearly 2½ seconds better than the first day when his progress had been affected by a misfiring engine. After having switched back to their older type of fuel injectors, Renault had also bounced back into contention somewhat. Prost had joined the elite sub-1 min 30 sec group with a time of 1 min 29.908 sec to clinch fourth spot on the grid, while Arnoux had improved by almost an incredible four seconds over the first day to 1 min 30.232 sec which moved him up to eighth place immediately behind Rebaque and de Angelis whose practice had been ended early through a rear suspension failure. Watson and Laffite were next and then came Villeneuve and Pironi in their Ferraris to neatly round off the front half of the grid, the French-Canadian being another to have been forced to stop early after spinning off into the barriers at the notorious flat-in-fifth kink just beyond the pits on his final set of qualifiers. Among the others, the Candy Toleman team were back in the doldrums with neither of their drivers having qualified after a variety of engine problems throughout the two days, and also taking no further interest in the weekend's proceedings were Rosberg, Serra, Gabbiani and, finally, Jacques Villeneuve whose hopes of qualifying for his first Grand Prix had been thwarted by near-continuous overheating and erratic brakes with the second Arrows.

On Sunday, prospects for the Grand Prix were looking glum indeed. Already the rains had returned, making conditions thoroughly wet and miserable, but now there was an even more worrying problem due to a wrangle over the circuit's insurance and the waivers that the teams were required to sign. Eventually, after several hours of discussion between Bernie Ecclestone and the organizers, and complete inactivity out on the track, an agreement was thrashed out, revised waivers were signed and, much to everyone's relief, preparations were finally under way for the race. But by then it was past 2.15 p.m., the scheduled start-time, and despite a shortened warm-up session it was almost another hour before the count-down began, causing panic and confusion amongst television and radio producers, and considerable frustration to the near-100,000 spectators waiting around in the unpleasant weather. Meanwhile, for the drivers, wet settings were obviously the order of the day as the rain persisted, but whilst everyone else seemed reasonably happy with their wet-weather tyres, the Goodyear runners were frantically trying to decide whether to rely on 13" or 15" diameter fronts and also which type of tread pattern to use at the rear. No-one was more concerned than Reutemann who went on to surprise everyone by leaping out of his car on the dummy grid, vaulting over the pit wall and promptly setting off on another warm-up lap in his spare car which, unlike his race car, had been kitted out with the smaller front tyres. Then, after completing the lap still undecided, he pulled up alongside his race car which meant that with Jones already in position there were three Williams on the grid! Minutes later, though, the spare car was wheeled away with Reutemann having finally made up his mind that the larger front tyres were a better proposition, and at long last, with everyone else ready, including Viellenuve who had opted to race the spare Ferrari, the field was flagged away on the pace lap prior to lining up on the grid again in readiness for the start which was now nearly 1½ hours late.

When the starting lights came on and red gave way to green it appeared that Reutemann had made the right choice of tyres as he slithered off the line and beat Piquet into the first right-hand turn. But then it all changed. First a hard-charging Jones bravely ran around on his outside at the next left-hander, briefly bumping wheels with his team-mate which caused Reutemann to momentarily lift off, and then Piquet, Prost and de Angelis all went by in quick succession to leave him down in fifth place ahead of the howling mob behind, most of whom were

barely discernible due to the vast quantities of water being flung up. Despite the atrocious conditions everything seemed to be going well as they all made their way down to the hairpin on the far side of the circuit, but as the mid-field runners were turning into the following right-hander Villeneuve suddenly nudged the back of Arnoux's Renault and pushed him into Pironi. That did it. In the next instant, while Villeneuve continued unabashed, albeit with his front wing now slightly cock-eyed, Arnoux was spinning off into the barriers and into retirement with damaged front suspension, and Pironi was dropping to the back of the field as he fought, successfully, to recover from a less harmful spin. On the second lap, with Jones making full use of the enormous advantage of clear visiblity, unlike his pursuers who were being blinded by the spray, there was another incident. This time it was Tambay whose Talbot aquaplaned off the track from eighth place, the Frenchman fortunately gathering it up without hitting anything as his compatriot in the Ferrari had done a couple of minutes earlier. Reutemann, meanwhile, was still losing places hand over fist as he struggled forlornly for grip on the saturated track, and it wasn't long before his team-mate started to go the same way, for on lap 7, as the rain intensified, the conditions finally got the better of Jones and he suddenly spun out of the lead. This really transformed the race order, for as the close-following Piquet was left having a busy moment avoiding the gyrating Williams, so Prost, Laffite and the fast-rising Villeneuve were all able to take advantage of the situation to nip by, and for Watson to close right up in fifth place before going past next time round. A Michelin 1, 2, 3, 4! In the mean-

time, other drivers were also having their moments in the worsening conditions, including Tambay who went off a second time with rather more dire consequences as he had to abandon his Talbot, after glancing the barriers, and Patrese who retired at the pits complaining that his Arrows was undriveable after he, too, had spun and knocked his nose cone askew. On lap 9, by which time Jones had dropped right away to a hopeless 14th place and Reutemann to an even more depressing 19th, Salazar disappeared under similar circumstances when the Ensign got away from him and the engine, which he stalled, refused to restart.

Although Prost was now leading the race he was ill-at-ease, for quite apart from the trying conditions his brakes were not behaving as they should have been and he had Laffite harrying him all the way around the circuit. Eventually, on lap 13, he was forced to concede to the Talbot team-leader, and within four more laps had dropped to fourth place behind the ever-enthusiastic Villeneuve, apparently unperturbed by the fact that his Ferrari was now running with a pronounced mid-range misfire, and Watson in his McLaren. Piquet, meanwhile, had been steadily losing contact with all four Michelin runners ahead of him owing to his obviously inferior wet-weather Goodyear tyres, and was now coming under intense pressure from none other than Pironi, the Frenchman having carved his way through the field in magnificent style since the first lap incident. He was not finished yet either, as on lap 19 he barged past Piquet and proceeded to reel in Prost to such good effect that just three laps later he was moving up yet another place. Sadly, though, that was to be Pironi's lot, as on lap 25 a brilliant drive

A particularly eventful race on home soil for Gilles Villeneuve saw the French-Canadian ultimately finish in a fine third place behind John Watson's McLaren, the pair of them shown at around half-distance and after having just lapped Eddie Cheever's Tyrrell. *(L.A.T. Photographic)*

was brought to an abrupt end by the Ferrari suddenly blowing up its engine! Minutes later, Jones, having only just rejoined the race after a pit stop for a different set of tyres, also retired when he returned to the pits to report that the handling of his Williams was such that it was a waste of time continuing, something which was quite understandable as he had been passed by everyone except an even more delayed Rebaque (two tyre stops and countless spins!) and any remaining hopes of retaining his World Championship crown had long since disappeared. All the while Laffite was steadily increasing his lead and as the 30-lap mark came up he was over 12 seconds clear of Villeneuve and Watson still vying for second place. Prost was now a distant fourth, albeit well clear of Piquet, and then came Giacomelli, Daly, doing wonders in the Avon-shod March, de Cesaris, de Angelis and Andretti, all still on the same lap as the leader. After that only seven others were left, as no sooner had Jones disappeared than Jarier had been forced off the track by an errant Rebaque who had spun (again!) right in front of him at the hairpin before the pits.

After following Villeneuve for what seemed an eternity, Watson finally made his move on lap 38 and immediately took off in pursuit of Laffite who was now barely 10 seconds away, the Frenchman having just spent five frustrating laps trying to lap Andretti's Alfa Romeo prior to finally getting past. Prompted by pit signals, however, Laffite responded to the challenge by speeding up and, even after Watson set what was to be the fastest lap of the race on his 43rd tour, continued to hold sway out in front. Villeneuve, on the other hand, dropped right away as whilst in the process of lapping de Angelis he ran into the back of the Lotus and the pair of them instantly spun before going on their way again with the Ferrari's front wing now not only bent, but looking decidedly second-hand. Nevertheless, the French-Canadian held on to his third place and was soon driving more determined than ever to keep clear of Prost. In the meantime, Piquet was having to keep a watchful eye on

Jacques Laffite drove superbly on the soaking wet track and came out a well-deserved winner. He is shown here soon after lapping Carlos Reutemann's Williams. (*L.A.T. Photographic*)

an advancing de Cesaris as already he had been forced to give up his fifth place to Giacomelli, and there was now an increasing danger of dropping out of the points altogether. As it happened he need not have worried, as on lap 49 he was moving back up into fifth place when Prost suddenly collided with Mansell's Lotus, after the young Englishman had inadvertently moved over on him, and ended his race (and his slim Championship hopes) with the Renault up against the barriers devoid of its nose wing. Mansell also retired, but he was about to do so in any case as on the previous lap he had gone into the pits to have a punctured tyre replaced, been sent out again on slick tyres as the rain had actually stopped some while earlier and then promptly spun off, damaging his rear aerofoil. Less than three laps later there was more drama when de Cesaris, who had behaved impeccably all weekend up to that point, suddenly became excited and decided to overtake Piquet when it just wasn't on. Again, there was a collision, but whereas the Italian slithered off the track to add his name to the casualty list with a stalled engine, Piquet succeeded in keeping his Brabham under control and went on his way in an even more secure fifth place, Daly having long since dropped away with fading

rear brakes. In the closing stages of what had obviously become a two-hour event due to the reduced pace, the rain returned with a vengeance. Even so, it had little effect on the final outcome, for Laffite continued to stay out of Watson's reach and eventually took the chequered flag, after 63 laps, with still more than 6 seconds in hand to conclude a memorable drive and keep his Championship hopes alive at the same time. Despite finishing second, Watson had done exceptionally well, too, but the real hero so far as the crowd was concerned was Villeneuve as he had pressed on regardless of the Ferrari's battered front wing gradually pulling away from its mountings, partially obstructing his view until breaking away completely, and held on to a particularly well-deserved third place. Lapped, but by no means disgraced, Giacomelli scored his first points of a difficult season by finishing fourth. Piquet was fifth and de Angelis sixth ahead of Andretti, Daly, Surer, a somewhat dejected Reutemann who at least had the consolation of knowing that he still led the Championship table, and, finally, Alboreto, the other retirements having been Cheever with a late engine failure and also Borgudd and Rebaque who had both spun out soon after half-distance.

Results			
1	J. Laffite (Talbot-Matra)	2 hr 01 min 25.205 sec (137.290 kph/ 85.308 mph)	
2	J. Watson (McLaren-Ford)	2 hr 01 min 31.438 sec	
3	G. Villeneuve (Ferrari)	2 hr 03 min 15.480 sec	
4	B. Giacomelli (Alfa Romeo)	1 lap behind	
5	N. Piquet (Brabham-Ford)	1 lap behind	
6	E. de Angelis (Lotus-Ford)	1 lap behind	

7	M. Andretti (Alfa Romeo)	1 lap behind
8	D. Daly (March-Ford)	2 laps behind
9	M. Surer (Theodore-Ford)	2 laps behind
10	C. Reutemann (Williams-Ford)	3 laps behind
11	M. Alboreto (Tyrrell-Ford)	4 laps behind
*12	E. Cheever (Tyrrell-Ford)	7 laps behind

* Not running at finish.

Fastest lap: J. Watson (McLaren-Ford) on lap

43 in 1 min 49.475 sec (145.019 kph/90.110 mph)

Retirements
R. Arnoux (Renault) accident on lap 1, R. Patrese (Arrows-Ford) handling on lap 6, P. Tambay (Talbot-Matra) spun off on lap 7, E. Salazar (Ensign-Ford) spun off on lap 9, A. Jones (Williams-Ford) handling on lap 24, D. Pironi (Ferrari) engine on lap 25, J. P. Jarier (Osella-Ford) accident on lap 27, H. Rebaque (Brabham-Ford) spun off on lap 36, S. Borgudd (ATS-Ford) spun off on lap 41, N. Mansell (Lotus-Ford) accident on lap 46, A. Prost (Renault) accident on lap 49, A. de Cesaris (McLaren-Ford) spun off on lap 52.

1981

1st United States (Las Vegas) Grand Prix

Las Vegas: October 17
Weather: Very hot
Distance: 75 laps of 3.650 km
circuit = 273.75 km (170.10 miles)

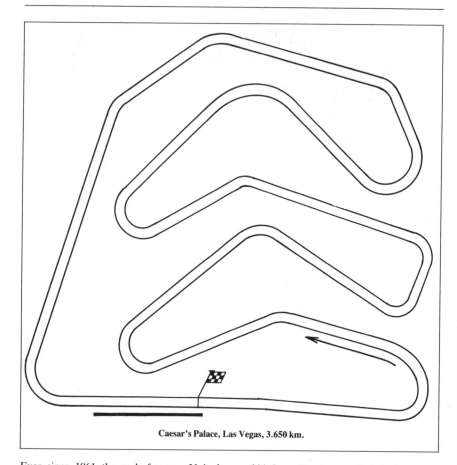

Caesar's Palace, Las Vegas, 3.650 km.

Ever since 1961 the end-of-season United States Grand Prix had always taken place at Watkins Glen but this year it was different. The organizers there had failed to come up with the financial payment due for the 1980 race by a date fixed by the Executive Committee of FISA, and as a result the 1981 race, due to have been run on 4 October, had been withdrawn from the World Championship calendar. As a replacement, FISA had then given its sanction for a new event to be held at a purpose-built circuit on land adjoining the Caesar's Palace Hotel in the tinsel city of Las Vegas, and to satisfy the rules concerning track approval for the Grand Prix a Can-Am Challenge race was to take place – just one day before the Grand Prix! The actual circuit, part of which was on an existing car park and the remainder on previously unused ground, was uninspiring to the extreme, for it was an entirely flat 'Mickey Mouse' affair, consisting of a succession of mainly tight turns – fourteen in all – interspersed by short straights, and was lined by tall concrete barriers throughout its full length of 3.65 kilometres. In fact, Jacques Laffite likened it to a Go-Kart track but for all that the organizers, aided by Chris Pook

and his Long Beach team, had obviously put an enormous amount of effort into the project, for quite apart from space limitations it also had to be borne in mind that one of the main considerations had been that of worldwide television coverage. In particular, a lot of attention had been paid to making the track wide enough so as to permit relatively easy over-taking, sandy run-off areas had been provided where considered necessary and the track surface was as smooth as any on the calendar. So it was certainly not all bad news. Of course, more important still, there was now the World Championship, itself, to be decided with three drivers, Carlos Reutemann (49 points), Nelson Piquet (48 points), and Jacques Laffite (43 points), all in with a chance of carrying off the coveted title.

To allow everyone an opportunity of learning their way around the new circuit, an unofficial practice session was held on the Wednesday before the race, scheduled for Saturday. From this it soon became evident that the track was much faster than the anticipated average speeds of 85–90 mph, for the front-runners were hovering around the 100 mph mark in no time at all. It also

became evident that the track was going to be extremely hard on drivers, as with the direction of travel being anti-clockwise there was a preponderance of left-hand turns and this was placing a heavy strain on neck muscles; Piquet, in particular, suffering noticeably badly and actually being physically sick. Fastest in this opening spell were the Williams FWO7Cs of Jones and Reutemann which was to be a pattern that was to continue once the official timekeepers took up duty for the first qualifying session on the following afternoon, for the cars from Didcot were quickly proving to be the ones to try to beat. Reutemann seemed to be in a particularly determined mood and in conditions that

Starting Grid

	C. Reutemann Williams-Ford (1 min 17.821 sec)
A. Jones Williams-Ford (1 min 17.995 sec)	
	G. Villeneuve Ferrari (1 min 18.060 sec)
N. Piquet Brabham-Ford (1 min 18.161 sec)	
	A. Prost Renault (1 min 18.433 sec)
J. Watson McLaren-Ford (1 min 18.617 sec)	
	P. Tambay Talbot-Matra (1 min 18.681 sec)
B. Giacomelli Alfa Romeo (1 min 18.792 sec)	
	N. Mansell Lotus-Ford (1 min 19.044 sec)
M. Andretti Alfa Romeo (1 min 19.068 sec)	
	R. Patrese Arrows-Ford (1 min 19.152 sec)
J. Laffite Talbot-Matra (1 min 19.167 sec)	
	R. Arnoux Renault (1 min 19.197 sec)
A. de Cesaris McLaren-Ford (1 min 19.217 sec)	
	E. de Angelis Lotus-Ford (1 min 19.562 sec)
H. Rebaque Brabham-Ford (1 min 19.571 sec)	
	M. Alboreto Tyrrell-Ford (1 min 19.774 sec)
D. Pironi Ferrari (1 min 19.899 sec)	
	E. Cheever Tyrrell-Ford (1 min 20.475 sec)
K. Rosberg Fittipaldi-Ford (1 min 20.729 sec)	
	J. P. Jarier Osella-Ford (1 min 20.781 sec)
D. Warwick Toleman-Hart (1 min 21.294 sec)	
	M. Surer Theodore-Ford (1 min 21.430 sec)
E. Salazar Ensign-Ford (1 min 21.629 sec)	

Did not qualify:
S. Borgudd (ATS-Ford) 1 min 21.665 sec
F. Serra (Fittipaldi-Ford) 1 min 21.672 sec
D. Daly (March-Ford) 1 min 21.824 sec
J. Villeneuve (Arrows-Ford) 1 min 22.822 sec
B. Henton (Toleman-Hart) 1 min 22.960 sec
G. Gabbiani (Osella-Ford) 1 min 26.634 sec

were cool and dry proceeded to lap the tightly-coiled circuit in an awe-inspiring time of 1 min 17.821 sec (168.849 kph/104.917 mph) to put himself firmly at the top of the time-sheets. Even his team-mate had no answer to that and had ultimately to settle for a time nearly ½ second slower, Jones' best run coming out at 1 min 18.236 sec. As for the opposition, only Prost (1 min 18.433 sec) and Villeneuve (1 min 18.457 sec), driving a Ferrari 126CK specially flown out from Maranello to replace his battered Canadian race chassis, were really anywhere near in contention, for the others were all at least a second away from Reutemann's time. Nevertheless, there were some particularly good individual performances, especially from Mansell who got stuck in with his Lotus 87 and recorded the afternoon's sixth fastest time of 1 min 19.044 sec, and from de Cesaris (keeping off the walls for a change) who finished up just one place lower with a creditable 1 min 19.338 sec in his McLaren MP4. Like Prost and Villeneuve, both drivers also beat their respective team-mates by a good margin, although this was not exactly surprising as de Angelis had his practice run spoiled by a broken front anti-roll bar, while Watson was hardly able to practise at all due to the effects of a bad cold. Reutemann's two Championship adversaries were rather unhappy as well, for whilst Piquet turned in a reasonable fifth fastest time of 1 min 18.954 sec it was at considerable personal discomfort owing to a a stiff neck, and Laffite, meanwhile, was having car problems. Primarily it was lack of grip, but in addition his V12 Matra engine was not picking up properly out of the numerous slow corners, and the net result was a disappointing tenth place on the time-sheets immediately behind Andretti and his only fractionally quicker team-mate, Tambay. Even so the unluckiest driver of all had to be Jarier. First an engine failure with the new Osella FAIC during the morning untimed session had left the Frenchman with no option other than to take over the Italian team's older spare car and then, because of a severe fuel pressure problem, he was prevented from doing even one decent timed lap all afternoon.

During the untimed session on Friday morning Arnoux really made himself popular in the Renault camp by spinning off into the barriers and wrecking the rear end of a brand new chassis (RE35) that had been brought in as a replacement for the car that he had damaged in Montreal. Furthermore, there was no hope of effecting repairs in time for the afternoon session which meant that for the second day running the Frenchman had to revert to the spare Renault, as on the previous morning the new car had been put out of action by a turbo failure and a resultant fire. Reutemann's confidence also received a jolt when he misjudged an over-

taking manoeuvre on Piquet, rode up over one of the Brabham's rear wheels and became momentarily airborne before crashing down on the track. Fortunately he managed to gather it up without hitting the wall and, unlike Arnoux's Renault, the Williams appeared to be perfectly alright after being examined. However, once final qualifying was under way the Argentinian was troubled by excessive understeer, which suggested that something had been bent after all and, despite having his second set of qualifiers fitted to his spare car, failed to make any improvement on Thursday's time. Even so it was to make no difference as far as pole position was concerned because only Jones broke the 1 min 18 sec barrier during the course of the afternoon, but at 1 min 17.995 sec this still left the outgoing World Champion in second place on the grid. Meanwhile, the next two places went to Villeneuve, after another impressive performance in his obviously inferior handling Ferrari produced a lap in 1 min 18.060 sec, and to Piquet who did extremely well to get down to 1 min 18.161 sec as, apart from gear selection problems forcing him to switch cars, the Brazilian was now in agony from a bruised back – the result of a visit to a masseur to relieve his neck muscles! Prost, on the other hand, slipped to fifth spot by being one of the few drivers, along with Reutemann, not to improve in this final hour when he, too, ran into gear selection problems with his Renault. After Prost, Watson managed to shrug off the effects of his cold to claim sixth spot at 1 min 18.617 sec. Then came Tambay (1 min 18.681 sec), Giacomelli (1 min 18.792 sec) and Mansell by reason of his Thursday time as all attempts by the young Englishman to find some extra speed were thwarted by ignition problems with his intended race chassis, and by a down-on-power engine in the spare Lotus. Andretti very nearly knocked Mansell even lower down the order in spite of a fuel pick-up problem but, instead, had to settle for an eventual tenth place on the grid immediately ahead of Patrese, benefiting from a fresh batch of Pirelli qualifying tyres, and Laffite who achieved his best, though not exactly impressive, time after taking over Tambay's car which he was subsequently to commandeer for the race. Like Laffite, Arnoux was way out of the picture with the spare Renault, and left facing the prospects of starting the race from an uncharacteristic 13th position, while Pironi finished up in an even more disappointing eighteenth slot following an afternoon spoiled by a turbo failure and both handling and fuel-injection problems with the spare Ferrari. In contrast, an extremely pleasant surprise was to see Warwick qualify for his first Grand Prix at long last. There was also a Fittipaldi in the race for the first time since the British Grand Prix, Rosbert having qualified in twentieth

position. Jarier, too, overcame his problems of the first day, and a down-on-power engine, to make the cut but his team-mate didn't even bother to go out to try, so yet again Gabbiani was left in the non-qualifying zone where he was joined by Borgudd, Serra, Daly (surprisingly!), Villeneuve (J.) and Henton.

On Saturday the weather was very hot indeed and by the time that the 24 starters had formed up on the dummy grid in readiness for the 1.15 p.m. start it had already become quite obvious that they were in for a long and extremely gruelling race. During the final count-down the Clerk of the Course laid down some strict instructions concerning the starting procedure, but in the heat of the moment Villeneuve subsequently lined up his Ferrari too far to the left of his starting box after completing the pace lap, with the result that the Stewards later decided to disqualify him. In the meantime, though, it was all eyes on the starting lights and at the green Jones timed everything to perfection to surge away into an immediate lead while his team-mate on pole position made such a tardy start that almost before realizing it he was being swallowed up by Villeneuve and Prost. Giacomelli, after a brilliant start from the fourth row, also quickly found a way way around the Williams, leaving the World Championship leader to complete the opening lap in a somewhat disheartening fifth place, with Watson now biting at his heels and looking all set to go by at any moment. The other two Championship contenders, Laffite (another to make a good start) and Piquet, were also tucked tightly up behind ahead of Mansell, Tambay and the other thirteen cars, for already the field was one short, Jarier having retired on the start-line with a broken drive-shaft. At the end of the second lap, with Jones now holding an astounding 5 second advantage, de Angelis also retired when he went into the pits to complain of poor handling only for the Lotus mechanics to discover that one of his water radiators had sprung a leak! Tambay didn't last long either as having just recovered from a spin, following a wheel-banging incident with de Cesaris, the Frenchman's Talbot suddenly careered off the track on one of the quicker left-handers and ploughed into the barriers. Such was the impact that the entire front end of the car, wheels included, was torn off, but to everyone's amazement Tambay subsequently stepped out of the wreckage with little more than a bruised leg.

By lap 10 Jones was almost as many seconds clear, for although Prost had barged past Villeneuve back on the third lap and since pulled away he was making no impression at all on the leader, his cause not being helped by increasing tyre vibrations owing to the Renault's Michelins picking up rubber off the track. In the meantime, Villeneuve had been left with the task of keeping Gia-

1981

After taking the lead at the start, 1980 World Champion Alan Jones went on to totally dominate the inaugural Caesar's Palace Grand Prix at Las Vegas. Here he has just lapped Andrea de Cesaris (McLaren) and Keke Rosberg (Fittipaldi) relatively early in the race with no-one else even in sight. *(L.A.T. Photographic)*

earlier than usual. Within another lap Andretti was also past, and again with such ease that it was difficult to believe that there was a World Championship title at stake! Meanwhile, with Andretti soon pushing him hard once more, Piquet immediately set about Watson until taking over sixth spot and, more significantly, a points position on lap 22. Then, on the very next lap, came unexpected drama. Having received word of Villeneuve's disqualification, the Ferrari team personnel were trying to decide whether to call in their driver or lodge an appeal after the race, when the matter was resolved by Villeneuve suddenly pulling off to the side of the track with the back of his car on fire – a fault had developed somewhere in the Ferrari's fuel-injection system and the French-Canadian was out of the race! At almost precisely the same moment Laffite overtook Giacomelli to find himself an unexpected third, and before the same lap was out Andretti moved past both Watson and Piquet to take over fifth place. So, in less than a minute, the race order had been transformed, except up front where Jones was now leading Prost by well over half a minute. Furthermore, the field was now down to only 16 runners as just prior to Villeneuve's abrupt departure Surer and Rebaque had both added their names to a growing retirement list by disappearing into the pits with handling problems caused by a broken rear suspension rocker arm and an overheating engine, the legacy of a spin, respectively.

On lap 27, as de Cesaris was in the pits a second time having a bent steering arm replaced to cure continuing handling problems, came the start of another major reshuffle in the order when Giacomelli suddenly spun and slipped from fourth place to tenth. This was followed two laps later by Watson stopping for a fresh set of tyres, dropping the Ulsterman even further back, and then, almost immediately, by Andretti's fine drive being ended by a bolt breaking in the right rear suspension of his Alfa Romeo. That was not all, as only a couple more laps passed before Mansell was in the process of overtaking the uninspired Reutemann, while Prost was seen heading for the pits. Again it was for fresh rubber, and again it was a Michelin runner, so it was now becoming clear that tyres were playing just as an important role here as in Montreal three weeks earlier, only this time Goodyear seemed to be holding the upper hand. Be that as it may, Prost rejoined the race in sixth place between Reutemann and a fast-recovering Giacomelli, just as Patrese was on his way into the pits for a change of Pirellis, and proceeded to put on a stirring drive which saw him move back into second place in just fourteen laps. Furthermore this virtually put paid to Laffite's faint Championship hopes, especially as by then he, too, was in trouble with his Michelin

comelli at bay. He was being so successful at it, too, that there was now a whole string of cars trailing along behind him with Laffite next in line after having made light work of picking off Reutemann, already experiencing a slight problem selecting gears, and then Watson. Piquet was still lying eighth but Mansell had dropped away to 12th place after losing out to Andretti, Arnoux and de Cesaris in quick succession. Arnoux, though, was now making for the pits and about to conclude a most unhappy weekend by being forced to retire with an obscure electrical fault. On the following lap Cheever also disappeared from near the back of the field when the engine in his Tyrrell suddenly let go, while de Cesaris, suffering handling problems since his bump with Tambay,

turned off into the pits to see whether a fresh set of Michelins would help. Salazar was already there, the Chilean having pitted several minutes earlier with fluid leaking from one of the Ensign's rear brake lines, and on lap 16 Pironi joined de Cesaris in being another to make an early tyre stop. While all this was happening the situation behind Villeneuve was becoming even more exciting for, with Andretti tagging on to the queue and moving right in on his tail, Piquet was growing more and more anxious to overtake Reutemann. Indeed, the Brazilian was now all but touching the Williams' gearbox and, as the two cars approached the last left-hander before the pits on lap 17, he finally made it through on the inside when, for no obvious reason, Reutemann hit the brakes tyres. Rather than stop, however, Laffite kept going and it was not until the end of lap 52 that he finally veered off into the pit lane by which time he had also seen Piquet, Mansell and Giacomelli go past on successive laps. Now Reutemann and Watson were able to take advantage of his plight as well so that when he eventually returned to the fray Laffite found himself down in a somewhat lowly eighth place. Lower down the order still, meanwhile, a disappointing race from Pironi had not been improved by a further delay at the pits to have a damaged skirt replaced, while Warwick's Grand Prix debut had been brought to a conclusion by a broken gearbox in the Toleman after experiencing problems with his rear brakes caused by an oil leak.

After sixty laps Jones was already pacing himself to the finish, for barring mechanical trouble he had the race well and truly sewn up, being over 40 seconds clear of Prost. In third place, however, it was now Giacomelli, the Italian driving superbly and more than

making up for his earlier mistake. Mansell was still there in fourth place as he had also overtaken Piquet who was not looking too comfortable at all for his head could be clearly seen lolling around in the Brabham's cockpit which was a sure sign that he was suffering from physical exhaustion. Consequently there was still some considerable doubt as to the final outcome of the World Championship with the big question mark hanging over the Brazilian's ability to keep going, for Reutemann, now driving without fourth gear, certainly wasn't doing anything and, in fact, had just given way to Watson. Laffite was not that far behind Reutemann either for ever since his tyre stop the Frenchman had been making up ground rapidly. This continued, and on lap 69 Laffite was not only roaring past the troubled Williams driver but giving chase to Watson. To add to the excitement of the closing stages Giacomelli was also homing in on Prost, suffering a recurrence of tyre problems, but whereas Liffite succeeded in overhauling

Watson on the last corner of the last lap, after they had both unlapped themselves from a cruising Jones, the Italian failed in his bid to snatch second place by just a few car lengths.

After the race the scenes were quite remarkable for nearly every one of the 13 drivers still there at the finish – Alboreto had been the last retirement with late engine problems – were suffering from varying degrees of heat exhaustion. Piquet was in a particularly sorry state and it was a full 15 minutes before he could be properly revived. Nevertheless, it had all been worthwhile, for by holding on to fifth place – just – he was now the 1981 World Champion! In the Williams camp, meanwhile, emotions were mixed to the extreme as Jones was in an understandably jubilant mood having just convincingly won what was ostensibly his last Grand Prix, while Reutemann was in an equally understandably dejected frame of mind having just seen the World Championship title slip from his grasp by a single point.

Results

1	A. Jones (Williams-Ford)	1 hr 44 min 09.077 sec (157.702 kph/ 97.992 mph)	7	J. Watson (McLaren-Ford)	1 hr 45 min 27.574 sec	
			8	C. Reutemann (Williams-Ford)	1 lap behind	
2	A. Prost (Renault)	1 hr 44 min 29.125 sec	9	D. Pironi (Ferrari)	2 laps behind	
			10	K. Rosberg (Fittipaldi-Ford)	2 laps behind	
3	B. Giacomelli (Alfa Romeo)	1 hr 44 min 29.505 sec	11	R. Patrese (Arrows-Ford)	4 laps behind	
4	N. Mansell (Lotus-Ford)	1 hr 44 min 56.550 sec	12	A. de Cesaris (McLaren-Ford)	6 laps behind	
5	N. Piquet (Brabham-Ford)	1 hr 45 min 25.515 sec				
6	J. Laffite (Talbot-Matra)	1 hr 45 min 27.252 sec				

Still running at finish: E. Salazar (Ensign-Ford) 14 laps behind.

Fastest lap: D. Pironi (Ferrari) on lap 49 in 1 min 20.156 sec (163.929 kph/101.861 mph)

Retirements
J. P. Jarier (Osella-Ford) drive-shaft on lap 1, E. de Angelis (Lotus-Ford) water radiator on lap 2, P. Tambay (Talbot-Matra) accident on lap 3, R. Arnoux (Renault) electrics on lap 10, E. Cheever (Tyrrell-Ford) engine on lap 11, M. Surer (Theodore-Ford) rear suspension on lap 19, H. Rebaque (Brabham-Ford) overheating on lap 20, G. Villeneuve (Ferrari) fuel-injection on lap 23, M. Andretti (Alfa Romeo) rear suspension on lap 30, D. Warwick (Toleman-Hart) gearbox on lap 43, M. Alboreto (Tyrrell-Ford) engine on lap 67.

Nelson Piquet won his first World Championship title driving the Ford-Cosworth-powered Brabham BT49C . . .

1981

1981 Points Tables

Driver	Nationality	Car	USA (West) (Long Beach) Mar 15	Brazilian (Rio de Janeiro) Mar 29	Argentine (Buenos Aires) Apr 12	San Marino (Imola) May 3	Belgian (Zolder) May 17	Monaco (Monte Carlo) May 31	Spanish (Jarama) Jun 21	French (Dijon-Prenois) Jul 5	British (Silverstone) Jul 18	German (Hockenheim) Aug 2	Austrian (Österreichring) Aug 16	Dutch (Zandvoort) Aug 30	Italian (Monza) Sep 13	Canadian (Montreal) Sep 27	USA (Las Vegas) Oct 17	Total points
N. Piquet	BR	Brabham-Ford	4	–	9	9	–	–	–	4	–	9	4	6	1	2	2	50
C. Reutemann	RA	Williams-Ford	6	9	6	4	9	–	3	–	6	–	2	–	4	–	–	49
A. Jones	AUS	Williams-Ford	9	6	3	–	–	6	–	–	–	–	3	4	6	–	9	46
J. Laffite	F	Talbot-Matra	–	1	–	–	6	4	6	–	4	4	9	–	–	9	1	44
A. Prost	F	Renault	–	–	4	–	–	–	–	9	–	6	–	9	9	–	6	43
J. Watson	GB	McLaren-Ford	–	–	–	–	–	–	4	6	9	1	1	–	–	6	–	27
G. Villeneuve	CDN	Ferrari	–	–	–	–	3	9	9	–	–	–	–	–	–	4	–	25
E. de Angelis	I	Lotus-Ford	–	2	1	–	2	–	2	1	–	–	–	2	3	1	–	14
R. Arnoux	F	Renault	–	–	2	–	–	–	–	3	–	–	6	–	–	–	–	11
H. Rebaque	MEX	Brabham-Ford	–	–	–	3	–	–	–	–	2	3	–	3	–	–	–	11
R. Patrese	I	Arrows-Ford	–	4	–	6	–	–	–	–	–	–	–	–	–	–	–	10
E. Cheever	USA	Tyrrell-Ford	2	–	–	–	1	2	–	–	3	2	–	–	–	–	–	10
D. Pironi	F	Ferrari	–	–	–	2	–	3	–	2	–	–	–	–	2	–	–	9
N. Mansell	GB	Lotus-Ford	..	–	–	–	4	–	1	–	–	–	–	–	–	–	3	8
B. Giacomelli	I	Alfa Romeo	–	–	–	–	–	–	–	–	–	–	–	–	–	3	4	7
M. Surer	CH	Ensign-Ford / Theodore-Ford	–	3	–	–	–	1	–	–	–	–	–	–	–	–	–	4
M. Andretti	USA	Alfa Romeo	3	–	–	–	–	–	–	–	–	–	–	–	–	–	–	3
P. Tambay	F	Theodore-Ford / Talbot-Matra	1	–	–	–	–	–	–	–	–	–	–	–	–	–	–	1
A. de Cesaris	I	McLaren-Ford	–	–	–	1	–	–	–	–	–	–	–	–	–	–	–	1
S. Borgudd	S	ATS-Ford	–	–	–	–	–	–	–	–	–	1	–	–	–	–	–	1
E. Salazar	RCH	March-Ford / Ensign-Ford	–	–	–	–	–	–	–	–	–	–	–	1	–	–	–	1

Constructors

	Mar 15	Mar 29	Apr 12	May 3	May 17	May 31	Jun 21	Jul 5	Jul 18	Aug 2	Aug 16	Aug 30	Sep 13	Sep 27	Oct 17	Total
Williams-Ford	15	15	9	4	9	6	3	–	6	–	5	4	10	–	9	95
Brabham-Ford	4	–	9	12	–	–	–	4	2	12	4	9	1	2	2	61
Renault	–	–	6	–	–	–	–	12	–	6	6	9	9	–	6	54
Talbot (Ligier)-Matra	–	1	–	–	6	4	6	–	4	4	9	–	–	9	1	44
Ferrari	–	–	–	2	3	12	9	2	–	–	–	–	2	4	–	34
McLaren-Ford	–	–	–	1	–	–	4	6	9	1	1	–	–	6	–	28
Lotus-Ford	–	2	1	–	6	–	3	1	–	–	–	2	3	1	3	22
Arrows-Ford	–	4	–	6	–	–	–	–	–	–	–	–	–	–	–	10
Alfa Romeo	3	–	–	–	–	–	–	–	–	–	–	–	–	3	4	10
Tyrrell-Ford	2	–	–	–	1	2	–	–	3	2	–	–	–	–	–	10
Ensign-Ford	–	3	–	–	–	1	–	–	–	–	–	1	–	–	–	5
Theodore-Ford	1	–	–	–	–	–	–	–	–	–	–	–	–	–	–	1
ATS-Ford	–	–	–	–	–	–	–	–	–	1	–	–	–	–	–	1

N.B. Although the S. African GP took place as planned on Feb 7 it was not granted World Championship status.
Cancellation: USA (East) GP (Oct 4)

... although for the second year running the Constructors' title went to the Williams team thanks to a string of consistent results recorded by Carlos Reutemann (car No. 2) and Alan Jones (car No. 1), depicted here driving to an impressive 1-2 victory in the early season Brazilian Grand Prix. (*Phipps Photographic*)

1982 One win – one championship

Following a year in which politics had stolen the headlines more often than the actual racing, the close season turned out to be a period of relative peace and calm. New rules announced by FISA were, in the main, accepted with little apparent disapproval and everyone devoted their energies rather more on generally preparing for the season ahead. Indeed, some of the changes brought about by the new rules were welcomed with open arms, in particular a decision to do away with the absurd business of ground-clearance checks which, in turn, meant that there was no longer any need for cars to have hydro-pneumatic suspension systems and the like. New rules concerning skirts also met with a favourable response as these were now officially permitted once more – somewhat ironic after the events of the previous winter – although they had to be fixed, not sliding, and the word 'skirt' was tactfully avoided. Instead, the official wording was that 'to the bottom of the two mandatory side panels may be attached a single piece of solid material of rectangular section'. This was to have a maximum height of 60 millimetres and a maximum uniform thickness of between five and six millimetres. In addition, it was now permissible to attach a single rubbing strip, although this, too, had to consist of a solid material (which would not produce dangerous fragments of debris on the track), fit within a rectangle of 30 × 15 millimetres and be rigidly secured to the 'single piece of solid material of rectangular section'. With the aim of affording better protection to the drivers' legs, another new rule (due to take effect by March 1982 at the latest) dictated a minimum width of 25 centimetres across the inside of the monocoque throughout the whole length of the cockpit, and the minimum weight limit for Formula 1 cars, previously set at 585 kg by the Concorde Agreement, was reduced to 580 kg. This last measure was not so popular amongst the FOCA-aligned teams as many of them still considered it to be too high. Meanwhile other, non-technical, changes were also announced at the same time. These included limiting teams to only one change of a car/driver combination during the season (except in a case of *force majeure*) once they had nominated their drivers for a season, raising the maximum number of entries acceptable for a Grand Prix from thirty to thirty-four and the number of starters from twenty-four to twenty-six, the one exception being Monaco. However, if more than thirty entries materialized at a Grand Prix, it was stipulated that pre-qualifying should take place and concurrently with the first official practice session, rather than holding special pre-qualifying sessions as in the past, to reduce the number of cars taking part in the remaining practice sessions to thirty. Those obliged to take part would be selected from teams who had failed to score any Championship points in 1981 and involved, initially, Warwick and Fabi (Toleman), Jarier and Paletti (Osella) and Boesel (March).

Certainly, one of the main talking points as the curtains had come down on the 1981 season centered around the prospects of seeing no less than three former World Champions making comebacks in 1982. Brabham had reportedly offered £2.6 million to James Hunt, 'someone' had reportedly offered £3 million to Jackie Stewart and Niki Lauda was actively in the throes of negotiating a deal with McLaren International and the team's sponsors, Marlboro, following renewed interest in the sport after having turned his back on it two years earlier. Ultimately Hunt and Stewart both declined their offers, but Lauda successfully concluded his deal to join McLaren where he was to partner John Watson in place of Andrea de Cesaris. Apart from this significant development in driving strength, McLaren made few changes during the winter and were to continue relying on subtly modified

Former double World Champion Niki Lauda returned to Grand Prix racing in 1982, following a two-year sabbatical, and drove the McLaren MP4B. *(Phipps Photographic)*

versions of John Barnard's MP4 design, now referred to as the MP4B. This included employing essentially the same successful carbon-fibre monocoque as in 1981 except for adaptations to conform to the new rule concerning width and stiffness around the footwell. Like an increasing number of other teams, McLaren were now also looking at the turbo-charged alternative and, towards the end of 1981, became involved in an ambitious and exciting new project by signing an agreement with Porsche Engineering for the exclusive rights to a specially commissioned turbo-charged V6 engine. However, the intention was for the engine to be built for use in 1983, so in the meantime the red and white cars from Woking were still to derive their power from the ubiquitous Ford-Cosworth DFV engine.

In direct contrast to McLaren, the Williams team had ended the 1981 season in the knowledge that they were losing the services of a former World Champion, as Alan Jones had given notice of his intention to retire from the sport owing, mainly, to growing disenchantment with the current breed of Grand Prix cars with their rock-hard suspensions. To make matters worse for them their other regular driver, Carlos Reutemann, subsequently announced that he, too, was retiring, and so for a while the World Champion constructors for the second year running (and winners of the Queen's Award for Export Achievement earlier in the year) were left high and dry. However, Reutemann was to change his mind shortly afterwards. Then, following a fruitless attempt to lure Jones out of retirement, as well as making an unsuccessful approach to Mario Andretti (he had now left Alfa Romeo but since committed himself to the Pat Patrick Indy car team in the United States), Frank Williams finally signed

The Williams FW08. *(Autosport)*

up Keke Rosberg as his second driver, the Finn having left the Fittipaldi team at the end of 1981. Meanwhile, on the technical side the winter months were spent carrying out considerable research and development on a new car which was originally designed to have two driving axles at the rear and four wheels of the same diameter as the two at the front. Like the six-wheeled cars produced by Tyrrell and March in 1976 and 1977, the main advantage that designer Patrick Head was trying to exploit was that of

The Williams FW08B (a late 1982 version of the FW07D), which was never raced. *(L.A.T. Photographic)*

improved aerodynamics achieved through a reduced frontal area, increased underbody venturi areas, and being able to mount the rear aerofoil much further back relative to the centre of gravity of the car – without infringing the regulations due to the rearmost axle being further back. However, despite extensive testing the team came to the conclusion that the project was not yet raceworthy and, instead, decided to go ahead with the production of a more conventional four-wheeled car, the FW08. Like the FW07 and its derivatives, including the six-wheeler (FW07D), this was built around a relatively simple and compact monocoque of aluminium honeycomb. An immediate difference, though, was its front suspension as this was by double wishbones with a push-pull-rod running diagonally down from the apex of the top wishbone across the centre of the base-line of the lower wishbone, and operating a bell-crank at the lower end of the inboard coil-spring/damper unit, the top end of which was fixed. Previously, of course, the team had employed the rather more orthodox rocker-arm type of suspension but due to the severe loads imposed by the current stiff suspensions the rocker arms, out of necessity, had been growing progressively heavier, added to which there was an aerodynamic advantage with the pull-rod suspension layout in as much as it permitted a cleaner flow of air into the side-pods. Compared to its predecessors, the new car was also generally much stiffer and considerably lighter. So light, in fact, that it weighed in at around only 540 kg and had to be ballasted to bring it up to the minimum weight. But here the original intention was to over-exploit a loophole in the regulations that allowed a car to be topped up with its normal quantities of lubricants and coolants

prior to post-race scrutineering. This was to be done by employing 'disposable ballast' in the form of water stored in plastic containers which, it was claimed, was for brake-cooling purposes. In reality, though, it was a means of enabling the car to be raced underweight so as to partially compensate for the power deficiency over the turbo-charged cars. The idea was that the water could quickly be jettisoned in the approximate direction of the brakes through small pipes early in a race and then topped up again at the end of the race to bring the car back up to weight. However, by the time that the FW08 was ready to make its debut in the Belgian Grand Prix, FISA had reacted to this blatant rule-bending and, amidst considerable controversy, had taken steps to end the practice. Consequently, the plastic water containers that had been brought into use had to remain full to keep the car up to the minimum weight limit until, later, being substituted for lead ballast. Meanwhile, prior to the Belgian Grand Prix, the team continued using their 1981 cars, the FW07Cs, which were suitably modified to conform to the new rules concerning footwells and skirts. These, like the new model, appeared in the team's familiar green and white livery but with the 'Leyland' lettering on the side-pods replaced by 'TAG' (Techniques d'Avant Garde) who remained the main sponsors along with Saudia Airlines, substantial trading losses having forced Leyland Vehicles to withdraw their support.

For the Parmalat Brabham team 1982 was to be a year of transition, a year in which they were to switch from Ford-Cosworth engines to BMW turbo-charged engines. Extensive testing and development of the turbo-charged project had, of course, already been taking place with the

The Ford-Cosworth-powered BT49D Brabham being driven by Riccardo Patrese. *(Phipps Photographic)*

1982

The BMW-powered BT50 Brabham, being driven by reigning World Champion Nelson Piquet. *(Dave Webb)*

The Harvey Postlethwaite-designed Ferrari 126C2, depicted here with Patrick Tambay on board during the French Grand Prix at Paul Ricard. *(Autosport)*

purpose-built BT50 for well over a year, and during the winter this continued with various detail modifications being incorporated into two brand new chassis to be built in readiness for the first race of the season in South Africa. Primarily these included the adoption of new fuel and oil systems and tanks, new radiators and new bodywork. Since the first brief public appearance of the original test-car during practice for the 1981 British Grand Prix the wheelbase had also been shortened to little more than that of the Ford-Cosworth-engined cars following a decision to substitute the slim Weismann transverse-shaft gearbox/final-drive unit (part of the original design) for a modified Hewland gearbox. Nevertheless, overall the BT50 was no more than a logical development of the original BT49 design and retained essentially the same basic monocoque of aluminium honeycomb as well as a similar pull-rod suspension system all round. Only the rear end was significantly different as here there was a tubular sub-frame extending rearwards from the rear bulkhead of the monocoque to carry the BMW engine as this, unlike the Ford-Cosworth engine, was not a fully stressed member. The engine, itself, was an in-line four cylinder unit of 1499 cc (89.2 × 60 mm) with Bosch fuel and ignition systems and a single KKK turbo-charger and was capable of producing 570 bhp at 10,800 rpm at this stage of its development. Unfortunately, whilst being extremely powerful, it was to suffer from poor reliability and it was because of this that Brabham were to continue campaigning Ford-Cosworth-engined cars in some of the early season races using up-rated versions of the successful BT49, now in 'D' specification. As in 1980 and 1981 Nelson Piquet, the new World Champion, was to remain as team leader, but his former number two, the wealthy Mexican Hector Rebaque, was replaced by the ex-Arrows driver Riccardo Patrese.

Of the three teams already using turbo-charged cars, only Ferrari made any major changes during the winter months by producing a completely new chassis, the 126C2. Designed by Harvey Postlethwaite, who had joined the Italian team from Fittipaldi midway through 1981, this featured a very neat and compact monocoque of bonded,

rather than riveted aluminium-skinned honeycomb sheeting and carbon-fibre bulkheads, which was not only stronger but also considerably lighter than traditional Ferrari designs. The bodywork, too, was all new and had a distinctly smooth aerodynamic shape devoid of ducts or louvres; although the suspension, whilst being new in design, was similar to that of the 1981 Ferrari and consisted, initially, of lower wishbones and fabricated top rocker arms operating coil-spring/damper units tucked neatly inboard. Considerable development work also continued on the V6 engine which still used twin KKK turbo-chargers and was now capable of producing around 580 bhp at 11,800 rpm. As before, this was attached directly to the rear of the monocoque as a fully stressed member, but now drove through a smaller and neater transversely-mounted gearbox and final-drive unit. In addition to the new car there was one other significant change made by Ferrari for 1982. That concerned tyres as, after having run his cars on Michelins since 1978, the Commendatore decided to switch back to Goodyears because the French firm had, of late, been tending to give rather more in the way of attention to the Renault team.

Unlike Ferrari, the Elf Renault team were content to continue relying on uprated versions of their 1981 cars, the RE30 series, which was not altogether surprising since apart from still being relatively new they had proved themselves to be extremely successful. Even so, the winter months saw the design undergo a total revision with the emphasis placed on weight reduction, and by the time that the cars, now referred to as RE30Bs, reappeared at the start of the new season numerous detail refinements had been carried out. Primarily these involved the monocoque being made both stiffer and lighter as well as having different bulkheads, the bodywork being tidied up and the suspension layout being altered, the front units being mounted lower in the monocoque than previously and the rear units being mounted on a cross-member in place of the hitherto tubular frame. More development work was also carried out on the V6 twin turbo-charged engine with the aim of improving reliability at a continuous output of some 550 bhp compared to the 540 bhp at 11,500 rpm previously quoted.

Following their rather unhappy first season in Formula 1, the Candy Toleman team were also to continue with their existing car throughout 1982 but in slightly uprated specification which led to it being referred to as the TG181B. It also had an alternative name – 'The Flying Pig' – in deference to its handling, while another nickname to be used, following the conflict over the Falkland Islands, was 'The General Belgrano' after the ill-fated Argentine battleship! In spite of the difficult transition from Formula 2 to Formula 1, however, the team were determined to persevere, and in this respect were considerably encouraged by the untiring efforts of Brian Hart who was now extracting around 580 bhp from his four cylinder 'Monobloc' engine, still using the Garrett AiResearch turbo-charger unit. Throughout 1982 more, mainly weight-saving, modifications were to follow and, eventually, a brand new car was built that made its debut in the Italian Grand Prix even though it was really intended for

Alain Prost captured at speed in the Renault RE30B. *(Dave Webb)*

1983. This was the TG183 designed by Rory Byrne and his design team, and although it was described as being no more than a refinement of the current car it immediately differed from it by having a monocoque comprising carbon-fibre inner and outer panels with Kevlar bar reinforcement and an aluminium honeycomb core. The bulkheads were also of carbon-fibre and at the rear the torsion boxes had been replaced by a triangular steel sub-frame to accommodate the engine which was now being used as a semi-stressed member following further revisions carried out by Brian Hart. Because of the extra space created by discarding the torsion boxes, the turbo-charger unit was now housed in the left-hand side-pod leaving just the inter-cooler above the engine where it was tucked in behind the fuel tank. This cooled the charge air from the compressor which, in turn, was cooled from water contained in separate twin radiators integral with two very large inclined radiators mounted in each of the two side-pods. Combined, these alterations and other detail refinements also permitted the use of much tidier bodywork which incorporated nose, cockpit and engine cover and was made in Kevlar composite. The suspension, too, was different as the rocker arms had been substituted for what had become the increasingly fashionable push-pull-rod arrangement, both at the front and the rear. Reverting back to the winter, another change was made to driving strength, for while Derek Warwick was to continue with the team, considerable pressure from their main sponsors, the Italian Candy Domestic Appliances firm, led to Brian Henton being elbowed out in favour of the former Italian Can-Am driver Teodorico Fabi.

Two other teams expected to join the growing list of turbo runners in 1982 were Alfa Romeo and Talbot-Ligier as the Autodelta firm had been developing and testing their own twin turbo-charged V8 engine since 1980 and,

For their second season of Grand Prix racing Toleman were to rely mainly on the TG181B, an uprated version of the team's 1981 car. This is Teo Fabi in action during the Swiss Grand Prix at Dijon. *(Autosport)*

more recently, the Matra designer, George Martin, had become involved in work on a new turbo-charged V6 engine. However, for reasons apparently associated with a marketing dispute over Matra wishing to sell their Mureno sports coupé through the Peugeot-Talbot retail chain the turbo-charged engine was withheld, while the Alfa Romeo engine was still not considered to be raceworthy: it was to appear in public just once during practice for the Italian Grand Prix installed in a brand new chassis almost identi-

The Marlboro Alfa Romeo Tipo 182. *(Autosport)*

cal to that of Autodelta's other 1982 cars. Consequently, in both instances, the ageing V12s were used once again and, at the start of the new season, these reappeared in cars that were largely unchanged from 1981 except for alterations to comply with the new rules. By then, though, work was already at an advanced stage on new cars with the first to appear, at the Brazilian Grand Prix, coming from the Autodelta factory. This was the Tipo 182

designed, to a large extent, by Gerard Ducarouge who had joined the team from Talbot-Ligier during the previous summer, and was a car that bore certain resemblances to the McLaren MP4. This was particularly true of the monocoque, as in common with the McLaren it was a carbon-fibre honeycomb structure, the only difference being that it had been manufactured by the British Advanced Composite Components company rather than by the Hercules company in the United States. Outwardly, too, there were similarities between the two cars, and compared to the older Tipo 179 and its derivatives it was not only much lighter but of an altogether much smarter appearance with a considerable amount of attention obviously having been paid to aerodynamics (even components like the team's developed Hewland gearbox had been made slimmer, as had the crankcase for the V12 engine) and also the bodywork, which was all new. Later in the season, at Monaco, it was the turn of Talbot-Ligier to unveil their new car, the JS19, which had originally been designed to accommodate the turbo-charged V6 Matra engine. Like the new Alfa Romeo, this also bore certain resemblances to another car, only it was more akin to the Lotus 80 in appearance for it had extremely sleek aerodynamic bodywork which extended beyond the rear wheels and around the engine bay, and featured, initially, narrow full-length side-pods and skirts. In addition to the new bodywork, the JS19 also had a new monocoque of aluminium honeycomb-Kevlar construction, which was riveted and glued together, and bulkheads made of solid alloy at the front, and of titanium at the rear. As with the earlier model, the suspension was tucked tightly inboard all round but this, too, was a new design and in its original form consisted of lower wishbones and top rocker arms activating the coil-spring/damper units with fabricated

The Gitanes Talbot-Ligier JS19. *(Autosport)*

Elio de Angelis hard at work in the John Player Special Lotus 91. *(Autosport)*

Michele Alboreto putting the Tyrrell 011 through its paces. *(Dave Webb)*

uprights front and rear, a system not dissimilar to that employed on the new Alfa Romeo. As well as their new cars both teams had a new driver as, following Mario Andretti's decision to leave Alfa Romeo at the end of 1981, Marlboro more or less 'arranged' for Andrea de Cesaris to join the team from McLaren, and for reasons that were less apparent Talbot-Ligier replaced Patrick Tambay with Eddie Cheever after his year-long stay at Tyrrell.

Of the remaining teams only John Player Team Lotus and Tyrrell were destined to enjoy any success in 1982, and even then it was to be rather spasmodic. For Tyrrell, the continuing lack of a major sponsor was the biggest problem as development work had to be closely allied to a limited budget and resulted in the team having to rely exclusively on their 1981 cars, the 011s, for another season, these being driven by Michele Alboreto and, initially, Slim Borgudd. Despite the lack of sponsorship, however, the winter months saw the basic design undergo numerous revisions, particularly to the suspension, which was changed to a push-pull-rod system, and also the aerodynamics, and this was a pattern that was to continue throughout much of 1982 with increasingly encouraging results. At the start of the new season Lotus also fielded revised versions of their 'legal' 1981 cars, the 87, which now, in 'B' specification, included the adoption of wider and longer side-pods, repositioned water radiators and a longer wheelbase to alter the weight distribution. This, however, was only an interim measure, and by the Brazilian Grand Prix the team were ready to race their new 1982 car, the 91. In most respects this was little more than a refined version of the older car using essentially the same monocoque of carbon-fibre/Kevlar Nomex honeycomb sandwich and a rocker arm suspension system all round, but with considerable emphasis placed on detail in the interests of reducing weight. The bodywork, on the other hand, was completely new and was distinguished by a long swept-down engine cover with air ducts protruding on either side of the roll-over bar, while other important

changes with the aim of improving the aerodynamics still further included a new, one-piece underbody pod with an adjustable leading edge. To drive his cars, Colin Chapman retained the services of Elio de Angelis and Nigel Mansell, despite strong speculation that the Italian would be moving over to Alfa Romeo for 1982, and Peter Warr was now competitions director once more after having rejoined the team from Fittipaldi at the end of the previous season.

For the other seven teams, all using conventional cars powered by the Ford-Cosworth DFV engine, 1982 was to be a year mainly of frustration and disappointment despite considerable efforts being made to improve their position. To summarize, Ragno Arrows started the year with a pair of brand new David Wass-designed, Pirelli-shod A4s

The Ragno Arrows A4. *(Autosport)*

which were a logical development of the A3s and entered for Brian Henton (until new team leader Marc Surer had recovered from a winter testing accident) and the Italian Formula 3 driver Mauro Baldi; ATS continued with uprated versions of their 1981 cars, now known as the D5 (sometimes D6!), but replaced Slim Borgudd with the former RAM and Ensign driver Eliseo Salazar (sponsored by the Chilean petroleum distribution company, Copec) 79

1982

and added German Manfred Winkelhock (sponsored by the German Liqui-Moly firm) to their line-up – the German team now also had the services of Alistair Caldwell, from Brabham, to assist on the technical side and Peter Collins, from Lotus, as manager; Mo Nunn's under-financed Ensign team struggled on with their N180B (MN15) and, after the South Africa Grand Prix, a slightly improved N181 (MN16), now in the hands of the Colombian Formula 2 driver Roberto Guerrero; the similarly under-financed Fittipaldi team persevered with a singleton entry for Francesco (Chico) Serra using a modified 1981 car, the F8D, and also a new Richard Divila/Tim Wright-designed F9 introduced at the British Grand Prix; the

Denim/S.A.I.M.A.-sponsored Osella team continued to rely on slightly modified versions of the George Valentini-designed FA1C introduced at the 1981 Italian Grand Prix for Jean-Pierre Jarier and new-boy Riccardo Paletti; John MacDonald's RAM team continued their association with March Engineering and entered a pair of Adrian Reynard-designed March 821s (revised versions of the 811) initially for Jochen Mass, making a Formula 1 comeback to replace Derek Daly, and the Brazilian Formula 3 driver Raul Boesel; finally Teddy Tip's Theodore outfit started out with their 1981 car before introducing the new TY02 at the Brazilian Grand Prix with Derek Daly initially as their driver in place of Marc Surer.

The ATS D5. *(Phipps Photographic)*

The Ensign N181. *(Phipps Photographic)*

The Fittipaldi F9. *(Phipps Photographic)*

The Denim/S.A.I.M.A. Osella FA1C. *(Dave Webb)*

The RAM March 821 *(L.A.T. Photographic)*

The Theodore TY02. *(L.A.T. Photographic)*

XXVIIIth South African Grand Prix

Kyalami: January 23
Weather: Warm and dry
Distance: 77 laps of 4.104 km
circuit = 316.01 km (196.36 miles)

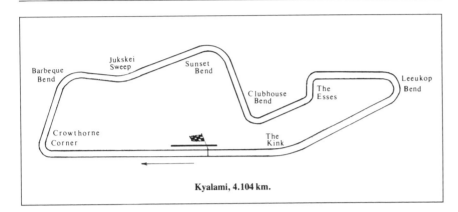

Kyalami, 4.104 km.

After a winter virtually devoid of any political bickering, a complete contrast to the situation 12 months earlier, everything seemed to augur well for the first race of the new season. All of the teams were ready with either brand new or modified cars, suitably adapted to conform to the new regulations concerning skirts and the abandonment of hydro-pneumatic suspension systems, and there was to be no longer any more of the fiasco witnessed throughout most of 1981 of cars having to undergo ground-clearance checks on each occasion that they appeared in the pit lane. For the fans there were also numerous different car/driver combinations to look forward to seeing in action for the first time, with the added interest of watching just how former double World Champion Niki Lauda would fare after his two-year sabbatical. The only problem was that when the time came round for the first official practice session on the Thursday morning there were no drivers present or, at least, none except for Jochen Mass. Instead, they had earlier all climbed aboard a coach (Mass had arrived late and missed it!) and twenty-nine of them were now in self-imposed exile in a hotel in Johannesburg, on strike and awaiting the outcome of discussions between their representative, Didier Pironi, and FISA President Jean-Marie Balestre. What was it all about? Well, it was to do with two specific clauses included in an application form for a 'super-licence' required for participation in the 1982 World Championship and which had been introduced mainly to prevent drivers from breaking existing contracts prematurely to join other teams, a recent case in point being Prost's acrimonious move from McLaren to Renault at the end of 1980. One of these clauses (clause 1) asked a driver to indicate the date on which his contract with his current team expired and to acknowledge that he was committed to that team exclusively in the World Championship until that date: the other clause

(clause 5) asked a driver to acknowledge that he would do nothing which would harm the moral or material interests or the image of International Motorsport or the World Championship. But to Niki Lauda, in particular, the implications were obvious. Team owners could start selling drivers and demanding transfer fees as in soccer, with the drivers themselves powerless to do anything about it. As a result Lauda was refusing to sign the form, as were some of the other drivers (the rest already had), and along with Pironi had made unsuccessful representation to Balestre on the previous day to have the wording changed to the effect that if a driver was not allowed to leave his team, then the team was not allowed to fire the driver. And, for once, there was solidarity amongst the drivers, or certainly very nearly.

Throughout Thursday there was deadlock, and complete inactivity out on the track. Eventually the spectators were sent home with refunds, while the Stewards of the Meeting issued a statement to the effect that the race was being postponed for eight days and that the international licences of all 31 drivers entered for the race were being suspended. Shortly afterwards it was also announced that FISA had withdrawn the licences of the 31 drivers and that none of them would ever be eligible for the World Championship again! Then, a meeting of the team managers prompted a second statement from the Stewards which said that the race would still be on if drivers wishing to participate reported to the circuit between 8 a.m. and 9 a.m. the following morning, and provided that at least fifteen cars were able to run in both the untimed and timed practice sessions. In the meantime, Pironi was keeping Lauda informed of the situation by telephone, but as there was no sign of any agreement the drivers locked themselves away in their hotel room, a large conference hall, and went on to spend the night refusing to speak to anyone, including irate team

managers and even tearful wives and girlfriends. The next morning 9 a.m. came and went and they were still there, except for Teo Fabi who had decided to opt out of the strike, sneaked out of the room and made his own way to the circuit. Pironi, meanwhile, was busy putting over the drivers' views to Balestre and also to representatives of the organizers and the teams until at around 10 a.m. with Mass starting to practise all on his own, it finally appeared that an agreement had at long last been reached – clause 1 was to be amended and clause 5 discussed or, apparently, so it was said. Whatever, Mass was black-flagged, Pironi telephoned Lauda once more and within an hour all 31 drivers were at the circuit, reporting for duty and,

Starting Grid	
R. Arnoux Renault (1 min 06.351 sec)	N. Piquet Brabham-BMW (1 min 06.625 sec)
G. Villeneuve Ferrari (1 min 07.106 sec)	R. Patrese Brabham-BMW (1 min 07.398 sec)
A. Prost Renault (1 min 08.133 sec)	D. Pironi Ferrari (1 min 08.360 sec)
K. Rosberg Williams-Ford (1 min 08.892 sec)	C. Reutemann Williams-Ford (1 min 09.306 sec)
J. Watson McLaren-Ford (1 min 09.736 sec)	M. Alboreto Tyrrell-Ford (1 min 10.037 sec)
J. Laffite Talbot-Matra (1 min 10.241 sec)	E. Salazar ATS-Ford (1 min 10.624 sec)
N. Lauda McLaren-Ford (1 min 10.681 sec)	D. Warwick Toleman-Hart (1 min 10.685 sec)
E. de Angelis Lotus-Ford (1 min 10.685 sec)	A. de Cesaris Alfa Romeo (1 min 10.952 sec)
E. Cheever Talbot-Matra (1 min 11.005 sec)	N. Mansell Lotus-Ford (1 min 11.227 sec)
B. Giacomelli Alfa Romeo (1 min 11.285 sec)	M. Winkelhock ATS-Ford (1 min 11.808 sec)
R. Boesel March-Ford (1 min 12.077 sec)	J. Mass March-Ford (1 min 12.100 sec)
S. Borgudd Tyrrell-Ford (1 min 12.366 sec)	D. Daly Theodore-Ford (1 min 13.418 sec)
F. Serra Fittipaldi-Ford (1 min 13.467 sec)	J. P. Jarier Osella-Ford (1 min 13.834 sec)

Did not qualify:
M. Baldi (Arrows-Ford) 1 min 13.976 sec
R. Paletti (Osella-Ford) 1 min 15.504 sec
B. Henton (Arrows Ford) 1 min 16.653 sec
T. Fabi (Toleman-Hart) No time
Withdrawn: R. Guerrero (Ensign-Ford)

1982

where necessary, signing the outstanding application forms, Lauda included.

When practice did eventually get under way with a 90 minute untimed session it took place with the notable absence of the reigning World Champion, and with an impressive-looking trio of BMW-powered Brabham BT50s all carrying the number 2.Quite simply an incensed Bernie Ecclestone considered that Piquet was in no fit state to drive due to an obvious lack of sleep, and had sent him off for a medical check-up! Also absent was the new Ensign recruit Roberto Guerrero as Mo Nunn had gone a stage further and withdrawn the Colombian's entry altogether, ostensibly for the same reason. Yet another team to be immediately affected by the strike was Arrows. Already they had temporarily lost the services of their new team leader Marc Surer because of broken ankles sustained in a pre-race testing accident at the circuit, and now his appointed deputy, Patrick Tambay, was so disillusioned with this latest round of politics that he had decided against taking up the post. It just so happened, though, that Brian Henton was on hand looking for a drive and, after being approached by Jack Oliver, he was only too happy to step in. Normally, of course, the loss of a full day's practice would have been considered quite critical but with all of the teams having spent at least two days at the circuit during recent pre-race testing it was of no great consequence. Nor did it have any effect on the overall scene, for as had been the case throughout the test days the Renault, Ferrari and Brabham turbocharged cars, less affected by the high altitude of the circuit (6000 feet above sea-level) than their normally-aspirated rivals, were proving to be uncatchable, and down the long straight leading to Crowthorne Corner were clocking up speeds of around 20 mph faster. Apart from Prost leaving the track at Sunset Bend and breaking a rear suspension upright on his Renault against the retaining wall when the car's left rear tyre suddenly deflated, the 90 minutes passed virtually free of incident, and everyone went away seemingly well prepared for the all-important hour of qualifying which was going to decide the grid positions.

About an hour later the serious business of qualifying was under way with Piquet now being allowed to join in at long last. It didn't take the Brazilian long to settle down, as in no time at all he produced a lap in 1 min 06.625 sec (this was well over 3 seconds inside Jabouille's pole-winning time for the 1980 race which had been achieved with the aid of sliding skirts) and then returned to the pits to complain that his Brabham was understeering! It transpired that one of the skirts had jammed under the corresponding side-pod, a problem that was soon rectified. Even so, Piquet was subsequently unable to make any further improvement and, more-

over, saw his hopes of remaining at the top of the time sheets shattered by Arnoux who went on to wrap up pole position with a blistering lap of 1 min 06.351 sec (222.670 kph) shortly before rain developed with just over 20 minutes of the session still to run. Like Piquet, the other four leading turbo runners also hit various problems, although none of these were serious enough to prevent the first three rows of the grid from being an all-turbo affair. Instead, they merely served to underline their superiority. As it was Villeneuve, winding up third fastest, had a retaining bolt break loose from one of his Ferrari's side-pods, upsetting the car's balance; Pironi's sister car gradually lost its boost pressure owing to a water leak causing overheating; Prost's Renault started losing losing power, almost certainly through dirt having found its way into the engine during the morning off-course excursion; and Patrese, trying to concentrate on the spare Brabham, was forced to switch to his proposed race car twice, first because of an electrical fault and then after a flap broke away from the rear aerofoil. In the meantime, it was the Williams drivers who came out best of the rest. Rosberg, who had obviously settled in well with his new team, posted seventh fastest time of 1 min 09.892 sec in spite of experiencing oversteer, while Reutemann, handicapped by a dud set of qualifying tyres and, like several others, losing the benefit of his second set due to the onset of the rain, finished up one place lower at 1 min 09.306 sec. After the Williams duo, Watson planted his McLaren MP4B in ninth spot before ending his practice on a rather low note by sliding off the wet track into the catch-fences at Crowthorne Corner and badly damaging the rear end of the spare MP4. Then came an inspired Alboreto, Laffite, Salazar, doing surprisingly well in the ATS, and Lauda who just managed to squeeze on to the front half of the grid after proving to everyone that he had lost none of his old flair and determination by recovering brilliantly from an early trip into the catch-fences at Crowthorne and pressing on regardless of a bent left front wishbone! Of the others, headed by Warwick's obviously much-improved turbo-charged Toleman-Hart and de Angelis' Lotus 87B, Winkelhock and Boesel had both done particularly well to qualify comfortably for what was to be their first Grand Prix, whereas Serra and Jarier (in considerable pain from ribs cracked in a winter testing accident with Williams at Paul Ricard) both only just made the cut thanks to the number of starters now being increased from 24 to 26. Those who failed, on the other hand, included Henton, whose Arrows had come to rest at Leeukop after only a few laps with a blocked fuel pressure relief valve, and Fabi after the former Can-Am driver had been constantly dashing in and out of the pits because of a

turbo-charger problem with the older and expermental Toleman-Hart.

After an overnight storm, the weather had cleared up somewhat by Saturday morning and although the skies were still fairly cloudy it was both warm and dry. During the 30 minute warm-up session, which saw the teams frantically trying to decide on the correct choice of tyres for the race, Mansell's Lotus 87B stopped out on the circuit with a dead engine, this coming after brake problems throughout the previous afternoon's qualifying run, and Warwick found the brake pedal going spongy on his Toleman. Otherwise there was little in the way of trouble and the only change in the line-up was Alboreto having opted to race the spare Tyrrell.

As the time approached for the start of the race, with the 26 starters already having left the pits and formed up on the dummy grid, it had long since become clear that any adverse publicity over the drivers' strike had done little harm so far as the spectators were concerned, for there were some 85,000 of them packed into various vantage points around the circuit. In fact, Lauda had almost certainly eased the situation by appearing on local television during the previous evening to apologize for any inconvenience caused and to emphasize how much the drivers enjoyed being at Kyalami. Now Pironi got in on the act as well by reiterating these comments over the PA system and adding that the first six finishers in the Grand Prix would be giving away their helmets to a public raffle after the race as a further gesture of goodwill. With that, the Frenchman climbed back into his Ferrari and a few minutes later Arnoux was leading the field away on the pace lap prior to bringing them back to their starting positions once more. Now the adrenalin was really flowing, the starting lights went on, red gave way to green, and at long last the 1982 Quindrink-Pointerware-sponsored South African Grand Prix was under way with Arnoux making the most of his advantageous pole position to storm away into an undisputed lead. Piquet, on the other hand, made a right mess of his start by allowing the revs to drop too low, and not only baulked his new team-mate but was swallowed up by car after car on the run down to Crowthorne, from where Prost emerged in second place followed by the two Ferraris of Villeneuve and Pironi. That was still the order at the end of the lap but already the two Renaults looked to be in command with even Villeneuve, his Ferrari running with more boost pressure that Pironi's sister car, struggling to maintain contact with them. Behind Pironi, Rosberg had slotted into fifth place with Patrese hard on his heels, followed by Laffite, Alboreto, Reutemann, Watson, Salazar, Cheever and the unhappy Piquet who was now lying thirteenth ahead of Lauda and the other ten cars, for already the field was two short. First

René Arnoux leads team-mate Alain Prost and the rest of the closely-bunched pack into Crowthorne Corner moments after the start of the race. *(Autosport)*

Mansell's engine had died on him again just over half way round the lap and then, in the confusion caused by the rapidly slowing Lotus, Jarier had spun off into the catch-fences at Clubhouse Corner.

On lap 4 Piquet made his second mistake of the afternoon, only this time it was to prove far more expensive. He had already followed Cheever past Salazar but now, in his eagerness to continue making up lost ground, he ran down the outside of the American on the approach to Crowthorne, overtook Alboreto as well and simply arrived too fast, locked up his brakes and spun off into the catch-fences. A fraction over three laps later Villeneuve also departed the fray dramatically when a turbo bearing suddenly failed and brought his Ferrari to a smoky halt just beyond Clubhouse Corner, an incident that left the two leading Renaults totally unchallenged as by this stage Pironi had dropped even further away than his unfortunate team-mate. Although he was still up amongst the other leading cars, Rosberg had run into a problem, too, for soon after being forced to give way to Patrese on the fifth lap his gear-lever knob had come off in his hand and was now unnervingly rolling around in the Williams' footwell. Furthermore, besides making the business of changing gear extremely difficult, this had also enabled Reutemann to nip past, and now Watson was threatening to do the same, both drivers having earlier disposed of Alboreto and Laffite without much trouble. In spite of his difficulties, however, Rosberg continued to cope with the situation admirably and on lap 18 actually found himself moving up a place when Patrese disappeared into the pits with hardly any oil pressure left due to a leak from

the turbo bearing in the number 2 Brabham. A few minutes earlier Cheever had been another retirement with his Talbot suffering from an apparent vapour lock, while Warwick had dropped to the back of the field after stopping for an early change of Pirellis. Up front, meanwhile, the two Renault drivers had already been starting to lap tail-enders, and on lap 14 this had resulted in a change of leadership as a moment's hesitation by Arnoux amidst the traffic had enabled Prost to take over the reins. Even so the pair of them were still running nose to tail and now well over 15 seconds clear of Pironi's third-placed Ferrari. Further back still, Reutemann was now running in a strong fourth place and driving really well, a complete contrast to his lack-lustre performance at Las Vegas at the end of the previous season, and then came the closely-matched duo of Rosberg and Watson. After a cautious start, Lauda had begun to speed up and was currently lying seventh ahead of Alboreto, Laffite and de Angelis who were the only others still on the same lap as the leader.

The next major change occurred at the end of lap 24 when Pironi, running into handling problems, suddenly veered off into the pits and took on a fresh set of Goodyears. The delay, accentuated by a troublesome left rear wheel nut, dropped the Ferrari driver to eighth place behind Alboreto, but once back out on the track he began to fly, repassing the Tyrrell on lap 30 and taking only a further seven laps before barging past Lauda's McLaren. Now he quickly homed in on Watson, although as he did so attention was suddenly diverted towards Prost when, on lap 41, the leading Renault slid very wide

coming out of the Jukskei Sweep and slowed dramatically. The left rear tyre had deflated and it seemed almost certain that Prost was out of the race. However, the little Frenchman obviously had other ideas about that, pulled off the racing line and gingerly eased his way round to the pits even though the punctured tyre rapidly disintegrated and eventually parted company with the rim completely. Once in the pits, the Renault mechanics immediately swooped on the stricken car, slapped on a new set of Michelins, inspected the rear suspension and slight bodywork damage and quickly sent their man back out into the fray, albeit now in eighth place behind Alboreto, just like Pironi earlier, and a whisker over a lap behind Arnoux. Nevertheless, from the point of view of the race this couldn't have been better. Apart from Pironi's sustained charge stalemate had set in, but with two drivers now out to make up lost ground, the situation could hardly have been more exciting. To add to the interest, Reutemann had now not only steadied what had become an over 40 second gap between himself and Arnoux but was actually gaining slightly, something which was not altogether surprising as apart from the Argentinian continuing to drive his heart out the leader was suffering from the effects of increasing tyre vibrations caused by his Michelins picking up rubber from the track. The rest of the field, meanwhile, was tending to be overlooked somewhat, but as it was there was little change apart from Borgudd having dropped even further back than Warwick after a pit stop for a new nose cone following a spin. For Warwick, though, the race was about to end spectacularly. On his 44th lap a loose rear suspension bolt pierced the Toleman's left rear tyre and caused a frightening accident at Barbeque Bend from which the Englishman was fortunate to escape unharmed.

By lap 50 the situation up front had become even more exciting as Reutemann was now little more than half a minute behind Arnoux and still gaining ground, while Pironi, having fought his way up to third place, was steadily reeling them both in. That was not all, for Prost, meanwhile, was lapping at a phenomenal rate and was easily the fastest man on the track. He had already dispensed with Alboreto and forged ahead of Arnoux to unlap himself and now, in the space of just five more laps, went by Lauda, Watson and Rosberg almost as if they weren't there to set about wiping out the deficit to Pironi. This didn't take him long either, as by lap 58 Prost had latched on to the tail of the Ferrari, and four laps later, almost immediately after the pair of them had sailed past Reutemann's Williams, sliced through into second place at Leeukop. All the while, Arnoux had gradually been lapping slower and slower due to the problem with his tyres becoming worse. Rather than stop for fresh rubber, however, Arnoux chose to stay out, with the result that the flying Prost closed up to him remorselessly until, on lap 68, he was once more leading the race. Quite incredible! After that the number 15 Renault quickly drew away with Prost reeling off the remaining nine laps effortlessly to record a brilliant and memorable victory. In the meantime, the other leading positions underwent a complete change in the closing stages as Lauda put on a late spurt and overtook both Watson and Rosberg, Reutemann caught and passed Arnoux with just over four laps to go, while Pironi saw an almost certain second place disappear when his Ferrari developed an engine misfire and brought him into the pits

soon after being overtaken by the eventual winner. Furthermore the delay, combined with the loss of power and a second pit stop in a vain attempt to find a cure, saw an afternoon's hard work come to nought, for not only did he finish out of the points but in a dejected eighteenth and last position, Laffite having become the eighth retirement back on lap 55 with his Talbot suffering from a similar problem to Cheever's earlier in the race.

Unfortunately, the afternoon ended on a bitter note as, shortly after Prost, Reutemann and Arnoux had mounted the rostrum, news came that the Stewards had issued a statement to each team during the race indicating that the licences of twenty-nine of

the drivers were being suspended indefinitely, including that of Tambay but not those of Mass, Fabi, or Henton. It also gave no indication of any agreement having been reached and merely referred to a temporary truce having been called for the purposes of running the race. Not long after, FISA also issued a statement supporting the Steward's action, the only difference being that their list of suspended drivers included the names of Mass and Fabi! Either way all of the drivers were naturally deeply incensed and immediately responded by lodging formal appeals to which FISA replied by announcing that a meeting of the Executive Committee would be held in Paris to discuss the business of the drivers' strike four days later.

Results

1	A. Prost (Renault)	1 hr 32 min 08.401 sec (205.769 kph/ 127.859 mph)	8	E. de Angelis (Lotus-Ford)	1 lap behind	17	F. Serra (Fittipaldi-Ford)	5 laps behind
2	C. Reutemann (Williams-Ford)	1 hr 32 min 23.347 sec	9	E. Salazar (ATS-Ford)	2 laps behind	18	D. Pironi (Ferrari)	6 laps behind
3	R. Arnoux (Renault)	1 hr 32 min 36.301 sec	10	M. Winkelhock (ATS-Ford)	2 laps behind			
4	N. Lauda (McLaren-Ford)	1 hr 32 min 40.514 sec	11	B. Giacomelli (Alfa Romeo)	3 laps behind			
5	K. Rosberg (Williams-Ford)	1 hr 32 min 54.540 sec	12	J. Mass (March-Ford)	3 laps behind			
6	J. Watson (McLaren-Ford)	1 hr 32 min 59.394 sec	13	A. de Cesaris (Alfa Romeo)	4 laps behind			
7	M. Alboreto (Tyrrell-Ford)	1 lap behind	14	D. Daly (Theodore-Ford)	4 laps behind			
			15	R. Boesel (March-Ford)	5 laps behind			
			16	S. Borgudd (Tyrrell-Ford)	5 laps behind			

Fastest lap: A. Prost (Renault) on lap 49 in 1 min 08.278 sec (216.385 kph/134.456 mph)

Retirements

J. P. Jarier (Osella-Ford) accident on lap 1, N. Mansell (Lotus-Ford) electrics on lap 1, N. Piquet (Brabham-BMW) accident on lap 4, G. Villeneuve (Ferrari) turbo-charger on lap 7, E. Cheever (Talbot-Matra) vapour lock on lap 12, R. Patrese (Brabham-BMW) turbo-charger on lap 19, D. Warwick (Toleman-Hart) accident on lap 44, J. Laffite (Talbot-Matra) vapour lock on lap 55.

XI° Grande Prêmio do Brasil

Rio de Janeiro: March 21
Weather: Very hot
Distance: 63 laps of 5.031 km
circuit = 316.95 km (196.95 miles)

The aftermath of the drivers' strike at Kyalami had dragged on for several weeks as the decision reached at the FISA Executive Committee meeting had incensed the drivers still further; fines of $5,000 had been imposed on the twenty-nine involved (Mass and Fabi had been exonerated), together with a two-race ban, suspended for two years, while those who had protested at Zolder in 1981 had each been given an additional $5,000 fine and a five-race ban, also suspended for two years. At the same time it had been stipulated that their licences would remain suspended indefinitely unless the fines were paid within 48 hours, although there was the right of appeal – once the fines had been paid! Severe treatment indeed, with the only sign of any reconciliatory action having been a vague promise to approach the F1 Commission with a view to redressing the imbalance between the drivers and the teams concerning clause 1 in the application form for a 'super-licence'.

Once again the reaction from the drivers had been one of solidarity. They had all

refused to pay the fines (some of the teams eventually paid up on behalf of their drivers) or to accept the threat of suspension. Instead, they had responded in two ways. First they had lodged appeals to the FIA International Court of Appeal and then, primarily as a show of strength, they had disbanded the Grand Prix Drivers' Association and formed the Professional Racing Drivers' Association (PRDA), electing Didier Pironi as their President and making membership available to all professional drivers, not only Grand Prix drivers. This had then been followed, in late February, by an appeal tribunal of the South African Automobile Sport Federation upholding the appeals made by the drivers after the Grand Prix and stating that the race stewards had no power to suspend their licences. More important still, just over a week later the FIA International Court of Appeal had convened and reached a verdict that had appeased the drivers. The fines had been reduced to $5,000 for everyone and the threat of suspension in the event of any

further trouble amended to apply to just one race over a much shorter period of six months. In addition, the Court had expressed its disapproval of the fact that the drivers had not been represented at the FISA Executive Committee meeting and of M. Balestre's and FISA's actions, which it considered had been too hasty and too heavy-handed. Of far greater significance, it had ruled that the drivers should henceforth have more say in the study of new Formula 1 regulations, for this had led to the controversial application form for a 'super-licence' being re-worded, and to the entire episode being brought to a conclusion.

An immediate casualty of the drivers' dispute had been the Argentine Grand Prix, due to have taken place on March 7, as the organizers, already extremely worried about the Republic's astronomically high rate of inflation, had decided against taking any chances and asked for their race to be postponed. Quite apart from anything else this meant that almost exactly two months had lapsed without a Grand Prix. Far from being idle, however, the teams had been busy carrying out various test programmes, both at Rio and elsewhere, and also preparing more new cars or carrying out further modifications to existing chassis: these included altering the footwell design, where it had not already been done, to comply with the rules that now demanded a minimum width across the inside of the monocoque to give better protection to the driver's legs. As a result of all the work the line-up for the Brazilian race was very impressive indeed and embraced a number of newly-designed cars, these being a trio of Alfa Romeo Tipo 182s, a pair of Lotus 91s, an Ensign N181 and a Theodore TY02. In addition, Brabham had produced two brand new Ford-Cosworth-powered BT49s, uprated to 'D' specification, as the BMW-powered BT50s had been temporarily put to one side on the alleged grounds that

the engine was too powerful for the chassis! For RAM March, meanwhile, there had been a change of another sort since the South African Grand Prix, as the team had attracted sponsorship from Rothmans to add to the support already being given to them by ICI, Newsweek and Rizla, with the result that the 821s were now finished off in a new blue and white colour scheme.

Unfortunately, the weekend started out under the strong possibility of yet another major confrontation. This time it stemmed from some of the FOCA-aligned teams, notably Williams and Brabham, trying to circumvent the rules concerning the minimum weight limit by employing 'disposable ballast' or, to be more specific, plastic water containers ostensibly required to store water for brake cooling purposes. Essentially, this situation had come about owing to the ability of some of the leading teams using the normally-aspirated Ford-Cosworth engines to design and build cars well below the weight limit through the extensive use of materials such as carbon-fibre and titanium, as this had led to the addition of lead ballast being necessary to render the cars legal. However, having examined the definition of weight in the Concorde Agreement – the weight of the car in running order with its normal quantities of lubricants and coolants but without any fuel or driver on board must not be less than 585 kg (580 kg for 1982) – it had occurred to some people that by adopting 'water-cooled brakes' it would be possible to carry sufficient water to bring a car up to the required weight without the need for lead ballast. Furthermore, the water could be quickly jettisoned in the approximate direction of the brakes through small pipes early in a race so as to reduce weight and thereby help to make up for the power deficiency over the turbo-charged cars, prior to the water being replaced again after a race to bring the car back up to the required weight for post-race scrutineering. In fact, experiments had already been carried out by Williams and Brabham towards the latter part of 1981 and again in South Africa but no-one had taken much notice. But now, with the water containers having become larger, rival teams had cottoned on to what they were really up to. Ferrari and Renault, whose cars were above the weight limit due to carrying turbo-charger units and associated ancillaries, had become particularly agitated over the matter, taking the view that cars should not be permitted to have their so-called brake cooling water containers refilled after a race as they did not consider them to be necessary adjuncts to the car's performance. Moreover, they were now threatening to lodge official protests, especially in the event of the race subsequently being won by an 'illegal' car.

Practice, itself, was a somewhat disjointed affair owing to the organizers' insistence on

bringing out the chequered flag on each occasion that there was even a minor incident. It also turned out to be a particularly tough experience for the drivers, as the cars, running with stiff suspensions so as to obtain maximum benefit from the fixed skirts, combined with a bumpy track surface, led to them receiving a dreadful pounding. Bruised backs were certainly a common complaint and so were aching neck muscles due partly to the preponderance of the left-hand turns caused by the direction of travel being, unusually, anti-clockwise, neck collars or support straps attached to helmets and cockpit sides only marginally easing the problem. In addition, when it came to the qualifying sessions, drivers were faced with taking unacceptably high risks in the quest for an optimum lap time, particularly if they came up behind a slower car and were to avoid being baulked, for such was the short life of the super-sticky qualifying tyres (limited to just two sets per car in each timed session) that they were really only worth one good lap. Consequently, the overall scene was one of both considerable frustration and irritation which was not helped at all by extremely humid conditions and a paddock where the Ferrari and Renault teams mumbled on about under-weight cars, and several of their rivals about the imbalance between the turbo and non-turbo cars in the current formula. Even the paying spectators were disenchanted. Apart from the constant interruptions caused by the organizers' over-exuberance, there were periods of almost complete inactivity out on the track due to the tyre situation. However, at the end of it all one clear fact to emerge was that the revised rules concerning skirts had helped to increase cornering speeds and to reduce lap times by a phenomenal amount. In fact, this had already been proved in South Africa and, more recently, during pre-race testing here when Piquet had bettered his pole position time of 1 min 35.079 sec for the 1981 race by well over the a massive five seconds, the local hero having been fastest during the test sessions. Now, though, in official qualifying, he had been one of a number of drivers to have failed to get in a clear lap and had had eventually to settle for seventh spot on the grid with a time of 1 min 30.281 sec, achieved on Friday afternoon. Instead it had been Prost's turn to steal the limelight by clinching pole position with a stupendous lap in 1 min 28.808 sec (203.941 kph). Like Piquet, the Frenchman had also recorded his best time on Friday after an engine misfire in his Renault had prevented any improvement on Saturday.

In spite of the various shortcomings of practice and a general lack of excitement the rest of the grid line-up was much as anticipated with just a few notable exceptions. One of these was Rosberg who had done extremely well. Not only was he the fastest

1982

non-turbo runner, as in South Africa, but he had also qualified in an excellent third place with a time of 1 min 29.358 sec. Indeed, had it not been for Villeneuve putting in another of his do-or-die efforts on his final set of qualifiers late on Saturday afternoon, and stopping the clocks at 1 min 29.173 sec, the Finn would have been on the front row. As it was he had still beaten the other two leading turbo runners, for Arnoux had ended up being fourth fastest at 1 min 30.121 sec after having indulged in a couple of spins, the first right at the start of practice when the rear aerofoil support had snapped on his Renault, while Pironi had come out only eighth fastest behind Lauda, Reutemann (his progress had been interrupted by gearbox and fuel pressure problems) and Piquet. Further down the order, meanwhile, de Cesaris had qualified his new Alfa Romeo in a fairly respectable tenth spot without too much fuss or bother to line up alongside Patrese, and de Angelis, in the first of the new Lotus 91s, had also made the front half of the grid along with Watson (troubled by understeer and the traffic) and Alboreto. Their respective team-mates, on the other hand, had both had more than their fair share of problems. Giacomelli, in one of the other new Alfa Romeos, had been plagued by poor handling and an engine misfire, added to which the fuel line had come off at one point and caused a small fire, while Mansell had had two off-course excursions in the second Lotus 91, plus the failure of a crown-wheel and pinion to contend with. The first incident had been caused by insecurely fastened bodywork lifting off soon after the start of practice and the second when the car had suddenly jumped out of gear. Problems of one sort or another had also affected a good number of the remaining drivers, not least Winkelhock who had hardly been able to practise at all on Saturday due to his ATS blowing up its engine in the morning and suffering an electrical failure on the first lap of final qualifying in the afternoon. Jarier was another to have had a particularly trying time of it due to his Osella running with a persistent fuel-feed problem. Nevertheless, the Frenchman had at least gone quick enough to scrape on to the back of the grid along with Serra, and also Laffite and Cheever in their obviously over-weight and misfiring Talbot-Matras, whereas his young team-mate had not even graduated beyond pre-qualifying on Friday morning. Not that this was surprising, as Paletti's hopes had been dashed first by a rear wishbone breaking loose and then by a wheel dropping off! What had been surprising, however, was to find the two Toleman drivers also being ruled out of the race at the end of practice, although both Warwick and Cheever had found their cars behaving terribly over the bumps, besides which the Englishman's efforts had been thwarted by his rear aerofoil breaking away from its

mounting and by minor engine disorders. Henton, after having been forced to complete practice in the spare Arrows following an engine failure, had not made the cut either, nor had Guerrero in the new Ensign.

After the sultry weather experienced throughout practice, conditions were much more pleasant on Sunday. It was still very hot, certainly, but now it was from a sun beating down from clear blue skies. During the morning warm-up session the appetites of the crowd, some 80,000 of them, were whetted nicely by Piquet turning in the fastest time, something that must have made the Brazilian World Champion confident of achieving a good result when he later took up his position on the grid for the start of the race. At the green Prost made one of his slower getaways, but Villeneuve was away like a bullet and so was Rosberg who quickly slotted into second place behind the Ferrari after sitting it out wheel to wheel with Arnoux going into the first right-hander. Not satisfied with that, the Finn then launched an attack on Villeneuve for the lead by attempting to run around on the outside of him as they hit the brakes for the left-hand hairpin leading on to the long back straight. However, Villeneuve had the line and held it with the result that Rosberg ran wide, exited the corner correspondingly slower and was left in no position to do anything at all to prevent Arnoux and a fast recovering Prost from steaming past along the straight that followed. Consequently instead of being in the hoped-for lead, Rosberg went on to complete the opening lap down in fourth place where he was followed over the line by Patrese (another to have made a very good start), Pironi, Piquet, Reutemann, Lauda, Alboreto, de Cesaris, Watson and the others who were being led by the Lotus 91s of de Angelis and Mansell.

The order on the second lap remained much the same but next time round Patrese powered past Rosberg, while Pironi dropped from sixth place to sixteenth when the back of his Ferrari suddenly got away from him at the last right-hander before the pits. Two laps later Piquet also rushed on ahead of Rosberg and by the end of lap 6 the two blue and white Brabhams were lying third and fourth with Prost, already suffering from a slight misfire at the top end of his Renault's rev band, simply unable to keep them out. By now the partisan crowd had become ecstatic and when, on lap 9, their hero swopped places with Patrese and immediately started closing the small gap to Arnoux and Villeneuve, still only a few car lengths apart, there was even more cheering and chanting to be heard. Meanwhile, it was no less hectic behind the leaders, for there was a lot of cut and thrust driving going on throughout most of the field. In particular, some of the scenes at the end of the back straight were quite incredible with cars arriv-

ing two, or even three, abreast. The battle for eighth place was certainly a no-holds barred affair, for although de Cesaris had earlier nipped past Alboreto and Lauda, they were now coming back at him, and Watson was there as well with de Angelis following closely in their wake. On the tenth lap it became even more hairy. First Lauda dived to the inside of the Alfa Romeo at the end of the back straight and, in being forced to back off, was nearly clouted up the rear by his team-mate who was in the midst of carrying out a somewhat more successful manoeuvre on Alboreto. Then, later on the same lap, Alboreto and de Angelis had a slight contretemps which dropped them both behind Mansell, Giacomelli, Winkelhock and Pironi, while de Cesaris eventually succumbed to the pressure from Lauda, rode over a kerb and ended up in the pits to check out a sudden deterioration in the Alfa's handling. The Italian's mechanics, however, could find nothing amiss and hurriedly sent their man on his way again, only for the car's undertray to break loose four laps later amidst a shower of sparks, and put de Cesaris out for good. By then there had also been two other retirements: Boesel had spun off the track when the rear suspension broke on his March, almost certainly as a result of an earlier bumping match with Daly, and then the Irishman, driving with a damaged front wing and side-pod as a consequence, had gone off as well, stalled his engine and been unable to restart. Laffite was another soon out of the race. He had already been delayed by a pit stop in a vain attempt to cure an engine misfire, and when the Talbot's handling became impaired following a trip over a kerb the amiable Frenchman decided to call it a day. Shortly afterwards his team-mate was forced out, too, with hot water leaking into his cockpit, while Giacomelli's work for the day was brought to an abrupt halt by an engine failure.

After 20 laps Villeneuve still led the race, but his advantage, as much as 5 seconds at one point, was now visibly being eaten away by Piquet, the Brazilian having finally got the better of Arnoux on lap 17 amidst another delirious outburst from the crowd. Since then Arnoux had also lost out to Rosberg and Patrese, just after they had swopped places, and was currently running only a short distance ahead of an epic struggle going on between Prost, Reutemann, Lauda and Watson. All four drivers were really hard at it, passing and repassing one another with gay abandon, and although Reutemann had just dropped to the back of the quartet he was making it quite obvious that he had no intention of staying there for long. In fact, on the very next lap, the 21st, he repassed Watson once more, just as Prost caught and passed Arnoux, and then dived to the inside of Lauda under braking for the last right-hander before the pits. This time, though,

End of the race for Gilles Villeneuve as he spins out of the lead on lap 30 and almost takes Nelson Piquet's Brabham with him. *(Autocar & Motor)*

Reutemann messed things up by colliding with the McLaren and bending its right rear suspension with the result that a furious Lauda was left with no alternative other than to drive round to the pits to retire at the end of the following lap. Reutemann, on the other hand, continued on his way only to disappear from the race even quicker than Lauda by almost immediately becoming involved in a similar argument with Arnoux, both cars being deposited in the catch-fences. At almost precisely the same moment there was another commotion when Baldi (lapped) moved over from Pironi and Alboreto at the end of the back straight but then swung right across into the path of de Angelis whom he had apparently not seen. Whatever, the Lotus rode up over the left rear wheel of the Arrows and careered off into the catch-fences, while Baldi was left trailing into the pits for a new rear aerofoil before continuing even further in arrears. Throughout all of this drama the three leading cars had become even closer to one another and by lap 24 were virtually nose to tail. Before Piquet could do anything about Villeneuve, however, it was Rosberg who made the first move by diving through on the inside of the Brabham at the end of the pits straight and momentarily nosing ahead. On this occasion the Williams drifted wide as it negotiated the right-hander that followed, enabling Piquet to forge on ahead once more, but on lap 27 Rosberg repeated the manoeuvre more successfully and emerged from the corner in second place. Naturally this silenced the crowd, although not for long as two laps later Piquet regained the place by running around on the outside of the Williams at the left-hander at the end of the back straight. That was not all as on the following lap Villeneuve left his braking a fraction too late for the right-hander before the hairpin

and ran just wide enough to enable Piquet to draw right up alongside, on the outside. Then, after being forced to put his two inside wheels on to the grass verge, the French-Canadian suddenly spun straight across the track and careered on into the catch-fences. He was out of the race! Meanwhile, after a busy moment avoiding the wayward Ferrari, Piquet automatically took over as the new leader and went on to complete the lap with about a second in hand over the ever-present Rosberg.

On lap 33, with Piquet and Rosberg still circulating only a few car lengths apart, attention was suddenly diverted towards the third-placed Patrese when he spun on the

way out of the last right-hander before the pits. At first it seemed inconsequential as he gathered it up and continued on his way apparently none the worse, but in reality he had reached a state of physical exhaustion due to a combination of the heat, the bumpy ride and the enormous G-forces. Fortunately he still had sufficient awareness to do the right thing and head straight for the pits where his condition was readily made apparent by the Brabham mechanics having to lift him out of the car and into the pit garage prior to eventually being revived. In the meantime, Pironi and Mass both stopped for fresh tyres at the end of the same lap and shortly afterwards Serra caused more dust to

An exhausted Nelson Piquet receives an arm of reassurance from Keke Rosberg on the rostrum after 'winning' his home Grand Prix. *(L.A.T. Photographic)*

rise by spinning off into the catch-fences in his Fittipaldi. Only a minute or so later Salazar was also forced out when he felt the engine start to tighten in his ATS, but none of this was of much consequence to the crowd for their eyes were glued on Piquet's progress as he struggled to stay clear of Rosberg. However, in spite of a few heart-stopping moments for them when Piquet occasionally ran wide on one or two of the corners as he, too, began to feel the effects of heat exhaustion, the blue and white Brabham continued to hold sway out in front. In fact, in the last dozen or so laps Piquet even started to extend his lead due to Rosberg having to ease up to conserve his tyres and eventually crossed the line for the final time a whisker under 12 seconds ahead of the Williams to conclude an extremely difficult and courageous drive. Almost half a minute later

Prost duly followed them home in third place despite the Renault's high-speed misfire, while Watson finished a close fourth after having been plagued by increasing under-steer during the latter half of the race. After that a battered and bruised Mansell took fifth place ahead of the only other driver to complete the full 63 laps, Alboreto, the Italian Tyrrell driver having caught and passed Win-kelhock's well-driven ATS back on lap 46.

After the race the scenes were even more remarkable than at the previous year's end of season Grand Prix in Las Vegas with just about all twelve drivers still there at the finish staggering out of their cars suffering from varying degrees of dehydration and heat exhaustion. Piquet was in a particularly sorry state as within moments of taking up his place on the rostrum he suddenly collapsed with fatigue and had to be supported by

Rosberg and Prost before being revived again in time to collect his trophy. Meanwhile, Renault's Jean Sage and Ferrari's Marco Piccinini were busy carrying out their earlier threats of lodging official protests against the legality of the first two cars due to the use of 'disposable ballast' only to have them rejected by the Stewards of the meeting. Not satisfied with that, however, both teams then subsequently appealed to FISA. At a hearing of the FIA International Court of Appeal almost exactly a month later Piquet and Rosberg were both disqualified on the grounds that their cars should have been up to the minimum weight limit at all times during the race when clearly this had not been the case, evidence having been produced to prove it. Consequently, Prost was declared the winner of the race and the other nine finishers all moved up two places.

Results

1	A. Prost (Renault)	1 hr 44 min 33.134 sec (181.891 kph/ 113.022 mph)
2	J. Watson (McLaren-Ford)	1 hr 44 min 36.124 sec
3	N. Mansell (Lotus-Ford)	1 hr 45 min 09.993 sec
4	M. Alboreto (Tyrrell-Ford)	1 hr 45 min 23.895 sec
5	M. Winkelhock (ATS-Ford)	1 lap behind
6	D. Pironi (Ferrari)	1 lap behind
7	S. Borgudd (Tyrrell-Ford)	2 laps behind
8	J. Mass (March-Ford)	2 laps behind
9	J. P. Jarier (Osella-Ford)	3 laps behind
10	M. Baldi (Arrows-Ford)	6 laps behind

Fastest lap: A. Prost (Renault) on lap 36 in 1 min 37.016 sec (186.687 kph/116.001 mph)

Retirements

R. Boesel (March-Ford) spun off on lap 12, D. Daly (Theodore-Ford) spun off on lap 13, A. de Cesaris (Alfa Romeo) loose undertray on lap 15, J. Laffite (Talbot-Matra) handling/ engine on lap 16, B. Giacomelli (Alfa Romeo) engine on lap 17, E. Cheever (Talbot-Matra) water leak on lap 20, R. Arnoux (Renault) accident on lap 22, C. Reutemann (Williams-Ford) accident on lap 22, E. de Angelis (Lotus-Ford) accident on lap 22, N. Lauda (McLaren-Ford) rear suspension on lap 23, G. Villeneuve (Ferrari) spun off on lap 30, R. Patrese (Brabham-Ford) driver fatigue on lap 35,

F. Serra (Fittipaldi-Ford) spun off on lap 37, E. Salazar (ATS-Ford) engine on lap 39.

Disqualified

N. Piquet (Brabham-Ford) who crossed the line in first place after 1 hr 43 min 53.760 sec (183.040 kph/113.736 mph) and who recorded the race's fastest lap on lap 4 in 1 min 36.582 sec (187.525 kph/116.523 mph), and also K. Rosberg (Williams-Ford) who crossed the line in second place after 1 hr 44 min 05.737 sec.

N.B. M. Winkelhock and S. Borgudd both took the chequered flag ahead of A. Prost and would, had they completed a further lap within the required time, have been on the same lap and one lap behind the winner respectively, although it would have made no difference to their final positions.

VIIth United States Grand Prix (West)

Long Beach: April 4
Weather: Warm and sunny
Distance: 75.5 laps of 3.428 km
circuit = 258.81 km (160.81 miles)

Just five days after Brazil Carlos Reutemann had dropped a bombshell on Frank Williams by announcing his decision to retire from the sport, this time for good. Although the reason was not made obvious, the Argentinian, like his erstwhile team-mate, had been growing increasingly disenchanted with the current breed of Grand Prix cars, and it seemed almost certain that his country's mounting antagonism with Britain over the sovereignty of the Falkland Islands (this was to lead to an invasion exactly a week after his announcement) had been an influencing factor. Whatever, Frank Williams had been caught completely off-guard. In response he had first made another unsuccessful attempt to lure Alan Jones out of retirement, and then contacted Mario Andretti who, fortunately, was free from any commitment to the

Patrick Racing Indy team during the Long Beach weekend and had agreed to a one-off drive. Apart from this sudden and unexpected reorganisation within the Williams team, the entry for the race was virtually identical to that of a fortnight earlier. There were no other driver changes and the only different car was the spare Williams which had been built up around the monocoque of the team's hitherto test car using parts off Rosberg's Brazilian race chassis, this having ended up with the underside of its monocoque damaged following the Finn's epic duel with Piquet. It was noticeable, though, that several more of the cars had developed a need for 'water-cooled brakes'. These included even the Renaults as the French team had now decided to join in with the cheating going on over the weight limit regulations

subject to the outcome of the impending Appeal Tribunal.

As usual, with Long Beach being a street circuit, pre-race testing had been out of the question and so when the track was opened for the first 90 minutes of practice on Friday morning everyone was anxious to get stuck in. This year the sense of urgency was more apparent than ever as since the 1981 race the circuit layout had undergone a number of modifications, partly to make way for the construction of a new hotel complex in the vicinity of what had previously been the Queens Hairpin. Now, instead of a sharp 180-degree right-hander here, there was a 90-degree right-hander located slightly further to the west and followed by a completely new section of track leading up to Ocean Boulevard. This consisted of a series of very demanding corners, both to the right and to the left, interspersed by short straights and a long ess-bend. On the other side of the circuit, too, the short straight at the bottom of the hill from Linden Avenue had been lengthened, making the right-hand and the left-hand corners that followed tighter, and there was now also a new chicane located about one-third of the way along the fast curving Shoreline Drive section, this latter addition being a preparatory step to move the pits away from Ocean Boulevard. Combined, these various alterations marginally extended the overall lap distance to 3.428 kilometres and it soon became apparent that they had a significant impact on lap times for even when some of the leading lights began to settle down the pace was still around 10 seconds slower than that of the previous year. A pleasant surprise was to see Giacomelli and de Cesaris both going well in their new Alfa Romeo 182s, the torque from

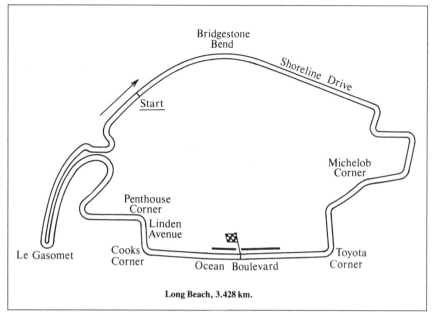

Long Beach, 3.428 km.

the V12 engine obviously proving its worth on this particular circuit. Rosberg and Piquet were also turning in good times, as was Lauda in spite of having to stop for a new nose cone at one point following a spin which had brought him into contact with a wall. Not that the former double World Champion was alone in overstepping the mark. On the contrary, throughout most of the morning numerous drivers seemed to be going off in all directions or taking trips up escape roads as they learned their way round the revised circuit. Fortunately, in the majority of cases little or no harm ensued, but when Patrese hit the wall at the new right-hander at the end of Shoreline Drive the impact not only bent the Brabham's right front wheel and suspension but also damaged the suspension pick-up points inside the monocoque. As a result the car was beyond immediate repair and the Italian was forced to take over the team's spare BT49C for the rest of the weekend. For Warwick, meanwhile, the morning ended on an even unhappier note as by coming out slowest of the five drivers obliged to take part in pre-qualifying, due to a persistent misfire from the Hart turbocharged engine, he was left with no further part to play in the proceedings.

The afternoon's hour of qualifying followed a similar pattern to that of the morning untimed session except that, if anything, it was even more hectic as was to be expected with grid positions at stake. Again a number of drivers had their 'moments' but they were all pretty harmless and certainly not enough to cause any major panic. Nor was there too much in the way of serious mechanical trouble; one of the few drivers out of luck being Watson who returned to the pits after only one slow lap and subsequently lost a lot of time while a troublesome fuel pump received attention. Even so, the Renault

team, unusually, seemed to be at sixes and sevens, with Prost getting nowhere and Arnoux not doing much better. Some of the other leading Michelin runners were failing to make the hoped-for impression as well and it was not until near the end of the session that a reason for this became apparent – the French tyre firm suddenly realized that they had issued an incorrect batch of tyres! The difference was staggering for once out on the correct rubber Prost started to fly and, despite a recurrence of the high-speed misfire that had plagued him in Brazil, rocketed from near the bottom of the time-sheets right up to fourth place with a lap in 1 min 29.935 sec. Unfortunately for Arnoux it was all too late, as just prior to the mistake being rectified his engine had let go with the result that he had been forced to call it a day. Consequently, he was left well down the order and in a rather appropriate thirteenth place immediately below de Cesaris, the Italian's hopes of maintaining the momentum displayed in the morning being dashed by the failure of the Alfa's distributor right in the midst of an all-out effort for a really quick lap. The three drivers to finish ahead of Prost, meanwhile, were Rosberg (1 min 28.576 sec), openly delighted to have come out fastest, Lauda (1 min 28.791 sec) and, despite losing an engine near the end of the session, Piquet (1 min 29.934 sec). Then, immediately behind him, it was Villeneuve (1 min 29.949 sec) followed by Mansell, Pironi, Patrese, de Angelis and Giacomelli who had all just failed to join the elite sub-1 min 30 sec group. Watson? Well, the unfortunate Ulsterman had managed to squeeze in barely a handful of laps towards the end of the session and was left way down in twenty-sixth place ahead only of Paletti, Salazar (he had lost most of the morning session because of an inoperative clutch),

Baldi and Fabi.

In the midst of another busy 90 minutes of testing on Saturday morning everyone thought that Ferrari were playing a joke or trying to outdo their rivals using 'water-cooled brakes' by fitting Pironi's car with a rather weird-looking double rear aerofoil. However, when Villeneuve's car also appeared in similiar configuration for the start of the final qualifying session it seemed as if it must be a serious ploy after all. Essentially this revised layout involved the adoption of two rear aerofloils, both mounted on a central pillar but staggered in front of one another with one offset to the left of the car's centre line and the other to the right. Each complied with the rules concerning the width of bodywork behind the rear wheels, limited to 110 centimetres, although combined, the overall width was well beyond this amount which, of course, was not what the rules intended at all! According to Pironi the effect was a slightly improved straight-line speed and marginally better traction through the quick corners, but any benefit was to be more than negated by the Goodyear tyres proving to have an inferior turning-in ability to the Michelin tyres as more and more rubber went down on the track. Consequently both Pironi and Villeneuve were soon finding themselves being left behind somewhat amidst a general lowering of lap times and so, too, were most of the other Goodyear runners. Rosberg certainly was as he was one of the few drivers destined to make no improvement at all on his Friday time. An eventful moment at the new right-hander at the end of Shoreline Drive in which he burnt out his clutch whilst recovering from a spin effectively saw to that, for although the Finn subsequently took over the spare Williams he was unhappy with its handling. Piquet's hopes of defending his grid position ended under similar circumstances when he virtually wrote off the

right front corner of his Brabham against the wall at the bottom of the hill in Linden Avenue. Furthermore, because there was no longer a spare Brabham available, this marked the end of the day's work for the Brazilian and left his mechanics with the task of trying to straighten out the car for the race. In the meantime, the Renault team were coming back with a vengeance after their problems on Friday, for Arnoux had quickly taken over Rosberg's position at the top of the time-sheets and Prost was lapping only fractionally slower in spite of still not being too happy with his car: overnight the high-speed misfire had been cured following the discovery of a small piece of heat resistant material blocking a filter in one of the inter-coolers, but now a new set of springs was upsetting the car's balance! Also featuring strongly were Giacomelli and de Cesaris in their Alfa Romeos, along with Lauda who was next to steal the limelight by being first to lap in the 1 min 27 sec bracket and achieving what almost certainly looked like being a pole-winning time of 1 min 27.436 sec. In fact, Lauda obviously thought so, too, as he sat out the final stages of practice only for de Cesaris to recover from an earlier excursion into a wall, which had led to a rear wheel having to be replaced, and to spring a real surprise just before the flag came out by stopping the clocks at 1 min 27.316 sec. A tremendous performance that left the Italian openly emotional when he returned to the pits with his first-ever pole position in the bag. By the close Arnoux (1 min 27.763 sec), after a stripped second gear had been replaced, and Prost (1 min 27.979 sec) had also broken the 1 min 28 sec barrier to line up in third and fourth places on the grid, while Giacomelli (1 min 28.087 sec) had only just failed to join them to take fifth spot immediately ahead of Piquet, the Brazilian having got down to 1 min 28.276 sec before his accident to wind

up being the fastest Goodyear runner. Rosberg, on the other hand, had slipped right back to eighth place, sandwiched between the Ferraris of Villeneuve and Pironi. Even so this was still a good deal better than his new temporary team-mate, as Andretti had qualified in a somewhat disappointing fourteenth spot with Jarier, Watson, Alboreto and Cheever being the others to finish ahead of the American. Mansell, Patrese and de Angelis had also slipped well down the order after failing to keep up with the increased pace on their Goodyear tyres. Nevertheless, all three were still safely ensconced on the grid, unlike Serra who had dropped into the non-qualifying zone to join Fabi, Paletti and Baldi as a spectator for the race.

On Sunday the weather was absolutely superb with clear blue skies accompanied by warm sunshine. Overnight the Brabham mechanics had completed repair work on Piquet's car and, with no further problems cropping up for anyone during the morning warm-up session, everything seemed to augur well for the 75½ lap race, the only question mark hanging over the ability of de Cesaris to cope with the responsibility of starting a race from pole position. As it happened no-one need have worried for after he had safely led the field around to the starting area along Shoreline Drive, and the starting lights had flicked from red to green, the Italian got away perfectly to take up an immediate lead from Lauda and Arnoux who were left disputing second place. Indeed, rather more in the way of concern drifted back to his compatriot in the Lotus 91 as, for reasons best known to himself, de Angelis had caused all kinds of confusion by lining up on the wrong side of the grid between Laffite and Mansell, an incident that was to lead to a Steward's enquiry and a fine of $2,000! Somehow, though, they all managed to keep out of one another's way, apart from the two ATS cars of Winkelhock and Salazar making light contact with Borgudd's Tyrrell, and went on to complete the first full lap (actually 1½ laps) intact with de Cesaris doing commendably well out in front.

Early on the second lap Winkelhock brought his ATS into contact with Borgudd's Tyrrell again, only this time the consequences were rather more severe as the German was forced to retire on the spot after bouncing off into the wall. His team-mate's race didn't last much longer either, as in a burst of over-exuberance just two laps later Salazar also finished up against the wall to conclude a pretty dismal day for Gunther Schmidt's outfit. In the meantime, the order of the leading cars was staying unchanged with de Cesaris, steadily pulling away on his own, still being pursued by Arnoux, Lauda and Giacomelli, all three remaining tightly bunched up together ahead of Villeneuve. Too tight it seemed, as on lap 6 Giacomelli made a run up on the inside of Lauda's

The surprise package at Long Beach was Andrea de Cesaris and the Alfa Romeo Tipo 182. Here the Italian leads René Arnoux's Renault during the early stages of the race. *(L.A.T. Photographic)*

McLaren approaching the hairpin, locked up his brakes and promptly slid into the back of Arnoux's Renault. The result, two more retirements and Lauda up into second place with Villeneuve a reasonably close third. Naturally the rest of the field also automatically moved up two places allowing Rosberg, next along, to take over fourth spot immediately in front of a hard-charging Watson, the Ulsterman, running on the softer of two types of Michelin tyres available, having earlier scorched past Alboreto, Piquet, Pironi and Prost in quick succession. Even fifth place was not enough to satisfy Watson's appetite, however, as he clearly demonstrated on the following lap by overtaking Rosberg and immediately giving chase to Villeneuve before going past him as well only two laps later. Further back, meanwhile, Pironi had just become another driver to have ended his race in a wall-banging incident, and Borgudd was in the pits for a new rear aerofoil following his earlier confrontations with the two ATS drivers. Prost was in trouble, too, as his brakes were playing up and rapidly dropping him out of contention. Worse still, the problem was soon to result in a trip up the escape road on Ocean Boulevard, contact with the wall and yet another retirement.

By lap 15 Lauda had steadily eaten away de Cesaris' advantage at the head of the race, which at one point had been as much as 5 seconds, and was looking all set to pounce at any moment. The change of leadership came even sooner than expected, however, for when de Cesaris arrived at the new chicane he suddenly found himself being held up by Boesel, whom he was about to lap, and lost sufficient momentum to enable Lauda to surge past as they accelerated away towards the end of Shoreline Drive. That settled it, for once out in front Lauda quickly pulled away and left a somewhat disillusioned Italian holding down a lonely second place, Watson being a distant third at this stage and already growing concerned about the state of his tyres after the early charge. Meanwhile, behind the Ulsterman, there was soon another battle shaping up as Villeneuve was gradually being reeled in by Rosberg and Piquet, and Alboreto was not exactly being left behind in seventh place. In fact, by lap 19 Rosberg was right up with the Ferrari and on the following lap actually managed to slip ahead on the short squirt between the hairpin and the new chicane. Once out of the chicane, though, Villeneuve immediately retaliated by using the Ferrari's superior power to blast past his rival on the approach to the right-hander at the end of Shoreline Drive. Undaunted, Rosberg had another stab at the same spot on the next lap and once again led the Ferrari through the chicane. Moreover, this time he stayed in front after a determined effort by Villeneuve to try to restore the status quo by charging down

on the outside of the Williams ended up with the French-Canadian overstepping his braking point for the right-hander and half spinning up the escape road. Piquet very nearly went on ahead of the Ferrari as well but just before he had the chance Villeneuve had slammed the car into first gear and was under way again, pressing on as hard as ever and even pulling away from his new pursuer within another lap or so. Rosberg, meanwhile, was immediately making inroads on Watson's third-placed McLaren and, by lap 27, had not only wiped out the deficit but was slicing past to take over the third spot. Not that this was particularly surprising as Watson was now suffering from quite acute handling problems caused by a broken skirt and also by his rapidly deteriorating tyres which was to lead to the inevitable pit stop for fresh rubber just two laps later. By then the field had dwindled to only fourteen cars following another spate of retirements. Much of the trouble had apparently been caused not so much by the track breaking up but by a layer of loose gravel forming off the racing line, particularly in the new section leading up to Ocean Boulevard. Whatever, this had just resulted in Guerrero's debut being ended after bringing his Ensign into contact with the wall, and for similar reasons Piquet and Daly had only minutes earlier also departed from the fray. Prior to that Andretti had retired at the pits with bent rear suspension after he, too, had hit the wall. In between all of this drama Jarier had gone out with a broken gearbox, while Laffite had been forced to abandon his Talbot due to spinning and stalling his engine in the midst of a heated mid-field scrap with Patrese. The Italian had spun as well but had been able to continue, albeit minus a nose fin!

On lap 34, with Watson now a lap down in eighth place following his tyre stop and still unhappy about the McLaren's handling, there was suddenly no de Cesaris. The Ital-

ian, after a faultless drive, had apparently looked in his mirrors, seen smoke issuing from the direction of his rear brakes and in a momentary lapse of concentration had gone off into the wall on the rise to Ocean Boulevard. At almost precisely the same moment Henton disappeared equally as abruptly from near the back of the field when he, too, put a wheel on the loose stuff whilst attempting to overtake Borgudd, so now there were just twelve cars left with the race still to reach the half-way mark. After that, though, it was relative calm – certainly as far as Lauda was concerned, for he was left enjoying a massive lead of very nearly a full minute over Rosberg with only Villeneuve, Alboreto and Cheever still on the same lap. Even so, for a while at least, there was still some racing going on as Alboreto had caught up with Villeneuve and was making spirited efforts to pass the Ferrari, while not far behind Cheever a similar dispute was in progress over sixth place between Patrese and de Angelis. Unfortunately, though, Alboreto was forced to ease off shortly afterwards due to the Tyrrell's left side-pod beginning to work loose, possibly the legacy of a brief wheel-banging incident with the Ferrari, and once Patrese had outwitted his compatriot on lap 38 there was not a lot of excitement left. Indeed, the only other changes of any significance to occur were Cheever being forced to stop and replace worn tyres on lap 45, before stopping for good fourteen laps later with oil leaking from the Talbot's gearbox, and Patrese catching and passing Alboreto's stricken Tyrrell in the closing stages of the race to snatch fourth place. All the while, Lauda continued serenely on his way, even allowing Patrese and Alboreto to unlap themselves before the finish, to eventually score a convincing victory just three races into his comeback: his only problem, which also applied to some of the other drivers, had been a busy moment

Niki Lauda sprays the champagne after achieving victory just three races into his comeback. (*L.A.T. Photographic*)

1982

avoiding a rather erratically driven breakdown truck collecting Piquet's damaged Brabham earlier in the afternoon. Less than 15 seconds behind the Austrian at the flag, underlining just how hard he had been trying, Rosberg had every reason to feel well satisfied with second place, while a reasonably contented Villeneuve duly took third spot ahead of the other eight finishers, only to find himself subsequently being excluded from the results following a successful protest from Ken Tyrrell against the Ferrari's double rear aerofoil! As in Brazil Ferrari's Marco Piccinini also protested the first two cars over the use of 'disposable ballast' but this was thrown out by the Stewards. And so ended another 'happy' weekend.

Results

1	N. Lauda (McLaren-Ford)	1 hr 58 min 25.318 sec (131.00 kph/ 81.40 mph)
2	K. Rosberg (Williams-Ford)	1 hr 58 min 39.978 sec
*	G. Villeneuve (Ferrari)	1 hr 59 min 29.606 sec
3	R. Patrese (Brabham-Ford)	1 hr 59 min 44.461 sec
4	M. Alboreto (Tyrrell-Ford)	1 hr 59 min 46.265 sec
5	E. de Angelis (Lotus-Ford)	1 lap behind
6	J. Watson (McLaren-Ford)	1 lap behind
7	N. Mansell (Lotus-Ford)	2 laps behind
8	J. Mass (March-Ford)	2 laps behind
9	R. Boesel (March-Ford)	5 laps behind
10	S. Borgudd (Tyrrell-Ford)	7 laps behind

* Disqualified

Fastest lap: N. Lauda (McLaren-Ford) on lap 12 in 1 min 30.831 sec (135.861 kph/84.420 mph)

Retirements
M. Winkelhock (ATS-Ford) accident on lap 2, E. Salazar (ATS-Ford) accident on lap 4, B. Giacomelli (Alfa Romeo) accident on lap 6, R. Arnoux (Renault) accident on lap 6, D. Pironi (Ferrari) accident on lap 7, A. Prost (Renault) accident on lap 11, M. Andretti (Williams-Ford) rear suspension on lap 20, D. Daly (Theodore-Ford) accident on lap 23, N. Piquet (Brabham-Ford) accident on lap 26, J. P. Jarier (Osella-Ford) gearbox on lap 27, J. Laffite (Talbot-Matra) stalled engine on lap 27, R. Guerrero (Ensign-Ford) accident on lap 28, B. Henton (Arrows-Ford) accident on lap 33, A. de Cesaris (Alfa Romeo) accident on lap 34, E. Cheever (Talbot-Matra) gearbox on lap 59.

II° Gran Premio di San Marino

Imola: April 25
Weather: Warm and dry
Distance: 60 laps of 5.040 km circuit = 302.40 km (187.90 miles)

On the Monday of the week leading up to the San Marino Grand Prix the appeals lodged by Renault and Ferrari against the first two cars in Brazil had finally been heard by the FIA International Court of Appeal in Paris, and both Piquet and Rosberg were disqualified. Of even greater significance (for FOCA had taken the view that this was the introduction of a new rule contrary to the terms of the Concorde Agreement and FIA statutes), the tribunal had declared that, in future, cars were to be weighed after a race in exactly the same conditions in which they had crossed the finishing line with no topping up of oil and water permitted. In consequence a hastily-convened meeting of FOCA's membership had taken place two days later in London and, following a vote, had come out in favour of boycotting the forthcoming race at Imola. Instead, though, the organizers were to be asked to postpone the event until July 3 (on the grounds that 'In order to disqualify Piquet and Rosberg from the Brazilian Grand Prix, the FIA appeal tribunal has sought to change the Formula One rules in a way which would render all our cars ineligible for Grand Prix racing') so as to allow an opportunity for the legal implications to be considered. In reality, FOCA was up in arms; first because it felt that the decision had been influenced by a threatened withdrawal of Renault and Ferrari unless the weight limit rules were clarified, and second because a ban on topping-up fluids meant that the plastic water containers used in conjunction with 'water-cooled brakes' were now useless and that a means of keeping pace with rival teams using turbo-charged engines was lost. There was also the additional concern that cars would now have to start a Grand Prix over the minimum weight limit of 580 kilogrammes to compensate for the weight loss during a race caused by the natural consumption of essential fluids and the like which, FOCA said, was a rule change in itself.

The outcome of FOCA's decision, which although by no means unanimous was supported by the vast majority of its membership, was that there were just 14 entries at Imola for a race that the organizers, understandably, had refused to postpone at such short notice. These consisted of the usual two entries from each of the FISA-aligned teams, Ferrari, Renault, Alfa Romeo, Osella and Toleman (Guy Ligier had recently switched allegiance to FOCA), plus two more from ATS and also Tyrrell who had both opted out of FOCA's 'strike', although for entirely different reasons. In the case of ATS, Gunther Schmidt felt that he had not really benefited from FOCA membership and had simply chosen to go his own way and attend the race. Ken Tyrrell, on the other hand, wholeheartedly supported the action but, at the same time, had had little option other than to break ranks as he had only recently negotiated two new sponsorship deals with former backers of his team, both of which were Italian! The first was a three-race agreement with the Candy Domestic Appliance firm, which had withdrawn its support from Toleman after Long Beach, and the second was a one-race deal with Imola Ceramica. Interestingly enough, the injection of this much-needed money into the Woking-based team had also led to a change of driver, as Slim Borgudd had been replaced by Brian Henton, the Englishman's stint at Arrows having ended due to the return of Marc Surer to the cockpit following his winter testing accident at Kyalami.

When it came round to the business of practice on Friday morning it was a rather odd experience seeing the pit lane half deserted and most of the pit garages closed up.

Starting Grid

R. Arnoux Renault (1 min 29.765 sec)	
	A. Prost Renault (1 min 30.249 sec)
G. Villeneuve Ferrari (1 min 30.717 sec)	
	D. Pironi Ferrari (1 min 32.020 sec)
M. Alboreto Tyrrell-Ford (1 min 33.209 sec)	
	B. Giacomelli Alfa Romeo (1 min 33.230 sec)
A. de Cesaris Alfa Romeo (1 min 33.397 sec)	
	*D. Warwick Toleman-Hart (1 min 33.503 sec)
J. P. Jarier Osella-Ford (1 min 34.336 sec)	
	T. Fabi Toleman-Hart (1 min 34.647 sec)
B. Henton Tyrrell-Ford (1 min 35.262 sec)	
	M. Winkelhock ATS-Ford (1 min 35.790 sec)
R. Paletti Osella-Ford (1 min 36.228 sec)	
	E. Salazar ATS-Ford (1 min 36.434 sec)

*Non-starter: D. Warwick (Toleman-Hart)

Nevertheless, everyone soon settled back to watch what was almost certainly going to be a battle between Ferrari and Renault, especially as Alfa Romeo were having to employ some 40 kilogrammes of lead ballast to bring their cars up to weight. During the untimed session lap times were of little consequence, even to the Osella and Toleman drivers because, of course, with such a small field there was no need for pre-qualifying. In spite of this, though, there was certainly no sign of anybody taking things easy for, as usual, there was the task of juggling with variables and generally setting up cars in readiness for the first hour of qualifying. For most of the seven teams present this appeared to be a relatively straightforward exercise as the only real problem to emerge away from the pits was a drive belt detaching itself from the front of the Hart engine in Fabi's Toleman which stranded the Italian out on the circuit. However, in the pits, the ATS team were in a state of perplexity as, despite having a contract with the Bernie Ecclestone-owned/Jean Mosnier-managed International Race Tire Service Ltd to supply them with Avon tyres, the tyre transporter had been ordered back to base! Consequently they had no fresh tyres, only three sets of partly worn covers left over from Long Beach, which meant that both Winkelhock and Salazar were hardly being able to practise at all.

In the afternoon it was the turn of Renault to run into trouble. First Prost returned to the pits with smoke belching from the back of his car, actually a brand new chassis (RE38B), following a head gasket failure. Then, not long afterwards, Arnoux came marching into the pits to report that he had abandoned his car at Tosa following a fire caused by an oil leak from one of the turbo units. As a result, with Prost having commandeered the team's only spare car, Arnoux had to sit out proceedings for a while and wait until his team-mate had finished his qualifying run before he could get back out on the track. By then Pironi had also switched to the spare Ferrari as earlier a punctured tyre had sent him careering off into the barriers and done sufficient damage to suggest that the Frenchman had been lucky to emerge from the incident unharmed. When it was all over, though, the situation was much as anticipated, with the two Renault and the two Ferrari drivers filling the first four places on the time-sheets, Prost coming out quickest at 1 min 31.169 sec followed by Villeneuve (1 min 31.541 sec), Pironi (1 min 32.020 sec) and Arnoux (1 min 32.628 sec). After that came de Cesaris (1 min 33.879 sec), Warwick and the first of the Ford-Cosworth runners, Alboreto, right back to Fabi who, not surprisingly, was last in the order after having had only a brief outing in Warwick's car towards the end of the afternoon due to his own car still undergoing an engine change;

both cars, incidentally, now being sponsored by Ted Toleman's firm, Cougar Marine, following the loss of support from Candy.

After a further 90 minutes of untimed practice on Saturday morning, which was relatively uneventful except for Villeneuve returning to the pits at one point with the fibre-glass air ducts to his front brakes on fire due to the brakes overheating, it was not long before the final battle for grid positions was under way. By then Gunther Schmidt had managed to persuade Pirelli to supply his team with some new tyres but, because the front wheels of the ATS cars were of the incorrect size for the Italian rubber, only the rear covers could be used. As a result the situation was still far from being satisfactory as it meant mixing crossply tyres (Avon) with radial tyres (Pirelli) and consequential handling difficulties, the only consolation for Winkelhock and Salazar, as they struggled on gamely, being the knowledge that a batch of unused Avon tyres were on their way from the team's headquarters in England for the race. Elsewhere everything seemed to be going much according to plan, apart from Pironi still being confined to the spare Ferrari. Following the off-course excursion of the previous afternoon subsequent examination had revealed his proposed race chassis to be a virtual write-off. Indeed, part of it had already been cannibalized to build up a new car around the monocoque of the car that the Frenchman had damaged at Long Beach (this had been straightened out in a jig at the team's factory overnight and then transported to the circuit) but the work took longer than anticipated and was not finished until barely 10 minutes before the end of practice. Even then it made no difference to Pirioni's grid position, as he still failed to improve on his Friday time in the few laps that he was able to cover in the 'new' car, and he eventually had to settle for fourth spot. In the meantime, pole position had developed into an exciting three-cornered contest between Villeneuve and the Renault duo, Prost and Arnoux, with all three drivers giving it all they had got, much to the delight of an extremely large crowd present. Naturally their hero was Villeneuve, but in the final reckoning his best lap of 1 min 30.717 sec proved sufficient for only third spot on the grid as Arnoux had managed to squeeze in a real flier at 1 min 29.765 sec, while Prost, now concentrating on his team's spare chassis as he preferred its handling to the new car, made it an all-Renault front row with a time of 1 min 30.249 sec. Behind them, Alboreto had once again come out as the fastest Ford-Cosworth runner and had actually gone one better than the first day by beating both Alfa Romeo drivers to clinch a well-earned fifth spot, leaving Giacomelli sixth and de Cesaris seventh. Warwick was next in spite of having had a frightening moment towards the end of the session when

the left front suspension collapsed on his Toleman and sent the car slewing across the track at Rivazza, fortunately without hitting anything, while Jarier, Fabi, Henton, Winkelhock, Paletti and Salazar, in that order, rounded off the small grid.

With practice over, Ken Tyrrell decided that it was time to lodge another protest. On this occasion it was nothing to do with Ferrari's double rear aerofoil as there was no sign of that, but rather against all of the turbo-charged cars on the grounds that they were fitted with turbines which, according to the rules, were not permitted. However, after considering the matter and examining the rules – these did make reference to turbines but in spirit if not in word referred to turbine engines such as the gas-turbined engine used by Lotus some ten years earlier, not exhaust-driven turbines used for turbo-charged engines – the Stewards threw out the protest on the following morning and pointed out that there was another rule which permitted supercharging to be done by whatever means were available. So that was that, and the possibility of having an even smaller field of just eight cars in the race dismissed.

As the morning wore on it became increasingly obvious that the lack of cars had in no way diminished interest in the race, for the spectators arrived at the circuit in their hordes, the 90,000 or so that eventually turned up no doubt relishing the prospect of a good scrap between Ferrari and Renault. For some of the teams, meanwhile, there was soon some extra work to be done, as during the customary warm-up session Arnoux's engine was running unduly hot, which led to his mechanics knuckling down to the unenviable task of carrying out a precautionary engine change at short notice, de Cesaris's Alfa Romeo briefly caught fire when a fuel line broke loose near the fuel pump and Warwick's Toleman coasted to rest out on the circuit with an electrical fault. Nevertheless, at the appointed hour in the afternoon all fourteen starters left the pits right on time, completed the warm-up lap and formed on the dummy grid in readiness for the 3 p.m. start. At this stage everything seemed to be nicely back under control, but when the field was eventually signalled away for the pace lap Paletti's Osella remained motionless with an engine that refused to fire up and had to be subsequently push-started. Worse was to follow when, just over half way round the lap, the engine in Warwick's Toleman cut out again due to a recurrence of the electrical problem that had struck in the morning, thus ending the unfortunate Englishman's race before it had even started. Consequently, just twelve cars actually took the start (Paletti was still on his way round when the green lights went on) and then only eleven of them got away as Henton's first Grand Prix drive for Tyrrell terminated within a matter of yards with his 011 suffering a transmission

1982

failure. Arnoux, meanwhile, got off the line splendidly to shoot straight into the lead, but although he was followed into second place by his team-mate the possibility of a Renault demonstration run quickly evaporated. By the time that the leaders had reached Tosa, Villeneuve had already put himself in between the two yellow and white cars, and before the end of the lap Pironi had elbowed Prost back to fourth place. Following hard on their heels, Alboreto was fifth, busy keeping the two Alfa Romeos at bay, while Fabi had slotted into eighth place ahead of Jarier, the two ATS cars and the delayed Paletti.

At the end of the second lap the first five cars roared across the line in unchanged formation, but de Cesaris was already heading for the pits, his Alfa Romeo misfiring badly due to fuel pump trouble which, two laps later, was to put him out for good. Prost was also in trouble with his engine. It just wasn't pulling properly, and after seven laps of steadily losing contact with the trio ahead of him he, too, veered off into the pits where the number 15 Renault was retired with a suspected head gasket or valve failure. Paletti's debut didn't last much longer either as on the following lap he became the third driver to retire at the pits with his Osella having suffered a rear suspension breakage. This reduced the field to just nine cars. Fortunately, though, the leadership struggle was developing into a really intriguing situation, for although Arnoux had pulled out as much as 4 seconds on the two Ferraris during the opening phase they were now gaining on him. Further back, too, behind Alboreto and Giacomelli, who were becoming increasingly spaced out in fourth and fifth places, Fabi,

Jarier, Winkelhock and Salazar were engaged in a captivating dice for what had become sixth place. As the Ferraris gradually homed in on the leader, so this continued with Winkelhock scrambling past Jarier on the tenth lap and then jumping to the head of the little group seven laps later when Fabi, obviously thoroughly enjoying his first Grand Prix up to that point, was finally forced to concede his place due to a sudden drop in boost pressure. A pit stop located the problem to a split union on the Hart engine's boost-control unit but by the time that this had been rectified the Italian was several laps down and effectively out of contention. All the while the two Ferraris had been drawing ever closer to the Renault and were now well within striking distance. In fact, Villeneuve had already just had one brief stab at wrestling the lead away from Arnoux but had been forced to back off, and on lap 22 even found himself being passed by his team-mate. Four laps later, though, Villeneuve regained the second spot and then immediately launched an all-out attack on Arnoux, aiming his Ferrari for the inside of the Renault as they charged up the hill after Tosa before forcing his way past into the lead on the approach to the fast Piratella left-hander that followed. Naturally the crowd went wild and in their excitement probably failed to notice that Giacomelli had just stopped out on the circuit with the surviving Alfa Romeo having suffered an engine failure!

On lap 31 the crowd fell silent again which left no-one in any doubt that Arnoux had retaken the lead. Even so it seemed to be of little consequence, for the two Ferraris con-

tinued to remain tightly bunched up behind the Renault and all three drivers put on a wonderful display of motor racing at its very best. Time and again they would arrive at corners almost two or even three abreast and, although the order went unchanged apart from Pironi taking over second spot for his team-mate again on lap 35 before being repassed five laps later, it was an absolutely gripping spectacle. Towards the end of lap 44, however, ominous-looking puffs of blue smoke started appearing from the back of the Renault and as the leading trio roared past the pits to start another lap it was even thicker. Then there were flames – a turbocharger had caught fire – and suddenly, amidst thunderous applause from the crowd, the Ferraris were first and second, the unlucky Arnoux being forced to pull off to the side of the track just before Tosa for his car to receive the attention of the marshals. It now seemed all over, for in spite of Alboreto lapping as impressively as ever, the Tyrrell was by this time well over half a minute in arrears, while Jarier's Osella was the only other car still on the same lap. Winkelhock having just gone into the pits with his ignition system playing up, and Salazar having already lost time there a few minutes earlier with a gear-change problem. On lap 46, however, Pironi gave the first indication that there was more to come after all by forging ahead of Villeneuve when the French-Canadian started easing off slightly in order to conserve fuel, and in response to pit signals telling both drivers to slow down. Naturally, though, on seeing his team-mate go by, Villeneuve immediately speeded up again and on lap 49 retook the lead up the

The battle for supremacy in the poorly-attended San Marino Grand Prix, René Arnoux shown here hanging on to a slender advantage over the two Ferraris of Gilles Villeneuve and Didier Pironi. *(Autosport)*

hill after Tosa whilst in the midst of lapping Winkelhock's ATS. After that he slackened off once more, expecting Pironi to do the same, only for their positions to change again on lap 53, at which point it became clear that team orders were being thrown out of the window. The next few minutes were quite incredible with both drivers fighting tooth and nail to outwit one another until eventually, on the penultimate lap, Pironi appeared to momentarily lift off on the approach to Tosa enabling Villeneuve to move back in front. For a moment or two

this led to strong speculation that perhaps they had been playing games after all. But it soon proved to be nothing of the sort. Going into Tosa for the final time Pironi suddenly dived to the inside of his team-mate's car, left his braking as late as he dared and scrambled out of the hairpin as the race leader yet again. After that it really was all over with one deeply-incensed Villeneuve (he had firmly believed that a 'SLOW' signal meant hold position – after the race Pironi and Piccinini were to emphatically deny that

there were any team orders!) unable to do anything more about it other than to settle for a close, very close, second place. Just over a minute later Alboreto took a fine third place, Jarier was fourth to give Osella their first-ever Championship points, and Salazar was fifth. In spite of crossing the line in sixth place, ahead of Fabi who was too far behind to be classified in any case, Winkelhock was excluded from the results when his ATS was found to be under the minimum weight limit after the race – by just two kilogrammes!

Results						
1	D. Pironi (Ferrari)	1 hr 36 min 38.887 sec (187.732 kph/ 116.651 mph)	4	J.P. Jarier (Osella-Ford)	1 lap behind	*Disqualified
			5	E. Salazar (ATS-Ford)	3 laps behind	Fastest lap: D. Pironi (Ferrari) on lap 44 in 1 min 35.036 sec (190.917 kph/118.630 mph)
2	G. Villeneuve (Ferrari)	1 hr 36 min 39.253 sec	*	M. Winkelhock (ATS-Ford)	6 laps behind	**Retirements**
3	M. Alboreto (Tyrrell-Ford)	1 hr 37 min 46.571 sec		Also running at finish: T. Fabi (Toleman-Hart) 8 laps behind		B. Henton (Tyrrell-Ford) transmission on lap 1, A. de Cesaris (Alfa Romeo) fuel pump on lap 4, A. Prost (Renault) engine on lap 7, R. Paletti (Osella-Ford) rear suspension on lap 8, B. Giacomelli (Alfa Romeo) engine on lap 25, R. Arnoux (Renault) engine on lap 45.

XL Grote Prijs van Belgie

Zolder: May 9
Weather: Warm and sunny
Distance: 70 laps of 4.262 km circuit = 298.34 km (185.38 miles)

During the week following the San Marino Grand Prix the FIA Plenary Conference had taken place in Casablanca, and the opportunity used to set up a working group to try to reach a compromise over the FIA International Court of Appeal's decision that resulted in Nelson Piquet and Keke Rosberg being disqualified from the Brazilian Grand Prix. However, Ferrari's Marco Piccinini had expressed the view that the decision could not be questioned and that FOCA had no grounds for demanding any change. Consequently no progress had ensued and, instead, FOCA had decided to refer the matter to the International Chamber of Commerce in Lausanne for an independent judgement under the terms set out in the Concorde Agreement. At the same time, though, it stated that the FOCA teams (under threat of reduced sponsorship in the event of another Grand Prix being disrupted because of disputes arising from technical regulations) would be discontinuing their boycott and going to Belgium as originally planned, but with their cars ballasted to 580 kg and with every intention of causing as much disruption as possible when it came down to the interpretation of rules! And so this was the setting of what promised to be yet another extremely 'happy' weekend, not helped at all by a very strained atmosphere in the Ferrari camp caused by Gilles Villeneuve and Didier Pironi still being at loggerheads with one another after Imola and not even on speak-

ing terms.

Since the 1981 race the hopelessly inadequate pit area, that had contributed to the death of one of the Osella mechanics, had been replaced by an entirely new pits/paddock complex and a much wider pit lane. As a result there was now ample room for everyone, even allowing for the fact that a total of 32 entries materialized. By and large the driver line-up was the same as at Long Beach a month earlier, except that Brian Henton had taken over from Slim Borgudd at Tyrrell, following the return of Marc Surer to fitness,and Derek Daly had been signed up by Frank Williams to make up for the loss of the now-retired Carlos Reutemann; the Irishman's vacated seat at Theodore, meanwhile, having been filled by Dutchman Jan Lammers. In addition, a third March 821 had been entered by Mike Earle's Sussex-based Onyx operation for the self-financing Spaniard Emilio de Villota which appeared to differ from the Rothmans March cars run by John MacDonald only by being painted in a black colour scheme rather than blue and white. On the technical front, too, most of the teams brought along familiar cars, but again there were a few important changes. Primarily these involved the TAG Williams team producing three examples of their new FW08 design, which they were now ready to race using large water tanks (these were to be kept full!) to bring them up to the legal weight, and the Parmalat Brabham team

arriving with a trio of BMW turbo-charged BT50s in response to an ultimatum issued by the German firm to race their engine at Zolder or face the consequences! Although they had built them around existing designs, Marlboro McLaren and John Player Team Lotus also each had a brand new chassis on hand, and just about all of the other cars had undergone further detail modifications. Of these the most obvious was the spare Alfa Romeo, as this now featured narrower sidepods, designed to work in conjunction with longer skirts, and also a revised, swept-up exhaust system. Finally, after the tyre supply problems at Imola, Gunther Schmidt had ended his contract with Avon, much to their chagrin, and now had his ATS cars running on Michelins once more, as in 1981.

With such a full entry list the opening practice session on Friday morning, which started some 20 minutes late due to a shortage of doctors, effectively saw drivers in one of two categories. The first group, made up of Warwick, Fabi, Jarier, Paletti, Boesel and de Villota, was faced with the task of having to pre-qualify, and was thus racing against the clock, while the second was faced with the somewhat more casual, though no less important, business of sorting cars as a prelude to the first qualifying session. Amidst all of the activity quite a number of problems emerged, not least so far as Brabham were concerned, for although the BMW engines were lacking nothing in outright power they were showing a reluctance to pick up cleanly out of the corners. Consequently both Piquet and Patrese were far from pleased about the situation. Prost was in trouble in the engine department, too, only in his case it was an

1982

overheating problem that eventually led to the spare Renault being wheeled out. Just prior to this Rosberg had also switched to the spare Williams due to the brakes playing up on his intended race chassis and, after having started out in the modified Alfa Romeo, Giacomelli didn't take long before he was another to swop cars which suggested that the revisions offered little or nothing in the way of improvement. Then, towards the end of the session, the engine in Pironi's Ferrari suddenly cut out half way round the circuit and effectively ended activities for the morning, as by the time that the car had been retrieved the heavens had opened and everyone was scurrying for the shelter of the pits. So that was that, and for Paletti and de Villota it was the end of their weekend's work already by dint of having recorded the two slowest times out of the six drivers obliged to take part in pre-qualifying.

Fortunately the rain passed over as quickly as it had come, and by the start of the qualifying session the track was all but dry again. Because his race car had been found to be in need of an engine change Prost was still confined to the spare Renault, but was soon using it to such good effect that it seemed to be of little consequence. Indeed, before long both he and team-mate Arnoux were completely dominating the scene and, certainly by the time that they had gone through their two sets of tyres, were securely ensconced at the top of the time-sheets with laps of 1 min 15.962 sec and 1 min 15.903 sec respectively. Such was their superiority that no-one else could even break the 1 min 17 sec barrier, although Piquet, despite still being unhappy with the low-speed pick-up of his BMW engine, came very close with a fine effort that netted third fastest time of 1 min 17.124 sec. Alboreto, following another superb performance in his Tyrrell, Villeneuve, Lauda, Mansell, Rosberg (he had once again swopped cars due to more brake trouble) and de Cesaris were also well up there with all six drivers covered by less than four-tenths of a second but the rest, headed by Daly on his first public outing in the Williams, were well over 2 seconds off the pace. These included the likes of Patrese, whose run in the number 2 Brabham had been interrupted by a troublesome turbo-charger unit having to be replaced on his BMW engine; Pironi, who had made little impression in either his proposed race chassis, which had been put right during the interval, or the spare Ferrari that he had subsequently taken over; and Watson, who was complaining of handling problems and a down-on-power engine. As it was, all three had just scraped into the top half of the time-sheets along with Giacomelli and de Angelis. For Henton, meanwhile, the first day's practice had come to nought. At the end of the afternoon his Tyrrell was found to be 3 kilogrammes underweight, after being one of two cars selected at random to be checked, with the result that his lap times were scrubbed.

The weather was still far from settled on Saturday but, despite an ever-present threat of rain, conditions remained dry for both the untimed session in the morning and the final hour of qualifying in the afternoon. As always it was the afternoon session that really mattered and once this was under way it became apparent almost immediately that the front row of the grid was not necessarily going to be an all-Renault affair after all. Rosberg and Lauda, in particular, were in tremendous form, with both coming ever nearer to joining Arnoux and Prost in the sub-1 min 16 sec bracket, while the very impressive Alboreto was lapping only fractionally slower in his Tyrrell. This continued until eventually Rosberg put the cat amongst the pigeons in the best possible manner by turning in the fastest time yet of 1 min 15.847 sec, only to find Prost and Arnoux responding with even quicker laps of 1 min 15.701 sec and 1 min 15.730 sec respectively to re-establish themselves in the first two places. After that it was effectively over, as Rosberg's hopes of doing any better were thwarted by a return of the brake gremlins, and Lauda gave up early after deciding that he was unlikely to progress beyond 1 min 16.094 sec. Piquet, meanwhile, was in no position to offer any challenge at all because, apart from having to contend with a soft brake pedal, his BMW engine was suffering from a severe lack of boost pressure, a problem that persisted even after a new turbo-charger unit had been installed. In fact, the Brabham pit was in shambles as Patrese was experiencing similar trouble with the spare car that he had been obliged to take over in the morning – as a result of an engine blow up! Even the BMW competitions director, Dieter Stappert, was becoming increasingly bemused, not to mention embarrassed, by their plight, while Bernie Ecclestone was probably wishing that he had ignored the ultimatum and continued running Ford-Cosworth engines. Nevertheless, the problems were by no means confined to the Brabham team, for several other drivers were having their progress hampered as well. Among them were Winkelhock and Guerrero, who had both stopped with clutch trouble during the morning and were left waiting around while repairs were being effected; Daly, who, after having been forced to abandon his Williams with a badly misfiring engine at the start of the afternoon's activities, was finding the team's spare chassis still short on brakes; and Laffite, who returned to the pits midway through the session with something obviously amiss with the electrics on his Talbot. Giacomelli was yet another having his practice severely curtailed, but this was due more to a personal problem as he had jarred his back earlier in the day and was now hardly able to drive at all because of the pain. Consequently the Autodelta team's hopes were resting firmly on the shoulders of de Cesaris who was responding well, and he eventually went around in 1 min 16.575 sec to move up to seventh place on the time-sheets where he was sandwiched by the Ferraris of a much-improved Pironi (1 min 16.501 sec) and Villeneuve (1 min 16.616 sec). At this point, though, Villeneuve had used only his first set of qualifying tyres and was sitting patiently in his cockpit waiting to go out again, no doubt intent on beating his 'team-mate'. However, when the moment came to go out, with just 10 minutes of practice remaining, it was to lead to dire consequences and to prove conclusively the dangers faced by drivers being limited to just two sets of short-life qualifying tyres which were really only worth one good lap apiece, a regulation openly criticized time and again by Villeneuve and numerous others.

In the midst of what was to be his quick lap Villeneuve crested the rise after the first chicane and came up behind a slower-driving Mass. Obviously with no intention of lifting off, he then moved over to the right-hand side of the track to go past on the outside of the March through the fast left-hander that followed. At precisely the same moment, though, Mass moved the same way with the intention of letting the French-Canadian through to his inside – a simple misunderstanding that led to the Ferrari's left front wheel making contact with the right rear wheel of the March and to the red car instantly becoming airborne at well over 200 kph. Then, after remaining off the ground for quite some considerable distance and somersaulting, the Ferrari nose-dived into the sandy run-off area. After that it struck the guard-rail, cannoned off the bank and rapidly disintegrated with parts flying off in all directions, its luckless occupant being hurled out and left lying prone by the catch-fences on the opposite side of the track, minus his crash helmet. Naturally Mass, who was fortunate not to have been struck again by the ill-fated Ferrari, stopped immediately on the grass verge. From there he rushed over to where Villeneuve lay and within moments was joined by Arnoux, Warwick and a doctor before arrangements were made for a helicopter to fly him off to a nearby hospital, unconscious and suffering from a broken neck as well as severe spinal injuries. In the meantime, of course, practice was stopped and although it was eventually allowed to resume once the track had been cleared only a handful of drivers had any inclination to go out again. Even then none of them made any hoped-for improvement on their lap times in the few minutes remaining, notably the Brabham duo and a few of the tail-enders, and the afternoon finally drew to a close on a very unhappy note for everyone.

On Saturday evening came the tragic, though not unexpected, news that Gilles Villeneuve had succumbed to his appalling injuries. Consequently, it came as no surprise to learn that by the following morning Enzo Ferrari had withdrawn both of his cars from the race as a mark of respect for his extremely talented and well-liked driver. There then followed a meeting to discuss the potential danger of having a large gap on the right-hand side of the grid where the two Ferraris would have been and eventually it was decided to draw up a revised starting

order. As a result de Cesaris was moved up to the third row alongside Alboreto; Mansell and Piquet were promoted to the fourth row, and so on right back to Mass and Baldi who were allowed to bring the field back up to twenty-six even though they had originally been ruled out as non-qualifers. So in the end, apart from Paletti and de Villota, only Guerrero and Lammers were left out in the cold, the Colombian Ensign driver being particularly unfortunate due to the clutch problem he had managed to squeeze in only two timed laps on Saturday whereas on Friday he had ended up 19th fastest.

The mid-day warm-up session produced late problems for Prost (turbo-charger failure) and Rosberg (high-speed engine misfire) but, that apart, everything went off reasonably well. This was particularly true so far as de Cesaris, Lauda and Watson were concerned, as they turned in the three fastest times; the Ulsterman, no doubt, hoping to quickly make up for his rather lowly grid position once the race was under way. The weather, meanwhile, had improved considerably after the dull and overcast conditions throughout practice as the skies had cleared and a warm sun was beating down. Even this, though, did nothing to dispel the gloom caused by the previous afternoon's accident but, as always, the show had to go on and a few minutes before 3.30 p.m. everyone was making final preparations for the start, Prost's Renault fitted with two new turbo-charger units and Rosberg's Williams with a fresh engine. But now there was soon to be another problem: Mansell's clutch mechanism failed on the pace lap and as the field returned to face the starting lights the young Englishman was unable to select first gear. Worse, in his efforts to try to force the Lotus into gear when the green lights went on, he stalled the engine and despite immediately raising his arm to warn the others was not spotted by Giacomelli until it was almost too late. Then, in abruptly swerving to the right to avoid the stationary car, the Italian forced Laffite over into Salazar's path, wheels touched and in the next instant the ATS was half spinning across the front of the Talbot and on into the Alfa Romeo, sending both cars skating off to the side of the track and out of the race. Somehow Laffite and the others that followed all managed to take evasive action amidst the confusion, made all the worse by Warwick also stalling his engine on the line, and were safely on their way with the two Englishmen eventually joining in after both receiving push-starts. In the meantime, Prost had just made one of his poorer starts and been elbowed back to third place by Arnoux and an impressive-looking Rosberg who had slotted his Williams into second place at the first corner. This was still the order at the end of the opening lap with Lauda well up in fourth place followed by de Cesaris, Alboreto, Patrese, Piquet, Watson,

de Angelis and Daly; this last pair about to swop places in front of Cheever who led the rest except for Winkelhock. Incredibly the second ATS was also out of the race already, with clutch failure.

Initially Arnoux gave every impression of pulling away from Rosberg but a small gap that appeared between them during the first couple of laps rapidly began to shrink again until by lap 5 there was nothing in it. Then, as they went through the double right-hander on the far side of the circuit, the Renault suddenly slowed owing to a loss of power, Rosberg flashed past into the lead and Arnoux ended the lap by diving into the pits. There a new set of tyres were slapped on, the engine quickly checked over and Arnoux sent back out into the fray only to stop again twice on successive laps before the Renault was finally retired with a broken spindle in the right-hand compressor unit. To make matters worse for the French team, Prost was losing ground hand over fist due to erratic handling. He had already dropped behind Lauda and de Cesaris just prior to his team-mate's demise, and on lap 9 was elbowed down to sixth place by Patrese and a fast-rising Watson, Alboreto having just slipped to seventh spot but still going well ahead of Piquet and Daly. Meanwhile, Rosberg was maintaining a 3 second advantage out in front with Lauda, who had de Cesaris hard on his heels, seemingly unable to do anything about it. As this continued, with little change, Mansell was forced to retire with a broken gearbox after nine laps as a result of changing gear without a clutch, and minutes later, in quick succession, the two Tolemans were also in the pits, both drivers complaining of being short on brakes. In fact, Fabi had already stopped once a few laps earlier and this time decided to give up the unequal struggle. Warwick, on the other hand, rejoined the race but quickly discovered that a fresh set of Pirellis was inducing chronic oversteer! At the end of lap 17, after having been passed by Alboreto, Prost veered off into the pit lane as well to see whether a change of Michelins would do anything to improve the handling of his Renault – just as the closely-following Piquet missed his braking point for the last chicane, shot across the grass and lost his place to Daly! After that the World Champion was soon struggling to stay ahead of Jarier, Cheever and Laffite due to the onset of gear-change problems.

By lap 20 Rosberg was already beginning to lap back-markers and for a minute or so it seemed as if this might well provide Lauda with the opportunity of mounting a serious challenge for the lead, as the gap started to come down. Once out of the traffic, though, Rosbert responded by pulling away again, and on lap 30 Serra helped him to extend his lead still further, to over 10 seconds, by spinning right in front of Lauda at the first corner. Fortunately, by standing on his brakes, the Austrian managed to avoid the gyrating Fittipaldi and was soon on his way again, but not before de Cesaris had made the most of the opportunity to slice past into second place. Any hopes that the Italian may have had of catching Rosberg, however, disappeared almost immediately as on lap 35 the Alfa Romeo suddenly went coasting to rest with broken gear linkage – the end of an impressive drive. Less than five laps earlier Alboreto's impressive drive in sixth place had also been ended abruptly by his Tyrrell blowing up its engine, and since then his team-mate had gone out for similar reasons, while Warwick had just retired the surviving Toleman with a broken drive-shaft. The field was thinning rapidly. It was also becoming increasingly spaced out, as prior to this latest string of retirements de Angelis, Jarier and Baldi had all been delayed at the pits having worn tyres replaced, Prost had stopped a second time for yet another set of Michelins (still to no avail) and, on lap 29, Piquet had also turned into the pit lane only to have carried on without stopping – it transpired that his Brabham had jammed in gear and that whilst he had been slowing down it had freed itself! Even so the gearbox was still playing up so it was hardly surprising that he was now a lap behind the leaders and down in ninth place between Mass and de Angelis. Ahead of him, meanwhile, his team-mate in the other BMW-powered Brabham had been doing an excellent job of keeping Watson at bay and, in spite of having finally succumbed to the Ulsterman's sustained pressure on lap 31, was still running strongly, now in fourth place and well clear of Daly and also the two Talbots of Cheever and Laffite who were right up together, and the only others not yet to have been lapped.

Although Lauda now had a clear run at Rosberg, he was again unable to offer any sort of challenge, as even before the incident with Serra he had been forced to ease off slightly to conserve his tyres, particularly the left front which was wearing badly. Consequently Rosberg continued to draw away and before long more attention was being focused on Watson, the Ulsterman having started out on a harder compound than Lauda and now steadily catching his team-mate. This continued until lap 46, by which time the two McLarens were running nose to tail. Then, as they arrived at the first corner at the start of the next lap, Watson neatly went by under braking and quickly knuckled down to the task of trying to reel in the leader. However, at this stage his chances of progressing any further looked remote, for Rosberg was now almost 20 seconds clear. In fact, though, the chances were better than they seemed as the Finn was also in trouble, his left rear Goodyear wearing away along with the Williams' rear brakes. Lower down the order, meanwhile, Jarier had just become the latest addition to a growing retirement list, with a buckled rear aerofoil resulting from taking off too soon from a second tyre stop and collecting an air-hose to one of the pneumatic spanners. On lap 53 Patrese also disappeared, the Italian being caught out on deteriorating tyres and spinning off into the catch-fences to end a certain finish in the points. Moments later Piquet very nearly went off at the same spot but, despite running wide and spinning, managed to regain the track and continued on his way. Just before this, Laffite had overdone things as well while having a spirited dice with his team-mate, and was about to undergo a lengthy stop at the pits having a damaged

skirt replaced. So one way and another the twisty little circuit was certainly taking its toll.

By lap 60 Watson had reduced the gap to Rosberg to a whisker over 10 seconds and was gaining on him by whole seconds each time round, bringing the race to a thrilling climax. To add to the excitement Cheever had earlier moved right in on Daly's tail and was now challenging hard for what had become fourth place. Like Rosberg, though, Daly was suffering from worn tyres and fading brakes, and on lap 61 finally overstepped the mark under braking for the first corner and slid gently off into the catch-fences leaving Cheever to continue on his own. Watson, meanwhile, had now brought the gap to Rosberg down to less than 8 seconds, but then it suddenly began to level out and even increase slightly which led to all kinds of speculation. In fact, Watson had eased up after incorrectly assuming that it was Rosberg's Williams that had gone off at the first corner and it was not until he had passed the pits a couple more times and read the signals that the message sank in. After that, of course, he immediately speeded up once more and, aided by a new fastest lap on his 67th tour, was soon within striking distance of the green and white car ahead of him. Then, on the penultimate lap, the chase was over. Rosberg, with his left rear tyre now virtually down to the canvas and coming up to lap Surer's Arrows, left his braking a fraction too late for the hairpin and slid just wide enough for Watson to squeeze by into the lead. In no position to retaliate, the disappointed Finn then had to settle for second place for his third race on the trot, finishing a shade over 7 seconds behind a very happy and satisfied Watson. A minute

John Watson, benefiting from comparatively hard Michelin tyres fitted to his McLaren MP4B, drove a well-judged race and took the lead on the penultimate lap. *(Phipps Photographic)*

or so later Lauda duly crossed the line in third place, but there was an even bigger disappointment in store for him as in post-race scrutineering the first seven cars were all weighed and his McLaren found to be 2 kilogrammes under weight. As a result the

Austrian was disqualified and his third place awarded to Cheever. After that only six others were left, including de Angelis' fourth-placed Lotus 91 which completed the race with a broken exhaust, as during the closing minutes Mass had dropped out

because of an engine failure, Baldi had spun off when the throttle stuck on his Arrows and Prost's miserable afternoon had also ended off the track after finally being caught out by the atrocious handling of his Renault.

Results

1	J. Watson (McLaren-Ford)	1 hr 35 min 41.995 sec (187.047 kph/ 116.225 mph)
2	K. Rosberg (Williams-Ford)	1 hr 35 min 49.263 sec
*	N. Lauda (McLaren-Ford)	1 hr 36 min 50.132 sec
3	E. Cheever (Talbot-Matra)	1 lap behind
4	E. de Angelis (Lotus-Ford)	2 laps behind
5	N. Piquet (Brabham-BMW)	3 laps behind
6	F. Serra (Fittipaldi-Ford)	3 laps behind
7	M. Surer (Arrows-Ford)	4 laps behind
8	R. Boesel (March-Ford)	4 laps behind
9	J. Laffite (Talbot-Matra)	4 laps behind

*Disqualified

Fastest lap: J. Watson (McLaren-Ford) on lap 67 in 1 min 20.214 sec (191.278 kph/ 118.854 mph)

Retirements

B. Giacomelli (Alfa Romeo) accident on lap 1, E. Salazar (ATS-Ford) accident on lap 1, M. Winkelhock (ATS-Ford) clutch on lap 1, R. Arnoux (Renault) turbo-charger on lap 8, N. Mansell (Lotus-Ford) gearbox on lap 10, T. Fabi (Toleman-Hart) brakes on lap 14, D. Warwick (Toleman-Hart) drive-shaft on lap 30, M. Alboreto (Tyrrell-Ford) engine on lap 30, B. Henton (Tyrrell-Ford) engine on lap 34, A. de Cesaris (Alfa Romeo) gear linkage on lap 35, J.P. Jarier (Osella-Ford) rear aerofoil on lap 38, M. Baldi (Arrows-Ford) spun off on lap 52, R. Patrese (Brabham-BMW) spun off on lap 53, A. Prost (Renault) spun off on lap 60, J. Mass (March-Ford) engine on lap 61, D. Daly (Williams-Ford) spun off on lap 61.

XLᵉ Grand Prix de Monaco

Monte Carlo: May 23
Weather: Changeable
Distance: 76 laps of 3.312 km circuit = 251.71 km (156.41 miles)

Apart from the sad absence of Gilles Ville-neuve, the driver line-up for the Monaco Grand Prix was the same as at Zolder a fortnight earlier and because only 26 cars were being allowed to take part in official practice a special 60 minute pre-qualifying session was held early on the Thursday morning to reduce the numbers accordingly. Selected for 'weeding-out' were the drivers of teams who had failed to score any Championship points in 1981 which meant Warwick and Fabi (Toleman), Jarier and Paletti (Osella), Mass, Boesel and de Villota (March) and Serra (Fittipaldi). It was then quite simply a case of the three fastest being granted the right to join the remaining twenty-three drivers to have a crack at qualifying for the 20-car grid, and to the other five being ruled out. Of course, in the current 'happy' state of Grand Prix racing it wasn't as simple as it might have been. At the end of the hour Toleman's Alex Hawk-ridge, peeved that Fabi had come out fourth fastest behind Jarier, Mass and Warwick, lodged a protest against the March team not presenting the car in which Mass had set his best time for weighing, and was suggesting that it was underweight. However, with no way of checking the car because by then it had been partially stripped down following a reported valve spring failure that had led to Mass swopping chassis in the first place, the organizers refused to take any action and the matter was dropped.

An hour later, at 10 a.m. it was time for the more serious part of the day's pro-gramme to begin. For the Ensign and Theo-dore teams, though, there were immediate problems – no tyres! Shortly after the Bel-gian Grand Prix Avon/IRTS had announced that they were pulling out of Formula 1 and had subsequently sold off their entire stock of tyres to John MacDonald, a test session at Croix-en-Ternois in northern France having seen the March 821s perform much better on Avon rubber than the Pirelli rubber pre-viously used. Consequently Mo Nunn and Teddy Yip had both been left high and dry and, in spite of being hopeful of obtaining tyres from Goodyear upon their arrival at Monaco, were finding that none were forth-coming. Fortunately the Ensign team at least had some partly worn covers with them left over from a previous race meeting which meant that Guerrero could do some practice, but Lammers was completely out of work as the Theodore team had no tyres whatsoever and demonstrated the fact by leaving their car jacked up in the pits with four bare wheels. Practice also started off on a low note for Talbot-Ligier. Having brought along two of their brand new and long-awaited JS19s the scrutineers determined that their long side-skirts infringed the rules, and they forced the French team to carry out hurried modifications so that these did not extend beyond the centre line of the rear axles. This, in turn, not only led to the loss of a considerable amount of down-force and to the cars' handling becoming unbalanced, but also to an incensed Guy Ligier threatening to withdraw from the race. The others, mean-while, were soon busy familiarizing them-selves and their cars with the surroundings,

as well as carrying out various running adjustments for the first hour of qualifying. Prost and Arnoux were particularly pleased with the way in which a new electronic fuel-injection system devised by their team was working, for this was making a signifi-cant improvement to throttle response and generally creating more torque from the V6 engine out of the corners which, of course, was of paramount importance on a circuit such as this. In fact, both drivers were brim-ming with more confidence than usual, even though Prost had to abandon his car out on the circuit at one point following an electrical failure. Since Belgium, revisions had also been carried out to the BMW-powered Brabham BT50s, again with the emphasis on improving engine torque only by modifying the turbo-charger units. Unlike the Renault duo, however, Piquet was still not very impressed and even less so at the end of the morning as by then both his proposed race car and the spare were out of action – one in need of a new turbo unit and the other a new engine! As if to rub the salt in, Patrese, back to using a Ford-Cosworth-powered BT49D while his team-mate carried out the develop-ment work of the turbo-charged project, had no trouble at all and was right up amongst the early pace-setters. Elsewhere, too, the only real problems seemed to be some of the drivers having difficulties in balancing their cars or complaining of lack of traction out of the corners, although Watson had the engine in his McLaren blow up in a big way coming out of the tunnel on one lap, Henton bent a rear rocker arm on his Tyrrell after clipping the chicane and Mansell underwent the somewhat painful experience of being hit in the eye by a small stone – after driving with his visor slightly raised to keep cool!

Prost's luck deserted him again soon after

the start of the afternoon's qualifying session when, on this occasion, his engine blew up. As a result he was obliged to concentrate his efforts on the team's spare car which was not yet fitted with the new electronic fuel-injection system. Shortly afterwards Cheever also had to abandon his new Talbot for similar reasons and take over the spare JS17, while Watson was already in the spare McLaren following his engine failure in the morning. Apart from the unemployed Lammers, though, the rest were in the cars that they intended using for the race, including Piquet whose mechanics had replaced the broken turbo-charger unit during the interval. As anticipated, with conditions remaining warm and dry, the pace out on the track now really began to hot up, the front-runners lapping well inside Piquet's pole-winning time of 1 min 25.710 sec for the 1981 race almost immediately and soon even hovering around Pironi's best practice lap of 1 min

24.813 sec set in 1980 in the days of full ground-effect. Leading the way was Arnoux, but Patrese was still looking most impressive as well and, along with de Cesaris, who had his Alfa Romeo well on song, spent much of the afternoon trading fastest times with the Frenchman. In the end, though, it was Arnoux who had the final word after finding a gap in the traffic and turning in a superb time of 1 min 24.543 sec compared to de Cesaris's and Patrese's best efforts of 1 min 24.928 sec and 1 min 24.929 sec respectively, Patrese complaining bitterly afterwards that his compatriot had held him up on at least two occasions! The new Williams FW08s of Rosberg and Daly were featuring strongly, too, with both drivers now happy with their brakes following further testing, but finding the cars lacking slightly in the handling department. Nevertheless, this did nothing to prevent Rosberg from achieving fourth fastest time of 1 min 25.125 sec or Daly from being next at 1 min 25.505 sec. Prost, Lauda (in spite of losing an engine towards the end of the afternoon) and Alboreto also achieved laps in the 1 min 25 sec bracket to take the next three places on the time-sheets, while Piquet, after a relatively trouble-free outing, finished up ninth fastest ahead of Giacomelli and the others. Once again Henton managed to clip the chicane but, apart from damaging a rear wheel, got away with it.

As usual, in Monaco, Friday was set aside for participants of various supporting events, including the prestigious Formula 3 race, but on Saturday the streets of the Principality were once again echoing to the sweet sound of Formula 1 engines. Since Thursday Renault had transported in their test car, RE34B, as Prost had expressed a preference to it rather than the two cars that he had been using and, similarly, Williams now had their test car (the second in the new FW08 series) available as a spare for Daly to use should he have need of it. Apart from this, everything was much as before except that Teddy Yip had finally managed to persuade Goodyear to supply his team with some tyres, which meant that Lammers could at last join in and set about trying to qualify for the race. During the morning the 90 minutes of untimed practice was supposed to provide everyone with the opportunity to carry out further testing, but for a number of drivers it didn't exactly go as planned owing to a magnitude of various problems. Some were more serious than others, with Piquet being one of the first to be afflicted when the drive-belt to the fuel-injection pump of his BMW engine broke and brought him to rest just beyond the swimming pool complex. Arnoux (electrical failure), Mansell (no fuel pressure) and Giacomelli (fuel pump trouble) also had to abandon their cars out on the circuit during the course of the morning but, whereas Arnoux and Mansell were subsequently able to join Piquet in taking

over their spare cars once they had walked back to the pits, Giacomelli was out of luck. De Cesaris had already commandeered the spare Alfa Romeo, with the narrower side-pods, after his car had developed a seemingly incurable misfire! In the meantime, Prost was having his progress in the Renault test car hampered by excessive skirt wear, Warwick made contact with the guard-rail at La Rascasse and put a kink in the monocoque of the Toleman that he had been hoping to use for qualifying, actually Fabi's car, and among others not having a particularly happy time of it, de Angelis found his proposed race car running with a persistent misfire and his spare Lotus understeering badly. Just before the end of the session Daly also struck trouble when his Williams broke a valve spring so it was just as well that his team had brought along their test car, for now he was going to need it for the final hour of qualifying.

When it came round to the all-important hour of qualifying, Piquet and de Cesaris were also still confined to their teams' spare cars, but the other ravages of the morning had all been put right, except for Warwick being forced to use his own Toleman. Fortunately, rather less in the way of trouble occurred this time round which meant that everyone was able to concentrate on the job in hand largely unimpeded. Arnoux's Renault was certainly back on song, as was Giacomelli's Alfa Romeo, both drivers out setting the fastest times along with a very on-form Patrese. Now that more and more rubber had been laid down, Thursday's times were soon looking slow by comparison as all three were comfortably lapping in the 1 min 24 sec bracket and setting a cracking pace. Once Arnoux had gone through his first set of qualifying tyres, though, it was Patrese who stole the limelight by setting an entirely new standard and going around in 1 min 23.791 sec which not only moved him to the top of the time-sheets but also looked unbeatable. Even so Arnoux took it all in his stride as he sat in the pits waiting to go out on his second set of qualifiers and then, after mentally preparing himself for a counter-attack, responded magnificently in the closing minutes of practice by finding the clear track that he needed and regaining the pole convincingly with a much superior time of 1 min 23.281 sec. Naturally the Renault pit was the scene of jubilation and although Patrese went away bitterly disappointed he at least had the consolation of knowing that he would be starting the race from the front row of the grid as the nearest anyone else came to beating him was Giacomelli at 1 min 23.923 sec. In fact, only three other drivers had even managed to break the 1 min 25 sec barrier by the end of the afternoon. These were Prost (1 min 24.439 sec), Pironi (1 min 24.585 sec) bringing a crumb of comfort to an understandably very subdued Ferrari pit, and Rosberg (1 min 24.649 sec) who duly filled the next three places on the grid, de Cesaris having slipped to seventh place after failing to improve in the spare Alfa Romeo. Piquet had also failed to improve in the spare Brabham-BMW which left the reigning World Champion faced with the prospects of starting the race in a lowly thirteenth position. However, an even bigger surprise, especially after his recent performance, was to find Lauda only one place higher after he, too, had failed to pick up his lap times for no obvious reason other than being unhappy with the handling of his McLaren MP4B. Among the rest, all of whom had found some extra speed, Laffite and Cheever had managed to qualify their new, hastily modified Talbots without too much difficulty, but those less successful were Warwick, after being plagued by engine pick-up problems with his Toleman, Baldi, Mass, Jarier and, not surprisingly, in view of their restricted practice, Lammers and Guerrero. Nevertheless, for a moment or two after practice it looked as if Baldi might be in the race after all – at the expense of his team-leader – as when Surer's Arrows was one of the cars selected at random for weighing the scrutineers discovered some loose lead ballast wrapped in plastic foam in the cockpit and this was against the rules. Fortunately the car was still over the minimum weight limit even without this and so it proved to be rather academic except that it cost the Arrows team a FF3,000 fine!

After a bright start, the weather gradually deteriorated on Sunday and, by the time that Prince Rainer and Princess Grace were officially opening the circuit in traditional manner by touring around in a Rolls Royce, conditions had already become dull and overcast. Nevertheless, it was remaining dry so slick tyres were the order of the day as the twenty starters began leaving the pits shortly afterwards to form up on the dummy grid; a few of the drivers, including Rosberg and Daly in their Williams, squeezing in a second lap by running through the pit lane. Earlier, during an otherwise trouble-free warm-up session, Cheever's new Talbot had suffered a drive-shaft failure but this had since been put right. Like the American, everyone else was in the cars that they had originally intended using for the race, with just one exception. That was Prost who had been fastest in the warm-up and was sticking to the Renault test car (RE34B) that had been specially brought in for Saturday's practice. On the dummy grid, final preparations were completed and then, just a couple of minutes or so before the appointed start time of 3.30 p.m. Arnoux led the field away on the pace lap. Round they went until they were all back on the grid once more, engine notes rose and seconds later the 40th Monaco Grand Prix was on with Arnoux making an absolutely impeccable start that saw him snap straight into the

lead and dispel any hope that Patrese may have had of beating him off the line immediately. For a change the entire field actually made it through Ste. Devote intact, although a highly frustrated de Angelis was left bringing up the rear after he had been badly boxed in behind Piquet, the World Champion having had difficulty in getting the Brabham-BMW under way. Naturally, though, it was all eyes on the leaders and on Arnoux in particular for he was really putting the hammer down with even Giacomelli, who took over Patrese's second place on the rise up to the Casino, unable to stay with him. Prost was looking very strong in the other Renault as well and as they roared past the pits to complete the first lap was already lining himself up to go through on the inside of Patrese under braking for Ste. Devote. Two laps later Prost also made it past Giacomelli's Alfa Romeo and before long it looked as if the two Renaults were going to have the race to themselves, especially when Giacomelli suddenly slowed and ended his fifth lap by turning off into the pits to become the first retirement with a broken drive-shaft. Behind Patrese, meanwhile, the order was staying much the same as on the first lap with Pironi, next along, being pursued by de Cesaris, Alboreto and Rosberg. Then, after a gap, came Mansell, Daly, Watson, Winkelhock and Lauda with the rest strung out behind including de Angelis who was busy picking off tail-enders after his delayed start.

The Renault demonstration run continued until lap 15 with Arnoux holding the gap

between himself and team-mate Prost to around 7 seconds. But then, as the leader arrived at the swimming pool complex, his car suddenly got away from him, spun round and subsequently came to rest almost in the middle of the track with a stalled engine. Somehow he had managed to avoid the barriers, but restarting the engine proved to be an impossibility and eventually, after the rest of the field had scrambled past, Arnoux began to make his way forlornly back to the pits while his car was unceremoniously hoisted off the track by a crane. So now Prost led, but within a couple of laps his position was not looking very secure either as a 6 second gap that had opened up to Patrese rapidly started to dwindle due to Salazar, whom he was about to lap, refusing to move over for almost half a lap even though the Chilean was about to stop and have his rear aerofoil adjusted. In fact, by the time that Prost had also lapped Henton's Tyrrell, which he came across limping round to the pits with a punctured left rear tyre, and Surer's Arrows, he was left with only a few car lengths leeway over Patrese. Pironi was right up there, too, as was de Cesaris, while Rosberg was not much further away in fifth place after having just found a way past Alboreto. Mansell was next and still being pursued by Daly, but the Lotus 91 was throwing out so much oil that the Irishman eventually fell behind Watson on lap 25 whilst in the midst of trying to clean his visor! At that point Salazar had just parked his ATS on the rise after Ste. Devote and scram-

Didier Pironi (Ferrari) and Andrea de Cesaris (Alfa Romeo) follow the Ford-Cosworth-powered Brabham of eventual winner Riccardo Patrese into Ste. Devote during the early stages of the race. *(Phipps Photographic)*

bled out at speed covered in foam after the on-board fire extinguisher had triggered itself. Not many more minutes passed before both of the new Talbots also departed the scene after making little impression: Cheever pulled out with his Matra engine lacking oil, and Laffite joined him in the pits almost immediately afterwards complaining that he had had enough of struggling against erratic handling. On lap 32 Winkelhock became yet another retirement when his ATS coasted to rest with a transmission failure at Casino Square, but this went largely unnoticed as all attention was fixed on the leaders for, having pulled away again slightly, Prost was once more losing ground due to being baulked, this time by de Angelis. For virtually the entire lap the Italian simply refused to move over as he chased after Piquet, and only as they filed out of the swimming pool complex could Prost do anything about it, by which time Patrese was close enough to follow him through. Pironi was there as well but this nearly ended in disaster for as the Frenchman drew alongside the Lotus de Angelis swooped back on to the racing line for La Rascasse and promptly tore off the Ferrari's nose cone with his left rear wheel, inducing understeer, though fortunately nothing worse. Piquet, next in line to be lapped with his Brabham-BMW now popping and banging as well as running into gearbox problems, was no easy proposition either, and again it took the best part of a lap for Prost and his immediate pursuers to get by. Once clear of the traffic, though, Prost quickly started to reassert himself and left Patrese and Pironi disputing second place, de Cesaris soon beginning to drop back into Rosberg's clutches after missing a gear change and taking the edge off his engine by letting the revs run wild. Watson, meanwhile, quietly disappeared into the pits after thirty-six laps to retire his McLaren with ignition trouble.

By lap 50 Prost had extended his lead to over 6 seconds and, although Patrese had now shaken off Pironi's understeering Ferrari, any chance of progressing beyond second place looked slim indeed. It seemed as if stale-mate had set in throughout the rest of the field, too, for apart from a minor reshuffle caused by Mansell having called at the pits at the end of lap 47 to replace the left front wheel of his Lotus after glancing the barriers, the order was staying completely unchanged. Only Rosberg was creating much in the way of excitement by making repeated, albeit abortive, attempts to displace de Cesaris, a situation that continued right through until lap 65 when the Finn finally got too close to the Alfa Romeo at the chicane, hit the kerb with the right front wheel of his Williams and broke the suspension. By then Piquet had given up the unequal struggle with his ailing Brabham-BMW and Lauda had retired the surviving McLaren when he felt the engine start to tighten after having been down on power all afternoon. Consequently, with just over eleven laps remaining only ten cars were left – and now it was raining! It was not a downpour but rather a steady light drizzle making the track just damp enough to be really treacherous. Even so, this sudden change in conditions appeared to make little immediate difference with everyone pressing on as hard as ever, and although Alboreto disappeared after only five laps of running in fifth place this was due entirely to the rear suspension breaking on his Tyrrell in the vicinity of the swimming pool. However, a few minutes later came the first sign of trouble when Daly's Williams lost adhesion on the slippery surface at Tabac, half spun and struck the guard-rail on the outside of the corner with such force that the entire rear aerofoil assembly of the car was torn asunder, along with the gearbox oil pump. The impact also cracked the gearbox casing, allowing the lubricant to start seeping away, but Daly kept the engine running and continued unaware of the full extent of the damage, still in fifth place. Prost, meanwhile, looked to be well on the way to notching up his sixth Grand Prix victory, the Frenchman now holding a near 10 second advantage and having lapped everyone bar Patrese, Pironi and de Cesaris. In fact, he had just lapped de Angelis for the second time in a somewhat fraught episode at Ste. Devote which had seen the two cars making contact and the Renault's left rear wheel glancing the barriers, an incident that may well have contributed to what was to happen only a couple of minutes later. Whatever, as Prost exited the chicane on lap 74 the Renault suddenly went out of control and charged the barriers on the right-hand side of the track. From there it rebounded backwards into the barriers on the opposite side, spun through 180 degrees and finished up sideways almost in the middle of the track amidst flying bodywork and minus its right front wheel. Fortunately, apart from hurting a foot, Prost emerged unscathed from the wreckage but, naturally, was absolutely furious with himself as Patrese went past the scene into the lead. However, it was not over yet by any means.

On the very next lap, the penultimate, Patrese was also caught out by the slippery surface. Going downhill from the Mirabeau the back of his Brabham suddenly snapped out of line, gently swopped ends and stopped just short of the barriers on the apex of the Loews hairpin with a stalled engine. Eventually, with the engine refusing to restart, some marshals arrived to push the Brabham out of what was considered to be a dangerous position. Then, after being able to take advantage of the downhill section leading to Portier, Patrese managed to bump-start the engine and was on his way again only now in third place behind Pironi and de Cesaris. But even at this late stage the final outcome was still not settled, as on the last lap the somewhat bizarre succession of events continued with first de Cesaris's Alfa Romeo spluttering to a halt at Massenet out of fuel and, then, incredibly, Pironi's Ferrari stopping in the tunnel with its electronic fuel-injection system no longer working due to the car's battery having gone flat. Suddenly Patrese was back in the lead! Furthermore, this time he stayed there and finally completed the 76th lap to clinch a somewhat bewildering, though nonetheless joyful, first Grand Prix victory. Despite failing to finish, Pironi and de Cesaris were classified second and third respectively, while fourth place went to a hard-charging Mansell after he had overtaken team-mate de Angelis's rough sounding Lotus (the exhaust manifold pipe had broken several laps earlier) on the last lap and then led him past Daly's Williams which had ground to a halt at La Rascasse moments earlier with a seized gearbox. After that Henton's Tyrrell and Surer's Arrows, running with a very off-colour engine, were the only other cars to take the chequered flag, and so ended a Grand Prix that had just produced the most dramatic climax seen in years.

Results

1	R. Patrese (Brabham-Ford)	1 hr 54 min 11.259 sec (132.262 kph/ 82.184 mph)	
*2	D. Pironi (Ferrari)	1 lap behind	
*3	A. de Cesaris (Alfa Romeo)	1 lap behind	
4	N. Mansell (Lotus-Ford)	1 lap behind	
5	E. de Angelis (Lotus-Ford)	1 lap behind	
*6	D. Daly (Williams-Ford)	2 laps behind	
*7	A. Prost (Renault)	3 laps behind	
8	B. Henton (Tyrrell-Ford)	4 laps behind	
9	M. Surer (Arrows-Ford)	6 laps behind	
*10	M. Alboreto (Tyrrell-Ford)	7 laps behind	

*Not running at finish

Fastest lap: R. Patrese (Brabham-Ford) on lap 69 in 1 min 26.354 sec (138.073 kph/85.794 mph)

Retirements

B. Giacomelli (Alfa Romeo) drive-shaft on lap 5, R. Arnoux (Renault) stalled engine on lap 15, E. Salazar (ATS-Ford) fire extinguisher on lap 22, E. Cheever (Talbot-Matra) engine on lap 28, J. Laffite (Talbot-Matra) handling on lap 30, M. Winkelhock (ATS-Ford) transmission on lap 32, J. Watson (McLaren-Ford) ignition on lap 36, N. Piquet (Brabham-BMW) engine/gearbox on lap 50, N. Lauda (McLaren-Ford) engine on lap 57, K. Rosberg (Williams-Ford) front suspension on lap 65.

1st United States (Detroit) Grand Prix

Detroit: June 6
Weather: Warm and dry
Duration: 2 hours (62 laps of 4.0126 km circuit = 248.78 km (154.58 miles)

from Toleman, who had been forced to give the race a miss due to problems with their transporter whilst on its journey home from Monaco (this had put them hopelessly behind schedule), they had all made special efforts to arrive early. Now, after a mad rush, it had proved futile.

Unfortunately the situation was little better on Friday as at 10 o'clock, when official practice was due to start, work was still in progress installing more guard-rail and

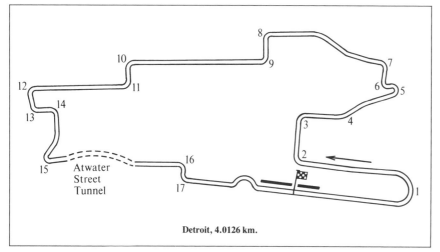

Detroit, 4.0126 km.

After just three races on the mainland of Europe the Grand Prix 'circus' returned to North America for a busy schedule that was to encompass two races on consecutive weekends. The first stop was of particular interest as it was a completely new venue – Detroit, the 'capital' of the United States automobile industry. It had all come about from an idea in 1981 to form part of a multi-million dollar campaign going on to try to restore the city's image which had been deteriorating rapidly since the early '70s due to a recession in the industry and problems associated with the resultant high unemployment. In fact, efforts to change things round had, by now, already been in progress for some five years under the auspices of the appropriately named Detroit Renaissance Group which had set about completely redeveloping a large area of land adjacent to the Detroit River, the focal point being a massive skyscraper complex of shops, offices, conference halls and luxury hotel. This, alone, had cost $350 million and was known as the Renaissance Centre. Discussions had then taken place on means of improving the city's image still further and of attracting trade and publicity which, in turn, had led to the idea of holding a Grand Prix around the streets bordering the Renaissance Centre. A committee had been formed, later to become the 'Detroit Renaissance Grand Prix Incorporated 1982' and an approach made to FOCA to sound out the idea. Then, after having received a favourable response, and subsequently been given the official blessing by FISA, the project had quickly gained momentum, no doubt greatly influenced by the fact that Henry Ford, himself, was involved in the management.

The actual circuit that materialized was a tight and twisty configuration consisting,

essentially, of no less than seventeen corners (these included two tight hairpins and several uniform 90 degree turns) interspersed by mainly short straights. Lined with a combination of concrete barriers, shielded by used tyres at the most precarious places, guardrail and wire catch fencing, it also featured a tunnel that curved gently to the right on the side nearest the river and a chicane (loosely referred to as Turns 18, 19, and 20) at the entrance to the open-air pits. These, again, were located on the riverside but on the inside of the track which ran in an anticlockwise direction and was almost exactly 2½ miles long. Although the streets had, necessarily, to be closed for the race, a somewhat clever concept of the overall design was that the main freeway, providing access to the Renaissance Centre and other parts of the city, was unaffected, for in spite of running straight through the middle of the circuit it dived underground at either end. A rather surprising aspect of the organizational side, however, was that there had apparently never been any mention of a race being held beforehand to comply with the rules concerning track approval for a Grand Prix. Quite how this had been allowed to come about was uncertain but on Thursday, when the streets were closed with the intention of allowing everyone a free practice session to become acclimatized to the new surroundings, the worse fears were confirmed. The circuit wasn't ready! Barriers were found to be inadequate, there were insufficient tyre walls, escape roads were neither long enough nor well enough protected and so on. As a result, because the various shortcomings could not be remedied in time, the whole idea of having any practice had to be scrubbed for the day. For the teams, in particular, this was frustrating to say the least as, apart tyre walls and generally bringing the circuit up to the required safety standard. Moreover, this went on and on until eventually, just before 4 o'clock, the drivers and FISA officials were finally satisfied that everything was in order. Because it was so late, though, it was decided to postpone qualifying until Saturday and, instead, there was just one hour of untimed practice. Bearing in mind that the drivers were all starting from scratch and that there were all of the natural hazards of a street circuit to contend with, such as manhole covers and even a railway crossing at one point, this went off reasonably well for most of them, the only real complaint being that the track was rather bumpy in spite of recent resurfacing work. There were exceptions, of course. One was Arnoux, who, after being one of several drivers having harmless spins or taking excursions down escape roads, overstepped the mark once too often about half way through the session, spun backwards into a wall and damaged the left rear corner of his Renault sufficiently to bring out the tow-truck. After that the Frenchman was forced to sit things out as Prost, still recovering from the foot injury sustained at Monaco, had, by then, already taken over the spare Renault due to an electrical problem. Earlier, Jarier had had his progress interrupted as well owing to his Osella suffering a rear suspension breakage, and then the team's spare car developing engine problems. Without doubt, though, the most unfortunate driver was Lammers as when the throttle jammed open on the Theodore not only did it send the Dutchman careering into a wall but the kick-back effect on the steering wheel broke his right thumb. Consequently, he had to go to hospital for treatment and was left in no fit state to play any further part in the proceedings.

On Saturday everything seemed to be under control at long last with practice starting reasonably promptly. Because of the problems on Friday, however, it had been agreed to dispense with any more untimed practice and to proceed with the business of qualifying immediately by having two one-hour sessions separated by an interval of four hours. This was all very well but it meant that the drivers, many of whom were still learning their way round and trying to sort cars, were faced with an enormous amount of work and, just to add to the pressure, there was understandable concern about the weather remaining dry as the skies were grey and overcast. In view of the overall situation it was hardly surprising that spins and trips down escape roads were soon once more a common sight but, again, most of them were pretty harmless and, in some instances, deliberate as a means of searching out the latest possible braking point at various locations. Indeed, about the only serious incident to occur was when Watson and Serra tangled following a misunderstanding in an overtaking manoeuvre in which the Ulsterman attempted to dive through on the inside of the Fittipaldi going into one of the left-hand turns and promptly found the door being slammed in his face. Serra continued apparently none the worse, but Watson's McLaren came to rest in the centre of the track looking decidedly second-hand with bodywork damage and its lower right front suspension broken. As a result practice had to be temporarily brought to a halt so that the car could be retrieved, while Watson made his way back to the pits to take over the spare McLaren. In the meantime, it was becoming clear that average lap speeds for the circuit were slower than even at Monaco, with anything much over the 80 mph-mark representing a pretty good effort. Given the nature of the circuit, though, this was much as had been anticipated but what had not been anticipated was Winkelhock being right up amongst the pace-setters, the German putting on an inspired performance in the yellow and white ATS. The two Alfa Romeo drivers, Giacomelli and de Cesaris, were demonstrating their recent good form as well and mixing it with the likes of Rosberg and Pironi who were both showing a preference to their respective teams' spare cars, the Williams being fitted with carbon-fibre brake discs for the first time at a race meeting, and the Ferrari running with revised front suspension featuring pull-rods in place of the previously used top rocker arms. This not only had the effect of making the steering lighter but also greatly improved the car's grip into slower corners, much to the obvious delight of its driver. At the end of the hour-long session, though, it was Prost who finished on top of the time-sheets after having taken his Renault around at an average speed of 82.7 mph (1 min 48.537 sec), Pironi's best lap coming out at 1 min 49.903 sec to place him fourth in the order behind de Cesaris (1 min 48.872 sec) and Rosberg (1 min 49.264 sec).

After these first four no-one had broken the 1 min 50 sec barrier, but the big surprise was to find that Winkelhock had come nearest in just joining them with fifth fastest time of 1 min 50.066 sec. Then came Giacomelli (1 min 50.252 sec), Mansell (1 min 50.294 sec) and de Angelis (1 min 50.443 sec) in their Lotus 91s, and Cheever (1 min 50.520 sec) who, like Laffite, was back in one of the older Talbot-Ligier JS17s after the rather unhappy debut of the new JS19s at Monaco. A further half a second away Lauda had come out tenth fastest after complaining of understeer and narrowly pipping Guerrero's well-driven Ensign, which was now running on Michelin tyres, while Daly rounded off the first dozen despite suffering from chronic handling problems with the second Williams that were later traced to a broken rear shock absorber. Lower down the order still there were some real surprises. The Monaco winner, Patrese, was one, for in the same car that he had used there he had come out only 14th fastest behind Laffite after difficulties getting through the traffic. Another was Arnoux finishing up a place lower – whilst his teammate had been out earning pole position he had spun away his chances again and then been plagued by gearbox trouble in the spare Renault. Watson, too, was right out of the picture, in 17th place behind Alboreto, after having experienced similar problems to Lauda and, of course, his accident with Serra. Without doubt, though, the biggest shock was to see Piquet at the very bottom of the list, the Brazilian having had a dreadful morning in which the BMW engine had cut out after only six laps in his proposed race car, and that in the spare Brabham had refused to pick up properly out of the many corners. Furthermore, hopes of doing anything about it in the afternoon were to be dashed by the weather as by then the threat of rain had become reality in the form of persistent drizzle. Indeed, Piquet didn't even bother to go out which meant that for the first time since the now-retired Jody Scheckter had failed to qualify for the 1980 Canadian Grand Prix, the reigning World Champion was destined to be a spectator on race day, along with de Villota who had come out 27th fastest after problems with loose bearings in the rear uprights of his March. Meanwhile, even for those who did venture out on the soaking wet track in the afternoon it was a pretty fraught experience, and for de Cesaris, in particular, as he spun and hit the wall by the entrance to the tunnel, fortunately whilst out in the spare Alfa Romeo which had been converted back to the same specification as the other Tipo 182s. Fastest in the wet, although, of course, it had no effect on the final grid order, was Lauda at 2 min 09.121 sec.

Thankfully the weather was warm and dry again on Sunday, despite being a bit cloudy, and by late morning a fair-sized crowd had gathered at various vantage points around the circuit, a good number having taken to the river in a flotilla of mainly small boats or in a large old-fashioned paddle steamer that had been hired for the occasion by Dodge Motors. The Grand Prix, itself, was not due to start until 2.20 p.m., but prior to this, and intermingled with various supporting events that included a Renault 5 saloon car race, there was the customary warm-up session. Not surprisingly, in view of the curtailed practice schedule, this was more welcome than usual and turned out to be a very busy 30 minutes indeed. It also turned out to be nothing short of a mitigated disaster for the little Italian Osella team as Jarier's car had a fuel line come adrift, caught fire and became hopelessly swamped in extinguisher foam, while Paletti crashed his car into a wall just beyond the tunnel. Unfortunately this was not to be the end of the hard-luck story either as some two hours later, when preparations got under way for the start of the race with the warm-up lap, not only was Paletti's car still undergoing repair work but, incredibly, Jarier contrived to spin off into a wall in the spare Osella due to a suspected deflating rear tyre. Whatever the reason, the damage was such that Jarier was eventually strapped into Paletti's car, in which he was destined to start the race from the pit lane, while his Italian team-mate was obliged to become a non-starter. Winkelhock – the fastest in the morning! – very nearly missed the start as well due to a steering arm breaking on his ATS, also on the warm-up lap. However, this was replaced quickly enough for the German to subsequently complete another warm-up lap and for him to make it around just in time to take up his place on the grid. As a result 24 cars finally set off on the pace lap and came round to face the starting lights whereupon the first Grand Prix through the streets of downtown Detroit was quickly set in motion. At the green Prost made another of his copybook starts but, with de Cesaris and Rosberg also getting away extremely well, he only just managed to hold them off to take the lead going into the first double left-hander. The rest followed, jostling wildly for position, and along with Jarier, who joined them from the pit lane, appeared to be all safely away on the first of the scheduled 70 laps, although simple arithmetic made it clear that the two-hour rule would take precedence.

At the end of the opening lap Prost still led from de Cesaris and Rosberg and even at this early stage was pulling away slightly. Pironi, using what had started out as being the spare Ferrari with the pull-rod front suspension, was hanging on well in fourth place and then came Mansell, Giacomelli, Cheever, Winkelhock, Lauda and Laffite occupying the remainder of the first ten positions, de Angelis having become bogged down at the start and lying fourteenth immediately ahead of Watson. Already there had been some trouble further down the field as Alboreto was on his way into the pits to have a bent steering tie-rod replaced on his Tyrrell; Boesel was following him in to retire his March with the right rear suspension broken, and Baldi had not even made it beyond the first tight hairpin (Turn 5) after having run into the back of the March and been eliminated on the spot. On the second lap, with the leaders maintaining their positions, there was also reason for despair in the ATS camp. First Winkelhock's promising weekend evaporated when another steering arm failed, sending him crashing into a tyre wall, and then Salazar arrived at the pits with a bent rear rocker arm in need of replacement. Even this, though, didn't put an end to the rot for on the very next lap de Cesaris went cruising into the pit lane with a broken

drive-shaft after clipping a wall, and Jarier promptly brought the retirement tally up to five – already – by stopping with a very sick-sounding engine, thus rounding off a thoroughly unhappy day for Osella. In the meantime, Prost had been building up an ever-increasing lead, but now Rosberg, with a clear road ahead of him and already dropping Pironi, began to steady the gap to around 3 seconds. Just when it looked as if the race was beginning to settle down, however, Guerrero suddenly slid wide at the first corner on lap 7 in his efforts to keep de Angelis at bay and then promptly ran over the right front wheel of the Lotus as it pulled alongside. That did it, for in the next instant the Ensign was partly in the air and subsequently skating off into the tyre wall, while de Angelis just managed to keep everything under control to continue on his way, albeit now with a bent steering arm. Fortunately Mass and Watson, following closely behind, managed to take evasive action but when Patrese arrived at the scene moments later the Italian locked his brakes and slid straight on into the tyre wall only a short distance away from the Ensign, the impact tearing away the Brabham's right front wheel. At the same time the Brabham's left rear brake cooling duct caught fire and whilst this was being attended to by a fire marshal – once he had recovered from very nearly tripping over his extinguisher! – a black flag suddenly appeared just before the chicane and a red flag at the start/finish line. The race was being stopped! With two damaged cars now parked near the apex of the first corner the organizers had simply decided against taking any chances.

Over an hour passed before preparations were in hand for the restart during which time cars were topped up with fuel, tyres were changed, adjustments made and even

items such as damaged skirts replaced in some instances. Then, eventually, the starting procedure was set in motion once more and the eighteen surviving cars formed on the grid in the order in which they had crossed the line after six laps of the original race, this being in accordance with the rules that also stipulated that the overall result of the Grand Prix would be determined by aggregating the times from the first part of the race with those of the second. Consequently, having been in the lead at the end of lap 6, Prost was again in pole position, Rosberg was second on the grid, and so on right back to Alboreto and Salazar who had been bringing up the rear after their pit stops.

As the green lights flashed on for the second time Prost repeated his excellent start earlier in the afternoon and went rushing into the first left-hander just in front of Rosberg and Pironi. Behind them, meanwhile, there was every bit as much jostling going on as at the first start, intensified by Mansell getting away rather hesitantly, but somehow they all kept it together and actually went on to complete the 'opening' lap without any serious mishaps. Across the line it was Prost, Rosberg, Pironi, Giacomelli, Cheever, Arnoux and Lauda, before Mansell who had slotted into eighth place ahead of Daly and the others. This was still the order next time round but Prost was really flying with even Rosberg, himself edging away from Pironi, simply unable to keep up. Indeed, within another couple of laps Prost had opened up a 3 second advantage and went on to completely dominate the early stages of the race leaving Rosberg to settle into a lonely second place well clear of Pironi, the Ferrari driver having a busy time keeping Giacomelli and Cheever at bay. In the meantime, Arnoux was soon in trouble

Part two of the first Grand Prix through the streets of Detroit gets under way with the two front row men, Alain Prost (Renault) and Keke Rosberg (Williams), leading away side by side. *(Autosport)*

with a slight engine misfire as a result of the Renault's fuel-injection system starting to play up, forcing the Frenchman to concede his place to Lauda on lap 12 (lap 6 of the re-started race), and Mansell was dropping even further down the field due to acute understeer caused, ironically, by new skirts fitted during the interval.

After fifteen laps (aggregate) Prost had extended his lead over Rosberg to a full 5 seconds but then it began to level out and before long even started shrinking slightly. Like Arnoux before him, Prost was running into trouble with his engine beginning to misfire slightly and refusing to pick up cleanly out of the corners, with the result that as the Renault slowed so Rosberg closed up, a situation that continued until lap 21 when the two cars were running nose to tail. Then, after spending another lap looking for a way past, Rosberg made his move in a breath-taking manner that saw the Williams driver pull up alongside Prost going into one of the tight right-handers, sit it out with him wheel to wheel on the outside and emerge, almost sideways, from the corner as the new race leader. Moreover, once ahead Rosberg immediately pulled clear and left Prost in the frustrating position of being unable to do a thing about it. By now there had also been a number of changes taking place lower down the order. De Angelis had just retired at the pits with gearbox trouble, Salazar had hit a wall following a steering breakage on his ATS, and Henton was in the midst of having a new rear aerofoil fitted to his Tyrrell after having been struck from behind and had the mounting broken by none other than his team-mate earlier in the race. Of far greater significance, however, was Watson's progress as, after having allowed himself a few laps to settle down, the Ulsterman was now really starting to make his presence felt. He had already swooped past the Lotus 91s of de Angelis (before he retired) and Mansell, Mass's March and Arnoux's ailing Renault in quick succession and was currently reeling in Laffite's eighth-placed Talbot at a prodigious rate. This continued, and by the end of lap 24 not only had he caught the French car but had gone past it with his sights now firmly set on Daly's Williams, taking less than another lap to displace that as well. From there he quickly homed in on the battle still raging over third place between Pironi, Giacomelli, Cheever and team-mate Lauda which was just about to undergo its first change, as on lap 26 a slight mistake from Giacomelli cost the Italian two places. That's how close it was! To add to the excitement they had now almost caught up with Prost but, with the Renault spluttering worse than ever, the Frenchman was in no position to put up a fight, continued to lose ground and then had to simply sit and watch as one by one the howling mob went on ahead. With his position having then become next to hopeless,

Prost veered off into the pits where he was destined to lose several laps having various components in the Renault's fuel system replaced in the hope of effecting a cure.

On lap 30, with Rosberg now leading the race by nearly 15 seconds, Watson continued his impressive climb through the field by overtaking Giacomelli. A few moments later, though, there was near disaster for him as when he slid fractionally wide through one of the tight turns Giacomelli immediately seized upon the opportunity to retaliate, aimed his Alfa Romeo for the outside of the McLaren on the approach to the right-hander that followed and then, with neither driver yielding an inch, brought his left front wheel into contact with Watson's right rear wheel. However, it was Giacomelli who came off worse when, after becoming partly airborne for a split second, the Alfa Romeo crashed down on the track and bounced off the barriers into retirement. Watson, on the other hand, casually kept his McLaren pointing in the right direction and continued totally unperturbed, demonstrating the fact emphatically two laps later in a succession of absolutely brilliant overtaking manoeuvres, all under braking, that carried him past Lauda, Cheever and Pironi and up into a splendid second place. Even Lauda must have been impressed with his team-mate's prowess and obviously decided that it was time that he did something as well by overtaking Cheever on lap 35 and Pironi a lap later. But it was still Watson who was attracting all of the attention for he was now reeling in the leader at an incredible rate, aided to some extent by Rosberg suffering

from a combination of his Goodyear tyres starting to go off, problems with locking rear brakes and a gearbox showing a reluctance to engage third gear. Consequently, like Prost earlier, the Finn was unable to do much about defending his position and on lap 37, while Cheever was in the throes of overtaking Pironi, he found himself becoming yet another victim of Watson's tenacity. Three laps later Lauda was also up with the Williams ready to pounce but then came an uncharacteristic error of judgement. Going into the first left-hander beyond the pits, the Austrian tried to squeeze between the inside of the Williams and the wall when there just wasn't the room, momentarily touched both and in the next instant was spinning out of the race. The end of an almost certain McLaren 1 – 2! Meanwhile, the closely-following Cheever safely swerved out of the way and by the end of the lap had moved from fourth place to second, the American passing Rosberg with rather less trouble. On the same lap Laffite, having long since overtaken Daly, also moved the other Talbot up a couple of places. This, though, was a somewhat more fraught business as shortly after following Pironi past Lauda's stationary McLaren he ran into the back of the Ferrari, wiping off the Talbot's nose cone as well as bending the right front fin out of shape, and only went ahead by reason of his compatriot being forced to take a brief, unscheduled trip down an escape road. A few minutes later there was yet another commotion, this time at the chicane due to Alboreto flying off into the tyre barrier after attempting to outbrake Daly, while not long after that Mansell dis-

---

A justifiably happy John Watson, after winning his second Grand Prix of the season and moving to the top of the Championship table, stood alongside a rather pensive-looking Eddie Cheever, who finished second, and the third-placed Didier Pironi. (*Autosport*)

appeared from seventh place when he stopped out on the circuit with engine trouble. So now there were only 12 cars left with the order behind Watson, steadily pulling away out in front, being Cheever, Rosberg, Laffite, Pironi, Daly, Mass, Surer, Henton, Serra and the two Renaults of Arnoux and Prost which were now both running perfectly again, Arnoux having just rejoined the race after he, too, had been into the pits to undergo similar treatment to that of his team-mate.

By lap 50 Watson had the race well and truly sewn up for not only was he still leading convincingly from Cheever but he was now also well ahead overall on aggregate times. Third place, on the other hand, was a different matter altogether for, although Laffite had just led Pironi past Rosberg's Williams, his Matra engine was suddenly starting to lose power. In fact, within a mere four laps Laffite was down to fourth place again, behind Pironi, and before long was dropping away at an even quicker rate than Rosberg in spite of the Finn suffering from sagging fuel pressure to add to his other problems. All the while Watson continued on his merry way, even affording himself the luxury of easing off a bit as the last few minutes ticked away, until eventually receiving the chequered flag after 62 laps (actually one lap early as the race had not quite reached the two-hour mark) to record a truly magnificent victory. To add to the obvious delight of the Ulsterman, the nine points that went with it also moved him to the top of the Championship table at the expense of Prost whose only consolation at the end of the afternoon was that of having set fastest lap.

Results

1	J. Watson (McLaren-Ford)	1 hr 58 min 41.043 sec (125.85 kph/ 78.20 mph)	7	J. Mass (March-Ford)	1 lap behind	
			8	M. Surer (Arrows-Ford)	1 lap behind	
			9	B. Henton (Tyrrell-Ford)	2 laps behind	
			10	R. Arnoux (Renault)	3 laps behind	
2	E. Cheever (Talbot-Matra)	1 hr 58 min 56.769 sec	11	F. Serra (Fittipaldi-Ford)	3 laps behind	
3	D. Pironi (Ferrari)	1 hr 59 min 09.120 sec				

Also running at finish: A. Prost (Renault) 8 laps behind.

Fastest lap: A. Prost (Renault) on lap 45 in 1 min 50.438 sec (130.801 kph/81.276 mph)

4	K. Rosberg (Williams-Ford)	1 hr 59 min 53.019 sec
5	D. Daly (Williams-Ford)	2 hr 00 min 04.800 sec
6	J. Laffite (Talbot-Matra)	1 lap behind

Retirements

M. Baldi (Arrows-Ford) accident on lap 1, R. Boesel (March-Ford) rear suspension on lap 1, M. Winkelhock (ATS-Ford) accident on lap 2, A. de Cesaris (Alfa Romeo) drive-shaft on lap 3, J.P. Jarier (Osella-Ford) engine on lap 3, R. Guerrero (Ensign-Ford) accident on lap 7, R. Patrese (Brabham-Ford) accident on lap 7, E. Salazar (ATS-Ford) accident on lap 14, E. de Angelis (Lotus-Ford) gearbox on lap 18, B. Giacomelli (Alfa Romeo) accident on lap 31, N. Lauda (McLaren-Ford) accident on lap 41, M. Alboreto (Tyrrell-Ford) accident on lap 41, N. Mansell (Lotus-Ford) engine on lap 45.

(Results given are the aggregate for the two-part race).

XX1st Canadian Grand Prix

Montreal: June 13
Weather: Overcast and cold, but dry
Distance: 70 laps of 4.410 km circuit = 308.70 km (191.82 miles)

For the second of the two mid-season North American rounds the venue was rather more familiar as it was the Ile Notre Dame circuit in Montreal, recently re-christened Circuit Gilles Villeneuve in memory of the much-missed local hero. In the past, of course, the Canadian event had very nearly always taken place late in the season but this year the addition of the inaugural Detroit Grand Prix to the calendar had made it convenient to go along with the wishes of the organizers and bring the date of the race forward. So far as the teams were concerned, though, it was all a bit of rush as it left only four clear days between packing up from one race and preparing for practice for the next and a good 500 miles road journey into the bargain. Nevertheless, at 10 a.m. on the Friday morning they were all ready to face the job in hand, with the only drawback being the weather. After several days of a virtual heatwave the skies had clouded over and it was drizzling. To make matters worse it soon developed into a downpour with the result that most drivers gave up after completing only a handful of laps or so, taking the view that it was a waste of time. Winkelhock probably wished that he had not even bothered to go out, as before he had gone very far he got all crossed up, slid into Arnoux's Renault and came off second best by putting a kink in the left-hand side of the monocoque of his ATS. For driver and team alike this couldn't have come at a worse time as the monocoque had only just been straightened out following the German's accident in Detroit, and as the other chassis damaged by Salazar had been sent back to base there was no longer a spare car available. Consequently, while arrangements were put in hand for the monocoque to be repaired again and the car rebuilt, Winkelhock had to face the prospect of becoming a spectator for the rest of the day, although as it happened he wasn't to miss much. The weather saw to that, for after clearing slightly and allowing the track to dry, within 15 minutes or so of the first qualifying session getting under way the rain returned. This meant that only those drivers who had gone straight out recorded anything like a decent time and even then it couldn't be taken too seriously. As it was de Cesaris came out quickest at 1 min 30.286 sec followed by Rosberg (1 min 30.963 sec) and Pironi (1 min 31.332 sec), the Frenchman still concentrating on the Ferrari with the pull-rod front suspension.

Much to everyone's relief the weather had turned a full circle by Saturday morning, with the clouds having dispersed to give way to clear blue skies. As a result the overall scene was completely transformed from that of the previous day with everyone going out as quickly as possible at the start of the untimed session and thrashing round trying to make up for lost time, the only exception being Winkelhock whose car was still not ready. In terms of lap times, although they weren't being officially recorded, Rosberg was still featuring very prominently indeed, but Friday's hero, de Cesaris, was out of luck as before he had really settled down a deflating rear tyre sent his Alfa Romeo spinning sideways over a kerb and led to the monocoque being damaged beyond immediate repair. Apart from the Italian, though, the vast majority of drivers managed to stay out of trouble despite the fact that many of the cars, with their stiff suspensions, were proving to be more than a bit of a handful over the bumps and undulations. There were also surprisingly few mechanical problems, especially in view of the enormous amount of activity. However, Salazar's ATS developed gearbox trouble to add to the German team's already heavy workload, besides keeping the Chilean in the pits for much of the morning, Mansell lost time having a leaking water radiator repaired on his Lotus 91 and Henton had his practice run cut short when the engine blew up in his Tyrrell. Then, just before the field was flagged off, Rosberg and Daly caused a mild panic in the Williams camp by both stopping in quick succession, the Finn to report that he felt his engine beginning to tighten and the Irishman with a broken valve spring.

For the final hour of qualifying Henton

1982

and Daly both had fresh engines installed in their cars, Rosberg took over the spare Williams with the carbon-fibre brakes and de Cesaris was using the spare Alfa Romeo. Patrese, meanwhile, had decided to concentrate on his spare Brabham BT49D out of choice rather than on a brand new chassis that had been built to replace the car wrecked at Detroit. As anticipated, with everything at stake and Friday's times now meaningless, life became even more hectic than in the morning, but this produced a problem in itself as, with so much traffic about, drivers were finding it next to impossible to get in a clear lap. Even so, Pironi

didn't seem to have much trouble, as after just four laps the Frenchman had whipped his Ferrari around in only 1 min 27.509 sec, and on race rubber at that. Furthermore, this was to go unbeaten giving Pironi his first pole position since joining Ferrari and only the third of his career. It was also the Italian team's first pole since Imola, 1981. Meanwhile, the BMW men were more than relieved to see Piquet also right up where it mattered in his Brabham BT50 after the disaster a week earlier. In fact, the Brazilian was fastest of all through the official speed trap and, thanks to much-improved throttle response following further development work carried out on the fuel system, went on to post a very respectable fourth fastest time of 1 min 28.663 sec. Apart from Pironi's Ferrari, only the Renaults were quicker. Arnoux eventually took the runner-up spot at 1 min 27.895 sec, although only after spending a lot of time having adjustments made to eliminate porpoising on a low fuel-load (he had spent the morning running on full tanks when the problem had not been apparent), while Prost came out third fastest at 1 min 28.563 sec in spite of still being in pain from his foot injury.

With the four turbo runners taking the first four places on the grid the situation was not looking at all promising for the rest, especially as qualifying had taken place in very hot conditions. Nevertheless, Giacomelli was reasonably pleased to have come out fifth fastest at 1 min 28.740 sec after finding a much sought after clear lap and Watson, despite being unhappy with the handling of his McLaren (again), had the distinction of being the fastest Ford-Cosworth runner. He, too, had managed to avoid the traffic at a crucial stage and produced sixth fastest time of 1 min 28.822 sec. His team-mate, on the other hand, was down in a frustrating eleventh spot behind Rosberg, Patrese, de Cesaris and de Angelis after having tried different settings in a vain attempt to iron out much the same handling problems with his McLaren. Also left frustrated at the end of the afternoon were Daly and Mansell who had finished up in thirteenth and fourteenth places respectively, immediately behind Cheever in the quicker of the two ageing Talbot-Ligier JS17s. Daly's chances of doing any better had been spoiled by a seized shock-absorber on his Williams, while Mansell had not only suffered from acute understeer with his Lotus but also from an engine that refused to pull properly due, as it was subsequently discovered, to incorrect mixture settings. Meanwhile, for three other drivers it was even worse as they had all failed to make the cut for one reason or another. These were Winkelhock, who had finally got his car back for the last 30 minutes or so of qualifying only to have found it lacking badly in the handling department; de Villota, who had never really looked like

qualifying in spite of trying hard; and Serra, whose hopes had disappeared after only three laps due to a fuel line coming adrift on his Fittipaldi and causing a small engine fire out on the circuit. Henton, though, had only just made it after losing his second engine of the day and found himself being joined on the back row of the grid by fellow countryman Geoffrey Lees who had done all that could be asked of him in the Theodore as stand-in for the injured Jan Lammers.

There was disappointment in store with the weather on race day for the hot sunshine, so apparent on Saturday, had disappeared behind a thick blanket of cloud and it had become decidedly chilly. For the organizers, already extremely worried that the loss of Gilles Villeneuve would have an adverse effect on the crowd attendance, this gave cause for even more anxiety and just to add to their concern there was a drivers' strike on the local Metro system which was usually the most popular means by which spectators made their way to the circuit. Rather than just sit and hope, though, they responded to the situation by making arrangements for a fleet of buses to be brought into service, providing free transport from the city, only to find that this still failed to bring the eventual size of the crowd up the level of expectations. Meanwhile, for the drivers there was an unusually long wait as, with the race not due to start until 4.15 p.m., to tie in with television schedules, even the warm-up session didn't get under way until 1.15 p.m. When this did eventually take place it produced more problems than usual as the engine of Giacomelli's Alfa Romeo cut out due to an electrical failure, Guerrero's Ensign snapped a drive-shaft, Henton's Tyrrell broke its gearbox and Jarier blew up the engine in his Osella. As ever, though, the mechanics proved equal to the task and by 4 p.m. all 26 starters had formed up on the dummy grid and were waiting the final countdown, the only change to the expected line-up being caused by Rosberg who had decided to use the spare Williams as he felt happier with it.

The waiting over, Pironi led the field away on the pace lap and a couple of minutes or so later they were all gently rolling into their starting positions. Some of the tail-enders, though, took longer than usual to pull up and before the red lights eventually came on Pironi found the Ferrari's clutch beginning to drag leaving him faced with the tricky business of endeavouring to keep the car in check by dabbing the brake pedal. Finally, with the car trying to creep more than ever, the engine stalled – just as the green lights flashed on! Consequently, all he could do was sit there with his arm in the air and while Arnoux took off into an immediate lead Prost swerved around to his left, as did most of the others queued up behind. Naturally, there were one or two anxious moments but no sign of any real trouble until the last few remaining cars came roaring up from further down the grid where a number of the drivers were totally unaware that anything was amiss. Boesel was one, and before realizing it he had clipped the right rear wheel of the stationary Ferrari to go skating off to the side of the track. Even so, this was inconsequential compared to what was to happen a split second later, for as Paletti arrived upon the scene he obviously didn't spot the Ferrari until it was too late and rammed the back of it at a speed of well over 100 mph, punting it across the track in front of Lees' Theodore which then, in turn, cannoned off into Salazar's ATS. Within seconds, Boesel, Pironi, Lees and Salazar were all stepping out of their damaged cars obviously none the worse for their ordeal, but in the Osella cockpit Paletti remaining absolutely motionless, trapped with the steering wheel against his chest and unconscious. On seeing this, Pironi immediately ran over to his aid and began tugging away at the remains of the Osella's front bodywork, whereupon he was quickly joined by some marshals and FISA's medical supremo Professor Watkins, while the organizers took hurried steps to stop the race. Before anyone could do very much, though, the car suddenly burst into flames (a fuel cell had ruptured) causing much greater anxiety until the fire was eventually extinguished by some very efficient work on the part of the fire marshals. Even then it took almost exactly half an hour before the young Italian could be freed and rushed off to hospital by helicopter where the worst fears were confirmed later that same evening when it was announced that he had succumbed to severe internal injuries.

Naturally the accident took away most of the enthusiasm for the race even before the full consequences were known, with Pironi being particularly upset over the affair, especially coming so soon after his teammate's tragic accident in Belgium. However, there was no question of not having a race so while the organizers made arrangements for the track to be cleared the teams prepared themselves for the restart, the only exceptions being Osella and Theodore. Quite understandably, Enzo Osella decided to withdraw his other car for Jarier, while Geoff Lees had damaged the only Theodore on hand beyond immediate repair. Pironi's Ferrari, Boesel's March and Salazar's ATS had also been put out of commission, but because the original race had been stopped before being in progress for more than two full laps, and was deemed to be null and void, all three drivers still had a role to play as each of their teams had other cars available which they were quite entitled to use. Consequently 23 cars finally lined up on the grid again, in qualifying order, apart from near the back where the gaps caused by the absence of Jarier, Lees and the unfortunate Paletti were

closed up. Then, almost exactly two hours after the first, Pironi led the depleted field around on another pace lap, they rolled into their positions once more, and everyone held their breath as the starting lights came on. Thankfully, this time they all got away without any mishaps, Pironi making an excellent start to lead the tightly-bunched pack into the first long right-hander and maintain his advantage throughout the rest of the opening lap. Almost immediately, though, the spare Ferrari, with its older-type front suspension, was proving to be a totally different proposition to that of his other car, added to which there was a slight engine misfire. As a result, instead of pulling away, Pironi was fighting a losing battle to even stay put, so when Arnoux drew alongside him just beyond the start/finish line at the beginning of the second lap there was nothing that he could do to prevent his compatriot from becoming the new race leader. Right behind them, Prost was not altogether happy with his engine either and was quickly elbowed back to fourth place by Piquet, while Giacomelli's Alfa Romeo was suffering from such a lack of power that the Italian was losing places hand over fist after a good start. In fact, towards the end of the second lap he had already made up his mind to go into the pits, so when Daly challenged him as they approached the last hairpin he had no hesitation in braking early so as to allow the Irishman to go through on the inside. Obviously Mansell, next along, had no idea that Giacomelli was heading for the pits and was caught completely unaware by his action, locked his brakes to try to avoid running into the back of him only to slide sideways and finish up by riding over the Alfa's right rear wheel. Both cars then immediately spun round before eventually coming to rest in the middle of the track, by which time other

drivers that had been following close behind were busy trying to dodge by on either side. Somehow they all safely made it and within a few seconds Giacomelli was stepping out of his car uninjured, even finding time to kick the Alfa's rear wheel! Mansell, on the other hand, took a good deal longer to move and when he did finally emerge was holding his left arm. Shortly afterwards it was learned that his hand had slipped through the steering wheel upon hitting the Alfa Romeo and had been badly wrenched as the front wheels of the Lotus had come crashing down on to the track. Eventually, because he was in so much pain, an ambulance was summoned to take him off to hospital, and while this was going on the marshals set about removing the two damaged cars under the presence of yellow flags. In the meantime, Guerrero found a less dramatic means of making his way into the pits to retire the Ensign with an inoperative clutch and Henton was already there having his Tyrrell checked over following a slight coming-together with Winkelhock's ATS which Salazar was now driving.

By the end of the third lap Pironi had lost two more places to Piquet and Prost to make it Renault, Brabham-BMW, Renault, Ferrari. Already dropping away, Watson was nonetheless holding on to fifth place as the leading non-turbo runner, but Rosberg, who had earlier been right up with the McLaren, had just dropped behind Cheever and de Cesaris and was in trouble with his Williams porpoising badly along the faster sections of the circuit. In fact, within another lap he was also forced to give way to Patrese, and before long was struggling even to hold on to ninth place. All the while the leaders were pulling further and further away with Arnoux dictating the pace out in front just over 2 seconds clear. However, with his BMW engine on full song, Piquet now began

Confusion on the second lap as Bruno Giacomelli's Alfa Romeo and Nigel Mansell's Lotus spin in the middle of the track after their coming-together. (*L.A.T. Photographic*)

1982

to press home the attack and by lap 9 had not only wiped out the deficit but was making for the inside of the Renault as they went into the fast ess-bend beyond the pits. There they stayed absolutely wheel to wheel until the Brabham nosed ahead on the way out of the turn to take over the lead. It was a moment to savour and one from which Piquet lost little time in consolidating his new position. There was no less excitement taking place behind them either, for while Prost was minding his own business in third place, Cheever, de Cesaris and Patrese had all just gone past Watson, rather surprisingly, in quick succession and were now also taking turns to pass Pironi's Ferrari. Further back, Lauda's McLaren was progressing backwards as well, the Austrian having been passed a few minutes earlier by Daly, de Angelis and even Laffite who had since gone into the pits to retire his Talbot on the grounds that it was undriveable! Obviously there had to be something wrong with Lauda's car, too, especially when Baldi also went on ahead shortly afterwards. Sure enough, at the end of lap 17, the number 8 McLaren was heading for the pits where it was discovered that he had been driving without a clutch, the second start having proved just too much for it.

After twenty laps there was little change up front with Piquet controlling the race beautifully, Arnoux doing his best not to be left behind and Prost still holding down third place but drifting even further into arrears due to his engine being off colour. However, in fourth place it was now Patrese, the Italian being in the midst of a sustained charge in the Ford-Cosworth-powered Brabham that had more recently carried him past de Cesa-

ris and Cheever in quick succession. Furthermore, he was now making noticeable inroads on the gap to the Renault ahead of him. Lower down the order, meanwhile, Mass stopped for a fresh set of Avons after making little impression near the back of the field in his March; Salazar had the engine blow up in the lone ATS and, at the end of lap 23, with Watson and Daly now also in front of him and his engine misfire growing worse, Pironi finally decided to see if anything could be done to cure the problem by making for the pits. While he was there having his fuel topped up and all four wheels changed, de Cesaris ousted Cheever from fifth place with a rather audacious manoeuvre under braking for the hairpin, and on lap 27 Patrese, having caught Prost, made light work of taking over third place. Then, just two laps later, third place suddenly became second! Incredibly, Arnoux had spun on his way into one of the tight left-handers on the return leg of the circuit due to a suspected broken skirt, stalled his engine and was unable to restart it just like the situation at Monaco three weeks earlier. This was bad enough for the French team, but minutes later they were in total despair when Prost also retired abruptly, his sick engine finally crying enough and blowing up in a big way along the fast straight early on lap 31. So now, with the race just short of the half-way mark, it was Piquet leading by almost half a minute from team-mate Patrese followed by de Cesaris, Cheever, Watson, Daly, de Angelis, Rosberg and Baldi. After that only six others were left and they had all been lapped, including Pironi who was about to go into the pits again with his engine still not right.

The race now settled down into a comparatively quiet phase with the only real excitement being provided by de Cesaris and Cheever still battling away with one another for what had become third place, the American pushing his adversary so hard that at times de Cesaris was quite literally sliding through some of the corners. As this continued so did the retirements with Alboreto next to disappear when, on lap 42, his Tyrrell coasted to rest at the entrance to the pit lane suffering from a broken gearbox and fuel starvation caused by an air leak in the fuel system. Six laps later Boesel was also out, the engine in his March blowing up out on the circuit, while only four more laps passed before Rosberg's miserable day, made all the worse by failing rear brakes, ended in the pits with his Williams now devoid of fifth gear. Even Piquet's immediate future was looking less assured at this stage as the BMW engine had suddenly started sounding less sweet due to the fuel mixture becoming too lean. However, by turning down the boost, the reigning World Champion managed to compensate for the problem and, although this enabled his team-mate to start closing up, it still did nothing to prevent him from going on to score a resounding victory, his first of the season discounting Brazil and the first ever for the turbo-charged BMW engine. He had also achieved something of a record by being a non-qualifier one week and a race winner the next! Meanwhile behind Patrese, who made it a splendid 1 – 2 for the Parmalat Brabham team, the situation changed dramatically in the last few minutes. First Cheever's fourth-placed Talbot spluttered out of fuel on lap 67 and then, on the penultimate lap, so did de Cesaris's third-

A non-qualifier in Detroit a week earlier, Nelson Piquet made amends in the best possible manner by driving superbly and giving the BMW-powered Brabham BT50 its maiden victory. *(L.A.T. Photographic)*

placed Alfa Romeo along with Daly's Williams which, until that point, had still been lying sixth even though its rear brakes had all but gone. Consequently Watson eventually came home a somewhat surprised third to extend his lead at the top of the Championship table to ten points, while de Angelis and Surer (he had caught and passed team-mate

Baldi thirteen laps before the finish despite the fact that his Arrows was plagued by a persistent misfire throughout most of the race) took the next two places ahead of a highly frustrated de Cesaris and Daly who were classified sixth and seventh respectively. A very unhappy Cheever, on the other hand, was classified an even more

disappointing tenth behind Baldi and Pironi, the Ferrari driver ending his race in style by setting the fastest lap on the penultimate tour: the engine misfire had been cured by a third pit stop just past half-distance when the black box had been changed along with adjustments being made to the fuel system.

Results

1	N. Piquet (Brabham-BMW)	1 hr 46 min 39.577 sec (173.655 kph/ 107.904 mph)
2	R. Patrese (Brabham-Ford)	1 hr 46 min 53.376 sec
3	J. Watson (McLaren-Ford)	1 hr 47 min 41.413 sec
4	E. de Angelis (Lotus-Ford)	1 lap behind
5	M. Surer (Arrows-Ford)	1 lap behind
*6	A. de Cesaris (Alfa Romeo)	2 laps behind
*7	D. Daly (Williams-Ford)	2 laps behind
8	M. Baldi (Arrows-Ford)	2 laps behind
9	D. Pironi (Ferrari)	3 laps behind
*10	E. Cheever (Talbot-Matra)	4 laps behind
11	J. Mass (March-Ford)	4 laps behind

Also running at finish: B. Henton (Tyrrell-Ford) 11 laps behind.

*Not running at finish.

Fastest lap: D. Pironi (Ferrari) on lap 66 in 1 min 28.323 sec (179.749 kph/111.691 mph)

Retirements
Original race:
R. Paletti (Osella-Ford) accident on lap 1,
G. Lees (Theodore-Ford) accident on lap 1,
J.P. Jarier (Osella-Ford) withdrawn before restart.

Restarted race:
N. Mansell (Lotus-Ford) accident on lap 2,
B. Giacomelli (Alfa Romeo) accident on lap 2,
R. Guerrero (Ensign-Ford) clutch on lap 3,
J. Laffite (Talbot-Matra) handling on lap 9,
N. Lauda (McLaren-Ford) clutch on lap 18,
E. Salazar (ATS-Ford) engine on lap 21,
R. Arnoux (Renault) spun and stalled on lap 29, A. Prost (Renault) engine on lap 31,
M. Alboreto (Tyrrell-Ford) gearbox on lap 42,
R. Boesel (March-Ford) engine on lap 48,
K. Rosberg (Williams-Ford) gearbox on lap 53.

XXX Grote Prijs van Nederland

Zandvoort: July 3
Weather: Overcast and cold, but mainly dry
Distance: 72 laps of 4.252 km circuit = 306.14 km (190.23 miles)

Originally there was to have been no Grand Prix in Holland in 1982. The organizers there had failed to make the payment due for the 1981 race by a date fixed by FISA's Executive Committee and this had resulted in it being relegated to the reserve list. So, too, had the Spanish Grand Prix for similar reasons. However, following the cancellation of the Argentine Grand Prix, the Spanish round had been reinstated and would have taken place on June 27 had the organizers not pulled out at short notice due, primarily, to financial problems. To fill the gap, negotiations had then proceeded between Bernie Ecclestone and the new Dutch organizer, Jim Vermeulen. Agreement had been reached, particularly regarding the financial aspect, and plans put in motion for the race to go ahead. However, because there were already three races on the calendar for August, the month in which the Dutch race had traditionally taken place in recent years, and because there was a large gap between the Canadian and British Grands Prix, it had been arranged for the first weekend in July. Even then there was a slight problem as due to a clash with the World Cup and the Wimbledon tennis finals, television schedules dictated that the race would start at 12.30 p.m. on the Saturday rather than on the Sunday. Nevertheless, no-one seemed unduly bothered, most only too happy to return to Zandvoort, and so on Thursday morning it was all systems go with a very full

entry of 31 drivers present and correct. Included in the line-up were a few changes, in addition to the reappearance of Derek Warwick and Teo Fabi marking the return of the Toleman team to the fold after missing the two North American rounds. First and foremost Ferrari were back to two drivers for the first time since the tragic loss of Gilles Villeneuve, the Commendatore having persuaded Frenchman Patrick Tambay to make a return to Grand Prix racing; for the 'locals', in particular, there was the good news that Jan Lammers was now fit enough to take up his place in the Theodore team once more after breaking his thumb in Detroit; finally Colin Chapman's test driver, Brazilian Roberto Moreno, was having his first big chance to prove himself behind the wheel of the second Lotus 91 due to Nigel Mansell still recuperating from the nasty arm injury sustained during the early stages of the Canadian Grand Prix. On the mechanical front, meanwhile, there was an even greater number of changes. To start with Ferrari, Brabham, Williams and March were all fielding brand new cars, each to the teams' existing designs, in addition to which the Italian marque had brought along an experimental car. This featured a longitudinal gearbox in place of the more familiar transverse unit and revised rear suspension inasmuch as the coil-spring/damper units had been moved further forward, the overall aim being to improve air-flow around the rear of the car.

All four Ferraris on hand also had the pull-rod front suspension as well as beefed-up front wishbones following a front suspension failure during recent testing at Paul Ricard that had caused Pironi to have a nasty accident from which he had been extremely fortunate to walk away unharmed. Elsewhere, too, there had obviously been a lot of work done between races as numerous other cars had undergone various detail modifications. These included the McLaren MP4Bs which had new underbody profiles, and, like the Williams FW08s, shallow rear aerofoils in the quest for more straight-line speed. Quite apart from all of this the Brabham team had entered both of their drivers in the BMW-powered BT50s and Talbot-Ligier were re-introducing their JS19s, so one way or another the paddock was the scene of considerable interest.

Practice started with the usual 90 minutes of testing, although for six drivers there was more to it than that as they were involved in the unenviable task of having to pre-qualify. Only the slowest of them was going to be eliminated, however, and that eventually turned out to be de Villota who was probably left wondering if he ever would actually start a race in 1982! Meanwhile, apart from some of the cars misbehaving themselves over the bumps, the session ran out with little in the way of trouble. Already the turbo-charged cars were looking dominant, with the Renaults, Brabham-BMWs and Ferraris reaching absolutely colossal speeds down the main straight, helped to no mean extent by the presence of a keen tail wind under cloudy skies. Naturally this was being reflected in overall lap times, and even before the official

1982

112

timekeepers took up duty for the first hour of qualifying it seemed certain that the opening battle for pole position would, at most, lay between six drivers. Sure enough, this proved to be the case only too well for it developed into a straight fight between Arnoux, Prost and Piquet, all three making comparatively light work of breaking the 1 min 15 sec barrier. In the end the matter was resolved by Arnoux stopping the clocks at 1 min 14.233 sec (206.205 kph) as any hopes that Prost had of improving beyond 1 min 14.660 sec were dashed by light drizzle developing just as he was about to set off on his second set of qualifiers, while the best

effort from a slightly embarrassed Piquet came out at 1 min 14.723 sec. Embarrassed, because earlier on the World Champion had spun off into the sand at Tarzan after he had mistakenly turned the brake balance knob, shifting all the emphasis to the front and causing the front wheels to lock, instead of the boost control knob next to it! Behind this high-speed trio, Pironi added to the turbo supremacy by posting fourth fastest time of 1 min 15.825 sec in his new Ferrari 126C2 rather than the experimental car that he had tried in the morning, but Tambay's first public appearance for the Italian team was hampered by an engine refusing to pick up cleanly out of the corners. Even so, this still didn't prevent the Frenchman from turning in a respectable 1 min 16.154 sec which placed him sixth fastest and left him sandwiched between the two fastest Ford-Cosworth runners, Lauda (1 min 15.832 sec) and Rosberg (1 min 16.260 sec). Patrese, on the other hand, had little chance to demonstrate his prowess behind the wheel of the second BMW-powered Brabham for the first time since Belgium as a broken skirt spoiled things on his first set of qualifiers and then, after covering a total of just four flying laps, he was sidelined through a broken turbo. Under the circumstances, he did well to finish up tenth fastest immediately behind the evenly-matched Alfa Romeos of Giacomelli and de Cesaris. In the meantime, it was also turning out to be an afternoon of mixed fortunes for the remaining team using turbo-charged engines, Toleman. First there was Warwick notching up a pleasing 13th fastest time and obviously benefiting from recent testing at the circuit as well as from a new batch of narrower and softer Pirellis which were working well. Then, in direct contrast, there was Fabi having a thoroughly miserable time of it with a rebuilt chassis that just could not be encouraged to handle properly. As a result, it was no surprise to see the Italian finish up in the non-qualifying zone where he found himself in the company of Guerrero, whose Ensign was bouncing alarmingly all over the track, Moreno, who was proving to be a disappointment in the second Lotus, and an openly disenchanted Cheever. Like team-mate Laffite, who was not much better off in winding up a disappointing 20th fastest, the American was finding the handling of the new Talbot-Ligier JS19 absolutely dreadful and, in desperation, had switched to the older spare JS17 only for that to have coasted to rest out on the circuit with ignition trouble!

For the final hour of qualifying on Friday afternoon conditions were much warmer than the previous day and, more significant still, the wind had changed direction. Now, instead of a tail wind on the main straight, there was a strong head wind. The combined effect of this was that lap times were increased by anything up to around 2 seconds

on average and resulted in only four drivers, Surer, Laffite, Cheever and Fabi, actually making any improvement. Even then it had little effect on the overall situation as Cheever, despite being allowed out in Laffite's car towards the end of practice, and Fabi still failed to hoist themselves on to the grid, while Laffite's improved time was so insubstantial as to be of no consequence. In fact, only Surer made any positive progress (he had been delayed by an engine misfire and gearbox trouble with his Arrows on the first day) for he went on to record the afternoon's 13th fastest time of 1 min 18.296 sec which moved him six places up the grid to seventeenth spot immediately behind team-mate Baldi. Meanwhile, although it was of no significance so far as the grid order was concerned, Arnoux once again came out fastest at 1 min 15.791 sec but Prost, confined to the spare Renault following an engine problem with his race car in the morning, had to give best to the Ferrari duo. First Pironi took the experimental car around in 1 min 16.655 sec and then Tambay produced third fastest time of 1 min 17.004 sec, the engine pick-up problem having finally been traced to the turbo wastegate which had subsequently been changed between sessions. Piquet would almost certainly have been up there as well but, because of the slower conditions, he was officially withdrawn from qualifying, as was Rosberg for the same reason, so as to be able to carry out experiments on some unmarked Goodyears in addition to his two allocated sets of qualifiers. As it was, Patrese came out fifth fastest despite having to use the spare Brabham-BMW after fuel-injection problems with the new car that he had been using, while Lauda, by finishing up two places lower behind de Cesaris, was once more the fastest Ford-Cosworth runner.

Just like the weather pattern in Montreal three weeks earlier, in which it had been bright and sunny one day and then overcast the next, so it was at Zandvoort for on Saturday the skies had clouded over again making conditions both cold and dreary, not least for the crowd which turned out to be disappointingly low. About the only unchanged aspect was the wind which was still blowing head-on down the main straight, a situation that led to the Toleman team changing the gear ratios in Warwick's car prior to the warm-up session. Having done that, they then sat back and watched their man set second fastest time, no less, to Piquet! The Alfa Romeo team were thinking ahead as well. In their case they had fitted rather crude and controversial auxiliary fuel tanks atop the main central fuel cell on each of the Tipo 182s to avoid the possibility of running out of fuel again as had happened to de Cesaris in Monaco and Canada. Meanwhile, Pironi was busy trying to decide which of his two Ferraris to race, eventually giving both cars an airing before finally making up his mind to play safe and use the new car with the transverse gearbox, and for a few of the drivers there were some unwanted dramas. Among those affected were Lauda, whose engine was consuming oil at such a worrying rate that the McLaren team decided to change it; Jarier, who suffered clutch failure in the lone Osella; and de Angelis whose Lotus started spraying out its fuel. However, no-one was in a worse state than poor old Laffite. First the engine in his proposed race car began spewing out oil when it was started up and then, after switching to Cheever's sister car, it was not long before the clutch failed. Consequently, while repairs began, the Frenchman was left with no option than to go out in the spare JS17 for what remained of the 30 minute session. Even then his troubles weren't over for the day, as when he subsequently joined the other 25 starters for the official warm-up lap just after noon he quickly discovered that the clutch in Cheever's car was still not right so in the end was reluctantly obliged to line up in the spare JS17.

At the green, with Winkelhock still on his way round the circuit after having been delayed by a recalcitrant engine, the two Renaults surged forward in unison and arrived at Tarzan virtually side by side. Prost, though, was already nosing ahead slightly and by staying off the brakes a fraction longer was able to cut across his team-mate's bows as they turned into the hairpin to take the lead. Pironi also got away extremely well to slot straight into third place but, in complete contrast, Piquet was slow off the mark and was elbowed back to seventh place in the initial rush by Tambay, Lauda and Giacomelli. Not that he was destined to stay there long as during a fast and furious opening lap, which saw Prost creeping away from Arnoux and Pironi up front, Piquet quickly began to make amends by overtaking Giacomelli. On the second lap he also quite literally powered past Lauda and Tambay in rapid succession, while ahead of him Pironi split the two Renaults by diving through on the inside of Arnoux under braking for the Marlborobocht. Thereafter, as Piquet settled down to the task of trying to catch Arnoux, so Pironi homed in on the other Renault until, at the start of the fifth lap, he neatly outbraked Prost going into Tarzan to take over the lead. Once in front, the Ferrari driver then immediately started to edge away and even by the end of the same lap was already a full second clear. Further back, meanwhile, Tambay was at the head of a whole string of cars and holding on to fifth place only through sheer determination and the Ferrari's superior straight-line speed, a fact that had been clearly illustrated on the third lap when Lauda had pulled right alongside him on the exit from Hunzerug, but then lost out on acceleration. Gia-

comelli, Rosberg (he had been boxed in behind Piquet at the start) and Patrese were right up there as well, although Watson, who had earlier been lying eighth, was dropping away with handling problems and had just lost another place to none other than Warwick's Toleman. Obviously the performance in the early morning warm-up session had not been the flash-in-the-pan that everyone thought, for the young Englishman had already systematically picked off Alboreto, de Angelis, Daly and de Cesaris and was really charging. Furthermore, he was soon moving up to join the queue behind Tambay, but on lap 8, after following Rosberg and Patrese past Giacomelli, came a serious setback – the Toleman's rear aerofoil suddenly flew off along the main straight! That, of course, immediately upset the car's balance and left Warwick spending the next lap gingerly making his way round to the pits for a complete new rear wing assembly, the mounting having broken. Undeterred, Warwick subsequently charged back out into the race seemingly more determined than ever and demonstrated emphatically just how hard he was trying by setting what was to be the afternoon's fastest time by going around in 1 min 19.780 sec (191.867 kph) on his thirteenth lap. Unfortunately, though, two laps later he was making for the pits again, this time to retire with a split oil union and to put an end to the British team's most encouraging performance to date. In the meantime, Patrese was also forced into the pits with gear selector problems that were traced to a bolt having dropped out of the linkage, Surer stopped for an early change of Pirellis and Laffite had retired even earlier than Warwick due to chronic handling problems. The rest, on the other hand, were all keeping hard at it with some really good scraps going on throughout most of the field, not least between Winkelhock and Salazar who were supposed to be team-mates! There had also been more changes taking place amongst the leading positions for Piquet had blasted past Arnoux along the main straight on lap 15;

and earlier, on lap 9, Rosberg had forced his way past Lauda under braking for the hairpin before dishing out the same treatment to Tambay just three laps later. Consequently, with the race now fast approaching the 20 lap mark, the leader-board read Pironi, Prost, Piquet, Arnoux, Rosberg, and Tambay.

On lap 22 came a very worrying moment indeed. Already concerned by a front-end vibration ever since the early stages of the race, Arnoux applied the brakes as usual for Tarzan only to see his left front wheel suddenly slew outwards before breaking away completely along with the hub and brake components. A lower wishbone had failed causing a fracture at the steering link and despite applying the brakes even harder, locking up the two rear wheels, the Frenchman (with no steering) was unable to prevent the Renault from careering straight across the sandy run-off area and on into the tyre wall beyond at almost unabated speed. Then, after scattering tyres in all directions and giving a group of nearby photographers a nasty shock, the Renault reared up on to two wheels and finally came to rest pointing skywards partly on top of the guard-rail. Amazingly, except for the front end being bent upwards, the aluminium monocoque had withstood the enormous impact and in virtually no time at all Arnoux was being helped out of the car, dazed and a little bruised around the right ankle, but otherwise totally unharmed. A lucky escape. For the French team, though, this was to be only the beginning of yet another troubled race, as Prost had already slipped some 10 seconds behind Pironi and was now rapidly being caught by Piquet. Worse still, his engine was starting to lose power and when Piquet finally overhauled him on lap 31 it was almost academic as two laps later Prost was turning into the pit lane trailing ominous-looking puffs of blue smoke. A cylinder head stud had broken. Apart from causing obvious disappointment in the Renault camp, this also reduced the field to nineteen cars as by now Serra, Boesel and Henton had

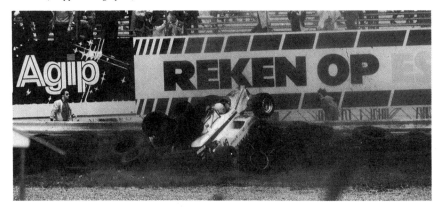

The end result of a lost wheel: René Arnoux's Renault comes to rest pointing skywards against the barriers at Tarzan. *(Phipps Photographic)*

also added their names to the retirement list, all three having gone out in quick succession at around the time of Arnoux's dramatic departure. Meanwhile, Rosberg automatically moved up into a secure-looking third place and Tambay was now fourth by reason of still keeping Lauda at bay. After that came Giacomelli, now being hampered by a broken exhaust and about to lose his place to Daly, followed by Watson, Alboreto and Baldi with everyone else having been lapped. These included Jarier and de Angelis, who had both been delayed by recent pit stops for fresh tyres and to replace a broken skirt respectively, Winkelhock, who was another about to stop for fresh tyres, and de Cesaris who had just begun a string of no less than three visits to the pits on successive laps prior to becoming the next retirement with some obscure electrical fault causing an incurable engine misfire.

By lap 40 the first three positions were looking settled for Piquet, whilst maintaining a useful 15 second cushion over Rosberg, was now very nearly half a minute behind the leading Ferrari and obviously driving to conserve fuel which it was known beforehand was going to be marginal. However, behind the leading trio the situation had just changed again as on lap 38, whilst his teammate was in the pits taking on a fresh set of Michelins, Lauda had finally scrambled past Tambay under braking for Tarzan to take over fourth place. Since then Daly had also gone ahead of the Ferrari which had suddenly developed an engine misfire a few minutes earlier. Naturally, with the problem not only persisting but growing worse, Tambay continued to drop away and by the end of lap 45 was down in a despondent seventh place behind Alboreto, the Italian having overtaken Giacomelli's rough-sounding Alfa Romeo earlier on the same lap. Lower down the order, too, there was still a lot of reshuffling going on as de Angelis had returned to the pits after completing 40 laps to complain that his Lotus was porpoising too badly to continue, Lammers had been forced out because of engine trouble with the Theodore and Mass had just lost time and tenth place due to a tyre stop. Instead, it was now

Watson who was lying tenth, the earlier change of rubber having unaccountably transformed the handling of his McLaren but seemingly too late for the Ulsterman to salvage any Championship points.

With twenty laps remaining the situation up amongst the leaders was still much the same. Pironi was completely untroubled out on his own and Piquet was staying well clear of Rosberg who, in turn, was having a lonely drive in third place ahead of Lauda. Even so the Finn had already made a small impression on the gap to the Brabham and was charging on as hard as ever despite having blistered his left front tyre early in the race. As a result the gap continued to come down and, just to add to the interest of the closing stages of the race, Alboreto was steadily gaining on the other, fifth-placed Williams of Daly who was also concerned about the state of his left front tyre as well as being troubled by his rear brakes. This last issue, however, was to be resolved in dramatic fashion: on lap 70 Daly was held up sufficiently by a back-marker to enable Alboreto to close right up and take a run at him from the outside going into Tarzan only for wheels to touch and the two cars to spin off. Nevertheless, they both subsequently rejoined the race but whereas Daly calmly reversed back on to the track, Alboreto put his right boot down too hard in a fit of temper and spun across to the inside of the hairpin before sorting himself out properly, by which time the Tyrrell's rear suspension had suffered from the unscheduled trip over the kerb.

Then, to make him even angrier (he was to have more than just a few words with Daly afterwards!), he quickly discovered that his right rear wheel had been knocked out of alignment and he was obliged to complete the race at a reduced pace with dense tyre smoke issuing from the back of the car. All the while Pironi had been lapping as regularly as clockwork and, despite easing right off with the end in sight, still went on to win by the handsome margin of very nearly 22 seconds, at the same time pruning Watson's lead at the top of the Championship table to just one point. Second place, on the other hand, was a different matter altogether as Rosberg had moved right in on Piquet's tail on the last lap, helped to a certain extent by the Brazilian being held up by Alboreto's Tyrrell through Hunzerug, and the two cars eventually crossed the line just 0.716 sec apart. Behind them, only Lauda was still on the same lap as the winner to take fourth place, Daly was fifth and Baldi sixth to score his first-ever Championship point after having earlier made light work of overtaking the ailing cars of Giacomelli and Tambay and then Alboreto's Tyrrell on the final lap. As for the rest, who no longer included Mass as he had gone out with an engine failure after 60 laps, Tambay completed his first race with Ferrari in eighth place, Watson was ninth and Surer tenth ahead of Giacomelli, Winkelhock, Salazar, Jarier and, finally, Patrese whose problems had continued with the Brabham's fuel system playing up in the latter stages of the race.

Didier Pironi raises an arm to acknowledge the chequered flag after dominating most of the race. (*Autosport*)

Results			
1	D. Pironi (Ferrari)	1 hr 38 min 03.254 sec (187.331 kph/ 116.402 mph)	
2	N. Piquet (Brabham-BMW)	1 hr 38 min 24.903 sec	
3	K. Rosberg (Williams-Ford)	1 hr 38 min 25.619 sec	
4	N. Lauda (McLaren-Ford)	1 hr 39 min 26.974 sec	
5	D. Daly (Williams-Ford)	1 lap behind	
6	M. Baldi (Arrows-Ford)	1 lap behind	
7	M. Alboreto (Tyrrell-Ford)	1 lap behind	
8	P. Tambay (Ferrari)	1 lap behind	
9	J. Watson (McLaren-Ford)	1 lap behind	
10	M. Surer (Arrows-Ford)	1 lap behind	
11	B. Giacomelli (Alfa Romeo)	2 laps behind	
12	M. Winkelhock (ATS-Ford)	2 laps behind	
13	E. Salazar (ATS-Ford)	2 laps behind	
14	J.P. Jarier (Osella-Ford)	3 laps behind	
15	R. Patrese (Brabham-BMW)	3 laps behind	

Fastest lap: D. Warwick (Toleman-Hart) on lap 13 in 1 min 19.780 sec (191.867 kph/ 119.221 mph)

Retirements

J. Laffite (Talbot-Matra) handling on lap 5, D. Warwick (Toleman-Hart) oil leak on lap 16, F. Serra (Fittipaldi-Ford) fuel pump on lap 19, R. Boesel (March-Ford) engine on lap 22, R. Arnoux (Renault) accident on lap 22, B. Henton (Tyrrell-Ford) throttle linkage on lap 22, A. Prost (Renault) engine on lap 34, A. de Cesaris (Alfa Romeo) electrics on lap 36, E. de Angelis (Lotus-Ford) handling on lap 41, J. Lammers (Theodore-Ford) engine on lap 42, J. Mass (March-Ford) engine on lap 61.

XXXVth British Grand Prix

Brands Hatch: July 18
Weather: Hot
Distance: 76 laps of 4.2061 km circuit -
319.66 km (198.63 miles)

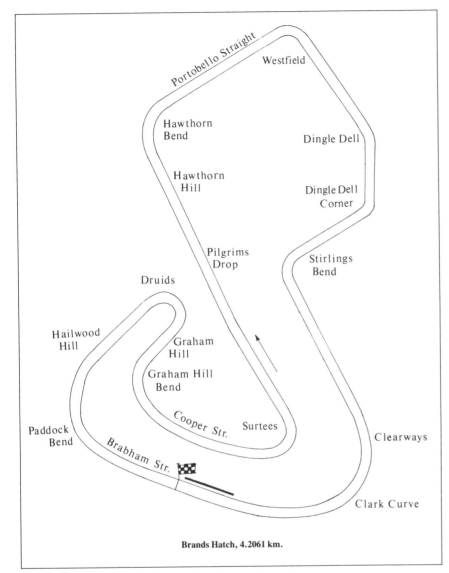

Brands Hatch, 4.2061 km.

strengthened lower front wishbones. In addition, the Fittipaldi team were in the midst of completing work on their brand new Richard Divila/Tim Wright-designed F9 – this was a logical development of the F8 and its derivatives but having a slim and more rigid monocoque, carbon-fibre bulkheads and pull-rod front suspension – and the Lotus team had an experimental car on hand, built around the monocoque of one of their ill-fated 88s. This also featured the now increasingly fashionable pull-rod front suspension. Meanwhile, other teams to have been particularly busy between races were Theodore, who had carried out a weight-saving programme on their

Starting Grid	
	K. Rosberg Williams-Ford (1 min 09.540 sec)
R. Patrese Brabham-BMW (1 min 09.627 sec)	N. Piquet Brabham-BMW (1 min 10.060 sec)
D. Pironi Ferrari (1 min 10.066 sec)	N. Lauda McLaren-Ford (1 min 10.638 sec)
R. Arnoux Renault (1 min 10.641 sec)	E. de Angelis Lotus-Ford (1 min 10.650 sec)
A. Prost Renault (1 min 10.728 sec)	M. Alboreto Tyrrell-Ford (1 min 10.892 sec)
D. Daly Williams-Ford (1 min 10.980 sec)	A. de Cesaris Alfa Romeo (1 min 11.347 sec)
J. Watson McLaren-Ford (1 min 11.418 sec)	P. Tambay Ferrari (1 min 11.430 sec)
B. Giacomelli Alfa Romeo (1 min 11.502 sec)	T. Fabi Toleman-Hart (1 min 11.728 sec)
D. Warwick Toleman-Hart (1 min 11.761 sec)	B. Henton Tyrrell-Ford (1 min 12.080 sec)
J.P. Jarier Osella-Ford (1 min 12.436 sec)	R. Guerrero Ensign-Ford (1 min 12.668 sec)
J. Laffite Talbot-Matra (1 min 12.695 sec)	F. Serra Fittipaldi-Ford (1 min 13.096 sec)
M. Surer Arrows-Ford (1 min 13.181 sec)	N. Mansell Lotus-Ford (1 min 13.212 sec)
E. Cheever Talbot-Matra (1 min 13.301 sec)	J. Mass March-Ford (1 min 13.622 sec)
M. Baldi Arrows-Ford (1 min 13.721 sec)	

Did not qualify:
M. Winkelhock (ATS-Ford) 1 min 13.741 sec
J. Lammers (Theodore-Ford) 1 min 13.815 sec
E. Salazar (ATS-Ford) 1 min 13.866 sec
R. Boesel (March-Ford) 1 min 13.968 sec

Because the French Grand Prix had been put back from its traditional date of the first weekend in July until the last for commercial reasons, in particular to avoid a clash with the World Cup soccer matches being televised, the next round of the 1982 World Championship was the Marlboro-sponsored British Grand Prix. This year, of course, that meant making the bi-annual trip to Brands Hatch and, with a British driver leading the points table for the first time since Jackie Stewart in 1973, interest was running at a very high level indeed even before the weekend started. Entry-wise, the situation was much the same as at Zandvoort a fortnight earlier with the only driver change being that of Nigel Mansell returning to the Lotus team even though he was still far from

being fully fit. However, the young Englishman was determined not to miss the chance of taking part in his first home Grand Prix and came prepared wearing a specially-made support cast over his left arm. On the mechanical front, too, nearly all of the teams brought along the same cars, although Ferrari had a new 126C2 for Tambay, Talbot-Ligier had produced the third of their new JS19s for Laffite with revised aerodynamics and a more conventional exhaust pipe layout (the pipes now extended rearwards over the top of the gearbox rather than through the side-plates of the rear aerofoil) and Renault had replaced the car damaged by Arnoux in his spectacular accident at Zandvoort by yet another chassis in their RE30B series, RE39B, which, like their other cars, had

TY02 that included the adoption of a carbon-fibre rear aerofoil, and also John Mac-Donald's RAM March outfit who had substantially modified their 821s. Primarily, they had strengthened the monocoques by riveting a carbon-fibre surround on to the aluminium, revised the front suspensions by using forward-biased rocker arms and fitted a spacer between the engine and gearbox of each of the cars to give them a longer wheelbase. Some of the remaining cars, too, had undergone further detail modifications of which none were more intriguing than the Brabham-BMWs as, for reasons that were not made readily apparent, these reappeared with three small built-in air-jacks and new, very large quick-release fuel fillers. In reality, though, Bernie Ecclestone's team were introducing a new tactical ploy. They were proposing to start their cars in the race on half-full fuel tanks and on soft compound tyres in the hope that their drivers would build up more than enough leeway to compensate for a pit stop at around half-distance. At that point the cars would then be replenished with enough fuel to see them through the rest of the race and be fitted with fresh soft tyres (pre-heated in a large oven to bring them up to the optimum working temperature), the aim, as always, being to gain an overall advantage on their rivals.

In all, 31 drivers should have been present at the start of practice on Friday morning, but because Emilio de Villota had withdrawn his entry and decided against continuing his involvement in the sport, the actual number that materialized was 30. Rather conveniently, this did away with the need for pre-qualifying which meant that the other drivers normally involved could settle down to the business of sorting cars along with everyone else, without being faced with the additional pressure of having to race against the clock. Naturally, the big question as things got under way was whether or not it was to be another show of turbo domination, for whilst being undeniably quick, the Kent circuit did not have any particularly long straights. This suggested that the non-turbo runners would be in with a reasonable chance of at least keeping pace with their more powerful rivals if not actually beating them, a fact that had been illustrated during recent pre-race testing when Rosberg had turned in the fastest time from de Angelis. In the event this was to prove to be the case but, meantime, the opening 90 minutes of practice were rather inconclusive as both Renault drivers were finding their cars behaving badly over the bumps, added to which Prost became stranded out on the circuit at one point with dead electrics, Tambay was experiencing acute understeer with the new Ferrari and Piquet was having a thoroughly frustrating time of it. First the drive-belt to the alternator broke on his proposed race chassis and then a blown head gasket ended his run in the

team's spare car. Consequently, of the leading turbo runners, only Pironi and Patrese were able to make much impression, but even they had to give best to de Angelis, the Italian Lotus driver starting the weekend in fine style by being quickest.

In the afternoon, with conditions remaining cloudy but warm, it was once again a normally-aspirated car that set the pace, only this time it was Rosberg's Williams. Slightly needled after having coasted to rest towards the end of the morning session when his fuel pumps had failed to function properly on a reducing fuel load, the Finn now put on a superb display of on-the-limit driving in the spare Williams (with the carbon-fibre brakes) and went on to be alone in breaking the 1 min 10 sec barrier at an astounding 1 min 9.540 sec (135.303 mph). Even more incredible, he achieved the time on a lap that saw him having a busy moment avoiding Arnoux's Renault which almost chopped him off as he ran up on the outside of it under braking for Druids. In fact, the Frenchman actually made contact, riding up over the Williams's left front wheel, but soon recovered only to nearly take the other Williams of Daly off going into Surtees a few minutes later. He apparently failed to notice him as well! Meanwhile, de Angelis was unable to maintain the same momentum as in the morning owing to losing some considerable amount of time when an electrical failure on the experimental Lotus brought him to rest out on the circuit. Nevertheless, once he had made his way back to the pits to switch to his more familiar car, the Italian certainly didn't disgrace himself and recovered sufficiently well to post a very respectable fourth fastest time of 1 min 10.650 sec. Only Pironi, after an engine misfire forced the Frenchman into the experimental Ferrari with the longitudinal gearbox (interestingly enough, this proved to be quicker than his regular car), and Piquet prevented him from taking the runner-up spot by turning in times of 1 min 10.066 sec and 1 min 10.418 sec respectively to lead the list of turbo runners. Despite a brief excursion on to the grass whilst keeping out of the way of Arnoux in addition to a problem with his clutch and brake pedals fouling one another because of a bent bracket, Daly was also well in the hunt after going around in joint fifth fastest time of 1 min 10.980 sec with Patrese. After that, though, only Lauda, Prost and the Alfa Romeo duo, de Cesaris and Giacomelli had lapped to within 2 seconds of Rosberg's time.

On Saturday it started all over again. First there were a further 90 minutes of testing in the morning which was highlighted by Giacomelli crashing heavily on the far side of the circuit when the carbon-fibre rear aerofoil mounting broke away from his Alfa Romeo, and also by Serra giving the new Fittipaldi an airing before spinning, harmlessly, on to the

grass and stalling the engine. Then there was the final hour of qualifying to savour in the afternoon. Unlike the first day, the skies were now clear and, if anything, conditions were too hot. Nevertheless, once the battle for grid positions resumed the majority of the drivers were soon making at least some improvement on their lap times with the two most noticeable exceptions, apart from Pironi and de Angelis who were both only marginally slower, being Rosberg and Daly. This was explained to a large extent, though, by both of them trying different set-ups which just didn't work. In Rosberg's case changes had been made to the suspension which were having an adverse effect on the car's handling, while Daly was trying a revised skirt system that was causing the steering to be too nervous going into the quick corners. The net result was that it made little difference so far as Rosberg was concerned as he still held on to his first-ever pole position by reason of the super-quick lap on the previous afternoon. Daly, on the other hand, slipped right back to tenth place on the grid as, in addition to the four drivers to have already beaten him, another five now also moved on ahead, these being a very on-form Patrese, who had rather less problems with the traffic than Piquet and produced an extremely impressive-looking second fastest time overall of 1 min 9.627 sec, Lauda (1 min 10.638 sec), Arnoux (1 min 10.641 sec), Prost (1 min 10.728 sec) and Alboreto (1 min 10.892 sec). Like the two Williams FW08s, Arnoux's Renault had also been set up differently for the second qualifying run, but in this instance it had made a noticeable improvement and enabled the Frenchman to move up from a rather hopeless fifteenth place after the first day to an eventual sixth spot on the grid. However, with Prost winding up a couple of places lower, separated from his team-mate by de Angelis, this was still a disappointment for the French team compared to their recent performances, in practice at least. There was disappointment in other quarters as well quite apart from that for the four drivers who had ultimately failed to qualify. First and foremost Watson, after complaining of lack of grip and problems with the traffic, had qualified in only twelfth spot; Tambay was one place lower when he should have been up near the front like his team-mate and probably would have been had his ignition not failed just as he was preparing for a quick lap on his second set of qualifiers; and both Alfa Romeo drivers had dropped back due to having been among the remaining few not to have improved, de Cesaris plagued by a misfiring engine and Giacomelli having had to start virtually from scratch in the team's spare car following his accident. On the other side of the coin, the Toleman team had both of their cars in a race for the first time, ignoring the ill-attended San Marino Grand

Prix, Mansell had done a commendable job by even qualifying after having effectively driven one-handed, and Cheever had spared the Talbot-Ligier team a certain amount of embarrassment by hoisting himself from the very bottom of the standings on Friday to 24th place on the grid. Even so, the French equipe were hardly bubbling with confidence as the American had resorted to the spare JS17 to achieve his best time, due to experiencing acute understeer with his JS19. Furthermore Laffite, whilst persevering with his new car despite being plagued by a similar problem, had made only a marginally better impression by finishing up just two rows higher alongside Guerrero's Ensign.

The sun was still bearing down on race day and although the Grand Prix was not scheduled to start until 3 p.m. the Kent circuit was alive with thousands of eager spectators from an early hour, many, no doubt, hoping that Watson would repeat his victory at Silverstone twelve months earlier. Prior to the main event the organizers laid on an absolutely superb supporting programme that included a race between representatives of the House of Lords and the House of Commons, a round of the Tricentrol RAC British Saloon Car Championship and seemingly endless demonstrations and parades, one of which was to mark the 75th anniversary of Shell. In addition, there was a magnificent and varied air display with appearances from the Marlboro Aerobatic team, Concorde, a Harrier jump-jet (this brought back vivid memories of the recent conflict in the Falkland Islands), a Sea King helicopter, a Douglas DC3 'Dakota' and the ever-popular Red Arrows. Amidst all the activity 30 minutes were set aside for the usual warm-up session which took place at mid-day. By then the Williams team had their FW08s back to the same specification in which they had started the weekend, Pironi had decided to rely on the 'old' Ferrari with the transverse gearbox, Serra was similarly intending to race the Fittipaldi F8D rather than the new, mainly untried, F9, and Cheever obviously wanted nothing to do with his Talbot-Ligier JS19 as he appeared in the older JS17 once again. Most intriguing of all was the situation in the Brabham pit for whilst it was still by no means clear whether or not they were going ahead with pre-planned pit stops it was certainly looking that way: pressurized fuel containers, ovens to heat tyres and flame-proof overalls were all at the ready, and lines had even been drawn on the pit apron to denote the exact spot where their cars were to stop. The warm-up, itself, saw Warwick spring another surprise, as in Holland, by setting third fastest time behind Piquet and Patrese. It also saw Rosberg have about the only problem when his Williams jumped out of gear and over-revved the engine sufficiently for a replacement to be considered necessary. This was to

prove significant some two hours later, for as the final minutes ticked away to 3 p.m. and everyone was preparing for the pace lap the fresh unit refused to fire up due to apparent fuel vaporization. Consequently it was left to Patrese to eventually lead the field around on the pace lap with Rosberg finally getting away after they had all gone. This, of course, meant starting the race from the back of the grid, a bitter blow for the Finn after the efforts made to secure pole position.

As the red lights glowed engine notes rose and then, seconds later, it was green for go. Patrese, though, didn't move and, instead, had his arm in the air to signify a stalled engine, the result of his Brabham having jumped out of gear. Directly behind him, Pironi took evasive action by moving to his right before charging off after Piquet and Lauda in third place but a split second later Arnoux collected the stationary Brabham's right rear wheel. He then lost his own left front wheel (again!) on impact and went sliding off to the outside of the track into retirement, taking the Brabham with him. That was not all, as in the confusion that followed Daly only just avoided making contact, Prost and Watson were both forced to take to the grass, the McLaren driver narrowly missing the guard-rail, and Fabi ran over the Renault's wheel to become the third

casualty with bent front suspension. More destruction was to quickly follow when, on only the third lap, Serra dived for the inside of Jarier under braking for Hawthorn Bend only to find himself riding up over the Osella's left front wheel due to the Frenchman inadvertently moving over on him. Again both retired, Serra being particularly fortunate to subsequently emerge from his car unharmed after some marshals had rushed to his aid, for the Fittipaldi had spun crazily in the air, careered backwards into the guard-rail, flipped over and briefly caught fire. This incident, too, had a dire effect on other people. First a closely-following Watson spun in trying to keep out of the way and was unable to restart after stalling his engine. Then Guerrero, who stood on his brakes, was struck from behind by Henton, the impact damaging the Tyrrell's nose cone and fracturing an oil pipe on the Ensign which was destined to retire on the following lap with a blown-up engine. So, in a race that was barely five minutes old, the field was already down to 19 cars, with the order behind Piquet, Lauda and Pironi (still occupying the three leading positions and putting increasing amounts of daylight between one another) being de Angelis, Alboreto (soon to become the first visitor to the pits to have a loose skirt rectified), Daly,

After a chaotic start, the leaders plunge down Paddock Bend with Nelson Piquet out in front and eventual winner Niki Lauda lying second ahead of Pironi, de Angelis, Alboreto, de Cesaris, Daly, Prost, Giacomelli and Tambay. *(Autosport)*

de Cesaris, Giacomelli, Prost, Warwick, Tambay and then Rosberg who had already carved his way up to twelfth place in magnificent style to lead the others.

By the start of lap 10 Piquet was as many seconds clear of Lauda and well on target to allow sufficient time for the speculative pit stop at around half-distance provided that he maintained the same pace. However, as the blue and white car climbed the hill to Druids it suddenly slowed, went coasting round the hairpin and down to Graham Hill Bend and was then seen turning off into the slip road behind the paddock. The belt driving the fuel-injection pump had broken so ending Piquet's race and all prospects of seeing the Brabham pit stop if, in fact, it had been planned. Meanwhile, Lauda took over the lead with a secure-looking 15 second advantage over Pironi, and Daly, who had barged past de Angelis during the previous lap, was now up into third place with the Ferrari right in his sights. The real surprise, though, was to see Warwick's Toleman now running in a strong fifth place, the young Englishman making an exceptionally good impression and presently giving chase to de Angelis after having earlier picked off Prost, Alboreto (before his pit stop) and both Alfa Romeo drivers. Rosberg, too, was coming more and more into the picture as he continued a sustained charge from the back of the grid. Currently lying ninth, he was not finished yet, either, and took only three more laps to make that sixth by going past Tambay, Prost and de Cesaris in quick succession. The only trouble was he was paying dearly for his forceful driving. His front tyres were becoming badly blistered. As a result it was only a question of time before he would have to stop for fresh rubber and, sure enough, at the end of lap 16, the Williams was seen making for the pits, bringing groans from an appreciative crowd. There, four new Goodyears were slapped on but by the time that Rosberg had rejoined the race to start all over again sixth place had become seventeenth and he was over a lap behind the leader. Nevertheless, from the point of view of the crowd, there was still plenty to cheer about elsewhere for Warwick was in no such trouble, had dispensed with de Angelis going

into Westfield Bend back on the twelfth lap and was soon outbraking Daly at Paddock Bend, on lap 19, to take over a superb third place. Furthermore, he then lost little time in not only attaching himself to the back of Pironi's Ferrari but going past that as well in another audacious outbraking manoeuve at Paddock Bend just seven laps later, accompanied by more roars of approval from the spectator stands. Second place! This was almost unbelievable but, at the same time, proved conclusively just what good progress the Toleman team had been making in recent weeks. In the meantime, Lauda, looking serenely confident out in front, had extended his lead to around 25 seconds and although Warwick quickly pulled away from Pironi, who was having to contend with a sticking throttle in addition to a shade more understeer than he would have liked, the gap between the first two cars remained almost constant over the next few laps. As it did so, Rosberg was forced to make a second pit stop for yet more new Goodyears and, at the end of lap 29, Daly was also heading for the pits for fresh rubber, handing fourth place back to de Angelis besides moving de Cesaris, Tambay, Laffite, a rather unimpressive Prost, Giacomelli and Cheever all up a place. Further back Mansell, after having stopped a few laps earlier to have a broken skirt replaced, quietly departed the fray on lap 30 saying that his left arm was hurting too much to continue, Mass and Surer were two others to stop for new tyres, and Alboreto seemed to be spending more time in the pits than out on the track having adjustments made to his Tyrrell to try to make it handle properly.

At half-distance (38 laps) most of the excitement seemed to be over as Lauda, Warwick and Pironi were well spread out in the first three places, while de Angelis, de Cesaris, Tambay, Laffite, Prost and Daly (he had already repassed Cheever and Giacomelli) were the only others still on the same lap as the leader. However, just when it looked as if stalemate had set in Warwick's Toleman suddenly slowed dramatically coming out of Druids on lap 41 and spent the rest of the lap touring around to the pits. A drive-shaft joint had failed. Quite apart from the obvious disappointment to driver, team

and spectator alike after such an outstanding performance, this automatically increased Lauda's lead to a massive 40 seconds and put the Austrian in an even stronger position. A lap later gearbox trouble also put Laffite out just when he seemed to be all set to score his first Championship points in the new Talbot JS19, and at almost the same time de Cesaris found his progress beginning to suffer because of his Alfa Romeo developing a pronounced engine misfire. As a result the Italian quickly began to slip back into Tambay's clutches, and before long Daly's as well, the Irishman continuing his fight-back after the tyre stop by overtaking Prost on lap 43. In fact, by lap 53 the ailing Alfa Romeo was behind them both and was about to be lapped by the leader who had just caused a certain amount of embarrassment in the Renault camp by going past Prost. Meanwhile, Rosberg's frustrating afternoon finally concluded when he was forced to retire his Williams with fluctuating fuel pressure, and de Angelis's hopes of finishing in third place received a setback due to the fuel system of his Lotus also starting to play up.

With sixteen laps remaining, and de Cesaris now down to seventh place behind Prost, Lauda began to ease off as he clearly demonstrated by allowing the Renault driver to unlap himself. Even so, such was his margin of superiority that he still went on to take the chequered flag more than 25 seconds ahead of Pironi to score a thoroughly convincing victory, the nineteenth of his career. Behind Pironi, whose six points for second place enabled him to take over from Watson at the top of the Championship table, de Angelis just failed to hold on to third place. Instead, in an exciting climax, Tambay caught and passed the Lotus on the last lap and so, very nearly, did Daly and Prost, both finishing less than half a second away in fifth and sixth places respectively. After that only Giacomelli, Henton (he had distinguished himself by setting fastest lap in the closing stages following a pit stop to change a blistered left front tyre), Baldi, Mass and Alboreto were still there at the finish as Surer and Cheever had both suffered late engine failures while de Cesaris's Alfa Romeo had ground to a half on lap 67.

Results		
1	N. Lauda (McLaren-Ford)	1 hr 35 min 33.812 sec (200.685 kph/ 124.700 mph)
2	D. Pironi (Ferrari)	1 hr 35 min 59.538 sec
3	P. Tambay (Ferrari)	1 hr 36 min 12.248 sec
4	E. de Angelis (Lotus-Ford)	1 hr 36 min 15.054 sec
5	D. Daly (Williams-Ford)	1 hr 36 min 15.242 sec
6	A. Prost (Renault)	1 hr 36 min 15.448 sec
7	B. Giacomelli (Alfa Romeo)	1 lap behind
8	B. Henton (Tyrrell-Ford)	1 lap behind
9	M. Baldi (Arrows-Ford)	2 laps behind
10	J. Mass (March-Ford)	3 laps behind

Also running at finish: M. Alboreto (Tyrrell-Ford) 32 laps behind.

Fastest lap: B. Henton (Tyrrell-Ford) on lap 63 in 1 min 13.028 sec (207.347 kph/128.840 mph)

Retirements
R. Patrese (Brabham-BMW) accident on lap 1, R. Arnoux (Renault) accident on lap 1, T. Fabi (Toleman-Hart) front suspension on lap 1, F. Serra (Fittipaldi-Ford) accident on lap 3, J.P. Jarier (Osella-Ford) accident on lap 3, J. Watson (McLaren-Ford) spun and stalled on lap 3, R. Guerrero (Ensign-Ford) engine on lap 4, N. Piquet (Brabham-BMW) fuel-injection on lap 10, N. Mansell (Lotus-Ford) handling on lap 30, D. Warwick (Toleman-Hart) drive-shaft on lap 41, J. Laffite (Talbot-Matra) gearbox on lap 42, K. Rosberg (Williams-Ford) fuel pressure on lap 51, M. Surer (Arrows-Ford) engine on lap 60, E. Cheever (Talbot-Matra) engine on lap 61, A. de Cesaris (Alfa Romeo) electrics on lap 67.

LXVIIIe Grand Prix de France

Paul Ricard: July 25
Weather: Hot
Distance: 54 laps of 5.810 km circuit = 313.74 km (194.95 miles)

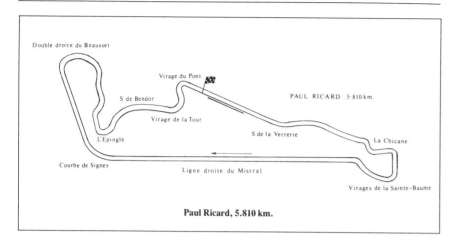

Paul Ricard, 5.810 km.

With the British and French Grands Prix taking place on consecutive weekends the teams were faced with a very tight schedule indeed for there were just four clear days before it was time to start all over again. Meanwhile, cars and equipment had to be loaded up at Brands Hatch, transported the best part of a thousand miles to Circuit Paul Ricard in the south of France, unloaded and everything prepared for the start of practice on the Friday morning. In addition, several cars had to be repaired or even replaced, so in many respects it was quite remarkable that everyone was more or less ready at the appointed hour, the only exception being Nigel Mansell. He had been advised to give the race a miss in order that his left wrist and arm injuries would have the chance to heal properly. Even so there was still a full quota of drivers present as Colin Chapman had invited Geoff Lees to take over his second car for the weekend, the 1981 European Formula 2 Champion, of course, having stood in for Jan Lammers under similar circumstances in Canada.

For Renault this was one race they really had to win to sustain their credibility after a succession of mainly disappointing results in a season that had promised so much. However, if the opening practice session was anything to go by they were in for another difficult time of it as both of their drivers were soon in trouble. First Arnoux, driving yet another replacement chassis (RE38B) following his start-line shunt at Brands Hatch, was dismayed to find his car porpoising badly down the exceptionally long and fast Mistral straight. Then Prost, who was trying out carbon-fibre brake discs as well as a new hydraulic suspension system designed to keep ride height at a constant level, returned to the pits on foot before covering many laps to report that he had been forced to abandon his car out on the circuit with a

dead engine. Fortunately, from the point of view of the team's morale, it turned out to be nothing worse than a broken electrical connection and thereafter the situation rapidly started to improve with Prost going out in the afternoon and setting the fastest time of 1 min 35.802 sec. Arnoux, too, was obviously making progress in the right direction by then, for despite still not being too happy about his car's behaviour he came to grips with the problem sufficiently well to wind up a very respectable third fastest at 1 min 36.548 sec, this reducing the tension within the French team still further. In the meantime, as had been anticipated, it was turning out to be a field-day for the turbo-charged cars with no less than six of them occupying the first eight places on the time-sheets. Splitting the Renaults, Pironi came out second fastest at 1 min 36.477 sec, Piquet was fourth fastest at 1 min 37.162 sec in spite of being forced to pack up early after losing his second engine of the day, and Patrese (1 min 38.541 sec) and Tambay (1 min 38.745 sec) were seventh and eight in the standings respectively behind the two very evenly-matched Ford-Cosworth-powered cars of Lauda (1 min 37.778 sec) and Rosberg (1 min 37.780 sec). Even then the situation might well have been different as Patrese also blew up his BMW engine during the afternoon, while Tambay, after having lost virtually the whole of the morning session due to a stone breaking the drive-belt to his Ferrari's fuel pump, lost yet more time when a leak in the car's recently devised water-cooled fuel-injection system allowed water to mix with the fuel! Meanwhile, so far as the remaining team using turbo-charged engines was concerned (Toleman), things were decidedly worse. For a start Fabi failed to record even one timed flying lap due to an oil leak setting his car ablaze along the Mistral straight and the Italian failing to

switch the engine off quick enough to prevent it from seizing. Then, to add to their problems, Warwick was simply unable to make his car handle properly with the result that in direct contrast to his performance at Brands Hatch (the subject of much unnecessary scorn from some rivals who were mumbling about him having raced on qualifying tyres and a low fuel load) he was making little or no impression whatsoever. Not that he was entirely alone in this respect as after Daly, ninth fastest at 1 min 38.767 sec, everyone was anything from at least three to nine seconds off the pace.

On Saturday morning Warwick didn't

Starting Grid	
R. Arnoux Renault (1 min 34.406 sec)	
	A. Prost Renault (1 min 34.688 sec)
D. Pironi Ferrari (1 min 35.790 sec)	
	R. Patrese Brabham-BMW (1 min 35.811 sec)
P. Tambay Ferrari (1 min 35.905 sec)	
	N. Piquet Brabham-BMW (1 min 36.359 sec)
A. de Cesaris Alfa Romeo (1 min 37.573 sec)	
	B. Giacomelli Alfa Romeo (1 min 37.705 sec)
N. Lauda McLaren-Ford (1 min 37.778 sec)	
	K. Rosberg Williams-Ford (1 min 37.780 sec)
D. Daly Williams-Ford (1 min 38.767 sec)	
	J. Watson McLaren-Ford (1 min 38.944 sec)
E. de Angelis Lotus-Ford (1 min 39.118 sec)	
	D. Warwick Toleman-Hart (1 min 39.306 sec)
M. Alboreto Tyrrell-Ford (1 min 39.330 sec)	
	J. Laffite Talbot-Matra (1 min 39.605 sec)
J.P. Jarier Osella-Ford (1 min 39.909 sec)	
	M. Winkelhock ATS-Ford (1 min 39.917 sec)
E. Cheever Talbot-Matra (1 min 40.187 sec)	
	M. Surer Arrows-Ford (1 min 40.335 sec)
T. Fabi Toleman-Hart (1 min 40.421 sec)	
	E. Salazar ATS-Ford (1 min 40.673 sec)
B. Henton Tyrrell-Ford (1 min 40.852 sec)	
	G. Lees Lotus-Ford (1 min 40.974 sec)
M. Baldi Arrows-Ford (1 min 40.997 sec)	
	J. Mass March-Ford (1 min 41.579 sec)

Did not qualify:
J. Lammers (Theodore-Ford) 1 min 41.714 sec
R. Guerrero (Ensign-Ford) 1 min 42.270 sec
F. Serra (Fittipaldi-Ford) 1 min 42.414 sec
R. Boesel (March-Ford) 1 min 43.099 sec

exactly help his chances by putting his Toleman out of action with extensive front-end damage after arriving too quickly at the fast left-hand turn leading on to the Mistral straight and spinning off into the catch-fences. Pironi also indulged in a quick, though less harmful, spin at Beausset, while amongst those to have mechanical problems were team-mate Tambay, Patrese and Lauda who all suffered engine failures. For the Renault team, on the other hand, there was no trouble whatsoever and both of their drivers were out setting a scorching pace. Furthermore, this pattern continued into the final hour of qualifying with Arnoux taking just two timed laps to record a magnificent pole-winning time of 1 min 34.406 sec (221.553 kph) and Prost, his car now fitted with conventional steel brake discs, turning in a very comfortable second fastest time of 1 min 34.688 sec. More than a full second slower than both of them, Pironi continued to lead the opposition by taking his familiar Ferrari 126C2 around in 1 min 35.790 sec, and then came Patrese (1 min 35.811 sec), Tambay (1 min 35.905 sec) and Piquet (1 min 36.359 sec) to make it six turbo-charged cars in the first six places on the grid. It was certainly no surprise, though, as all of them had been consistently reaching speeds of around 200 mph down the long back straight throughout both days of practice. Nevertheless, it was still a demoralizing sight for the other teams using normally-aspirated engines and to the Ford-Cosworth brigade, in particular, as even the quickest amongst their number, Lauda, finished up in only ninth place on the grid, the Austrian lining up behind the two evenly-matched Alfa Romeos of de Cesaris (1 min 37.573 sec) and Giacomelli (1 min 37.705 sec) who were both obviously benefiting from overnight changes to gear ratios and aerodynamic appendages on their cars. Lauda, in fact, failed to improve on his Friday time as did team-mate Watson (driving a brand new chassis this weekend) and both Williams drivers, neither of whom had a very happy afternoon. First Rosberg ran out of fuel at one point besides complaining, afterwards, that Lauda had blocked him on a quick lap. Then Daly also coasted to rest out on the circuit after being forced to switch off when an oil pipe came adrift on his car. However, as no-one else beat their existing times Rosberg lined up alongside Lauda, while Daly rounded off the front half of the grid in company with Watson and a much-improved de Angelis whose first day had been spoiled somewhat by the same fuel system problem that had struck at Brands Hatch. Meanwhile, amongst the drivers to finish up lower down the order, one of the most pleasing aspects was Warwick's performance in the closing ten minutes of practice. After waiting around for repairs to be completed on his car, and undergoing the frustrating experience of

having to watch Friday's time slip from being 19th fastest to 25th up until that point, the young Englishman responded magnificently when he did finally go out again and leap-frogged over no less than eleven drivers to wind up in 14th spot on the grid. Naturally the Toleman team was overjoyed, not least the mechanics, and to add to their obvious delight Fabi had qualified as well after his disaster of the previous afternoon. Lees, who had blown up an engine in each of Friday's sessions, the first when he selected an incorrect gear, also hoisted himself out of the non-qualifying zone but Serra, concentrating on the new Fittipaldi F9 until gearbox trouble forced him into the older F8D, was less successful, and so was Boesel. Both were ultimately joined by Lammers and also by Guerrero whose hopes of holding on to a grid position had been dashed by a recalcitrant gearbox as well as a tired engine.

Following two days of mainly clear blue skies and hot sunshine, the weather on Sunday was no exception. In fact, if anything, it was even hotter, but fears on the part of the organizers that the heat would have an adverse effect on the size of the crowd proved unfounded as the number of spectators that ultimately turned up was claimed to be an all-time record for the circuit. Because the Grand Prix was due to start at 1.30 p.m., the warm-up session took place comparatively early and, just like the previous week at Brands Hatch, much of the attention was diverted towards the Brabham pit. Here, once again, there was every indication that pit stops were being planned during the race. All the necessary equipment was at the ready and even wheel changes were being practised. Apart from this, the 30 minutes were fairly uneventful with the only obvious problem to show up being a water leak on Daly's Williams. Pironi, though, was

complaining of poor throttle response out of the slower corners (this led to the Ferrari mechanics changing the turbo units on his car) and the Talbot–Ligier team, concentrating entirely on their JS19s this weekend, were dismayed to find that overnight changes to the suspension settings of their cars were proving to be a step in the wrong direction. This was in spite of the fact that Laffite and Cheever had both found it virtually impossible to balance the cars for the mixture of slow and fast corners throughout practice.

Due to recent problems, even tragedy, caused by cars stalling on the grid a revised starting procedure was being adopted. This provided that in the event of such an occurrence the start would be aborted by the appearance of flashing yellow lights. Everyone would then be obliged to switch off and the sequence begun all over again with a second pace lap matched by a corresponding reduction of one lap in the race distance to avoid any problems regarding fuel. However, on this occasion it was not needed as when the 26 cars lined up to face the starting lights there was no last-minute trouble. Instead, apart from a bit of weaving near the back of the grid caused by Jarier's Osella breaking a drive-shaft as the Frenchman let out his clutch, it was a good clean start and particularly so for the two Renault drivers as Arnoux took off into an immediate lead and Prost neatly slotted into second place ahead of Pironi's Ferrari. The pair of Brabham-BMWs weren't exactly slow off the mark either, Patrese and Piquet snapping straight into fourth and fifth places respectively in front of Tambay in the other Ferrari, while Daly quickly moved up into seventh place to head the non-turbo brigade after making what was almost certainly his best start ever. This was still the order as the leaders roared down the long back straight, but then Patrese

Eventual winner René Arnoux comes under pressure from Nelson Piquet's Brabham during the early stages of the French Grand Prix which, this year, returned to the Paul Ricard circuit. (*L.A.T. Photographic*)

jinked out of Pironi's slip-stream and an instant later was powering past the Ferrari to take over third place as they went into Signes. After that the Italian's progress was rapid indeed. On the second lap he dispensed with Prost, took only another lap to see off Arnoux as well and from there immediately began to pull away to consolidate his new position at the front of the race. Piquet, too, was making much the same sort of impression and although it took him a little longer to find a way past Arnoux, after displacing Pironi and Prost on the second lap, it was still only the fifth lap before the Brabhams were lying first and second, at this stage 5 seconds apart. Lower down the order, meanwhile, there had already been two more retirements. First Fabi had seen his oil pressure warning light come on half way round the opening lap – the Toleman's oil pump had stopped working – and he had immediately switched off the engine following the unfortunate incident in practice. Then Salazar had completed only two laps before spinning off into the catch-fences at the ultra fast ess-bend just beyond the pits. Although he was still in the race, de Cesaris was not having a very happy time of it either as his engine was misfiring badly. In fact, after having ended the opening lap in ninth place behind his team-mate, he'd already been overtaken by Lauda and Watson and on seeing Rosberg (he had made a poor start), Alboreto and de Angelis go by on the sixth lap, he finally made for the pits to have the Alfa's fuel system checked over.

By the eighth lap the two Brabhams were already beginning to look invincible with both of them now pulling away from the Renaults at a prodigious rate and leaving the rest of the field, including the Ferraris, even further behind. However, just when it looked as if the race was settling down a puff of blue smoke suddenly appeared from the back of Patrese's car as he lifted off for Signes and by the time that he had reached Beausset it was obvious that there was a major problem, the Brabham visibly slowing and the smoke intensifying. In fact, the BMW engine had holed a piston. Unaware that an oil fire was developing, Patrese kept going as best he could until finally pulling up at the entrance to the pits. By that stage the fire had really taken hold and the Brabham's rear bodywork was ablaze, although almost before the Italian had stepped out of the cockpit some marshals were on the scene with extinguishers and quickly had the situation under control. Piquet, meanwhile, had already swept past into the lead and now had a useful, if uneasy, looking 7 second advantage over Arnoux which was soon increasing still further. As he continued to draw away, Lees crawled into the pits at the end of lap 9 to have a punctured right rear tyre replaced on his Lotus, a lap later Cheever also broke out of formation for a fresh set of Michelins

as well as adjustments to try to improve the handling of his Talbot and then, on lap 11, came an accident of near-catastrophic proportions which could have had a profound effect on the future of motor racing as a whole. It all came about as a result of Mass and Baldi, vying for eighteenth place, colliding with one another going into Signes at a speed approaching 300 kph after the Italian had darted out of the March's slip-stream towards the end of the Mistral straight and attempted to go through on the inside. Without apportioning any blame, it appeared that Mass then moved over on him but, whereas the Arrows spun off into the catch-fences, from where its occupant subsequently emerged unharmed, the March became airborne, cartwheeled over the catch-fences, struck the tyre-lined barriers and ricocheted into a debris fence at the edge of a spectator enclosure where it landed upside down. Mercifully, though, the consequences were nowhere as serious as they might have been for whilst around a dozen spectators were involved, the injuries, apart from broken bones in one instance, were confined to minor abrasions, bruises and also burns caused by the March briefly catching fire. Despite being trapped for several minutes, Mass escaped serious injury as well but was in a state of considerable shock and also complaining that his back and shoulders were hurting. Nevertheless, it was still remarkable and, indeed, fortunate that no-one was killed.

As the rescue services sped to the scene of the accident and started to do what was necessary, the situation behind the five leading turbo-charged cars continued to change quite dramatically, only now because of a succession of pit stops. They began on lap 13 when Daly, who had been more than holding his ground as the leading non-turbo runner up until that point, took on four fresh tyres after having picked up a puncture. Then, moments later, he was followed by Watson, whose McLaren had developed a pronounced misfire, and also by Laffite who was in much the same sort of trouble as Cheever in the other Talbot. After that only another lap passed before there was more activity caused by Warwick stopping to report that he had lost the use of his clutch, and while the Toleman mechanics were busy freeing it Lauda found himself in need of a change of rubber. Unbeknown to the Austrian, though, the McLaren mechanics were still milling around Watson's car as he headed down the pit road and so, on seeing this, he drove straight back out on to the track before trying again next time round. By then his team-mate's car had been wheeled away into retirement with a broken electrical lead, so Lauda eventually got his fresh tyres and charged back out into the fray in twelfth place just as de Angelis pulled in to complain that the fuel system on his Lotus was playing

up yet again. Like Watson, he, too, was destined to retire. All the while Piquet was up an ever-increasing lead and after twenty laps was almost as many seconds clear of Arnoux who, in turn, was now beginning to draw away from Prost due to his team-mate having slowed slightly as he learned to live with a broken skirt. Further back, the two Ferraris of Pironi and Tambay were still pounding along in fourth and fifth places but becoming increasingly spaced out, while Rosberg was now running in a lonely sixth spot ahead of Alboreto, Giacomelli, Daly and Lauda, the Austrian having already regained a couple of places since his tyre stop at the expense of Henton and Winkelhock who were left leading the others still in the race.

Attention now became focused on the Brabham pit where preparations were being made for the much-publicized tyre and fuel stop. Rough calculations suggested that this would cost Piquet about half a minute in which case the race was heading for an exciting climax for he would almost certainly rejoin in third place and be left with approximately 10 seconds to make up in order to regain the lead. Alas, the pit stop never materialized as on lap 24 a puff of blue smoke appeared from the back of Piquet's Brabham as he lifted off for Signes and that heralded the end of yet another BMW engine, the Brazilian pulling off to the side of the track just beyond the right-hander. Apart from the obvious disappointment to driver and team alike, this effectively put an end to the race as such, as from then on it became a rather tedious procession with Arnoux steadily increasing his lead and Prost, in spite of his broken skirt, coming under no threat whatsoever from the two Ferraris which were running on too conservative a tyre choice and lacking grip. About the only bit of light relief came during the final ten laps. At that point the Renault management, having already decided that Prost was now their main hope of winning the Championship, held out a pit board to Arnoux indicating that his team-mate was to win only to find that it brought no response. On seeing this, they repeated the signal but again it achieved nothing as Arnoux was taking the view that having built up an advantage of more than 20 seconds it was too much to ask of him. Consequently he drove on to a comfortable victory while a somewhat peeved Prost made it a magnificent Renault 1 – 2 to give the French team just the sort of fillip that they had so badly needed, the two yellow, white and black cars separated by a fraction over 17 seconds at the finish. Almost 25 seconds later Pironi duly followed them home in third place to extend his lead over Watson at the top of the Championship table to nine points. Tambay completed his race with a misfiring engine in an even more distant fourth place, and Ros-

1982

berg just held off Alboreto to take fifth spot, the Finn having had to work really hard to defend his position in the latter stages of the race because of a blistered left rear tyre. After that everyone else was at least a lap in arrears, but there were still 16 of the original 26 cars running at the finish as only one other retirement had occurred. That was de Cesaris who had spun off almost exactly at half-distance when a front tyre deflated on his Alfa Romeo. Warwick, though, only just made it for no sooner had he crossed the line, after having lost the use of his clutch again, than the Toleman's transmission broke!

<table>
<tr><td colspan="4">Results</td></tr>
</table>

1	R. Arnoux (Renault)	1 hr 33 min 33.217 sec (201.215 kph/ 125.029 mph)		
2	A. Prost (Renault)	1 hr 33 min 50.525 sec		
3	D. Pironi (Ferrari)	1 hr 34 min 15.345 sec		
4	P. Tambay (Ferrari)	1 hr 34 min 49.458 sec		
5	K. Rosberg (Williams-Ford)	1 hr 35 min 04.211 sec		
6	M. Alboreto (Tyrrell-Ford)	1 hr 35 min 05.556 sec		
7	D. Daly (Williams-Ford)	1 lap behind		
8	N. Lauda (McLaren-Ford)	1 lap behind		
9	B. Giacomelli (Alfa Romeo)	1 lap behind		
10	B. Henton (Tyrrell-Ford)	1 lap behind		
11	M. Winkelhock (ATS-Ford)	2 laps behind		
12	G. Lees (Lotus-Ford)	2 laps behind		
13	M. Surer (Arrows-Ford)	2 laps behind		
14	J. Laffite (Talbot-Matra)	3 laps behind		
15	D. Warwick (Toleman-Hart)	4 laps behind		
16	E. Cheever (Talbot-Matra)	5 laps behind		

Fastest lap: R. Patrese (Brabham-BMW) on lap 4 in 1 min 40.075 sec (209.003 kph/ 129.868 mph)

Retirements
J.P. Jarier (Osella-Ford) drive-shaft on lap 1, T. Fabi (Toleman-Hart) oil pump on lap 1, E. Salazar (ATS-Ford) spun off on lap 3, R. Patrese (Brabham-BMW) engine on lap 9, J. Mass (March-Ford) accident on lap 11, M. Baldi (Arrows-Ford) accident on lap 11, J. Watson (McLaren-Ford) electrics on lap 14, E. de Angelis (Lotus-Ford) fuel pressure on lap 18, N. Piquet (Brabham-BMW) engine on lap 24, A. de Cesaris (Alfa Romeo) spun off on lap 26.

XLIV Grosser Preis von Deutschland

Hockenheim: August 8
Weather: Overcast but dry
Distance: 45 laps of 6.797 km
circuit = 305.86 km (190.05 miles)

From Paul Ricard it was now time to move on to another venue ideally suited to the turbo-charged cars, the Hockenheim-Ring near Heidelberg in West Germany. Here, some quite significant changes had taken place since the 1981 race. The first chicane had been tightened and a new, additional chicane inserted immediately before the hitherto very quick and extremely demanding Ostkurve on the far side of the circuit. Apparently the changes had come about owing to growing concern over ever-increasing speeds but the new chicane, in particular, was such a tight and narrow little affair that instead of making the track safer, which was supposed to be the object of the exercise, several of the drivers considered it to be downright dangerous. Either way, the fact remained that one of the fastest (and most exciting) corners on the Grand Prix calendar had been lost and now become a tricky second gear ess-bend through which there was barely enough room for one car.

As practice got under way with 90 minutes of testing on Friday morning the line-up was very similar to that seen at Paul Ricard a fortnight earlier. There were just two new cars in evidence and only one driver change apart from that of Nigel Mansell returning to take up his place in the Lotus team once more. Renault had completed work on the tenth chassis in their RE30B series, which was intended for Prost, and Williams had put together another FW08, their sixth, for Daly to use, while the change of driver was to be found at Theodore. Here, for no obvious reason, Jan Lammers had been dropped in favour of the current leader of the Marlboro British Formula 3 Championship, Irishman Tommy Byrne, who was making his first public appearance in a Grand Prix car aided by sponsorship from Rizla. Unfortunately, though, things didn't get off to the best of starts for him as after only about half an hour he became the first victim of the new Ost-kurve chicane by arriving a fraction too quickly, bouncing over the kerb and striking the tyre barrier. Even so it was not exactly a disaster for, in spite of practice having to be interrupted so that the barrier could be replaced and the Theodore towed back to the pits, damage was confined mainly to the car's left front suspension and Byrne, uninjured, was able to go straight out again in the team's spare chassis. Meanwhile, Mass had already withdrawn from the weekend's activities by then after quickly discovering that he was in no fit state to drive due to still suffering from the consequences of his high-speed accident at Paul Ricard. In fact, this was to be the German's last appearance in a Grand Prix car as following a disappointing run of results and his unhappy episode in France, coming so soon after his involvement in Villeneuve's tragic accident at Zolder, he was subsequently to discontinue his participation in the sport. For the time being, though, John MacDonald had covered the eventuality of Mass not being able to take part here by inviting along Rupert Keegan who, of course, had already driven for him in Formula 1 towards the latter part of 1980. Transferring the Englishman to Mass's car was not as straightforward as MacDonald had anticipated, however, for within a couple of laps of going out Keegan was black-flagged. MacDonald was then informed that his replacement driver could only take part if he obtained the signed agreement of all of the other team managers, and although this was eventually achieved it was not until early afternoon that Keegan was officially allowed to join in. In the meantime, the morning session ran out reasonably smoothly for just about everyone else apart from Fabi, whose practice was cut short by an oil leak and a resultant fire on the Toleman, and also Arnoux who had to spend most of his time in the pits owing to a fuel-injection problem: this was allowing the engine to run on too lean a mixture and had resulted in a turbo-charger unit overheating.

Because of the interruption in the morning the first hour of qualifying was some 15 minutes late in starting and was only just about in full swing when Lauda's McLaren suddenly flew off into the catch-fences at the first right-hander beyond the pits. At the previous corner he had been forced off line to get by Keegan's March and it appeared that his sticky Michelin tyres had picked up some sand and lost much of their adhesion. Whatever, Lauda was soon out of the car and switching to the team's spare chassis only to find shortly afterwards that his right arm, which had been wrenched by the steering wheel, was becoming rather painful. Minutes later, Daly was involved in an even more bizarre incident at the Ostkurve chicane. The left front wheel suddenly dropped off his new Williams! Quite simply it had not been fixed properly following a tyre change but, fortunately, in this instance the chicane was a blessing in disguise as due to the enforced reduction in speed the Irishman was able to gather it up without hitting anything. Furthermore, because of the current stiff suspensions he then found it possible to drive back to the pits on three wheels and was soon under way again in the spare Williams leaving his somewhat embarrassed mechanics to check the new car over for any damage. Yet another driver soon taking over his team's spare car was Salazar when his ATS developed a bad oil leak, while a blown-up engine after just one lap in his Talbot led to Laffite having to share team-mate Cheever's car. However, when Guerrero had a drive-shaft let go on his Ensign he was even less fortunate as there was no alternative car available. Consequently the Colombian was

forced to become a spectator along with Fabi who was waiting around in the vain hope that the Toleman mechanics would complete an engine change and repair the fire damage on his only car before the end of the session. Meanwhile, amongst the drivers avoiding the worst of the trouble, the pace was really warming up with the front-runners already approaching Prost's pole-winning time of 1 min 47.50 sec for the 1981 race even with the additional chicane. Pironi, in particular, was in stunning form in his familiar Ferrari 126C2, after having given the experimental car with the longitudinal gearbox an airing during the morning, and eventually rocketed around the revised 6.797 km circuit in just 1 min 47.947 sec (226.678 kph). Not only was this to be the fastest time of the afternoon but convincingly so, for by the end of the hour-long session even his nearest challenger was very nearly a full second away. That was Prost who, having earlier reverted to the spare Renault for a few laps while his mechanics tried to cure a high-speed misfire on his new car (like Arnoux's proposed race car this had the hydraulic ride height control system), had then swopped back again and produced a lap in 1 min 48.890 sec. Third fastest, Arnoux had achieved his best time of 1 min 49.256 sec in the spare Renault due to the fuel-injection problem persisting on his own car. Then, closely bunched up behind, came Piquet (1 min 49.415 sec), using the spare Brabham-BMW with the carbon-fibre brakes, Tambay (1 min 49.570 sec) and Patrese (1 min 49.760 sec) to make it six turbo-charged cars in the first six places on the time-sheets. It was just like Paul Ricard all over again, except that the order was slightly different, the BMW engines were proving to be much more reliable owing, it appeared, to the provision of additional exterior cooling aids and the margin of superiority over the normally-aspirated cars was far greater. In fact, it was so great as to be almost ridiculous. Even Patrese's time was the best part of a massive 3 seconds quicker than the leading non-turbo runner which had ultimately turned out to be none other than Alboreto's Tyrrell, the Italian narrowly pipping Lauda who had achieved his best time just before the off-course excursion. De Cesaris, Rosberg and Watson were not that far behind him either but the situation was looking really depressing for the rest, including Daly whose hopes of doing anything in the spare Williams had been dashed by a persistent misfire.

After pleasant conditions throughout Friday's practice, the next day was completely the opposite with near-incessant rain. As a result, when the circuit was opened for the 90 minute untimed session in the morning there was a distinct lack of enthusiasm with a good number of the drivers staying put in the hope, vainly as it happened, that it would eventually clear up. Other drivers, however,

were keen to press on if only to try out wet settings and to evaluate different types of wet-weather tyres available, there being no guarantee that race day would be any better. Pironi was one and obviously taking matters more seriously than most as he clearly demonstrated by recording a succession of fastest laps. Sadly, though, his brave performance was to end in disaster. Running down the fast section of track between what was now the third chicane and the entrance to the stadium, he was confronted by a massive ball of spray which he mistook to be all coming off Daly's Williams looming in front of him. In fact, another car was there as well, Prost's slower-travelling Renault which Daly now proceeded to overtake by going past on its right-hand side. Because of all the spray, though, Pironi still failed to spot the Renault, assumed Daly had moved over for him and went to go past on his inside only to run into the back of the concealed French car, collecting its right rear wheel with his left front. Somehow Prost managed to bring the Renault to a halt without losing control in spite of its right rear corner having been torn away by the impact. The Ferrari, on the other hand, shot straight up into the air, somersaulted, crashed down on to the track and then charged the guard-rail on the right-hand side with a sickening thud before finally coming to rest a short distance away with its front end smashed and buckled almost beyond recognition. In many respects it was very similar to Villeneuve's dreadful accident at Zolder but, unlike the French-Canadian, Pironi had, mercifully, survived the ordeal and was still conscious as he lay trapped in the wreckage. Even so it was obvious that he was in a bad way by the reactions of other drivers who stopped at the scene and ran to his aid before the rescue services arrived. His legs, which had both been shattered, were of particular concern and when he was eventually released from the cockpit, well over half an hour later and whisked off to the nearby Heidelberg University Clinic by helicopter to undergo an emergency operation there were fears that he might even have to have his right leg amputated below the knee. That, at least, was to prove unnecessary, although tragically not only had his Championship hopes been brought to an abrupt end but also his Grand Prix career for in spite of constant rumours of a subsequent comeback he was never to regain the strength and movement in his right leg needed to drive again right up until his untimely death five years later in a powerboat accident off the Isle of Wight.

Although practice eventually resumed for what was left of the 90 minute untimed session, the lack of enthusiasm was, understandably, more apparent than ever. Much the same applied to the final hour of qualifying in the afternoon, for with the rain continuing to pour down a lot of the drivers took the view that it was pointless going out. Nevertheless, Tambay did his best to dispel some of the obvious despondency in the Ferrari pit with a spirited display of on-the-limit driving that kept him at the top of the time-sheets throughout most of the session, his best lap coming out at 2 min 04.090 sec which went unbeaten until the closing minutes when Piquet did an even quicker 2 min 03.434 sec. Naturally, though, not even these impressive performances had any bearing on the final grid order. What did change the situation was the McLaren team officially withdrawing their entry for Niki Lauda as owing to his arm injury causing so much discomfort, the Austrian had decided to give the race a miss so as not to jeopardize his chances of taking part in his home Grand Prix scheduled for the following weekend. As a result everyone behind him was moved up a place which meant that Surer, who had ended the first day 27th fastest, found himself with a further role to play after all. Ferrari, on the other hand, failed to officially withdraw their entry for Didier Pironi until after the grid was published and despite representations made to the organizers from the Theodore team to allow Byrne to bring the starting field back up to 26, supported by a signed statement from all of the other team managers to the effect that they had no objections, the request was turned down. So, in the end, the Irishman had to face up to being a spectator on race day along with Keegan and also the unlucky Fabi whose hopes of hoisting himself onto the grid had, of course, vanished with the rain.

The skies were still grey and overcast on Sunday but at least the rain had stopped with the result that the warm-up session, held up for half an hour because of an accident at the new chicane during a supporting race, took place on a dry track. Naturally, with everyone having effectively lost a day's practice because of the rain, this was more welcome than usual and turned out to be an extremely busy 30 minutes. There were also a couple of dramas as Surer blew up the engine in his Arrows, and Watson inadvertently tried to take a short cut through one of the chicanes. He, too, finished up in need of an engine change due to sand finding its way in all of the wrong places! Fastest, and alone in planning to make the long-awaited Brabham pit stop during the race, was Piquet followed by Tambay who was obviously still doing his best it keep up spirits in the Ferrari pit. Meanwhile, because the day's programme was running in arrears, the organizers were fretting over television schedules, and later it was agreed to do away with the regulation two hours and thirty minutes interval between the end of the warm-up and the start of the race and to keep to the original time-table of a 3 p.m. start. Consequently, barely two hours passed before the first cars were leaving the pits and forming on the

dummy grid, a process that was considerably enlivened by Rosberg stepping straight out of his Williams, leaping over the pit wall and setting off on another lap in the team's spare car owing to a high-speed engine misfire being apparent. Needless to say, his original car was soon wheeled away. All was not well with Watson's McLaren either. None of the instruments were working, and although strenuous efforts were made to remedy the situation in the few minutes that remained they were to no avail, which left the Ulster-man faced with the prospects of having to drive 'blind'. Then, to add to the last-minute drama, the engine in Baldi's Arrows refused to fire up immediately prior to the pace lap. So, while Prost (he was using the spare Renault even though his new car had been repaired since the previous morning's accident) took on what should have been the unfortunate Pironi's responsibility of leading the rest of the field around the circuit, the Italian dashed into the pits and prepared to join the race in the spare Arrows from the pit lane.

When the moment came that everyone was waiting for it was a good clean start and particularly so for Arnoux as he made the most of the vacant pole position in front of him, nosed ahead of his team-mate and took the lead as they arrived at the first right-hander. Right behind the two Renaults, and despite developing a lot of wheelspin, Piquet just held off Alboreto and Tambay for third place and the rest followed busily trying to sort themselves out, Cheever making a brilliant run down the inside from his twelfth position on the grid to eventually slot into

seventh place between de Cesaris and a rather hesitant Patrese. Even by the first chicane, though, the order was changed with Piquet moving ahead of Prost to give chase to the leader and Patrese quickly making up for his sluggish start by overtaking Cheever before following Tambay and de Cesaris past Alboreto's Tyrrell later on the same lap. On the second lap Patrese continued to make up lost ground by using the superior power of his BMW engine to blast past de Cesaris' Alfa Romeo, while his team leader attracted even more attention by wrestling away the lead from Arnoux and immediately putting daylight between himself and the Renault. Indeed, by the end of the lap the reigning World Champion was already as much as 2 seconds clear and proceeded to continue pulling away at a phenomenal rate in the 'light-weight' Brabham. Meanwhile, Cheever's promising start came to nought when a trip up over a kerb at one of the chicanes broke the Talbot's left-hand skirt and sent him into the pits for a replacement. Here, he was soon to be joined by Baldi, de Angelis and Winkelhock. Baldi's problem was a badly running engine in the spare Arrows, which was to result in retirement after three more fruitless visits to the pits on successive laps, de Angelis had done more or less the same as Cheever, and Winkelhock, much to the dismay of the large crowd, had to give up with broken transmission after having cooked his clutch at the start. On lap 4 there was also no Jarier, the Frenchman spinning off at the third chicane just after there had been another reshuffle amongst the leaders caused by Tambay finding a way

After Didier Pironi's dreadful practice accident, Patrick Tambay did much to restore morale in the Ferrari camp by scoring the first Grand Prix victory of his career. Here he leads Alain Prost's Renault and Riccardo Patrese's Brabham through the stadium during the opening laps of the race whilst lying third. *(L.A.T. Photographic)*

past Prost's third-placed Renault and by Rosberg taking over Alboreto's role as the leading Ford-Cosworth runner in seventh place.

The situation amongst the five leading turbo-charged cars now began to show signs of settling down a little and rather more in the way of attention became fixed on Watson's progress after an understandably cautious start due to the lack of even a rev-counter. First he caught and passed Alboreto on lap 6, swallowed up Rosberg two laps later and then quickly moved up to challenge de Cesaris. So quickly, in fact, that as the two Marlboro-sponsored cars hurtled down towards the first chicane on lap 9 not only were they together but Watson was jinking out from behind the Alfa Romeo and drawing alongside as they arrived at the braking area. For a moment it looked as if de Cesaris would stave off the attack but Watson was having none of it and quite literally barged past into sixth place, the light contact between the two cars having a profound effect on the Italian's race. He was to complete the lap by crawling into the pits to retire with a fractured oil radiator! At about the same time Prost's race also started to turn sour owing to his engine developing a misfire. Initially it was barely discernible but then the situation rapidly deteriorated until at the end of lap 11, the Frenchman decided to make for the pits where he was to undergo a lengthy stop having a broken fuel-injection pipe repaired. Meanwhile, on the previous lap, Arnoux had finally been forced to give way to sustained pressure from Tambay, but if Renault fortunes were no longer looking good that was nothing compared to what lay around the corner for the Brabham team. Their problems started on lap 13 when Patrese's promising run in what had just become fourth place ended in the pits with smoke belching out from underneath the engine cover of his car to signify a piston failure. That was bad enough for them, but six laps later their day turned into yet another total disaster when Piquet, leading the race by a massive 27 seconds, came up to lap Salazar's ATS at the new chicane. Normally, this should have proved a relatively

straightforward exercise but as Piquet drew alongside the yellow and white car and both drivers applied their brakes Salazar found his rate of retardation slower than he had anticipated owing to having moved off the normal racing line where there was much more grip. As a result, when Piquet started turning into the first part of the chicane Salazar was still going at a fair rate of knots on his inside and promptly collected the Brabham's left rear wheel with the ATS's right front. Not surprisingly, this led to dire consequences for both of them, Piquet striking the tyre wall before spinning across the track and eventually coming to rest on the left-hand side with a stalled engine and Salazar slewing to a halt in the middle of the track with the front of the ATS too badly crumpled to continue. What was surprising, however, was Piquet's subsequent behaviour. Understandably deeply incensed, he leapt out of his car, rushed over to Salazar, who was already out of his ATS, and began to openly give vent to his feelings by punching and kicking the Chilean in a frenzied outburst that lasted for several seconds in full view of the television cameras, a spectacle that not only did nothing to improve Grand Prix racing's already tarnished image but also dispelled any sympathy for the World Champion.

By the time that this rather unsavoury episode had drawn to a conclusion – Piquet eventually stalked away after flinging his gloves on the ground as a final gesture of frustration – Tambay had already gone by into the lead and Arnoux into second place six seconds later. Watson moved up into third place, albeit half a lap behind, and then came Rosberg a further 20 seconds in arrears before Alboreto and Laffite who were about to swop places, the Frenchman having steadily climbed up the lap charts ever since the start, and finding the handling of his Talbot much better than of late owing to it having revised suspension pick-up points all round. Cheever's JS19 had been similarly modified but the American had broken another skirt shortly after rejoining the race and had then stopped again prior to giving up altogether with only eight laps to his credit owing to the car's balance being upset. Prost

had also retired by now, for in spite of his lengthy pit stop the Renault had still not been running properly. Consequently there were now only sixteen cars left but even that quickly dwindled to thirteen: on lap 21 de Angelis picked up a puncture and decided against continuing once he had limped into the pits owing to having been sick in the cockpit, a lap later Boesel disappeared out on the circuit, also with a flat tyre, and on lap 26 Daly bowed out of seventh place by hurriedly switching off his engine when a valve spring broke. While all this was happening Tambay was steadily increasing his lead over Arnoux, and as he obviously had the situation nicely under control most of what little interest remained centred around Laffite's efforts to reel in Rosberg's Williams. In fact, he was now all but up with the green and white car and on the following lap, lap 27, wiped out the deficit completely prior to making comparatively light work of taking over the fourth spot. Alas, it was to be shortlived. As the Frenchman entered the stadium section next time round he came up behind Mansell's Lotus, pulled over to the inside of the track to lap him along the pit straight but then made a rare error of judgement by going into the right-hander that followed too fast. Somehow, despite sliding off the track and having a very busy moment indeed, Laffite managed to avoid the catchfences but by the time that he had sorted himself out both Rosberg and Alboreto had gone on ahead of him again. Furthermore, the trip over the kerb had damaged the Talbot's skirts and thereafter Laffite quickly fell away until at the end of lap 36, with Giacomelli and Surer now also ahead of him, he finally peeled off into the pits with every intention of having the skirts replaced. When he arrived there, however, he found to his dismay that Cheever had already gone through the team's supply of skirt material so was left with little choice other than to call it a day. At almost exactly the same moment Watson also retired when the front suspension suddenly broke on his McLaren as he braked for the Ostkurve chicane, sending him gently spinning off into the tyre barrier. Post-race examination suggested that this

---

Results

1	P. Tambay (Ferrari)		1 hr 27 min 25.178 sec (209.929 kph/ 130.443 mph)
2	R. Arnoux (Renault)		1 hr 27 min 41.557 sec
3	K. Rosberg (Williams-Ford)		1 lap behind
4	M. Alboreto (Tyrrell-Ford)		1 lap behind
5	B. Giacomelli (Alfa Romeo)		1 lap behind
6	M. Surer (Arrows-Ford)		1 lap behind
7	B. Henton (Tyrrell-Ford)		1 lap behind
8	R. Guerrero (Ensign-Ford)		1 lap behind
9	N. Mansell (Lotus-Ford)		2 laps behind
10	D. Warwick (Toleman-Hart)		2 laps behind
11	F. Serra (Fittipaldi-Ford)		2 laps behind

Fastest lap: N. Piquet (Brabham-BMW) on lap 7 in 1 min 54.035 sec (214.576 kph/133.331 mph)

Retirements

M. Winkelhock (ATS-Ford) transmission on lap 4, J.P. Jarier (Osella-Ford) spun off on lap 4, M. Baldi (Arrows-Ford) engine on lap 7, E. Cheever (Talbot-Matra) handling on lap 9, A. de Cesaris (Alfa Romeo) accident damage on lap 10, R. Patrese (Brabham-BMW) engine on lap 14, A. Prost (Renault) fuel-injection on lap 15, E. Salazar (ATS-Ford) accident on lap 18, N. Piquet (Brabham-BMW) accident on lap 19, E. de Angelis (Lotus-Ford) driver unwell on lap 22, R. Boesel (March-Ford) tyre failure on lap 23, D. Daly (Williams-Ford) engine on lap 26, J. Laffite (Talbot-Matra) handling on lap 37, J. Watson (McLaren-Ford) front suspension on lap 37.

was almost certainly connected with the off-course excursion during the morning warm-up but, whatever, the Ulsterman had lost a secure third place and walked away from the scene bitterly disappointed.

After Watson's bad luck the race ran its course without any further drama, Tambay scoring his first-ever Grand Prix victory in splendid fashion and giving Ferrari just the sort of result that they needed after the events of the previous day. At the finish the amiable Frenchman had lapped everyone apart from Arnoux who duly followed him across the line in second place just over 16 seconds later. Despite having had to contend with a stiffening gear-change and misfiring engine in the latter stages of the race, Rosberg held off Alboreto to take what should have been Watson's third place and behind them Giacomelli, trailing a broken skirt, and Surer completed the list of point scorers by finishing fifth and sixth respectively. Further back still Henton was seventh, Guerrero was eighth after having driven most of the race without a clutch and Mansell, still wearing a wrist support and having lost time in the pits quite early on for a new skirt, was ninth. After that only two others were left, these being Warwick, who had also lost time because of a punctured left front tyre, and Serra who had completed a non-stop run in the new Fittipaldi F9 but had been troubled by a recalcitrant fourth gear most of the way.

XX Grosser Preis von Österreich

Österreichring: August 15
Weather: Hot
Distance: 53 laps of 5.9424 km
circuit = 314.95 km (195.70 miles)

Twelve months earlier the future of the Austrian Grand Prix had looked bleak. Dwindling attendance figures matched by rising costs had no longer made it a viable proposition and it had seemed that the 1981 race would be the last. But then, during the winter, and no doubt strongly influenced by Niki Lauda's proposed comeback, Bernie Ecclestone had entered into discussions with local businessman Ernie Huppert (a keen supporter of Grand Prix racing) and between them they had come up with a rescue package whereby a new company was specially formed to take over the financial responsibilities of the event. As a result the race, after initially having been scrubbed from the calendar, was on again and the possibility of losing one of the finest venues of them all was avoided.

Immediately following the German Grand Prix the BMW personnel had returned to their factory in Munich and collected a new batch of engines that incorporated a revised exhaust system. Essentially, this involved the adoption of an entirely separate exhaust pipe from the blow-off valve (or waste-gate) instead of the previous arrangement whereby it exhausted into the main exhaust pipe. The idea behind it was to improve the engine's torque characteristics rather than its power output, which had never been lacking in any case and was an aspect that was soon being made apparent all over again during the opening practice session on Friday morning. Almost from the word go Piquet and Patrese were easily the two quickest drivers out on the circuit and thoroughly enjoyed themselves in the magnificent setting. Both of their cars (Piquet was using the spare BT50) were running with carbon-fibre brakes and, later, as conditions became hotter, with dry-ice packed around the BMW inter-coolers. This was done to reduce the charge temperature in the interests of sustaining engine reliability, and it seemed to be having the desired effect for there was no sign of any problems whatsoever. However, whilst everything was starting off well in the Brabham camp, quite a number of frailties were showing up elsewhere. Lauda, still nursing his arm injury but determined not to miss his home Grand Prix, had struck trouble almost immediately. Just before the circuit had been officially opened for practice he had gone out to do some filming, had had the camera removed and then promptly blown up an engine! Fortunately this had occurred in the spare McLaren so the situation was not as serious as it might have been for him as he was able to continue practice in his proposed race chassis. De Cesaris, who came to rest out on the circuit with a broken throttle cable quite early on, was also reasonably fortunate inasmuch as the organizers temporarily suspended proceedings so that his Alfa Romeo could be retrieved. But when Arnoux pulled up with a dead engine shortly afterwards it was a different story. Quite simply, the organizers declined to intervene as the stationary Renault was not considered to be in a dangerous position. Consequently, the Frenchman waited to be towed back to the pits in vain and spent the rest of the morning an unhappy spectator. Perhaps he should have stopped in the middle of the track! In the meantime, the dramas continued with Henton suffering an engine failure and both Daly and Warwick arriving at the pits on foot. Amazingly the Irishman's Williams had shed another wheel, just like in Germany, and for a similar reason, only this time its left rear; while Warwick's problem was a bolt having sheared in the right rear suspension of his Toleman. Needless to say Daly was hardly amused, nor for that matter was Frank Williams, but, like Warwick, was obviously none the worse for the ordeal, both drivers having avoided hitting anything as they had skated to a halt.

Despite the morning's problems, which had also included several drivers having difficulties in encouraging their cars to behave properly over the bumps and undulations, everything had more or less been sorted out again come the start of the first timed session. About the only exception was Arnoux's Renault, for this was still being worked on and so, as an interim measure, the French-man was sent out in the team's spare chassis. This, however, proved to be a virtual waste of time. First he was constantly dashing in and out of the pits on every lap in a fruitless

Starting Grid	
N. Piquet Brabham-BMW (1 min 27.612 sec)	R. Patrese Brabham-BMW (1 min 27.971 sec)
A. Prost Renault (1 min 28.864 sec)	P. Tambay Ferrari (1 min 29.522 sec)
R. Arnoux Renault (1 min 30.261 sec)	K. Rosberg Williams-Ford (1 min 30.300 sec)
E. de Angelis Lotus-Ford (1 min 31.626 sec)	M. Alboreto Tyrrell-Ford (1 min 31.814 sec)
D. Daly Williams-Ford (1 min 32.062 sec)	N. Lauda McLaren-Ford (1 min 32.131 sec)
A. de Cesaris Alfa Romeo (1 min 32.308 sec)	N. Mansell Lotus-Ford (1 min 32.881 sec)
B. Giacomelli Alfa Romeo (1 min 32.950 sec)	J. Laffite Talbot-Matra (1 min 32.957 sec)
D. Warwick Toleman-Hart (1 min 33.208 sec)	R. Guerrero Ensign-Ford (1 min 33.555 sec)
T. Fabi Toleman-Hart (1 min 33.971 sec)	J. Watson McLaren-Ford (1 min 34.164 sec)
B. Henton Tyrrell-Ford (1 min 34.184 sec)	F. Serra Fittipaldi-Ford (1 min 34.187 sec)
M. Surer Arrows-Ford (1 min 34.422 sec)	E. Cheever Talbot-Matra (1 min 34.620 sec)
M. Baldi Arrows-Ford (1 min 34.715 sec)	R. Keegan March-Ford (1 min 34.770 sec)
M. Winkelhock ATS-Ford (1 min 34.984 sec)	T. Byrne Theodore-Ford (1 min 34.985 sec)

Did not qualify:
R. Boesel (March-Ford) 1 min 35.149 sec
J.P. Jarier (Osella-Ford) 1 min 35.206 sec
E. Salazar (ATS-Ford) 1 min 35.271 sec.

attempt to have a fault cured with the car's electronic fuel-injection system. Then the engine cut out completely and brought him to a standstill out on the circuit – again. Rather than lose more time, though, Arnoux walked back to the pits to take over his original car once it had been made ready only to find that still not running properly either. As a result he ultimately failed to chalk up even one timed flying lap all afternoon. Meanwhile, Watson's progress received a serious setback when his engine blew up in a big way as the spare McLaren was found to be down on power and handling badly, both Fabi and Serra were frustrated by their cars running with persistent misfiring engines, as were Giacomelli and de Cesaris to only a slightly lesser extent in their Alfa Romeos. Tambay, the sole Ferrari representative for obvious reasons, had his qualifying run ended early when his clutch gave out at the Boschkurve. So, too, did Henton when he ran out of fuel! Consequently, it was a pretty fraught afternoon and a demoralizing one as well for many of them when they saw their lap times and compared them to those of Piquet and Patrese, the difference, even over the other front-runners, being absolutely astounding. In fact, only three of them had lapped to within even 4 seconds of Piquet's best lap of 1 min 27.612 sec (Patrese had turned in 1 min 27.971 sec) and even then they looked hopelessly outclassed, Tambay winding up third fastest at 1 min 29.522 sec followed by Prost on 1 min 29.867 sec and Rosberg, the fastest non-turbo runner, on 1 min 31.108 sec.

After an overnight thunderstorm, the weather had cleared again by the following morning, and when practice resumed at 10 a.m. for a further 90 minutes of testing, conditions were both warm and dry. Although most drivers were able to carry on largely unhindered it was not all plain sailing by any means, for during the course of the morning's activities Alboreto understeered off the track and damaged his Tyrrell beyond immediate repair, Boesel and Keegan both had their March 821s come to rest out on the circuit due to an engine failure and an electrical fault respectively and Salazar also blew up the engine in his ATS. In addition, Arnoux's appalling run of bad luck continued when a turbo let go which not only damaged the engine in his Renault but also put further strain on his hopes of actually qualifying for the race. However, as Prost had now switched to the spare Renault and was showing a preference to it, arrangements were made for Arnoux to take over his team-mate's abandoned car for the final hour of qualifying and, as a precautionary measure, the electronic fuel-injection system was discarded in favour of the older mechanical injection. In the meantime, the two Brabham-BMWs were running as fast and as reliable as ever, but when it came round to

the afternoon session, with conditions now really hot, Piquet and Patrese were both quite happy to bide their time in the pits watching the opposition. Only in the last remaining 15 minutes or so did the situation change when Patrese finally decided to go out and was followed shortly afterwards by his team leader. Even then they needn't have bothered as no-one approached their Friday times let alone beat them. Nevertheless, as a means of spreading more gloom and despondency it was certainly successful, as once again they set the two fastest times, albeit fractionally slower, at 1 min 28.296 sec (Patrese) and 1 min 28.398 sec (Piquet) respectively. As it was Prost put up the best challenge on this occasion by getting down to 1 min 28.864 sec prior to being sidelined by a broken turbo just as he was setting off on his second set of qualifying tyres. Tambay, on the other hand, failed to improve in the hot conditions and for the second day running was complaining of a slight lack of grip through the faster corners. In the closing minutes of practice he also suffered turbo failure after having had the boost pressure turned right up in a vain attempt to do something about the Brabhams, and ultimately had to settle for fourth fastest time of 1 min 29.856 sec immediately ahead of Arnoux. At long last the little Frenchman had kept out of trouble and, despite not being too happy with the handling of Prost's car, had responded with a lap in 1 min 30.261 sec to move up to fifth fastest overall. So, at the end of the day, the leading turbo runners had the front of the grid to themselves for the third race in a row. Behind them, Rosberg was still the quickest driver in a normally-aspirated car after having improved to 1 min 30.300 sec, but Alboreto, who had ended the first day next in line, had been right out of the picture in the heavier and less developed spare Tyrrell. As a result, the Italian had to rely on his Friday time for an eventual eighth spot on the grid where he was sandwiched between de Angelis's well-driven Lotus 91 and the second Williams FW08 of Daly. After that there were a few surprises, not least the starting order of the two McLaren drivers as Lauda had qualified in only 10th place and Watson in a really disappointing 18th place. Both of them, however, had found it virtually impossible to balance their cars, with Watson, in particular, complaining of severe understeer. To make matters worse, the Michelin qualifying tyres that they had been using had proved virtually worthless after less than one lap. On a brighter note, Guerrero had qualified his Ensign in a most encouraging 16th place between Warwick and Fabi in their Tolemans, Byrne had qualified (just!) for his first-ever Grand Prix and, despite indulging in a quick spin at the chicane, Keegan got himself into a Grand Prix for the first time since 1980 somewhat to the embarrassment

of team-mate Boesel who had failed to make the cut along with Jarier and Salazar.

After yet another thunderstorm on Saturday evening, it was back to clear blue skies again on Sunday and certainly by early afternoon, with a massive crowd anxiously awaiting the start of the race, it had become really hot. During the warm-up session, which had taken place at mid-day, everything had gone off well except for the Renault team. First Prost had returned to the pits with oil leaking from the vee of the engine in the spare car that he had been hoping to race. Then, not long afterwards, Arnoux, who was back in his own car once more, had followed him in with a stripped fourth gear. Fortunately the gearbox in Arnoux's car had soon been repaired, but the oil leak on the spare car had proved impossible to cure in the amount of time available and so, as the other 25 starters left the pits for the warm-up lap, Prost had no choice other than to set off in his original car. Amongst the others, meanwhile, Alboreto was still confined to the spare Tyrrell following his off-course excursion during the previous morning, Rosberg had opted to race the spare Williams that he had used throughout most of practice and both Piquet and Patrese were starting out with their Brabham-BMWs on soft compound tyres as well as on half-full fuel tanks with the obvious intention of making pit stops at around half-distance. However, just as everything seemed all settled, Surer suddenly came running down the hill from the Hella-Licht Schikane and into the pits to report that he had been forced to abandon his Arrows with a dead engine. Consequently his team had to hurriedly wheel out their spare car and the Swiss was left facing the prospects of taking the start from the pit lane due to it having been officially closed by now. This, of course, was in accordance with the rules, which were eventually enforced – but not until Surer had been incorrectly waved out on to the track, completed a warm-up lap and joined the others waiting on the dummy grid!

Almost as soon as Surer's Arrows had been wheeled back into the pit lane the rest of the field was signalled away on the pace lap and a couple of minutes or so later all twenty-five cars were back on the grid. Then, after a brief pause, on went the starting lights and at the green they were away with Piquet snapping straight into the lead and Rosberg making a real demon of a start by pulling over to the right and charging between Tambay's Ferrari and the pit wall. In complete contrast, team-mate Daly made an unusually slow start to which de Cesaris, immediately behind him, responded by attempting to go by on his outside. Unfortunately for the Italian, though, Lauda was already there and by trying to squeeze between the two cars, de Cesaris brought the left rear wheel of his Alfa Romeo into contact with the Williams' right front wheel, was thrown sharply to the left and promptly ran into the side of Giacomelli's sister car, which was coming through on Daly's inside. The result, chaos and three instant retirements. Giacomelli slammed into the barriers, de Cesaris bounced off his team-mate's car before sliding across to the other side of the track and Daly pulled up with a broken tie-rod. That was not all, as in the confusion that arose behind them Keegan brushed the pit wall and quickly discovered that the March had broken a steering arm as he continued on his way. At this point, however, it seemed certain that the race would be stopped, especially when the red warning lights flashed on at the start-line, but as no-one had been injured and the track was quickly cleared a decision was taken to let it continue – just as the leaders were streaming out of the Jochen Rindt Kurve! Out in front it was still Piquet but Rosberg's excellent start had come to nought as apart from having been beaten in the initial rush up to the Hella-Licht Schikane by the other leading turbo runners, Patrese, Prost, Tambay and Arnoux, he had also been edged out by de Angelis. As a result the Finn was now back in seventh place where he was lying immediately ahead of Alboreto, Mansell, Lauda, Warwick and Laffite. After that came Fabi followed by the rest of the survivors right back to Watson (he had been badly baulked at the start) and the delayed Surer who was left bringing up the rear once Keegan had disappeared into the pits to retire.

On the second lap the two Brabham drivers swopped places but rather more in the way of attention was diverted towards Tambay, when the Ferrari slowed dramatically with a flat right rear tyre, and also towards Alboreto who suddenly spun off into the guard-rail at the entrance to the Bosch-kurve. In both instances they had picked up punctures after running over debris at the scene of the start-line shunt but whereas Tambay's tyre had gone down quickly, Alboreto's tyre, also the right rear, had been losing air much more slowly and caught him completely unawares. Fortunately, in spite of the Tyrrell being quite badly damaged, the Italian subsequently emerged unharmed but was obviously bitterly disappointed. So, too, was Tambay to only a slightly lesser extent as by the time that he had crawled round to the pits and taken on a new tyre he had lost the best part of two laps. In the meantime, the Brabham duo was already pulling out a considerable advantage, even over Prost's third-placed Renault, and most of the excitement was coming from further down the field where positions were changing one after another. Warwick and Fabi, in particular, were making an exceptionally good impression in their Tolemans, and by lap 5 had not only worked their way through to sixth and seventh places respectively but were also

showing signs of catching de Angelis. Sadly, though, three laps later it all became meaningless, as within the space of just a few seconds Fabi coasted to rest with broken transmission and then Warwick suffered a rear suspension failure, similar to that in practice and with much the same consequences. Naturally this was a bitter blow to the British team, and the situation was no longer looking too good from the point of view of the race either, for with Guerrero having also gone out only a minute or so earlier, due to the Ensign breaking a driveshaft, there had now been a total of eight retirements in as many laps. Even so it was not all bad news for there were still several interesting little scraps going on, and over the next few minutes it was the turn of Henton to steal some of the limelight. First he whipped past Mansell's Lotus, which had earlier been running as high as sixth but was now dropping away with a slight engine misfire, and then he caused an even bigger surprise (and dismay to the crowd!) by overtaking Lauda's McLaren. Moreover, he quickly pulled away from the Austrian and before long was securely ensconced in eighth place behind Rosberg and Laffite.

By lap 15 the two Brabham-BMWs were over 20 seconds clear and well on schedule to allow for their planned pit stops. Prost was still pounding along in third place but Arnoux had started visibly falling away and ended the lap by going into the pits to complain of a loss of power. Despite the Renault undergoing a thorough examination, however, nothing much could be done as the problem lay with the turbo compressor, and after subsequently trying one more lap the Frenchman had to call it a day. Meanwhile, at the end of lap 16, Mansell took his misfiring Lotus into the pits as well and underwent much the same sort of treatment before retiring at the end of the next lap with a suspected broken valve spring. Winkelhock was yet another to retire about now due to spinning off at the Jochen Rindt Kurve and stalling his engine, while Piquet sprung a real surprise by dashing into the pits at the end of lap 17, which was much earlier than had been expected. So early, in fact, that the Brabham pit crew were caught on the hop, and by the time that they had changed all four wheels, hauled out the fuel containers from the pit garage and topped up the fuel load half a minute had gone by, twice as long as it would have been had they been ready. Later, Piquet claimed to have indicated his intention to come in whilst passing the pits on the previous lap as his rear tyres had blistered but obviously no-one had noticed! As it was, valuable time had now been lost and when Piquet eventually charged back out into the fray a solid second place had become a distant fourth, immediately in front of Rosberg. Worse still, his engine was no longer feeling so responsive

and instead of being able to make the hoped-for charge, Piquet soon found himself struggling to even maintain the small gap to the Williams which now, with a reducing fuel load, was handling much better than it had been earlier in the race. All the while Patrese was moving further and further ahead and this continued right through until the end of lap 24 when, with a 33 second cushion over Prost, he made for the pits – as planned. This time everything went off to perfection and in just 13.8 seconds the well-drilled Brabham mechanics had changed all four wheels, added around 100 litres of fuel and had their man ready to charge back out into the fray. Furthermore, he was still leading the race when he regained the track, despite the additional time lost travelling into and out of the pit lane, although Prost was now a mere 3 seconds away. Nevertheless, after taking a lap or so to grow accustomed to some harder compound tyres that had been fitted as a precaution following Piquet's earlier problems, Patrese soon looked to have the measure of the Renault and by lap 28 was even starting to ease away again slightly. But then disaster struck him. Entering the fast downhill Texaco Schikane, smoke suddenly appeared from the back of the Brabham and in the next instant the blue and white car was careering off the track with its rear wheels locked solid due to a gudgeon pin having failed and the con-rod having punched a hole in the block. It then spun hopelessly out of control across the grass for what seemed an eternity before finally stopping, backwards, against an earth bank – immediately in front of a spectator fence! Mercifully, Patrese subsequently stepped out of his car none the worse for the ordeal apart from being visibly shaken and suffering from the understandable frustration of having just had an almost certain victory taken away from him.

On lap 31, with Prost now leading by the very comfortable margin of almost half a minute over de Angelis, the Brabham team were in for another nasty shock when Piquet's engine suddenly cut out as he came up towards the start/finish line. The drive-gear between the crankshaft and the camshafts at the front of his BMW engine had failed, so all that Piquet could do was to pull over to the inside of the track and stop just beyond the pits as Rosberg sailed past into third place. Incredibly, only a lap later, and having just automatically moved up into a fine fifth place, Henton also suffered an engine failure and he, too, went coasting out of the race. As a result there were now just nine cars left, since only a few minutes before Patrese's dramatic exit Cheever had retired his Talbot with engine trouble, while shortly afterwards Byrne had ended his debut by spinning off in the Theodore, and then Surer had bowed out with something obviously amiss with the fuel system in the spare Arrows after having made three pit stops on successive laps. Moreover, only Prost, de Angelis, Rosberg and Laffite were now still on the same lap and well spaced out at that. In fact, about the only interesting aspect remaining at this stage was Tambay's efforts to haul his Ferrari into the points. Ever since his early pit stop the Frenchman had really been motoring and, having just moved up into eighth place at the expense of Serra, was currently giving chase to Baldi and Watson who were running virtually nose to tail a short distance behind Lauda. Both McLaren drivers were suffering from lack of grip due to running on too conservative a tyre compound and were doing little more than just driving round, but the Ferrari was causing its driver no problems at all and by lap 44 Tambay had not only caught Watson but was slicing past him into seventh place – just as smoke appeared from the back of the Ulsterman's car prompting him to hurriedly switch off before the engine blew up. Eight cars left!

As Tambay's impressive drive continued by taking his Ferrari past Baldi's Arrows on lap 47, and Lauda's McLaren two laps later, the race suddenly took on a new dimension. Already it had become noticeable that Rosberg was steadily gaining on de Angelis, and had now closed to within 5 seconds of the Lotus, but just when the crowd was relishing the prospects of a close finish for second place so the engine in the leading Renault cut out at the Hella-Licht Schikane. This had actually also happened momentarily on the previous lap (lap 48) but this time it was accompanied by a sheet of flames shooting

The exciting finish to the race as Elio de Angelis's Lotus just holds off Keke Rosberg's Williams to the line. It was the Italian's first-ever Grand Prix victory, the first for the Lotus team since 1978 and a result that marked the 150th Grand Prix win for the remarkable Ford-Cosworth DFV engine. *(Phipps Photographic)*

out from the car's exhaust pipes and Prost rolled to a halt just around the corner, the flames vanishing as soon as he had turned off the ignition. Once again the Renault team's fuel-injection system had gone on the blink leaving the Frenchman to walk, disconsolately, back to the pits. In the meantime, of course, Rosberg's pursuit of de Angelis had taken on greater significance than ever for now victory was at stake. To make matters even more interesting they were coming up to lap Laffite's third-placed Talbot but this was to make no difference, the experienced Frenchman reading the situation well and keeping out of the way of both of them. So it was now a straight fight to the flag and what a superb climax it produced with Rosberg moving ever closer until just over half way round the 53rd and final lap he was tucked right under the Lotus's gearbox. However, in spite of the enormous pressure, and a couple of worrying moments when his engine missed

a beat as if running low on fuel, de Angelis kept his head and made sure that he stuck firmly to the racing line. As a result Rosberg had more or less to sit there until the two cars exited the Jochen Rindt Kurve when he finally made his move by jinking out of his rival's slipstream and attempted to pull alongside. For a moment it looked as if it might work but de Angelis kept the hammer down and just held off the Finn as he crossed the line – by 0.125 sec! That's how close it was, and for the first time since Holland 1978, when the Lotus team had last savoured victory, Colin Chapman was able to go through the once familiar routine of jubilantly throwing his cap in the air. The result also gave de Angelis his first taste of a Grand Prix victory as well as marking the 150th Grand Prix win for the remarkable Ford-Cosworth DFV engine. So, at the end of a dramatic and exciting afternoon it was time to celebrate – for some people, at least!

Results				
1	E. de Angelis (Lotus-Ford)	1 hr 25 min 02.212 sec (222.219 kph/ 138.080 mph)		

7   F. Serra (Fittipaldi-Ford) — 2 laps behind
*8   A. Prost (Renault) — 5 laps behind
* Not running at finish.

Fastest lap: N. Piquet (Brabham-BMW) on lap 5 in 1 min 33.699 sec (228.315 kph/141.868 mph)

Retirements
B. Giacomelli (Alfa Romeo) accident on lap 1, D. Daly (Williams-Ford) accident on lap 1, A. de Cesaris (Alfa Romeo) accident on lap 1, R. Keegan (March-Ford) accident damage on lap 2, M. Alboreto (Tyrrell-Ford) spun off on

2	K. Rosberg (Williams-Ford)	1 hr 25 min 02.337 sec
3	J. Laffite (Talbot-Matra)	1 lap behind
4	P. Tambay (Ferrari)	1 lap behind
5	N. Lauda (McLaren-Ford)	1 lap behind
6	M. Baldi (Arrows-Ford)	1 lap behind

lap 2, R. Guerrero (Ensign-Ford) drive-shaft on lap 7, T. Fabi (Toleman-Hart) transmission on lap 8, D. Warwick (Toleman-Hart) rear suspension on lap 8, M. Winkelhock (ATS-Ford) spun and stalled on lap 16, R. Arnoux (Renault) turbo-charger on lap 17, N. Mansell (Lotus-Ford) engine on lap 18, E. Cheever (Talbot-Matra) engine on lap 23, R. Patrese (Brabham-BMW) engine on lap 28, M. Surer (Arrows-Ford) engine on lap 29, T. Byrne (Theodore-Ford) spun off on lap 29, N. Piquet (Brabham-BMW) engine on lap 32, B. Henton (Tyrrell-Ford) engine on lap 33, J. Watson (McLaren-Ford) engine on lap 45.

XVI Grosser Preis der Schweiz

Dijon-Prenois: August 29
Weather: Hot
Distance: 80 laps of 3.800 km
circuit = 304.00 km (188.90 miles)

Ever since the Le Mans disaster of 1955, when Pierre Levegh's Mercedes-Benz had crashed into the crowd during the 24-hour race and killed the hapless Frenchman along with over eighty spectators, the Swiss Government had maintained a permanent ban on motor racing in their country. As a

result the Swiss Grand Prix, that had first started in 1934 and been a round in the World Championship up to and including 1954, had ceased to exist. But then, in 1975, the Swiss Automobile Club had taken positive steps to resurrect their Grand Prix by forming a liason with the owners of the

Dijon-Prenois circuit (about 200 km north of the Swiss border) and holding a non-Championship Formula 1 race there. Now, seven years later, they had come to a similar arrangement and, moreover, this time the race had been granted World Championship status. So, after an absence of 28 years, the Swiss Grand Prix was back on the calendar – even if it was being held in France!

In spite of the atrociously high attrition rate in Austria, hardly surprising when bearing in mind that there had been four Grands

1982

Starting Grid

R. Arnoux
Renault
(1 min 01.740 sec)

A. Prost
Renault
(1 min 01.380 sec)

N. Lauda
McLaren-Ford
(1 min 02.984 sec)

R. Patrese
Brabham-BMW
(1 min 02.710 sec)

N. Piquet
Brabham-BMW
(1 min 03.183 sec)

A. de Cesaris
Alfa Romeo
(1 min 03.023 sec)

K. Rosberg
Williams-Ford
(1 min 03.589 sec)

D. Daly
Williams-Ford
(1 min 03.291 sec)

*P. Tambay
Ferrari
(1 min 03.896 sec)

B. Giacomelli
Alfa Romeo
(1 min 03.776 sec)

M. Alboreto
Tyrrell-Ford
(1 min 04.069 sec)

J. Watson
McLaren-Ford
(1 min 03.995 sec)

M. Surer
Arrows-Ford
(1 min 04.928 sec)

J. Laffite
Talbot-Matra
(1 min 04.087 sec)

E. Cheever
Talbot-Matra
(1 min 05.001 sec)

E. de Angelis
Lotus-Ford
(1 min 04.967 sec)

B. Henton
Tyrrell-Ford
(1 min 05.391 sec)

J. P. Jarier
Osella-Ford
(1 min 05.179 sec)

M. Winkelhock
ATS-Ford
(1 min 05.451 sec)

R. Guerrero
Ensign-Ford
(1 min 05.395 sec)

R. Keegan
March-Ford
(1 min 06.011 sec)

D. Warwick
Toleman-Hart
(1 min 05.877 sec)

R. Boesel
March-Ford
(1 min 06.136 sec)

T. Fabi
Toleman-Hart
(1 min 06.017 sec)

N. Mansell
Lotus-Ford
(1 min 06.211 sec)

E. Salazar
ATS-Ford
(1 min 06.168 sec)

Did not qualify:
F. Serra (Fittipaldi-Ford) 1 min 06.339 sec
T. Byrne (Theodore-Ford) 1 min 06.990 sec
M. Baldi (Arrows-Ford) 1 min 07.836 sec

*Withdrawn: P. Tambay (Ferrari) 1 min 03.896 sec.

Prix in just five weeks, everyone had soon reorganized themselves and appeared to be in reasonably good shape at the start of practice on Friday morning. Most of the entry was totally familiar, for there were no changes on the driver front and what few new cars were on hand were all further examples of existing designs with just one exception. That was the brand new, Dave Wass-designed Arrows A5, a car which bore a striking resemblance to the Williams FW08, complete with pull-rod front suspension, although it did have a narrower front track and wider rear track. The car was so new, in fact, that apart from a brief shake-down run at Donington immediately prior to

being transported over to France, it had yet to turn a wheel and so Surer, who was to drive it, was particularly keen to make the most of the opening 90 minute session. The rest were soon settling down to the job in hand as well and before long the circuit was alive with activity, both out on the track and in the pits as drivers began stopping for various adjustments. Certainly the most common complaint emerging was that of cars understeering badly, which was not altogether unexpected given the numerous downhill twists and turns that fell away, but apart from this everything seemed to be starting off relatively smoothly with no major disasters. Following their recent performances, in practice at least, it was the leading turbo runners that were, understandably, attracting most of the attention, although among them only Arnoux was making any real impression. This was in spite of the fact that he was not exactly receiving priority treatment from his team due to an impending move to Ferrari for 1983. Prost, meanwhile, was unhappy with the way in which his car was behaving over the bumps, as were Piquet and Patrese with their Brabham-BMWs, and Tambay, in the lone Ferrari, was in real trouble. Quite simply the constant battering from driving the current breed of Formula 1 cars, with their rock-hard suspensions, had taken its toll on the Frenchman and just over a week earlier he had awoken to severe neck and back pains caused by a pinched nerve. Since then the pain had extended down his right arm and he was now barely able to change gear. Even having his helmet strapped to the cockpit sides of the Ferrari did little to alleviate his obvious discomfort and at the end of the morning Tambay was only too glad to be able to take a rest. By then Arnoux had made the headlines for two reasons. First he had recorded the fastest time, unofficially. Then he had brought the session to a close a few minutes early by losing control of his Renault through the fast and demanding Courbe de Pouas due to a suspected deflating left rear tyre.

Despite the Renault having been extensively damaged after spinning off, backwards, into the catch-fences and on into the guard-rail, Arnoux had walked away from the scene unharmed, and come the start of the first qualifying session was soon lapping faster than ever in the team's spare car. In the meantime, a change of springs and skirts had apparently transformed the handling of Prost's car for he was now beginning to lap every bit as quick as his team-mate. Indeed, before long the two of them were trading fastest times one after another and engaged in a tremendously exciting tussle that went on until Prost finally scorched around in just 1 min 01.380 sec (222.874 kph), Arnoux turning in a personal best of 1 min 01.740 sec. Amazingly, both were well over a massive 4 seconds quicker than the fastest

practice lap for the last Grand Prix to be held at this particular circuit just over twelve months earlier when Arnoux had started from pole position with a time of 1 min 05.95 sec. In addition, they had overwhelmed the opposition in no uncertain terms as even their nearest challenger was more than a full second away from either of them. That was Lauda who, after having been well off the pace throughout the Austrian weekend, was absolutely delighted with how his McLaren was performing here and had responded accordingly. His only bone of contention, and that of a lot of the others, was problems getting through the traffic. Nevertheless, one clear lap that produced a time of 1 min 02.984 sec had proved enough to put him into a fine third place on the time-sheets just ahead of Patrese (1 min 02.997 sec) and de Cesaris (1 min 03.023 sec), both of whom were less than 0.1 sec slower. Piquet, on the other hand, was still far from happy with his Brabham, actually a brand new chassis, and was also complaining that the Goodyear qualifying tyres were blistering with worrying alacrity. As a result the reigning World Champion had to eventually make do with sixth place in the standings after going around in 1 min 03.366 sec – almost exactly 2 seconds slower than Prost! Seventh fastest, and complaining of vicious understeer with his Williams, was Rosberg at 1 min 03.589 sec. Then came Giacomelli, despite having had to contend with two broken exhausts, a brave Tambay and Watson who had just scraped into the top ten after handling and tyre problems, the Ulsterman narrowly pipping Alboreto, driving a new and lighter Tyrrell 011, and also Laffite whose Talbot was sporting new side-pods designed to improve the car's handling still further. After that the rest of the order looked pretty familiar except that Surer was well up in mid-field with the new Arrows and, in contrast, Mansell was near the bottom of the list of times, actually only 24th fastest. Like his team-mate, though, the young Englishman had switched to his spare Lotus for qualifying due to the gear ratios being all wrong in his proposed race chassis – only to have had his progress seriously hampered by a down-on-power engine!

By the time that it came round to the final hour of qualifying on Saturday afternoon conditions were quite a bit warmer than the previous day and the general consensus of opinion was that the track was slower. This, in turn, led to the Renaults being officially withdrawn from qualifying so that Prost and Arnoux, confined to the spare car for the rest of the weekend, could concentrate on testing a new batch of Michelin tyres as well as spend some time running on full tanks. Lauda, too, was so convinced that he would be unable to improve on his Friday time that he decided to bow out completely, while another absentee was Tambay due to the pinched nerve causing him even worse pain than before. Consequently a lot of the usual excitement associated with the final battle for grid positions was lost, and although Patrese and Piquet went on to set the two fastest times of 1 min 02.710 sec and 1 min 03.183 sec respectively, after taking turns behind the wheel of the spare 'light-weight' Brabham, it did nothing to prevent the front row from being an all-Renault affair. It also did little to affect their own grid positions as Piquet remained sixth fastest overall, while Patrese moved up just one place, to third on the grid, by beating Lauda's existing time. Meanwhile, the Williams FW08s of Rosberg and Daly had spouted nose fins to improve their turning-in ability in spite of the fact that it meant sacrificing a certain amount of straight-line speed. So far as Rosberg was concerned, however, it made little difference to lap times for, like the majority of drivers, the Finn failed to make any improvement. Interestingly enough, though, Daly picked up almost exactly a full second on his previous best by recording the afternoon's third fastest time of 1 min 03.291 sec. As a result he not only fiished up by out-qualifying his team-mate for the very first time but also made up no less than six places to earn an eventual seventh spot on the grid. This apart, the only other change of any consequence was brought about by Boesel. He had improved sufficiently to hoist himself out of the non-qualifying zone to the detriment of fellow-countryman Serra who had not exactly helped his chances by spinning off in the Fittipaldi F9 during the morning untimed session, this coming after a similar incident in the older F8D on the previous day. Mansell, though, had only just gone quick enough to avoid being bumped off the grid after another frustrating afternoon, this time plagued by chronic handling problems. In addition, towards the end of practice, he had spun off into the catch-fences at one of the downhill left-handers due to a misunderstanding whilst attempting to overtake Henton's Tyrrell which had been travelling much slower after having just left the pits on a fresh set of tyres. In fact, he was openly blaming his compatriot for not having moved over soon enough and practice ended with the pair of them involved in a heated argument over the affair!

On Sunday morning Tambay was suffering as badly as ever so Ferrari's Marco Piccinini was left with little choice other than to officially withdraw the Frenchman from the race. However, as the grid had already been published it was too late for Serra to be allowed in as the fastest non-qualifier with the result that the Brazilian had to remain a spectator along with Byrne and Baldi, who had also failed to qualify. The others, meanwhile, were soon taking to the track for the warm-up session which was starting at the comparatively early hour of 10 a.m. owing to

the race being scheduled for 1 p.m. Interestingly enough, the Brabham team had now joined Williams in running their cars with nose fins in the hope of eliminating the handling imbalance that had been so apparent throughout practice. But for Piquet, alone in planning a pit stop during the race on this occasion, there was soon another problem to worry about. Before he had covered many laps he felt his clutch beginning to slip. This, though, was just one of several problems to crop up, for while Prost was thoroughly enjoying himself and setting the fastest time, Cheever's Talbot coasted to rest with a broken fuel metering unit, Henton's Tyrrell stopped through lack of fuel pressure and, similarly, Rosberg had to park his Williams when the throttle cable snapped. Worst of all, Guerrero returned to the pits to report that a replacement engine fitted to his Ensign overnight had started to tighten leaving Mo Nunn's under-financed team no alternative other than to fall back on the engine (their only other!) that the Colombian had already used in Austria and throughout practice. Needless to say this was now well past its best. Furthermore, when the remaining 24 starters began leaving the pits for the warm-up lap some two hours later, the engine change was still in progress and Guerrero was left facing the prospects of starting the race from the pit lane which was officially closed just prior to the job being completed. Apart from this, and the Lotus team deciding the fit nose fins to their cars at virtually the last minute even though neither of their drivers had tried them before during the weekend, everything else appeared to be auguring well. The other problems of the morning warm-up had all been quickly rectified, tyres had been carefully chosen to take into account what was quite an abrasive track surface, the weather was doing its bit with the circuit bathed in hot sunshine and there were some 60,000 spectators filling just about every conceivable vantage point, by now all anxiously awaiting the start.

When the green light did go on Prost and Arnoux both made their now customary good starts with Arnoux just getting the jump on his team-mate to take the lead as they headed towards the first right-hander. Behind the two Renaults, Patrese held off Lauda for third place but de Cesaris and Daly were both beaten in the initial rush by Piquet and Rosberg, and were down in seventh and eighth places respectively as the rest of the field rounded the first turn, Guerrero being allowed to join in as soon as they had all gone. This remained the order of the leaders throughout the opening lap, but Prost was shadowing his team-mate (running on slightly more conservative tyres) all around the circuit, and at the start of the second lap almost effortlessly took over the lead towards the end of the main straight. Once in front, Prost then immediately began

to edge away and soon appeared to have the race nicely under control by extending his advantage at the rate of around half a second per lap. Piquet, on the other hand, was making nowhere near the hoped-for progress bearing in mind that he would be stopping for fresh tyres and more fuel somewhere at around half-distance. Although he quickly disposed of Lauda on the second lap, it took him another two laps to overtake his team-mate and considerably longer to deal with Arnoux. In fact, on lap 6 the World Champion didn't exactly improve his chances by sliding very wide on the way through the left-hander at the end of the loop after finding some oil that had just been deposited by the tired engine in Guerrero's Ensign, which had already blown up, as another four laps went by before he could make up the ground lost on Arnoux. Moreover, by the time that Piquet had finally caught and passed the Frenchman on lap 11, Prost was some 6 seconds clear and looking totally unassailable. Further back, meanwhile, Rosberg had now come through to fourth place after brief skirmishes with Lauda and Patrese, who had just swopped places following a somewhat longer engagement, and Watson had tigerishly fought his way up to an impressive-looking seventh place by overtaking Surer, Alboreto, Giacomelli, Laffite, de Cesaris and Daly in rapid succession. Now he, too, was looking for a way past Patrese's Brabham but, like Lauda, was soon finding that no easy task due to its vastly superior straight-line speed more than compensating for an obvious shortage of grip through the twists and turns.

By lap 20, quarter-distance, Prost was still holding sway out in front and keeping the gap to Piquet almost constant even though they were now beginning to lap tail-enders. Behind them, Arnoux was maintaining a healthy-looking third place from Rosberg and Lauda, but Watson, who had finally scrambled past Patrese three laps earlier, had just veered off into the pits to begin a lengthy stop from a new skirt. He had been forced over the kerbing whilst in the throes of overtaking the Italian! As a result, Patrese found himself in sixth place once more but apart from having lost contact with the five leading cars he was now coming under considerable pressure from Daly who, in turn, was being hotly pursued by de Cesaris, Laffite, Alboreto, Warwick, Fabi and de Angelis. Earlier, Giacomelli had been right up amongst them as well but had ended his seventeenth lap by becoming the first visitor to the pits for fresh tyres, and it was for the same reason that Warwick's promising run was interrupted at the end of lap 21. This, however, proved to be the beginning of the end for the Englishman. Within just four laps of rejoining the race his Hart engine suddenly cut out and left him stranded out on the circuit along with Keegan who, moments later, inadvertently touched his accelerator pedal as he braked for one of the corners, spun, stalled his engine and was unable to restart. Not long afterwards both of their respective team-mates were also sidelined. Fabi, whose engine had started misfiring, pulled into the pits at the end of lap 32 with his water temperature rising dramatically and almost before he had stepped out of the Toleman, along came Boesel to retire his March with a slipping clutch caused by oil leaking from the gearbox. Only two more laps passed before both Talbots were in the pits as well, Laffite to retire with handling problems caused by a damaged skirt, and Cheever to replace worn tyres which was something that was soon to bring in Salazar and Jarier. While all this was happening the situation amongst the five leading cars was staying largely unchanged apart from the gaps fluctuating slightly as they moved in and out of the traffic. Lauda, though, was gradually moving ever closer to Rosberg, which suggested that there could well be a good scrap in the offing here later in the race, and, of course, Piquet had yet to make his planned pit stop. In sixth place, too, it was still Patrese, but here the situation was as tense as ever with Daly, de Cesaris, Alboreto and de Angelis all remaining tightly bunched up behind the Brabham and looking all set to be shortly joined by none other than Mansell who had been quietly climbing up through the field from the back of the grid ever since the start.

At the end of lap 40, half-distance, the Renaults were lying first and second as Piquet was finally making for the pits. This time, unlike Austria, the Brabham pit crew was ready and waiting for him and, after being stationary for barely 14 seconds while all four wheels were changed and the fuel was topped up, Piquet was able to rejoin the race in fifth place ahead of team-mate Patrese and his entourage. Here, things were becoming even more hectic as Alboreto had now forced his way through into seventh place and Daly had been elbowed back to ninth behind de Cesaris, the Irishman having spent a number of laps struggling to keep up due to his Williams running a shade too much rear wing, and its left rear tyre having blistered early in the race. To add to the excitement the leaders were now starting to lap them all. However, whilst this was to prove a relatively straightforward exercise for Prost and Arnoux by being able to make full use of their superior power along the main straight, Rosberg and Lauda (they were now running virtually nose to tail) later ran into all sorts of problems so far as getting by de Cesaris was concerned. For reasons best known to himself, the Italian quite simply refused to move over for them and, instead, proceeded to put on a quite disgraceful exhibition of blatantly blocking the track. In the end, after almost pulling alongside the Alfa Romeo on one

occasion only to find himself having to back off, Rosberg had to quite literally barge his way past. Even so, by the time that he had eventually made it and shaken himself clear of Patrese some four laps had passed and the Renaults had both pulled a further 10 seconds clear. Lauda, too, had much the same sort of problem with the ill-mannered Italian which, in turn, caused him to lose most of the ground that he made up on Rosberg. Furthermore, any hopes of making it up again once out of the traffic vanished almost immediately as before many more minutes had passed the Austrian started suffering from the effects of an ever-increasing front wheel vibration. As a result, he was more or less forced to settle down to a lonely drive in fourth place, well clear of Piquet who was doing little more than holding his ground despite being on fresh rubber. Meanwhile, the situation behind Patrese had changed yet again as Alboreto had spun and dropped to tenth place after making an unsuccessful stab at the Brabham driver on lap 49 and shortly afterwards Daly had been overtaken by de Angelis who, consequently, was now lying eighth. Further back still, Surer's first race in the new Arrows A5 had just been interrupted by a tyre stop, and Jarier had suffered an engine failure. Nevertheless, even at this comparatively late stage, there were still 18 of the original 25 cars circulating, including Watson's McLaren which was being driven as hard as ever in spite of the Ulsterman having lost three laps whilst in the pits.

With 20 laps remaining Prost's advantage over Arnoux had dwindled to little more than 5 seconds and speculation was rife that the leader had a problem. Sure enough, his left-hand skirt was disintegrating which was not only having an adverse effect on the Renault's handling but also on Prost's lap times. Consequently, Arnoux continued to steadily close up but just when it looked as if he was about to press home the attack his Renault suddenly developed a pronounced

misfire and fell away dramatically. At first, Arnoux was convinced that he was running low on fuel and responded by dashing into the pits screaming for more. Sadly for the Frenchman, though, that was not the problem as when he took off again the engine was misfiring as badly as ever. Instead, it was more or less a repeat of the fuel-injection problem that had cost his team-mate victory in Austria, and with much the same consequences, as almost immediately afterwards Arnoux was coasting to rest with a dead engine. By then Rosberg, who had been steadily gaining on both Renaults even before Arnoux's problem, had already gone through into second place and was now driving harder than ever with his sights firmly set on the leader. For the crowd the tension was becoming almost unbearable and the same seemed to be true of the man with the chequered flag for after Prost and Rosberg had crossed the line to start their 78th lap, now only a few car lengths apart, he was already preparing to unfurl it. Fortunately, the Williams team manager, Peter Collins, saw what was happening, rushed over to the official and restrained him which was just as well from Rosberg's point of view for the Finn was still behind the Renault as he came round to complete the lap. He was now closer than ever, though, and mid-way round the following lap, as the two cars approached the downhill left-hander at Bretelle, Prost ran just wide enough turning into the corner for Rosberg to be able to slam through on the inside. From then on the Williams quickly drew away, with Prost in no position to respond, and although the confused organizers failed to hold out the chequered flag at the correct time – it appeared at the end of lap 81! – Rosberg drove on to his long-awaited first Grand Prix victory in style, a result that moved him to the top of the Championship table at the expense of the unfortunate Pironi, and fully vindicated a late tyre gamble in which a harder left rear had been fitted to that of his team-mate's car.

Keke Rosberg on the way to scoring his long-awaited first Grand Prix victory, a result that moved the Finn to the top of the World Championship table. (*L.A.T. Photographic*)

Although somewhat disappointed, Prost at least had no trouble in holding on to second place as only one other driver was still on the same lap and almost a full minute away in any case. That was Lauda who duly brought his vibrating McLaren home in third place ahead of the Brabham-BMWs of Piquet and Patrese, the Italian just holding off a strong challenge from de Angelis who, in turn, finished just in front of Alboreto, Mansell, Daly and, after having recovered from a quick spin in the closing stages, de Cesaris.

After that there were still another six cars running at the finish as the only other retirement had been Winkelhock with a broken engine mounting, although Cheever was too far behind to be classified due to two further pit stops with tyre and skirt problems.

Results			
1	K. Rosberg (Williams-Ford)	1 hr 32 min 41.087 sec (196.796 kph/ 122.283 mph)	
2	A. Prost (Renault)	1 hr 32 min 45.529 sec	
3	N. Lauda (McLaren-Ford)	1 hr 33 min 41.430 sec	
4	N. Piquet (Brabham-BMW)	1 lap behind	
5	R. Patrese (Brabham-BMW)	1 lap behind	
6	E. de Angelis (Lotus-Ford)	1 lap behind	
7	M. Alboreto (Tyrrell-Ford)	1 lap behind	
8	N. Mansell (Lotus-Ford)	1 lap behind	
9	D. Daly (Williams-Ford)	1 lap behind	
10	A. de Cesaris (Alfa Romeo)	2 laps behind	
11	B. Henton (Tyrrell-Ford)	2 laps behind	
12	B. Giacomelli (Alfa Romeo)	2 laps behind	
13	J. Watson (McLaren-Ford)	3 laps behind	
14	E. Salazar (ATS-Ford)	3 laps behind	
15	M. Surer (Arrows-Ford)	4 laps behind	
*16	R. Arnoux (Renault)	5 laps behind	

Also running at finish: E. Cheever (Talbot-Matra) 10 laps behind.

* Not running at finish.

Fastest lap: A. Prost (Renault) on lap 2 in 1 min 07.477 sec (202.735 kph/125.973 mph)

Retirements

R. Guerrero (Ensign-Ford) engine on lap 5, D. Warwick (Toleman-Hart) engine on lap 25, R. Keegan (March-Ford) spun and stalled on lap 26, T. Fabi (Toleman-Hart) engine on lap 32, R. Boesel (March-Ford) gearbox oil leak on lap 32, J. Laffite (Talbot-Matra) handling on lap 34, J.P. Jarier (Osella-Ford) engine on lap 45, M. Winkelhock (ATS-Ford) engine mounting on lap 56.

LIII° Gran Premio d'Italia

Monza: September 12
Weather: Hot
Distance: 52 laps of 5.800 km
circuit = 301.60 km (187.40 miles)

Monza – Ferrari country – and it was the Italian team that made the early headlines. After the obvious disappointment caused by Patrick Tambay being unable to take part in the so-called Swiss Grand Prix, the Commendatore was taking no chances and had successfully concluded a deal for Mario Andretti (free from any CART commitments over this particular weekend) to drive for him on a one-off basis in much the same manner that he had done for Frank Williams at Long Beach earlier in the year. For the many thousands of fanatical Italian supporters the news was greeted with near-delirium as the American-domiciled Italian had always been one of their heroes ever since he had driven for Ferrari back in the early '70s. To add to their open delight, Tambay was also fit enough to drive again following intensive treatment at a clinic in Switzerland which meant that for the first time since Didier Pironi's dreadful accident at Hockenheim two Ferraris would be in action. Meanwhile, with the aim of increasing still further the already excellent chances of carrying off the Constructors' Championship, the team had produced lighter versions of the successful V6 turbo-charged engine, made possible by the extensive use of new alloys, and were bringing into use new cylinder heads with revised water channels designed to improve the flow of water through them. In addition, work had also been completed on another new chassis which was fitted with the longitudinal gearbox and the corresponding revised rear suspension. This was to serve as a new spare car as Tambay was using the chassis that he had driven briefly at Dijon, also newly built, and Andretti was consigned to what had previously been the spare car, this, like Tambay's, appearing with the more familiar transverse gearbox. Some quite important changes had taken place amongst the lesser teams as well. For a start the hitherto unsponsored, dark blue Tyrrells were now in a predominantly dark green livery to signify a new sponsorship tie-up (provisionally on a one-race basis) with Denim to coincide with the launch of a new range of Denim Musk men's toiletries. John MacDonald had his March 821s running on Michelin tyres rather than on Avons as previously used. And Toleman were now ready to race their brand new Rory Byrne-designed TG183. This appeared in a dark grey and white colour scheme as distinct from the red, white and blue colours of the British team's earlier model and was being entrusted to Derek Warwick. In the Arrows camp, too, there was a slight reorganization as the new A5 car had been passed over to Mauro Baldi due to reasons that were almost certainly associated with the fact that this was the Italian's home Grand Prix and that the team's sponsors were Italian.

Fine weather helped everything off to a good start for the opening 90 minutes of practice on Friday morning, and before long it became evident that, even with three chicanes, Monza was yet another circuit well suited to the turbo-charged cars. The Brabham-BMWs of Piquet and Patrese were certainly on song with no sign at all of the handling problems that had beset the team at Dijon, even though the cars were essentially unchanged apart from being fitted with fresh engines. In the Ferrari camp Tambay was making back to back comparisons between the new car and his proposed race chassis and Andretti, who had arrived in Italy a week earlier to spend some time testing at the Fiorano track, was looking remarkably at home in the other 126C2. All seemed to be going well for Renault, too, although neither Prost nor Arnoux were over-enthusiastic with how their cars were handling, and they were busily juggling with variables trying to arrive at the best possible compromise, something that equally applied to a number of the others. Warwick, in particular, was openly dismayed with the new Toleman, especially as it had performed well in recent testing, but since then Pirelli had introduced a new batch of tyres with stiffer sidewalls which didn't seem to be working too well, not on the Toleman at least! To compound the team's misery Fabi's older car, which was fitted with a new, experimental 6-speed gearbox, became stranded out on the circuit with a dead engine after covering only a handful of laps. Fortunately, once the car had been retrieved at the end of the session, this turned out to be nothing worse than the battery having packed up but in the meantime, of course, the Italian lost a lot of valuable time. So, too, did Cheever when his Talbot similarly came to a rest with seized transmission, while Alboreto and Serra both had their runs interrupted by clutch trouble. Two other drivers, meanwhile, both ended their practice early owing to errors in the cockpit. Salazar, plagued by a bout of porpoising, glanced the barriers at the second

1982

frustrated by a seized rear shock-absorber. Cheever and Salazar, on the other hand, were able to go straight out in their teams' spare cars and were joined in this respect by Fabi who had switched to the spare Toleman. Elsewhere everyone was using their proposed race cars, although just when all appeared to be running reasonably smoothly Mansell's Lotus developed clutch trouble whilst out on its first set of qualifying tyres, and Rosberg, after covering only eight laps on race tyres, had the engine blow up in his Williams. Furthermore, whereas Mansell went on to enjoy a relatively trouble-free ride in his spare Lotus, Rosberg lasted barely half a lap in the spare Williams before silently rolling to a halt in the vicinity of the Ascari chicane soaked in foam. An electrical short had not only cut out the engine but also triggered off the on-board fire extinguisher! His team-mate was not much better off either, for when Daly did eventually join in, over half an hour late, his Williams persisted in jumping out of fifth gear. Others not having a particularly happy time of it included Lauda and Watson, whose McLarens were suffering from an acute lack of grip through the three chicanes, and also de Angelis who, apart from being plagued by poor handling, went on to end his afternoon's work early by flying off into the catch-fences at the Curva Parabolica, the incident tearing away the right front corner of his Lotus. Meanwhile, amongst those avoiding the worst of the trouble, the pace was really warming up, with Tambay and Piquet leading the way and engaged in an exciting duel for the provisional pole. Eventually this was resolved in favour of Tambay with a time of 1 min 29.275 sec, in spite of his Ferrari stopping out on the circuit with a broken turbine blade towards the end of the session, as Piquet was unable to progress beyond 1 min 29.709 sec. Although they both appeared to be concentrating rather more on achieving a good race set-up than on optimum lap times, Prost and Arnoux were next with evenly matched times of 1 min 30.488 sec and 1 min 30.520 sec respectively. Then came Patrese (1 min 30.818 sec) and Andretti (1 min 31.474 sec) to make it six turbo-charged cars in the first six places on the time-sheets, the fastest normally-aspirated car being Rosberg's Williams which had gone around in 1 min 32.340 sec just before the engine failure. After that, about the only surprise in the order, apart from Lauda winding up only 11th fastest and Watson a totally despondent 19th, was to find Jarier lying ninth, sandwiched between de Cesaris and Alboreto. This, in fact, led to all kinds of allegations being brandished about and, eventually, to the Frenchman's engine being measured, but the truth of the matter was that the Osella was performing well on the new Pirelli tyres and Jarier had been able to respond accordingly.

On Saturday morning much of the attention was briefly diverted towards the Alfa Romeo pit when the Autodelta team wheeled out their long-awaited, turbo-charged car, the 182T. After Friday's practice de Cesaris had put the car through its paces at the Balocco test track with reasonably encouraging results. But now, just when it mattered most, the Italian ran over a kerb almost as soon as he went out and returned to the pits with part of a side-pod scraping along the ground. As a result he had to spend the rest of the morning in his more familiar V12 while repairs were being effected. Although this was an untimed session there was still a lot of fast motoring going on, and for some the pace became a little too hectic: Arnoux and de Angelis eventually tripped over one another at the second chicane, while Mansell had an accident of his own making at the first chicane. Fortunately all three drivers escaped injury but the Renault sustained quite substantial damage around its right front corner, and both Lotus 91s were also left looking rather second-hand. Nevertheless, by early afternoon everything had been patched up again only for Arnoux to quickly run into more trouble at the start of final qualifying when a turbo let go and forced him to sit things out for half an hour or so. Once again the battle for pole position seemed to be turning out to be a straight fight between Tambay and Piquet, with both of them recording some quite phenomenal lap times, especially when taking into account the hot conditions. Eventually, after going through his allocated two sets of tyres, Tambay appeared to have settled the matter with a lap in 1 min 28.830 sec but then Piquet suddenly turned the tables on his rival by producing an even faster time of 1 min 28.508 sec. That really did seem to be it, but then Andretti, having held back on his second set of tyres and having the boost pressure on his Ferrari turned up about as high as it would go, ventured out and eclipsed them both with an eventual pole-winning time of 1 min 28.473 sec (236.004 kph). A fantastic achievement which not only brought a state of euphoria to the Ferrari pit but also sent the many thousands of patriotic Italian supporters present crazy with excitement. Indeed, after that everything else seemed to be of little consequence. By the end of the afternoon, though, Patrese had improved sufficiently to move ahead of the two Renault drivers to take fourth place on the grid, in spite of his engine having gone off colour in the closing stages, and Rosberg had successfully defended his position as the fastest non-turbo runner with an improved time of 1 min 31.834 sec. Further back, too, Watson had improved by over 1½ seconds following an overnight change of settings on his McLaren to hoist himself up to a slightly more respectable 12th place on the grid, two places lower than team-mate Lauda. In con-

chicane which resulted in the Chilean having to abandon his ATS with deranged front suspension, and Daly, having similar problems with his Williams, as well as being unhappy with the brakes, also briefly left the track and returned to the pits with a badly wrinkled side-pod.

At the start of the first qualifying session work was still in progress repairing Daly's Williams, and Warwick was also left waiting around while his mechanics finished altering the suspension settings of the new Toleman in the vain hope of adapting the chassis to the latest Pirelli tyres, earlier efforts having been trast, Jarier had been unable to repeat Friday's performance and had slipped to 15th spot in the final reckoning. In the meantime, there had been a good scrap going on amongst the tail-enders even to get on to the grid and the four finally destined to miss the race were Winkelhock, Byrne and the two March drivers, Keegan and Boesel, both of whom had had problems acclimatizing to the change of tyres, and had been wearing out skirts at a rather alarming rate. Amongst the remaining drivers, Warwick had qualified the new Toleman in 16th spot despite having suffered a turbo seizure in the morning and still having made little progress on the latest Pirelli tyres which were now being discarded in favour of the older ones; Fabi finished up six places lower after engine problems during the morning had forced him into the spare Toleman once again; de Cesaris had abandoned another run in the Alfa Romeo V8 turbo owing to further trouble, in particular fluctuating boost pressure. Finally Laffite, following a generally disappointing couple of days, found his afternoon's lap times being scrubbed after practice when his Talbot, one of two cars selected at random for weighing, failed – just – to come up to the minimum weight limit. As a result the Frenchman slipped from 18th to an even more lowly 21st place on the grid.

By the time that it came round to the start of the race on Sunday afternoon Piquet had been forced to take over the spare Brabham as during the warm-up session an obscure electrical fault had caused the engine to cut out in his race chassis. Otherwise everyone was settled in the cars that they had intended using in the first place, for although Tambay's engine had also cut out at more or less the same time this had since been replaced, while one or two less serious problems to have cropped up had, similarly, all been put right by now. Being on pole position (for the first time since Watkins Glen 1978), Andretti had the responsibility of leading the field around on the pace lap and as he did so, in hot sunshine and in front of a capacity crowd, it was already patently clear what was expected. Overnight someone had painted messages on the track which, translated, read 'Mario and Patrick – win for Gilles'. However, after the American had brought them all safely back to their starting positions and the lights had changed from red to green, he allowed his engine to race up against the rev-limiter, had to momentarily dip the clutch and was beaten in the rush to the first chicane by Piquet, team-mate Tambay and Arnoux. Prost very nearly made it past him as well after making a bold run down the outside of the track but, instead, finished up with all four wheels on the grass and having a busy moment gathering it up. Meanwhile, Piquet's lead proved to be a very short-lived affair for no sooner had he exited the chicane than his clutch began to slip.

Consequently, he was quickly swallowed up by the other leading cars and when Tambay's Ferrari was first to appear out of the Curva Parabolica towards the end of the lap the spectators were beyond themselves with delight. Unfortunately for them, though, it was only a matter of seconds before Arnoux was darting out from behind the Ferrari's slip-stream, drawing alongside and nosing ahead as the two cars raced across the line – instead of an outburst of hysteria there were audible groans! Behind these first two, Patrese had come through to third place at the expense of Andretti and Piquet after recovering from a rather slow start, and then it was de Cesaris and Giacomelli in their V12 Alfa Romeos followed by Rosberg, Watson, Prost, Alboreto, Lauda, Cheever, Jarier and de Angelis. After that there was already a sizeable gap before Surer appeared in 16th place, but this was hardly surprising as there had been bedlam at the second chicane caused by Daly losing control of his Williams. At the first chicane the Irishman had been struck from behind by Guerrero's Ensign and had continued unaware that something was amiss with the Williams' rear suspension until after exiting the Curva

Grande. Then, in applying the brakes for the second chicane, the green and white car had suddenly snapped sideways into Henton's Tyrrell which, in turn, had sent to Englishman spinning into the path of Warwick's new Toleman with dire consequences to them both. Daly was soon out of the race as well, retiring at the pits at the end of the lap with the Williams' lower left rear wishbone broken, while Guerrero followed him in to begin a lengthy stop having the Ensign's front bodywork patched up.

On the second lap Piquet continued losing places hand over fist because of his clutch problem, and it was clear that Brabham's hopes rested fairly and squarely on the shoulders of Patrese who quickly followed Arnoux past Tambay to take over second place. Both Brabham-BMWs had come to the grid in 'sprint form' due to pit stops being on the agenda, so the Italian now not only had to get past the leading Renault but also pull away from it as quickly as possible to allow for his stop. This, however, soon proved to be easier said than done, for Arnoux was flying and it was as much as Patrese could do to even catch the Renault let alone get by. Then on lap 6, just when it

On lap 2 of the Italian Grand Prix René Arnoux has just moved into the lead at the expense of Patrick Tambay. *(Autosport)*

1982

Nelson Piquet, after being first away at the start, has already dropped to tenth spot on lap 2 because of a slipping clutch and is now coming under pressure from Michele Alboreto, Niki Lauda and Eddie Cheever, watched only a short distance away by Jean-Pierre Jarier. *(Autosport)*

was becoming interesting, the number 2 Brabham suddenly started to drop away and went on to complete the lap down in fifth place before touring into the pits next time round. Incredibly, Patrese had run into a similar problem to that of his team-mate and retired with clutch failure. At the end of the following lap Piquet was in the pits as well and for the Brabham team it was all over. The same applied to the Toleman team as after Warwick had been punted out of the race through no fault of his own, only two more laps had passed before Fabi's engine had inexplicably cut out. Meanwhile, Laffite had become yet another retirement due to his Talbot developing gearbox trouble. So already the field was thinning fast and, moreover, becoming increasingly spread out. Even the leading positions were no longer the source of any real excitement. With Patrese gone, Arnoux now had a clear advantage, while Tambay was well beyond the reach of Prost who had quickly recovered from the excursion on to the grass at the start and steadily worked his way up into third place in front of Andretti's Ferrari, troubled by a sticky throttle pedal. Only fifth place held much in the way of interest where de Cesaris was being kept on his toes by team-mate Giacomelli, Rosberg and Watson, all four tightly bunched up together. Even this soon started fizzling out, though, as on lap 11, while Jarier was having a busy moment

bringing the Osella to rest when a rear suspension breakage led to the left rear wheel flying off, de Cesaris felt his engine start to misfire, plummeted to the back of the quartet and disappeared into the pits. There, he was to lose over a lap having the Alfa's ignition coil replaced. In the meantime Watson, absolutely delighted with how his McLaren was performing, made comparatively light work of overtaking Rosberg and, two laps later, on lap 13, was not only taking over Giacomelli's brief role as the leading non-turbo runner, but quickly consolidating fifth place. All the while Lauda was getting nowhere in the other McLaren, merely trailing around behind Alboreto due to experiencing acute understeer and trouble with erratic front brakes. Furthermore, the handling problem was steadily growing worse owing to a skirt wearing away and eventually, at the end of lap 22, the Austrian turned off into the pits to give up the unequal struggle, by which time de Angelis, making even less of an impression in his Lotus, had taken on a fresh set of tyres in the vain hope of curing similar handling deficiencies.

At the start of lap 25 of what was turning out to be a rather dull and uninteresting Italian Grand Prix, attention suddenly became fixed on Rosberg's Williams when first the rear aerofoil tilted over as the car roared past the pits and then flew off completely. The Finn, however, failed to notice

and, instead, made full use of a sudden and unexpected surge of power to finally blast past Giacomelli's Alfa Romeo on the approach to the first chicane. But then, through the chicane, Rosberg found himself weaving all over the road and as he eased off so Giacomelli repassed him, pointing vigorously to the back of the Williams as he did so. Convinced that he had picked up a puncture, Rosberg responded by driving carefully around to the pits and, following a certain amount of confusion caused by a momentary breakdown in communications until he had been told precisely what had happened, eventually rejoined the race with a new rear aerofoil assembly. Even so all hopes of picking up any Championship points had now been lost as seventh place had become 15th and he was over two laps in arrears. Meanwhile, for the crowd there was something to cheer about at long last. After being steadily reeled in by Prost, and looking in increasing danger of losing his second place, Tambay was suddenly alone once more and the Renault was seen spluttering into the pits. It was a recurrence of the electronic fuel-injection problem that had been plaguing the French team over the previous few months and, in spite of adjustments being hurriedly carried out, they were to no avail for no sooner had Prost rejoined the race than the engine cut out completely, ending his last remaining hopes of winning the 1982 World Championship. On the following lap Surer was in the pits as well, with his engine sounding decidedly off colour, and after subsequently trying just one more lap he, too, was forced to call it a day, while only a few more minutes passed before Giacomelli and de Angelis were both climbing out of their cars. Giacomelli's problem was a broken side-pod which was having a dire effect on the Alfa's handling and de Angelis simply gave up, a sticking throttle to add to the already bad handling of his Lotus being the final straw. After that, though, there were no further changes except for Rosberg and de Cesaris picking off one or two of the tail-enders following their pit stops, and it was a relief when the chequered flag finally appeared to bring the whole dreary affair to a conclusion. Nevertheless, at the end of it all, the fact remained that Arnoux had driven to a resounding victory, his second of the season, and that Tambay (still far from fully fit) and Andretti (plagued by that sticking throttle) had certainly not disgraced themselves by finishing in second and third places respectively, especially as they had been running on what had turned out to be too conservative a tyre choice. On the contrary they had more or less assured Ferrari of the Constructors' Championship, so that, at least, made up for much of the disappointment of not actually winning the race. Behind them, and the only other driver to complete the full distance, Watson had done just about as much as he could have hoped for by finishing in a solid-looking fourth place to score his first points since Canada, as well as keeping his faint Championship hopes alive. Alboreto was fifth, Cheever, who had been named as Arnoux's replace-ment at Renault in 1983 on the previous day, was sixth and Mansell finished just out of the points in seventh place after an uncomfortable ride caused by his Lotus 91 porpoising badly throughout most of the race. After that the remaining six finishers, headed by Ros-berg's Williams, were all at least two laps behind the winner, including Salazar who deserved a medal for perseverence as the Chilean's ATS had been bouncing around so violently all afternoon that even the engine cover had been shaken off during the race!

Results		
1	R. Arnoux (Renault)	1 hr 22 min 25.734 sec (219.534 kph/ 136.412 mph)
2	P. Tambay (Ferrari)	1 hr 22 min 39.798 sec
3	M. Andretti (Ferrari)	1 hr 23 min 14.186 sec
4	J. Watson (McLaren-Ford)	1 hr 23 min 53.579 sec
5	M. Alboreto (Tyrrell-Ford)	1 lap behind
6	E. Cheever (Talbot-Matra)	1 lap behind
7	N. Mansell (Lotus-Ford)	1 lap behind
8	K. Rosberg (Williams-Ford)	2 laps behind
9	E. Salazar (ATS-Ford)	2 laps behind
10	A. de Cesaris (Alfa Romeo)	2 laps behind
11	F. Serra (Fittipaldi-Ford)	3 laps behind
12	M. Baldi (Arrows-Ford)	3 laps behind

Also running at finish: R. Guerrero (Ensign-Ford) 12 laps behind.

Fastest lap: R. Arnoux (Renault) on lap 25 in 1 min 33.619 sec (223.031 kph/138.585 mph)

Retirements
B. Henton (Tyrrell-Ford) accident on lap 1, D. Warwick (Toleman-Hart) accident on lap 1, D. Daly (Williams-Ford) rear suspension on lap 1, T. Fabi (Toleman-Hart) engine on lap 3, J. Laffite (Talbot-Matra) gearbox on lap 6, R. Patrese (Brabham-BMW) clutch on lap 7, N. Piquet (Brabham-BMW) clutch on lap 8, J.P. Jarier (Osella-Ford) rear suspension on lap 11, N. Lauda (McLaren-Ford) handling on lap 22, A. Prost (Renault) fuel-injection on lap 28, M. Surer (Arrows-Ford) engine on lap 29, B. Giacomelli (Alfa Romeo) handling on lap 33, E. de Angelis (Lotus-Ford) sticking throttle/handling on lap 34.

IInd United States (Las Vegas) Grand Prix

Las Vegas: September 25
Weather: Overcast but dry
Distance: 75 laps of 3.650 km
circuit = 273.75 km (170.10 miles)

With the curtains coming down on the European season at Monza it was soon time for everyone to make their third visit in less than six months to North America for the final round of the 1982 World Championship. This, for the second year running, was to take place on the uninspiring but, nonetheless, extremely demanding little circuit laid out on land adjoining the Caesars Palace Hotel in Las Vegas and, just like 11 months earlier, had the added importance of being the Championship decider or, at least, as things stood: Rosberg, the clear favourite for the title, had accumulated 42 points and Watson, the only other remaining contender with the unfortunate Pironi out of action, had 33 points to his credit. However, it was not as simple as saying that Watson had to win the race and Rosberg had to finish lower than sixth if the Finn was to be denied, as there were other factors to be taken into consideration. These concerned the outcome of two important appeal hearings to have recently taken place. The first was an appeal lodged by Williams Engineering against the FIA International Court of Appeal's decision to exclude Rosberg (and Piquet) from the results of the Brazilian Grand Prix following the use of 'disposable ballast', for which judgement was still being awaited from a French civil court in Paris. The other was an appeal lodged with the FIA International Court of Appeal by McLaren International against Lauda's disqualification from third place in the Belgian Grand Prix on the basis that his MP4B had been 2 kilogrammes below the minimum weight limit when, in the

team's view, the scales had been inaccurate. Here again, no decision had been announced as yet. Consequently, it was quite conceivable that Rosberg had already won the World Championship on the assumption that the Williams' appeal would be upheld. On the other hand, if it was rejected but the appeal lodged by McLaren was successful, Lauda was still in with a chance as this would increase his points tally from thirty to thirty-four and mean that a victory by him here with Rosberg finishing lower than fifth would change things around completely. As it happened both appeals were to be subsequently turned down but, in the meantime, there was obviously no way of knowing this so Rosberg arrived at the circuit with every intention of doing his utmost to settle the matter conclusively by being amongst the first five finishers, preferably as the winner. Naturally, these same factors also affected the final outcome of the Constructors' Championship, and when taking into account all of the mathematical possibilities no less than three teams (McLaren, Renault and Williams) could still pip Ferrari, the firm favourites, to the post.

Contrary to original expectations the driver line-up for the race was identical to that at Monza a fortnight earlier, as Andretti had once again obtained the agreement of his CART entrant, Pat Patrick, and his sponsors to drive for Ferrari, although it was on the strict understanding that he would still take part in a race at Michigan over the weekend. This was scheduled for Sunday whereas the Grand Prix was taking place on Saturday.

Needless to say, Ferrari, was delighted with the arrangement in view of the extra impetus that this would give towards clinching the Constructors' Championship; and so, too, were the organizers. The previous year's race had been a near-disaster financially and it was hoped, vainly as it happened, that Andretti's presence would stimulate much more interest in the event. So far as the first day's practice on Thursday was concerned, however, the American must have been left wondering whether he had done the right thing (he would be obliged to start the Michigan race from the back of the grid due to missing qualifying there) as the Ferraris were in dire trouble with fuel vaporization problems owing to what was extremely hot weather. The heat was also affecting a number of the other runners, notably the Alfa Romeos of Giacomelli and de Cesaris, but the Ferraris, in particular, just could not be encouraged to run properly. To make matters worse for the team, both Andretti and Tambay had their cars splutter to a halt out on the circuit during the first qualifying session so, at the end of the day, it was hardly surprising that they were languishing in only ninth and 24th places respectively on the time-sheets. Meanwhile, the situation was little better in the Brabham camp, only here the reasons were more to do with their drivers being unable to achieve any sort of reasonable handling balance with their cars, a situation not helped by the absence of Gordon Murray. He had taken such a dislike to Las Vegas in 1981 that he had decided to stay at home! Consequently they, too, were well off the pace with Piquet winding up seventh fastest and Patrese 12 places lower. In fact, of all the leading turbo runners only Arnoux was enjoying a trouble-free ride as Prost was yet another having a frustrating

1982

Starting Grid

A. Prost
Renault
(1 min 16.356 sec)

R. Arnoux
Renault
(1 min 16.786 sec)

M. Alboreto
Tyrrell-Ford
(1 min 17.646 sec)

E. Cheever
Talbot-Matra
(1 min 17.683 sec)

R. Patrese
Brabham-BMW
(1 min 17.772 sec)

K. Rosberg
Williams-Ford
(1 min 17.886 sec)

M. Andretti
Ferrari
(1 min 17.921 sec)

**P. Tambay
Ferrari
(1 min 17.958 sec)

J. Watson
McLaren-Ford
(1 min 17.986 sec)

D. Warwick
Toleman-Hart
(1 min 18.012 sec)

J. Laffite
Talbot-Matra
(1 min 18.056 sec)

N. Piquet
Brabham-BMW
(1 min 18.275 sec)

N. Lauda
McLaren-Ford
(1 min 18.333 sec)

D. Daly
Williams-Ford
(1 min 18.418 sec)

*R. Guerrero
Ensign-Ford
(1 min 18.496 sec)

B. Giacomelli
Alfa Romeo
(1 min 18.622 sec)

M. Surer
Arrows-Ford
(1 min 18.734 sec)

A. de Cesaris
Alfa Romeo
(1 min 18.761 sec)

B. Henton
Tyrrell-Ford
(1 min 18.765 sec)

E. de Angelis
Lotus-Ford
(1 min 19.302 sec)

N. Mansell
Lotus-Ford
(1 min 19.439 sec)

M. Winkelhock
ATS-Ford
(1 min 19.767 sec)

M. Baldi
Arrows-Ford
(1 min 20.271 sec)

R. Boesel
March-Ford
(1 min 20.766 sec)

R. Keegan
March-Ford
(1 min 21.180 sec)

T. Byrne
Theodore-Ford
(1 min 21.555 sec)

*Non-starter:
R. Guerrero (Ensign-Ford) 1 min 18.496 sec
**Withdrawn:
P. Tambay (Ferrari) 1 min 17.958 sec
J.P. Jarier (Osella-Ford) 1 min 19.222 sec

Did not qualify:
T. Fabi (Toleman-Hart) 1 min 21.569 sec
E. Salazar (ATS-Ford) 1 min 21.583 sec
F. Serra (Fittipaldi-Ford) 1 min 22.387 sec.

What was a surprise, though, was to find Alboreto and Cheever trading second fastest times behind Arnoux, both drivers putting on an inspired display and making the most of good handling and plenty of grip. Eventually, after going around in a very impressive-looking 1 min 18.842 sec, Cheever had his prowess halted by the Talbot stopping with an electrical fault, leaving Alboreto, his Tyrrell still painted in the dark green colours of Denim Musk and in wide track configuration, to take the honour of driving the fastest normally-aspirated car at 1 min 18.756 sec. Almost half a second slower, Rosberg and Lauda turned in closely-matched times of 1 min 19.162 sec and 1 min 19.171 sec respectively to finish up between Prost and Piquet. Then, after that, there was another surprise in the shape of Jarier who had done exceptionally well to have come out eighth fastest in the Osella. This put him just in front of Andretti and also Watson who had had to rely on the spare McLaren for qualifying following an eventful morning in which he had spun on no less than three occasions before stopping with a suspected broken valve spring. Like Watson, numerous other drivers had been having their moments as well, most of them pretty harmless except for Warwick damaging the right front suspension of the new Toleman – twice! First, soon after the start of qualifying, he had tangled with Byrne's Theodore whilst attempting to overtake the Irishman. Then, later, he had spun off into the catch-fences when a broken battery terminal led to the engine cutting out at an inopportune moment.

For the final hour of qualifying on Friday afternoon conditions were slightly cooler, but it was still warm by any standards. Overnight the Ferrari team had taken steps to overcome the fuel vaporization problems and the 126C2s now not only had extra ducting but also a generous quantity of dry-ice packed around their inter-coolers. Most of the other teams, too, had taken various measures to combat the heat, and so everyone was now keeping their fingers tightly crossed that all would be well, including Patrese who had already lost an engine in the morning untimed session. Although Arnoux had ended the first day comfortably fastest, pole position was by no means a foregone conclusion as during the morning Prost, with the boost pressure problem now cured, had been lapping every bit as quickly as his team-mate, and some of the normally-aspirated cars had also gone extremely well. Indeed, there was an early rude awakening for the Frenchman for, just as everything was warming up nicely, Cheever suddenly whistled around in 1 min 17.683 sec which was the fastest lap of all up to that point, even quicker than Reutemann's pole-winning time of 1 min 17.821 sec for the 1981 race. Alboreto was looking as menacing as

ever, too, but then he finally overdid things, clipped a wall and went limping into the pits to have a broken steering arm replaced, whereupon Jarier conveniently brought proceedings to a temporary halt. Amazingly, the Osella had suffered another suspension failure and shed a wheel, just as it had done at Monza, only this time it was the right front. Furthermore, the consequence could have been far more serious as it had happened at one of the worst possible spots, on the fast straight leading to the final left-hander. Fortunately, though, Jarier had subsequently stepped out of the car uninjured after careering straight off into a sandy run-off area and coming to rest just short of a concrete retaining wall. It had still been a frightening moment for him, nevertheless, and one that was to lead to his entry being withdrawn from the race later in the afternoon. Meanwhile, the delay caused in retrieving the badly damaged Osella enabled the Tyrrell mechanics to complete repairs to Alboreto's car and in the closing minutes of practice the Italian repaid their efforts in the best possible way by reinstating himself as the fastest non-turbo runner with a superb performance that produced a lap in 1 min 17.646 sec. In fact, had it not been for the Renaults, he would have been in pole position, but by then Prost and Arnoux had both set an entirely new standard with laps in the 1 min 16 sec bracket, Prost achieving the faster time, 1 min 16.356 sec, compared to his team-mate's 1 min 16.786 sec. With Cheever's earlier time holding good for fourth place on the grid, Patrese lined up in fifth place after making a vast improvement of over 2½ seconds on the first day to 1 min 17.772 sec, and the two men in the spotlight, Rosberg and Watson, were left facing the prospects of starting the race from sixth and ninth places respectively, separated by the much-improved Ferraris of Andretti and Tambay. This was in spite of the American losing a turbo late in the session and his team-mate covering a bare minimum of laps due to a recurrence of the pain, particularly in his right arm, that had been troubling him since shortly after the Austrian weekend. Behind Watson, Warwick had recovered well enough from his dramas of the previous afternoon to qualify the new Toleman TG183 in tenth spot, Laffite was in eleventh place and then, completing the top half of the grid, came Piquet and Lauda, both of whom had had problems. In Piquet's case it was turbo-charger trouble to add to the already poor handling of his car, while Lauda had been forced to bow out early when he felt the engine start to tighten in his McLaren. A few of the others had also run into trouble. Henton had bent a rocker arm on his Tyrrell, which had curtailed his practice as the team's spare car was being kept to one side should Alboreto have need of it, and similarly Boesel and Salazar had both

time of it, fluctuating boost pressure being his major bone of contention. Even so, the Frenchman still managed to put in one quite reasonable lap of 1 min 18.922 sec which, although over a full second slower than his team-mate's best run of 1 min 17.868 sec, was more than sufficient to place him fourth in the standings. In the meantime, of course, some of the normally-aspirated runners were getting a look in for a change which was not altogether unexpected on a circuit with so many tight turns and no really long straights.

brought their cars into contact with the wall during the afternoon. Furthermore, whilst Henton had already gone fast enough to be sure of getting into the race, and Boesel had been able to borrow his team-mate's car to scrape on to the back of the grid, Salazar was not so fortunate and was left a non-qualifier along with Fabi, Serra and, until subsequently being reprieved by Jarier's withdrawal, Byrne.

Only 24 cars left the pits and took their places on the assembly grid prior to the start of the race on Saturday afternoon. During the morning warm-up session three laps had been enough for Tambay, still in considerable pain, to realize that it would be foolish even to attempt starting what was generally considered to be the most arduous race of the season. Then Guerrero had pulled up with the Ensign team's only engine on the point of seizing due to a poorly fitted jubilee clip on a water hose allowing all of the coolant to escape. Yet another casualty of the warm-up had been Laffite, an electrical fault stranding his Talbot out on the circuit, but this had since been rectified. Now, though, it was the turn of Boesel to have a problem. When the time came round for the pace lap his engine refused to start. As a result, the Brazilian had to sit there while the other 23 starters went on their way, and although the March was eventually coaxed into life it was little more than half way round the circuit when the starting lights came on. At the green Prost made the most of his pole position to take off into an immediate lead closely followed by teammate Arnoux, but it was Cheever who attracted most of the attention by making a determined bid to beat Alboreto's Tyrrell into the first tight left-hander. On went the brakes, the Tyrrell on the inside and the Talbot on the outside, and with neither driver obviously prepared to yield an inch there was the almost inevitable clash of wheels. Nevertheless, they both kept it under control and emerged from the corner, Alboreto first, apparently none the worse, although the Talbot's left front wheel had been knocked slightly out of true, causing a steering vibration, and the Tyrrell now had the tell-tale signs of their coming-together – a black tyre mark on its right-hand side-pod, blue paint on its right rear tyre and a slight cut on its right front tyre! Directly behind them, Rosberg had deliberately run wide to avoid the possibility of any involvement, but despite the momentary confusion everyone subsequently kept out of one another's way and went on to complete the first full lap of the tightly-coiled circuit intact. Across the line it was still the two Renaults of Prost and Arnoux being pursued by Alboreto, but Cheever was now down in fifth place behind Patrese. Sixth was Andretti, and then it was Rosberg, Piquet, Warwick, Daly, Watson, Laffite, de Cesaris and Lauda before Surer

and the others right back to the delayed Boesel.

By the end of the second lap the two Renaults were already moving clear of Alboreto and leaving the rest of the field even further behind, only it was now Arnoux who was dictating the pace. Patrese, Cheever, Andretti, Rosberg and Piquet were all still running nose to tail but Warwick was really struggling to hold on to ninth place and visibly dropping away, the new Toleman proving to be quite a handful on full tanks, as well as suffering from poor throttle response and indifferent brakes. This, in turn, was causing a queue to build up behind him and, on the third lap, led to Daly's Williams losing its right-hand nose fin. The Irishman, becoming increasingly agitated, had made an abortive attempt to dive through on the inside approaching one of the many corners and clipped the Toleman's left rear wheel! Meanwhile, Watson's already faint hopes of carrying off the Championship were looking even slimmer, for apart from having slipped to 12th place behind Laffite he now had de Cesaris crawling all over him. The situation here, though, was soon to change. First the Matra engine in Laffite's Talbot started misfiring so badly that the Frenchman made straight for the pits to have the problem investigated – he was later to complete one more lap before the engine cut out completely just as it had done in the morning warm-up. Then Watson began to speed up, and after making comparatively light work of slicing past Daly and Warwick on successive laps was soon homing in on Piquet. Before long de Cesaris was also past Daly but there then seemed to be nothing at all that the Italian could do about Warwick with the result that the queue of cars behind the Toleman became even longer. Furthermore, this indirectly led to another collision shortly afterwards when, on lap 9, Baldi inadvertently ran into the back of Mansell's Lotus as they arrived at the braking area for one of the left-handers and punted the black and gold car off the track into retirement with deranged rear suspension. On the following lap, however, the queue finally subsided somewhat. Warwick slid wide on one of the faster turns, got on to the loose stuff and by the time that he had sorted himself out de Cesaris, Daly, Lauda and Surer had all been able to take advantage of his predicament to charge past. Tenth place had become 14th!

After ten laps the gap that had steadily been growing between Alboreto and the two Renaults started levelling out and before long even began to come down again, giving rise to speculation that Arnoux had run into a problem. Sure enough, his engine was no longer pulling properly and, after losing the lead to Prost on lap 15, Arnoux rapidly slipped back into the clutches of Alboreto until dropping behind him as well. This happened on lap 20 when Arnoux was seen

heading for the pits where he was destined to retire with the Renault refusing to run on six cylinders, thus ending his four-year old career with the French team on a rather unhappy note. By then Patrese had also disappeared from fourth place, his Brabham having stopped out on the circuit two laps earlier with clutch trouble similar to that at Monza, and Warwick had been delayed by a pit stop for a broken spark plug to be replaced. Watson, though, was pressing on as hard as ever and bringing the Championship battle to life with a stirring drive which had carried him past Piquet on lap 12 and then Rosberg, Andretti and Cheever on successive laps. In fact, the Ulsterman was now up into third place no less and already settling down to the task of trying to wipe out a near-half minute deficit to the two leading cars. His team-mate, on the other hand, was making nowhere near the same impression and, instead, was languishing in tenth place seemingly unable to find a way past de Cesaris even though Daly had succeeded in repassing the Alfa Romeo a few laps earlier. The outgoing World Champion, Piquet, was another having a rather uninspiring race, merely driving around in what had now become seventh place, so it was just as well that the Brabham team had dispensed with the idea of including planned pit stops for this particular race owing to the comparatively long and slow entrance to the pits. Even so, at the end of lap 26 Piquet had little choice other than to veer off into the pit lane, for the BMW engine in his Brabham suddenly developed a chronic misfire. Moreover, he was to retire as the problem was traced to a broken spark plug, parts of which had found their way into the cylinder. Barely half a lap later there was also no Andretti, much to the consternation of the Ferrari pit. A rear suspension link had broken and sent the American sliding off the track – directly in front of Rosberg! Now this was really significant, not so much from the point of view of the outcome of the Constructors' Championship as this seemed to be a foregone conclusion, but more from the point of view of the Drivers' title, for Rosberg was now able to take over that all-important fifth place. Meanwhile, only a few more minutes passed before an unhappy weekend for the Lotus team was brought to a conclusion by de Angelis blowing up his engine in a big way, and this was quickly followed by Warwick taking the new Toleman into the pits for the third and final time, its Hart engine still showing a healthy appetite for spark plugs.

The next retirement came with Byrne ending only his second Grand Prix by spinning off on lap 40. Of far greater significance at this stage, however, was the situation amongst the leaders, as after gradually dropping away from Prost, Alboreto was now showing signs of catching him again and Watson was reeling them both in. Further

1982

Michele Alboreto, who put the Tyrrell team back into the winner's circle for the first time since 1978 by driving to a well-judged first-ever Grand Prix victory. (*L.A.T. Photographic*)

Alboreto had not only been taking great chunks out of Prost's advantage but had just moved to the front of a Grand Prix for the very first time. Once again Prost, looking a certain winner, had struck trouble and been forced to ease up due to his Michelin tyres picking up rubber and causing a severe vibration, particularly under braking. Within another four laps Watson was also in front of the Renault but his Michelin tyres were now also going out of balance due to picking up rubber and although he was able to outpace the Renault he could make no further impression on the Tyrrell. Consequently all hopes of an exciting climax gradually disappeared and the race more or less fizzled out with Alboreto romping home to a comfortable and thoroughly well-deserved victory, his first ever and the first for Ken Tyrrell since the late Patrick Depailler won at Monaco in 1978. Behind a philosophical Watson, Cheever ended his year-long association with the Talbot Ligier team in a splendid third place after overhauling Prost's ailing Renault just over nine laps from home. Then, less than 3 seconds away from the yellow, black and white car at the finish, and the only other driver to complete the full 75 laps, came an openly ecstatic Rosberg to claim fifth place and the World Championship irrespective of what the courts were to decide – a string of consistent drives highlighted by just one outright victory had been enough.

back, Cheever was still looking good in fourth place, Rosberg seemed to have settled for a finish rather than attempting any heroics and Lauda had finally worked his way up into a distant sixth place following an epic struggle with de Cesaris and also overcoming brief resistance from Daly. This was in spite of the Williams driver having to contend with ever-worsening understeer caused, largely, by the loss of the nose fin early in the race. Unfortunately for Lauda, though, the lengthy spell behind the Alfa Romeo had led

to the McLaren's water temperature rising to a worrying level and although he had dropped back a bit to allow things to cool off prior to launching an all-out attack on the Italian going into the first left-hander on lap 34 – amidst a certain amount of wheel-banging! – this had taken the edge off his engine. Worse, the oil pressure warning light was now starting to flicker and eventually, after 53 laps, Lauda was forced to call it a day with the engine showing signs of seizing. However, this went largely unnoticed as by then

---

Results		
1	M. Alboreto (Tyrrell-Ford)	1 hr 41 min 56.888 sec (161.111 kph/ 100.109 mph)
2	J. Watson (McLaren-Ford)	1 hr 42 min 24.180 sec
3	E. Cheever (Talbot-Matra)	1 hr 42 min 53.338 sec
4	A. Prost (Renault)	1 hr 43 min 05.536 sec
5	K. Rosberg (Williams-Ford)	1 hr 43 min 08.263 sec
6	D. Daly (Williams-Ford)	1 lap behind
7	M. Surer (Arrows-Ford)	1 lap behind
8	B. Henton (Tyrrell-Ford)	1 lap behind
9	A. de Cesaris (Alfa Romeo)	2 laps behind
10	B. Giacomelli (Alfa Romeo)	2 laps behind
11	M. Baldi (Arrows-Ford)	2 laps behind
12	R. Keegan (March-Ford)	2 laps behind
13	R. Boesel (March-Ford)	6 laps behind

Also running at finish: M. Winkelhock (ATS-Ford) 13 laps behind.

Fastest lap: M. Alboreto (Tyrrell-Ford) on lap 59 in 1 min 19.639 sec (164.993 kph/ 102.522 mph)

Retirements

J. Laffite (Talbot-Matra) electrics on lap 6, N. Mansell (Lotus-Ford) rear suspension on lap 9, R. Patrese (Brabham-BMW) clutch on lap 18, R. Arnoux (Renault) engine on lap 21, N. Piquet (Brabham-BMW) engine on lap 27, M. Andretti (Ferrari) rear suspension on lap 27, E. de Angelis (Lotus-Ford) engine on lap 29, D. Warwick (Toleman-Hart) engine on lap 33, T. Byrne (Theodore-Ford) spun off on lap 40, N. Lauda (McLaren-Ford) engine on lap 54.

The 1982 World Champion, Keke Rosberg, in his Williams – a string of consistent drives highlighted by just one outright victory had been enough. (*Phipps Photographic*)

The Constructors' title, however, went to Ferrari after a season marred by the dreadful accidents befalling Gilles Villeneuve and Didier Pironi, the latter pictured during practice for the British Grand Prix at Brands Hatch. (*Dave Webb*)

1982 Points Tables

Driver	Nationality	Car	S. African (Kyalami) Jan 23	Brazilian (Rio de Janeiro) Mar 21	USA (West) (Long Beach) Apr 4	San Marino (Imola) Apr 25	Belgian (Zolder) May 9	Monaco (Monte Carlo) May 23	USA (Detroit) Jun 6	Canadian (Montreal) Jun 13	Dutch (Zandvoort) Jul 3	British (Brands Hatch) Jul 18	French (Paul Ricard) Jul 25	German (Hockenheim) Aug 8	Austrian (Österreichring) Aug 15	Swiss (Dijon-Prenois) Aug 29	Italian (Monza) Sep 12	USA (Las Vegas) Sep 25	Total points
K. Rosberg	SF	Williams-Ford	2	–	6	–	6	–	3	–	4	–	2	4	6	9	–	2	44
D. Pironi	F	Ferrari	–	1	–	9	–	6	4	–	9	6	4	–	–	–	–	–	39
J. Watson	GB	McLaren-Ford	1	6	1	–	9	–	9	4	–	–	–	–	–	–	3	6	39
A. Prost	F	Renault	9	9	–	–	–	–	–	–	1	6	–	–	6	–	–	3	34
N. Lauda	A	McLaren-Ford	3	–	9	–	–	–	–	–	3	9	–	–	2	4	–	–	30
R. Arnoux	F	Renault	4	–	–	–	–	–	–	–	–	9	6	–	–	–	9	–	28
P. Tambay	F	Arrows-Ford / Ferrari	–	–	–	–	–	–	–	–	–	4	3	9	3	–	6	–	25
M. Alboreto	I	Tyrrell-Ford	–	3	3	4	–	–	–	–	–	1	3	–	–	–	2	9	25
E. de Angelis	I	Lotus-Ford	–	–	2	–	3	2	–	3	–	3	–	–	9	1	–	–	23
R. Patrese	I	Brabham-Ford / Brabham-BMW	–	–	4	–	–	9	–	6	–	–	–	–	2	–	–	–	21
N. Piquet	BR	Brabham-Ford / Brabham-BMW	–	–	–	–	2	–	–	9	6	–	–	–	–	–	3	–	20
E. Cheever	USA	Talbot-Matra	–	–	–	–	4	–	6	–	–	–	–	–	–	–	1	4	15
D. Daly	IRL	Theodore-Ford / Williams-Ford	–	–	–	–	–	1	2	–	2	2	–	–	–	–	–	1	8
N. Mansell	GB	Lotus-Ford	–	4	–	–	–	3	–	–	–	–	–	–	–	–	–	–	7
C. Reutemann	RA	Williams-Ford	6	–	–	–	–	–	–	–	–	–	–	–	–	–	–	–	6
G. Villeneuve	CDN	Ferrari	–	–	–	6	–	–	–	–	–	–	–	–	–	–	–	–	6
A. de Cesaris	I	Alfa Romeo	–	–	–	–	–	4	–	1	–	–	–	–	–	–	–	–	5
J. Laffite	F	Talbot-Matra	–	–	–	–	–	–	1	–	–	–	–	–	4	–	–	–	5
M. Andretti	USA	Williams-Ford / Ferrari	–	–	–	–	–	–	–	–	–	–	–	–	–	–	4	–	4
J.P. Jarier	F	Osella-Ford	–	–	–	3	–	–	–	–	–	–	–	–	–	–	–	–	3
M. Surer	CH	Arrows-Ford	–	–	–	–	–	–	–	2	–	–	–	1	–	–	–	–	3
M. Winkelhock	D	ATS-Ford	–	2	–	–	–	–	–	–	–	–	–	–	–	–	–	–	2
E. Salazar	RCH	ATS-Ford	–	–	–	2	–	–	–	–	–	–	–	–	–	–	–	–	2
B. Giacomelli	I	Alfa Romeo	–	–	–	–	–	–	–	–	–	–	–	–	–	2	–	–	2
M. Baldi	I	Arrows-Ford	–	–	–	–	–	–	–	–	–	–	–	1	–	1	–	–	2
F. Serra	BR	Fittipaldi-Ford	–	–	–	–	1	–	–	–	–	–	–	–	–	–	–	–	1

Constructors

	Jan 23	Mar 21	Apr 4	Apr 25	May 9	May 23	Jun 6	Jun 13	Jul 3	Jul 18	Jul 25	Aug 8	Aug 15	Aug 29	Sep 12	Sep 25	Total
Ferrari	–	1	–	15	–	6	4	–	9	10	7	9	3	–	10	–	74
McLaren-Ford	4	6	10	–	9	–	9	4	3	9	–	–	2	4	3	6	69
Renault	13	9	–	–	–	–	–	–	1	15	6	–	6	–	9	3	62
Williams-Ford	8	–	6	–	6	1	5	–	6	2	2	4	6	9	–	3	58
Lotus-Ford	–	4	2	–	3	5	–	3	–	3	–	–	9	1	–	–	30
Tyrrell-Ford	–	3	3	4	–	–	–	–	–	1	3	–	–	–	2	9	25
Brabham-BMW	–	–	–	–	2	–	–	9	6	–	–	–	2	–	3	–	22
Talbot (Ligier)-Matra	–	–	–	–	4	–	7	–	–	–	–	–	4	–	1	4	20
Brabham-Ford	–	–	4	–	–	9	–	6	–	–	–	–	–	–	–	–	19
Alfa Romeo	–	–	–	–	–	4	–	1	–	–	–	–	–	2	–	–	7
Arrows-Ford	–	–	–	–	–	–	–	2	–	–	–	2	–	1	–	–	5
ATS-Ford	–	2	–	2	–	–	–	–	–	–	–	–	–	–	–	–	4
Osella-Ford	–	–	–	3	–	–	–	–	–	–	–	–	–	–	–	–	3
Fittipaldi-Ford	–	–	–	–	1	–	–	–	–	–	–	–	–	–	–	–	1

Cancellation: Argentine G.P. (Mar 7)

1983 A time of change

Throughout most of the 1982 season seemingly never-ending meetings and discussions, punctuated by proposals and counter-proposals, had taken place between just about everyone involved in Grand Prix racing. These cornering speeds), of relieving the physical stress of drivers resulting from the current breed of cars with their with particular emphasis placed on means of improving safety (allied to growing concern over vastly-increased cornering speeds), of reliving the physical stress of drivers resulting from the current breed of cars with their rock-hard suspensions and of maintaining a sporting balance between the turbo-charged and the normally-aspirated cars. However, whilst it had been generally accepted that something needed to be done, especially after the tragic death of Gilles Villeneuve at Zolder and other subsequent worrying incidents such as spectators being injured by a wayward car at Paul Ricard, the FOCA-aligned teams and the 'Grandee' constructors (Ferrari, Renault, Alfa Romeo, Osella, Toleman and ATS) had remained in total disaccord with one another over various proposals put forward both by FISA's Jean-Marie Balestre and the two opposing sides. As a result, deadlines for instigating changes had come and gone, and at the end of the season nothing of any substance had been achieved whatsoever, one of the main stumbling blocks having been the 'unanimous agreement' clause for any major rule changes contained in the Concorde Agreement. Early in October, though, the situation had changed dramatically. First a meeting had taken place between Enzo Ferrari and Bernie Ecclestone which had led to a new list of proposals being drawn up advocating minor changes to wing dimensions and a reduced minimum weight limit for 1983, as well as rather more substantial measures for 1984, including a ban on skirts and under-car aerodynamics. Then, during the following week Jean-Marie Balestre, who had been given a copy of the proposals, even though not all of the FOCA-aligned teams were in agreement with them, had presented most of the proposals at a meeting of the FISA Executive Committee with a view to having them implemented – immediately! – 'due to a case of *force majeure* and for the safety of the drivers and the spectators'. By then the Executive Committee had only just received two official reports. One was from the Medical Commission stating, amongst other things, that a high proportion of

the drivers had back and neck problems caused by driving the solidly suspended cars: the other was from the Circuit and Safety Commission stating that modern Grand Prix cars had outgrown many of the present circuits and that unless cornering speeds were considerably reduced some circuits may have to be denied their licences. At the same time Niki Lauda and John Webb, on behalf of the drivers and the circuit owners respectively, had presented the unanimous views that the cars had to be slowed down. Consequently, it was not surprising that after taking everything into consideration, the Executive Committee had subsequently voted to approve the proposals made by Balestre. After that only another day had passed before the FISA President had sought and obtained the permission of the FIA to go ahead with the changes accordingly, which had resulted in the issue of the following Press Release:

The FISA Plenary conference and the FISA Executive Committee met in Paris on October 11, 12 and 13 within the framework of the FIA October Congress. During these meetings, the following decisions were taken:

FORMULA 1
Due to a case of *force majeure* and for the safety of the drivers and the spectators, the following modifications to the Formula 1 World Championship Technical Regulations shall come into force on January 1, 1983 or as from the first European Grand Prix, if the constructors request this from the FISA.
1. Introduction of a full flat bottom on the car between the rear tangent of the front wheels and the front tangent of the rear wheels.
2. Banning of skirts and any systems used to fill the gap between the bodywork and the ground.
3. Height of the rear wing increased by 10 cms to increase the rear visibility of the driver.
4. Reduction of the width of the rear wing from 110 cms to 100 cms and of the overhang from 80 cms to 60 cms to reduce the aerodynamic downforce.
5. Increase in the frontal protection of the drivers' feet from 30 cms to 50 cms (survival cell).
6. Improvement of the tank protection and the side panels of the car.

7. Improvement of the rear red lights (power increased from 15 to 25 watts).

8. New system of checking the weight of the cars during practice, at the entrance to the pits and after the race.

9. New definition of the weight of the car (the minimum weight is the weight of the car with the petrol on board, in order to simplify checks).

10. Minimum weight: 540 kgs.

11. Banning of four-wheel drive cars.

12. Banning of cars with more than four wheels.

13. Obligation for the competitor to prove eligibility of his car(s) to the scrutineers.

1984

1. Reduction of the fuel tank capacity from 250 to 220 litres.

2. No refuelling during the race.

FISA, Paris, October 14.

Not surprisingly, the initial reaction from the teams at the announcement of such sweeping changes, combined with the very short notice given, was one of shock and, in some instances, outright disapproval of what was considered to be a flagrant breach of the Concorde Agreement. Nevertheless, after lengthy discussions everyone (some reluctantly!) agreed to accept the changes and, furthermore, decided that they would modify existing cars, or design and build new ones, for the first race of 1983 rather than wait until the start of the European season – subject to two conditions. The first was that the opening event in South Africa scheduled for February 12 should be postponed until the end of the season to allow them an extra month in which to prepare and test their cars: the second was that there should be a two-year extension of the Concorde Agreement. Both were subsequently agreed, the first following consultations with the organizers of the South African Grand Prix, although Balestre announced at a specially convened meeting of the Formula 1 Commission in Paris on November 3 that a new agreement known as the 'Formula 1 Convention' would be drawn up between the FIA, FOCA and the 'Grandees' to cover the 1985 and 1986 seasons. This would include everything contained within the Concorde Agreement, but with a few changes. Of these the most important were to be the substitution of the 'unanimous agreement' clause by a new rule stating that changes to stability rules must be agreed by 85% of the ten top teams in each of the previous two years and also the provision to permit greater possibility for intervening in matters of safety. At the same meeting the proposals listed on the October Press Release were ratified as coming into effect on January 1, 1983, accompanied by definitions of flat-bottoms and skirts, and it was also announced that the regulations regarding engines would remain stable until the end of 1985. There would, however, be a progressive reduction in the maximum permissible fuel capacity – 250 litres for 1983 (as before),

220 litres for 1984 and 195 litres for 1985 – as an initial means of limiting power.

Naturally, several of the teams had already been well advanced with their preparations for 1983 by the time that the new rules were announced, which meant that a lot of work counted for nothing. This was particularly true for Brabham as Gordon Murray and his design team had been developing a new ground-effect car (the BT51) to supersede the BT50 throughout most of the year. Rather than attempt to adapt it, however, the decision was made to start afresh on designing and building a car to exploit the new rules to the full. The outcome was the strikingly elegant BT52, a car that was almost arrow-like in appear-

The strikingly elegant Brabham BT52 – this is actually a 'B' version pictured during practice for the British Grand Prix at Silverstone, by which time the team's colour scheme had been transposed whereby dark blue had become white and vice versa. *(C.R. Foxworthy)*

ance due to the lack of side-pods (no longer necessary) and the adoption of an incredibly slim monocoque, that combined a lower section of aluminium honeycomb with an upper section of moulded carbon-fibre composite, together with a very large delta front wing. As well as that, the BT52 differed from its predecessor in just about every other respect, with particular emphasis placed on transfering as much weight as possible to the rear. This included the driving position being moved a foot further back which, in turn, provided greater driver protection as his feet were now behind the centre line of the front wheels, the mounting of the inter-cooler for the BMW turbo-charged engine and matching water radiator at an angle immediately ahead of the rear wheels (left and right-hand sides respectively) and both the exhaust system and the single KKK turbo-charger unit being repositioned much further back on the left-hand side. Although the same four-cylinder BMW engine was retained this, too, underwent considerable development work during the winter months and was now capable of producing some 640 bhp at 11,000 rpm. As before it was mounted on a steel sub-frame behind the rear bulkhead of the monocoque but now drove through a completely redesigned transmission featuring a slimmer, Brabham/Weismann/Alfa Romeo/Getra-designed, gearbox based on the Hewland FG unit. At the same time it was quite apparent that the team were going to be continuing with the refuelling stops that they had introduced in 1982, as the fuel tank capacity was only 191 litres, more than 20% less than the limit. For the suspension, Gordon Murray once again introduced a new line of thinking from his previous car by bringing into use push-rods, as distinct from pull-rods, to operate inboard-mounted coil-spring/damper units all round; and in order to facilitate quick repairs in the event of a minor accident, he had the front suspension and nose box of the car contained within one easily removable section that was bolted on to the front bulkhead. A similar idea also existed at the rear where the suspension, gearbox and radiators were again contained within one section so that the engine could be replaced with the minimum of inconvenience. After that the last major change concerned tyres as, in common with a lot of other designers, Gordon Murray was convinced that the new rules would favour radials and so, in consequence, the team switched from Goodyear to Michelin. Weighing in right on the new minimum weight limit of 540 kg, the BT52s (three examples were made ready for the first race of the new season) were finished off in the team's familiar dark blue and white colour scheme, ran with financial support from Parmalat in conjunction with the Italian Fila sportswear concern (the team's new co-sponsor) and were handled by the same drivers as in 1982, Nelson Piquet and Riccardo Patrese.

In complete contrast to Brabham, the Ferrari team (winners of the Constructors' Championship in 1982) were to start the new season using cars that were largely unchanged from the previous year. Obviously, modifications had been necessary so as to enable them to conform to the new rules, and on their first appearance at the Brazilian Grand Prix the 126C2/Bs (as these revised cars were designated) also had their water radiators and inter-coolers located further back which, in turn, had made way for shorter side-pods. Otherwise, everything was much as before, including the 120-degree, V6 engine which was now capable of producing 620 bhp at 11,500 rpm. However, problems associated with lack of traction were to quickly bring about more modifications, primarily the adoption of a massive rear aerofoil, in which the outer edges extended forwards and met side-plates at the rear of the car's side-pods, and also a revised rear suspension whereby the rocker arm arrangement was replaced by a new system employing very wide-base wishbones and pull-rods. In the meantime, designer Harvey Postle-thwaite was already hard at work on an entirely new car for 1983 that was destined to make its debut at the British Grand Prix in July. Designated the 126C3, this immediately differed from its predecessor by having a monocoque constructed of Kevlar and carbon-fibre composite

as opposed to aluminium-skinned honeycomb sheeting. Produced in two sections, upper and lower, it was bonded together, complete with magnesium bulkheads, to form a single structure with the nose cone, cockpit surround and fuel cell all integral, and was both lighter and stiffer than that of the C2. Orginally, the car had been designed to have the inter-coolers and water radiators housed in very small side-pods but overheating problems during shake-down tests had led to a re-think and, instead, these were replaced by the C2/B-type side-pods and radiator installation prior to its race debut. This, in turn, made the car that was already similar in appearance to the C2/B even more of a look-alike, for apart from the monocoque there were no other radical differences between them at all. So far as drivers were concerned 1982 had, of course, been a dreadful year for the Italian team. The extremely talented Gilles Villeneuve had lost his life in a practice accident at Zolder, and Didier Pironi had had his Grand Prix career brought to an abrupt end through sustaining appalling leg injuries in another practice accident at Hockenheim. At this point in time there was still a distinct possibility that Pironi would eventually be able to stage a comeback and, indeed, Enzo Ferrari had promised that there would be a car waiting for him as soon as he was able and ready to return to racing. Meanwhile, the Commendatore had already made a successful approach to René Arnoux towards the end of the previous season to join his team for 1983 and was more than happy to retain the services of Patrick Tambay, who had been brought in as a replacement for Villeneuve mid-way through 1982.

René Arnoux, new to Ferrari in 1983, pictured behind the wheel of the 126C3, which was built around a unitary integrated monocoque moulded in carbon-fibre composite reinforced with Kevlar. *(Phipps Photographic)*

The move by Arnoux to Ferrari had come as no surprise as, ever since the 1982 French Grand Prix when he had ignored pit signals indicating that he should concede victory to Prost, the relationship between the two Renault drivers had deteriorated rapidly. In fact, it had reached the point where Prost had left no-one in any doubt that he would not be prepared to tolerate Arnoux as his team-mate for another year and it was this that had led to the inevitable split. Consequently, the French team also had to find a new driver for 1983 and, after intense speculation that this would be Derek Warwick, the final choice was Eddie Cheever – the American moving over from Talbot-Ligier. In most other respects, though, Renault-ELF were initially to carry on more or less from where they had left off at the end of 1982 by relying on their RE30 series of cars, suitably modified so as to comply with the revised rules. Whilst appearing outwardly the same as the previous year's chassis, these revamped versions (RE30Cs) also incorporated a number of minor revisions as a result of extensive winter testing, among which was the introduction of new front and rear uprights that not only provided improved rigidity but were also more adaptable for brake cooling purposes. Throughout the winter months considerable efforts were also made to improve the reliability of the 90-degree, V6 twin turbo-charged engine (now capable of producing nearly 650 bhp and featuring water-injection) with particular emphasis placed on the electronic fuel-injection system, which had given so much trouble in the past. At the same time a lot of other work went into the completion and testing of a brand new car that, contrary to original plans, was to be brought into use for the second race of the season at Long Beach due to the RE30Cs proving uncompetitive. This, in fact, was the prototype for a new RE40 series of cars and, just like Ferrari with their 126C3, represented the first move by Renault into carbon-fibre composite chassis besides featuring a fashionable pull-rod suspension system. Otherwise, it was very similar to the RE30C in mechanical layout and even retained full length side-pods, despite its flat bottom, to house the engine ancillaries. The carbon-

Apart from Brabham, Ferrari and Renault, only the Toleman team had raced turbo-charged cars in 1982, albeit rather unsuccessfully in terms of achieving results. Even so they had still made noticeable progress compared to their first season of Grand Prix involvement in 1981 and this was a pattern that was to continue throughout 1983. Originally, the intention was to carry on using the TG183 that had made its debut at the 1982 Italian Grand Prix and just to enter the one car for Derek Warwick, Teodorico Fabi having now left the team and about to embark on a new career in North American Indy car racing. However, during the close season, all that changed. First came the announcement of the new Formula 1 technical regulations. Then, much later, the team decided to enter a second car after all, for Alfa Romeo refugee Bruno Giacomelli, which was almost certainly tied up with the fact that Candy was showing an interest in returning as sponsors once more. Whatever, the Italian domestic appliance firm did, indeed, renew its association with the team and was joined in its financial support by the Italian Sergio Tacchini sportswear concern and also by Iveco, the international truck consortium through their German subsidiary Magirus-Deutz. In the meantime, to meet the change of circumstances a completely new car was built and the original TG183 converted to the same specification. Designated the TG183B, this represented a major redesign by Rory Byrne for – apart from the front suspension, the retention of a carbon-fibre/Kevlar bar monocoque, now incorporating a lower and longer fuel tank, and the four-cylinder Hart engine – just about everything was

Like Ferrari, Renault also made the move into carbon-fibre composite chassis in 1983 and produced the RE40, depicted in the hands of Alain Prost. *(Autosport)*

The distinctive appearance of the Candy/Magirus Toleman TG183B is clearly evident from this photograph of Derek Warwick in action at Monaco. *(L.A.T. Photographic)*

fibre monocoque tub, manufactured by the French aerospace firm Hurel-Dubois, also had the same dimensions as the aluminium monocoque of the RE30 series but, of course, was both stiffer and lighter. This, in turn, played an important role in bringing the overall weight of what was both an attractive and aerodynamically efficient car down to near the 540 kg limit.

changed. Certainly the most notable features of the new car were the oil and water radiators being contained within a somewhat bulky full-width nose section, where the under-body ahead of the front axle line was shaped to provide a limited amount of additional downforce, stubby side-pods, which housed air to air rather than the previous air to water inter-coolers, and a double rear aerofoil

1983

arrangement. This consisted of two separate aerofoils running parallel with one another (the most rearward was mounted right on the limit so far as the regulations were concerned) and linked by massive side-plates that merged on either side of the rear bodywork. Consequently, it was hardly surprising that when the TG183B was first unveiled it caused a minor sensation. By taking the new regulations to their extremes – even the rear under-tray had been shaped behind the rear axle line to achieve a modest amount of down-force to supplement the double rear aerofoil – Rory Byrne had produced a car that was entirely different in appearance from any of the others.

As if to underline the shift of emphasis to more powerful engines, no less than five more of the established teams were to join the ranks of the turbo runners in 1983, although two – McLaren International and Williams Grand Prix Engineering – were not to make the changeover until near the end of the season. Of the others, ATS and Lotus came to arrangements with BMW and Renault, respectively, for the supply of turbo-charged engines, while Alfa Romeo had their own, which they had been developing and testing ever since 1980. However, the Autodelta branch of Alfa Romeo S.p.A. officially withdrew from racing at the end of 1982 for financial reasons and, instead, was leaving it largely to Gianpaulo Pavanello's Euroracing organization (new to Formula 1 but well known in Formula 3 circles) to carry on the grand old name of the sport's past. Under this arrangement Autodelta were still to remain responsible for the manufacture of the cars and engines, and most of the Alfa Romeo racing personnel were retained, including Carlo Chiti and Gerard Ducarouge. The main sponsors, too, were still Marlboro (now joined by Nordica) but one immediate casualty was Bruno Giacomelli as Euroracing were keen to have their former Formula 3 driver, Mauro Baldi, in the team and, indeed, signed him up from Arrows to drive alongside Andrea de Cesaris. Prior to this reorganization Alfa Romeo had, of course, already produced a new prototype turbo-charged car based around the same British-built carbon-fibre composite monocoque as the Tipo 182 and given the 182T, as it was called, its first public appearance during practice for the 1982 Italian Grand Prix. Since then modifications had been carried out to make it comply with the new rules, but fundamentally the overall design was otherwise unchanged. In fact, the updated version, known as the 183T, even retained full-length side-pods like the new Renault as these were required to house the inter-coolers for the twin Italian Sylo turbo-charger units and also the water radiator (on the right-hand side) and oil radiator (on the left-hand side) for the 90-degree, V8 engine of 1496 cc (74 × 43.5 mm). This, complete with its Marelli/Weber engine management system, was capable of producing 620 bhp at 11,500 rpm, which compared favourably with the 535 bhp quoted for the older normally-aspirated V12 unit, even though it was at the cost of far greater fuel consumption.

The long-awaited Alfa Romeo turbo-charged project finally came to fruition in 1983 with the arrival of the Marlboro/Nordica-sponsored Tipo 183T, although by now Gianpaulo Pavanello's Euroracing organization had stepped in to carry on the grand old name of the sport's past. *(Phipps Photographic)*

Consequently, with no immediately plans to make refuelling stops during races, a larger fuel tank with the maximum permitted capacity of 250 litres was adopted until being superseded by a smaller fuel tank immediately prior to the British Grand Prix at Silverstone. Meanwhile, despite the corresponding need for higher bodywork behind the cockpit, the overall weight of the car was still only around 10 kg above the new weight limit due to the extensive use of Nomex sandwiched in Kevlar honeycomb. Compared to its predecessor, the new car also had revised suspension geometry (the suspension, itself, was still by lower wishbones and top rocker arms activating in-board mounted coil-spring/damper units all round), as well as larger nose fins and extended bodywork around the gearbox as a means of achieving as much down-force as possible without infringing the regulations.

Unlike Alfa Romeo, under the new Euroracing banner, both ATS and John Player Team Lotus had virtually to start from scratch on chassis to accommodate their new engines. In the event ATS designer Gustav Brunner came up with a very purposeful-looking car indeed, the D6. It was based around a carbon-fibre composite monocoque, manufactured by the Swiss firm Seger & Hoffmann and similar in structure to that of the new Ferrari 126C3 inasmuch as the upper section at the front doubled as the bodywork. This, in turn, meant that the only separate

Manfred Winkelhock hard at work in the BMW-powered ATS D6. *(Phipps Photographic)*

bodywork panels required were for the tops of the side-pods and the engine cover. The engine installation followed much the same principles employed by Brabham, for the four-cylinder unit was mounted on a tubular sub-frame behind the rear bulkhead of the monocoque, but an immediate difference was the layout for the inter-coolers and radiators as, initially, these were housed in almost full-length side-pods. To cater for the extra power delivered by the BMW turbo-charged engine, as opposed to the Ford-Cosworth DFV, the team also produced their own modified version of the Hewland gearbox, which combined to form the oil tank, while other features of the new ATS included the use of carbon-fibre for the front and rear wings and undertray and the adoption of the now fashionable pull-rod suspension all round. Finished off in the familiar ATS yellow and black colour scheme, the D6 was to be driven by the German driver Manfred Winkelhock (the only entry from the team in 1983), who not only had to acclimatize himself to a turbo-charged car for the first time but also to Goodyear cross-ply tyres due to Gunther Schmidt's association with Michelin having finished at the end of the 1982 season.

The first turbo-charged Lotus, the 93T, was another purposeful-looking car when it was unveiled and, whilst having been designed by the team's extremely experienced Martin Ogilvie, had actually been styled by Colin Chapman along the sharp angular lines of the Lotus road cars. Chapman had also been responsible for conducting the negotiations with Gerard Larrousse in 1982 for the supply of Renault engines and, more recently, had con-

cluded a deal with Pirelli to use their radial tyres, convinced, like so many others, that cross-plies would be inferior under the new rules. Tragically, though, the Lotus team chief was never to see the project reach its completion as in mid-December (1982) he suffered a heart attack at his home and passed away at the comparatively early age of 54. Needless to say, this was a terrible shock, not only to his family but also to the Lotus organization and the sport as a whole. Nevertheless, in spite of the immense loss the team was to carry on under the jurisdiction of competitions director Peter Warr. The new car, meanwhile, was built around a monocoque based on that of the 87/88/91 chassis, although entirely different in the method of construction: the carbon-fibre and Kevlar materials were pre-soaked in resin and then assembled in layer form, with a Nomex paper honeycomb forming the meat in a sandwich, prior to being baked at 125 degrees Centigrade in the team's recently installed oven at Ketteringham Hall. This, in turn, resulted in an even stronger and stiffer chassis than its predecessor, besides being lighter, notwithstanding the fact that it was necessarily larger to incorporate a bigger fuel cell with the maximum permitted capacity of 250 litres. Because the deal with Renault included a contractual right for the French firm to dictate the method of engine installation (Renault were also to be responsible for engine rebuilds), this aspect was virtually identical to that of the Renault RE30C/RE40 and, similarly, involved the use of full-length side-pods to house the ancillaries. At the rear of the car fabricated steel uprights were employed and the suspension was by wide-

Elio de Angelis poses for the cameras in the cockpit of the Renault-powered Lotus Type 93T. (*Autosport*)

base lower wishbones and top rocker arms operating inboard-mounted coil-spring/damper units, but at the front the uprights were of cast magnesium and the suspension was by a pull-rod system. A lot of attention had also been paid to detail, particularly in catering for the more powerful turbo-charged engine. This included the adoption of larger brakes to compensate for the lack of engine 'braking', as well as beefed up drive-shafts that worked in conjunction with the team's own modified Hewland gearbox. In the meantime, because Renault would initially be supplying engines for only one car, which was being entrusted to Elio de Angelis, the team also produced a revised version of the Ford-Cosworth-powered Lotus 91, known as the Lotus 92. This was to serve as an 'interim' car for Nigel Mansell and was built around the same basic monocoque as the 91, but featured a computer-controlled 'active' suspension system whereby the car rode on hydraulic jacks rather than on conventional coil-spring/damper units. Designed by the team's research and development director, Peter Wright, the idea behind it was to give the car a self-levelling ride while, at the same time, maximize its cornering ability. However, the system failed to come up to expectations and this, combined with the extra weight entailed, led to the 92 appearing more often than not with conventional suspension similar to that employed on the 93T. Furthermore, the original intention of subsequently using the 'active' suspension on the turbo-charged car was dropped altogether and, in fact, the 93T itself was to be pensioned off after the German Grand Prix following a succession of rather dismal performances. Instead, at the British Grand Prix in July, the team introduced another new Renault-powered car, the 94T. Designed by Gerard Ducarouge, who had only joined Lotus some six weeks earlier after unexpectedly being given marching orders by Euroracing, this was smaller and lighter than the rather ungainly 93T and was built around the carbon-fibre/Kevlar composite monocoque of the Lotus 91/92. This, in turn, meant that the team would now be committed to refuelling stops during races owing to the smaller fuel cell. The engine installation, too, was slightly different from that of the earlier model following updated advice given by Renault, and the mounting and positioning of the radiators and inter-coolers was such that narrower, albeit full length, side-pods were in evidence. Interestingly enough, the suspension was completely the reverse of the 93T in that rocker arms were used at the front and pull rods at the rear, but the uprights, whilst all new, were still of cast magnesium and fabricated steel respectively. Numerous other differences also existed between the two cars, particularly in bodywork and weight distribution, and in appearance it was neater and tidier altogether.

As already mentioned, McLaren International and Williams Grand Prix Engineering were not to join the ranks of the turbo runners until near the end of the season. Of the two, McLaren were to be first to make the transition, which was not altogether surprising as Ron Dennis had signed an agreement with Porsche Engineering for the exclusive rights to a specially commissioned turbo-charged V6 engine towards the end of 1981 and by March (1983) this had been made ready for testing in a purposely adapted MP4 chassis, dubbed the MP4/1D. However, it was only after pressure from Niki Lauda through Marlboro that the first turbo-charged McLaren appeared at all at a Grand Prix in 1983. Both Ron Dennis and John Barnard, who were now in full control of McLaren International due to Teddy Mayer and Tyler Alexander both disposing of their interests in January (because of 'an unnecessary overlap of management abilities'), would have preferred to start from scratch with a brand new car in 1984. Lauda, on the other hand, was convinced after encouraging test results that it would be beneficial to test the engine under race conditions as quickly as possible to iron out any teething problems that might arise before it came to the new season. So, amidst a certain amount of political unease, John Barnard reluctantly designed an 'interim' car to accommodate the new engine and this, the MP4/1E, was subsequently completed just in time for it to make its debut in the Dutch Grand Prix at the end of August. There was certainly nothing startling new about the actual chassis as it was built up around the same moulded carbon-fibre/honeycomb composite monocoque as one of the team's early 1983 Ford-Cosworth-powered cars (the MP4/1C) which, itself, was merely a revamped version of the MP4B. The main difference between the MP4/1C and the MP4B, apart from the modifications required by the new rules and the adoption of a new pull-rod front suspension system, was reprofiled side-pods that tapered inwards at the rear so as to create down-force on part of the top surface of the flat undertray in the vicinity of the rear suspension. Consequently, it was the new engine that attracted most of the attention and quite rightly so for it was a very neat and compact affair indeed. Although it had been designed and built by Porsche Engineering under the surveillance of the firm's deputy head of engine and research development, Hans Mezger, the cam covers carried the 'TAG turbo' label with the only indication that the engine was the work of Porsche being a small 'Made by Porsche' label on the air-intakes. This was because the project was being financed by Techniques d'Avant Garde (a major sponsor of the Williams team) following a successful approach made by Ron Dennis to the Saudi company's president Mansour Ojjeh shortly after he had commissioned the engine, the Porsche family treating it very much as a customer contract due to their already heavy involvement in endurance and sports car racing. Indeed, owing to the commercial nature of the arrangement a new company had been formed in 1982 known as TAG Turbo Engines (Mansour Ojjeh was the president and Ron Dennis was the vice-president) with a view to opening up other commercial ventures at some future date. Reverting to the actual engine, which carried the destination TTE-PO1, it had six cylinders in 'V' formation – the first time for a Porsche-built engine – with an aluminium/magnesium alloy cast crankcase at an 80-degree angle, unusual but due to the engine being designed during the ground-effect era when slimness was all important. With a bore of 82 mm and a stroke of 47.3 mm to give it a capacity of 1499 cc, the engine was actuated by four gear-driven camshafts with the gear train also driving twin oil and water pumps at the front, had four valves per cylinder and, with specially-designed twin KKK turbo-charger units, was capable of producing a minimum of 600 bhp at 11,700 rpm. Weighing in at a modest 150 kilogrammes, this all-new V6 unit was atta-ched to the rear bulkhead of the monocoque by a four-point fixing and was used as a fully stressed member. The KKK turbo-charger units were mounted on either side of it and twin oil coolers, water radiators and water/air inter-coolers were housed one behind the other in each of the car's two side-pods, with the vents at the front being split into three sections so that the air was channelled to the three cooling aids separately. The car was also fitted with a purpose-built and brand new Bosch Motronic engine management system that incorporated two inter-linked microprocessors (one for each bank of cylinders) to monitor every aspect of engine/turbo-charger perform-ance, including fuel mixture, ignition and turbo boost pressure, and also to make any necessary compensatory adjustments between the two banks of cylinders. Like the Ford-Cosworth cars, this first turbo-charged McLaren was finished off in the red and white colours of Marlboro and also carried 'Unipart' and 'SAIMA' lettering, the Italian freight forwarding company, which had sponsored Osella during 1982, having changed allegiances at the end of the season. As in 1982 the team's drivers were Niki Lauda who, incidentally, had been obliged to undergo minor plastic surgery during the winter to rectify problems with an over-active tear duct, and John Watson for whom a second MP4/1E was completed immediately prior to the Italian Grand Prix.

Whereas McLaren had the Porsche-designed, TAG-financed engine to power their first turbo-charged car, the Williams team came to an arrangement with Honda, but were to wait until the rearranged South African Grand Prix before making the transition. Prior to that the Didcot-based team continued to rely on Ford-Cosworth V8 engines (developed by John Judd's Swindon-based firm) installed in cars based around the successful FWO8 chassis introduced at the 1982 Belgian Grand Prix. Now updated to 'C' specification, these were outwardly similar apart from the side-pods, which were much shorter due to the water and oil radiators being mounted further back, the adoption of larger wings (initially) and the appearance of additional sponsors' names (Denim and ICI) on the bodywork. Naturally, modifications had been necessary to satisfy the new rules, and among a few other changes apparent were the rear aerofoil now being horizontally mounted and also new suspension incorporating pull-rods at the front and upper rocker arms at the rear. In addition, the team had originally hoped to have eventually raced their six-wheeled car that had now been undergoing a programme of development and testing for well over a year. However, despite having grafted the rear end on to a

The Honda-powered Williams FW09. *(Autosport)*

FWO8 monocoque during the latter part of 1982 and re-christened the car the FWO8B, the team were caught out by the change of rules banning cars with more than four wheels, so consequently had to abandon the project. The tie-up with Honda, meanwhile, was not officially announced until the weekend of the Austrian Grand Prix, even though Frank Williams had begun talks with the Japanese firm over a year earlier. Nevertheless, it seemed fairly obvious that a firm deal had been concluded well before the announcement, as within only a couple of weeks of it the team were testing a brand new car designed by Patrick Head with assistance from aerodynamicist Frank Dernie. This was the FWO9, but whilst being new in conception it was still based around an aluminium honeycomb monocoque, the only hint of the increasingly popular carbon-fibre composite being found around the central fuel cell. The suspension, too, was similar to that employed on the FWO8C but the new car, which also had

The TAG-Porsche-powered McLaren MP4/1E being driven by Niki Lauda on its race debut in the Dutch Grand Prix. *(Phipps Photographic)*

1983

a fractionally longer wheelbase along with numerous other detail changes, was easily distinguishable from its predecessor by having a faired-in roll-over hoop and longer side-pods so as to house not only the water and oil radiators but also the inter-coolers for the Honda turbocharged engine. The actual engine supplied by Honda, the RA163-E, was a 1500 cc version of a 2-litre, V6 unit that they had introduced to Formula 2 racing some three years earlier and this, for much the same reasons as the TAG-Porsche engine, had the crankcase (of cast iron) at an 80-degree angle. It was fitted with twin KKK turbocharger units and, with Honda's own developed electronic fuel-injection system, was capable of producing somewhere in the region of 600 bhp, no official figures being quoted or, indeed, little else in the way of specification. To drive his 1983 cars, Frank Williams retained the services of Keijo (Keke) Rosberg, the new World Champion, but dropped Irishman Derek Daly in favour of the former Talbot-Ligier driver Jacques Laffite who had, of course, driven for him once before in 1974 and 1975.

Ordinarily, the race debut of the new Williams FWO9 would have marked the return of Honda to Grand Prix racing for the first time since 1968 but in actual fact the new Japanese turbo-charged engine had already made its first Grand Prix appearance earlier in the year at Silverstone, installed in the back of a car that introduced a completely new name to the sport – Spirit. Even the name, itself, was relatively new as it had first appeared only at the beginning of 1982 following the formation of a team by former March Formula 2 team manager John Wickham and the ex-McLaren designer Gordon Coppuck to run Formula 2 cars, using the Honda 2-litre V6 engines and with Stefan Johansson and Thierry Boutsen as the

drivers. Since then, and because Spirit Racing had enjoyed a considerable amount of success at its first attempt, Honda had awarded the team a one-year contract to test and develop their new 1.5-litre V6 turbocharged engine and it was this that eventually led to the Goodyear-shod Spirit-Honda making its Grand Prix debut. To accommodate what was a very heavy Formula 1 engine and all of its ancillaries, Gordon Coppuck (with assistance from John Baldwin) initially built up a chassis around the aluminium honeycomb monocoque from one of the team's Formula 2 cars and brought it up to Formula 1 specification by using revised bodywork, beefed up suspension components and so on. Certainly by Formula 1 standards the result was a very small and compact car indeed and one that bore a striking resemblance to the Toleman TG183B so far as the aerodynamics were concerned for it, too, had a double rear aerofoil arrangement linked by massive side-plates that blended into the rear bodywork. Originally, the intentions were to employ the car, known as the 201, merely as a test hack for the team's retained driver Stefan Johansson and, indeed, shortly after giving it an initial run in the non-Championship Race of Champions at Brands Hatch in April work commenced on the design and construction of a new car. Designated the 201C, this was still based on the team's Formula 2 chassis but, whilst being outwardly similar to the 201, incorporated a number of detail improvements such as a slimmer nose section, a new adaptor plate for the team's own cast magnesium oil tank/bellhousing and revised suspension geometry. However, because the newer car developed engine problems during the morning of the British Grand Prix the team had unexpectedly to rely on the 'test hack' for their Grand Prix debut. Later in the

The Spirit 201, which not only brought a completely new name into the sport but also marked the return of Honda to Grand Prix racing after an absence of 15 years. (*Autocar & Motor*)

season the team also produced the first pukka Formula 1 Spirit, the 101, which featured a different monocoque, revised bodywork and aerodynamics and a supposedly improved inter-cooler and exhaust installation for the Honda engine. However, this was never actually raced in 1983 due to overheating problems occurring on its only appearance during practice for the European Grand Prix at Brands Hatch.

One other team initially expected to field a turbo-charged car in 1983 were Talbot-Ligier, but for the second year running the project failed to get off the ground. On this occasion agreement was reached in principle between Guy Ligier and Gerard Larrousse for the supply of Renault turbo-charged engines following Governmental pressure emanating from the news that the French firm would be supplying engines to John Player Team Lotus in 1983: Renault were apparently less than enthusiastic about becoming involved with a second team, but the company was, of course, Government owned and French president François Mitterand, a close friend of Guy Ligier, took the view that if Renault could supply a British team there was no reason why they should not supply a French one. However, after all that, Guy Ligier ultimately decided that there was neither the time nor the money available to go ahead with such an arrangement in 1983. Instead, he abandoned the Matra V12 engine in favour of becoming a Ford-Cosworth user once more, a situation made possible because of Talbot severing all ties with the Vichy-based team at the end of 1982 for reasons almost certainly due to Matra having withheld their V6 turbo-charged engine earlier that year. Meanwhile, preparations for the new season also included the signing up of new drivers, following the departure of Jacques Laffite and Eddie Cheever to Williams and Renault respectively, and the building of a new car to accommodate the different engine as well as to take into account the rule changes. So far as the drivers were concerned Guy Ligier had already snapped up Jean-Pierre Jarier from Osella for 1983 towards the end of the previous season, and eventually opted for the former RAM driver Raul Boesel to be the Frenchman's team-mate, the Brazilian having obtained the necessary sponsorship from Cafe do Brasil and Fly Brasil. For the new car the team's designers, Michel Beaujon and Claude Galopin, started virtually from scratch and placed particular emphasis on transferring as much weight as possible to the rear along similar lines to those employed by Gordon Murray with the Brabham BT52. The result was the pencil-slim Ligier JS21 which, like the Brabham, had no side-pods due to the water radiators being mounted at an angle immediately ahead of the rear wheels and the oil coolers being located even further back on either side of the Hewland gearbox. Although it was based around a similar aluminium honeycomb monocoque to the JS19, the new Gitanes-sponsored car also had a totally enclosed rear end behind the engine, with the aim of providing extra down-force to supplement

The Gitanes Ligier JS21. *(Phipps Photographic)*

the rear aerofoil, and featured an intriguing Citroen-based hydraulic suspension system. This was controlled by a belt-driven pump and was designed to bring the car up to its correct ride height and to keep it there. Like the 'active' suspension of the Lotus 92, this did away with the need for conventional coil-spring/damper units and was, overall, to prove more effective than an optional suspension system employing upper and lower wishbones and pull-rods.

Of the remaining teams already relying on Ford-Cosworth engines (there were now only five of them as Fittipaldi Automotive had folded at the end of 1982 and Mo Nunn's little Ensign outfit had combined forces with Theodore), Arrows started the season with two new, but unsponsored, Dave Wass-designed, Goodyear-shod A6s, which were similar in appearance to the Williams FWO8 and entered for Marc Surer and, initially, the ex-Fittipaldi driver Francesco (Chico) Serra – Jack Oliver and Alan Rees had nominated former World Champion Alan Jones as their second driver but he was still recovering from a broken leg after being thrown from a horse on his farm near Melbourne during the winter. John MacDonald's Rizla/Newsweek-sponsored RAM organization began with a new and very neat Dave Kelly-designed, Pirelli-shod March RAM 01 (also similar in appearance to the Williams) with former ATS driver Eliseo Salazar (personally sponsored by the Chilean petroleum distribution company, Copec) behind the wheel. The reconstituted Theodore team ran Goodyear-shod, Ensign-based N183s for Roberto Guerrero (sponsored by Cafe de Colombia) and the former Venezuelan motorcycle rider and Formula 2 driver Johnny Cecotto (sponsored by Sanyo and the Conte of Florence clothing firm). Osella, now sponsored by a herbal cosmetics firm operated by a friend of Enzo Osella known as Kelémata and using Michelin tyres, first relied on updated versions of their 1982 cars (now in the hands of the 1982 European Formula 2 Champion Corrado Fabi and Lancia sports car driver Piercarlo Ghinzani) before coming to an arrangement with Alfa Romeo for the supply of the ageing V12 engines and producing suitably

1983

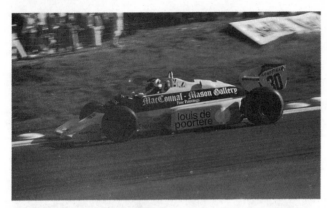

The Arrows A6. *(Phipps Photographic)*

The March RAM 01. *(Phipps Photographic)*

The Theodore N183. *(Phipps Photographic)*

adapted cars (designed by Tony Southgate) known as the FA1Es. Finally, Tyrrell continued for the major part of the season with revamped versions of the Goodyear-shod 011 that had won the last race of the ground-effect era, but now running in the light green and yellow colours of the Italian clothing group, Benetton, and with American Can-Am driver Danny Sullivan taking over from Brian Henton as team-mate to Michele Alboreto. However, the Tyrrell designer Maurice Phillippe had already begun work on a brand new car over the winter and this was finally made ready for its first appearance during practice for the Austrian Grand Prix. Designated the 012, it was built around a carbon-fibre/aluminium honeycomb monocoque in close collaboration with the carbon-fibre division of Courtaulds and included the upper section doubling as the bodywork in similar fashion to that of the new Ferrari 126C3 and ATS D6. Other than that, the 012 was little more than a logical development of its predecessor in most respects, but pull-rod suspension was now employed all round and the upper and lower wishbones at the rear were mounted on a new Tyrrell-designed gearbox casing that also incorporated the oil tank. Like the revamped version of the 011, this new Tyrrell was devoid of side-pods, although was even smaller overall and markedly different in its aerodynamics. This was particularly true at the rear of the car, for here there was a reverse-vee delta aerofoil with two very large side-plates and a secondary aerofoil mounted low down immediately behind the rear wheels, which gave it a very distinctive appearance.

The Kelémata Osella FA1E. *(L.A.T. Photographic)*

The revamped Tyrrell 011 in its new Benetton livery. *(Autosport)*

1983

XII° Grande Prêmio do Brasil

Rio de Janerio: March 13
Weather: Hot
Distance: 63 laps of 5.031 km
circuit = 316.95 km (196.94 miles)

The first race of a new Grand Prix season always generates a lot of interest and this year that applied to an even greater extent. For a start there had been an unusually long gap of over five months since the last race of 1982, but of rather greater significance was the fact that every single car was either new or heavily modified to comply with the sweeping rule changes made by FISA during the winter. In addition, there were major driver changes, new engine installations, new colours and a number of other differences, quite apart from the intriguing prospects of watching drivers adjusting to the altered characteristics of their cars brought about by the introduction of flat bottoms and the ban on skirts. In fact, it was almost like the beginning of a new era, accompanied by a very welcome and much-needed atmosphere of political calm.

A total of 28 drivers were present for the start of practice on Friday morning when the weekend's activities got under way with a 90 minute untimed session. After extensive pre-race testing at the circuit, the most recent having taken place over the previous weekend, this hardly seemed necessary but it was welcomed all the same as a number of teams were still busy trying out fresh ideas. During the test sessions one of the most surprising aspects had been the performance of the new Toleman TG183B with its four cylinder Hart turbo-charged engine, for Warwick had all but dominated proceedings with some truly magnificent efforts. Now it just remained to be seen whether the Hampshire lad could repeat this superb showing when it mattered most. Meanwhile, with everyone soon out thrashing around once more and by no means taking things easy the first, almost inevitable, problems began to show up with the Brabham and Ferrari teams seemingly suffering the most. In the case of Brabham, rather more than Ferrari, this was hardly surprising after a rush to have three brand new BMW-powered BT52s prepared for the event, and their problem was primarily associated with heat build-up from the turbo-charger units, which were mounted low down and well back on the left-hand side of the chassis. This was not only causing the cars' gearboxes to run very hot – Patrese eventually stopped with his gearbox on the point of seizing – but also upsetting their handling due to the heat affecting the left rear dampers. Ferrari's problems, too, were partly associated with excessive heat, although this was more to do with the high ambient temperature (well over 100°F/38°C) affecting the performance of extremely low-mounted radiators. The

126C/Bs were also suffering from a pronounced lack of rear-end adhesion and, just to add to the team's troubles, Tambay's car went on to shear its distributor drive as a result of jerky throttle response caused by a bout of fuel vaporization, this bringing out the spare Ferrari for a few laps. Elsewhere, too, the heat was causing a few problems and a number of other drivers were also complaining of poor traction or of difficulties in obtaining a good handling balance. Nevertheless, about the only one amongst them to have his progress seriously interrupted was the new Arrows recruit, Serra, who was sidelined with a broken valve spring in his new, unsponsored, A6 before he had had an opportunity to learn very much.

By 1 p.m., the start of qualifying, it was hotter than ever, but everything seemed to be in order with each driver's chosen two sets of tyres matched to his number and all of them preparing to begin battle for grid positions. The new Tyrrell recruit, Sullivan, was first away and before long the rest followed, some waiting behind longer than others. It was pointless looking back at Prost's year-old pole position time of 1 min 28.808 sec for comparison purposes as by now it was abundantly clear that no-one would approach it with the new breed of cars. Nevertheless, the overall pace was soon becoming pretty hectic with the turbo-charged cars looking all set to dominate the hour-long session notwithstanding the problems being experienced by Ferrari and Brabham, the latter team keeping the boost pressure turned down on their cars somewhat to ease matters. Having come out fastest during the previous weekend, a lot of attention was fixed on Warwick's progress, but Prost was soon attracting just as much, and so was Tambay thanks to plenty of boost and Goodyear's qualifying tyres affording better traction. Their respective team-mates, on the other hand, were not making anywhere near the same sort of impression – hardly surprising in Arnoux's case as before he had covered many laps a mistake led to his Ferrari spinning off and becoming stranded out on the circuit for the remainder of the afternoon. Giacomelli, meanwhile, was still trying to sort the second Toleman, which was actually the original TG183 that had first appeared at the 1982 Italian Grand Prix, and Cheever had his hopes of bringing the second Renault into the picture dashed by a loose plug lead just as he was all wound up for a really quick lap. In the meantime, the John Player Lotus team were having a terrible time of it as de Angelis was forced to abandon the Renault-powered 93T with the engine refusing to run properly

and, for similar reasons, Mansell's Ford-Cosworth-powered 92 came to rest out on the circuit. As a result the pair of them had to take turns behind the wheel of the team's spare car (an updated, flat-bottomed 91) and were way off the pace, as was Alboreto when engine problems forced the Italian into the spare Tyrrell. Others also out of luck included Jarier, who blew up the engine in his Ligier JS21 and then found the clutch inoperative in the team's spare car, Guerrero and Winkelhock, who were both forced to give up early, also because of engine problems, and de Cesaris who lost a turbo on his Euroracing Alfa Romeo 183T before promptly spinning off in his team's spare car. Amidst all of this trouble came the totally

Starting Grid

	K. Rosberg Williams-Ford (1 min 34.526 sec)
A. Prost Renault (1 min 34.672 sec)	
	P. Tambay Ferrari (1 min 34.758 sec)
N. Piquet Brabham-BMW (1 min 35.114 sec)	
	D. Warwick Toleman-Hart (1 min 35.206 sec)
R. Arnoux Ferrari (1 min 35.547 sec)	
	R. Patrese Brabham-BMW (1 min 35.958 sec)
E. Cheever Renault (1 min 36.051 sec)	
	N. Lauda McLaren-Ford (1 min 36.054 sec)
M. Baldi Alfa Romeo (1 min 36.126 sec)	
	M. Alboreto Tyrrell-Ford (1 min 36.291 sec)
J.P. Jarier Ligier-Ford (1 min 36.393 sec)	
	E. de Angelis Lotus-Ford (1 min 36.454 sec)
R. Guerrero Theodore-Ford (1 min 36.694 sec)	
	B. Giacomelli Toleman-Hart (1 min 36.747 sec)
J. Watson McLaren-Ford (1 min 36.977 sec)	
	R. Boesel Ligier-Ford (1 min 37.729 sec)
J. Laffite Williams-Ford (1 min 38.234 sec)	
	J. Cecotto Theodore-Ford (1 min 38.378 sec)
M. Surer Arrows-Ford (1 min 38.468 sec)	
	D. Sullivan Tyrrell-Ford (1 min 38.686 sec)
N. Mansell Lotus-Ford (1 min 39.154 sec)	
	F. Serra Arrows-Ford (1 min 39.965 sec)
C. Fabi Osella-Ford (1 min 40.309 sec)	
	M. Winkelhock ATS-BMW (1 min 41.153 sec)
E. Salazar March-Ford (1 min 41.478 sec)	

Did not qualify:
P. Ghinzani (Osella-Ford) 1 min 42.267 sec

Excluded:
A. de Cesaris (Alfa Romeo) No time.

unexpected news that defending World Champion Rosberg, after switching to the spare Williams FWO7C, had just whistled around in 1 min 34.526 sec to shoot to the top of the time-sheets. What was surprising about this, quite apart from the fact that he had gone quicker than any of the turbo runners, was that during pre-race testing the Williams team had not featured at all strongly in terms of lap times – deliberately holding back, so it now appeared! Furthermore, by the end of the session the time had still gone unbeaten leaving Rosberg on the provisional pole immediately ahead of five turbo runners, these being Prost (1 min 34.672 sec), Tambay (1 min 34.993 sec), Warwick (slightly disappointed to have wound up fourth fastest at 1 min 35.206 sec after an inlet pipe to the compressor unit had failed whilst out on his second set of Pirellis), Piquet (1 min 35.815 sec) and Patrese (1 min 35.958 sec). After that came Lauda as the second fastest non-turbo runner at 1 min 36.054 sec, despite having spent much of his time concentrating on achieving a good race set-up and finding the Michelin qualifying tyres little better than race rubber, followed by Baldi, Arnoux, Giacomelli, Jarier and de Cesaris who had also recorded laps in the 1 min 36 sec bracket.

Conforming to the now long-established format of practice, there was another 90 minute untimed session on Saturday morning followed by the all-important final hour of qualifying in the afternoon. If anything, it was now even hotter than the first day and the general concensus of opinion was that the track was marginally slower. Even so, once the battle for grid positions resumed it was nonetheless exciting, for pole position was by no means a foregone conclusion and everyone was obviously determined to at least try to pick up on their lap times, including Salazar and Ghinzani who had yet to qualify for the race. There were also a number of dramas, two of which could have been rather more serious than turned out to be the case. First Cheever, on a quick lap, came across Salazar's rather slower travelling RAM March and clipped its front wing with a rear wheel, which sent the Renault limping into the pits with a flat tyre. Then, later, Mansell was inadvertently chopped off by Surer going into the fast right-hander at the end of the pits straight when he, too, was on a flat-out lap and was forced to take to the grass where he spun, finished up sideways across the track and almost collected Serra's Arrows. Meanwhile, for the Candy Toleman team the afternoon was turning out to be a disaster with Warwick and Giacomelli both suffering engine failures in rapid succession before achieving even one timed flying lap between them. Warwick, in fact, had stopped out on the circuit during the morning with what was thought to have been an electrical fault, but subsequent diagnosis suggested that the

engine had begun to run on too lean a mixture and this, in turn, had led to a piston being damaged. Giacomelli's problem, on the other hand, was caused by the turbo waste-gate sticking and producing a sudden and dramatic surge in boost pressure. Shortly afterwards Winkelhock was also reduced to the role of spectator, temporarily, when a turbo let go on his ATS. Cecotto, who had survived a frightening moment during the morning when a wheel flew off his Theodore, was now having his progress hampered by a down-on-power engine, and Patrese was obliged to switch to the spare Brabham due to an oil line coming adrift on his proposed race chassis. Yet another extremely frustrated driver was de Cesaris who was spending his afternoon continually driving in and out of the pits with engine and turbo problems, both with his own and the spare Alfa Romeo. Eventually, in the dying minutes of practice, he even took over team-mate Baldi's car but still failed to squeeze in a timed flying lap and, moreover, incurred the wrath of the stewards by ignoring a signal to stop at an area specially set aside for cars to be weighed at random: this was all part and parcel of the new rules concerning the minimum weight limit whereby drivers were required to stop during timed practice, if so requested by the appearance of a red light, to have their cars weighed with the driver on board. The driver's weight, which had been officially recorded before practice for use during the first half of the season prior to each driver being weighed again, was then deducted from the gross weight and if the net figure was below 540 kg (or the driver failed to stop when requested) the rules stipulated that the car/driver would be excluded from the meeting. Obviously, de Cesaris was aware of this but, being in a highly emotional state because of his problems, and having already been selected for weighing on the previous lap, had driven straight into his pit. As a result the stewards had little alternative other than to abide by the rules, leaving the Italian faced with the prospects of being a spectator on race day.

Away from this rather unhappy episode, practice ended with the front row of the grid going unchanged, for although Rosberg and Prost had both failed to improve on their existing times no-one had beaten them, Tambay having come closest with the afternoon's fastest time of 1 min 34.758 sec. Consequently the French Ferrari driver was still in third place on the grid, but in fourth spot it was now Piquet who had moved up at the expense of Warwick after benefiting from an additional cooling duct attached to the left rear bodywork of his Brabham BT52 and getting down to 1 min 35.114 sec in the closing minutes of practice. Immediately behind Warwick, Arnoux had hauled the second Ferrari up into sixth place despite a turbo failure whilst out on his second set of

qualifiers and similarly Cheever had improved sufficiently in the second Renault to line up in eighth place where he was sandwiched between Patrese and Lauda, both of whom had been amongst others not to have found any extra speed. After that there were quite a number of surprises for whilst Alboreto had improved by some 2½ seconds over the first day and de Angelis by an even greater margin of over 3½ seconds in the Lotus-Renault to round off the top half of the grid in company with Baldi and Jarier, the likes of such notables as Watson and Laffite had failed to make any impression whatsoever. Instead, the Ulsterman had qualified in only 16th place between Giacomelli's Toleman and Boesel's ill-handling Ligier after being unable to set up his new McLaren to his liking, while the new Williams recruit had finished up two places lower even though he had been given a chance behind the wheel of the spare FWO7C in which Rosberg had wrapped up the pole. In complete contrast, Guerrero had done well to qualify the new Theodore in 14th spot and Cecotto, Sullivan and Fabi had certainly not disgraced themselves by all qualifying reasonably comfortably for their first Grand Prix in amongst the two Arrows drivers, Surer (suffering from a tummy bug) and Serra, and also Mansell in the Lotus 92. Right at the back, Winkelhock had just scraped on to the grid at the last possible moment after his troubled practice in the ATS-BMW, made all the worse by handling problems, and he was subsequently joined by Salazar, another to have suffered from poor handling, following de Cesaris's exclusion. As a result the only driver to be left behind as a non-qualifier was Ghinzani in the second of the two Osella FA1Ds which had also both been running with deficiencies in the handling department.

After the sizzling heat of the two days of practice, Sunday was slightly cooler and instead of a blazing hot sun beating down from clear blue skies it had become rather overcast. For the 26 drivers preparing for the 63-lap race this was a welcome relief, but there was still considerable concern over tyre wear as quite apart from anything else heavy overnight rain had washed much of the rubber off the track surface and left it rather abrasive. The turbo teams were particularly concerned, not least Ferrari as the 126C2/Bs had already shown a healthy appetite for tyres during testing. However, contrary to original intentions, Brabham were preparing to go ahead with the pre-planned pit stop routine that they had introduced mid-way through the previous season for both of their drivers. Williams, too, were planning to start Rosberg on half-full fuel tanks and on comparatively soft tyres, careful calculations having suggested that if all went well the Finn could build up sufficient leeway in the first part of the race to more than compen-

1983

sate for a pit stop at around half-distance to take on fresh tyres and more fuel. As a result both teams, along with one or two others for that matter, took the opportunity of practising pit stops during the customary 30 minute warm-up session that get under way at 10.30 a.m. owing to the start of the race being scheduled for 1.30 p.m. After the numerous problems that had cropped up during practice this was virtually trouble-free, apart from Boesel's Ligier breaking a rear anti-roll bar. But, just over two hours later, when the cars started leaving the pits for the warm-up lap prior to forming on the grid, there was real consternation in the Lotus camp: de Angelis' 93T began belching out ominous-looking blue smoke from one of its exhaust pipes. Furthermore, after being driven around for two warm-up laps, the car had to be wheeled away with a broken turbo-charger and de Angelis strapped into the spare Lotus in which he was obliged to take the start from the pit lane as by then this had been officially closed. In the meantime, final preparations for the remaining 25 starters proved to be somewhat more straightforward and, after the usual count-down, they were eventually signalled away for the pace lap whereupon Rosberg led them around and carefully brought them back to their grid positions once more to face the starting lights.

As the red light gave way to green the entire field got away well and none better than Rosberg whose 'light-weight' Williams just held off Prost's more powerful Renault to lead into the first right-hander. From there Rosberg then quickly began easing away and went on to completely dominate the opening lap by pulling out a clear advantage of more than 2 seconds over the French car, which ended the lap with the two BMW-powered Brabham BT52s of Piquet and Patrese hard

on its heels. Only a short distance away, Tambay was fifth with team-mate Arnoux and Cheever right up with him and then came Warwick, Baldi and the others being led by the two Marlboro McLarens of Lauda and Watson, the Ulsterman having already come through to 11th spot from his rather lowly grid position. Alboreto, on the other hand, had dropped right to the back of the field, apart from the delayed de Angelis, after having just recovered from a spin caused through being nudged from behind by Baldi's Arrows under braking for one of the left-handers. However, this was of little consequence to the huge Brazilian crowd for their attention was firmly fixed on local hero Piquet, who soon gave them plenty to cheer about by making comparatively light work of displacing Prost half way round the second lap. Furthermore, by being able to capitalize on his superior horse-power, Piquet immediately began reeling in Rosberg's Williams and took only until lap 7 before neatly slicing past on the inside of it at the end of the long back straight to become the new race leader, accompanied by an even more vivacious outburst from the obviously delighted crowd. By then Patrese was also rapidly closing in on the Williams after having followed his team leader past Prost back on the third lap, but just when he looked all set to take over second place on lap 10 the Italian suffered a sudden loss of power and began to drop away again. An exhaust pipe had broken and caused a marked reduction in boost pressure. At this stage Prost was lying a distant fourth and Tambay was still fifth but Arnoux, having to contend with quite a severe tyre vibration, had just been elbowed back to seventh place by none other than Watson who was making outstanding progress in his McLaren and overtaking cars almost as if they weren't there. Nor was he finished yet.

On the next lap he flew past Tambay's Ferrari, also in tyre trouble, took only a further three laps to overhaul Patrese's ailing Brabham and then followed that up by giving chase to Prost's Renault, which he finally caught and passed under braking going into one of the left-handers on lap 17. After that, though, Watson could hope to do little more than consolidate his excellent third place as Piquet and Rosberg, now running 9 seconds apart, were both around half a minute away and well on schedule to allow for their planned pit stops. In the meantime, Arnoux was rapidly progressing in the opposite direction with his tyre vibration now being made all the worse by a wheel balance weight having flown off. In fact, since being forced to give way to the impressive Watson he had already lost three more places to Baldi, Warwick and Lauda and was currently lying tenth just ahead of Cheever, the American being another to have faded away after a promising start due to experiencing an acute lack of grip caused by too conservative a choice of tyres. Patrese was now losing places hand over fist as well but this soon became academic as at the end of lap 18 the Brabham driver turned off into the pits with his engine sounding worse than ever and subsequently retired after trying just one more lap. At least he was not alone as Alboreto had been forced to bow out after only seven laps due to losing oil from an oil cooler damaged in the first lap incident with Baldi, and since then Giacomelli had spun harmlessly out of the race in his Toleman while Fabi's debut in the Osella had been ended by engine trouble. Guerrero was not much better off either as he was now in the midst of a lengthy pit stop having a faulty left rear brake caliper attended to on his Theodore, the delay leaving the Colombian well and truly bringing up the rear. Later, a

---

Keke Rosberg's Williams leads into the first right-hander seconds after the start. *(Autosport)*

similar problem was also to interrupt a promising debut by his team-mate, Cecotto.

With the leading positions becoming settled, much of the attention now drifted back to a really epic struggle going on for what had become sixth place between Baldi, Warwick and Lauda. Warwick, in particular, was trying just about everything he knew to find a way round the Alfa Romeo but Baldi, who had passed the Englishman back on the second lap, was blocking every move even though it frequently meant taking rather unconventional lines through some of the corners. However, the situation was shortly to change dramatically. First Lauda, growing increasingly agitated, made a successful stab at Warwick on lap 21 prior to taking just two more laps to outwit Baldi going into one of the left-handers. Then Warwick, who attempted to follow Lauda through, suddenly found Baldi closing the door on him and subsequently climbing over one of his front wheels, an incident that led to the Toleman momentarily taking to the grass before continuing in seventh place and to the Alfa Romeo spinning and coming to rest in the middle of the track with a stalled engine. Furthermore, the collision had damaged its rear suspension and although Baldi was push-started back into the race (this was later to lead to him being disqualified!) he was obliged to complete the lap by pulling off into the pits to retire. At around the same time both Ligiers also disappeared in quick succession from mid-field, Jarier stopping with a broken wheel bearing and Boesel with an electrical problem, but almost before they had been missed there was a flurry of excitement caused through Rosberg coming round to complete his 28th lap by diving into the pits for the pre-planned tyre and fuel stop. At first all seemed to be going well as the Williams mechanics fell on the car but then it turned into a near-disaster due to a small amount of fuel trickling down on to the hot exhaust pipes and causing a flash fire. Not surprisingly, Rosberg reacted immediately by unfastening his harness and hurriedly

leaping out of the cockpit only to find Patrick Head instructing him to get back into the car, the flames being extinguished very efficiently indeed by one of the Williams' pit crew. Nevertheless, by the time that the fuel had finally been replenished and Rosberg had been push-started back into the race, well over a minute had lapsed and second place had become ninth where he was exactly a lap behind Piquet.

Apart from Lauda moving up to challenge Tambay until taking over fifth place on lap 34 and Rosberg quickly following Piquet past a good scrap going on between Surer and Laffite to regain two of his lost places, the next major change came on lap 35. Up to that point Watson had still been driving superbly and even looked to have an outside chance of taking over the lead when the time came round for Piquet to make his pit stop, the gap between them having levelled out at just over half a minute. But then it was suddenly all over for him. The McLaren's engine started to tighten and the Ulsterman wisely decided to switch off before it seized completely. A bitter blow. Consequently, Prost unexpectedly found himself in second place once more, while Piquet was left leading the race by a massive 84 seconds. Morover, even after making his pit stop on lap 40 Piquet was still 55 seconds to the good due to the well-drilled Brabham mechanics changing all four wheels and topping up the fuel load in just 17 seconds, and from then on was able to drive at his own pace without coming under any pressure whatsoever. Thankfully, from the point of view of the race, the situation behind him was not nearly so clear cut, for Lauda was now rapidly gaining on Prost, starting to feel the first effects of a worrying rear-end vibration to add to an already unpredictable handling problem, and further back Rosberg was absolutely flying on his fresh tyres. In fact, the Finn was already back in a points-winning position – now lying fifth ahead of Warwick – and during the final twenty laps went on to reel in Tambay, Prost and even

Lauda to finish in an excellent second place a fraction over 20 seconds behind the victorious Piquet. In complete contrast, Prost continued falling away dramatically, and in the end only just held off Warwick, himself hampered by increasing understeer caused by the earlier wheel-banging incident with Baldi, to wind up an unhappy seventh. Tambay, nursing a badly blistered rear tyre, fell away to only a slightly lesser extent, losing fourth place to a late-charging Laffite a little over four laps from home and very nearly fifth place to Surer, who crossed the line less than a tenth of a second away at the finish. Further back, behind Prost and Warwick, Serra brought the second Arrows home in ninth place, a totally exhausted Arnoux was tenth in his vibrating Ferrari and Sullivan, the last driver not to have been delayed for one reason or another, completed his first Grand Prix by finishing in 11th place ahead of the other six cars still there at the finish, the only other retirement having been Cheever's Renault which had gone out with a broken turbo-charger after 41 laps.

Unfortunately, after the race the situation became rather reminiscent of 1982 when the stewards announced that Rosberg (for the second year running!) and de Angelis were both being disqualified. In Rosberg's case it was because of the push-start, while the decision to penalize de Angelis was based on the fact that he had switched from a Renault-engined car to a Ford-Cosworth-engined car prior to the start of the race, even though he had driven both cars during practice. Naturally, with more at stake, the Williams team were particularly incensed and Frank Williams subsequently filed an appeal through the RAC to go before the FIA International Court of Appeal. At a specially convened hearing in May, however, the FIA Court rejected the appeal but in doing so also stated that second place would remain 'vacant' which meant, unusually, that the drivers who had finished behind Rosberg would not automatically be moved up a place.

Results

1	N. Piquet (Brabham-BMW)	1 hr 48 min 27.731 sec (173.334 kph/ 108.947 mph)
*	K. Rosberg (Williams-Ford)	1 hr 48 min 48.362 sec
3	N. Lauda (McLaren-Ford)	1 hr 49 min 19.614 sec
4	J. Laffite (Williams-Ford)	1 hr 49 min 41.682 sec
5	P. Tambay (Ferrari)	1 hr 49 min 45.848 sec
6	M. Surer (Arrows-Ford)	1 hr 49 min 45.938 sec
7	A. Prost (Renault)	1 lap behind
8	D. Warwick (Toleman-Hart)	1 lap behind
9	F. Serra (Arrows-Ford)	1 lap behind
10	R. Arnoux (Ferrari)	1 lap behind
11	D. Sullivan (Tyrrell-Ford)	1 lap behind
12	N. Mansell (Lotus-Ford)	2 laps behind
*	E. de Angelis (Lotus-Ford)	3 laps behind
13	J. Cecotto (Theodore-Ford)	3 laps behind
14	E. Salazar (March-Ford)	4 laps behind
15	M. Winkelhock (ATS-BMW)	4 laps behind

Also running at finish: R. Guerrero (Theodore-Ford) 10 laps behind

* Disqualified

Fastest lap: N. Piquet (Brabham-BMW) on lap 4 in 1 min 39.829 sec (181.426 kph/112.733 mph)

Retirements

M. Alboreto (Tyrrell-Ford) oil cooler on lap 8, B. Giacomelli (Toleman-Hart) spun off on lap 17, C. Fabi (Osella-Ford) engine on lap 18, R. Patrese (Brabham-BMW) broken exhaust on lap 20, J.P. Jarier (Ligier-Ford) wheel bearing on lap 23, M. Baldi (Alfa Romeo) rear suspension/disqualified on lap 24, R. Boesel (Ligier-Ford) electrics on lap 26, J. Watson (McLaren-Ford) engine on lap 35, E. Cheever (Renault) turbo-charger on lap 42.

1983

VIIIth United States Grand Prix (West)

Long Beach: March 27
Weather: Warm and sunny
Distance: 75 laps of 3.275 km
circuit = 245.62 km (152.62 miles)

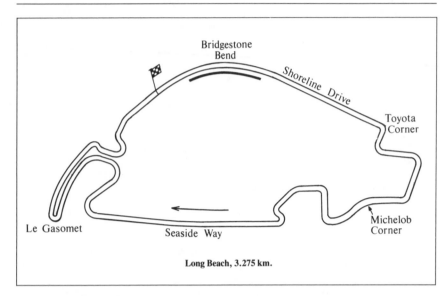

Bridgestone
Bend

Shoreline Drive

Toyota
Corner

Michelob
Corner

Le Gasomet

Seaside Way

Long Beach, 3.275 km.

landing heavily on the track surface amidst a shower of sparks, but very unsettling for the drivers. To make matters more difficult still the second bump was just short of the braking area for the sharp right-hander at the end of the straight and so was throwing cars off line just when it was least needed. In addition, there was considerable concern over the pounding that suspension systems were receiving, something that was justified all too quickly by Warwick returning to the pits after completing less than a handful of laps with the top right wishbone broken in the rear suspension of his Toleman. Subsequent examination also revealed the suspension on the left-hand side of the car to be on the way out as well, and when Giacomelli's sister car was found to be on the point of suffering a similar fate, after the Italian had been called

From South America it was soon time for the teams to head off to North America or, more precisely, to Downtown Long Beach for the 8th United States Grand Prix (West). This year there was a touch of sadness about the event as strong rumours persisted indicating that it would be the last for Formula 1 cars in the foreseeable future. Sure enough, on the day following the race these were to be confirmed when British entrepreneur Chris Pook announced that he and his Long Beach Grand Prix Corporation had entered into a three-year agreement, due to come into effect in 1984, for the race to become a less expensive and almost certainly more popular (locally speaking that is) round in the American CART Championship for Indy cars. Quite simply the cost of staging the Grand Prix, in particular the astronomically high amount of expenditure incurred in transporting the Formula 1 'circus' from Europe to California, made it an uneconomic proposition, a situation aggravated by declining spectator and television interest. For the time being, though, it was down to business as usual come the start of practice on Friday morning with the first priority so far as the drivers were concerned being to acclimatize themselves to the surroundings due to the lack of any pre-race testing at the circuit. Since the previous year work had been completed on a lengthy project to modify the track layout to make way for an extensive building development programme taking place, and to overcome local opposition to the closure of Ocean Boulevard, one of the town's main thoroughfares, for the duration of the meeting. Now, instead of the track winding its way up the rise to Ocean Boulevard, it turned sharply to the right rather

than to the left on reaching Pine Avenue, and from there swung sharp left into a car parking area and on through a tight ess-bend before rejoining the 'old' circuit at Linden Avenue by means of a comparatively long straight, Seaside Way. This ran parallel to Ocean Boulevard but at a lower level and was routed underneath the Long Beach convention centre through a tunnel. Naturally, with Ocean Boulevard no longer forming part of the circuit, the pits had had to be relocated and these were now situated behind the long, curving Shoreline Drive section with the inner lane of the dual-carriageway being utilized as the pit lane from the chicane that had been installed for the 1982 race to just beyond the right-hander at the far end. The changes also meant that for the first time since 1977 the start and finish areas were once more in the same place, the start/finish line now being in front of the pits.

The immediate result of the modifications, which took away little of the spectacular nature of the circuit, was to marginally reduce the overall lap distance to 3.275 kilometres but, unfortunately, they were soon to become the source of a major bone of contention. For a start the run-off area at the end of the new straight was no longer considered to be adequate due to the much faster approach speeds of the cars. Even worse was the existence in close proximity of two bumps that had apparently arisen due to slight subsidence caused by several weeks of quite appalling weather. Both of these bumps were barely discernible to the eye but were enough to make the modern-day Grand Prix cars behave like kangaroos, spectacular to watch as they became airborne before

Starting Grid

P. Tambay
Ferrari
(1 min 26.117 sec)

R. Arnoux
Ferrari
(1 min 26.935 sec)

K. Rosberg
Williams-Ford
(1 min 27.145 sec)

J. Laffite
Williams-Ford
(1 min 27.818 sec)

E. de Angelis
Lotus-Renault
(1 min 27.982 sec)

D. Warwick
Toleman-Hart
(1 min 28.130 sec)

M. Alboreto
Tyrrell-Ford
(1 min 28.425 sec)

A. Prost
Renault
(1 min 28.558 sec)

D. Sullivan
Tyrrell-Ford
(1 min 28.833 sec)

J.P. Jarier
Ligier-Ford
(1 min 28.913 sec)

R. Patrese
Brabham-BMW
(1 min 28.958 sec)

A. Jones
Arrows-Ford
(1 min 29.112 sec)

N. Mansell
Lotus-Ford
(1 min 29.167 sec)

B. Giacomelli
Toleman-Hart
(1 min 29.266 sec)

E. Cheever
Renault
(1 min 29.422 sec)

M. Surer
Arrows-Ford
(1 min 29.521 sec)

J. Cecotto
Theodore-Ford
(1 min 29.559 sec)

R. Guerrero
Theodore-Ford
(1 min 29.585 sec)

A. de Cesaris
Alfa Romeo
(1 min 29.603 sec)

N. Piquet
Brabham-BMW
(1 min 30.034 sec)

M. Baldi
Alfa Romeo
(1 min 30.070 sec)

J. Watson
McLaren-Ford
(1 min 30.100 sec)

N. Lauda
McLaren-Ford
(1 min 30.188 sec)

M. Winkelhock
ATS-BMW
(1 min 30.220 sec)

E. Salazar
March-Ford
(1 min 31.126 sec)

R. Boesel
Ligier-Ford
(1 min 31.759 sec)

Did not qualify:
C. Fabi (Osella-Ford) 1 min 31.901 sec
P. Ghinzani (Osella-Ford) 1 min 32.182 sec.

in as a precautionary measure, the team announced that they were not prepared to take any further part in the proceedings until something was done. Moreover, as the day wore on there seemed to be a distinct possibility that other teams would follow suit, for although there were no other reported suspension failures a growing band of drivers were becoming increasingly incensed over the situation, many expressing the view that under race conditions cars' suspensions could be expected to last only a few laps which, in turn, was liable to result in numerous accidents. The organizers, of course, were only too aware of what was happening and, under the guidance of FISA's safety inspector, Derek Ongaro, responded positively by making arrangements to have the track smoothed out between the two offending bumps at the end of the day's activities using quick-drying concrete. In the meantime the drivers, Warwick and Giacomelli apart, were left to persevere as best they could, and by the end of the first qualifying session there had been some particularly creditable performances, not least from new-boy Cecotto and Guerrero who had taken their Theodore N183s around in sixth and eighth fastest times of 1 min 29.559 sec and 1 min 29.585 sec respectively. Alboreto, fastest of all during the morning untimed session, had every reason to feel pleased with his efforts as well for he was still the quickest non-turbo runner at 1 min 29.066 sec and, ultimately, had been beaten only by a very on-form Arnoux (now comfortably fastest at 1 min 26.935 sec), Prost (1 min 28.558 sec), Tambay (1 min 28.598 sec) and Patrese (1 min 28.958 sec). Rosberg, too, was well placed with seventh fastest time of 1 min 29.577 sec in spite of having been forced to abandon the spare Williams FWO7C, his favoured qualifying car, with a broken electrical connection. Some of the other notables such as Piquet, Lauda and Watson, on the other hand, had made virtually no impression at all and were complaining bitterly not only of the track conditions but also that the Michelin qualifying tyres were virtually useless and even inferior to race rubber.

On Saturday morning it didn't take long at all for the drivers to discover that the efforts made to solve the bump problem had been successful. Consequently, the atmosphere became more relaxed altogether with the only person not happy now being Ken Tyrrell. For reasons that were almost certainly associated with the fact that his cars had been riding the bumps almost as if they hadn't existed, he was now arguing that the circuit should have been left untouched – on the grounds that if it was necessary to adapt a circuit to the cars then it was time to do something about the long straight at Paul Ricard so as to reduce the advantage of the turbo-charged cars over those with normally-aspirated engines! However, no-one seemed

interested in Uncle Ken's views, and certainly none of the drivers who were too busy sorting cars for the final hour of qualifying, Warwick and Giacomelli now included. As on Friday all of them were still using the same chassis seen at Rio, with just one exception – that being Prost, as following the rather disappointing performances of the RE30Cs there the Renault team had brought forward their plans and flown out the new prototype RE40 for the Frenchman. However, after the promising showing on Friday, which had enabled Prost to clock up second fastest time in spite of experiencing too much oversteer and problems with the Michelin qualifying tyres, the car now developed an erratic misfire that refused to go away even when the fuel-injection pump was changed. As a result a frustrating morning for Prost was followed by more of the same in the afternoon and, even on the odd occasion that the misfire momentarily disappeared, a really quick lap proved an impossibility. Instead, he wound up having a harmless spin due to trying a shade too hard at one point accompanied by a slower time of 1 min 29.765 sec. After being sidelined by a broken gearbox during the morning, Arnoux was unable to make quite the same sort of impression as on the first day either but unlike his compatriot in the Renault, who was elbowed back to eighth place on the grid, the Ferrari driver still managed to record a very respectable third fastest time of 1 min 27.628 sec. Moreover, his Friday time was beaten only by team-mate Tambay who, having been troubled by a misfiring engine with both his race car and the team's spare chassis on the previous day, now used just one set of Goodyear's obviously superior qualifying tyres to notch up a splendid pole-winning time of 1 min 26.117 sec and make it an all-Ferrari front row. This was in spite of the 126C2/Bs still being short of traction even with large revised rear aerofoils in which the outer edges extended forwards and met side-plates at the rear of the cars' side-pods.

Behind the Ferraris, Rosberg set the afternoon's second fastest time of 1 min 27.145 sec to move up to third place on the grid after a spirited display of opposite-lock motoring to combat understeer problems, while Laffite certainly made up for his lacklustre practice performance in Brazil by joining his team-mate on the second row with fourth fastest time of 1 min 27.818 sec. He, in turn, was closely followed by de Angelis (1 min 27.982 sec) in the Renault-powered Lotus 93T, which was now running with a longer wheelbase in an effort to improve its weight distribution but proving to be quite a handful through the numerous twists and turns, Warwick (he did particularly well to come out sixth fastest at 1 min 28.130 sec in view of his lack of practice), Alboreto and Guerrero. Later in the afternoon, however,

the Colombian was in for a nasty shock when the organizers scrubbed his second day's lap times due to the bodywork of his Theodore being too wide – by just over a centimetre! Ironically, the team had pointed this out to the scrutineers prior to the start of practice, explaining that a side-pod had become distorted by the heat in Rio, and had been given the all clear. As it was the unfortunate Guerrero now found himself being relegated from eighth place on the grid to 18th by reason of his slower Friday time and the intervening drivers all moving up a place. Among them were Prost, Sullivan, Jarier, Patrese (another of the very few not to have improved) and the man of the moment, former World Champion Alan Jones, who had declared himself fit enough to make his comeback for the Arrows team following his horse riding accident and had acquitted himself well in a cockpit that was by no means ideally suited to his now somewhat bulky frame. Mansell, Giacomelli, Cheever (now confined to the spare Renault after bending the left front corner of his race chassis against a wall during the afternoon) and Surer also moved up a place at the expense of Guerrero, as did his team-mate, Cecotto, who had had a disappointing second day compared to Friday with his chances having been spoiled somewhat by gear-linkage trouble and a wall-banging incident in the morning. Amazingly, though, both Theodores were still higher up the grid than Piquet, as well as Lauda and Watson in their McLaren MP4/1Cs and the two Euroracing Alfa Romeo drivers, de Cesaris and Baldi, all of whom had had a very frustrating couple of days on their Michelin tyres added to which de Cesaris's practice had been cut short by a turbo fire caused by a bearing failure. Indeed, things were so bad that only Winkelhock's ATS, Salazar's RAM March, Boesel's Ligier and the two Osella FA1Ds of Fabi and Ghinzani, who had both failed to qualify, had ultimately gone slower than them!

Although local forecasts suggested otherwise, the warm and sunny weather enjoyed throughout practice continued into Sunday making conditions very pleasant indeed, both for the teams as they started preparing for the race and for the spectators who were out in their numbers – in spite of the fact that the Americans were supposed to be no longer interested in Grand Prix racing! The morning warm-up session did nothing to spoil the happy scene except for Toleman and Lotus not being over-impressed with Pirelli's race rubber and Prost being rather perplexed at finding the new Renault still suffering from a slight misfire. This was in spite of the engine having been changed overnight. With conditions staying the same there was also no last-minute dithering over choice of tyres, although some of the Michelin runners were trying to make up their minds whether to use a new tyre recently developed by the French firm or to stick to an older one. Interestingly enough, opinions were evenly divided in the McLaren camp as Lauda eventually went to the grid on the new rubber and Watson on the older type which he had already used to good effect at Detroit in the previous year. Either way it seemed pretty academic in view of their desperately low starting positions.

When it came to the start Tambay did everything right as he blasted away into an immediate lead from his first-ever pole position, but Rosberg nearly messed things up completely. In a determined bid to charge between the two front row Ferraris, he put his boot hard down on the accelerator only for the rear end of his Williams to snap out of line and its left rear wheel to clout Arnoux's right front wheel. Nevertheless they both continued apparently none the worse, Rosberg roaring off in pursuit of Tambay, while Arnoux slotted into fourth place behind Laffite as the field headed towards the end of Shoreline Drive. Here they somehow all subsequently rounded the sharp right-hander intact, but seconds later there was more drama when Rosberg overdid things again, this time by locking up his rear wheels under braking for the right-hander at the end of Seaside Way. Luckily, through a combination of good fortune and cockpit skill, the Finn merely spun through 360 degrees and was able to carry on as if nothing had happened, albeit now in third place after his team-mate had taken the opportunity to nip past. Obviously, though, Tambay was left with a bit more breathing space and went on to complete the lap several car lengths clear. Further back, behind the two green and white Williams, Alboreto had by then taken over fourth place from Arnoux, while Sullivan, in the other Tyrrell, had come through to sixth place ahead of Patrese, Prost, Cheever and Jarier. Warwick, on the other hand, had dropped right back to 11th spot after a very disappointing opening lap from his third row grid position and de Angelis to an even more lowly 13th where he was sandwiched between the two Arrows A6s of Surer and Jones, both cars, incidentally, now running with Valvoline sponsorship following the arrival of the former World Champion to the team.

Although Rosberg quickly repassed Laffite, the next four or five laps saw Tambay steadily pulling away and opening up a good 2 second advantage. But then, with his front tyres starting to show signs of overheating, the Ferrari driver eased off slightly which enabled his immediate pursuers, Rosberg, Laffite, Alboreto and Arnoux, to gradually close up once more, not enough to pose an immediate threat but sufficient to make the situation decidedly interesting. Patrese, Cheever and Jarier were not exactly being left behind either but Sullivan, who had

earlier been elbowed back to ninth place, was losing ground, as was Prost to an even greater extent owing to a return of the mysterious misfire. In fact, the Frenchman was currently losing places hand over fist and this eventually prompted him to make for the pits at the end of lap 16 where over two laps were to be lost while the Renault mechanics struggled in vain to effect a cure, the misfire still persisting when Prost finally rejoined the race. Whilst he had been stationary, de Angelis had stopped for a fresh set of Pirellis after suffering from an acute lack of grip in his Lotus 93T and Cheever had also gone into the pits with every intention of changing his Michelins only to have been quickly sent on his way again by the busy Renault mechanics. Meanwhile, Mansell and Baldi (after clipping a wall) had both been delayed by even earlier tyre stops, and there had already been two retirements. First Winkelhock had slid off into the wall at the end of Shoreline Drive on lap 4 when his ATS suddenly turned sharp left under braking. Then, only eight laps later, Warwick had gone out no less spectacularly when the left rear Pirelli on his Toleman threw its tread and led to the car spinning off backwards into the barriers at the end of Seaside Way. Since then, on lap 13, Arnoux had also very nearly let his Ferrari get away from him, but apart from losing out to Cheever (before his abortive trip into the pits), Patrese and an impressive-looking Jarier had been able to gather it up again without suffering any adverse consequences.

By lap 20 the battle up front had become even more interesting for not only were the first six cars now running virtually nose to tail but Rosberg was darting and weaving all over the road behind Tambay's Ferrari in an effort to find a way past. In fact, on the previous lap he had even momentarily pulled alongside it only for the unflustered Tambay, driving to preserve his tyres, to have out-accelerated him. Jarier, though, had just been rather more successful in dealing with Patrese and on lap 23 he attempted to pass Alboreto as well by making a run up on the inside of the Tyrrell approaching one of the tight right-handers. Unfortunately, this time it didn't come off so smoothly, for the two cars made contact and slithered up an escape road, an incident that allowed Patrese to go on ahead once more and one that brought Alboreto into the pits to have a bent steering arm replaced. Shortly afterwards Cheever also went into the pits to make a second, more successful, attempt at having his tyres changed, and was followed in quick succession by Arnoux, another in need of fresh rubber, Jones, to have a steering arm replaced after an argument with a wall, and Salazar to retire the RAM March with broken gear linkage. All the while Rosberg was trying harder than ever to take over the lead, and on lap 26 finally decided that he

had waited long enough by diving down on the right-hand side of the Ferrari on the approach to the hairpin before the pits when Tambay, apparently, was least expecting it. Whatever, the Frenchman stuck to his normal line and as he turned into the tight turn so his right rear wheel struck the Williams' left front wheel. This then acted like a launching pad and led to the Ferrari bouncing up into the air before spinning, backwards, out of the race with a stalled engine. Rosberg, on the other hand, was subsequently able to drive around the back of the stricken car and continue on his way only to find his team-mate racing alongside him and Jarier, who had quickly caught and repassed Patrese, immediately behind the pair of them. There then followed another commotion, for as the two green and white cars reached the braking area for the chicane, still side by side, they momentarily touched and in the slight confusion that resulted Jarier inadvertently ran into the back of Rosberg, causing the reigning World Champion to retire on the spot. Jarier didn't last much longer either, as soon afterwards he was forced to call it a day at the pits with the handling of his Ligier impaired by a damaged front wing. Everything now seemed to be happening at once, for during the next few minutes Giacomelli stopped for fresh tyres, stalled his engine and was unable to restart, Guerrero pulled up with a broken gearbox, Baldi disappeared out on the circuit after hitting another wall when the throttle stuck open in his Alfa Romeo, Jones lost more time at the pits due to the replacement steering arm not being in alignment and then the two Lotus drivers followed one another into the pits, de Angelis having had enough of sliding around on his Pirelli tyres and Mansell, in much the same trouble, to try another set. The result of all this meant that the race order was undergoing a complete reshuffle. Already, of course, Laffite had taken over the lead and Patrese had moved up to a close second place but, in the meantime, Lauda and Watson had come through to third and fourth places no less and were both flying, as they had been ever since the start. Although they had just been overtaken by the McLaren duo, shortly after having swopped places, Surer and Sullivan were now also on the leader-board, while close behind them, in seventh place, was none other than Cecotto in only his second Grand Prix. Only a further couple of seconds away, Arnoux was eighth and then, spread out behind, came Piquet, suffering from lack of grip and a sticky throttle pedal, the delayed Cheever, de Cesaris and the last driver still on the same lap as the leader, Boesel.

As Laffite continued to maintain a small advantage over Patrese, a highly impressive Cecotto went charging past Sullivan and Surer in quick succession and, on lap 33, Watson carried out a superb overtaking

three laps from home, he had crawled into the pits with a broken distributor. Laffite, meanwhile, had lost two more places on lap 67 after being overwhelmed at the end of Shoreline Drive by an almighty scrap that had suddenly developed between Cheever and Arnoux (following a second tyre stop). Here all three cars had arrived together with Arnoux making the most of the situation to move up from sixth place to fourth in one fell swoop. At the time Cheever had relatiated almost immediately only to have been re-passed by the Ferrari prior to pulling off the track with a broken gearbox on the following lap. As a result Arnoux had then been able to consolidate his new position, which became an eventual third because of Patrese's misfortune, while Laffite had unex-pectedly regained two of his lost places to finish fourth ahead of the other point scorers, Surer and Cecotto, the Venezuelan having been justly rewarded for a splendid drive

Watson accelerates away from one of the many tight turns during the closing stages of the race. *(L.A.T. Photographic)*

manoeuvre on Lauda at the end of Shoreline Drive. At this stage the Ulsterman was nearly 20 seconds behind the two leading cars but that now began to come down dramatically. Consequently Patrese, being kept informed of the situation by pit signals, decided that he had had better start looking for a way past Laffite, who was unable to respond to the growing threat since his tyres were going off. However, in a rather desper-ate attempt to outbrake the Williams driver at the end of Shoreline Drove on lap 43, Patrese overdid things, went scurrying up the escape road and was unable to rejoin the race until after Watson and Lauda had both gone through. Laffite, meanwhile, succeeded in holding on to the lead for just two more laps before Watson sliced past him followed, moments later, by Lauda. Incredibly, the McLarens were first and second – from 22nd and 23rd positions on the grid respectively! After that they quickly pulled away and went on to completely dominate the rest of the race with Watson chalking up his fifth Grand Prix success in resounding style by finishing nearly half a minute clear of Lauda, the Austrian being hampered slightly by a bout of cramp in his right leg, and the new Miche-lin tyre not proving to be quite so effective as the older type that his team-mate had chosen. Either way it was clear that whereas Goodyear had had the edge over Michelin during practice it had turned out to be a different story in the race or, at least, so far as the McLarens were concerned.

Behind the victorious McLaren duo, the closing stages of the race had continued to provide drama and excitement throughout almost the entire field. Initially, Patrese had looked all set to finish in third place after making a more successful attempt at over-taking Laffite on lap 52 but then, just over

Lauda works his way round the second lap in an unpromising 21st position ahead of Giacomelli's Toleman, Piquet's Brabham (almost hidden), Winkelhock's ATS and Boesel's Ligier. *(Autosport)*

spoiled somewhat by a recalcitrant gearbox during the last 20 laps or so. Boesel, delayed by a comparatively late pit stop to have a damaged rear wheel replaced on his Ligier after striking the barriers, Sullivan, hampered by a worsening tyre vibration,

Alboreto, Prost and Mansell in his tyre troubled Lotus 92 also made it to the finish but no less than three other drivers had long since joined the retirement list. These were de Cesaris, because of gearbox trouble, an unhappy Piquet, who had struck the barriers

when his throttle stuck open completely, and Jones who, having dropped to the back of the field after his second pit stop, had later decided to give up when his left leg, which was still being held together by two steel pins, started giving him a lot of pain.

Results		
1	J. Watson (McLaren-Ford)	1 hr 53 min 34.889 sec (129.753 kph/ 80.624 mph)
2	N. Lauda (McLaren-Ford)	1 hr 54 min 02.882 sec
3	R. Arnoux (Ferrari)	1 hr 54 min 48.527 sec
4	J. Laffite (Williams-Ford)	1 lap behind
5	M. Surer (Arrows-Ford)	1 lap behind
6	J. Cecotto (Theodore-Ford)	1 lap behind
7	R. Boesel (Ligier-Ford)	2 laps behind
8	D. Sullivan (Tyrrell-Ford)	2 laps behind
9	M. Alboreto (Tyrrell-Ford)	2 laps behind
*10	R. Patrese (Brabham-BMW)	3 laps behind
11	A. Prost (Renault)	3 laps behind
12	N. Mansell (Lotus-Ford)	3 laps behind

* Not running at finish.

Fastest lap: N. Lauda (McLaren-Ford) on lap 42 in 1 min 28.330 sec (133.477 kph/82.939 mph)

Retirements
M. Winkelhock (ATS-BMW) accident on lap 4, D. Warwick (Toleman-Hart) tyre failure on lap 12, E. Salazar (March-Ford) gear linkage on lap 26, P. Tambay (Ferrari) accident on lap 26, K. Rosberg (Williams-Ford) accident on lap 26, J.P. Jarier (Ligier-Ford) accident damage on lap 27, B. Giacomelli (Toleman-Hart) electrics on lap 27, M. Baldi (Alfa Romeo) accident on lap 27, R. Guerrero (Theodore-Ford) gearbox on lap 28, E. de Angelis (Lotus-Renault) handling on lap 30, A. de Cesaris (Alfa Romeo) gearbox on lap 49, N. Piquet (Brabham-BMW) accident on lap 52, A. Jones (Arrows-Ford) driver gave up on lap 59, E. Cheever (Renault) gearbox on lap 68.

LXIXe Grand Prix de France

Paul Ricard: April 17
Weather: Overcast but dry
Distance: 54 laps of 5.810 km
circuit = 313.74 km (194.95 miles)

After having put their race back from its traditional date of the first weekend in July until the last in 1982, the organizers of the French Grand Prix had, this year, brought it forward to mid-April. The reason behind this, prompted because of recent heavy financial losses incurred by the circuit owners, was to try to boost spectator attendances through avoiding the holiday season when people were seemingly more interested in soaking up the sun on the nearby Mediterranean beaches. In the event it was to make no appreciable difference, but for all that the fact remained that the race had now become the opening round of the European season and had attracted a very fine entry indeed that included a number of new cars and a couple of driver changes. In this latter respect John MacDonald had entered a second car for Frenchman Jean-Louis Schlesser (nephew of the late Jo Schlesser), who had made his Formula 1 debut at Brands Hatch the previous weekend in the resurrected, though poorly supported, Race of Champions, and the Arrows team had reinstated Francesco (Chico) Serra in their second car in place of Alan Jones. Naturally, this last move was by no means a reflection of Jones' driving but, rather, a reflection of the team's current financial situation due to the continued lack of a major sponsor materializing, and one that had come about by mutual agreement between the Australian and Jack Oliver: both had felt that it was in the team's best interests to direct what money was available on developing cars

instead of on paying a realistic wage to a top flight driver. Among the cars, meanwhile, were a pair of brand new Renault RE40s for Prost and Cheever, the prototype now being relegated to the 'muletta'; a new Euroracing Alfa Romeo 183T for Baldi to replace the chassis damaged at Long Beach; a new Tyrrell 011 for Alboreto; a new March-RAM 01 for Salazar; a new Williams FW08C, which was being earmarked as a spare car for Rosberg; and a new Toleman TG183B for Giacomelli – which Warwick had already crashed during Michelin and Pirelli tyre testing at the circuit over the previous weekend when a small stone had jammed open the throttles! Needless to say, it had subsequently been repaired. Since Long Beach the John Player Lotus team had also produced the second of their Renault-powered 93Ts, which Mansell had driven in the Race of Champions. However, this was now being set aside as a spare car for de Angelis and, instead, the Englishman had been allocated the team's pair of Ford-Cosworth-powered 92s, both of which were running on conventional suspension as the 'active system' on the newer car had now been discarded due, apparently, to any benefits derived from it being more than negated by the extra weight. As if to underline the enormous amount of work that had taken place during the previous three weeks, numerous other cars had undergone various modifications as well. These included the trio of Brabham BT52s, which reappeared with new engine covers and wings, stronger final-drive units and

on-board hydraulic jacking systems, and also the Ferrari 126C2/Bs, which had undergone a weight-saving programme made possible by the adoption of new carbon-fibre aerofoils and lighter bodywork in addition to having had the on-board electric starters replaced by new gearbox-driven pneumatic systems activated by external air-starters. In common with Renault, Euroracing Alfa Romeo and Ligier, Ferrari had also fitted their cars with quick-action refuelling nozzles on the right-hand side of the fuel tanks, all four teams joining Brabham and Williams in considering the possibility of making pre-planned pit stops during the race: at Long Beach this had not been apparent due to the awkward pit lane exit where cars were liable to have been delayed by the controlling marshal in the event of the track being busy in the immediate vicinity.

During the previous weekend's tyre test sessions Andrea de Cesaris and his Euroracing Alfa Romeo V8 turbo had come out fastest on both days, and this was a pattern that continued on the first day of official practice. Running a comparatively modest amount of boost pressure (to avoid a recurrence of engine problems caused by anything higher) and finding the Michelin qualifying tyres working considerably better than at Long Beach, the Italian proved uncatchable as he went on to stop the clocks at a most impressive 1 min 38.099 sec. Then came the bad news! At the end of the day's activities car number 22 was ushered into the scrutineering bay and, although there were no problems with weight, the on-board fire extinguisher bottle was found to be empty. Quite why this latter item was checked in the first place was uncertain but rumours seemed to suggest that there had been a tip-off from someone within the team as a means of conspiring against Gerard Ducarouge. Whatever, the Frenchman was to find himself out of work the following week, even though he remained adamant that it was an oversight rather than a deliberate ploy to save a few kilos, and de Cesaris had his lap times scrubbed. Apart from this rather unhappy affair, the main aspect of Friday's practice was the manner in which the turbo-charged cars completely dominated proceedings. Not that this was in any way unexpected given the nature of the circuit and its exceptionally long Mistral straight, but what was surprising was to find only one normally-aspirated car in the first ten places on the time-sheets – Lauda's McLaren. Fastest, following de Cesaris's exclusion, were the two new Renault RE40s of Prost and Cheever at 1 min 38.358 sec and 1 min 38.980 sec respectively, both cars obviously benefiting from extensive testing at the circuit and from a new, super-sticky, batch of Michelin qualifying tyres that were being made available at this stage to only the French team, Brabham and McLaren. Neither driver had any major problems, although Prost endured a nasty moment through the twisty infield section before the pits whilst out on his second set of qualifiers when an apologetic Boesel inadvertently moved over on him, causing a quick spin, and Cheever was forced out a few minutes early by a turbo failure. Despite the leading edge of a side-pod working loose late in qualifying, de Angelis also had the Renault-powered, Pirelli-shod Lotus 93T well up in the reckoning with third fastest time of 1 min 39.512 sec, while Piquet persevered with handling problems in the spare Brabham BT52, that he had taken over following a turbo failure, to post fourth fastest time of 1 min 39.601 sec. After that no-one had broken the 1 min 40 sec barrier, but Arnoux was only just outside, as were Winkelhock, coping admirably with unpredictable handling in his ATS, and a highly frustrated Tambay who was having the worst possible time imaginable with engine and turbo problems. Twice in the morning he had had to return to the pits on foot due to the engine cutting out in his proposed race car and a turbo letting go on the spare Ferrari, and this was followed by more of the same in the afternoon. In the circumstances, to wind up seventh fastest had to be a pretty good effort. Meanwhile, Warwick was another out of luck as right at the start of qualifying his Toleman had also come to rest out on the circuit when its electronic fuel pump seized, breaking the drive cable into the bargain. Consequently, instead of being able to get up amongst the front-runners he had to content himself with a few comparatively slow laps in Giacomelli's car, which was set up differently, with the result that he was left well down the order, actually 17th fastest – nearly 5 seconds slower than Prost!

On Saturday morning much of the attention was directed towards the McLaren pit when Lauda's MP4/1C was wheeled out fitted with a brand new engine, the long-awaited successor to the ultra-successful Ford-Cosworth DFV. Designated the DFY, this was still a normally-aspirated, 90-degree, V8 affair but had different bore and stroke dimensions of 90.0 × 58.8 mm (2994 cc) as well as redesigned cylinder heads, valve gear, camshafts, fuel-injection system and the like. Combined, together with other refinements such as the use of magnesium alloy for the inlet manifolds and water-pump housings, the overall package was not only some 15 kilogrammes lighter than the older unit but more efficient, particularly in mid-range power, although maximum power output was only marginally higher at around 520 bhp at the same 11,000 rpm. In all, four such units were on hand, McLaren having two and Lotus and Williams one apiece, and by the start of final qualifying Watson (following an engine failure!) had had one fitted to his car, as had Mansell. Even so it didn't have any dramatic effect on their lap times as Mansell went on to improve by just over half a second on the previous day to wind up in 18th place on the grid at 1 min 42.650 sec, while Lauda and Watson were both marginally slower than before in what, admittedly, were slightly more windy conditions. Nevertheless, they still came out fastest among the non-turbo brigade by narrowly pipping Race of Champions winner Rosberg – troubled by lack of grip with his Goodyear qualifiers – and the impressive Cecotto in his similarly shod Theodore. Such was the domination of the turbo-charged cars, though, that their efforts were rewarded with only 12th and 14th positions on the grid, while Rosberg and Cecotto had to make do with 16th and 17th behind Alboreto, the Italian, suffering from a bug, being another not to pick up on his Friday time following delays with engine problems in the morning. Meanwhile, the battle for pole position was turning out to be a non-event. Prost saw to that by having the boost pressure in his Renault turned up about as high as it would go and storming around the 5.81 km circuit in 1 min 36.672 sec (216.360 kph). Futhermore it was an all-Renault front row, for although Cheever failed to improve after being forced into the team's spare car, due to his proposed race chassis developing an incurable misfire earlier in the day, no-one beat his existing time from Friday. As it happened, Patrese came nearest to move up to third place on the grid at 1 min 39.104 sec, closely followed by Arnoux, who suffered a turbo fire in the closing minutes of practice just after he had been clocked at 1 min 39.115 sec, and de Angelis (1 min 39.312 sec). Not far behind them, de Cesaris (hampered by his car constantly jumping out of gear) and Baldi turned in almost identical times of 1 min 39.611 sec and 1 min 39.618 sec respectively, with Piquet next up at 1 min 39.746 sec but still ahead of both Alfas on the grid by reason of a slightly superior time on Friday. However, like his team-mate, the former World Champion was far from happy with how his car was performing, as for the second day in a row the BMW engines were seldom running cleanly and the chassis were proving virtually impossible to balance, the team even having resorted to putting lead ballast into the nose sections as a means of achieving more front end grip. In addition, Piquet had undergone a rather harrowing experience during the morning when an exhaust pipe had cracked and resulted in his rear aerofoil flying off – the heat build-up had melted the carbon-fibre central support pillar! Tambay had another frustrating day of it as well, his proposed race car pumping out all its coolant at the start of practice, and the spare Ferrari that he took over for qualifying, suffering its third turbo failure, all of which added up to a disappointing 11th place on the grid. Without doubt, though, the worst incident of all had come midway through the afternoon when the left rear Goodyear on Serra's Arrows came off its rim just beyond the pits and sent the Brazilian's car hurtling, upside down, into the catch-fences after running over the high kerbing. Mercifully, Serra survived the ordeal unscathed as he later demonstrated by going out in his team's spare car in a desperate bid to avoid being bumped off the grid. In the event he needn't have bothered as Salazar, Ghinzani and Schlesser, the three eventual non-qualifiers, all failed to beat his Friday time and, not surprisingly, so did Serra, himself.

After two days of mainly clear blue skies and reasonably warm sunshine, race day was grey and overcast which, together with the presence of a keen wind, made conditions decidedly chilly. During the morning the usual 30 minutes of free practice came and went without any major dramas, apart from Arnoux's Ferrari running into turbo-charger trouble, but the amount of activity in the pits was phenomenal with various teams all practising wheel changes against the clock. The outcome of this was that Brabham, Williams, Renault and Ferrari all decided, conclusively, to go ahead with the pre-planned pit stop routine during the race, but Euroracing Alfa Romeo, the other team looking most likely to join them, subsequently opted out for no obvious reason. Nevertheless, even with four teams – in adjoining pits – about to embark on hurried refuelling stops, the organizers, understandably, were still concerned about the potential hazards and only too happy to comply with instructions issued beforehand by FISA to declare the pit lane a restricted area for the duration of the race. The mechanics, in particular, certainly had no qualms about that, but when the time approached to position the cars for the warm-up lap there still wasn't enough room in spite of the extra breathing space – or, at least, not in the Lotus pit, so it seemed. Quite simply, as de Angelis' 93T was being moved around on slave wheels Mansell failed to notice what was happening as he stood chatting to the team's chief mechanic and promptly found the big toe on his left foot being squashed! Naturally, this put him in agony, but after receiving first-aid treatment the plucky Englishman insisted on racing and eventually joined the other 25 starters on the grid, all of them keeping their fingers tightly crossed. First they were hoping that the rain would hold off and second that they had made the right choice of tyres from the numerous different types available, not only from Michelin and Goodyear but also from Pirelli who had produced no less than three new race compounds following the problems at Long Beach.

Within seconds of Prost leading the field around on the pace lap and bringing them all back to their grid positions once more the starting light came on, red gave way to green and they were on their way, the number 15 Renault surging forward into an undisputed lead made to look all the more impressive by the other Renault momentarily hanging back with spinning wheels. Patrese, having switched to the spare Brabham BT52 for reasons that were not obviously apparent, followed it into second place, while Piquet went charging between Arnoux and the pit wall to take up station in fourth spot, directly behind a recovering Cheever. Further back Lauda and Watson also used the inside of the track in a similar ploy to try to gain a few places, but so far as the Ulsterman was concerned it was soon to prove a wasted effort. Down at the far end of the circuit leading round to the long back straight Baldi's Alfa Romeo, immediately in front of him, suddenly hesitated slightly and almost before realizing it Watson had run into the back of it, smashing his nose cone and causing the Italian to have a brief off-course excursion. However, they both gathered themselves up and after subsequently driving round to the pits, the McLaren to have a new nose cone fitted and the Alfa Romeo for fresh rear tyres, eventually rejoined the race. Even now, though, Watson's problems weren't over as less than three laps later a fault with the McLaren's throttle assembly, accompanied by strange noises, led him to believe that his new DFY engine was about to blow up so he hurriedly switched off and parked out on the circuit. Shortly afterwards Mansell retired as well, the Englishman disappearing into the pits after six laps with the pain from his foot injury coming on worse as the effects of the pain-killing spray, that had been applied earlier, gradually started wearing off. The end of a brave effort. In the meantime, Prost was literally running away with the race, being already a good 4 seconds clear; and with Cheever having repassed Patrese on the third lap the situation for Renault was looking very encouraging indeed. Since then Patrese had lost another place to Piquet, but the surprising aspect was the progress being made by Rosberg who had obviously worked out a good race set-up and was using it as only he knew how through the twistier parts of the circuit to compensate for the lack of power over the turbo-charged cars along the very fast straight. As a result, not only had the World Champion come through as the best-placed non-turbo runner but to an excellent sixth between the Ferraris of Tambay (another to have made an excellent start in the spare car that he was using) and Arnoux (unhappy on

harder tyres than those of his team-mate). In complete contrast, Warwick was falling away quite dramatically after a promising start and struggling for grip even though the Tolemans were running plenty of wing to encourage the Pirelli tyres to run at their optimum working temperature. Unbeknown to the Englishman, though, a water pipe had split, allowing some of the coolant to find its way on to his left rear tyre. Consequently, the Toleman's handling continued to deteriorate rapidly until, at the end of lap 13, Warwick made for the pits to change what he thought to be a punctured tyre. Here, the leak was still not noticed but just over a lap later rising water temperatures said it all and Warwick wisely switched off to become the third retirement.

On lap 18 the Renault 1 – 2 was interrupted by Piquet forcing his way past Cheever but any hopes that the Brazilian had of catching the leader seemed to depend on the outcome of the impending pit stops, for it soon became apparent that he could make no impression at all on Prost, who was now almost 10 seconds clear. Meanwhile, Patrese disappeared from fourth place by veering off into the pits at the end of lap 19 to retire due to his BMW engine having blown out all its coolant, and this was followed almost immediately by de Angelis rolling to a halt out on the circuit with a dead engine caused by the electronic fuel-injection system having gone on the blink. By then, though, the Lotus team leader had already dropped away to a pretty hopeless-looking 12th place despite several, yet ultimately unsuccessful, efforts to defend his position from Rosberg, Winkelhock, de Cesaris, Laffite and more latterly, Lauda, the handling of the Renault-powered 93T still leaving a lot to be desired on its Pirelli tyres. Other drivers were running into trouble now as well. Cecotto, after making little impression near the back of the field, was in need of fresh tyres, de Cesaris, who had earlier worked his way up to eighth place after a sluggish start, followed the Venezuelan into the pits with a gear-linkage problem and dropped right to the back of the field in the ensuing delay, and there were also two more retirements in quick succession. First Sullivan's clutch exploded, which damaged both the flywheel and an oil pipe causing a lot of smoke as the oil found its way on to the Tyrrell's hot exhausts. Then, only moments later, a good mid-field scrap involving Guerrero and Surer came to an abrupt end when the Theodore limped into the pits with suspected valve failure – just as Arnoux was about to attract rather more in the way of attention by making Ferrari's first-ever pre-planned pit stop.

Despite being new to the game, the Ferrari pit crew did an admirable job and kept their driver waiting just 15.7 seconds while they replenished the fuel and changed all four wheels. Even so the delay, combined with the time lost travelling into and out of the pit lane, cost Arnoux no less than five places as in the meantime Laffite (yet to stop, of course), Winkelhock, Lauda, Alboreto and Jarier all rushed on ahead of him. When Cheever took his turn to stop on the very next lap, though, it was a different story for in spite of being stationary a slightly longer 17.6 seconds in what was also Renault's first pre-planned pit stop, the American was overtaken only by Tambay due to being that much further ahead. Moreover, it took him only four laps to regain the place as at the end of lap 29 it was time for Tambay, preceded by Prost, to go into the pits to take on his fuel and tyres. Once again the Ferrari pit crew carried out their well-rehearsed routine with precision but the Renault mechanics found their job being made extra difficult by Prost stalling his engine and then, after restarting it, allowing the rear wheels to turn before the right rear wheel had been properly tightened. In his anxiety to keep the engine from stalling again by blipping the throttle he had taken his foot off the brake pedal! As a result 24.6 seconds were lost before Prost could set off once more, during which time Piquet had become a clear leader, and team-mate Cheever a close third. Nevertheless, this was still quicker than Rosberg's stop that had taken place two laps earlier. A slight problem over fitting the left front wheel had meant the Finn having to sweat it out for 26.1 seconds and slipping from fifth place to eighth behind Laffite, Winkelhock and Lauda. That was bad enough but on lap 30, moments after Lauda had spun harmlessly out of a promising sixth place when a rear wheel bearing seized on his McLaren, Rosberg nearly met with disaster. Coming on to the pits straight he suddenly found himself being confronted by Baldi's delayed Alfa Romeo, which had just been forced into the gravel on the left-hand side of the track by a rather unruly Winkelhock and gone out of control. Eventually it was to finish up against the guard-rail on the opposite side of the track with its right rear corner badly damaged and momentarily on fire but, in the meantime, Rosberg was showered with flying stones, smashing the Williams' windscreen besides scratching his helmet, and was somewhat fortunate in being able to carry on otherwise unscathed. Winkelhock, avoiding the worst of the drama that he had caused, also continued only to end the lap by beginning a succession of pit stops with a broken exhaust pipe that was to result, ultimately, in another retirement.

At the end of lap 32 attention became focussed on the pits once more when Piquet, another nearly to have suffered from Winkelhock's behaviour, finally made his stop. Now this, of course, was really crucial but despite being turned around in only 16.1 seconds the Brazilian still lost his brief lead to Prost and was left to rejoin the race in second place just ahead of Cheever – an

Alain Prost cruises on to victory, the fourth for Renault on home soil in five years. *(Phipps Photographic)*

identical situation to that before the round of pit stops had begun! Similarly, Tambay was lying fourth once more, although in fifth place it was now Laffite, a position that he maintained even after his pit stop on the following lap when Patrick Head, having examined Rosberg's discarded tyres and discovered that they would have lasted the race distance, instructed the Williams' mechanics to merely top up the Frenchman's fuel. However, whilst this took only 13.8 seconds the delay was more than sufficient for Rosberg to close right up on his team-mate, and on lap 36 the two green and white cars swopped places just as Prost was coming up to lap them both. After that, or at least once Arnoux had repassed Alboreto to move up

into seventh place on lap 40 – he had already long since disposed of Jarier by then – the race more or less fizzled out as such. In fact, the only other changes to occur throughout the entire field came about only as a result of the retirements of Fabi and Boesel, both with engine problems, and also Giacomelli, who abandoned his Toleman out on the circuit in the closing minutes with gearbox trouble. All the while Prost drove on in impeccable style and, with Piquet unable to mount any sort of challenge due to experiencing a worrying amount of understeer, ran out a very comfortable winner indeed to give the Renault team their fourth victory on home soil in five years.

Time to celebrate. After the race Alain Prost holds his trophies aloft, flanked by an apparently tired team-mate, Eddie Cheever, and a smiling Nelson Piquet, who split the Renault duo by finishing second. *(Autosport)*

Results

1	A. Prost (Renault)	1 hr 34 min 13.913 sec (199.866 kph/ 124.191 mph)	
2	N. Piquet (Brabham-BMW)	1 hr 34 min 43.633 sec	
3	E. Cheever (Renault)	1 hr 34 min 54.145 sec	
4	P. Tambay (Ferrari)	1 hr 35 min 20.793 sec	
5	K. Rosberg (Williams-Ford)	1 lap behind	
6	J. Laffite (Williams-Ford)	1 lap behind	
7	R. Arnoux (Ferrari)	1 lap behind	
8	M. Alboreto (Tyrrell-Ford)	1 lap behind	
9	J.P. Jarier (Ligier-Ford)	1 lap behind	
10	M. Surer (Arrows-Ford)	1 lap behind	
11	J. Cecotto (Theodore-Ford)	2 laps behind	
12	A. de Cesaris (Alfa Romeo)	4 laps behind	
*13	B. Giacomelli (Toleman-Hart)	5 laps behind	

* Not running at finish.

Fastest lap: A. Prost (Renault) on lap 34 in 1 min 42.695 sec (203.671 kph/126.555 mph)

Retirements

J. Watson (McLaren-Ford) engine on lap 4, N. Mansell (Lotus-Ford) foot injury on lap 7, D. Warwick (Toleman-Hart) water pipe on lap 15, R. Patrese (Brabham-BMW) engine on lap 20, E. de Angelis (Lotus-Renault) fuel-injection on lap 21, D. Sullivan (Tyrrell-Ford) clutch on lap 22, R. Guerrero (Theodore-Ford) engine on lap 24, F. Serra (Arrows-Ford) drive-shaft on lap 27, M. Baldi (Alfa Romeo) accident on lap 29, N. Lauda (McLaren-Ford) wheel bearing on lap 30, M. Winkelhock (ATS-BMW) broken exhaust on lap 37, C. Fabi (Osella-Ford) engine on lap 37, R. Boesel (Ligier-Ford) engine on lap 48.

III° Gran Premio di San Marino

Imola: May 1
Weather: Warm and mainly sunny
Distance: 60 laps of 5.040 km
circuit = 302.40 km (187.90 miles)

Twelve months earlier the organizers of the San Marino Grand Prix had been on the receiving end of the dispute between FOCA and FISA over the disqualifications of Piquet and Rosberg from the Brazilian Grand Prix and found the FOCA-aligned teams, or at least the vast majority of them, boycotting their event. This year, though, the world was at peace again with the result that the race had attracted a full entry of 28 drivers, the only absentee from the line-up at Paul Ricard being Frenchman Jean-Louis Schlesser who had decided against continuing his brief association with John MacDonald's RAM team. Most of the cars were the same as for the French round of the Championship as well, although several of them had undergone further detail modifications. Serra's Arrows had been completely rebuilt following the rather spectacular practice shunt there, and three were brand new: Renault had built up another chassis in their RE40 series for Prost and set aside his Paul Ricard-winning car as a spare, Brabham had completed work on their BT52 for Patrese, and Gunther Schmidt's ATS outfit were putting the finishing touches to a second D6 for Winkelhock. This, rather interestingly, besides being around 25 kilogrammes lighter than the German team's original 1983 car was fitted with refuelling nozzles, as now indeed were the Lotuses of de Angelis and Mansell. Although not correct in the strict sense of the word, the little Italian Osella team also had a new car on hand as having recently taken delivery of the first batch of V12 Alfa Romeo engines from the Autodelta factory they had stripped down one of their 1982 FA1Cs and rebuilt it around the same aluminium monocoque so as to accommodate one of these along with an Alfa Romeo gearbox, transmission and rear suspension. Dubbed the FA1E, this was due to be driven by Piercarlo Ghinzani while Corrado Fabi was to continue persevering with the Ford-Cosworth-powered FA1D. Meanwhile, of the various cars to have undergone modifications, the most obvious changes had been made to the trio of Ferrari 126C2/Bs. In addition to reappearing with very large rear aerofoils and massive fibre-glass air ducts to the front brakes, all three cars now had new pull-rod rear suspension systems that were not only lighter and more rigid than the previous rocker-arm arrangement but also offered better traction by encouraging more rubber to stay in contact with the ground. Toleman were another team to have carried out suspension changes between races, both at the front and at the rear of their cars, but here rather more in the way of interest was attracted towards Brian Hart's latest version of his four cylinder turbo-charged engine as this had two plugs per cylinder and a new Hart/Lucas-conceived electronic fuel-injection system. At this stage only one such 'development' engine was available and this was installed in the back of Warwick's TG183B.

The track was still damp from heavy overnight rain when the circuit opened for the start of practice on Friday morning, but conditions rapidly improved and before long things were warming up nicely, both with the weather and the amount of activity taking place. As always the first priority was for drivers to acclimatize themselves and their cars to the surroundings which was a fairly straightforward exercise for most of them owing to the amount of pre-race testing that had taken place here recently. Nevertheless, there were still a lot of adjustments being made to suspension settings and the like, and tyres, in particular, were coming under a lot of close scrutiny as all three tyre firms had brought along massive stocks for the

Starting Grid

R. Arnoux Ferrari (1 min 31.238 sec)	
	N. Piquet Brabham-BMW (1 min 31.964 sec)
P. Tambay Ferrari (1 min 31.967 sec)	
	A. Prost Renault (1 min 32.138 sec)
R. Patrese Brabham-BMW (1 min 32.969 sec)	
	E. Cheever Renault (1 min 33.450 sec)
M. Winkelhock ATS-BMW (1 min 33.470 sec)	
	A. de Cesaris Alfa Romeo (1 min 33.528 sec)
E. de Angelis Lotus-Renault (1 min 34.332 sec)	
	M. Baldi Alfa Romeo (1 min 35.000 sec)
K. Rosberg Williams-Ford (1 min 35.086 sec)	
	M. Surer Arrows-Ford (1 min 35.411 sec)
M. Alboreto Tyrrell-Ford (1 min 35.525 sec)	
	D. Warwick Toleman-Hart (1 min 35.676 sec)
N. Mansell Lotus-Ford (1 min 35.703 sec)	
	J. Laffite Williams-Ford (1 min 35.707 sec)
B. Giacomelli Toleman-Hart (1 min 35.969 sec)	
	N. Lauda McLaren-Ford (1 min 36.099 sec)
J.P. Jarier Ligier-Ford (1 min 36.116 sec)	
	F. Serra Arrows-Ford (1 min 36.258 sec)
R. Guerrero Theodore-Ford (1 min 36.324 sec)	
	D. Sullivan Tyrrell-Ford (1 min 36.359 sec)
J. Cecotto Theodore-Ford (1 min 36.638 sec)	
	J. Watson McLaren-Ford (1 min 36.652 sec)
R. Boesel Ligier-Ford (1 min 37.322 sec)	
	C. Fabi Osella-Ford (1 min 37.711 sec)

Did not qualify:
E. Salazar (March-Ford) 1 min 38.097 sec
P. Ghinzani (Osella-Alfa Romeo) 1 min 38.873 sec.

weekend. Among them was yet another completely new range of Pirelli 13-inch diameter rear covers and fractionally wider fronts. For Tambay, though, it was turning out to be every bit as bad as his first day in France a fortnight earlier, for no sooner had he begun to settle down than he found himself coasting to rest out on the circuit, his engine having cut out due to a suspected ignition fault. Then, after walking back to the pits and eventually being strapped into the spare Ferrari, he set off again only to come to another grinding halt just beyond the exit from the pit lane. On this occasion he managed to restart the engine but it still refused the run cleanly, with the result that any hopes that the Frenchman might have had of learning very much completely evaporated. Moreover, his luck continued to desert him in the afternoon, for having had his proposed race car retrieved and put right he almost immediately ran into another, even bigger, problem – the engine blew up! Consequently, his second set of qualifying tyres had to be slapped on to the spare Ferrari, but with that still persisting in popping and banging it was a wasted effort. Meanwhile, in the unlikely event of it being any consolation to him, he was now not the only driver in trouble. For a start, Warwick's first qualifying run with the new Hart 'development' engine lasted a mere three laps before he returned to the pits with something obviously amiss with the turbo-charger unit, and this was followed by the spare Toleman, that he took over, developing a seemingly incurable oil leak. Patrese, too, had to resort to the spare Brabham due to engine problems, while de Angelis was similarly obliged to switch to the spare Lotus 93T after suffering a turbo failure. Later de Cesaris and Baldi also ran into turbo-charger trouble in their Alfa Romeos but at least they both had a fair crack of the whip and certainly no reason to feel dispirited as by then they had recorded what were to be sixth and seventh fastest times of 1 min 34.345 sec and 1 min 35.000 sec respectively. Even Tambay must have felt a little happier when it was all over for just prior to his engine blowing up he had gone around in 1 min 34.221 sec and this had subsequently been bettered only by team-mate Arnoux (he had sent the many thousands of fanatical Ferrari supporters present crazy with excitement by producing the afternoon's fastest lap of 1 min 33.419 sec), Piquet (1 min 33.542 sec), Prost (1 min 33.653 sec) and Cheever (1 min 33.888 sec). In the meantime, with Winkelhock, after fighting vicious oversteer in the new ATS, de Angelis and Warwick filling up the first ten places on the time-sheets the situation for the non-turbo runners was looking just as hopeless as in France. As it was, a particularly enthusiastic performance from Surer in his Arrows A6 had resulted in the Swiss being fastest amongst their number, but even his best lap of 1 min 35.723 sec was only 11th fastest overall.

At 10 o'clock on Saturday morning it was time to start all over again in conditions that were even better than the previous day for now the circuit was bathed in warm sunshine from clear blue skies whereas it had been rather hazy. The surprising aspect was the size of the crowd for there were more spectators gathered at the various vantage points than one would normally have expected to see on race day at a lot of venues, the vast majority obviously turning out to urge on their beloved Ferraris. For a change things now went well for Tambay and, instead, it was Arnoux's turn to strike trouble by blowing up his engine, which left the Ferrari mechanics faced with the unenviable task of having to replace it in time for final qualifying. Amidst all of the activity, which saw a number of drivers still fiddling with variables or giving their spare cars an airing and so on, there were also a few other mechanical disasters. These included Patrese's Brabham and Guerrero's Theodore both stopping with broken drive-shaft joints, Alboreto's Tyrrell blowing up its engine, de Cesaris' Alfa Romeo losing another turbo, accompanied by a brief fire, and both Tolemans rolling to a halt out on the circuit with engine problems. For Warwick this was particularly infuriating as he had only just got back into the car after having earlier baled out of it rather smartly when the electrics short-circuited and caused a small fire to develop in the cockpit. Worse still, the Toleman mechanics were beaten by the clock in their efforts to rectify matters so at the start of the all-important hour of final qualifying Warwick was strapped into the spare Toleman with the intention of letting Giacomelli use it later in the afternoon, the Italian's proposed race chassis still being in bits and pieces as well. Unfortunately, though, that didn't work out either – after just one timed flying lap the spare car broke its differential output shaft! Consequently, Warwick had to become a spectator and Giacomelli never had the chance to go out at all, leaving both drivers relying on Friday's times for their ultimate grid positions. Apart from this unhappy state of affairs in the Toleman camp, the situation elsewhere was now more or less back to normal as the other teams to have suffered problems in the morning had all been able to render their cars mobile again. Even so, a rather intriguing sight was that of Ferrari, Renault and Brabham all showing no sense of urgency whatsoever, notwithstanding the fact that with only two sets of tyres allocated to each driver it was usual for some of them to hold back longer than others. But here there was almost complete inactivity for at least the first ten minutes of qualifying until Arnoux finally stepped aboard his Ferrari and then, one by one, Piquet, Patrese, Tambay, Cheever and

Prost all followed him out on to the track. Initially, it looked as if pole position was settled when Arnoux proceeded to slice four-tenths off his previous best time from Friday and the spectators obviously thought so, too, judging by their reactions at the news. However, this proved to be just the beginning of an absolutely enthralling battle for the coveted spot as only minutes later Tambay lapped quicker still, although at a price for this ended with him returning to the pits trailing a haze of ominous-looking blue smoke to signify an engine failure. Then Piquet and Patrese made their presence felt by recording two more breath-taking laps to split the Ferraris, both drivers absolutely delighted with the handling of their Brabhams after extensive testing had ironed out the understeer so apparent at Paul Ricard. To add to the drama, the Renault duo were soon getting into the act as well, but whereas Prost stirred things right up by achieving yet another fastest lap, Cheever found himself unable to make quite the same impact owing to having gone the wrong way in setting up his car. Nevertheless, this in no way diminished the tenseness of the situation, which continued with Piquet winning the pole on his second set of qualifiers only to lose it, finally, to Arnoux who sent the crowd wild, just as he had done on the previous day, with an absolute flyer in 1 min 31.238 sec (198.864 kph). Moreover Tambay, taking to the spare Ferrari for his second run and improving to 1 min 31.967 sec, only just failed – by four-thousandths of a second! – to make it an all-Ferrari front row. Instead, he had to settle for third spot on the grid behind Piquet, while Prost (1 min 32.138 sec), Patrese (1 min 32.969 sec) and a slightly disappointed Cheever (1 min 33.450 sec) were left to complete the first three rows. Naturally, with so much excitement among the leading lights, the rest of the field went virtually unnoticed but when all of the lap times had been collated and the grid was drawn up it was no surprise to find Winkelhock, de Cesaris, de Angelis and Baldi (even though he had not improved following more turbo-charger trouble) filling the next two rows to just about complete the turbo rout. Only Warwick and Giacomelli had failed to make it a total walk-over but this was understandable, of course, in view of what had happened. Even they, though, were better placed than many of their normally-aspirated rivals for Warwick had wound up in 14th spot behind Rosberg, the on-form Surer and Alboreto, while Giacomelli was just three places lower and separated from his team-mate by Mansell and Laffite. In fact, about the only real surprise was the final positions of the Marlboro McLaren drivers. After two days of struggling for grip on what for a non-turbo car were comparatively hard Michelin qualifying tyres, Lauda had qualified a disappointing 18th and Watson an even more lowly 24th, the Ulsterman having lapped quicker than only Boesel, Fabi and the two non-qualifiers – Salazar in the lone RAM March and Ghinzani in the Alfa Romeo-powered Osella.

On Sunday morning the spectators absolutely poured into the Imola Autodromo until by 11.30 a.m., when the 30 minute warm-up session began, there were already over 100,000 of them positioned around the 5.04 km circuit, few leaving any doubts of what they wanted to see going by the number of Ferrari slogans and banners being waved. There was even a red and white Canadian maple leaf painted just ahead of Tambay's starting position, not only serving as a poignant reminder of past exploits of the much-lamented Gilles Villeneuve in car number 27 but also as a clear indication of exactly what was expected of his successor. The warm-up, itself, saw the Ferraris only third and fourth fastest behind Cheever's Renault and Patrese's Brabham, although an encouraging sight for the 'Tifosi' was that of Prost coasting to rest out on the circuit with a seized fuel-injection pump and Piquet having to take over the spare Brabham because of his engine going off-colour. The Hart 'development' engine in Warwick's Toleman also refused to run cleanly owing to something still obviously awry with the electrics, while Winkelhock, already using the spare ATS because of the new car springing a fuel leak, pulled up with a broken turbo. The worst incident, however, came in the closing minutes of the session when de Cesaris had the throttle stick open on the spare Alfa Romeo that he was hoping to race, for this led to the car skating off the track at the Acque Minerali and flipping over before landing, upside down, atop the tyre barrier. Mercifully, the Italian subsequently scrambled out unhurt, and damage to the car was such that some two hours later, when the time came for the warm-up lap, he was able to climb aboard it once more – in conditions that were warm and sunny after earlier heavy clouds had looked like upsetting the fine weather. By now Piquet's Brabham had undergone an engine change, and a new fuel-injection pump had been fitted to Prost's Renault. On the other hand, Warwick and Winkelhock (after the turbo-charger problem had proved somewhat easier to cure than the fuel leak) both had to face the prospects of racing their teams' spare cars, as did de Angelis when a turbo suddenly let go in his Lotus 93T on its way round to the grid. Furthermore, this last problem led to a change of plans in the Lotus camp as earlier the decision had been taken to join Brabham, Williams, Ferrari, Renault and Euroracing Alfa Romeo in making pre-planned pit stops during the race. Now, though, the idea had to be abandoned so far as de Angelis was concerned as the spare 93T had yet to be fitted with a quick-action refuelling

Excitement for the Italian spectators as the two Ferraris of René Arnoux and Patrick Tambay lead the field around on the opening lap. *(Autosport)*

nozzle, and only Mansell be included – the Englishman, incidentally, running a Ford-Cosworth DFY for the second successive day in common with Lauda and Watson in their McLarens.

A great cheer went up as Arnoux led the field around on the pace lap and this was followed by an even bigger one at the start of the race when the two Ferraris roared off the line in first and second places, Piquet's Brabham barely moving. Incredibly, the Brazilian had stalled his engine! Naturally, this instantly brought memories flooding back of Montreal 1982, but somehow the rest of the closely-bunched pack all managed to scramble past the obstacle without coming to any grief, and after they had gone Piquet was push-started into the race. His team-mate, meanwhile, had followed the Ferraris away in third place ahead of Prost and de Cesaris, and judging by the manner in which he was almost immediately darting about behind Tambay there seemed to be little doubt that he was looking for even better things. Sure enough, on the third lap, Patrese made a successful run up on the inside of Tambay going into Tosa and just three laps later carried out an equally effective manoeuvre on Arnoux under braking for Rivazza to take over the lead. At this point the crowd fell silent, the fact that Patrese was Italian obviously carrying no weight whatsoever. Nevertheless, the Ferraris did, at least, have the edge over the rest of the field for Prost was only just about keeping up with Tambay, while the others, apart from de Cesaris, were being left hopelessly behind. In addition, there had already been two retirements. First an extremely disappointed Cheever had gone out on only the second lap with a broken turbo-charger, an incident that had also brought Cecotto into the pits owing to some of the Renault's oil finding its way on to his

visor – indifferent brakes had convinced the Venezuelan that the oil was brake fluid from his Theodore! Then, only two laps later, Guerrero had gone off into the barriers at the very fast right-hander before Tosa after being forced to put his inside wheels on to the grass by Sullivan's Tyrrell, which he had been attempting to overtake. Apparently the young American, who was still in the race, had failed to spot him making a run up on his inside and had inadvertently moved over on him. Whatever, Guerrero was livid about the affair but, at the same time, could consider himself fortunate in having survived the high-speed shunt intact, which was certainly more than could be said for his car.

After ten laps it was still Patrese leading from Arnoux, Tambay and Prost, and with the Brabham driver looking serenely confident out in front, already pulling away slightly, there seemed little likelihood of any further change in the immediate future, especially as Prost was no longer really keeping up with Tambay. Now completely on his own, de Cesaris was similarly still holding down fifth place but Winkelhock, who had initially been lying sixth, had dropped completely out of the picture and was visibly struggling to keep his ill-handling ATS pointing in the right direction. Instead, after having earlier followed Baldi past Cheever's ailing Renault, de Angelis' Lotus 93T and the unhappy German's car, it was now Rosberg who had come through to a distant sixth spot, with Baldi, his Alfa Romeo smoking rather a lot, seventh and de Angelis eighth. Then came Lauda, Laffite, Alboreto, Mansell and two drivers in the midst of a sustained charge, Watson and Piquet. Even Piquet, though, was not lapping so quickly as his team-mate, for after the problem at the start he had over-revved his engine and this had taken the edge off it. Nevertheless, he continued to follow Watson up through the field until overtaking the Ulsterman shortly afterwards, their passage being made all the easier by Alboreto sliding off the track on lap 11 when a rocker arm failed in the Tyrrell's rear suspension and also by Lauda lasting just one more lap prior to making a rare error at the chicane before Acque Minerali. Here, the Austrian simply left his braking a shade too late, struck the kerb and went spinning off into the tyre barrier to retire with the front of his McLaren looking the worse for wear. Only a couple of minutes later Cecotto disappeared from the back of the field under similar circumstances (at least he was in good company!), which not only brought the casualty list up to five – already – but also ended a disastrous day for the little Theodore team.

At the end of lap 20 the spectators were holding their breath – Arnoux had suddenly pulled off into the pits. However, they had nothing to worry about. It was just that he was making his fuel/tyre stop earlier than expected due to his Goodyears having gone off, and in exactly 16 seconds the Ferrari was on its way again only now in fifth place, close behind de Cesaris's Alfa Romeo. Almost unnoticed in the excitement, Fabi spun off in his Osella on what was becoming an increasingly slippery track surface due to a build-up of gravel on many of the corners, and Giacomelli trundled quietly into the pits to retire with a bolt having sheared in the left rear suspension of his Toleman. Up front, meanwhile, Patrese was now leading Tambay by almost 6 seconds, and when Prost's turn came to pull off into the pits on lap 27, followed moments later by de Cesaris, these two were left completely out on their own. Even so this situation was obviously not going to last long for they had yet to make their pit stops, which they finally did on laps 32 (Tambay) and 34 (Patrese). The effect, though, was greater than expected for whereas the Ferrari pit crew had their man away again in exactly 15 seconds without losing his place, the Brabham pit crew took an agonisingly long 23.3 seconds to complete the same task thanks to Patrese pulling up about a metre past his stopping point and causing, indirectly, one of the air-lines to the pneumatic wheel hammers to become disconnected after being overstretched. In the circumstances, they did well to recover as quickly as they did but by the time that Patrese finally regained the track Tambay had already gone by into a 10 second lead, bringing a rather subdued crowd back to life once more. By now Mansell, Rosberg and Baldi had also been into and out of the pits for their fuel and tyres, all without any real drama, and once Laffite and Piquet, who had hoisted himself right up to fifth place a few laps earlier, had done likewise shortly afterwards the overall picture became somewhat clearer. Already Arnoux had long since

The sorry sight at Rivazza just moments after Danny Sullivan's Tyrrell had crashed into the abandoned Toleman of Derek Warwick. *(Autocar & Motor)*

settled into third place behind Tambay and Patrese, while Prost had resumed in fourth place after his pit stop. However, in spite of having nearly messed up his fuel/tyre stop by overshooting his pit, it was now de Cesaris in fifth spot once more, followed by Piquet and, the last driver still on the same lap as the new leader, Rosberg. For Piquet, though, a hard afternoon's work and a fantastically quick pit stop lasting just 11.2 seconds was to count for nothing as on lap 42 his Brabham trickled into the pits with a suspected broken valve. Prior to this there had also been three more retirements lower down the order so the field was now dwindling rapidly. On lap 28 Warwick had put a wheel on to the 'marbles' at Rivazza and careered off into the tyre barrier, ten laps later Sullivan had done exactly the same thing at the same spot and ploughed into the abandoned Toleman, which had done neither car any good at all, and a few minutes after that Jarier had ended his race in the pits with an overheating engine caused by a stone-pierced water radiator. De Angelis and de Cesaris didn't last much longer either. Having stopped for a new set of Pirellis at the end of lap 38, almost immediately after being lapped by Tambay, de Angelis completed only another six laps before returning to the pits saying that it was pointless continuing due to the handling of his Lotus rapidly deteriorating on a reducing fuel load. De Cesaris, on the other hand, didn't have any choice in the matter as his problem was an engine failure, possibly as a result of having over-revved it earlier whilst reversing back to his pit. Rather surprisingly, Mansell also brought his Lotus into the pits about now – with tyre problems – but, despite dropping to the back of the field, he took a rather more philosophical approach than his team-mate and subsequently continued on fresh rubber.

With ten laps remaining the tension was becoming almost unbearable so far as the crowd was concerned for Patrese had steadily brought the gap down to Tambay to less than 3 seconds and was now closing up fast, the Ferrari having developed an erratic misfire each time that it went through the long left-handed Tamburello. In fact, within another couple of laps the two cars were running nose to tail and early on lap 55 it was no real surprise to see the Brabham taking over the lead after drawing alongside the Ferrari just beyond Tamburello. As earlier, the crowd fell silent again but then, half a minute later, an enormous cheer went up. Unbelievably, Patrese had crashed and Tambay was leading once more. In his efforts to consolidate his new position as quickly as possible, the Italian had arrived at the chicane before Acque Minerali too fast, got hopelessly off line for the right-hander that followed and skated off into the tyre barrier. To add to the confusion, only a few more seconds lapsed before Arnoux also arrived at the corner off line and he, similarly, finished up on the grass. However, unlike Patrese, Arnoux somehow managed to avoid the barriers and eventually succeeded in rejoining the race just after Tambay had come round again to lap him and some way behind a surprised Prost, his compatriot in the Renault moving up from fourth place to second in one fell swoop even though he was now nursing a down-on-power engine besides having to contend with understeer and a reluctant fourth gear. Meanwhile, as Tambay proceeded to reel off the few remaining laps at his own pace, more drama quickly followed. First Mansell's Lotus shed its rear aerofoil (a massive four-tier affair that his team had been experimenting with on and off recently) along the very fast section of track after Tamburello, which sent 169

1983

his car spinning wildly into the barriers; its driver, mercifully, surviving the frightening ordeal unscathed. Then, in the dying minutes, Baldi and Winkelhock both disappeared from the lap charts because of late engine failures, leaving just nine cars still there at the finish. Even Tambay only just made it as on the slowing down lap his Ferrari stuttered to a halt at Acque Minerali – seemingly out of fuel! Nevertheless, this did nothing to hide his obvious joy at winning the race and after being rescued from

some of the now hysterical spectators, who had rushed over to lift their new hero out of his car, he eventually took his place on the rostrum, flanked by Prost and team-mate Arnoux. Behind this happy trio of Frenchmen, Rosberg had kept going as hard as ever to finish in fourth place, and Watson, struggling for grip throughout the latter half of the race, had seen his perseverance rewarded with a satisfying fifth place. The Arrows team, sponsored on a one-race basis by the

Italian Marilena sportswear firm, had every reason to feel pleased as well. Surer, after an early pit stop to replace a punctured tyre had dropped him to the back of the field, had recovered sufficiently to take a well-deserved Championship point for sixth place, while Serra had completed a generally tidy nonstop drive to finish two places lower between the only other finishers, Laffite (who had had a clutch problem most of the way) and Boesel.

Results					
1	P. Tambay (Ferrari)	1 hr 37 min 52.460 sec (185.480 kph/ 115.251 mph)	8	F. Serra (Arrows-Ford)	2 laps behind
2	A. Prost (Renault)	1 hr 38 min 41.241 sec	9	R. Boesel (Ligier-Ford)	2 laps behind
3	R. Arnoux (Ferrari)	1 lap behind	*10	M. Baldi (Alfa Romeo)	3 laps behind
4	K. Rosberg (Williams-Ford)	1 lap behind	*11	M. Winkelhock (ATS-BMW)	3 laps behind
5	J. Watson (McLaren-Ford)	1 lap behind	*12	N. Mansell (Lotus-Ford)	4 laps behind
6	M. Surer (Arrows-Ford)	1 lap behind			
7	J. Laffite (Williams-Ford)	1 lap behind			

* Not running at finish.

Fastest lap: R. Patrese (Brabham-BMW) on lap 47 in 1 min 34.437 sec (192.128 kph/ 119.383 mph)

Retirements
E. Cheever (Renault) turbo-charger on lap 2, R. Guerrero (Theodore-Ford) accident on lap 4, M. Alboreto (Tyrrell-Ford) rear suspension on lap 11, N. Lauda (McLaren-Ford) accident on lap 12, J. Cecotto (Theodore-Ford) accident on lap 12, B. Giacomelli (Toleman-Hart) rear suspension on lap 21, C. Fabi (Osella-Ford) accident on lap 21, D. Warwick (Toleman-Hart) accident on lap 28, D. Sullivan (Tyrrell-Ford) accident on lap 38, J.P. Jarier (Ligier-Ford) water radiator on lap 40, N. Piquet (Brabham-BMW) engine on lap 42, E. de Angelis (Lotus-Renault) handling on lap 44, A. de Cesaris (Alfa Romeo) engine on lap 46, R. Patrese (Brabham-BMW) accident on lap 55.

XLIᵉ Grand Prix de Monaco

Monte Carlo: May 15
Weather: Changeable
Distance: 76 laps of 3.312 km
circuit = 251.71 km (156.41 miles)

After the exciting and incident-packed San Marino Grand Prix the next stop on the 1983 Championship trail was almost certainly the most popular of them all – Monaco. One of the drawbacks of the annual 'race round the houses' event, however, was the limitations placed on the number of cars allowed to take part, and once again this had produced an immediate problem. There were too many entries. As a result the local automobile club, resorting to its own rules as usual, declared that there would be a special hourlong pre-qualifying session starting at 8 o'clock on Thursday morning, the first day of official practice. Nominated to take part were drivers of the three teams not to have scored Championship points in 1982, which meant Warwick and Giacomelli (Toleman), Guerrero and Cecotto (Theodore) and Salazar (RAM). Of these, the three fastest would be permitted to join the remaining 23 drivers entered for the race to have a crack at trying to qualify for one of the 20 available starting places on the grid, while the other two would be ruled out. As it happened it couldn't have been much more straightforward thanks to both of the Theodore N183s becoming stranded out on the circuit before either of their drivers had really settled in. Guerrero, using what had previously been the spare chassis because of his unhappy experience at Imola, stopped at Casino Square with a broken

drive-shaft after initial problems with a recalcitrant fifth gear, and Cecotto crashed into the guard-rail on his way through the tunnel. Nevertheless, it was still a close run thing so far as Warwick was concerned as he had to use all three Toleman TG183Bs on hand before graduating, his proposed race car suffering an almost immediate turbo failure and the spare car, after first of all being plagued by a compressor problem, breaking a steering joint. Even after taking over Giacomelli's car, once it was clear that the Italian had gone quick enough, Warwick still had problems to contend with. The support bracket to the front underwing snapped, causing excessive oversteer, and, at almost exactly the same moment, the turbo wastegate became jammed open by a small piece of broken exhaust pipe which resulted in a substantial amount of throttle lag. And all this before official practice had even begun!

When, at 10 a.m., the main part of the day's programme did begin with 90 minutes of testing there was another local rule to bear in mind. This concerned the amount of fuel that could be stored in the pits, actually no more than 50 litres per car. Consequently, any idea of going ahead with pre-planned pit stops during the race was a non-starter: beforehand, Bernie Ecclestone had made strong representations to the organizers to rescind the rule, even to the point of suggest-

ing that the race would not carry World Championship status, but they had refused to retract. Naturally, for Bernie's team, this was of particular concern as the fuel consumption figures of the BMW engines, combined with the restricted fuel tank capacity of the BT52s, indicated that it might well be touch and go as to whether or not their cars would last the race distance. Be that as it may, with no pre-race testing possible around the street circuit and a lot to be learned owing to everything from gear ratios to suspension settings, aerodynamics and all of the other variables having been arrived at by little more than guesswork, there was soon a lot of activity. Mechanically, there were few changes from the last race in spite of the high number of cars that had been damaged. In fact, apart from the unfortunate Theodore outfit, who were already packing up, all of the remaining teams had been able to glue everything back together again, and the only actual new car was to be found in the McLaren pit where a virtually untried MP4/1C was ready for Watson to use, complete with a Ford-Cosworth DFY engine. Further testing between races, however, had resulted in a number of existing cars having undergone further modifications. Among them were the Renault RE40s of Prost and Cheever, all four Ferrari 126C2/Bs that the Italian team had brought along to avoid Tambay and Arnoux having to share only one spare car, the trio of Ligier JS21s and also Alboreto's Tyrrell 011 which reappeared with new front suspension designed to improve the car's turning-in ability on this

Starting Grid

	A. Prost
	Renault
R. Arnoux	(1 min 24.840 sec)
Ferrari	
(1 min 25.182 sec)	E. Cheever
	Renault
P. Tambay	(1 min 26.279 sec)
Ferrari	
(1 min 26.298 sec)	K. Rosberg
	Williams-Ford
N. Piquet	(1 min 26.307 sec)
Brabham-BMW	
(1 min 27.273 sec)	A. de Cesaris
	Alfa Romeo
J. Laffite	(1 min 27.680 sec)
Williams-Ford	
(1 min 27.726 sec)	J.P. Jarier
	Ligier-Ford
D. Warwick	(1 min 27.906 sec)
Toleman-Hart	
(1 min 28.017 sec)	M. Alboreto
	Tyrrell-Ford
M. Surer	(1 min 28.256 sec)
Arrows-Ford	
(1 min 28.346 sec)	M. Baldi
	Tyrrell-Ford
N. Mansell	(1 min 28.639 sec)
Lotus-Ford	
(1 min 28.721 sec)	F. Serra
	Arrows-Ford
M. Winkelhock	(1 min 28.784 sec)
ATS-BMW	
(1 min 28.975 sec)	R. Patrese
	Brabham-BMW
R. Boesel	(1 min 29.200 sec)
Ligier-Ford	
(1 min 29.222 sec)	A. de Angelis
	Lotus-Renault
D. Sullivan	(1 min 29.518 sec)
Tyrrell-Ford	
(1 min 29.530 sec)	

Did not qualify:
B. Giacomelli (Toleman-Hart) 1 min 29.552 sec
N. Lauda (McLaren-Ford) 1 min 29.898 sec
J. Watson (McLaren-Ford) 1 min 30.283 sec
C. Fabi (Osella-Ford) 1 min 30.495 sec
E. Salazar (March-Ford) 1 min 31.229 sec
P. Ghinzani (Osella-Alfa Romeo) 1 min 35.572 sec.

tight little circuit. Like Williams, McLaren and Lotus, the Tyrrell team had now also been supplied with the short-stroke DFY engines. Renault, meanwhile, had introduced new low-line exhaust systems in which the exhaust pipes, rather than protruding from the top rear edge of each of the sidepods directly in front of the rear wheels, had been re-routed under the rear of the car to eliminate excessively high tyre temperatures; Ferrari had fitted a driver-controlled knob in the cockpits of their cars which activated a valve in the fuel system to dispel any unwanted air bubbles, the cause of Tambay's erratic misfire at Imola; and Ligier, besides adopting double rear aerofoils, in company with Osella, were once more using the Citroen-based hydraulic suspension system following encouraging results achieved in testing. Finally, the only other major change was to be found in the Arrows pit. Here the previously all-white A6s had been repainted in a smart cream, brown and white livery to

signify a new sponsorship tie-up with Barclay cigarettes, a British-American Tobacco brand sold only in Switzerland, which had already been sponsoring Surer on a personal basis.

Although the 1½ hours of untimed practice produced no serious mechanical disasters, apart from de Angelis suffering two turbo failures, few drivers were happy with how their cars were performing and many were constantly dashing into the pits for various adjustments. Even at the end of it all it was much the same story, with the result that a lot more work went on during the interval between sessions. By 1 p.m., though, everyone was more or less ready to go out again and just had to hope that they had now gone the right way in choice of settings. One of the first to take to the track was Arnoux, and – having started the 1982 race from pole position, in a Renault, of course, as opposed to a Ferrari – it was clear that the Frenchman was intent on letting history repeat itself if at all possible. He was setting a cracking pace. Tambay, staying out of trouble for a change, had the other Ferrari well on song, too, and Rosberg was obviously doing his best to keep up by almost literally throwing his Williams through the numerous twists and turns. This was in spite of the fact that he was feeling a bit off-colour because of some virus infection. His teammate, meanwhile, was soon back in the pits with two bent wheel rims on the left-hand side of his car as a result of having glanced the barriers in the vicinity of the swimming pool. Luckily, there was no other damage and, after the tyres had been carefully removed and fitted to new rims, Laffite was able to join in once more. Prost was another soon destined to return to the pits owing to his rev-counter no longer working properly, thanks to an electrical short circuit, while Patrese was even more unfortunate, as within minutes he was forced to abandon his Brabham out at Portier with a dead engine. In this instance, the carbon-fibre air-collector box to the fuel-injection had come detached and blown away, leaving the Italian to walk in before taking over his team's spare car. All the while, life in the McLaren pit was becoming more fraught by the minute with both Lauda and Watson complaining bitterly that their MP4/1Cs were almost undriveable. Already the suspension settings had been adjusted to provide a softer ride but nothing would seem to bring their Michelin tyres up to working temperature. To make matters even more galling for them the similarly-shod Ligiers, which had been in much the same sort of trouble as the McLarens at Imola, were performing much better after the modifications with Jarier, in particular, making quite a good impression. However, this fact went largely unnoticed due to a superb scrap that developed over the provisional pole between Arnoux and Prost

once the Renault's rev-counter had been put right. Three times they traded fastest laps, and it was only in the closing minutes when Prost, on his second set of qualifying tyres, went around in 1 min 24.840 sec that the issue was finally resolved, Arnoux's best lap coming out at 1 min 25.182 sec. Despite being well over a second slower than both of them, Cheever saw an enthusiastic performance in the second Renault rewarded with third fastest time of 1 min 26.279 sec, while Tambay and Rosberg were handily placed with fourth and fifth fastest times of 1 min 26.298 sec and 1 min 26.307 sec respectively. After that, though, the rest were faced with a lot of catching up to do as they were all over 2 seconds or more off the pace, including Piquet, never the most happy of drivers on street circuits, who had come out sixth fastest at 1 min 27.273 sec and both McLaren drivers who had not yet even qualified.

For the drivers, at least, Friday was a rest day owing to the circuit being set aside for participants of the various supporting events included on the weekend's programme. Consequently, it was not until Saturday morning that attention became focused on the Formula 1 cars once more when practice resumed at 10 o'clock with a further 90 minutes of testing. In the McLaren pit confidence was now running a little higher as a fresh batch of Michelin tyres had arrived on Friday of the same construction as a new type that the team had tested at Clermont-Ferrand over the previous weekend and found to be a noticeable improvement. It had obviously been no flash in the pan either. Once everything was in full swing both Lauda and Watson were clocking up times, unofficially, at around 2 seconds quicker than on Thursday and looking better altogether. Naturally, with conditions remaining dry, albeit now rather overcast, the others were all hard at it as well, busily preparing themselves for the final hour of qualifying or, in some instances, trying to find a decent race set-up. Invariably, though, with so much activity going on there were a few unwanted dramas. Among them were Piquet pulling up just before Ste. Devote with a broken driveshaft, Boesel returning to the pits with the control pump to the hydraulic suspension of his Ligier having failed, and Arnoux creating what must have been one of the biggest smoke-screens seen for a long time when a turbo-charger let go in his Ferrari. De Cesaris and Salazar, meanwhile, didn't exactly help themselves by coming into contact with the guard-rail near the harbour chicane at different times, the front of the RAM March being left looking decidedly second-hand. Mansell had a slight problem as well, which saw the Englishman vacating the cockpit of his Lotus 92 in what must surely have been record-breaking time – his battery had suddenly short-circuited and sent a heavy current of electricity through the carbon-fibre seat pan! Nevertheless, this obviously did him no harm as later, after the battery had been replaced and the electrics checked over, he went out again and recorded, unofficially, the morning's third fastest time. This was a real surprise but it was not the only one as Winkelhock, his ATS now sporting a massive Ferrari-like rear aerofoil, finished up by setting the fastest time of all which really put the cat amongst the pigeons. Indeed, as everyone went away to prepare for the final hour of qualifying it seemed certain that there was an exciting climax in store. But it was not to be. Soon after mid-day the weather decided to intervene with rain developing and then intensifying to such an extent that by 1 p.m. the circuit was awash. Furthermore, it refused to let up, so as time wore on it became increasingly obvious that the entire grid was going to be decided by Thursday's times. Consequently practice, as such, more or less just fizzled out with the frustration and disappointment nowhere more apparent than in the McLaren pit where Lauda and Watson (both potential race winners taking into account their drives at Long Beach) had to face up to the fact that their work was over for the weekend. So, too, did Giacomelli, Fabi, Salazar and Ghinzani who were the others to have finished outside the top 20 on Thursday. About the only useful aspect of the rain was that it did provide the Goodyear runners with an opportunity to try out some newly-developed wet-weather tyres which, unusually for the American firm, were of radial construction as opposed to their more familiar range of cross-plies. Rosberg was one of the drivers to use them and in a spirited display of opposite-lock motoring had actually recorded the session's fastest time of 1 min 52.030 sec, just pipping Arnoux who had lapped in 1 min 52.183 sec using his spare Ferrari – heroic performances from them both, but totally meaningless in real terms.

Ironically, almost as soon as practice had ended the weather cleared up but overnight another belt of rain came through and on the following morning it was still tipping down. Only as mid-day approached was there any sign of an improvement, although even this proved to be no more than a brief respite. No sooner had what turned out to be a fairly uneventful 30 minute warm-up session taken place than the rain returned with a vengeance. It then continued on and off right through until just before 3 p.m. when the cars were about to leave the pits prior to lining up on the dummy grid, de Cesaris's Alfa Romeo now fitted with a fresh engine following problems with an oil leak during the warm-up session and Warwick's Toleman with a new turbo-charger unit after he, too, had been sidelined. Consequently, once the cars were on the grid and with the rain still spitting, the deliberations began in earnest with teams frantically trying to make up their minds whether they should opt for slicks or wet-weather tyres, and whether their cars should have wet or dry settings. It was confusing to the extreme and totally dependent on which way the weather would turn next. Would it clear or would there be another downpour? Eventually, decisions had to be made and in the final reckoning the vast majority of the turbo teams decided to play safe by choosing to use wet-weather tyres, some, such as Renault, with their cars on wet settings, others not. In fact, of the turbo-charged cars only Warwick's Toleman and de Angelis' Lotus 93T set off on the pace lap fitted with slick tyres, after 'James Bond' (Roger Moore) had cruised around the circuit in an open-topped sports car alongside Jackie Stewart, although Tambay's Ferrari (fastest in the warm-up session) would certainly have been another if the Frenchman could have had his way. Opinions amongst the teams using normally-aspirated cars, on the other hand, were about evenly divided with Rosberg, Laffite, Alboreto, Sullivan and Surer (Arrows were hedging their bets) all setting off on slick tyres in the hope that it would be a worthwhile gamble should the rain hold off and their rivals have to stop and change tyres.

When Prost brought them all safely back to their starting positions once more the cars on the right-hand side of the track appeared to have a slight advantage due to the overhanging trees there having kept the road surface relatively dry. Indeed, this was something that was made only too apparent a few seconds later. As the green starting lights lit up Arnoux's Ferrari hung back badly with spinning wheels whereas Prost's Renault took off with only the slightest hint of wheelspin and was away into an undisputed lead. The best start of all, however, came from Rosberg who saw a gap appearing in front of him caused by Cheever's Renault veering towards the centre of the track, went for it and in a perfectly executed overtaking manoeuvre slammed his Williams straight into a magnificent second place. Arnoux, meanwhile, also lost out to Tambay and de Cesaris before getting properly under way, and only just held off Jarier going into the Ste. Devote chicane, the Ferrari and the Ligier arriving virtually side by side. Miraculously, everyone subsequently filed through the tight turn intact, despite the extremely slippery surface, but still only 18 cars went on to complete the opening lap due to Alboreto and Mansell having an argument over the same piece of road on the approach to the swimming pool complex. Here, Mansell had tried to squeeze past on the inside of the Tyrrell, which had slid fractionally wide on its way out of Tabac, only for wheels to have touched and both drivers to finish up with their cars against the barriers. Ahead of this early drama, Rosberg was not only keeping right up with Prost but was really pushing him hard in spite of being on slick tyres. Moreover, as they accelerated past the pits to start the second lap Rosberg aimed his Williams for the dry inside line under the trees and sailed past the Renault into the lead with no apparent trouble whatsoever. A couple of seconds behind them Arnoux, having already fought his way up to fourth place, tried a similar tactic on Cheever just beyond the pits. However, unlike Rosberg, the Frenchman only just squeezed through at the last possible moment and then, because of being off line, slid wide enough through Ste. Devote to enable his adversary to repass him going up the hill to the Casino. On the fourth lap, though, Arnoux finally got his third place, while later on the same lap a fast-rising Laffite also made it past Cheever to relegate the American to fifth. In the meantime, Rosberg was putting on a masterful display, deliberately avoiding the wettest parts of the circuit wherever possible, even though it meant taking unconventional lines through some of the corners, yet still managing to pull away from Prost at around two seconds per lap and leaving the rest hopelessly behind. The weather was doing its bit as well for the rain had now dispersed completely and the track was already starting to dry. In fact, the wet-weather tyres were turning out to be a dead loss as Piquet more or less confirmed by turning off into the pits as he came round to complete his fourth lap to change to slicks. Boesel and Winkelhock, on the other hand, never had the opportunity to change tyres. They had just tripped over one another on the approach to the harbour chicane when the German had tried, unsuccessfully, to squeeze past the Ligier after it had slid to the outside of the track on its way out of the tunnel. Sixteen cars left!

On lap 6, with other drivers now starting to discard their wet-weather tyres, there was more drama. This time it was over on the far side of the circuit at Portier where Arnoux's Ferrari suddenly glanced the barriers after being forced off line by Laffite charging down on his outside. Nevertheless, in spite of the impact damaging the left rear wheel rim and puncturing the corresponding tyre, Arnoux quickly sorted himself out and continued on his way almost as if nothing had happened with every intention of making it back to the pits. Even when the rim began to fragment he still carried on at a fair rate of knots before finally coming to rest by the entrance to the pit lane. From here the stricken car was subsequently pushed into the Ferrari pit – rather handily located at that end of the pit lane – and then, after all four wheels had been changed and the damage hastily patched up, Arnoux was sent back out into the fray. But it was to no avail. Within less than a lap he was forced to park out on the circuit, the damage being worse than at first appreciated. His team-mate, meanwhile, had been frantically waiting to join in the rush going on to change tyres and it was not until the end of lap 10 that Tambay eventually achieved his ambition, by which time he had already lost all contact with the leaders and now dropped to a pretty hopeless-looking 11th place. At this stage it was obvious that the tyre gamble by the brave-hearted had really paid dividends, for Rosberg's lead had mushroomed to over 25 seconds, Laffite, running on harder compound tyres than his team-mate, was now lying a very comfortable second, Surer was similarly on his own in a fine third place and Warwick was up to fourth immediately ahead of Prost, the French Renault driver having stopped to change his tyres at the end of lap 7. De Angelis, too, had come right through to sixth place but Piquet was now reeling him in fast and on the 12th lap it was no surprise to see the Brazilian go charging past the Lotus to join Prost in his pursuit of Warwick. Before long Cheever, who had changed tyres at the end of lap 8 and was now the only other driver still on the same lap as the leader, was also bearing down on de Angelis, to which the Italian responded by obligingly pulling off into the pits to complain that his Pirelli tyres had gone off. This was at the end of lap 18, just four laps after de Cesaris had become the sixth retirement with gearbox trouble.

With Rosberg and Laffite so far apart and completely out on their own relative to the rest of the field the focal point of attention was now the scrap for fourth place where Warwick was fighting to hold off Prost and Piquet. If practice form was anything to go by then it seemed to be only a question of time before Prost would overtake the Toleman. But the Englishman continued to defend his position magnificently, helped to some extent by some quick adjustments made to the Renault's suspension settings at the time of Prost's pit stop proving to be more of a handicap than an improvement on the drying track. Piquet was not in an ideal position to launch an all-out attack either due to the ban on refuelling forcing him to run with only a modest amount of boost pressure in the interests of lasting the race distance. Even so, with Prost obviously getting nowhere and Cheever's Renault starting to loom ever larger in his mirrors, the Brazilian decided on lap 22 that it was time to make a move and went swooping past Prost on the inside line going through the tunnel of all places. Now he, too, began looking for a way past the impressively-driven Toleman but with an equal lack of success due to Warwick remaining totally unflustered and steadfastly hugging the racing line. Prost, meanwhile, soon found himself losing further ground to team-mate Cheever, the two Renaults swopping places on their way past the pits going into lap 28. Any joy that the American might have derived from that, however, turned to bitter disappointment

just over three laps later when he suddenly put his left arm in the air at the harbour chicane to signify that his engine had cut out. The cause was apparently electrical but, whatever, he had to sit and watch as Prost repassed him before eventually rolling to a halt in the vicinity of the swimming pool. Only minutes later Jarier, who had been running strongly in tenth place behind Patrese and Tambay, also had to park his Ligier when the control pump to the car's hydraulic suspension system failed and allowed the suspension units to collapse. So now, with the race fast approaching half-distance, the field had dwindled to just twelve cars.

Shortly after the half-way mark the epic duel going on between Warwick and Piquet started to take on even greater significance for they were fast coming up to within striking distance of Surer's third-placed Arrows. Indeed, by lap 43 the deficit had been wiped out completely, and during the next six laps the three cars ran absolutely nose to tail with Surer really having to drive his heart out to stay in front. Only at the start of lap 50 did the situation change. Then it changed dramatically. Approaching Ste. Devote, Warwick moved over to the outside of the track as if feinting to overtake and just as he was about to turn into the chicane inadvertently brought his right front wheel into contact with the Arrows' left rear wheel when the Swiss moved over to claim the line. That, unfortunately, immediately resulted in the Arrows being spun around and making contact with the guard-rail on the left-hand side of the track, where its nose cone was torn away, before careering, backwards, into the guard-rail on the other side, its driver unharmed but out of the race. Meanwhile, Warwick skated off to the left-hand side, but

by keeping his engine running was able to rejoin the race in fifth place, after Piquet and Prost had managed to thread their way through the debris, only to complete the lap by touring into the pits to retire because of the Toleman's left rear suspension being too badly damaged to continue. De Angelis retired about this time as well, the Lotus-Renault suffering a drive-shaft failure as the Italian accelerated along the pit lane after another stop for more Pirellis, and this was quickly followed, on lap 54, by Laffite being forced to bow out of a very secure second place with a broken gearbox. Earlier Rosberg's immediate future had not been looking too good either. His Williams had developed a slight misfire, and on one lap, as he had negotiated the swimming pool complex, the engine had cut out completely. Fortunately, by keeping the car in gear and letting out the clutch, he had been able to restart it and whilst the engine had still shown a tendency to cut out occasionally as he lifted off for some of the corners the problem had since all but dissipated. Consequently he was now pressing on as hard as ever and with Laffite, (who had steadily been gaining on him) no longer there his lead had suddenly grown from a shade over 20 seconds to almost exactly a minute. Up into second place now, Piquet was still having to keep a watchful eye on Prost even though the Frenchman was finding fourth gear increasingly difficult to engage, while a further 15 seconds adrift Patrese and Tambay were similarly running in close formation after having unlapped themselves on lap 42 when Rosberg's problem had been at its worst. In fact, these last two had been trading fastest laps for quite some time in spite of the Ferrari having shed one of its rear aerofoil side supports early in the race. Unfortu-

Reigning World Champion Keke Rosberg drove brilliantly in the Ford-Cosworth-powered Williams FW08C and scored what, surprisingly, was only the second Grand Prix victory of his career in convincing style. (Autosport)

nately, though, Patrese's efforts were to go unrewarded as within a few more laps the Brabham's fuel-injection system started playing up and on lap 65, following a pit stop to take on a few extra litres of fuel, he went coasting to rest just beyond Portier with a dead engine. The end of another good drive.

During the closing stages Piquet really turned on the tap as he gave chase to the leader but, despite being in considerable discomfort from badly blistering hands caused by kick-back through the steering wheel as well as being badly held up by Sullivan's Tyrrell when he came up to lap the American for the second time, Rosberg proved uncatchable. Instead he went on to conclude a brilliant drive and worthwhile tyre gamble by scoring what was only his second Grand Prix victory with a final winning margin of just over 18 seconds. Behind the second-placed Piquet, Prost was reasonably satisfied to finish third in view of his problems, Tambay was a distant fourth in a race that he might well have won had he been allowed to start on slick tyres and, after a careful drive spoiled only by his ill manners in delaying Rosberg, Sullivan scored his first-ever World Championship points by coming home in fifth place ahead of the only other survivors, Baldi and Serra.

Results			
1	K. Rosberg (Williams-Ford)	1 hr 56 min 38.121 sec (129.586 kph/ 80.521 mph)	
2	N. Piquet (Brabham-BMW)	1 hr 56 min 56.596 sec	
3	A. Prost (Renault)	1 hr 57 min 09.487 sec	
4	P. Tambay (Ferrari)	1 hr 57 min 42.418 sec	
5	D. Sullivan (Tyrrell-Ford)	2 laps behind	
6	M. Baldi (Alfa Romeo)	2 laps behind	
7	F. Serra (Arrows-Ford)	2 laps behind	

Fastest lap: N. Piquet (Brabham-BMW) on lap 69 in 1 min 27.283 sec (136.603 kph/84.881 mph)

Retirements
M. Alboreto (Tyrrell-Ford) accident on lap 1, N. Mansell (Lotus-Ford) accident on lap 1, R. Boesel (Ligier-Ford) accident on lap 4, M. Winkelhock (ATS-BMW) accident on lap 4, R. Arnoux (Ferrari) accident damage on lap 7, A. de Cesaris (Alfa Romeo) gearbox on lap 14, E. Cheever (Renault) electrics on lap 31, J.P. Jarier (Ligier-Ford) suspension on lap 33, M. Surer (Arrows-Ford) accident on lap 50, D. Warwick (Toleman-Hart) rear suspension on lap 50, E. de Angelis (Lotus-Renault) drive-shaft on lap 50, J. Laffite (Williams-Ford) gearbox on lap 54, R. Patrese (Brabham-BMW) fuel system on lap 65.

XLI Grote Prijs van Belgie

Spa-Francorchamps: May 22
Weather: Warm and sunny
Distance: 40 laps of 6.949 km
circuit = 277.960 km + 0.662 km = 278.622 km (173.127 miles)

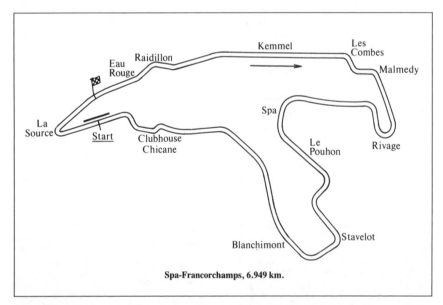

Spa-Francorchamps, 6.949 km.

There was rather more excitement than usual surrounding this year's Belgian Grand prix as for the first time in 13 years it was being held on the historic Circuit Nationale de Spa-Francorchamps, situated in a deep and heavily wooded valley in the beautiful Ardennes. It had all come about as a deliberate plan on the part of the organizers to attract the race back to their circuit by embarking on an ambitious modernization programme five years earlier. Previously they had lost the race becaue many people had considered the original circuit to have become too fast and dangerous for Formula 1 cars, and so they had responded by making substantial alterations that effectively cut the circuit in half by means of a new 'link road' and reduced the overall lap distance from 14.10 to 6.949 kilometres. Now, instead of the track following the line of the main Francorchamps to Malmedy road from La Source to Burnenville, it swung sharp right just before the left-handed Les Combes to join an entirely new and extremely demanding section that meandered its way down the valley and up the other side, concluding with a relatively long sweeping right-hander that met up with the original circuit once more along the Francorchamps-Stavelot road just short of Blanchimont. From there it then followed the line of the main road back to La Source as before except for a slight deviation through a new chicane designed to reduce approach speeds for the hairpin. Really it was no more than a short, sharp layby at the side of the main road and because of this had already been nick-named 'The Bus Stop'! Once it had become known for sure that the Belgian Grand Prix was returning to what was largely considered to be its rightful home, a great deal of effort and money had also gone into the building of a brand new pits complex and paddock on the area of land on the inside of the track before La Source hairpin. Previously the pits had been located on the hill leading down to Eau Rouge but now they were on the level immediately prior to La Source with the paddock, a split level affair, directly behind them. This was fine in principle but not quite so good in practice due to recent heavy rain having turned the paddock area into a mud-bath, added to which the business of transferring tyres, in particular, to the pits was a rather arduous affair owing to the uphill gradient. Nevertheless, it was the track, itself, that really mattered and this had already met with the overwhelming approval of the drivers during recent pre-race testing when just about all of them had expressed outright pleasure at being faced with a real challenge, unlike that provided by some of the newer, modern-day venues.

Reasonably fine weather got everything off to a good start on Friday morning and it was obvious that the drivers were bubbling with enthusiasm by the manner in which they were quickly getting stuck in. The entry, not surprisingly in view of there having been only four clear days in which to pack everything up at Monaco and transport it to Belgium, was virtually identical to the previous weekend, with the only major changes apparent being almost totally confined to the Arrows team. Here, besides having built up a brand new A6 for Surer to replace the chassis badly damaged in the unfortunate incident with Warwick's Toleman, they had now released Chico Serra and signed up 'local' Formula 2/Formula 3 exponent Thierry Boutsen to drive their second car. This had come about following a successful test session completed by the young Belgian at Silverstone recently and because he had attracted considerable sponsorship money

from Louis de Poortere carpets, Diners Club International and one or two other sources. Meanwhile, one other important development to have occurred since Monaco was the introduction of an improved version of the recently released Ford-Cosworth DFY engine which, with completely new elektron cylinder heads and revised valve gear, was expected to perform more efficiently as well as providing an increase in power output across its entire rev range. Only two such units had been released so far, and both to the Benetton Tyrrell team, one having been installed in Alboreto's car for immediate use and the other put to one side for the time being. Unfortunately, though, the new engine was suffering from a fuel mixture problem with the result that the Italian was constantly dashing into the pits for adjustments to try to eliminate a persistent misfire. This apart, most drivers were finding their progress going largely unimpeded, although Piquet suffered an early engine failure before coming to rest out on the circuit in the spare Brabham when its transmission broke and the Candy Toleman team seemed to be having more problems than they could cope with. First Giacomelli joined Piquet in losing an engine and then Warwick had a turbocharger unit let go. Even the team's spare car that Giacomelli had taken over in the meantime was not turning out to be of much use as that was plagued by clutch trouble. Towards the end of the 90 minutes of testing Cecotto also ran into a spot of bother. But this was under rather different circumstances as it emanated from driver error when Jarier, having just followed Patrese out of the pits, moved over to pass the Brabham at precisely the same moment that the Venezuelan came charging up behind them at Eau Rouge. Consequently, Cecotto was forced completely off line, spun and was able to do nothing to prevent his Theodore from crashing into the guard-rail on the outside of Raidillon. Luckily the damage, mainly around the left front corner of the car, turned out to be less than at first feared. Nevertheless, Cecotto was absolutely livid about the affair and later proceeded to make a point of giving Boesel a piece of his mind in the pits, not realizing until afterwards that the transgressor had actually been Jarier. Um . . . well . . . !

Throughout the morning, and during the recent pre-race testing for that matter, the pace-setter had been Andrea de Cesaris in his familiar Euroracing Alfa Romeo V8 turbo. However, when it came round to the first hour of qualifying in the afternoon the Italian found himself being eased out of the limelight by Prost and Tambay. Even so he was certainly not left behind. On the contrary, through being able to run a bit more boost than of late, thanks to modifications carried out to the Alfas' turbo compressor units, combined with a superb display of car

control, de Cesaris clocked up a well-deserved third fastest time of 2 min 04.840 sec. Tambay also looked to be working really hard in the cockpit of his Ferrari and nowhere more so than through the dauntingly quick Eau Rouge and the long uphill right-hander that followed where the sudden change in direction was obviously upsetting the car's balance. By comparison, Prost's Renault appeared to be causing its driver no problems at all through this tricky section apart from bottoming out slightly and, in fact, was one of the most stable cars out on the circuit. Cheever's Renault was the same but, unfortunately, the American's engine had lost its edge. Consequently, whilst his team leader went on to set the afternoon's fastest lap of 2 min 04.615 sec (200.749 kph) with little apparent effort, albeit a mere 0.011 sec quicker than Tambay, it was no real surprise to see Cheever come out over 2½ seconds slower at 2 min 07.294 sec. Almost exactly a full second slower than Prost with a time of 2 min 05.628 sec, after a fresh BMW engine had been installed in his Brabham, Piquet was next up, but here again this seemed mainly due to sheer horse-power and cockpit skill overcoming chassis instability. Much the same applied to team-mate Patrese and Winkelhock in the other two BMW-powered cars who wound up in sixth and seventh places on the time-sheets immediately behind Arnoux. Meanwhile, with Cheever's time turning out to be eighth in the standings, any lingering doubts about this not being yet another turbo circuit had now been dispelled completely. Even a typically enthusiastic performance from Rosberg, the fastest normally-aspirated runner at 2 min 07.975 sec, despite complaints of understeer, was more than 3 seconds off the pace, while most of the other Ford-Cosworth users were virtually nowhere. These included both McLaren drivers, Lauda and Watson, and also Alboreto who had lost so much time in the morning whilst efforts were being made to encourage the new DFY engine to run properly that he had not really had an opportunity to set up his Tyrrell to his liking. Surer, on the other hand, had been making noticeably good progress in his well-balanced Arrows and ended up by pipping Laffite's well-driven Williams as the second fastest non-turbo runner, tenth fastest overall and eight places higher than his impressive-looking new team-mate. As in the morning there were few serious mechanical problems and the only driver to have his qualifying run badly affected was Baldi due to his Alfa Romeo blowing up its engine after only three laps. This obviously went a long way to explaining why he was over 4 seconds slower than his hard-charging team-mate. De Angelis, though, lost a considerable amount of time when a trip up over the kerb at the chicane broke the right front upright on his very poorly-handling Lotus 93T, as did Cecotto when a front aerofoil support broke on his repaired Theodore, while the Toleman team never seemed to recover from their problems earlier in the day. Giacomelli was only 16th fastest after going out late because of the length of time it took to complete his engine change, and Warwick, confined to the spare Toleman, was a thoroughly disappointing 22nd, the Englishman complaining that the engine was hopelessly down on power due to turbo boost trouble and that the Pirelli qualifying tyres were going off within less than a lap.

As Saturday dawned wet, and the rain came on progressively worse as the day wore on, the first day's times stood for the grid for the second weekend running, leaving Ghinzani and Salazar as the two non-qualifiers. In spite of the dismal conditions, which were absolutely appalling for what was supposed to be the final hour of qualifying, every driver ventured out on wet-weather tyres at some time or another during the day, and again there was plenty of enthusiastic driving to savour. Without doubt, though, the most inspiring performance of all came from Cheever. He really excelled himself on the soaking wet track in the afternoon by reeling off a succession of fastest laps, his best coming out at 2 min 25.700 sec – almost a full 5 seconds quicker than anyone else! As it was Rosberg came closest to him with yet another of his spectacular performances that produced a lap in 2 min 30.151 sec and he, in turn, was followed by Warwick and de Angelis with almost identical times of 2 min 30.477 sec and 2 min 30.478 sec respectively. Little wonder that some people went away in the hope that it might be a wet race!

Much to the relief of most of the drivers it was dry once more on Sunday and this led to the late morning warm-up session being very busy indeed due to everyone trying to make up for the loss of time caused by the previous day's wet practice. During the 30 minutes Prost lapped well over half a second clear of the field, but while he was out enjoying himself some of the others ran into trouble. These included Warwick, when another turbo-charger unit broke in his Toleman, and also Laffite and Patrese who were perplexed at finding their engines misbehaving due to what was subsequently diagnosed to be fuel pump and electrical trouble respectively. Worst of all, the second of the two brand new DFY engines that had been installed in Alboreto's Tyrrell overnight lasted barely two laps before blowing up, leaving the Italian's mechanics faced with the unenviable task of having to replace it – with one of the first generation DFY units. Nevertheless, everything was sorted out in good time and shortly past 2 p.m. all 26 drivers were leaving the pits and subsequently forming on the dummy grid in conditions that had now become extremely pleasant. As they sat back

to await the start a lot of interest centred around the teams planning refuelling/tyre stops during the race and, in all, there were eight – Brabham, Williams, Ferrari, Renault, Euroracing Alfa Romeo, Lotus, ATS and Toleman. Earlier, the Ligier team had considered the possibility of joining them but, despite having arrived at the circuit with their JS21s equipped with refuelling nozzles, they had now apparently decided against it. Not that this was in any way surprising after a disappointing practice in which the French cars, no longer fitted with the double rear aerofoil layout used at Monaco, had been lacking badly in the handling department, the Citroen-based hydraulic suspension systems having proved less than effective on this fast circuit.

After the field had gone around on the pace lap and lined up on the grid once more for the 2.30 p.m. start there was confusion to say the least. Surer was in trouble with a stripped first gear, while de Angelis had stalled his engine, and as the red starting lights went on both drivers had their hands in the air. On spotting that there were problems the official FISA starter, Derek Ongaro, responded by switching on the flashing yellow lights to indicate 'start delayed'. But, as the red lights went out, de Cesaris instinctively took off, as did Prost, and both went charging into La Source with the others half-heartedly in pursuit except for Surer, de Angelis and Laffite, the Frenchman having correctly switched off. The officials, though, quickly took steps to stop the 'race' and a few minutes later the transgressors had all re-assembled on the grid, by which time Surer's Arrows had been wheeled away into the pits and the disappointed Swiss was preparing to take the second start from the pit lane in the team's spare car. Meanwhile, in the delay that arose, the Ferrari and Renault mechanics were seen stepping over the barriers in front of the pits armed with churns of petrol and showing every sign of proposing to top up their cars' fuel tanks. Now this was strictly forbidden by the rules and led to an incensed Frank Williams lodging official protests over the matter. Later, after Ferrari's Marco Piccinini had convinced him that he had called his mechanics back before they had reached either Tambay or Arnoux's cars, Williams withdrew the protest against the Italian team but, in spite of Jean Sage insisting that no fuel had been added to the pair of RE40s, Renault were fined $5,000 for taking fuel out on to the grid. An expensive exercise, and a rather pointless one for while preparations were being made for the restart the organizers announced that the race distance was to be reduced from the original 42 laps to 40 so as to allow for the abortive lap and a second pace lap.

At the restart, which came some 15 minutes after the false start, de Cesaris took off like a scalded cat and went squeezing

between Prost's Renault and Tambay's Ferrari in a most forceful manner to once again lead the pack into La Source. Here, all 25 cars (Surer's Arrows was being held back in the pit lane) subsequently rounded the extremely tight turn in one piece despite Piquet and Arnoux bumping wheels, which forced Cheever to run very wide, and were soon crossing the timing/finishing line to start the first lap proper, this, unlike the start-line, still being situated opposite the old pits on the hill leading down to Eau Rouge. For Patrese, though, the Belgian Grand Prix was to be a very brief affair. As the field plunged through Eau Rouge and tore up the hill towards Les Combes the BMW engine in his Brabham suddenly blew up. Consequently, Patrese could do no more than pull off to the side of the track prior to beginning a lonely walk back to the pits. Meanwhile, the rest of the field were soon coming round to complete the opening lap with de Cesaris still leading and having already pulled three or four car lengths clear of Prost, in second place. Third was Tambay and he, in turn, was being hotly pursued by team-mate Arnoux, Piquet, Winkelhock, Rosberg, Laffite, Cheever, Baldi, de Angelis and the impressive Guerrero who had qualified well in his Theodore and was now holding 12th place in the race ahead of the others. Naturally, though, it was the leaders who were attracting the attention and de Cesaris, in particular, for there was no doubt about it the Italian was driving superbly and making the most of what appeared to be a very strong engine. Furthermore, he continued steadily building up his lead in spite of Prost seemingly pushing his Renault to the limit, and after five laps had opened up a clear advantage of more than 2 seconds. By then his team-mate's race had already ended, Baldi having turned off into the pits on lap 4 to retire the other Alfa Romeo with a throttle linkage problem. Boutsen, too, had stopped at the same time to complain that the back of his Arrows felt unstable and although he had since gone out again on fresh tyres only another lap passed before the Belgian concluded his debut by returning to the pits for good – when the problem was finally traced to a broken rear rocker arm.

After ten laps there was no change up front except that de Cesaris had now extended his lead over Prost to almost 5 seconds and was looking totally unassailable. A further couple of seconds away, Tambay was still holding on reasonably well in third place but Arnoux, who had earlier been pressing his team-mate quite hard, had dropped back a bit because of his engine losing its edge. Instead, the Frenchman was, himself, now coming under increasing pressure from Piquet, with Winkelhock and the irrepressible Rosberg, doing wonders in the normally-aspirated Williams, watching it all from a short distance away. There was a lot

The opening lap of the re-started Belgian Grand Prix as the cars stream down the hill past the old pits into Eau Rouge, led by the Euroracing Alfa Romeo 183T of Andrea de Cesaris. *(Autocar & Motor)*

of close racing taking place lower down the order as well, nowhere more so than in mid-field where de Angelis, Guerrero, Lauda and Giacomelli, all running in tight formation, had recently been joined by a fast-rising Warwick obviously intent on making up for his lowly starting position. In fact, the Englishman was already working his way through this group, having swopped places with his team-mate on lap 9 and just blasted past Lauda and Guerrero in quick succession on the rise from Eau Rouge. Further back, Jarier had also been picking up a few places in his Ligier, but a recent attempt to go round Watson on the outside at La Source had ended in disaster due to the Frenchman clouting the McLaren's left front wheel with his right rear wheel and putting both of them out on the spot with suspension damage. Meanwhile, it was not long before Winkelhock's good drive in sixth place started to turn sour. First his BMW engine began popping and banging as he came round to complete his 11th lap, which enabled Rosberg to

overtake him prior to stopping off at the pits on lap 12. Then, after eventually rejoining the race well and truly in last place with a broken fuel-injector pipe having been replaced, only another seven laps passed before he underwent the terrifying experience of his ATS shedding its right rear wheel. It happened on the way through the fast double-apex left-hander at the bottom of the new section of track and led to his car careering off, backwards, through the catchfences and on into the guard-rail beyond from where, much to everyone's relief, the German subsequently walked away completely unharmed.

After several laps of visibly struggling to keep Piquet at bay, clearly illustrated by his Ferrari constantly riding up over the kerbs (this had already led to its left front brake duct breaking away!), Arnoux finally lost his fourth place to the Brazilian on the way down the hill from La Source on lap 17. However, this was soon to become academic as after being amongst the first to stop for

fuel and tyres two laps later, the Frenchman disappeared from the lap charts altogether on lap 23 when his engine suddenly blew up out on the circuit – just one lap before Guerrero suffered a similar fate in his well-driven Theodore. In the meantime, de Cesaris had also made his pit stop on lap 19 and an agonisingly long delay of 25.3 seconds, resulting from nothing more than sheer inefficiency, had not only cost the Italian his lead, which had previously grown to 7 seconds, but dropped him to sixth place behind Prost, Tambay, Piquet, Rosberg and Cheever. Furthermore, even after the others had taken their turn to stop, he was still left in a distant second place, 10 seconds behind Prost. That was bad enough but much worse was to follow when, on lap 26, and still pressing on as hard as ever to try to wipe out the deficit, de Cesaris had a fine drive brought to an unhappy end when the Alfa V8 expired at the top of the hill from Eau Rouge. Unfortunately, this incident also ended any real hopes of an exciting climax for it left Prost 27 seconds clear of Piquet, who automatically took over the second spot, and all the Frenchman had to do now was to keep going. Even so, there was still some close racing to savour, for now that the order had settled down again somewhat after the round of pit stops Tambay was only a couple of seconds behind Piquet, following a marginally slower stop, while Cheever was not that much further away in fourth place after having just beaten the still hard-charging Rosberg out of the pits back on lap 20. To add to the interest a non-stop run in his McLaren had moved Lauda right on to Laffite's tail in sixth place, and further back still Warwick was starting to enliven proceedings all over again with another charge, from 12th place, after being forced to stop twice for fuel because of considerable problems in the Toleman pit caused by a troublesome fuel-line nozzle.

As the race entered its final phase Piquet's hopes of holding on to second place received a severe setback when he lost the use of fifth gear in his Brabham. Nowhere was the effect more apparent than on the long uphill section leading to Les Combes, and it was here that he eventually had to more or less sit and watch as first Tambay and then Cheever took advantage of his predicament to go rushing past on laps 34 and 38 respectively. All the while Prost was stroking home to a most comfortable second victory of the season, easing off and yet still going on to take the chequered flag at the end of the 40 laps with over 23 seconds in hand. Only 8 seconds behind Piquet at the finish, Rosberg crossed the line in a thoroughly well-deserved fifth place, team-mate Laffite was a distant sixth and the result of a hard afternoon's work from Warwick was scantly rewarded with an eventual seventh place. Lauda, meanwhile, had been forced to retire at the pits on lap 34

1983

The champagne flows after the race as Alain Prost celebrates his second victory of the season in the company of team-mate Eddie Cheever and Patrick Tambay, who finished in second place in his Ferrari. *(Autosport)*

with a broken valve and an attempt by Giacomelli to catch Laffite in the closing stages had ended on the last lap by the Italian spinning, lightly glancing the barriers and losing his place to Warwick before recovering to wind up eighth. After that the remaining six runners still there at the finish (Fabi and Mansell had been the only other retirements with broken rear suspension and a broken gearbox oil pump respectively) were all at least a lap down, including Alboreto who had dropped to last place following a late pit stop in a fruitless effort to cure worsening gearbox trouble.

Regrettably, a fine afternoon's racing ended in considerable controversy and confusion. Already, of course, there were the protests against Ferrari and Renault for allegedly topping up their cars' fuel tanks on the grid, but now Brabham had also lodged a protest against Renault. This concerned the revised exhaust system introduced on the RE40s immediately prior to Monaco as it was being argued that the exhaust gases from the re-routed exhaust pipes were being used to reduce the turbulence of the air around the back of the cars and thus improving the under-car aerodynamics. In other words, the exhaust gases were considered to be a 'moveable aerodynamic device' and as such there was some doubt as to whether this was illegal or not. To add more fuel to the fire, Renault joined in the action by pointing out to the organizers that the Williams team had not acted in accordance with the regulations after the race. First Rosberg and Laffite had both failed to complete a slowing-down lap – apparently because they were both very low on fuel – and neither car had been taken to the parc fermé for possible scrutineering within the allotted time. However, after a couple of hours of deliberations the organizers eventually issued a Press Release to the effect that all three protests had been withdrawn, that no-one was being disqualified and that, in consequence, the results stood. In fact, the only positive action taken was to fine Renault $5000 for taking fuel out on to the grid, as already mentioned.

Results						Retirements
1	A. Prost (Renault)	1 hr 27 min 11.502 sec (191.729 kph/ 119.135 mph)	8	B. Giacomelli (Toleman-Hart)	1 hr 29 min 49.775 sec	R. Patrese (Brabham-BMW) engine on lap 1, M. Baldi (Alfa Romeo) throttle linkage on lap 4, T. Boutsen (Arrows-Ford) rear suspension on lap 5, J. Watson (McLaren-Ford) accident on lap 9, J.P. Jarier (Ligier-Ford) accident on lap 9, M. Winkelhock (ATS-BMW) accident on lap 19, C. Fabi (Osella-Ford) rear suspension on lap 20, R. Arnoux (Ferrari) engine on lap 23, R. Guerrero (Theodore-Ford) engine on lap 24, A. de Cesaris (Alfa Romeo) engine on lap 26, N. Mansell (Lotus-Ford) gearbox on lap 31, N. Lauda (McLaren-Ford) engine on lap 34.
2	P. Tambay (Ferrari)	1 hr 27 min 34.684 sec	9	E. de Angelis (Lotus-Renault)	1 lap behind	
3	E. Cheever (Renault)	1 hr 27 min 51.371 sec	10	J. Cecotto (Theodore-Ford)	1 lap behind	
4	N. Piquet (Brabham-BMW)	1 hr 27 min 53.797 sec	11	M. Surer (Arrows-Ford)	1 lap behind	
5	K. Rosberg (Williams-Ford)	1 hr 28 min 01.982 sec	12	D. Sullivan (Tyrrell-Ford)	1 lap behind	
6	J. Laffite (Williams-Ford)	1 hr 28 min 44.609 sec	13	R. Boesel (Ligier-Ford)	1 lap behind	
7	D. Warwick (Toleman-Hart)	1 hr 29 min 10.041 sec	14	M. Alboreto (Tyrrell-Ford)	2 laps behind	

Fastest lap: A. de Cesaris (Alfa Romeo) on lap 17 in 2 min 07.493 sec (196.217 kph/ 121.923 mph)

IInd United States (Detroit) Grand Prix

Detroit: June 5
Weather: Warm and sunny
Distance: 60 laps of 4.0233 km
circuit = 241.40 km (150.00 miles)

From the wide open spaces of the magnificent Spa-Francorchamps circuit it was now time to go street-racing again with the Grand Prix scene moving on to Detroit, in spite of the fact that 12 months earlier the future of this then new addition to the calendar had looked decidedly shaky. For the teams it was

all a bit of a rush as there had not been much more than a week in which to return home from Belgium and crate everything up for air-freighting across the Atlantic. And, because the Canadian Grand Prix was scheduled for the following weekend, it had meant packing sufficient cars, spare parts and

equipment to see them all through both races. Consequently, in view of such a tight time-table, it was no surprise to find the bulk of the entry totally familiar as preparations began for the start of practice on the Friday morning, the only really noticeable aspect being the absence of John MacDonald's RAM team. Quite simply they had been forced to withdraw their entry because of financial problems arising from Salazar's recent lack of success in achieving the results necessary to continue attracting the support of his Chilean sponsors. Otherwise, it was very much a case of the same drivers in the same cars with just the odd modification here and there, although one team to have been particularly busy since Belgium were ATS. In addition to having completely rebuilt Winkelhock's race car after the frightening accident caused by the right rear wheel dropping off, they had carried out major alterations to their older, spare car in order to try out a new and lower turbo-charger installation and exhaust system. This revised layout also included moving the radiators and intercoolers further back, and it made way for the car to have shorter, Williams-like, side-pods to give it a much tidier appearance altogether. Because there had been insufficient time to do much in the way of testing, however, the German team were proposing,

initially at least, to still concentrate on their regular race chassis.

Since the inaugural race in 1982 the organizers had responded to criticism over their circuit by making one or two small, though nonetheless important, alterations. Primarily, these were the easing of the chicane before the pits, extending the pit lane so that the entrance was now before the chicane rather than beside it – a much safer arrangement – and the replacement of Turns 5 and 6 (the ridiculously tight hairpin and 90-degree right-hander that immediately followed on the outward leg) by a short, new section of track. This left the original circuit by means of a gentle left-hander just before the start of the old hairpin and continued straight across the dual-carriageway to link up with the existing straight leading to Turn 7. Naturally these improvements were openly welcomed, and even a delay of some 50 minutes before practice could actually commence (this was due to work still being in progress to seal off the circuit from any potential non-paying members of the public) was being looked at in much the same light: in the previous year the circuit had not been ready until late afternoon. As luck would have it, though, by the time that the all-clear had been given rain was falling and this, together with the fact that the pits were out in the open, resulted in a distinct lack of enthusiasm being apparent to begin with. Nevertheless, it wasn't long before the first engines were being fired up and, eventually, drivers started taking to the track only to find their chances of learning very much being thwarted by the rain continuing, intermittently, throughout the whole 90 minutes. To make matters worse the rain later came on harder than ever so that when it came round to the first hour of qualifying the already difficult conditions had become next to impossible. But, as was to be expected with no guarantee that the weather would be any better over the rest of the weekend, everyone went out on rain tyres at some time or another and between them put on a wonderful display as they slid and slithered around the tight confines. Spins were also a common occurrence. Even so, apart from Prost, Tambay and Guerrero all winding up with dented nose cones and Winkelhock marking up the bodywork of his ATS after a slight contretemps with Sullivan's Tyrrell, the only damage of any consequence was to the right rear corner of Laffite's Williams when the Frenchman lost adhesion on his way through the chicane and spun into the wall in front of the pits. Meanwhile Rosberg, in the other Williams, was putting on a particularly spectacular performance, and by somehow keeping off the walls saw his efforts ultimately rewarded with the afternoon's fastest time of 2 min 06.382 sec. Although this represented an average speed of only 114.604 kph (71.212 mph), it was still mighty impressive

under the circumstances besides being well over a second quicker than anyone else; Jarier and Mansell, rather surprisingly, being next up at 2 min 07.652 sec and 2 min 07.792 sec respectively after two more particularly courageous efforts. For a change the turbo-charged cars were largely out of the picture. Indeed, just about all of them looked to be a real handful on the soaking wet track and at the finish only de Cesaris's well-driven Alfa Romeo (fourth fastest at 2 min 08.034 sec), Cheever's Renault and Arnoux's Ferrari featured in the first ten places on the time-sheets.

The skies were still grey and overcast on the following morning, but at least the rain had stopped, and when practice resumed at 10 a.m. with a futher 90 minute untimed session the track was virtually dry. As a result the overall scene immediately became one of frantic activity, for not only were drivers anxious to make up for lost time but they now had to try to quickly sort their cars on dry settings in readiness for what was going to be an even more important final hour of qualifying than usual – assuming that the rain continued to hold off. Some drivers were obviously more successful than others if the unofficial lap times were anything to go by and a real surprise was to see Rosberg being left behind somewhat, the World Champion complaining of lack of grip besides suffering from a heavy head cold which the wet practice had obviously done nothing to improve. Instead it was Piquet who came out on top this time, closely followed by Alboreto, after finding the latest Ford-Cosworth DFY engine offering good acceleration out of the many tight turns, and Prost. De Angelis, fastest of all during the previous morning, was also well in the running and driving with much more enthusiasm than of late, stronger wishbones in the rear suspension of his Lotus 93T, combined with stiffer Pirelli tyres and a large double rear aerofoil (a similar set-up was also being tried on Mansell's only fractionally slower Lotus 92), having apparently transformed the handling of the car.

By 1 p.m. clear patches of blue sky were beginning to appear so it now became obvious that for the third race on the trot the entire grid would be decided by just one hour of qualifying. Although there had been a few mechanical problems during the morning most of them had since been rectified and the only driver confined to his team's spare car was Cecotto after having damaged the left rear corner of his Theodore against a wall too badly for the necessary repair work to be completed in time. As usual, once the action started some drivers were seen holding back in the pits longer than others, and on this occasion it was to prove crucial. For some strange reason, after the first 15 minutes or so the track conditions gradually changed but instead of becoming faster as more and

Starting Grid

R. Arnoux Ferrari (1 min 44.734 sec)	
	N. Piquet Brabham-BMW (1 min 44.933 sec)
P. Tambay Ferrari (1 min 45.991 sec)	
	E. de Angelis Lotus-Renault (1 min 46.258 sec)
M. Surer Arrows-Ford (1 min 46.745 sec)	
	M. Alboreto Tyrrell-Ford (1 min 47.013 sec)
E. Cheever Renault (1 min 47.334 sec)	
	A. de Cesaris Alfa Romeo (1 min 47.453 sec)
D. Warwick Toleman-Hart (1 min 47.534 sec)	
	T. Boutsen Arrows-Ford (1 min 47.586 sec)
R. Guerrero Theodore-Ford (1 min 47.701 sec)	
	K. Rosberg Williams-Ford (1 min 47.728 sec)
A. Prost Renault (1 min 47.855 sec)	
	N. Mansell Lotus-Ford (1 min 48.395 sec)
R. Patrese Brabham-BMW (1 min 48.537 sec)	
	D. Sullivan Tyrrell-Ford (1 min 48.648 sec)
B.Giacomelli Toleman-Hart (1 min 48.785 sec)	
	N. Lauda McLaren-Ford (1 min 48.992 sec)
J.P. Jarier Ligier-Ford (1 min 48.994 sec)	
	J. Laffite Williams-Ford (1 min 49.245 sec)
J. Watson McLaren-Ford (1 min 49.250 sec)	
	M. Winkelhock ATS-BMW (1 min 49.466 sec)
R. Boesel Ligier-Ford (1 min 49.540 sec)	
	P. Ghinzani Osella-Alfa Romeo (1 min 49.885 sec)
M. Baldi Alfa Romeo (1 min 49.916 sec)	
	J. Cecotto Theodore-Ford (1 min 51.709 sec)

Did not qualify:
C. Fabi (Osella-Ford 1 min 53.516 sec

rubber went down they became slower. The most logical explanation was that the warm afternoon sun began drawing moisture from the track surface and produced an invisible film of water which, in turn, led to tyres losing a certain amount of grip. Whatever, the effect was quite dramatic, for it resulted in the fastest times all coming in the opening spell and those drivers to go out early deriving an appreciable advantage over their more tardy rivals, a fact clearly confirmed by Arnoux. He recorded a pole-winning time of 1 min 44.734 sec almost immediately on his first set of qualifying tyres, in spite of making light contact with the guard-rail, yet was more than 2 seconds slower when he later went out on his second set. Naturally, it also produced a number of anomalies, for whilst its was reasonable enough to see Piquet (1 min 44.933 sec) and Tambay (1 min 45.991 sec) snatch the next two places on the grid immediately ahead of a pretty consistent de Angelis, after all three had also more or less gone straight out, some of the other drivers normally associated with the front end of the grid lost out badly. This was particularly true of the Renault duo, who soon realized their mistake in waiting around in the hope that the rising temperature would encourage their Michelin tyres to perform better. As it was, Cheever had to work really hard to qualify seventh fastest behind the two nimble and well-driven Ford-Cosworth-powered cars of Surer and Alboreto, while Prost, failing to come to terms with a handling imbalance, was left to line up in an uncharacteristically low 13th place on the grid. The Williams team, too, made the understandable mistake of running their harder tyres first, saving their softest qualifiers for later. Consequently, although Rosberg and Laffite, back in his original car following overnight repairs, both set their best times towards the end of the session it meant virtually nothing: Rosberg was a disappointed 12th in the standings immediately behind Boutsen (belying his lack of experience) and Guerrero, while Laffite finished up no less than eight places lower in amongst Jarier's Ligier and the two tyre-troubled (as usual!) McLarens of Lauda and Watson. There were other hard-luck stories as well. Amongst them were Patrese who, having opted to use the spare Brabham that he had taken over earlier in the day following problems with a fuel leak, had qualified in only 15th place after being unable to find a clear lap; Winkelhock who had been forced to resort to the largely untried spare and heavily-modified ATS soon after the start of qualifying because of a broken oil pipe and come out a pretty despondent 22nd; and Fabi who had tried just about everything he knew to overcome engine problems with both Ford-Cosworth-powered Osella FA1Ds on hand but still wound up as the only non-qualifier. For the Osella team, though, there

was at least some consolation as Ghinzani had finally qualified the Alfa Romeo-powered FA1E and was now looking forward to taking part in only his second-ever Grand Prix.

Following the rather unseasonable weather experienced throughout much of practice, race day was absolutely superb, and this obviously helped to attract a sizeable crowd (estimated at over 70,000) to the circuit during the morning in addition to numerous other spectators out in a large flotilla of boats bobbing about on the Detroit River. In many ways the atmosphere was not unlike that normally associated with Monaco, for there were various parties in progress and everyone seemed to be thoroughly enjoying themselves as they awaited the start of the Grand Prix. The teams were all in a fairly relaxed mood as well with final preparations having been made all the more straightforward by a virtually trouble-free warm-up session that had got under way at the early hour of 9.15 a.m. owing to the race being scheduled for 12.15 p.m. Only the final choice of tyre compounds was causing any sort of problem, and this was not being made any easier by a certain amount of indecision by some of the teams over whether or not to go ahead with refuelling/tyre stops during the race. Renault seemed to be particularly unsure of which was the right way to go but, like everybody else, eventually had to make up their minds and in the end came to the conclusion that the RE40s would be too hard on their brakes and tyres to risk a full-tank run. Rather more sure of themselves, Ferrari, Euroracing Alfa Romeo and Toleman were also proposing to go ahead with the pit stop routine. But others, such as Brabham and Williams, were unforthcoming as to precisely what they intended doing, and even when the cars started leaving the pits for the warm-up lap just before noon their plans were still not clear, which was all rather intriguing.

After the usual countdown, Arnoux led the field around on the pace lap, and soon the 26 cars were forming on the grid once more to face the starting lights. Just as Derek Ongaro was about to put on the red light, however, he noticed that de Cesaris suddenly had his hand in the air to signify a stalled engine, so promptly held up the 'start delayed' board instead. At that point the other drivers all followed the correct procedure by switching off and prepared themselves to undergo the starting procedure again which, in accordance with the rules, meant that there would be a five-minute delay and that the race distance would be reduced by one lap, from 61 to 60, to allow for another pace lap. Even after that, though, the start still proved to be a bit chaotic for when the green light eventually came on nearly 10 minutes later Tambay's Ferrari barely moved. Incredibly, the

Frenchman had now stalled his engine! This time, of course, it was too late to do anything about it – the race had started – with the result that Tambay had to sit there holding his breath while the drivers behind him scrambled past, fortunately without resulting in any untoward incidents. After they had gone Tambay fully expected to be push-started, instead of which he found his car being hitched up to a tow-truck and being unceremoniously removed from the circuit. Now this was not at all what was supposed to happen under such circumstances, as had already been indicated by the officials at the Drivers' Briefing in the morning, so when the normally placid Tambay eventually stepped out of his car he was absolutely furious over the treatment that he had just received. In the meantime, the others were soon filing through the chicane and blasting past the pits to complete the opening lap with Piquet clearly leading after having beaten Arnoux away at the start. Behind the sole surviving Ferrari, de Angelis was in third place, but only on the road as he had been adjudged to have jumped the start and was being penalized one minute for his over-exuberance, as was Winkelhock, driving the more familiar of the two ATS D6s, for similar reasons. After de Angelis came de Cesaris, Alboreto, Warwick, Rosberg (already up to seventh place), Cheever and then Boutsen and Surer in their two Arrows before Prost and the rest of the field.

Piquet and Arnoux went on to completely dominate the early stages of the race and were soon entirely out on their own, engaged in an exciting leadership tussle. Even so, this was by no means the only point of interest for whilst de Angelis appeared to be having little difficulty in holding down third place, Alboreto, Warwick and Rosberg were running absolutely nose to tail behind de Cesaris with the World Champion all but climbing over the back of the Toleman in his efforts to get by. Prost, too, was leaving no-one in any doubts that he was intent on making up for his low grid position as quickly as possible by sailing past Surer on the second lap and immediately launching an all-out attack on Boutsen. Unfortunately, though, in his haste to overtake the Belgian, Prost made a rare error of judgement under braking for one of the many tight turns, touched the back of the Arrows and tore away the right-hand nose fin of his Renault against its left rear wheel. Needless to say, this instantly upset the car's handling and effectively ended the Frenchman's hopes of hoisting himself up amongst the leaders, although he did at least dispose of Boutsen shortly afterwards without too much difficulty. His team-mate, meanwhile, was soon in far worse trouble as on the fifth lap Cheever suffered an ignition failure and went coasting to rest out on the circuit with a dead engine. At the end of the same lap de Angelis was also forced to park his Lotus

René Arnoux takes a look down the inside of Nelson Piquet's Brabham as they head towards the first double left-hander after the pits during the midst of their early leadership tussle. The abandoned car is the Lotus 93T of Elio de Angelis. *(Autosport)*

when its crown-wheel and pinion broke on the way out of the chicane, and only a few moments later Ghinzani went limping into the pits to retire his Osella, the V12 Alfa Romeo engine overheating badly besides being low on oil pressure. All the while Piquet and Arnoux were leaving everyone else further and further behind with nothing to choose between them. At the start of the tenth lap, however, Arnoux finally decided that he had had enough of following the Brabham and made a successful stab at wrestling the lead away from his adversary going into the first double left-hander after the pits. Once in front, Arnoux then immediately began to draw away dramatically, which suggested that Piquet had been holding him up. Either way it was of little consequence to the Brazilian as he knew only too well that Arnoux would be stopping for fuel and tyres later in the race whereas, contrary to expectations, he was proposing to go through non-stop.

As Arnoux continued to power away into the distance, more and more attention became focused on Rosberg who, by the end of the lap 11, had come through to third place and was now beginning to eat into a near-15 second deficit to Piquet. Alboreto was another worth keeping an eye on, especially as his Tyrrell had started out on full tanks, for not only was he still running ahead of Warwick, but he was also looking all set to take over fourth place from de Cesaris at any moment. There was still a lot going on further down the field as well where Laffite was making particularly good progress, as he had been ever since the start. In fact, by lap 13 the French Williams driver had worked his way up to eighth place and was hard on

the heels of Prost's Renault. With his front tyres going off due to vicious understeer caused by the loss of the nose fin, there was not a lot that Prost could do about it either, so it came as no real surprise on lap 16 to see him being overhauled by his compatriot. Furthermore, whilst Laffite charged off in pursuit of de Cesaris (he had just dropped behind Alboreto and Warwick in quick succession with his tyres also starting to go off), Prost lasted only another three laps before veering off into the pits for fresh rubber and in the hope of having a new nose fin fitted to his car. However, it was decided that the task of replacing the lost part would take too long and so, once all four wheels had been changed and the fuel topped up, Prost was sent on his way again to persevere as best he could – only now in an even more hopeless-looking 14th place after Boutsen, Guerrero, Sullivan, Watson, Mansell and Winkelhock had all gone on ahead whilst he had been stationary. By this time Jarier, already on his third set of Michelins, Patrese, Lauda and Baldi had also been into the pits for fresh rubber and what had promised to be a good race for Surer, after his superb performance in final qualifying, had gone from bad to worse. At the start he had been badly boxed in behind Tambay and then, after only a few laps, some paper had partially blocked off one of the Arrows' water radiators, causing an overheating problem and leading to the Swiss being black-flagged on the misunderstanding that water dripping out of the radiator overflow pipe had been oil! He would have had to have stopped in any case in order that the offending paper could be removed but the extra time lost in convincing the officials that there was no oil leak had cost

him well over a lap and put him right out of the picture.

By lap 20 Rosberg had completely wiped out the deficit to Piquet and before the lap was over went by him with surprising ease to take up station in second place. At this point he was around 20 seconds behind Arnoux but any prospects of catching him were soon looking pretty remote: instead of the gap coming down it increased until at the end of lap 29 when the Ferrari was seen heading for the pits to undergo its scheduled refuelling/tyre stop. Almost exactly 25 seconds later, Rosberg also turned off the track for the same reason, thus ending any further speculation over his intentions. However, whereas Arnoux succeeded in rejoining the race without losing his lead (just!) a slight problem with the Williams' right rear wheel, combined with the fact that he was that much further in arrears, resulted in Rosberg slipping back to fifth place behind Piquet, Alboreto and Laffite. It would have been seventh but a few minutes earlier Warwick had gone into the pits with his engine misfiring and had subsequently retired with just one more lap under his belt, while de Cesaris was now in the process of making his planned pit stop. Even so, Rosberg was soon moving up again, as on lap 32 Arnoux saw an almost certain victory disappear when the Ferrari's electronic fuel-injection system suddenly failed, bringing him to a halt out on the circuit with a dead engine, and at the end of the same lap it was time for Laffite to stop for his tyres and fuel. Consequently, Rosberg automatically moved up into third place where he was some 25 seconds behind Piquet who, in turn, was left holding a precarious lead over Alboreto. In the meantime, the drama and excitement was by no means confined to the leaders for all manner of things had been happening lower down the order. For a start Guerrero had been obliged to relinquish a strong mid-field position at the end of lap 22 because of broken gear linkage; on the following lap Lauda and Jarier had both followed him into the pits for yet more tyres; and two laps after that Warwick had pulled up with his engine problem only to have found himself being joined in retirement by Patrese due to the spare Brabham that the Italian had chosen to race having used up its brakes. More recently, on lap 27, Winkelhock had crawled into the pits with both the front and the rear suspension damaged on the right-hand side of his ATS, the result of having glanced the barriers at the exit from the Atwater tunnel, and since then there had been two more retirements in quick succession. First Sullivan had parked his Tyrrell out on the circuit with a dead engine – the problem was later traced to no more than a loose electrical connection. Then Jarier, intending to try his fifth set of Michelins, had been forced to call it a day when the Ligier mechanics discovered that

The surprise winner of the race, Michele Alboreto in the Benetton-sponsored Tyrrell 011. *(L.A.T. Photographic)*

the retaining nut for his car's right front wheel was jammed. As a result of all of this it was now almost like a different race with the order behind Rosberg having become Watson, in fourth place, followed by Laffite (after his pit stop), a tiring Boutsen (he had earlier only just survived a big moment through the chicane), Mansell, Prost and Cecotto. Then, in tenth place and having just rejoined the race a lap behind the leaders after his planned pit stop, it was Giacomelli with de Cesaris, Boesel, Surer, Lauda and Baldi all strung out behind. Even this situation didn't last long, though, as at the end of lap 34 de Cesaris retired at the pits with a turbo failure after having just recovered from a spin three laps earlier whilst attempting to repass Boutsen. Then, at the end of the following lap, Cecotto was also forced to retire at the pits with similar gear-linkage problems to those of his team-mate, which the Theodore mechanics were still trying to repair along with a broken engine mounting.

Over the next dozen or so laps the race finally did settle down again with the only changes coming on lap 39, when Mansell caught and passed Boutsen for sixth place, and shortly afterwards when Guerrero made a surprise reappearance in his Theodore

despite having lost around twenty laps while repairs were being carried out in the pits. Even so it was certainly no less interesting for, apart from slight variations caused by the lapping of slower cars, the gap between Piquet (running only a modest amount of boost pressure to conserve fuel) and Alboreto was seldom more than a couple of seconds. Watson, too, was staying well within striking distance of Rosberg's third-placed Williams, even mounting a serious challenge at one point before dropping back a bit. Indeed, everything augured well for a really exciting finish in spite of the fact that Piquet appeared to be in full control of the situation. But then, on lap 51, came another dramatic twist to the race: Piquet suddenly slowed as he felt the first effects of a punctured left rear tyre, and went on to spend the rest of the lap limping round to the pits as first Alboreto and then Rosberg surged past him, with Watson also moving ahead as he made his way along the pit lane. In the pits all four wheels were changed and a few litres of fuel added but even though the Brabham mechanics carried out the job with their usual efficiency Piquet could do little more than to drive for a finish in fourth place after that. Meanwhile, as Alboreto reeled off the

final nine laps at his own pace to come out a happy and surprised winner, Watson put on a real spurt in the closing stages and only just failed in his efforts to catch Rosberg. Instead, the Ulsterman had to settle for a close, though nonetheless satisfying, third place ahead of a rather dejected Piquet. After that only Laffite, in fifth place, completed the full 60 laps, but there were still another eight cars running at the finish as no other retirements had occurred apart from Lauda pulling out late in the race with his McLaren having become virtually undriveable because of a seized shock-absorber.

Almost as soon as the race had ended the Brabham team followed up their action at Spa-Francorchamps a fortnight earlier by lodging another protest against Renault's revised exhaust system. In response, the French team also protested Piquet's Brabham on the grounds that the car's rear aerofoil exceeded the maximum permitted height on one side. The organizers, however, subsequently turned down both protests – any infringement by the Brabham team was found to be immeasurable – so, once again, nothing was achieved other than to delay the official confirmation of the results.

Results		
1	M. Alboreto (Tyrrell-Ford)	1 hr 50 min 53.669 sec (130.611 kph/ 81.158 mph)
2	K. Rosberg (Williams-Ford)	1 hr 51 min 01.371 sec
3	J. Watson (McLaren-Ford)	1 hr 51 min 02.952 sec
4	N. Piquet (Brabham-BMW)	1 hr 52 min 05.854 sec
5	J. Laffite (Williams-Ford)	1 hr 52 min 26.272 sec
6	N. Mansell (Lotus-Ford)	1 lap behind
7	T. Boutsen (Arrows-Ford)	1 lap behind
8	A. Prost (Renault)	1 lap behind
9	B. Giacomelli (Toleman-Hart)	1 lap behind
10	R. Boesel (Ligier-Ford)	2 laps behind
11	M. Surer (Arrows-Ford)	2 laps behind
12	M. Baldi (Alfa Romeo)	4 laps behind

Also running at finish: R. Guerrero (Theodore-Ford) 22 laps behind.

Fastest lap: J. Watson (McLaren-Ford) on lap 55 in 1 min 47.668 sec (134.525 kph/83.590 mph)

Retirements

P. Tambay (Ferrari) stalled at start, E. Cheever (Renault) ignition on lap 5, P. Ghinzani (Osella-Alfa Romeo) engine on lap 5, E. de Angelis (Lotus-Renault) crownwheel and pinion on lap 6, R. Patrese (Brabham-BMW) brakes on lap 25, D. Warwick (Toleman-Hart) engine on lap 26, M. Winkelhock (ATS-BMW) accident damage on lap 27, J.P. Jarier (Ligier-Ford) wheel nut on lap 30, D. Sullivan (Tyrrell-Ford) electrics on lap 31, R. Arnoux (Ferrari) fuel-injection on lap 32, A. de Cesaris (Alfa Romeo) turbocharger on lap 34, J. Cecotto (Theodore-Ford) gear linkage on lap 35, N. Lauda (McLaren-Ford) shock-absorber on lap 50.

1983

XXIInd Canadian Grand Prix

Montreal: June 12
Weather: Hot
Distance: 70 laps of 4.410 km
circuit = 308.70 km (191.82 miles)

Just five days after the incident-packed Detroit Grand Prix the teams had completed the 500-odd mile trek to Montreal and were ready to start all over again on the 4.41 kilometre Circuit Gilles Villeneuve, situated on the man-made Ile Notre Dame in the St Lawrence Seaway. Naturally, with such a short gap between the two races, combined with the amount of travelling involved, nobody had had the time to do very much other than to dust down their cars and carry out essential repairs, so the entry was virtually identical to that of the previous weekend. In fact, the only obvious change apart from the outward appearance of Surer's Arrows, which was being sponsored on a one-off basis by decaffeinated Pepsi (the sponsorship tie-up with Barclay cigarettes had ended after Detroit), was the return of the RAM team to the fold. Here, following Eliseo Salazar's cash-flow problems, John MacDonald had invited Jacques Villeneuve to drive for him over the weekend, the North American Formula Atlantic Champion, who had tried, unsuccessfully, to qualify the second Arrows for the same race (and Las Vegas) two years earlier, having received the necessary sponsorship from Canadian Tires and Avis.

The first day's practice took place in mainly cool and overcast conditions and turned out to be a Ferrari benefit with Tambay and Arnoux both taking to the circuit like the proverbial duck and setting the pace virtually from the word 'go'. In the morning, when drivers were concentrating on trying to sort their cars, Tambay was fastest, unofficially, and looked to be carrying on in the same authoritative manner during the afternoon until Arnoux stepped in and eventually stopped the clocks at an unbeaten 1 min 28.984 sec. This was an absolutely splendid performance, marred only by the Frenchman making himself extremely unpopular with Piquet, Cheever and de Angelis after moving over on them at different times when he had apparently failed to look in his mirrors whilst taking things comparatively easy. Fortunately, all three drivers had managed to keep their cars under control, despite having been forced badly off line, but no-one was left in any doubts as to their views on the matter – least of all Arnoux! His equally impressive team-mate, meanwhile, conducted himself in a rather less controversial manner and overcame a slight handling deficiency (this was particularly pronounced through the bumpy ess-bend after the pits where his Ferrari was tending to skip off line rather alarmingly) to end the afternoon a mere eight-thousandths slower, Tambay's best lap coming out at

1 min 28.992 sec. True to form, the main opposition to the Ferraris came from Renault and Brabham even though both teams had their share of problems. At Renault, Prost had his engine blow up in a big way on his first set of qualifying tyres, and was forced to complete practice in his team's spare car; while at Brabham, who had carried out subtle aerodynamic revisions to the BT52s, Piquet had taken over his spare car even earlier after having experienced poor throttle response out of the slower turns during the morning. That was not all, as following a brief shower of rain mid-way through the timed hour, which sent everyone scurrying for the shelter of the pits for a few minutes, Patrese later went out on the quickly drying track and promptly understeered off into the barriers. Consequently he, too, had to complete practice in his spare Brabham due to the impact badly damaging both the front and the rear suspension on the left-hand side of his proposed race chassis. At the end of the day, though, the Italian's best lap of 1 min 31.227 sec was still sixth fastest, behind the Ferrari duo, Prost (1 min 29.942 sec), Cheever (1 min 30.255 sec) and Piquet (1 min 30.366 sec). In the meantime, following the brief respite provided by the somewhat tighter confines of Detroit, the non-turbo runners were largely out of the picture once more. Only Rosberg, fighting as hard as ever to try to keep up with his more powerful rivals, was really anywhere near in contention with a most creditable seventh fastest time of 1 min 31.583 sec, although team-mate Laffite did well to finish up just three places lower behind Winkelhock and, the other major casualty of the afternoon, de Cesaris. Like Prost, the Italian also blew up his engine in a big way and had arrived in the pit lane with the rear of his Alfa Romeo almost totally enshrouded by smoke – only to have found his car being selected by the computer to be weighed at random! Not surprisingly, on seeing the amount of smoke pouring from the car's exhausts, the officials had quickly decided to forget all about that and had lost no time in waving him straight past the weighing area.

The weather was both brighter and hotter on the second day but it seemed to make no difference to the Ferrari drivers who were once again prominent in both sessions. However, during the final hour of qualifying, when Arnoux made sure of retaining the pole with an improved time of 1 min 28.729 sec (178.927 kph), Tambay was unable to make quite the same sort of impact owing, mainly, to making the self-confessed mistake of choosing qualifying tyres that

were too soft. In addition, a turbo failure whilst out on his first run meant taking over the spare Ferrari, which didn't handle so well, and in the final reckoning Tambay's best lap of 1 min 29.658 sec was more than half a second slower than that achieved on Friday besides being only fifth fastest. Instead it was Prost, still using the spare Renault as he preferred the feel of it to his proposed race chassis, who eventually came out second fastest on this occasion after making a determined effort to pip Piquet for the other front row spot on the grid on his final set of qualifiers. This produced a lap in 1 min 28.830 sec whereas Piquet, having gone through his quota of tyres a bit earlier, had turned in a marginally slower 1 min

Starting Grid

	R. Arnoux Ferrari (1 min 28.729 sec)
A. Prost Renault (1 min 28.830 sec)	N. Piquet Brabham-BMW (1 min 28.887 sec)
P. Tambay Ferrari (1 min 28.992 sec)	R. Patrese Brabham-BMW (1 min 29.549 sec)
E. Cheever Renault (1 min 29.863 sec)	M. Winkelhock ATS-BMW (1 min 30.966 sec)
A. de Cesaris Alfa Romeo (1 min 31.173 sec)	K. Rosberg Williams-Ford (1 min 31.480 sec)
B. Giacomelli Toleman-Hart (1 min 31.586 sec)	E. de Angelis Lotus-Renault (1 min 31.822 sec)
D. Warwick Toleman-Hart (1 min 32.116 sec)	J. Laffite Williams-Ford (1 min 32.185 sec)
M. Surer Arrows-Ford (1 min 32.540 sec)	T. Boutsen Arrows-Ford (1 min 32.576 sec)
J.P. Jarier Ligier-Ford (1 min 32.642 sec)	M. Alboreto Tyrrell-Ford (1 min 33.175 sec)
N. Mansell Lotus-Ford (1 min 33.588 sec)	N. Lauda McLaren-Ford (1 min 33.671 sec)
J. Watson McLaren-Ford (1 min 33.705 sec)	R. Guerrero Theodore-Ford (1 min 33.721 sec)
D. Sullivan Tyrrell-Ford (1 min 33.791 sec)	J. Cecotto Theodore-Ford (1 min 34.314 sec)
R. Boesel Ligier-Ford (1 min 34.486 sec)	C. Fabi Osella-Ford (1 min 34.544 sec)
M. Baldi Alfa Romeo (1 min 34.755 sec)	

Did not qualify:
J. Villeneuve (March-Ford) 1 min 35.133 sec
P. Ghinzani (Osella-Alfa Romeo) 1 min 35.171 sec

28.887 sec. Patrese, confined to his spare Brabham again owing to the BMW engine in his repaired race chassis having started showing signs of tightening up in the morning, was next with another improved time of 1 min 29.549 sec – fourth fastest on the day but not enough to join his team leader on the second row of the grid because of the superior time set by Tambay on Friday. As a result, Patrese had to make do with a spot on the third row next to a slightly disappointed Cheever, who had slipped back to sixth place simply through being unable to progress beyond 1 min 29.863 sec. Even the American, though, was well over a second clear of the rest of the field as the next best time was 1 min 30.966 sec, achieved by Winkelhock in the newer of the two ATS D6s (with the older-style turbo-charger installation and long side-pods) rather than in the heavily-revised spare car that he had also been trying on and off during practice.

For the normally-aspirated runners the situation was now looking worse than ever with the only one amongst their number to prevent a complete turbo walk-over, apart from Baldi's most unimpressively-driven Alfa Romeo, being the consistently hard-trying Rosberg. Even with an improved time of 1 min 31.480 sec, though, the reigning World Champion still had to face the prospects of starting the race from ninth spot on the grid, where he was sandwiched between de Cesaris and Giacomelli. Team-mate Laffite, meanwhile, was among the very few drivers not to have improved on their lap times, but he was still the second fastest non-turbo runner overall by reason of his Friday time. As a result, the Frenchman just squeezed into the top half of the grid behind de Angelis and a disgruntled Warwick who had lost a turbo in final qualifying and found the handling of the spare Toleman absolutely dreadful even though he had ultimately set his best time in it. Among the others the only really notable aspect had been Boutsen's driving, especially when bearing in mind that this was only his third Grand Prix. Furthermore, he had been sidelined for most of the morning untimed session because of an engine failure, and yet still wound up a mere 0.036 sec slower than his team leader with 15th fastest time overall of 1 min 32.576 sec. An excellent performance by any standards and one that must have caused considerable embarrassment to the McLaren team for the second time in a week as the Belgian newcomer had beaten Lauda and Watson by well over a second. As usual, the main problem here was lack of grip but Watson, celebrating the news that he had just been awarded the MBE in the Queen's Birthday Honours List, had also had to contend with broken transmission soon after the start of practice on Friday morning as well as a new Ford-Cosworth DFY engine blowing up on him during final qualifying. Alboreto, too, had

had a rather unhappy second day, blowing up one of the new DFY engines in each session before setting his best time (still only 17th fastest) in the spare Tyrrell fitted with a standard DFV unit, while Mansell had fared little better. On the first morning he had stopped with a broken crown-wheel and pinion, a problem that had been overcome by grafting on the rear end of the spare Lotus 92 to his race chassis only for it to have resulted in poor traction. Then during final qualifying, with his car back in normal configuration and fitted with a new DFY engine, he had seen any hopes of picking up on his lap times dashed by an inexplicable loss of revs. Problems of one sort or another, mainly associated with poor handling or lack of traction, had also affected most of the tail-enders, including Villeneuve, who had never really looked like qualifying the RAM March in spite of trying extremely hard, and also Ghinzani whose chances of getting the Alfa Romeo-powered Osella into its second race had effectively been ended by clutch trouble.

Although it had been predicted otherwise, the weather on Sunday turned out to be hot and sunny after a damp start, and by the time that it came round to the 30 minute warm-up session in mid-morning there was already a healthy-sized crowd in attendance. Once again it was a Ferrari that headed the time-sheets but whereas Tambay went away feeling justifiably confident, Arnoux had rather less cause for optimism as he had turned off into the pits early with smoke issuing from the back of his car. The engine had blown up! As Patrese and Mansell were not enamoured with their engines the Brabham and Lotus mechanics also had to knuckle down to the task of carrying out unscheduled engine changes, while yet more work was

provided by Warwick damaging the underside of his Toleman after momentarily leaving the track, Giacomelli's Toleman breaking a bellhousing joint and the fuel-injection pump seizing on de Angelis' Lotus 93T. However, the various jobs were all completed in good time, teams made their final choice of tyres and soon after 1 p.m. the 26 starters were lined up on the grid patiently awaiting the final count-down. Nearly an hour later they were still there! Incredibly, as the minutes were ticking away towards 1.30 p.m., there was a sudden power failure which, in turn, meant no starting lights, no computerized timing, no PA system, no television and so on. Naturally, this caused all sorts of confusion and so it was with some considerable relief that power was restored again after about 45 minutes. Thereafter everything ran smoothly, the final count-down was completed, Arnoux led the field around on the pace lap and then they were all back on their grid positions once more ready for the start.

When the green light finally did come on Arnoux made rather better use of his pole position than he had done at Detroit by timing everything to perfection and surging forward into an undisputed lead. Most of the others also got away well, none better than Patrese who flew past the outside of Tambay before squeezing between Prost and Piquet and then outbraking the Renault team leader going into the chicane to take up a splendid second place. That then remained the order of the leaders for the rest of the opening lap with Arnoux crossing the line at the end of it already three or four car lengths clear. Behind them, Cheever was chasing hard in sixth place, then came de Cesaris, Giacomelli, Winkelhock, Rosberg, de Angelis, Boutsen, Laffite, Warwick and the others all

Eventual winner René Arnoux leads Riccardo Patrese, Alain Prost and Nelson Piquet during the opening stages of the race. (Autosport)

tightly strung out behind, except for Jarier and Surer who were both missing. After a pause they eventually came round but drove straight into the pits to retire their cars, the Ligier going out with a broken gearbox and the Arrows with a broken output flange between its differential and a constant velocity joint. On the second lap de Angelis also went missing from 11th place and he, too, subsequently disappeared into the pits to retire his Lotus-Renault with deranged throttle linkage, so it was not exactly turning out to be a very auspicious start. Arnoux, though, probably had other ideas about that, for he already appeared to have the race under control with the gap between himself and Patrese now well over a second. At this stage Prost, still driving what had started the weekend as the spare Renault, was holding on well in third place but he was far from happy as his engine was suffering from a sudden loss of power since the morning. Nor was his gearbox by any means perfect, especially when it came to changing down, and after two more laps he finally had to give way to sustained pressure from Piquet. Now a long way back behind Tambay and Cheever, de Cesaris was another not to be over-impressed with the way his engine was performing, but of far greater concern to the Italian was the sight of Rosberg looming in his mirrors, the World Champion having already dealt with Winkelhock and Giacomelli very effectively indeed. It soon became clear that he had no intention of staying behind the Alfa Romeo any longer than necessary by the manner in which he moved in on its tail and enthusiastically began looking for a way past. At the hairpin before the pits, in particular, Rosberg would repeatedly dive for the inside under braking only to find de Cesaris claiming the line and firmly closing the door on him each time. Eventually, on lap 11, Rosberg made an even more determined effort to get by here but still de Cesaris remained unimpressed and so the inevitable happened. Wheels touched! Fortunately, nothing much came of it. De Cesaris continued none the worse with his seventh place still intact and, although the Williams skipped up over the kerb, Rosberg quickly gathered it up and charged on as hard as ever, albeit now in tenth place behind Winkelhock and Laffite caught up in a similar dispute. While this was happening Watson continued what was already looking to be another promising drive by forcing his way past Warwick's Toleman to take over 11th spot, and only a short distance away Lauda was hard on the heels of Giacomelli in the other Toleman, who was slipping down the field quite dramatically. However, unlike Boutsen, who had overtaken the Italian with comparative ease on the previous lap, Lauda messed things up completely when he attempted to go past on the 12th lap by locking up his brakes, spinning and stalling

his engine. Furthermore, he was unable to restart it and, instead, wound up as the fourth retirement, a fact that went largely unnoticed due to rather more attention being focused on Tambay taking over fourth place from Prost under braking for the final hairpin.

On lap 16, with Arnoux now almost exactly 10 seconds clear of Patrese, there was disappointment in store for Piquet. As he came round to complete the lap the Brabham's throttle cable suddenly snapped, a problem that sent him coasting into the pits to retire. Consequently, Tambay automatically took over third place ahead of Cheever and Prost, who had swopped places a couple of laps earlier, while Winkelhock, after having caught and passed de Cesaris on the previous lap, now found himself in the top six. For the German, though, it was to be a brief moment of glory as on lap 18 Rosberg, who had already repassed team-mate Laffite and made a rather more successful job of dispensing with de Cesaris, went flying past him. Furthermore, he had now shot his tyres and after completing the following lap by turning off into the pits for fresh rubber dropped right out of contention. By then Sullivan and Cecotto had also pulled up at the pits, the Tyrrell driver stopping for repairs to a broken rear aerofoil and his opposite number at Theodore to retire with a broken differential, while not long afterwards Mansell was in for what was already his third set of Pirellis. Unfortunately, after practice the Lotus team had altered the settings of his 92 and whereas a similar set-up previously tried on de Angelis' Renault-powered 93T had worked quite well it had made the Ford-Cosworth-powered car virtually undriveable. In fact, the Englishman was destined to stop on no less than another four occasions for tyres prior to finally giving up the unequal struggle after 44 laps. Meanwhile, as he was left trailing along at the back of the field, all eyes became fixed on Tambay as he closed up to Patrese's second-placed Brabham. However, just when it seemed to be only a question of time before the Ferraris were lying first and second, the Frenchman's engine suddenly developed an erratic misfire with the result that he began to fall away again, even losing his place to Cheever on lap 29. Soon Prost was looking all set to pounce as well but then Tambay tried using the cockpit control introduced just prior to Monaco which activated a valve in the fuel system to dispel any unwanted air bubbles and, much to his relief, found that this did the trick. Thereafter, with the engine coming back on full song once more, Tambay immediately started pulling away from Prost, and he set about catching Cheever whilst cursing himself for not having tried the control earlier.

Between laps 32 and 39 most of the attention became centred on the pits when de

Cesaris, Warwick, Prost, Laffite, Arnoux, Cheever, Rosberg, Patrese, Giacomelli, Baldi and Tambay all took turns to make their scheduled refuelling/tyre stops. However, as the various pit crews all carried out their work without running into any major problems the overall pattern of the race remained largely unaffected, for when everything had settled down again Arnoux was still leading by just over 10 seconds from Patrese, and similarly Cheever was still a close third ahead of Tambay, Prost and Rosberg. Laffite, who had earlier lost little time in following his team leader past de Cesaris, had also rejoined the race still in seventh place, but the unlucky Frenchman had since been forced to bow out with a stripped third gear. So, instead, it was now Watson who was seventh followed by Boutsen and Alboreto, de Cesaris having slipped to tenth place and about to join the growing retirement list with his engine showing signs of overheating. In fact, with Fabi, Guerrero and Boesel all having disappeared from lower down the order for various reasons just before half-distance and both Tolemans coming to rest out on the circuit over the course of the next few minutes, due to a blown-up engine (Giacomelli) and a quite spectacular turbo-charger failure (Warwick) respectively, there were soon only 12 cars left. Before Warwick's eventual demise, Patrese ran into trouble as well. His gearbox started playing up. Consequently, not only did he drop further and further away from Arnoux but he also steadily fell back into the clutches of Cheever and a hard-charging Tambay, who was currently the fastest driver on the track. For a while, of course, the sight of the three cars converging on one another produced considerable excitement but, unfortunately, any prospects of seeing a real battle develop failed to materialize. First Patrese, in no position to put up a fight, had more or less to sit and watch as both the Renault and the Ferrari sailed past him in quick succession on lap 49. Then, shortly afterwards, Tambay had his hopes of launching an all-out attack on Cheever dashed by his car beginning to oversteer, a problem almost certainly caused by the Frenchman having tried too hard after his pit stop and blistering his rear tyres. Whatever, Cheever was able to start creeping away from him and from that point on the first three places never really looked in doubt for no-one was going to catch Arnoux, as was clearly demonstrated by the little Frenchman continuing to extend his lead until taking the chequered flag at the end of the 70 laps over 42 seconds clear. It was a most resounding victory, the fifth of his career and the first since joining Ferrari, added to which the result also marked the 150th Grand Prix win for Goodyear tyres.

Behind Tambay, who duly brought the other Ferrari home in third place, Rosberg finished in a strong fourth place in spite of completing the race with slight brake problems and being in pain from an inflamed right foot; Prost was fifth after an unhappy afternoon not helped by a late pit stop to replace a punctured left front tyre; and Watson, whose front brakes faded near the end, took the final point by finishing sixth after withstanding a strong challenge from Boutsen in the closing stages until the Belgian had been forced to back off due to removing the

left-hand nose fin of his Arrows against the McLaren's right rear wheel. That's how close it had been! After that only Alboreto, Sullivan (later to be disqualified when his Tyrrell was found to be 4 kilogrammes below the minimum weight limit following a loss of coolant) and Baldi were still there at the finish as Patrese's race had ended in the pits after 57 laps with his gearbox virtually useless, and Winkelhock had coasted to rest on the final lap with something obviously amiss

with the ATS-BMW's fuel system. Even this was not quite the end of the day's story, though. On the slowing-down lap Giacomelli hitched a ride back to the pits with Rosberg and promptly slid off the side of the Williams to wind up lying injured on the track. Thankfully, after being whisked off to the medical centre, he later emerged perfectly all right apart from having a badly bruised arm. Even so, it was still a rather unhappy way to end the afternoon.

Results		
1	R. Arnoux (Ferrari)	1 hr 48 min 31.838 sec (170.661 kph/ 106.044 mph)
2	E. Cheever (Renault)	1 hr 49 min 13.867 sec
3	P. Tambay (Ferrari)	1 hr 49 min 24.448 sec
4	K. Rosberg (Williams-Ford)	1 hr 49 min 48.886 sec
5	A. Prost (Renault)	1 lap behind
6	J. Watson (McLaren-Ford)	1 lap behind
7	T. Boutsen (Arrows-Ford)	1 lap behind
8	M. Alboreto (Tyrrell-Ford)	2 laps behind
*	D. Sullivan (Tyrrell-Ford)	2 laps behind
**9	M. Winkelhock (ATS-BMW)	3 laps behind
10	M. Baldi (Alfa Romeo)	3 laps behind

*Disqualified
**Not running at finish

Fastest lap: P. Tambay (Ferrari) on lap 42 in 1 min 30.851 sec (174.747 kph/108.583 mph)

Retirements
J.P. Jarier (Ligier-Ford) gearbox on lap 1, M. Surer (Arrows-Ford) transmission on lap 1, E. de Angelis (Lotus-Renault) throttle linkage on lap 2, N. Lauda (McLaren-Ford) spun and stalled on lap 12, N. Piquet (Brabham-BMW) throttle cable on lap 16, J. Cecotto (Theodore-Ford) differential on lap 18, C. Fabi (Osella-Ford) gearbox on lap 27, R. Guerrero (Theodore-Ford) engine on lap 28, R. Boesel (Ligier-Ford) wheel bearing on lap 33, J. Laffite (Williams-Ford) gearbox on lap 38, A. de Cesaris (Alfa Romeo) engine on lap 43, B. Giacomelli (Toleman-Hart) engine on lap 44, N. Mansell (Lotus-Ford) handling/tyres on lap 44, D. Warwick (Toleman-Hart) turbocharger on lap 48, R. Patrese (Brabham-BMW) gearbox on lap 57.

XXXVIth British Grand Prix

Silverstone: July 16
Weather: Hot
Distance: 67 laps of 4.7185 km
circuit = 316.14 km (196.44 miles)

Although the Swiss Grand Prix had originally been included on the calendar, and was scheduled to have taken place at Dijon on July 10, a lack of television coverage – considered essential to make it a viable proposition – had led to its cancellation. Quite simply, the Swiss television authorities had refused to cover an event outside their own territory and French TV had not been prepared to incur the expense of televising a second Grand Prix in France. As a result over a month had gone by without a race, but despite this unusually long gap in mid-season the teams, almost without exception, had certainly not been idle. On the contrary, there had been test sessions to attend at Silverstone, Hockenheim and the Österreichring, and development work had continued unabated as was clearly evident from the entry that materialized for the Marlboro-sponsored British Grand Prix. Virtually every single car had undergone some form of modification or another, while no less than nine teams – Euroracing Alfa Romeo, Arrows, ATS, Brabham, Ferrari, Lotus, Osella, Renault and Toleman – all arrived at Silverstone with at least one brand new chassis. Moreover, four of them had been built to completely new designs. These were a pair of Harvey Postlethwaite-designed Ferrari 126C3s and also a pair of Renault-powered Lotus 94Ts, the work of Gerard

Ducarouge who, following his unceremonious sacking by Euroracing earlier in the year, had joined the British team just prior to Detroit. In addition to this already impressive line-up, the Spirit team were now ready for their first taste of Grand Prix racing following the brief appearance in the non-Championship Race of Champions at Brands Hatch back in April. Obviously their arrival also marked the serious return of Honda to Formula 1 racing after an absence of almost 15 years, so was an entry that, understandably, stimulated a lot of interest. Finally, one other change to the regular line-up had been brought about by John MacDonald acquiring the services of the Formula 2 driver, Kenny Acheson, to drive the RAM March for the remainder of the season, the Ulsterman having secured the necessary support from the RMC Group (his existing sponsors) in association with the Valvoline oil company.

With the British Isles currently enjoying a mini heat-wave, practice started in hot and dry conditions on Thursday morning but for two drivers there were immediate problems. First Alboreto arrived in the pit lane after just one lap with the back of his Tyrrell on fire due to a fuel-line having become disconnected. Then, whilst this was being attended to, Tambay pulled off the track at Chapel Curve in his brand new Ferrari 126C3 with a dead engine caused by an apparent electrical

fault. Consequently, both of them had to resort to their teams' spare cars, the Frenchman after hitching a ride back to the pits. This, however, turned out to be just the beginning of an absolutely hectic opening 90 minutes of testing. Most of it was caused by drivers simply dashing in and out of the pits for all manner of adjustments as they endeavoured to set up cars to their liking, or to try out different tyre compounds, but as the morning wore on more and more of them also ran into trouble. Among those affected were Boesel, whose Ligier coasted to rest in the vicinity of Stowe with fuel metering problems; Giacomelli, Jarier and Watson, who all lost engines; Winkelhock, who had a turbo-charger let go on his new ATS, and both Mansell and Johansson who were plagued by misfiring engines in their new cars. However, it was certainly not all bad news, and for de Angelis, in particular, the morning couldn't have ended on a much happier note. Whilst his team-mate had spent most of the time frustratingly sitting around in the pits, he had eventually clocked up the fastest time, unofficially, of 1 min 11.632 sec, his new Lotus 94T performing perfectly and already proving to be a different proposition altogether than its bulky and unloved predecessor.

At 1 p.m. it was time for the more serious part of the day's programme to begin, the first hour of qualifying. By now most of the morning's problems had received attention, although Giacomelli was waiting around for the job of installing a fresh Hart engine in his Toleman to be completed, Tambay was having to rely on the spare Ferrari 126C2/B once more because the engine in his new car was still refusing to run properly and Boesel had been obliged to switch to the spare Ligier. So far as Mansell was concerned, however, all efforts made by the Lotus mechanics to rid the Renault engine in his 94T of its irksome misfire were soon proved to have been a waste of time. It was as bad as ever. Consequently, he went on to spend most of the session in the pits once again where work continued, in vain, to effect a cure. Similarly, the Honda engine in Johansson's new Spirit 201C could not be encouraged to run cleanly. But, whereas Mansell seemed determined to

persevere with his new car, the Swede carried on hopping in and out of his team's older and heavier spare chassis every so often until eventually pulling off the track at Copse Corner – out of fuel! By that stage Fabi's qualifying run in a new Alfa Romeo-powered Osella FA1E had also ended out on the circuit, with a broken throttle cable, and Lauda had just arrived at the pits with a blown-up engine in his McLaren, while not long afterwards Boesel and Winkelhock were both forced to give up a few minutes early: the engine in the spare Ligier had blown a head gasket and the ATS-BMW had suffered another turbo failure. So, one way or another, there was still a fair amount of trouble about, but this in no way detracted from an exciting battle that developed between the Ferraris, the Brabham-BMWs, the Renaults and de Angelis' Lotus-Renault for the leading grid positions. Far from it. With all seven absolutely flying and clocking up average lap speeds that were nudging the 150 mph-mark, the tension was almost unbearable right up until the field was finally flagged off, by which time Silverstone was buzzing with the news that Prost had just broken the magical 150 mph barrier. He had gone around in 1 min 10.170 sec – 150.423 mph! After that everything else seemed to be of secondary importance, but when the other lap times had been collated Arnoux (1 min 10.436 sec), de Angelis (1 min 10.771 sec), Tambay (1 min 10.874 sec), Cheever (1 min 11.055 sec) and Piquet (1 min 11.098 sec) had all lapped less than a second slower, and so very nearly had Patrese at 1 min 11.246 sec. As had been anticipated, the normally-aspirated cars were virtually nowhere, with only one of them in the first 13 places on the time-sheets. That was Rosberg's hard-driven Williams, but even the reigning World Champion's untiring efforts had produced a best lap of only 1 min 13.755 sec – 11th fastest and over 3½ seconds off the pace!

On Friday conditions were hotter than ever and after another extremely busy, though largely trouble-free, 90 minutes of testing in the morning the general concensus of opinion was that the track was marginally slower than the first day. Even so, when the time came round for the afternoon's final qualifying session, this did nothing at all to prevent it from being an absolutely enthralling hour. Initially, after the leading lights had all used up their first sets of qualifying tyres, it appeared that pole position was a foregone conclusion as the nearest anyone had come to beating Prost's incredible lap of the previous afternoon was Tambay, the Frenchman, using his new Ferrari at long last following an overnight engine change, setting what was now third fastest time overall of 1 min 10.588 sec. However, as if this was merely a warning shot, Tambay then took to the track on his second set of tyres and

suddenly changed the situation completely by whistling around in 1 min 10.145 sec. Not finished yet, he returned to the pits, had the worn tyres on the left-hand side of his car replaced by the less hard-worked right-hand covers from his first set and went out to squeeze in one more flying lap. The result, an even quicker 1 min 10.104 sec. Amazingly, though, this was still not enough to clinch the coveted pole position. Almost unnoticed in the excitement, especially as his Ferrari had earlier been wheeled away into the shade of its pit garage, Arnoux had yet to make his final run, and when he did eventually go out in the closing minutes of the session the outcome was almost unbelievable – a lap in 1 min 09.462 sec (151.956 mph)! Needless to say the Ferrari team were ecstatic, with the possible exception of Tambay who appeared to be rather bemused by it all even though he was still on the front row of the grid.

Of the other front-runners on Thursday only the Brabham duo, Piquet and Patrese, had ultimately improved on their lap times. They, too, were both driving new cars which were being referred to as BT52Bs owing to having a number of detail changes to their predecessors. These included slightly different bodywork, improved aerodynamics, revised suspension geometry and a transposed colour scheme in which dark blue had become white and vice versa. Initially, both cars had also appeared with shorter nose cones. But, after being plagued by understeer during the first day, and having tried the spare Brabham still fitted with an older and longer nose cone, and found it more responsive, Piquet had had the longer nose cone fitted to his car for final qualifying. Even so, apart from still being slower than the times set by Prost and de Angelis on Thursday (they had seen their hopes of improving dashed by an intermittent engine misfire and by a bad choice of qualifying tyres respectively), his best lap of 1 min 10.933 sec had, somewhat ironically, been beaten by his team-mate, Patrese having turned in a marginally quicker 1 min 10.881 sec. Consequently, Piquet had to settle for an eventual sixth place on the grid immediately ahead of Cheever and a much-improved Winkelhock who had hoisted his new ATS-BMW up to eighth spot with a time of 1 min 11.687 sec. Almost exactly a further half a second away, de Cesaris had qualified ninth and then, completing the front half of the grid, came Warwick, Baldi, Giacomelli and, finally, Rosberg who had remained the fastest non-turbo runner. This was in spite of the fact that the World Champion, confident that he could go no faster than on Thursday, had been officially withdrawn from final qualifying in order that extra time could be spent on finding a decent race set-up using unmarked tyres. Next up, Johansson had qualified in an encouraging 14th spot for his first Grand Prix, having relied mainly on the spare Spirit-Honda in final qualifying due to its engine proving to be stronger than a replacement unit installed in the new chassis, but Mansell had wound up in a disappointing 18th place behind Lauda, Alboreto and Boutsen. Not that this was in any way surprising. First his new Lotus 94T had still refused to run properly in spite of a fresh Renault engine having been installed overnight. Then, after reluctantly switching to the team's spare 93T for the afternoon, he had only just set off on his second set of qualifying tyres when the engine in that blew up. For Watson, who had won the last British Grand Prix to be held at Silverstone in 1981, it had also been a particularly frustrating couple of days. Following the engine failure on Thursday morning, a replacement fitted for the afternoon had been well down on power, while part way through final qualifying yet another fresh engine installed overnight had begun to tighten up, forcing the Ulsterman to complete practice in the spare McLaren. The outcome of this was a pretty hopeless-looking 24th place on the grid and a lap time that was faster than only that set by Jarier, whose first day's times had been scrubbed for ignoring a red light directing him into the weighing area, Ghinzani and the three drivers who had ultimately failed to qualify for the race, Cecotto, Fabi and Acheson.

The fine weather was still very much in evidence on Saturday, and from early morning spectators arrived at the Northamptonshire circuit in their thousands, a large proportion of them having made use of the specially provided camping areas overnight. Prior to the Grand Prix, which was scheduled to start at 2.30 p.m., there was a very full and varied programme of supporting events that included a round of the Marlboro British Formula 3 Championship (won by a fast-rising star from Brazil called Ayrton Senna), numerous parades and a magnificent air display highlighted by an appearance of the inimitable Red Arrows. In amongst this there was also the customary 30 minute warm-up session for the Formula 1 cars which went off particularly encouragingly for the John Player Lotus team: de Angelis lapped more than a second clear of the field and Mansell at last had a trouble-free run following the fitting of a complete new wiring loom to his 94T. Johansson, on the other hand, was forced to switch to the spare Spirit-Honda when he found that the engine in the new, lighter, car was still not right and Patrese, with his Brabham BT52B now in long nose cone configuration, like Piquet's sister car, pulled off into the pits early because of an engine failure. At the end of it engine changes were also found to be necessary in Tambay's Ferrari, which had developed a slight high-speed misfire, and in Laffite's Williams, which had gone decidedly

off-colour, so while the large crowd basked in the hot sunshine there was a lot of activity going on behind the scenes. Nevertheless, apart from Johansson relying on the older Spirit-Honda for his debut, everything was back to normal when it was time for the official warm-up lap at 2 p.m. – only for Ghinzani's Alfa Romeo-powered Osella to come to rest out on the circuit moments later because of an electrical failure. As a result, the Italian had to sprint back to the pits and take over the car that his team-mate had failed to qualify, but the ensuing delay meant that he was left facing the prospects of starting the race from the pit lane. In the meantime, the remaining 25 starters were soon away on the pace lap and returning to their grid positions once more to face the starting lights, the adrenalin now really flowing.

Seconds later the waiting was over, the red lights changed to green and they were on their way with the two front row Ferraris rushing off towards Copse Corner virtually side by side and the rest fanning out all over the track behind them, jostling wildly for positions. Initially, Arnoux appeared to have the slight advantage as the leaders arrived at the right-hander but Tambay, on the outside, kept off the brakes a fraction longer, sat it out wheel to wheel with his team-mate and nosed into the lead as they headed off towards Maggotts. Hard on their heels, Prost did much the same to Patrese after being beaten off the line by the Italian, while Cheever had already surged through to fifth place ahead of Piquet and a somewhat tardy de Angelis. The others, meanwhile, quickly sorted themselves out with no real dramas and from there they all went on to safely complete a tense and exciting opening lap which Rosberg did his best to enliven still further by sliding very wide coming out of Becketts and momentarily taking to the grass. Across the line it was still Tambay out

in front from Arnoux, Prost, Patrese and Cheever. De Angelis, though, had just slipped ahead of Piquet on the approach to Woodcote to take over sixth spot and they, in turn, were being hotly pursued by de Cesaris, Winkelhock, Warwick, Johansson, Mansell (already up to twelfth place), Baldi and the rest being led by Lauda, proposing to make a planned pit stop for the first time, in the leading normally-aspirated car.

Early on the second lap Lotus fortunes suddenly took a nose-dive when de Angelis slowed and pulled off the track at Becketts with the rear bodywork of his 94T on fire. Although there was some doubt as to the precise cause of the problem, all the indications were that a turbo-charger unit had expired. Whatever, the flames were quickly extinguished by some marshals and the Italian walked away from the scene unharmed, though obviously bitterly disappointed. At the end of the same lap, with Tambay now edging away from his team-mate out in front, there was also consternation in the Toleman camp when Giacomelli pulled into the pits to complain of a loss of power from his Hart engine. He, too, was to retire after subsequently trying one more slow lap, by which time Cheever had disappeared from fifth place with a badly overheating engine and Johansson's promising debut in the Spirit-Honda had effectively been ended by a broken fuel pump belt: after a lengthy pit stop for repairs the Swede was to rejoin the race only for the fuel pump to fail completely moments later and bring him to rest at Becketts. Meanwhile, Tambay was still controlling the race beautifully, but Arnoux was under all kinds of pressure from Prost and having to fight every inch of the way to defend his position. Furthermore, soon after Patrese was forced out of a strong fourth place on lap 9, when a turbo failure sent the Brabham-BMW trickling into the pits, Arnoux found his Goodyear tyres rapidly

Copse Corner on the opening lap with the two leading Ferraris absolutely wheel to wheel and Alain Prost snatching third place from Riccardo Patrese. *(Autocar & Motor)*

losing their grip. Consequently, the job of staying ahead became that much harder, even though the Ferrari was clearly faster in a straight line. Prost, of course, could sense what was happening only too well and after spending a few more minutes looking this way and that for a way past finally made a decisive move going into Copse Corner at the start of lap 14 by diving for the inside line under braking and nosing ahead on acceleration. Five laps later Piquet caught and passed the Ferrari as well, while just ahead of him Prost took only until Copse Corner (again!) at the start of the following lap to become the new race leader, Tambay now in similar tyre trouble to his team-mate in spite of taking rather more care in trying to preserve them. By this stage no-one else was really in it as these first four had long since dropped the rest of the field. As it was de Cesaris (automatically promoted to fifth place following the retirements of de Angelis, Cheever and Patrese) still had Winkelhock pounding along behind him and a little further back Mansell had just won a long battle with Warwick by overtaking the Toleman going into Copse Corner on lap 17 to move up into seventh place, notwithstanding the fact that he was being troubled by severe oversteer and a bad vibration caused by the loss of a wheel balance weight early in the race. Further back again, Lauda was still leading the normally-aspirated contingent, now in ninth place immediately ahead of Baldi and team-mate Watson, and then came Rosberg and Jarier running in close formation followed by the last driver still on the same lap as the leaders, Laffite.

Once in the lead Prost immediately began to draw away from Tambay and left his compatriot at the mercy of Piquet. Despite the tyre problem steadily growing worse, however, Tambay proved to be no easy meat and even when the Brabham moved right in on to his tail he still refused to give up without a fight. Only on lap 31 did the situation change when Piquet finally squeezed through on the inside under braking for the Woodcote chicane, by which time Prost had pulled over 10 seconds clear. Nevertheless, it was not necessarily over yet by any means as there were still the refuelling/tyre stops to come. In fact, they were already under way with Winkelhock the first to have stopped at the end of lap 29, just two laps after Warwick had withdrawn from the contest because of a broken fifth gear. Over the next couple of minutes Watson and Arnoux also went into the pits and soon the rush was really on with Jarier, de Cesaris and Lauda all dropping out of formation in quick succession followed, on lap 36, by Prost and Tambay. Naturally, this changed the order completely and left Piquet leading the race, Prost rejoining in second place after being stationary for 14.5 seconds and Tambay in fourth spot between Mansell and Arnoux

following a slightly longer delay of 17.7 seconds. In the meantime, the excitement in the pits continued with Laffite, Baldi and Boesel each taking their turns to stop and then, at the end of lap 41, in went Piquet. Now this was really crucial but, in spite of the Brabham team turning their man around in just 12.26 seconds, Prost was over 15 seconds up the road before Piquet regained the track, so now it really did look to be all over. Mansell was ahead of him as well, although only for two laps as then it was time for the Englishman to make what was actually the last scheduled stop, Rosberg having gone in a lap earlier. Like their opposite numbers at Brabham, the Lotus pit crew did a magnificent job, taking exactly 13 seconds to change all four wheels and to top up the fuel, which enabled Mansell to rejoin the race in fifth place and only a comparatively short distance behind Arnoux. Furthermore, on discovering that the wheel-change had transformed the handling of his car, as well as having eliminated the vibration, Mansell responded by driving harder than ever and in no time at all was right up with the Ferrari, looking for a way past. For the crowd this was a real treat and although Arnoux, already short of grip once more, tried desperately to stave off the challenge by employing blocking tactics Mansell soon found an answer to that. Going into Abbey Curve on lap 48 he feinted to the right and then, after a quick flick of the steering wheel, slammed through on the inside before Arnoux really knew what had happened. It was a moment to savour, and the sight of the black and gold Lotus ahead of the Ferrari met with the vociferous approval of the spectators all around the circuit.

The closing stages of the race, unfortunately, became little more than a high-speed procession with Prost never putting a foot wrong and driving on to a third victory of the season unchallenged, the little Frenchman

completing the 67 laps a shade under 20 seconds clear of Piquet's second-placed Brabham. A further 7 seconds away, Tambay crossed the line in a convincing third place in spite of experiencing a gradual loss of grip, and 12 seconds later a jubilant Mansell brought his extremely well-driven Lotus 94T home in a fine fourth place a long way ahead of a disgruntled Arnoux. In sixth place, however, it was Lauda, as de Cesaris had lost any chance of a points finish because of a disastrous pit stop, made all the worse by a clutch problem contributing to a stalled engine, and Winkelhock had been forced to retire after 49 laps with an overheating engine. Ghinzani and Boesel had also been forced to retire from amongst the tail-enders at about the same time, but there were still another 11 cars running at the finish, including Rosberg's Williams – a disappointing 11th on a day that conditions had obviously suited Michelin tyres somewhat better than Goodyear.

Within moments of the race ending came news of a protest. For a change it was not against the Renault exhaust system as problems with handling and high engine temperatures during recent testing (held in hot weather) had led to the French team reverting to a layout similar to that seen earlier in the season. In any case this matter had now been referred to the FIA International Court of Appeal. Instead, it was against water-assisted fuel-injection systems being used by both Renault and Ferrari and had been lodged by Ken Tyrrell shortly after the start of the race. Essentially, he was contending that by adding water to the fuel before it entered the combustion chamber both teams were contravening Article 14 of the Formula 1 technical regulations (this concerned usable fuel) in four ways. First, the addition of water increased the octane rating of the fuel beyond the maximum permitted level. Second, it increased the oxygen

The end of a successful afternoon's work as Alain Prost takes the chequered flag to chalk up his third victory of the season. *(Autosport)*

content to more than the permitted 2%. Third, the fuel was no longer exclusively made up of hydrocarbons as stipulated.

Fourth, the fuel contained an illegal power-boosting additive. After considering the matter, however, the Stewards obviously did not

share Tyrrell's views as they subsequently turned down the protest and confirmed the results.

Results			
1	A. Prost (Renault)	1 hr 24 min 39.780 sec (224.049 kph/ 139.218 mph)	
2	N. Piquet (Brabham-BMW)	1 hr 24 min 58.941 sec	
3	P. Tambay (Ferrari)	1 hr 25 min 06.026 sec	
4	N. Mansell (Lotus-Renault)	1 hr 25 min 18.732 sec	
5	R. Arnoux (Ferrari)	1 hr 25 min 38.654 sec	
6	N. Lauda (McLaren-Ford)	1 lap behind	
7	M. Baldi (Alfa Romeo)	1 lap behind	
8	A. de Cesaris (Alfa Romeo)	1 lap behind	
9	J. Watson (McLaren-Ford)	1 lap behind	
10	J.P. Jarier (Ligier-Ford)	2 laps behind	
11	K. Rosberg (Williams-Ford)	2 laps behind	
12	J. Laffite (Williams-Ford)	2 laps behind	
13	M. Alboreto (Tyrrell-Ford)	2 laps behind	
14	D. Sullivan (Tyrrell-Ford)	2 laps behind	
15	T. Boutsen (Arrows-Ford)	2 laps behind	
16	R. Guerrero (Theodore-Ford)	3 laps behind	
17	M. Surer (Arrows-Ford)	3 laps behind	

Fastest lap: A. Prost (Renault) on lap 32 in 1 min 14.212 sec (228.897 kph/142.230 mph)

Retirements
E. de Angelis (Lotus-Renault) turbo-charger on lap 2, E. Cheever (Renault) engine on lap 4, B. Giacomelli (Toleman-Hart) turbo-charger on lap 4, S. Johansson (Spirit-Honda) fuel pump on lap 6, R. Patrese (Brabham-BMW) turbo-charger on lap 10, D. Warwick (Toleman-Hart) gearbox on lap 28, P. Ghinzani (Osella-Alfa Romeo) fuel pressure on lap 47, R. Boesel (Ligier-Ford) suspension on lap 49, M. Winkelhock (ATS-BMW) engine on lap 50.

XLV Grosser Preis von Deutschland

Hockenheim: August 7
Weather: Overcast but dry
Distance: 45 laps of 6.797 km
circuit = 305.86 km (190.05 miles)

Ten days after the British Grand Prix the FIA International Court of Appeal had convened to hear the appeal lodged by the Brabham team following the rejection of their protest in Detroit against the exhaust system used by Renault. The outcome of this was that the Court stated that the moving parts of the engine and turbo-charger did not 'of themselves have an aerodynamic effect on the behaviour of the car', although it also stated that 'on the other hand, the exhaust gases may have such an effect and it's obvious that all constructors tend to use the burnt gases in the best possible conditions to achieve the effect mentioned above'. Essentially, though, the Court concluded that the exhaust gases were no more than the combustion residue from the engine and not developed for an aerodynamic purpose, and dismissed the appeal accordingly. So that, at least, cleared one outstanding matter. But now there was another, as following the rejection of his protest at Silverstone against the water-assisted fuel-injection systems being used by Renault and Ferrari, Ken Tyrrell had also lodged an appeal to the FIA, for which judgement was still awaited. Furthermore, as the teams reassembled at Hockenheim for the German Grand Prix he lodged another protest on the same basis, which had also been signed by Frank Williams. The organizers, however, refused to be drawn into the controversy and, instead, indicated that the affair should be decided by the FIA Court of Appeal. Nevertheless, it did lead to repercussions for while Renault and Ferrari were busy defending their pos-

ition by stating that water was being used solely to cool the air-intake charge, the marketing director of ELF, François Guiter, announced that his firm was terminating its agreement to supply Tyrrell with petrol forthwith – even though Tyrrell stressed that it was not the petrol that he was claiming to be illegal, merely the way in which Renault was using it. Tyrrell was also adamant that he did not wish to affect the outcome of the 1983 World Championship and stated that his main concern was for 1984 when fuel tank capacity was to be reduced to a maximum of 220 litres as a means of limiting power output because, in his view, systems of water-injection would compensate for this reduction in fuel capacity. In spite of these comments, however, the fact remained that for the time being, at least, the position at the top of the Championship table, with Prost now leading Piquet by 6 points, could still be considered only provisional.

In stark contrast to Silverstone, grey and overcast skies were the prevailing conditions at the start of practice on Friday morning, making the vast concrete stadium that formed the major part of the circuit seem even more forbidding than usual. However, the important aspect was that the track was dry and, with drivers obviously intent on making the most of the 90 minutes of testing in the hope of being in good shape for the afternoon qualifying hour, everything was soon in full swing. Whilst there were no alterations to the driver line-up or anything completely new in the way of cars one surprise was to see the pair of Ferrari 126C3s fitted with the

massive rear aerofoils previously used on the C2/Bs. Naturally, there had to be a reason for this, and it transpired that much of the tyre trouble experienced in the previous race had subsequently been attibuted to lack of downforce due to using much smaller rear aerofoils. Even so, it still seemed a trifle odd at a fast circuit such as this but the Italian team were convinced that they were doing the right thing, particularly as wind tunnel tests had shown up no appreciable difference in the amount of drag. Like the Ferraris, which had also been refurbished with slightly revised and lighter bodywork, some of the other cars were sporting minor changes as well, notably Prost's Renault, which now had shortened under-body panels at the rear, and the newer of the two Spirit-Hondas, which had been given a longer wheelbase. In addition, Goodyear had brought along a new batch of slick tyres of radial construction in order that comparisons could be made with their more familiar range of cross-plies. This, of course, was of considerable interest, but little was to come of it. After the Ferrari and Williams teams had both tried the new tyres there were complaints from the drivers of understeer and by the end of the morning Goodyear had decided, temporarily, to shelve the project. In the meantime, tyres were probably the last thing on the minds of some of the other teams, as throughout the morning problems of one sort or another had been constantly cropping up. Lotus were in a particular sorry state, for de Angelis had damaged the nose cone and steering rack of his 94T after sliding off into the barriers at the Sachskurve, apparently because of going too fast on cold tyres, while Mansell's similar car had been plagued by persistent water leaks caused by a troublesome water hose joint. It was not much better in the Brabham pit either, for Piquet's proposed race chassis had suffered an electrical failure out on the circuit and the spare BT52B, that he had subsequently taken over, had promptly run into overheating problems owing to pumping out all of its water. A lot of other things had gone wrong as well, of which the more serious were a gearbox pinion shaft breaking on the newer Spirit-Honda, a turbo oil pipe repeatedly coming detached on Winkelhock's ATS, Warwick's Toleman suffering from clutch and engine problems and the Ford-Cosworth DFY engine in Lauda's McLaren blowing up. For some it had been testing in more than one sense of the word!

When, at 1 p.m., it was time to start

<table>
<tr><td colspan="2" align="center">Starting Grid</td></tr>
<tr><td></td><td>P. Tambay
Ferrari</td></tr>
<tr><td>R. Arnoux
Ferrari
(1 min 49.435 sec)</td><td>(1 min 49.328 sec)</td></tr>
<tr><td></td><td>A. de Cesaris
Alfa Romeo</td></tr>
<tr><td>N. Piquet
Brabham-BMW
(1 min 51.082 sec)</td><td>(1 min 50.845 sec)</td></tr>
<tr><td></td><td>A. Prost
Renault</td></tr>
<tr><td>E. Cheever
Renault
(1 min 51.540 sec)</td><td>(1 min 51.228 sec)</td></tr>
<tr><td></td><td>M. Baldi
Alfa Romeo</td></tr>
<tr><td>R. Patrese
Brabham-BMW
(1 min 52.105 sec)</td><td>(1 min 51.867 sec)</td></tr>
<tr><td></td><td>D. Warwick
Toleman-Hart</td></tr>
<tr><td>B. Giacomelli
Toleman-Hart
(1 min 54.648 sec)</td><td>(1 min 54.199 sec)</td></tr>
<tr><td></td><td>E. de Angelis
Lotus-Renault</td></tr>
<tr><td>K. Rosberg
Williams-Ford
(1 min 55.289 sec)</td><td>(1 min 54.831 sec)</td></tr>
<tr><td></td><td>S. Johansson
Spirit-Honda</td></tr>
<tr><td>T. Boutsen
Arrows-Ford
(1 min 56.015 sec)</td><td>(1 min 55.870 sec)</td></tr>
<tr><td></td><td>J. Laffite
Williams-Ford</td></tr>
<tr><td>M. Alboreto
Tyrrell-Ford
(1 min 56.398 sec)</td><td>(1 min 56.318 sec)</td></tr>
<tr><td></td><td>N. Mansell
Lotus-Renault</td></tr>
<tr><td>N. Lauda
McLaren-Ford
(1 min 56.730 sec)</td><td>(1 min 56.490 sec)</td></tr>
<tr><td></td><td>J.P. Jarier
Ligier-Ford</td></tr>
<tr><td>M. Surer
Arrows-Ford
(1 min 57.072 sec)</td><td>(1 min 57.018 sec)</td></tr>
<tr><td></td><td>D. Sullivan
Tyrrell-Ford</td></tr>
<tr><td>J. Cecotto
Theodore-Ford
(1 min 57.744 sec)</td><td>(1 min 57.426 sec)</td></tr>
<tr><td></td><td>J. Watson
McLaren-Ford</td></tr>
<tr><td>R. Guerrero
Theodore-Ford
(1 min 57.790 sec)</td><td>(1 min 57.776 sec)</td></tr>
<tr><td></td><td>R. Boesel
Ligier-Ford</td></tr>
<tr><td>P. Ghinzani
Osella-Alfa Romeo
(1 min 58.473 sec)</td><td>(1 min 58.413 sec)</td></tr>
</table>

Did not qualify:
K. Acheson (March-Ford) 1 min 59.003 sec
C. Fabi (Osella-Alfa Romeo) 2 min 01.113 sec
M. Winkelhock (ATS-BMW) No time

thinking about qualifying for grid positions several of the long-suffering mechanics were still toiling away trying to bolt everything back together again, which meant that not everyone was able to go out as early as they would have liked. Even some of those who did get out with reasonable promptitude were soon in trouble, and for Mansell it was beginning to look like Silverstone all over again. His Lotus 94T, fitted with a new water pump since the morning, now refused to pull beyond 6000 rpm. Consequently, the Englishman had to make his way back to the pits and pin his hopes on the unloved spare 93T. Johansson, too, was soon in much the same boat for, having set off in the newer Spirit 201C once more, he quickly discovered that his progress was being hampered by an engine misfire and had reluctantly to revert to his team's spare car, as did Piquet in similar trouble with his Brabham BT52B. While this was happening the Ferrari drivers were almost immediately establishing themselves at the top of the time-sheets, the pair of them out on their own in breaking the 1 min 50 sec barrier. Moreover, it was achieved after just one timed flying lap apiece due to the short life of the Goodyear qualifying tyres. Later, on his second set of tyres, Tambay went quicker still and produced a lap in 1 min 49.328 sec (this was in spite of inadvertently switching off the water-injection instead of the rev-limiter in his car!) although Arnoux, using race rubber for his second run, was unable to improve on his earlier time of 1 min 49.435 sec. Nevertheless, he still wound up second fastest as the next best time, achieved by de Cesaris driving a slightly revised Alfa Romeo 183T with larger turbo-charger units and improved aerodynamics, was 1 min 50.845 sec. Piquet, meanwhile, took the spare Brabham-BMW around in fourth fastest time of 1 min 51.082 sec, but his team-mate, by being over a second slower after suffering a loss of boost pressure, finished up four places lower behind the two Renault drivers and Baldi in the second of the Euroracing Alfa Romeos. Like Piquet, Prost relied on his team's spare car for his best time owing to the modifications on his own car causing a worrying amount of oversteer, while Cheever's efforts to go any quicker were thwarted by a loss of power, possibly as a result of having damaged the turbos after running out of fuel during the morning. Further down the order, behind the two closely-matched Toleman-Harts of Warwick and Giacomelli, de Angelis clocked up 11th fastest time even though most of the session was spent waiting around in the pits for repairs to be completed on his Lotus 94T, quite apart from a further handicap caused by the car's nose cone working loose on his quick lap. Then came Rosberg in the fastest of the hopelessly out-classed normally-aspirated cars – almost exactly 6 seconds slower than Tambay's Fer-

rari yet, at the same time, ahead of the three remaining turbo runners, Johansson, Mansell and an unfortunate Winkelhock. Unfortunate, because the German failed to achieve even one timed flying lap due to his ATS being sidelined by a broken turbo-charger, a legacy of the oil pipe problem in the morning, and the spare car being plagued by an incurable engine misfire. Some of the non-turbo runners had problems to contend with as well. Among them were Surer being plagued by a down-on-power engine in his Arrows (running this weekend with sponsorship from Leonardo – a firm specializing in leather goods), which went a long way to explaining why he was over a second slower than his impressive team-mate, and also Fabi whose efforts to hoist himself from the bottom of the time-sheets were dashed by a persistent high-speed engine misfire. Without doubt, though, the most unfortunate of them all was Boesel. His afternoon's work ended early by ploughing off into the barriers at the Sackskurve when the rear brakes failed on the spare Ligier that he was driving at the time, an incident that led to the car being virtually demolished and to the Brazilian being taken off to a nearby hospital for treatment to a neck injury.

That, unfortunately, proved to be the end of practice so far as any further battle for grid positions was concerned, as on Saturday both the morning untimed session and the final hour of qualifying took place in near-continuous rain. For ATS, of course, this was a bitter blow as it left the German team facing up to the reality of not taking part in their home Grand Prix, Winkelhock automatically joining Fabi and Acheson as a non-qualifier. In fact, conditions were so bad that some drivers didn't bother to go out at all during the afternoon, and among those who did several had spins or were forced to take to the escape roads at the chicanes, including the normally impeccable Prost. His team-mate, meanwhile, treated the bedraggled spectators to some superb opposite-lock power slides and only just failed to notch up fastest time, Cheever's best lap of 2 min 09.752 sec being just 0.158 sec slower than that set by Arnoux. Rosberg, too, put on another of his impressive displays of wet-weather driving and finished up in fourth place on the time-sheets behind Tambay who was now assured of starting the race from pole position.

In spite of the lack of a German driver in the race and the weather remaining rather unfriendly, if no longer actually raining, the spectators turned out in force on Sunday morning and before long the vast concrete stadium (containing seating accommodation for over 100,000 people) was just about crammed to capacity. With the Grand Prix scheduled for 2.30 p.m. the half-hour warm-up session should have started at 11.30 a.m. but, owing to some over-enthusiastic competitors in one of the supporting events damaging the catch-fences, the day's programme slipped some 30 minutes in arrears. Then, when the Formula 1 cars did eventually put in an appearance, there seemed to be nothing but trouble. For the John Player Lotus team it was more than that. It was nothing short of a disaster. First de Angelis rolled to a halt out on the circuit after just one lap with the control box for the electronic fuel-injection system having failed on his car: later he was to give vent to his feelings by ordering the *Motor Sport* correspondent, Denis Jenkinson, out of the Lotus pit in a rather unruly manner after complaining about something that had been written about him. Then Mansell, who had already had another trying time of it on Saturday with his 94T plagued by more overheating problems and a persistent engine misfire, quickly discovered that a fresh engine installed overnight had made no difference whatsoever. As a result, he could do little more than pull, dejectedly, into the pits where he was left facing up to the rather unhappy prospect of having to use the spare 93T for the race. About the only thing that could be said of it was that the British team was at least in good company as Prost ran into similar overheating problems to those of Mansell with his Renault RE40, Tambay blew up what was a new engine in his Ferrari 126C3 and Piquet ended the session saying that his BMW engine was down on power. The organizers, meanwhile, were hoping to do away with the regulation 2½-hour interval between the end of the warm-up and the start of the race in in order to keep abreast with television schedules but with so much mechanical mayhem it became increasingly obvious that the start would have to be delayed. Nevertheless, the mechanics knuckled down magnificently to the task of sorting everything out and, through everyone subsequently agreeing to reduce the amount of time between the opening of the pit lane and the start of the final count-down, the overall delay was limited to barely a quarter of an hour. This was in spite of Prost having to switch to the spare Renault at the end of of his warm-up lap – after finding a replacement engine, that had since been fitted to his original car, overheating badly!

The start proved to be a relatively clean and tidy affair, particularly up at the front where Tambay got away perfectly in his Ferrari 126C3 to emphatically beat his teammate into the first right-hander. Directly behind the two scarlet cars, de Cesaris similarly had little apparent trouble in slotting straight into third place but then, as the leaders rushed off towards the forest and to the first of the three chicanes, Piquet went steaming past the Italian in the spare Brabham that he had chosen to race with what looked to be consummate ease. Before long Prost, in spite of having had to set off in

second gear, was also moving up to challenge him and, indeed, ended the opening lap almost touching the Alfa's gearbox. Cheever was right up there as well, in sixth place, and then it was Baldi from Patrese, Johansson (he had made a particularly good start), Rosberg, Warwick, de Angelis, Laffite, Boutsen, a very tardy Giacomelli and Mansell before the main part of the non-turbo contingent. Already one car was out, Guerrero having pulled off the track at the Sachskurve with a blown-up engine in his Theodore, and part-way round the second lap there was another when Mansell's unhappy weekend was made complete by the Lotus 93T grinding to a silent halt. More engine gremlins! This latter incident, however, almost passed unnoticed due to a flurry of excitement caused by Arnoux taking over the lead from Tambay in a rather forceful manner and also by the two Renault drivers taking turns to elbow de Cesaris back to sixth spot. For Cheever, though, this was a particularly fraught business. At his first attempt to get by the Alfa Romeo he finished up momentarily on the grass after its occupant moved over on him – apparently inadvertently – and at the second attempt, on the approach to the third chicane, there was a brief clashing of wheels, fortunately with no serious consequences. Meanwhile, on the same lap, Patrese had rather less difficulty in overtaking Baldi in the other Alfa Romeo, and a little further back both Warwick and de Angelis surged past Rosberg's Williams under sheer horse-power advantage to give chase to Johansson in the Spirit-Honda.

With a clear track ahead of him, Arnoux began to really pile on the coal and was soon even pulling away from his team-mate who was rather more concerned about conserving his tyres, yet, at the same time, consistently

extending the gap between himself and Piquet's third-placed Brabham. Indeed, within half a dozen or so laps everything was pointing towards a Ferrari walk-over but then, on lap 10, the picture suddenly changed when Tambay went missing until eventually being seen crawling into the pits, his engine sounding decidedly off-colour. Moreover, efforts made by his mechanics to rectify matters by changing the plugs and other electrical ancillaries were to prove futile as the engine was still far from right when Tambay subsequently rejoined the race, and after completing just one more lap he retired the car with suspected valve failure. This was now actually the sixth retirement, for since Mansell's departure back on the second lap Alboreto's Tyrrell had stopped out on the circuit three laps later with a broken fuel pump drive, de Angelis' Lotus 94T had gone out with severe overheating problems after ten laps and Johansson had just abandoned the Spirit at the Sachskurve with its Honda V6 engine having blown up. In the meantime, Arnoux was pressing on as hard as ever as he clearly illustrated by setting a new fastest lap of 1 min 53.938 sec on his 12th tour, besides already beginning to lap tail-enders. At this stage Piquet was some 10 seconds adrift in his newly-acquired second place, while Prost, finding fifth gear becoming increasingly difficult to select in his Renault, was a further 5 seconds away in third place, still running immediately ahead of team-mate Cheever. There was then another sizeable gap to Patrese and de Cesaris, who had swopped places back on the eighth lap, and they, in turn, were being followed at varying intervals by Warwick, Baldi and the others, now being led by a very on-form Lauda. Like the Austrian, Watson was also climbing up through the field in the

René Arnoux, the eventual winner, leads team-mate Patrick Tambay and Nelson Piquet into the stadium during the early stages of the race. *(Phipps Photographic)*

other McLaren in his usual forthright manner and was currently lying eleventh, sandwiched between the two Williams FWO8Cs of Rosberg and Laffite. However, Rosberg, after leading the normally-aspirated brigade earlier in the race, was running into tyre problems caused partly by starting out on too soft a compound and partly through the need to run a minimum amount of wing in the interests of achieving reasonable straight-line speed. The result of this was that through the twisty stadium section his Williams was almost literally sliding all over the road by ever-increasing amounts and, although he tried desperately to defend his position, Watson finally got the better of him at the first right-hander going into lap 14. Five laps later Laffite, running on harder tyres, also made it through but by then there had been yet another change in the order due to a good drive from Warwick having ended in the pits after 17 laps because of engine trouble. Giacomelli, plagued by a lack of boost pressure for much of the race, didn't last much longer in the other Toleman either as on lap 20 he rolled to a halt out on the circuit with a broken turbo-charger, this bringing the retirement tally up to eight.

At the end of the 20th lap, just short of half-distance, the routine fuel and tyre stops began with Prost setting the ball rolling by bringing his Renault into the pits. In spite of a moment or so fishing in vain for first gear, as at the start, he was on his way again in almost exactly 13 seconds and rejoined the race in sixth place between the two Euroracing Alfa Romeos of de Cesaris and Baldi. On the following lap Rosberg was also in and then, two laps after that, even more excitement was brought about by the leader stopping, Arnoux subsequently rejoining in third place behind Piquet and Cheever thanks to more efficient pit work from the Ferrari team (13.1 seconds). Baldi also stopped on this lap but within a few minutes of resuming in eighth place his engine blew up and stranded him out on the circuit where he was soon to be joined by Boesel, in similar trouble. Meanwhile, the activity in the pits continued with Cheever, Jarier, Watson, Laffite and de Cesaris all taking on fresh tyres and more fuel in quick succession followed, on lap 28, by Patrese and also by Lauda who slid past his pit with his front wheels locked up and lost valuable time having to reverse into his correct place. The Brabham pit stop, on the other hand, was a real cracker, taking less than 10 seconds, and enabled Patrese to rejoin in fifth place directly in front of a rather bemused de Cesaris, who had repassed his compatriot just prior to making his own pit stop only to now find himself behind him once more. All the while Piquet was still driving around in the lead, but at the end of lap 30 he, too, turned off into the pits where he was destined to undergo a slightly longer delay than his team-mate of 11.1 seconds, yet still quicker than any of the others. Nevertheless this, together with the time lost travelling into and out of the pit lane, was still more than enough to allow Arnoux to take over the lead once again, and when Piquet finally regained the track, in second place, the Ferrari was almost 15 seconds clear. The two Renaults were next, but whereas Cheever was now in a strong third place, Prost was dropping away due to no longer being able to engage fifth gear at all. In fact, by lap 33 the Frenchman had been forced to give way to de Cesaris and Patrese, who had swopped places yet again, and was left persevering as best he could in what, at least, was a pretty secure-looking sixth place, everyone else having been lapped. Like Prost, Rosberg was also having a rather subdued race, for apart from his Williams still not handling very well, despite being sent out on harder tyres following the pit stop, his front brakes were now gradually going away. Consequently, instead of being able to set about regaining lost places, the World Champion was merely struggling around in a disappointing 13th place behind Lauda, Watson, Laffite, Surer, Jarier and another driver experiencing similar trouble, Boutsen.

At Silverstone there had been a distinct lack of pit signals from the Brabham pit and Piquet, unaware of how far he was behind Prost, had wound down the boost and concentrated on finishing second. On this occasion, however, he was being kept well informed of the situation and was responding by making a determined bid to snatch victory, closing up to the leading Ferrari at the rate of around a second per lap. Naturally, this produced a considerable amount of excitement in what had otherwise become a rather dull race. But, after reducing the gap to barely 5 seconds with just 6 laps remaining, Piquet seemed unable to make any further impression due to losing out a bit in traffic and to Arnoux speeding up to counter the challenge. In fact, the gap even began to increase again slightly until lap 43 when the rear of the Brabham suddenly shot up in flames as it went through the first chicane: a fuel filter had cracked, allowing fuel to seep on to the hot BMW engine. At first Piquet was convinced that it was a turbo failure, especially as the engine had cut out, but with his back becoming rather too warm for comfort he soon realized it was more than that, quickly pulled off to the side of the track, baled out and left some nearby fire marshals to deal with the conflagration. Obviously it was a bitter blow for him but then Cheever knew all about that as only four laps earlier he had seen a certain third place go down the drain, his Renault having expired out on the circuit with an inoperative fuel-injection pump caused by a broken control rod in the throttle mechanism. So now, with just over two laps to go, Arnoux could well afford to slacken right off, which was precisely what he did before happily acknowledging the chequered flag to score his second victory of the season and put himself back in the hunt for the World Championship.

Behind Arnoux, only de Cesaris, Patrese and Prost completed the full race distance and then they were a long way in arrears at that. Nevertheless, all three were only glad to have made it home as, in addition to Prost's gearbox trouble, Patrese had been short on revs ever since his pit stop and de Cesaris had been bothered by peculiar noises emanating from his engine for the last five minutes or so as if something was about to blow up at any moment. Fortunately for him

Results						
1	R. Arnoux (Ferrari)	1 hr 27 min 10.319 sec (210.524 kph/ 130.813 mph)	7	M. Surer (Arrows-Ford)	1 lap behind	
2	A. de Cesaris (Alfa Romeo)	1 hr 28 min 20.971 sec	8	J.P. Jarier (Ligier-Ford)	1 lap behind	
3	R. Patrese (Brabham-BMW)	1 hr 28 min 54.412 sec	9	T. Boutsen (Arrows-Ford)	1 lap behind	
4	A. Prost (Renault)	1 hr 29 min 11.069 sec	10	K. Rosberg (Williams-Ford)	1 lap behind	
*	N. Lauda (McLaren-Ford)	1 lap behind	11	J. Cecotto (Theodore-Ford)	1 lap behind	
5	J. Watson (McLaren-Ford)	1 lap behind	12	D. Sullivan (Tyrrell-Ford)	2 laps behind	
6	J. Laffite (Williams-Ford)	1 lap behind	**13	N. Piquet (Brabham-BMW)	3 laps behind	

*Disqualified
**Not running at finish

Fastest lap: R. Arnoux (Ferrari) on lap 12 in 1 min 53.938 sec (214.758 kph/133.444 mph)

Retirements

R. Guerrero (Theodore-Ford) engine on lap 1, 1, N. Mansell (Lotus-Renault) engine on lap 2, M. Alboreto (Tyrrell-Ford) fuel pump drive on lap 5, E. de Angelis (Lotus-Renault) engine on lap 11, P. Tambay (Ferrari) engine on lap 12, S. Johansson (Spirit-Honda) engine on lap 12, D. Warwick (Toleman-Hart) engine on lap 18, B. Giacomelli (Toleman-Hart) turbo-charger on lap 20, M. Baldi (Alfa Romeo) engine on lap 25, R. Boesel (Ligier-Ford) engine on lap 28. P. Ghinzani (Osella-Alfa Romeo) engine on lap 35, E. Cheever (Renault) fuel-injection pump on lap 39.

it didn't and, instead, he was now able to celebrate his best-ever Grand Prix result – after a rather unhappy weekend off the track in which he had been arrested, released on bail of DM15,000 and fined $10,000 by FISA for bringing the sport into disrepute by knocking over a police officer whilst attemp-

ting to barge his way into the circuit on Friday morning! He had forgotten his circuit passes. Meanwhile, there was also some rather bad news in store for Lauda as after crossing the line in a splendid fifth place – the first normally-aspirated runner – he learned that he was being disqualified for reversing

his McLaren in the pit lane. As a result, the remaining eight finishers (Ghinzani had been the only other retirement with engine trouble late in the race) were all moved up a place and Laffite unexpectedly found himself being awarded a Championship point by being classified sixth behind Watson.

XXI Grosser Preis von Österreich

Österreichring: August 14
Weather: Warm and sunny
Distance: 53 laps of 5.9424 km
circuit = 314.95 km (195.70 miles)

Following one week after the German Grand Prix, most teams arrived at the Osterreich-ring with the same cars that they had used at Hockenheim, but Ferrari had gone home to Maranello and returned with a brand new 126C3 for Tambay, and the Benetton Tyrrell team had rushed out the first example of the long-awaited successor to their 011 series of cars, the 012. In addition, because the car raced by Piquet in Germany had been damaged by the fire more than at first thought, the Fila/Parmalat Brabham team had transported out their original BT52 chassis (uprated to 'B' specification) from base to act as a replacement spare chassis. Otherwise, it was all much of a likeness when practice began on Friday morning under warm sunshine on the fast and spectacular Austrian circuit, for there were no changes in the driver line-up at all.

The hour and a half from 10 a.m. to 11.30 a.m. was supposed to have been a time for drivers to settle in and to set up cars to their liking, preparatory to the one hour of qualifying in the afternoon. As nearly always, though, it didn't quite work out like that, not for some of them at least. Alboreto set off in the new Tyrrell with its distinctive reverse-vee delta rear aerofoil only to return to the pits after barely a handful of laps with the car suffering from a serious water leak; Johansson had to abandon the newer of the two Spirit-Hondas out on the circuit, a gear-box pinion shaft having broken again as on the first morning in Germany; Patrese blew up the BMW engine in his Brabham pretty comprehensively; and Renault were plagued by high engine temperatures which, in the case of Cheever, who also suffered from a lack of turbo boost pressure, was explained to a large extent by the subsequent discovery of a cracked water radiator on his car. How-ever, the worst incident to occur came from a cockpit error when de Angelis arrived too fast at the Texaco Schikane on one lap and careered off the track in his Lotus 94T, the car travelling some considerable distance across the grass before finally being arrested by an earth bank. Fortunately the Italian survived the ordeal unscathed, but the car, apart from having its nose cone ripped off, also finished up with its undertray damaged. Furthermore, because there was insufficient

time to carry out the necessary repairs, he had to fall back on the team's unloved spare 93T for the afternoon qualifying session – only to find himself being sidelined again when the bodywork began to work loose and severely restrict his vision! The afternoon also failed to produce any change of fortune in the Spirit camp, for the newer car, its gearbox now repaired, promptly suffered an engine failure and then the older car that Johansson subsequently took over once more developed a persistent misfire. As a result, the Swede failed to achieve even one decent timed flying lap and was left lan-guishing at the bottom of the time-sheets. In complete contrast, the Ferrari team were having no problems at all and dominating proceedings with Arnoux and Tambay both lapping well clear of the rest of the field. Arnoux, in particular, was in absolutely splendid form and was alone in breaking the 1 min 30 sec barrier with a lap in 1 min 29.995 sec. Even so, Tambay was not that far away and might well have eclipsed his team-mate had it not been for a deer wandering from the woods and bringing out the yellow flags on his final lap. As it was he had to settle, somewhat frustrated, for the runner-up spot at 1 min 30.358 sec, still the best part of half a second quicker than Prost who came out comfortably third fastest with a time of 1 min 30.841 sec. Mansell, having a trouble-free practice in his Lotus 94T for once, was well in the reckoning with fourth fastest time of 1 min 31.263 sec and he, in turn, was closely followed by Cheever, Patrese, Baldi and Piquet, the Brabham duo sharing their team's spare car due to Patrese's car still being out of commission because of the engine failure earlier in the day and Piquet's proposed race chassis being down on boost pressure. Of the non-turbo runners, Lauda was quickest with 13th fastest time overall of 1 min 34.518 sec, while Alboreto finished up four places lower behind an unhappy de Angelis, Watson and Rosberg after once again resorting to his more familiar Tyrrell 011, this time because of the newer 012, fitted with a conventional rear aerofoil between sessions, giving problems in the brake department.

The final qualifying session on Saturday afternoon, preceded by another busy 90

minutes of testing in the morning, was delayed nearly half an hour due to problems with a Harrier Jump Jet, which had treated the many thousands of spectators present to a breath-taking demonstration just before-hand. Normally no-one would have been too bothered but, unlike the previous day, there

Starting Grid	
P. Tambay Ferrari (1 min 29.871 sec)	R. Arnoux Ferrari (1 min 29.935 sec)
N. Mansell Lotus-Renault (1 min 30.457 sec)	N. Piquet Brabham-BMW (1 min 30.566 sec)
A. Prost Renault (1 min 30.841 sec)	R. Patrese Brabham-BMW (1 min 31.440 sec)
B. Giacomelli Toleman-Hart (1 min 31.693 sec)	E. Cheever Renault (1 min 31.695 sec)
M. Baldi Alfa Romeo (1 min 31.769 sec)	D. Warwick Toleman-Hart (1 min 31.962 sec)
A. de Cesaris Alfa Romeo (1 min 32.359 sec)	E. de Angelis Lotus-Renault (1 min 32.451 sec)
M. Winkelhock ATS-BMW (1 min 33.211 sec)	N. Lauda McLaren-Ford (1 min 34.518 sec)
K. Rosberg Williams-Ford (1 min 35.380 sec)	S. Johansson Spirit-Honda (1 min 35.892 sec)
J. Watson McLaren-Ford (1 min 36.059 sec)	M. Alboreto Tyrrell-Ford (1 min 36.079 sec)
T. Boutsen Arrows-Ford (1 min 36.357 sec)	J.P. Jarier Ligier-Ford (1 min 36.435 sec)
R. Guerrero Theodore-Ford (1 min 36.532 sec)	M. Surer Arrows-Ford (1 min 36.619 sec)
D. Sullivan Tyrrell-Ford (1 min 36.772 sec)	J. Laffite Williams-Ford (1 min 37.017 sec)
P. Ghinzani Osella-Alfa Romeo (1 min 37.117 sec)	C. Fabi Osella-Alfa Romeo (1 min 37.217 sec)

Did not qualify:
R. Boesel (Ligier-Ford) 1 min 37.400 sec
J. Cecotto (Theodore-Ford) 1 min 37.497 sec
K. Acheson (March-Ford) 1 min 38.974 sec

was a distinct possibility of rain so not unnaturally some of the drivers became rather agitated. In the event it was to remain dry, or at least until much later in the afternoon, and worries that another grid might be decided by just one hour of qualifying went unfounded. Since the day before Tyrrell had put away their new car for further testing but otherwise everything was back to normal again except that Prost and Warwick had both elected to use their teams' spare cars as a result of developments during the morning. In the case of Prost it was because his proposed race chassis, fitted with a fresh engine overnight, had been going so well that he simply wanted to save it for the race. Warwick, on the other hand, had gone out in the spare Toleman in order to try yet another revised version of Brian Hart's four cylinder engine (this had various internal modifications and a different type of turbocharger manufactured by the British firm, Holset) and had been sufficiently impressed as to rely on it for qualifying. However, just when it mattered most, the engine began losing power and Warwick, instead of being able to hoist himself up amongst the front-runners as had been hoped, was not even able to match the lap times being set by his team-mate. Much the same applied to de Angelis, for after a trouble-free morning with a fresh Renault engine installed in his Lotus 94T, this also began losing power. The big difference, though, was that whereas Warwick was only around a quarter of a second slower than Giacomelli, de Angelis was over two seconds slower than Mansell who was once again driving superbly and now turning in the next best times to Arnoux and Tambay in their seemingly all-conquering Ferraris. As on the first day Arnoux was proving to be fractionally the quicker of the pair and, with a slightly improved time of 1 min 29.935 sec, looked to have pole position wrapped up. But then, in the closing minutes of the session, the situation suddenly changed when Tambay, after experimenting with different rear springs in a fruitless attempt to iron out a touch too much understeer, had subtle changes made to his car's aerodynamics, went out on his second set of qualifying tyres and whistled around in 1 min 29.871 sec (238.021 kph). Convinced that he could do even better, he then allowed his tyres to cool and attempted to squeeze in one more flying lap. Unfortunately, this was to be in vain as his efforts ended in an almighty spin at the long left-handed Texaco Schikane, but at least there was the consolation for him of subsequently finding out that he had already done enough to wrestle away the pole from his team-mate – and that counted for a lot as Tambay had not been at all impressed by Arnoux's tactics in overtaking him on the second lap of the German Grand Prix!

Just over half a second slower than Tam-bay at 1 min 30.457 sec, Mansell earned a well-deserved third place on the grid but Prost, following more problems with high engine temperatures in the spare Renault, failed to improve on his Friday time and slipped back to fifth spot, sandwiched between the Brabham-BMWs of Piquet (1 min 30.566 sec) and Patrese (1 min 31.440 sec). Like his team leader, Cheever also failed to find any improvement after being troubled by a misfiring engine and was now down in eighth place, directly behind Giacomelli in the quicker of the two Toleman-Harts. Then came Baldi, Warwick, de Cesaris (he had lost a lot of time waiting around for an engine change to be completed from the morning), a disgruntled de Angelis and Winkelhock to round off the top half of the grid, the German having had his qualifying run curtailed by a turbo failure and resultant fire around the rear bodywork of his ATS. Lauda was next, still the fastest non-turbo runner by reason of his Friday time after spending the afternoon concentrating on achieving a decent race set-up, while Rosberg, in spite of losing his second engine of the day, finished up one place lower immediately ahead of a somewhat relieved Johansson, who had finally got the Spirit-Honda into the race. Among the others, Acheson's third attempt to qualify the RAM March had once again ended in failure and neither Boesel nor Cecotto (hampered by gearbox trouble) had gone quickly enough, but the Kelemata Osella team had cause for celebration as both of their cars were in a race for the first time all season. Ghinzani had qualified in 25th spot and Fabi had just scraped on to the back of the grid at virtually the last moment after earlier being stranded out on the circuit with a broken throttle cable until carrying out temporary repairs and driving around to the pits to have it replaced.

After practice the Renault team took steps to try to get to the bottom of their overheating problems and discovered that in one of the inter-coolers the flow of water was being restricted by an accumulation of calcium. Consequently, they thoroughly cleaned out the inter-coolers on all three of their cars and next morning were somewhat happier when Prost and Cheever both returned to the pits at the end of the 30 minute warm-up session reporting that all was well. In fact, Prost set the fastest time in conditions that were absolutely superb, while Cheever's only complaint stemmed from a slight handling imbalance. The Toleman team, too, had obviously found a cure for the loss of power from their revised Hart engine as Warwick lapped only fractionally slower than Prost, and to add to their obvious delight Giacomelli had the other TG183B well on song, this having been fitted with one of the new Holset turbo-charger systems overnight. Elsewhere, there was a mild panic in the

Euroracing Alfa Romeo camp caused by de Cesaris suffering an engine failure, as on the previous morning, and Winkelhock had another turbo let go on his ATS. Otherwise, apart from the usual vexed question of tyre choice, preparations for the race were relatively straightforward. That is until after lunch when Johansson left the pits along with the other 25 starters for the warm-up lap and found to his dismay that the Honda engine in his Spirit was no longer running properly. Moreover, it felt as if it was about to expire at any moment, so after coasting into his grid position the Swede hurriedly stepped out of the car, sprinted across to the pit lane and climbed aboard the spare chassis. Then, as he set off on another warm-up lap just prior to the pit lane being officially closed, arrangements were made to wheel the abandoned car off the grid – a task that had to be carried out with the aid of a trolley-jack following the discovery that a rear wheel bearing had seized!

By 2.30 p.m. everything was under control again. Tambay had led the field around on the final warm-up lap in front of a very large crowd enjoying the warm sunshine, and all 26 cars were back in their grid positions ready to face the starting lights. Prost had very nearly lined up on the wrong side of the track but, despite his Renault being at a rather peculiar angle after having corrected himself at the last moment, the official FISA starter, Derek Ongaro, had no hesitation in pressing the button for the green light and so away they went. Initially it appeared to be a good clean start with Tambay taking up an immediate lead and Arnoux slotting into second place after staving off a determined challenge from Piquet, the Brazilian trying unsuccessfully to run past on his outside by using the gap between the Ferrari and the pit wall. However, as the rest of the pack followed them up the hill towards the Hella-Licht Schikane things began to go wrong. First de Angelis lost control of his Lotus 94T and suddenly swung sharp left, making light contact with the front of Giacomelli's Toleman before sliding off to the side of the track into retirement. Then, almost certainly as a result of the confusion causing the tail-enders to bunch up, more drama quickly followed on the exit from the chicane when Ghinzani, on the inside, bounced off the kerbing into the side of Laffite's Williams which, in turn, ricochetted into Surer's Arrows and spun the unfortunate Swiss to the right, straight into the path of Sullivan's Tyrrell. To add to the commotion, only moments later Watson ran into the back of Fabi's Osella due to the Italian braking rather abruptly to avoid becoming involved in the mêlée. The end result of this was that Surer and Sullivan both had to abandon their cars on the spot, too badly damaged to continue, and Watson was left limping away from the scene with the right-hand nose fin of his McLaren torn and

1983

Patrick Tambay goes into the second lap a clear leader from team-mate René Arnoux and Nelson Piquet. *(Autocar & Motor)*

twisted, the others seemingly getting away with it. By now Giacomelli had also got under way again in his Toleman but, unfortunately, the impact from de Angelis's Lotus had smashed its left-hand water radiator. Consequently, at the end of the lap, the Italian had little alternative other than to retire the car at the pits where he was followed in by Watson for a new nose cone. In the meantime, the leaders were blissfully unaware of the carnage that had just taken place and were already into their second lap, Tambay still setting the pace from Arnoux and Piquet. Prost was fourth, having moved up a place at the expense of Mansell on the opening lap, and Patrese was right up there in sixth place ahead of Cheever, Warwick, Baldi, de Cesaris, Johansson and Winkelhock before Alboreto in the leading normally-aspirated car. Next time round, though, Patrese was ahead of Mansell, Winkelhock had overtaken Johansson, and Warwick was missing altogether until eventually being seen heading for the pits. A turbocharger unit had failed and so in less than five minutes it was all over for the Toleman team on a weekend that had promised considerably better.

The race now at last began showing signs of settling down a bit with the first seven cars forming a high-speed procession, and the two Alfa Romeos of Baldi and de Cesaris gradually losing contact yet, at the same time, staying well out of the reach of Winkelhock's ATS. Further back, Lauda was making good progress following a poor start and after moving up to lead the non-turbo brigade on the third lap was soon homing in on

Johansson's overweight Spirit, eventually passing the Swede on lap 7. Within another lap Alboreto was also right up with the Honda-powered car, and as the two of them arrived at the right-hander on the top part of the circuit mid-way round lap 9 the Tyrrell driver tried to squeeze through on the inside. Instead of making it past, though, he collected the Spirit's right front wheel and finished up on the grass with the Tyrrell's left rear wheel all but torn off. At first it seemed that Johansson's race was also over as he spun to a halt and began climbing out of the car. However, after quickly assessing the damage and discovering that only the nose section was missing, he stepped aboard once more, rolled down the grass to restart the engine and drove around to the pits prior to going out again with his car fitted with a fresh nose cone. While this was happening the important part of the race was going largely unchanged except that Tambay (controlling things beautifully at his own pace), Arnoux, Piquet and Prost were now beginning to drop Patrese and leave Mansell and Cheever even further behind, both of whom were unhappy with their tyres. Mansell's Pirellis were steadily losing their grip, while Cheever was paying the price for having started out on what was proving to be too conservative a choice of Michelins. Even so the American certainly wasn't having any trouble in keeping up with the Lotus and, indeed, was making concerted efforts to find a way past it. As this continued Baldi disappeared with a broken engine on lap 14, leaving his team-mate on his own in eighth place, and Rosberg, fighting back from a terrible start

caused by a recalcitrant first gear, made further progress by overtaking Jarier to move up into 11th place behind Lauda.

Apart from a hectic moment at the Hella-Licht Schikane on lap 15, when Prost briefly snatched third place from Piquet, only to lose it again after bouncing over the kerbing and unavoidably bringing the left rear wheel of his Renault into contact with the Brabham's right front wheel, the first real change in the tense leadership battle came on lap 22. By then Tambay had already lapped several back-markers and now came up behind Jarier's Ligier just before the right-hander where Johansson and Alboreto had earlier tangled. Instead of allowing the leader through, though, Jarier stuck rigidly to the racing line and then continued to thwart every attempt made by Tambay to get past, both along the entire length of the top straight and again going into the Bosch-kurve. Naturally, this enabled Tambay's immediate pursuers to close right up and as they all exited the long right-hander so Arnoux, holding a tight line, took full advantage of his team-mate's predicament by sailing past into the lead – just as he was about to pull out from behind the Ligier! Consequently, Tambay had to back off, and by the time that he had finally nipped through on the inside of Jarier at the Texaco Schikane – shaking his fist as he did so – the loss of momentum had also given Piquet the opportunity of moving on ahead of him. So the order was now Arnoux – Piquet – Tambay, with Prost still in fourth place until peeling off into the pits at the end of the lap to undergo his scheduled refuelling/tyre stop.

In the pits the Renault was serviced in only 11.7 seconds and when Prost charged back out into the fray he was in seventh place between de Cesaris and Mansell, the Englishman having just lost two places in as many laps because of his tyre problem steadily growing worse. By now Laffite had made his scheduled pit stop as well but, after completing just one more lap, the Williams driver was back in to retire his car after hoping, in vain, that the change of rubber would eliminate a worsening vibration that had been apparent ever since the first lap fracas. This was followed, in quick succession, by Boutsen arriving at the pits with the Ford-Cosworth engine in his Arrows misfiring badly – a problem that was traced to a broken spark plug and one that dropped the Belgian to the back of the field before setting off again with a fresh set of plugs – and by Guerrero retiring his Theodore with a broken gearbox. In the meantime, other drivers were making their routine stops and at the end of lap 28 it was the turn of the leader to come in, along with the fourth-placed Patrese. After being stationary for just 11.2 seconds, Arnoux rejoined the race in third place and Patrese (held up for a mere 10.2 seconds) took off in sixth place ahead of Cheever, who had stopped two laps beforehand. However, so far as the Italian was concerned, it was all but over as on lap 30 the BMW engine in his Brabham suddenly expired and he was obliged to pull off the track. All the while Tambay had been setting about making up lost ground following Jarier's inexcusable behaviour and on the same lap seized upon the opportunity to regain the lead when Piquet ran wide on his way out of the Hella-Licht Schikane and put a rear wheel on to the grass. Unfortunately, it was to count for nothing. By the time that Tambay had reached the Texaco Schikane the Ferrari was losing its oil pressure and he ended the lap by touring into the pits, his second engine failure on successive weekends. So now Piquet led once more, almost exactly 30 seconds clear of Arnoux, but yet to stop.

When Piquet did pull into the pits at the end of lap 31 his mechanics responded with their usual precision and had him on his way again in a whisker over 10 seconds. This, as it turned out, was just quick enough to prevent Arnoux from going by into the lead, the Ferrari roaring past the pits as the Brabham accelerated up the hill to the Hella-Licht Schikane. At this point, with Piquet on comparatively cold tyres, it still seemed likely that Arnoux would regain the lead but the Brazilian obviously had other ideas about that and defended his position magnificently throughout the rest of the lap. Then, with his tyres up to optimum working temperature once more, Piquet even began pulling away a little and looked to have the situation under control, although to add to the excitement

Prost was now only a few car lengths adrift in third place. Meanwhile de Cesaris, who had momentarily been lying third, suffered the ignominy of running out of fuel after being kept out longer than had originally been planned (the pits had been particularly busy at that time) and, on lap 34, Winkelhock disappeared from seventh place with the BMW engine in his ATS overheating badly. As a result Cheever, on softer tyres than previously, was now up into fourth place, Mansell was a distant fifth and, a lap down, Lauda was sixth after being last to stop for tyres and fuel. Then it was Jarier from Rosberg (no longer able to select third gear in his Williams), Fabi, Watson, Ghinzani, Johansson and Boutsen. No-one else was left.

Piquet continued to hold sway out in front until lap 38 when Arnoux and Prost both went by him in quick succession. Although there was no obvious sign of any problem, the Brazilian was, in fact, now feeling the effects of a slight loss of power from his BMW engine, so rather than try to stay with his two adversaries he turned down the boost

and concentrated on finishing third. Arnoux, meanwhile, tried desperately to break free of Prost's Renault by driving as hard as he knew how. But it was to little avail. His erstwhile team-mate simply kept on coming and for the next nine laps it was a really thrilling situation with barely anything to choose between them. On lap 48, however, Arnoux suddenly found that he could no longer select fourth gear as he accelerated away from the Hella-Licht Schikane, and that did it. As the Ferrari momentarily hesitated so Prost pounced by moving over to the inside of the track and blasting past into the lead before the two cars reached the next right-hander. After that Arnoux gradually fell away over the remaining five laps (his Ferrari was to roll to a halt out on the circuit during the slowing-down lap, the gearbox broken completely!) leaving Prost to notch up his fourth victory of the season almost 7 seconds clear and extend his lead at the top of the Championship table to a most comfortable-looking 14 points over Piquet, who duly completed the race in third place. Less than a second away from the Brazilian at the finish, after a

Alain Prost wins the race, and takes a 14-point lead in the World Championship table. *(Autocar & Motor)*

splendid charge in the closing stages, Cheever brought his Renault home in fourth place, Mansell was fifth, a lap behind and

blaming his tyres for not having finished higher, while Lauda rounded off the point scorers with another good drive in sixth

place, a further lap in arrears but, at the same time, well clear of Jarier and the remaining six finishers.

Results						
1	A. Prost (Renault)	1 hr 24 min 32.745 sec (223.494 kph/ 138.872 mph)	7	J.P. Jarier (Ligier-Ford)	2 laps behind	
2	R. Arnoux (Ferrari)	1 hr 24 min 39.580 sec	8	K. Rosberg (Williams-Ford)	2 laps behind	
3	N. Piquet (Brabham-BMW)	1 hr 25 min 00.404 sec	9	J. Watson (McLaren-Ford)	2 laps behind	
4	E. Cheever (Renault)	1 hr 25 min 01.140 sec	10	C. Fabi (Osella-Alfa Romeo)	3 laps behind	
5	N. Mansell (Lotus-Renault)	1 lap behind	11	P. Ghinzani (Osella-Alfa Romeo)	4 laps behind	
6	N. Lauda (McLaren-Ford)	2 laps behind	12	S. Johansson (Spirit-Honda)	5 laps behind	
			13	T. Boutsen (Arrows-Ford)	5 laps behind	

Fastest lap: A. Prost (Renault) on lap 20 in 1 min 33.961 sec (227.660 kph/141.461 mph)

Retirements
E. de Angelis (Lotus-Renault) accident on lap 1, M. Surer (Arrows-Ford) accident on lap 1, D. Sullivan (Tyrrell-Ford) accident on lap 1, B. Giacomelli (Toleman-Hart) accident damage on lap 2, D. Warwick (Toleman-Hart) turbo-charger on lap 3, M. Alboreto (Tyrrell-Ford) accident on lap 9, M. Baldi (Alfa Romeo) engine on lap 14, J. Laffite (Williams-Ford) handling on lap 22, R. Guerrero (Theodore-Ford) gearbox on lap 26, R. Patrese (Brabham-BMW) engine on lap 30, P. Tambay (Ferrari) engine on lap 31, A. de Cesaris (Alfa Romeo) out of fuel on lap 32, M. Winkelhock (ATS-BMW) engine on lap 34.

XXXI Grote Prijs van Nederland

Zandvoort: August 28
Weather: Overcast but dry
Distance: 72 laps of 4.252 km
circuit = 306.14 km (190.23 miles)

For McLaren International the Dutch Grand Prix was of particular significance as it marked the beginning of a new era for the British-based team. It was the first public appearance of their new turbo car, the MP4/1E, with its Porsche-designed, TAG-financed V6 turbo-charged engine. Originally it had been hoped that two such cars would be available for the race but whilst a second chassis had been brought over from England it was only partly completed. Consequently, there was just a singleton entry for Niki Lauda, his team-mate being left to persevere with a Ford-Cosworth-powered MP4/1C for another weekend. In fact, even Lauda's car was not quite ready when practice began under warm sunshine on Friday morning – even though the team's mechanics had been trying to finish it on the ferry over to Holland! So, as an interim measure, the Austrian started out in one of the more familiar MP4/1Cs prior to switching over to the new car part-way through the untimed session and then concentrating on it for the rest of the weekend. Not surprisingly, with a completely new package, there were teething problems apparent almost immediately, mainly with throttle lag and handling, but in terms of straight-line speed the car was very impressive and in amongst the best of them. Furthermore, the engine was soon proving to be extremely reliable, for after an otherwise trouble-free morning Lauda went on to enjoy more of the same in the afternoon qualifying session and was well pleased to end the day half way up the time-sheets, his best lap of 1 min 20.169 sec (the best part of a full second quicker than Watson could manage in his MP4/1C) placing him 16th fastest.

With so much attention being attracted

towards the McLaren pit it was easy to overlook the rest of the field but there were certainly some interesting things going on. Not least was that of Mansell heading the time-sheets for the first half-hour or so of qualifying after going out on his first set of Pirellis and turning in a lap of 1 min 16.721 sec. Indeed, had he not had the misfortune to come up behind Johansson's slower-moving Spirit-Honda through the series of corners leading on to the main straight whilst out on his second set of tyres, Mansell might well have earned the provisional pole. Instead, he saw his chance of improving slip away and wound up slightly disappointed to find his earlier time ultimately beaten, first by Prost (1 min 16.611 sec) and then by team-mate de Angelis who, after having taken the edge off the engine installed in a brand new Lotus 94T during the morning, made amends by charging around in what had now become the spare chassis in 1 min 16.411 sec. Nevertheless, from the point of view of the Lotus team as a whole, this was a most encouraging situation and seemed to fully vindicate a decision to fit their cars with the experimental four-tier rear aerofoils which, apart from a brief appearance during practice in Austria, had not been seen since Imola. Meanwhile, the usually dominant Ferrari 126C3s were being rather overshadowed, although Tambay was certainly well in the hunt with fourth fastest time of 1 min 16.857 sec and overcoming a slight handling deficiency through the slower turns by some quiet spectacular opposite-lock driving. Arnoux, on the other hand, was way off the pace by his normal standards (only 12th fastest) and having a most frustrating day, a turbo failure sidelining his proposed race chassis during the morning and the spare C3,

that he took over for qualifying, developing a seemingly incurable fault in its fuel-injection system. The two Brabham drivers were not too happy with their progress either, only in this instance the problem was that of being unable to find a good handling balance. Piquet, though, did at least manage one reasonable lap in 1 min 17.194 sec to narrowly pip Warwick, going well in his Toleman, for fifth place in the standings, while Patrese eventually salvaged eighth spot where he was sandwiched between the two reliably-running Euroracing Alfa Romeos of de Cesaris and Baldi. After that there were few surprises at the end of the day for, as usual now, the normally-aspirated runners were in a different league with even the best amongst them coming out only 14th fastest overall. That was Alboreto (now concentrating on the new Tyrrell 012 – with a conventional rear aerofoil), who just pipped Surer's Arrows for the dubious honour by 0.004 sec with a time of 1 min 20.149 sec.

After being troubled by more indifferent handling during the untimed session on Saturday morning, the Brabham team finally traced the cause to their cars' rear shock-absorbers, which were found to have been binding. This, it was thought, had probably occurred because of changes made to suspension settings and so, as a means of preventing a recurrence of the problem, the team altered the settings of their cars back to a previous configuration. However, for the final qualifying session it was decided to concentrate solely on the spare BT52B in order to take advantage of further development work recently carried out at the BMW factory in Munich. All three team cars had arrived at Zandvoort with a new water-spray system designed to reduce the temperature of the air entering the inter-cooler. But, in addition, the spare chassis had a modified exhaust system and a revised turbo-charger unit employing a larger turbine as well as a different boost control valve – supplied by Brian Hart! – to improve the low-speed

Starting Grid

Starting Grid

	N. Piquet
	Brabham-BMW
P. Tambay	(1 min 15.630 sec)
Ferrari	
(1 min 16.370 sec)	E. de Angelis
	Lotus-Renault
A. Prost	(1 min 16.411 sec)
Renault	
(1 min 16.611 sec)	N. Mansell
	Lotus-Renault
R. Patrese	(1 min 16.711 sec)
Brabham-BMW	
(1 min 16.940 sec)	D. Warwick
	Toleman-Hart
A. de Cesaris	(1 min 17.198 sec)
Alfa Romeo	
(1 min 17.233 sec)	M. Winkelhock
	ATS-BMW
R. Arnoux	(1 min 17.306 sec)
Ferrari	
(1 min 17.397 sec)	E. Cheever
	Renault
M. Baldi	(1 min 17.676 sec)
Alfa Romeo	
(1 min 17.887 sec)	B. Giacomelli
	Toleman-Hart
M. Surer	(1 min 17.902 sec)
Arrows-Ford	
(1 min 19.696 sec)	J. Watson
	McLaren-Ford
S. Johansson	(1 min 19.787 sec)
Spirit-Honda	
(1 min 19.966 sec)	J. Laffite
	Williams-Ford
M. Alboreto	(1 min 19.979 sec)
Tyrrell-Ford	
(1 min 20.149 sec)	N. Lauda
	McLaren-TAG
R. Guerrero	(1 min 20.169 sec)
Theodore-Ford	
(1 min 20.190 sec)	T. Boutsen
	Arrows-Ford
J.P. Jarier	(1 min 20.245 sec)
Ligier-Ford	
(1 min 20.247 sec)	K. Rosberg
	Williams-Ford
R. Boesel	(1 min 20.391 sec)
Ligier-Ford	
(1 min 20.660 sec)	C. Fabi
	Osella-Alfa Romeo
D. Sullivan	(1 min 20.815 sec)
Tyrrell-Ford	
(1 min 20.842 sec)	

Did not qualify:
P. Ghinzani (Osella-Alfa Romeo)
1 min 20.926 sec
J. Cecotto (Theodore-Ford) 1 min 20.955 sec
K. Acheson (March-Ford) 1 min 23.093 sec

engine response. That this latest specification was effective was soon made pretty obvious by Piquet not only being fastest of all through the speed-trap at the start/finish line but also turning in lap times that were immediately nearly a full second quicker than the day before. Moreover, when he went out on his second set of tyres, Piquet shot right to the top of the time-sheets with a lap in 1 min 16.132 sec before putting in a real flier at 1 min 15.630 sec (202.395 kph). After that Patrese took over the car and he, too, began to pick up on his lap times, ultimately improving to 1 min 16.940 sec. Unfortunately, though, his afternoon turned into a somewhat fraught affair owing to inadver-

tently baulking de Cesaris, on a quick lap, through the Hugenholtzbocht. Normally, drivers accept this as all part of the game, but not de Cesaris, not on this occasion at least. First he waited until Patrese was on a quick lap and deliberately gave his compatriot an unscheduled 'brake-test' and then, later, lashed out at him as he arrived at the pits – still sitting in the car and with his helmet on, of course! Away from this totally unnecessary and rather pathetic episode, practice ended with Piquet securely on pole position as no-one else had even approached his time, let alone beat it. As it was, Tambay had come nearest to him by improving to 1 min 16.370 sec, which moved the Ferrari driver up into second place on the grid and left the overnight pole-sitter, de Angelis, in third spot, the Italian, back in his new car, having failed to achieve a single timed lap all afternoon. On his first qualifying run the right front tyre of his Lotus had started losing air through a leaking wheel rim, while on his second run he had been so badly held up by Sullivan's Tyrrell that he had simply given up in frustration. His team-mate, using the spare 94T this time out after his own car had been wheeled away for an engine change in the morning owing to a spark plug breaking up, had also had problems with the traffic. Nevertheless, Mansell had at least made some improvement – to 1 min 16.711 sec – and finished up in a fine fifth place on the grid between Prost, marginally slower than the first day, and Patrese. For Arnoux, meanwhile, it had been another disastrous afternoon with more turbo trouble sidelining his proposed race chassis for the second day running followed by the engine blowing up in the spare Ferrari. Somehow, in between this, he had managed to improve to 1 min 17.397 sec but, even so, it still left the Frenchman facing the prospects of starting the race from an uncharacteristically low tenth position, Warwick, de Cesaris and Winkelhock being the others to wind up ahead of him. Cheever, too, found himself further down the grid than usual after complaining that the Michelin qualifying tyres had caused his Renault to oversteer badly, and was actually in 11th spot, just ahead of Baldi (in considerable pain and discomfort from an inflamed tendon in his right arm) and Giacomelli. There was then a gap of nearly 2 seconds separating the rest of the field, but a rather surprising aspect was to find them all covered by little more than a second. The only exception was Acheson, whose confidence had been shattered somewhat by his RAM March suffering a complete brake failure at the Marlborobocht during the morning and who had ended up at the bottom of the time-sheets for the second day running. Consequently, the Ulsterman was yet again a non-qualifier and was joined, on this occasion, by Ghinzani and Cecotto. Among the others, Johansson had qualified

the Spirit-Honda (now sporting a new red, white and blue livery) in 16th spot, behind Surer and a much-improved Watson (the two quickest normally-aspirated runners), in spite of a practice plagued by a misfiring engine and poor throttle response most of the time; Lauda had qualified the new McLaren-TAG three places lower after a turbo failure had killed his hopes of improving on the first day's performance; and Rosberg, blaming the traffic and a bad choice of tyres, had qualified only 23rd – by far his lowest starting position since joining the Williams team!

Unlike Friday, Saturday's practice had taken place under grey and overcast skies and it was the same on race day except that the clouds looked even more menacing. The wind had got up, too, and was doing its best to cover the surface of the track with fine particles of sand, which was obviously going to make it a bit slippery in places. Nevertheless, when it came round to the 30 minute warm-up session just past mid-day the drivers appeared to have little difficulty in adjusting to the change in conditions as there were no untoward incidents. Nor was there much in the way of mechanical mayhem, although Arnoux and Piquet were both unhappy with their engines, and Patrese, fastest in the warm-up, ended his run with an oil leak. For the Ferrari team this was no real problem as Arnoux simply elected to take over the well-used spare 126C3. The Brabham team, on the other hand, not only had to find a cure for Patrese's oil leak but also carry out an engine change as Piquet decided that he would rather stick to his own car but have it fitted with the engine from the spare chassis with the revised turbo-charger and exhaust systems. Furthermore, because of local noise restrictions on Sunday mornings delaying the warm-up session there was only 1½ hours or so in which to do the work before the start of the race, scheduled for 2.30 p.m. However, the Brabham mechanics rose to the occasion magnificently and had both of their drivers mobile again with just a few minutes to spare before the pit lane was officially closed. A pleasing aspect for the organizers, meanwhile, was the size of the crowd as in direct contrast to the previous year, when the race had necessarily been brought forward to early July and attracted a poor response, the spectators had returned in their numbers once more with the figure quoted at a much healthier 61,000.

As the field set off on the final warm-up lap, led by Piquet, Winkelhock's ATS was left behind on the dummy grid with its engine refusing to start. Eventually it was coaxed into life but the German, after catching up the others, then completely overlooked the rule about not overtaking and lining up at the back of the grid and, instead, proceeded to thread his way through the cars so as to take up his original starting position. Of much greater concern, however, was the length of time that some of the drivers took to form up at the back for this led to an inordinately long start and anxiety about clutches overheating. For Tambay, in particular, this was something that became only too apparent, and when the green light finally did come on it resulted in the Frenchman making a real mess of his start by very nearly stalling. Fortunately, he had the good sense to pull over to the left to allow as much room as possible for the cars immediately behind him to squeeze past but, for all that, there were still one or two hectic moments and it seemed to be more by luck than judgement that no-one came to any grief. Meanwhile, Piquet got away beautifully to snap straight into an undisputed lead. Without doubt, though, the most impressive start of all came from Cheever, who pulled over to the right before charging down the inside, almost brushing the pit wall, to take up second place – from 11th on the grid! In spite of the slow-moving Ferrari in front of them, Prost, Patrese and de Cesaris also made good starts to slot into the next three places directly ahead of the two black and gold Lotus 94Ts of de Angelis and Mansell, who arrived at Tarzan virtually side by side. Mansell, on the outside, then tried unsuccessfully to overtake his team-mate as they exited the hairpin and although he finally made it round the outside of him at the next corner he almost immediately slid wide, lost his momentum and had more or less to sit and watch as de Angelis, Arnoux, Warwick and Johansson (another to have made a good start) all rushed past him. Further back, Guerrero was already in trouble with a damaged nose cone after being struck by Jarier's Ligier, and Tambay was almost bringing up the rear, the opening lap ending with the Ferrari crossing the line in only 21st position as the Theodore was being driven straight into the pits for repairs.

Having got away to such a comfortable start, Piquet was obviously determined to make the most of it and went on to completely dominate the early stages of the race by pulling away at the rate of almost a second per lap. Cheever, on the other hand, soon began to lose the benefit of his superlative start. After just four laps Prost neatly slipped past him going into Tarzan and then, at the end of lap 8, he was elbowed back another place by Patrese, who pulled out of his slip-stream along the main straight and nipped through on the inside as they roared past the pits. However, whereas Prost had already pulled clear in second place and was giving chase to the leader, Patrese seemed unable to make any significant headway over Cheever. In fact, before long the pair of them were being caught by a hard-charging Arnoux, the Frenchman having disposed of de Angelis back on the second lap and taken over fifth place three laps later when smoke had started pouring out from the right-hand

turbo-charger unit of de Cesaris' Alfa Romeo and ended the Italian's race in the pits. By now Jarier had also retired, the front suspension of his Ligier having collapsed back on the fourth lap, but otherwise there seemed to be few problems cropping up and, instead, the spectators were being treated to lots of really close racing going on throughout most of the field. Amidst all of the excitement that this was causing, one driver to be making particularly good progress, apart from Warwick, who was now up into a fine sixth place ahead of de Angelis and Mansell, was Watson. Putting on another of his typical charges, he had already overtaken Laffite, Surer, Rosberg, Alboreto and Baldi, and was now coming up to challenge Johansson for ninth place. Tambay, after having allowed his clutch to cool down, was beginning to carve his way up through the field as well and was currently in the throes of following Winkelhock and Lauda past Alboreto and Rosberg, all five running virtually nose to tail. As these little battles continued to rage lower down the order, de Angelis disappeared from eighth place when the Renault engine in his Lotus suddenly cut out on lap 13 due to a fault developing in the fuel-metering unit, which left Mansell with a clear run at Warwick, and Arnoux took only until the start of lap 15 to oust Cheever from fourth place going into Tarzan prior to dishing out similar treatment to Patrese seven laps later.

After 25 laps Piquet was still looking as comfortable as ever out in front, although it had already become noticeable that the gap between himself and Prost's Renault, which at one point had been around 7 seconds, was slowly shrinking and was now down to little more than 5 seconds. A further 10 seconds away or thereabouts, Arnoux was steadily consolidating third place, but Patrese was now looking to be in real danger of being repassed by Cheever, the American coming

back at him with a vengeance. Warwick's sixth place was no longer looking very secure either for Mansell had now moved to within striking distance of the Toleman, and Watson, having long since dealt with Johansson, was catching them both. Further back, Tambay had just overtaken Winkelhock after being stuck behind the ATS for some ten laps, so was now up into tenth place behind Baldi, but Lauda, who had only moments earlier been lying 12th after following Baldi, Winkelhock and Tambay past Johansson, had suddenly been repassed by the Swede and was heading down the pit lane. At first it appeared that it might only be an early routine stop for tyres. Unfortunately, though, it was to be the end of an extremely promising debut for the McLaren-TAG turbo. It was not the engine as that had been running reliably throughout. Instead, it was the brakes, the fluid having boiled as a result of a lot of relatively late braking and the extra weight and speed of the turbo. Meanwhile, before Lauda had even stepped out of the cockpit, there was unexpected drama at Tarzan. This time it centered around Mansell who, despite having just received a signal to stop at the end of the following lap for his tyres and fuel, tried a hopelessly late outbraking manoeuvre on Warwick as they went into the hairpin and spun straight off into the sand, stalling his engine and putting paid to what had hitherto been such a promising weekend for the John Player Lotus team. Fortunately, Warwick kept well clear of the black and gold car as it careered off the track in front of him and continued with his sixth place intact for another five laps prior to Watson making a somewhat better job than Mansell of overtaking him on lap 32 – the same lap that Cheever scythed past Patrese to take over fourth spot and only moments after Tambay had caught and passed Baldi for eighth. At that point Warwick then made for the pits for

---

The incident that changed the entire complexion of the race: Alain Prost, with his Renault already sideways, about to collect the right front wheel of Nelson Piquet's Brabham. (*Autosport*)

fresh tyres and more fuel from where, after a comparatively long stop, he eventually rejoined the race in 12th position between Alboreto in the sole surviving Tyrrell (Sullivan had quietly disappeared from near the back of the field with an engine failure on lap 21) and Rosberg.

By half-distance (36 laps), with an increasing amount of activity taking place in the pits as other drivers began making their scheduled stops, the situation at the front of the race had become decidedly interesting: Prost was almost up with Piquet and now visibly gaining on him. For several laps the Brazilian had found his Brabham developing an increasing amount of oversteer as the tyres wore down and the fuel load lightened, but rather than bring forward his pit stop he continued to press on regardless, even when Prost moved right in on his tail. Meanwhile, Cheever's race turned really sour. At the end of lap 38 he made his routine pit stop in a reasonably quick 12.6 seconds only to find that on rejoining the race his engine was no longer pulling properly and was misfiring. Then, on returning to the pit lane at the end of the next lap to have the problem investigated he was waved straight on through as his team was busy preparing to receive Prost, whereupon his Renault continued to cough and splutter until the engine cut out completely part-way round lap 40 due to an electrical failure. That was bad enough, but to make matters worse for him on his way out of the pit lane the second time he had unavoidably run over the ATS designer, Gustav Brunner, who had failed to spot the Renault in the midst of overseeing Winkelhock's stop and was now on his way to the medical centre with a broken leg and ankle. The irony of it all was that Winkelhock should no longer have been in the race following the incorrect procedure taken by him on the pace lap – he was eventually to be black-flagged for this on lap 50 (almost exactly an hour after the infringement!) – while Prost was destined never to make his pit stop. Incredibly, in his efforts to wrench away the lead from Piquet, the Championship leader proceeded to put himself and his arch-rival out of the race by a most uncharacteristic error of judgement under braking for Tarzan at the start of the forty-second lap. Immediately prior to this he had aimed his Renault well over to the inside of the track but then, as he drew alongside Piquet, he momentarily locked up his rear wheels, which caused the back of his car to slide out of line, tried in vain to correct it, collected the right front wheel of the Brabham and promptly sent it skating off the track and on into the tyre barrier. At this point Prost appeared to have got away with it as he merely cannoned off the blue and white car and continued. However, the impact had damaged the Renault's left-hand nose fin and later on the same lap it turned upwards on its

René Arnoux drives on to a comfortable and somewhat fortuitous victory. *(Phipps Photographic)*

mounting as Prost approached the fast right-hander leading on to the main straight and sent the French car understeering off into the guard-rail at the side of the track. It then spun round to a halt, its left front suspension damaged but its occupant, mercifully, uninjured. Naturally, this changed the entire complexion of the race and left a surprised Arnoux in the lead, having taken on fresh tyres and more fuel only minutes earlier in a whisker over 10 seconds without losing his place. Behind him, Watson was now up into an incredible second place and Tambay was third, but by lap 44, when they, too, had made their tyre and fuel stops, the order was Arnoux, Patrese (he had stopped at the end of lap 40), Tambay, Watson. After that only Warwick, Baldi and Alboreto were still on the same lap as the unfortunate incident in the pit lane had seriously delayed Winkelhock, while Johansson had dropped right away owing to having lost even more time in the pits because of some petrol being inadvertently spilled around the back of his Spirit which had briefly caught fire.

Arnoux was now in the happy position of leading the race by well over 40 seconds, but there was never any question of it becoming a boring procession. Patrese and Tambay saw to that, for they were only some 3 seconds apart and became involved in an absolutely enthralling 'cat and mouse' battle for second place, the Brabham-BMW enjoying a slight power advantage along the straights, but the Ferrari compensating for

this by being quicker through the corners and gaining a bit of ground under braking. Over 20 laps later it was still much the same, making it seem increasingly likely that Tambay would have to settle for third place. Then came lap 67, and more bad luck for Patrese. The Brabham-BMW suddenly lost its turbo boost pressure and slowed dramatically which, of course, was all it needed for Tambay to go surging past. With less than six laps to go there was obviously little point in Patrese going into the pits, so he stayed out in the hope of still being able to finish in the points. Unfortunately for him, even this was to be too much to ask as within just two more laps he had been elbowed down to seventh place and eventually crawled across the line a dejected ninth. In the meantime, Arnoux had eased right off in the closing stages yet still went on to win the race by a very healthy 20 seconds from his team-mate, who finished in a comfortable second place to give the Ferrari team a superb, if extremely fortuitous, 1–2 victory. Still on the same lap at the finish, Watson followed the two scarlet cars home in a superb third place, Warwick was a jubilant fourth, having just scored the very first Championship points for himself and his team, and Baldi completed a difficult afternoon's work, because of his painful right arm, in fifth place. Then, a lap down, Alboreto concluded an encouraging race debut for the new Tyrrell 012 by finishing sixth, in spite of a very late fuel stop. Johansson, Surer, the unfortunate Patrese, 201

Boesel, Guerrero and Giacomelli (he had recovered from a quick spin in the closing stages) were also still running at the finish but both Williams drivers had packed up early after an altogether dismal weekend, Laffite going out with handling problems and Rosberg with a misfiring engine, while Fabi and Boutsen had both suffered late engine failures.

Results		
1	R. Arnoux (Ferrari)	1 hr 38 min 41.950 sec (186.107 kph/ 115.641 mph)
2	P. Tambay (Ferrari)	1 hr 39 min 02.789 sec
3	J. Watson (McLaren-Ford)	1 hr 39 min 25.691 sec
4	D. Warwick (Toleman-Hart)	1 hr 39 min 58.789 sec
5	M. Baldi (Alfa Romeo)	1 hr 40 min 06.242 sec
6	M. Alboreto (Tyrrell-Ford)	1 lap behind
7	S. Johansson (Spirit-Honda)	2 laps behind
8	M. Surer (Arrows-Ford)	2 laps behind
9	R. Patrese (Brabham-BMW)	2 laps behind
10	R. Boesel (Ligier-Ford)	2 laps behind
*11	C. Fabi (Osella-Alfa Romeo)	4 laps behind
12	R. Guerrero (Theodore-Ford)	4 laps behind
13	B. Giacomelli (Toleman-Hart)	4 laps behind
*14	T. Boutsen (Arrows-Ford)	7 laps behind

*Not running at finish

Fastest lap: R. Arnoux (Ferrari) on lap 33 in 1 min 19.863 sec (191.668 kph/119.097 mph)

Retirements
J.P. Jarier (Ligier-Ford) front suspension on lap 4, A. de Cesaris (Alfa Romeo) turbocharger on lap 6, E. de Angelis (Lotus-Renault) fuel-metering unit on lap 13, D. Sullivan (Tyrrell-Ford) engine on lap 21, N. Lauda (McLaren-TAG) brakes on lap 26, N. Mansell (Lotus-Renault) spun off on lap 27, J. Laffite (Williams-Ford) handling on lap 38, E. Cheever (Renault) electrics on lap 40, N. Piquet (Brabham-BMW) accident on lap 42, A. Prost (Renault) accident damage on lap 42, M. Winkelhock (ATS-BMW) disqualified on lap 51, K. Rosberg (Williams-Ford) engine on lap 54.

LIVº Gran Premio d'Italia

Monza: September 11
Weather: Warm and hazy
Distance: 52 laps of 5.800 km
circuit = 301.60 km (187.40 miles)

Early September meant Monza and in the light of recent results, in particular the outcome of the Dutch Grand Prix, Italian passions were running at an even higher level than usual. Not only had Ferrari flown past Renault in the Constructors' Championship to take a 12 point lead but both of their drivers were now in with a very real chance of clinching the Drivers' title, Arnoux having moved up into second place in the table just 8 points behind Prost (51 points), while Tambay was only a further 6 points adrift in joint third place with Piquet. The Italian team were taking no chances for their home race either and came armed with their usual trio of 126C3s plus a brand new chassis for Tambay so that both drivers had a spare 126C3 for the first time. Since Zandvoort, Renault had also built up a new RE40 for Prost as subsequent examination of his race car, following its dramatic off-course excursion there, had revealed slight damage to the monocoque; McLaren International had now completed work on their second MP4/1E and entered it for Watson; and Spirit had brought along a partly completed brand new car, the 101, in the vain hope of finishing it off in the paddock over the weekend. This apart, the line-up for the race was pretty familiar, although amongst modifications carried out to existing cars were all three Brabham-BMWs now appearing with the larger turbocharger units and Brian Hart-developed boost control valves seen only on the spare BT52B at Zandvoort, the trio of Toleman-Harts all being fitted with the British Holset turbo-charger units and the new Tyrrell 012 reappearing with revised front suspension.

During recent testing at the Autodromo the fastest time (1 min 31.53 sec) had been put up by the Euroracing Alfa Romeo driver, Andrea de Cesaris, and it was the 'local lad' who set the ball rolling at the start of official practice on Friday morning by recording the fastest time again. However, once the first qualifying session was in progress in the afternoon he soon found himself being outpaced by the Ferraris and the Brabham-BMWs but not, surprisingly, by the Renaults. In fact, the French team were all at sixes and sevens with engines that refused to rev properly, and just to add to their problems Prost was complaining of lack of grip from his Michelin tyres. Even the spare chassis that he tried was no better and this, coupled with earlier vague threats against his life (almost certainly as a ploy to distract him from the job in hand rather than being of malicious intent), accounted for an unusually grim-faced Frenchman. Mansell, too, had problems with the Renault engine in his Lotus 94T losing power during the afternoon, in addition to which he was finding the comparatively narrow rear Pirelli tyres affording little traction out of the three chicanes in common with team-mate de Angelis and the Toleman duo, Warwick and Giacomelli. It was the chicanes that were also causing Lauda and Watson their biggest headache in the McLaren MP4/1Es for whilst both drivers were enjoying good reliability and plenty of punch from the TAG-Porsche V6 turbo-charged engines, the road-holding of the cars, running with comparatively small rear aerofoils, and the braking was something else. Nevertheless, the pair of them were well in amongst the mid-field runners as regards overall lap times, so were not too

unhappy with what, after all, was a new project that still needed a lot of development and testing. In many respects, of course, this was something that equally applied to the still relatively new Spirit-Honda project. The big difference here, though, was that engine reliability was still a major source of concern, which Johansson did nothing to alleviate by blowing up his second V6 of the day even before he had settled down to any really quick laps. This, in turn, resulted in the Swede ultimately finishing up as not only being the sole turbo runner to be beaten by any of the seemingly outclassed normally-aspirated cars but also at the bottom of the time-sheets apart from Fabi, who had similarly had his qualifying run curtailed by an engine failure. In the meantime, the battle for the provisional pole position had gone hopelessly wrong so far as the 'Tifosi' was concerned as their beloved Ferraris had been well and truly seen off by the two Brabham-BMWs, Piquet topping the time-sheets at 1 min 30.202 sec and Patrese (fastest for the first half-hour or so of qualifying) taking the runner-up spot at 1 min 30.253 sec. The fact that Arnoux (1 min 30.799 sec) and Tambay (1 min 31.036 sec) had beaten everyone else was just not good enough – not in their eyes, at least!

On Saturday morning there was rather more cause for despondency among the many thousands of fanatical Ferrari supporters when, after about only half an hour of the second untimed session, proceedings were brought to a halt so that not one, but two of the scarlet cars could be retrieved from out on the circuit. Arnoux had come to rest with a broken turbo-charger, while Tambay had gone off at the second chicane and bent a steering arm against the guard-rail after attempting a late outbraking manoeuvre on Laffite's Williams. Almost as soon as the track had been re-opened, though,

29.122 sec and produced an outburst of jeers and cat-calls from the spectator stands. Piquet, on the other hand, ran into all sorts of trouble and ultimately failed to improve on his Friday time. First the spare Brabham BT52B that he was using for qualifying lost power. Then the engine in his proposed race chassis almost immediately blew up. Finally, in a last-ditch attempt to regain the pole, he climbed aboard his team-mate's car only to be confronted by the chequered flag to signify the end of practice as he powered out of the Parabolica to begin what should have been his quick lap. Meanwhile, Tambay had seen his hopes of replying to Patrese dashed by a turbo failure and Arnoux, on race tyres after finding on the previous afternoon that there was little to choose between them and Goodyear's qualifying rubber, had been unable to progress beyond 1 min 29.901 sec. So, at the end of the day, it was Brabham – Ferrari – Ferrari – Brabham and an Italian was on pole position for the Italian Grand Prix for the first time since the late Alberto Ascari in 1953. That, on the face of it, should have been a very satisfactory outcome but not, apparently, so far as the spectators were concerned who, in the main, drifted away from the circuit unusually subdued – Patrese, after all, was driving for the opposition!

Throughout this absorbing battle between the Ferraris and the Brabham-BMWs the other Championship contenders, Renault, had still been in the doldrums somewhat with both of their drivers a full 2 seconds off the pace. Nevertheless, a change of turbos and inter-coolers in the morning had, at least, helped Prost to move up into fifth place on the grid with an improved time of 1 min 31.144 sec, while Cheever had finished up two places lower between a pretty consistent de Cesaris and de Angelis in the quicker of the two Lotus-Renaults. Further back, Winkelhock and Baldi had both done comparatively well to qualify in the next two places immediately ahead of Mansell and Warwick, after a couple of frustrating days caused by a string of turbo failures and other niggling problems, and Lauda, having switched over from carbon-fibre to ventilated steel brake discs for the second day, had gone quick enough to just scrape into the top half of the grid. Once again the TAG-Porsche engines had maintained their excellent reliability record but, apart from the shortcomings of their chassis, the McLaren team had now run into a problem with their Bosch Motronic engine management systems causing a lack of fuel pressure, particularly when it came to starting the engines once they were hot. Both drivers had experienced it, and Watson particularly so as it had proved impossible to restart the engine in his car after its first qualifying run. As a result the Ulsterman had spent most of the afternoon in the pits (along with Ghinzani, whose practice had been ended in the morning by an engine failure)

just when he could have done with the extra time out on the track to continue acclimatizing himself to the vastly superior power and different driving technique required from the MP4/1E compared to that of the MP4/1C. Even so he had certainly not disgraced himself for he was only two places away from his team-mate on the grid and sandwiched between Giacomelli's Toleman and Rosberg's Williams, the fastest normally-aspirated car for the second successive day thanks mainly to the Finn's ability to cope with handling deficiencies caused by running virtually no rear wing in the interests of obtaining maximum straight-line speed. Rosberg's team-mate, on the other hand, had caused a real upset by failing to qualify for the race, possibly through spending too much time trying out Goodyear's latest batch of radial tyres to little avail. Boesel had also failed to make the cut, as had Acheson in spite of having the benefit of a short-stroke Ford-Cosworth DFY engine for the first time, but Johansson had improved sufficiently before yet another Honda V6 engine had blown up to hoist himself on to the grid and so, too, had Fabi. Apart from Laffite, the only other major surprise among the non-turbo runners was that of Alboreto being out-qualified by his team-mate for the first time all season and finishing up only 24th fastest. However, in addition to experiencing handling problems with the Tyrrell 012, his hopes of improving on the first day had been dashed by a seemingly incurable engine misfire.

Following two days of overcast skies and rather cool conditions, the weather on race day was a good deal brighter and warmer, although by the time that the 26 starters were leaving the pits and forming on the grid in readiness for the 3.30 p.m. start the sun had disappeared behind a thin haze. During the warm-up session just over two hours earlier Prost, having reverted to the spare Renault (but fitted with the lighter bodywork from his new chassis), had suddenly found himself back in the ball-park with no engine or handling problems whatsoever and had gone on to record the fastest time. Consequently, the Frenchman was now in a much more confident frame of mind whereas over at Ferrari things had gone the other way. With equal suddenness Arnoux and Tambay had both found their 126C3s lacking grip, almost certainly because of the hotter weather changing the track conditions. Not only that but now, after just a single warm-up lap, there were already signs of a blister appearing on one of Arnoux's rear tyres which, although promptly changed along with the other rear tyre, gave even more cause for concern. That apart, everything seemed to be running smoothly, and as soon as the final count-down had been completed Patrese, on pole position for only the second time in his career, led the field away on the pace lap.

both drivers went out in their spare 126C3s, Tambay taking over the brand new chassis for the first time. Thereafter things began to pick up somewhat and by the half-way point of the final qualifying session in the afternoon there was even a ray of hope for the 'Tifosi' when Tambay suddenly became the first driver to break the 1 min 30 sec barrier over the weekend by setting a new fastest time of 1 min 29.650 sec. Naturally, the news was greeted with near-delirium, a complete contrast to the mood beforehand. But alas, the joy was to be short-lived. Both Brabham drivers, playing the waiting game in the pits, had yet to show their hand and by the time that Patrese had eventually gone through his two sets of tyres he had lapped over half a second quicker than Tambay at 1 min

1983

Riccardo Patrese's Brabham streaks away into the lead at the start of the race. *(Autosport)*

Then, after bringing them all safely back to their starting positions once more, and refusing to be ruffled by more jeers and cat-calls from the packed public enclosures and grandstands, he patiently awaited the green light whereupon the Brabham lit up its wheels and was away like a jack-rabbit. Behind him there was the usual mad scramble for positions, which included Piquet driving around Arnoux before drawing alongside Tambay in the rush towards the first chicane, and also Cheever, after another superb start, going squeezing between Prost and de Cesaris and only just failing to follow Piquet past Arnoux's Ferrari. In fact, the Renault almost made contact with the Brabham as they went charging down the middle of the two rows of cars. For a moment or so everyone held their breath as the closely-bunched field converged for the chicane but, somehow, they all managed to sort themselves out and from there went on to complete the rest of the opening lap without any major dramas. Across the line it was still Patrese out in front with Piquet right up with him in second place followed, after several car lengths, by the two Ferraris of Tambay and Arnoux. Then, strung out behind them, came Cheever, de Cesaris, Prost, de Angelis, Mansell, Baldi, Warwick, Winkelhock and Watson before Rosberg in the leading normally-aspirated car. Unfortunately, though, the outgoing World Champion had already incurred the wrath of the officials by blatantly ignoring an instruction not to cross the white line marking the edge of the 'usable' track at the wide starting area. In the heat of the moment he had apparently forgotten all about that and had pulled out to go past Giacomelli's rather sluggish Toleman. Either way it was a costly move as he was later to find himself on the receiving end of a one minute penalty and a fine of $2,000!

On the second lap the two Brabham-BMWs pulled even further ahead, which was not altogether surprising as Tambay's Ferrari was already beginning to suffer from a mysterious loss of power. Indeed, by the time that the leaders were streaming out of the Parabolica again the Frenchman had slipped behind his team-mate and was now about to lose another place to Cheever, the Renault driver subsequently going past in a neat outbraking manoeuvre on the approach to the first chicane. An over-enthusiastic de Cesaris then decided that he would like to do the same. But it just wasn't on. He arrived far too quickly, locked up his brakes, creating dense tyre smoke, gently nudged the rear of the Ferrari and went spinning off into the sandy run-off area. This, in turn, caused the closely-following Prost to flat-spot his tyres as he, too, locked up to avoid the wayward Alfa Romeo. However, like Tambay, Prost was at least able to continue whereas de Cesaris, despite energetically trying to extricate his car from the sand, was forced to become the first retirement. Before he had finally accepted defeat, though, there was more drama unfolding on the other side of the circuit caused by the BMW engine in the leading Brabham suddenly belching out great clouds of white smoke on the approach to the Parabolica. A piston had burned out and as Patrese slowed before subsequently crawling into the pit lane, accompanied by a vociferous outburst from the crowd, so Piquet surged past into the lead. At the end of this same eventful lap Lauda followed the stricken Brabham into the pit lane to begin a lengthy stop for attention to a badly misfiring engine and while he was there no less than three other drivers struck trouble. First, on lap 5, Johansson pulled off the track with the Honda engine in his Spirit no longer delivering any power owing to a broken distributor, followed almost immediately by Baldi suffering an extremely smoky turbo-charger failure and ending a very unhappy afternoon for Euroracing Alfa Romeo. Then, only a lap later, Ghinzani was in the pits with a recalcitrant gearbox, a problem that was to end his race as well after just four more subsequent laps.

By lap 10 Piquet had steadily built up a cushion of more than 5 seconds over Arnoux and was obviously well in command of the situation. Cheever was still third, hanging on really well to the Ferrari in front of him, and then, after another sizeable gap, came Tambay, Prost and de Angelis running in tight formation with Watson looking all set to join them in the not too distant future. The Ulsterman, having already worked his way up to seventh place, was absolutely flying in his first race with the new McLaren-TAG and lapping only fractionally slower than the leader. Sadly, it was to end all too soon. Early on lap 14 his engine suddenly cut out due to some internal failure, and moments later Watson was pulling off the track to become the next retirement. As a result Warwick, also driving hard in the Holset turbo-charged, twin-plug Hart-engined Toleman, was once more able to take over the seventh place that he had lost to Watson six laps earlier, while Winkelhock automatically moved up into eighth place ahead of Mansell, Giacomelli and easily the fastest non-turbo runner, Rosberg. At almost exactly the same time fourth place also changed hands when de Angelis followed up a successful stab at overtaking Prost's tyre-troubled Renault on the 11th lap by making a somewhat less popular move from the point of view of the crowd in blasting past Tambay's Ferrari. Thereafter, or at least for the next ten laps, the race settled into an orderly procession interrupted only by the leaders gradually picking their way through tail-enders and by a heart-stopping moment on lap 22 when Tambay arrived at the first chicane a little too quickly and shot across the sand – without losing his place! However, at the end of lap 24 attention became focused on the pits when the refuelling/tyre stops were set in motion by Cheever and de Angelis both dropping out of formation: the Renault was stationary for 11.6 seconds and the Lotus for a slightly longer 14.2 seconds, slipping to fifth and seventh places respectively. On the following lap Arnoux also stopped and, interestingly enough, rejoined the race still just in front of Cheever following a delay of almost exactly 12 seconds, albeit now in fourth place behind Piquet, Tambay and Prost. So far as the Championship leader was concerned, though, the race was all but over. For several laps he had been steadily losing turbo boost pressure, and although he went ahead with his scheduled pit stop at the end of lap 26 it was already patently obvious that something was seriously amiss. Indeed, one more slow lap was enough to convince him that it was pointless continuing so, for the second time in a fortnight, Prost was to come away with nothing.

The activity in the pits continued with Warwick, Jarier, Tambay, Rosberg, Mansell and Winkelhock all stopping in quick succession and being serviced without any major hiccups, but when Lauda pulled in on lap 30 (actually his 24th lap due to the earlier pit stop) it led to near pandemonium. As he was about to set off once more the TAG-Porsche engine, still not running all that cleanly, stalled and brought his McLaren to rest right beside the Brabham pit where preparations were in progress to receive Piquet, the Brazilian being due in at the end of lap 31. Reactions were swift to the extreme. Never before had Lauda had so many willing volunteers to give him a push-start! Even Bernie Ecclestone joined in, but so far as the Austrian was concerned it was to little avail as within less than another lap he had switched off, the engine now showing every indication of being on the point of seizure. Meanwhile, when Piquet did go in at the end of lap 31, little realizing just how close he had been to finding his pit entrance blocked, everything went off superbly well with fuel being added and all four wheels changed in just 10.1 seconds, which enabled him to charge back out into the fray still a clear leader – by over 20 seconds. Behind him, Arnoux had automatically moved back up into second place from Cheever, Tambay was fourth in front of de Angelis once more thanks to a quicker pit stop and Warwick was now in sixth place ahead of Winkelhock, Giacomelli (he had

stopped off at the pits at the end of lap 30) and Mansell. After that everyone else – all non-turbo runners – was at least a lap down, including Rosberg's tenth-placed Williams, although Alboreto's Tyrrell was no longer amongst them as he had just gone out with clutch trouble.

For a while the crowd now became increasingly of the opinion that Piquet was running into trouble as the exhaust note from his BMW engine became decidedly flat and his lap times began to grow longer. In reality, though, the Brazilian had merely turned his turbo boost pressure control right down and was already pacing himself to the finish. Meanwhile, the BMW engine in Winkelhock's ATS did go off because of a broken exhaust, ending the German's race in the pits after 35 laps, and not long afterwards fourth gear broke on Cheever's Renault. This latter incident, unfortunately, put paid to some truly gallant efforts made by the American to find a way past Arnoux as it caused him to gradually drop away. It also removed most of what little excitement there was left in the race, for although Arnoux was now able to concentrate more freely on trying to reel in the leader he could make no real impression. Piquet made sure of that by stepping up the pace a little in the closing stages before cruising home to score a most convincing victory, the gap between himself and the Ferrari still being over 10 seconds at the finish. A further 8 seconds adrift, Cheever followed them over the line in a fine third place in spite of his gearbox problem and Tambay held on to fourth place in his underpowered Ferrari after a game attempt by de Angelis to catch and repass him had been thwarted by deteriorating brakes. In fact, the Italian very nearly failed to complete the race as during the last couple of laps his gearbox also began to disintegrate and he drove with the Renault engine in his Lotus up against the rev-limiter due to the lack of third and fifth gear. However, not only did he eventually make it to the finish but he also scored his first Championship points of the season by holding on to fifth place ahead of

Warwick, Giacomelli and a rather unhappy Mansell, who lost his seventh place on the finishing straight simply through lifting off to avoid hordes of undisciplined spectators running on to the track. Behind the Englishman, and lapped, Rosberg comfortably led home the normally-aspirated contingent in ninth place only for his afternoon also to end on an unhappy note when he learned of the one minute penalty. As a result of this the Finn eventually found himself being classified in only 11th spot due to Jarier's Ligier and Surer's Arrows (running in the distinctive green and white colours of the Golia confectionary firm this weekend) both being ahead of him on his revised time. After that only the two Theodore N183s of Cecotto and Guerrero were left as Boutsen, Sullivan and Fabi had all gone out with engine problems in quick succession during the closing stages.

It may not have been among the most exciting of races but the result couldn't have been much better so far as keeping the Championship title chase alive, for the situation was now Prost-51 points, Arnoux-49 points, Piquet-46 points, Tambay-40 points. Of course, at this stage much still depended on the outcome of Ken Tyrrell's appeal following the rejection of his protest at Silverstone against the water-assisted fuel-injection systems being used by Renault and Ferrari. Fortunately, it was to make no difference: eight days later, when the FIA International Court of Appeal finally covened to hear the matter, the case was subsequently adjourned pending an investigation into the technical implications by Professor Lenz of the University of Vienna but, at the same time, the Court announced that the 1983 World Championship would remain unaffected – whatever the outcome! In the event, at a further sitting of the Court in November the appeal was rejected in any case on the grounds that water, itself, contained neither energy nor the ability to increase engine power and, as such, could not be considered as a power-boosting additive under Article 14 of the Formula 1 Technical Regulations.

Results							Retirements
1	N. Piquet (Brabham-BMW)	1 hr 23 min 10.880 sec (217.548 kph/ 135.178 mph)	8	N. Mansell (Lotus-Renault)	1 hr 24 min 46.915 sec		A. de Cesaris (Alfa Romeo) spun off on lap 3, R. Patrese (Brabham-BMW) engine on lap 3, S. Johansson (Spirit-Honda) distributor on lap 5, M. Baldi (Alfa Romeo) turbo-charger on lap 6, P. Ghinzani (Osella-Alfa Romeo) gearbox on lap 11, J. Watson (McLaren-TAG) engine on lap 14, N. Lauda (McLaren-TAG) engine on lap 25, A. Prost (Renault) turbo-charger on lap 28, M. Alboreto (Tyrrell-Ford) clutch on lap 30, M. Winkelhock (ATS-BMW) exhaust on lap 36, T. Boutsen (Arrows-Ford) engine on lap 43, D. Sullivan (Tyrrell-Ford) engine on lap 45, C. Fabi (Osella-Alfa Romeo) engine on lap 46.
			9	J.P. Jarier (Ligier-Ford)	1 lap behind		
			10	M. Surer (Arrows-Ford)	1 lap behind		
2	R. Arnoux (Ferrari)	1 hr 23 min 21.092 sec	11	K. Rosberg (Williams-Ford)	1 lap behind		
3	E. Cheever (Renault)	1 hr 23 min 29.492 sec	12	J. Cecotto (Theodore-Ford)	2 laps behind		
4	P. Tambay (Ferrari)	1 hr 23 min 39.903 sec	13	R. Guerrero (Theodore-Ford)	2 laps behind		
5	E. de Angelis (Lotus-Renault)	1 hr 24 min 04.560 sec					
6	D. Warwick (Toleman-Hart)	1 hr 24 min 24.228 sec					
7	B. Giacomelli (Toleman-Hart)	1 hr 24 min 44.802 sec					

Fastest lap: N. Piquet (Brabham-BMW) on lap 20 in 1 min 34.431 sec (221.113 kph/ 137.393 mph)

1983

XXXVth Grand Prix of Europe

Brands Hatch: September 25
Weather: Warm and sunny
Distance: 76 laps of 4.2061 km
circuit = 319.66 km (198.63 miles)

Originally, after Monza, the Grand Prix teams should have been preparing for their third trip of the year to North America to attend an inaugural New York Grand Prix on September 25 and the Caesar's Palace Grand Prix at Las Vegas a fortnight later. However, contrary to categoric assurances given by Bernie Ecclestone (on behalf of FOCA) earlier in the year that all 17 events included on the 1983 World Championship calendar would take place, in response to rumours that certain races were in doubt, both had subsequently been deleted as, of course, had the Swiss Grand Prix. The New York Grand Prix had been postponed until 1984 due to a lack of time in which to complete the circuit following bureaucratic delays in obtaining permission for the event from the city authorities, while the Caesar's Palace Grand Prix had simply been cancelled due to the organizers failing to attract the television coverage considered necessary to make it a viable proposition. It so happened, though, that back in June, by which time it had become known for sure that the Swiss and New York Grands Prix were not going to take place, John Webb of Brands Hatch had seized upon the opportunity to apply through the RAC Motor Sports Association for a second Grand Prix to be held in Great Britain as a replacement for the New York race. From there things had then proceeded very quickly indeed. FOCA and FISA had more or less immediately approved the idea and given the necessary go-ahead and John Player & Sons through Imperial Tobacco Ltd, the sponsors of the British Grand Prix from 1972 to 1978, had agreed to provide the necessary financial support. Obviously, there was no way in which the race could be called the British Grand Prix and so, instead, it was to be the 'Grand Prix of Europe', a hitherto somewhat meaningless title that had frequently been bestowed upon one of the major Grands Prix to take place in Europe each year. It was also one that had been tagged on to the ill-fated Swiss Grand Prix some months earlier in a fruitless attempt to generate more interest. The title, in fact, had first been used as long ago as 1923 for the Italian Grand Prix at Monza and, since then, on a further 33 occasions, the most recent being for the 1977 British Grand Prix. Consequently, this was actually the 35th time that a race had carried the title, although it was only the first time that it was being used in its own right.

Warm and sunny weather helped the weekend off to a good start when the track opened for the first practice session at 10 o'clock on Friday morning, and before long the Kent circuit was alive with activity as drivers knuckled down to the usual routine of sorting cars for the more important hour of qualifying in the afternoon. In most respects the line-up was the same as at Monza a fortnight earlier, although for reasons that were not obviously apparent (there were rumours of problems with sponsorship and some argument over a $2,000 fine imposed by FISA at the Italian race for arriving late at the mandatory drivers' briefing) Johnny Cecotto was watching from the side-lines, his entry having been withdrawn. Nevertheless, there were still 29 drivers taking part as the Williams team had entered a third car for the new 1983 European Formula 2 champion, Dr Jonathan Palmer. This had been done as a gesture of appreciation for the enormous amount of testing that the Englishman had carried out for them and in the hope that it might influence another team to offer him a permanent drive in 1984. Naturally, an extra driver meant that the team could expect to have a busy time of it but by mid-morning it was turning out to be even busier than anticipated. First, after completing barely a handful of laps, Laffite returned to the pits with a broken valve spring in the engine of his FWO8C. Then, only minutes after that, Rosberg arrived there on foot to report that he had spun off at Dingle Dell and badly damaged the left front corner of his FWO8C – the very chassis that he had only just agreed to purchase from Frank Williams as a souvenir to remind him of his World Championship title! Consequently, there was no choice other than to strap the Finn into the team's only spare car and for Laffite to become a spectator for the rest of the morning while his engine was being changed. In the meantime, de Angelis swapped over to the spare Lotus 94T because of his proposed race car constantly jumping out of fifth gear, and Johansson's hopes of racing the new Honda-powered Spirit 101 disappeared through the engine installation causing an excessive build up of heat so he, too, had to switch cars. Later, Sullivan became yet another driver in need of his team's spare car when the Ford-Cosworth DFY engine blew up in a brand new Tyrrell 012 that he was using for the first time, and before the morning was out both Mansell and Lauda had been forced to join Laffite as spectators due to a broken gear selector and an engine failure respectively.

One particularly noticeable aspect of the morning session, apart from the various problems that had arisen, had been the number of cars running with huge 'table-top' rear aerofoils similar to those employed for most of the season by Ferrari and ATS. The logic behind it was obviously to generate more down-force and for this particular circuit, at least, Brabham and Renault, along with McLaren, who had also modified the turbo-charger and radiator layout on their MP4/1Es, were evidently sharing the same view as the other two teams inasmuch as it took priority over maximum speed. Certainly so far as Renault were concerned the larger wing seemed to be producing the right results, for Prost had been quickest of all, unofficially, and was absolutely delighted with the revised set-up. Using the RE40 that he had last raced at Zandvoort, rather than the new chassis prepared in time for Monza, he had gone around in 1 min 13.473 sec and that, of course, was only on race rubber. Even Prost, though, had to take something of a back seat once the opening qualifying session was under way, for now de Angelis and Mansell, after the earlier gearbox problems, began to get into their stride in the John Player Lotus 94Ts, fitted with the four-tier rear aerofoils. For once both of them were comparatively happy with their Pirelli tyres and went on to completely dominate proceedings by recording the two fastest times. Initially it was Mansell who set the pace, the Englishman using up his quota of qualifying tyres relatively early and shooting to the top of the time-sheets with a lap in 1 min 12.623 sec. But then, following an interuption caused by de Cesaris bouncing off the barriers just beyond Westfield Bend in his Alfa Romeo, de Angelis went out on his second set of tyres during the remaining 20 minutes, overcame a slight high-speed engine misfire and wrestled away the provisional pole from his team-mate by producing an even quicker lap in 1 min 12.342 sec. It was a superb performance and, with Mansell's time otherwise going unbeaten, the Lotus team were justifiably jubilant. Prost, meanwhile, had lapped only fractionally quicker than in the morning at 1 min 13.342 sec and was now fourth in the standings between the two purposeful-looking Brabham-BMWs of Piquet (1 min 12.724 sec) and Patrese (1 min 13.475 sec). Nevertheless, this still kept the Championship leader well in the hunt whereas his closest rival, Arnoux, was only seventh fastest behind Cheever after finding his Ferrari short of grip on the Goodyear qualifying tyres. Tambay, second fastest in the morning, had experienced much the same trouble in the other Ferrari but, in addition, he had been obliged to switch to his spare 126C3 for his second qualifying run due to a dramatic loss of turbo boost pressure in his proposed race car. The result was an even more disappointing ninth fastest time, which left the Frenchman only five places higher on the time-sheets than Rosberg in the quickest non-turbo car.

The weather was less settled on Saturday and during the untimed session in the morning conditions changed to the extreme, starting wet and ending in warm sunshine. This, not unnaturally, made the going quite tricky and accounted for an exceptionally high number of spins. Fortunately most of them were pretty harmless with drivers merely pointing their cars back in the right direction and continuing on their way. However, Lauda lost a lot of time in the pits having his McLaren checked over after going off at Druids, and when de Angelis later went off at the same spot the Italian was forced to abandon his Lotus – the team's spare car – due to mowing down the catch-fences and finishing up against the wooden barriers with the front of the monocoque damaged. Meanwhile, the changing conditions also had an interesting effect on lap times as at one point Warwick was the fastest driver out on the circuit when the track was at its wettest and Cheever, after complaining of a slight handling imbalance with his Renault on Friday, was right up there, too. Then later, as the track gradually dried, Tambay began to feature much more strongly only for the situation to change again in the dying minutes of the session when de Angelis (back in his proposed race chassis once more) had the final say by narrowly pipping Piquet and team-mate Mansell for the fastest lap of all, 1 min 14.126 sec. Furthermore, at the start of the final qualifying session, with the track now completely dry, de Angelis carried on in the same fashion and went even quicker than the previous afternoon, setting everyone a new target of 1 min 12.092 sec (130.512 mph). He then returned to the pits, had his second set of tyres slapped on to his Lotus and patiently waited for a challenge to emerge. But none materialized, the nearest anyone came to beating him being Patrese at 1 min 12.458 sec prior to a shower of rain in the last remaining 10 minutes or so putting paid to any more really quick laps. And so, for the first time in his career, de Angelis was on pole position whereupon he immediately went away and dedicated it to the memory of the late Colin Chapman, accompanied by a moving tribute to his former boss. The achievement also marked the first pole position for the Lotus team since Montreal 1978 as well as the first for Pirelli in modern-day Grand Prix racing and, of course, for John Player and Sons it was a sponsor's dream come true.

Whilst pole position had been a relatively straightforward affair for de Angelis the final battle for grid position had certainly not been lacking in drama or excitement. On the contrary there had been more harmless spins from Mansell, Piquet and Arnoux, which only served to underline just how hard they had been trying, and Tambay had survived a particularly alarming moment: as he had lifted off for Paddock Bend on one lap the engine had suddenly cut out in his Ferrari and, simultaneously, the on-board fire extinguisher had gone off. Consequently, as he had braked for the downhill right-hander so he had been sprayed with extinguisher foam! Nevertheless, after stopping at the bottom of the hill, Tambay had then walked back to the pits, calmly stepped aboard his spare 126C3 and had gone on to improve sufficiently to move up into sixth place on the grid at 1 min 13.157 sec, just one place lower than Arnoux who had lapped a mere 0.044 sec quicker. Mansell, Piquet and Prost, on the other hand, had been among a number of drivers not to have improved on their Friday times which, in the case of the Englishman, was hardly surprising. Not only had his efforts been scuppered by his own spin but, later, also by Piquet's due to the Brazilian's Brabham scattering earth and other debris on to the track at Surtees just before he had arrived there on what should have been his best lap. However, whereas Mansell and Piquet were still very well up the order – on the second row of the grid – a disappointed Prost (he had tried a different type of Michelin qualifying tyre from the first day only to have found his Renault suddenly lacking grip) had dropped back to eighth spot. Indeed, the Championship leader was now even behind team-mate Cheever who, in spite of using up only one set of tyres following an early turbo-charger failure, had improved to 1 min 13.253 sec. After that most of the final grid order was pretty much to the usual pattern. Among the line-up, Winkelhock had qualified in ninth spot by reason of his Friday time owing to problems with a misfiring engine in the final hour; Warwick and Giacomelli, after finding the Pirelli qualifying tyres no better than race rubber on their Tolemans – a complete contrast to the Lotus team – were 11th and 12th respectively between the two McLaren-TAGs of Watson and Lauda; Rosberg, consistently the fastest non-turbo runner from Surer and Boutsen in their Arrows A6s (running with one-off sponsorship from the MacConnal-Mason art gallery), was down in 16th place behind the two Euroracing Alfa Romeo drivers, de Cesaris (whose race chassis had been repaired overnight) and Baldi; and Johansson had the Spirit 201C in 19th spot after two days of grappling with more throttle lag problems and an erratic misfire from the Honda V6 engine. In fact, the only real upset, apart from Alboreto being out-qualified by his team-mate again and only just scraping on to the back of the grid, was to find Laffite being one of the three non-qualifiers for the second race on the trot, the others being Acheson and Fabi. The main reason on this occasion was a problem shared by virtually all of the Goodyear runners, that of generating sufficient heat into the front tyres. The big difference, though, was that whereas most of them had overcome this with varying degrees of success by adjusting their driving style, including Palmer, who had qualified with little fuss or bother at his first attempt, Laffite had obviously failed.

It was difficult to believe that it was early autumn on Sunday for the skies had cleared once more and Brands Hatch was bathed in warm sunshine. The Grand Prix, itself, was not due to start until 2.45 p.m. but for the 65,000 or so spectators who turned out – not quite up to usual British Grand Prix standards but very healthy nonetheless – there was certainly no shortage of activity beforehand. There were races for Formula Ford 2000 cars, ThunderSports cars and Ford Escort XR3is, the latter driven by represen-

1983

tatives of the House of Lords and the House of Commons, as well as a quite fantastic and varied lunch-time air and track display. In amongst all of this there was also the customary 30 minute warm-up session for the Formula 1 cars, which started at the comparatively early hour of 10.30 a.m. As nearly always, this produced a few late problems, for whilst Prost (in a position of conceivably becoming the new World Champion later in the day) was out setting the fastest time from de Angelis and Mansell in their Lotus 94Ts, Tambay and Cheever were troubled by a lack of turbo boost pressure and an engine misfire respectively, which saw them revert to their spare cars, and Winkelhock's ATS suffered a turbo-charger failure. The McLaren team, too, had more difficulty starting the engine in Watson's MP4/1E (a similar situation had arisen during practice) and both Arnoux and Patrese completed their runs by complaining that the engines in their cars were not quite right. Nevertheless, with nearly four hours between the end of the warm-up and the start of the race, there was ample time to sort everything out and by 2.15 p.m. all 26 starters were ready to leave the pits for the official warm-up lap. In fact, the only change to the expected line-up was that the two Tyrrell drivers had swapped cars due to Alboreto trying the new 012 in the warm-up session and finding it handling much better than his own car. On completing his warm-up lap, though, Patrese drove straight back into the pits to report that his BMW engine was still misfiring, despite a

change of electrical components, and subsequently set off on another lap in the team's spare chassis prior to joining the others waiting on the grid. Then, during the brief lull to the final count-down, the Brabham mechanics hurriedly carried out some cockpit adjustments for him due to the car having previously been set up for Piquet.

With the time fast approaching 2.45 p.m. de Angelis led the field away on the final warm-up lap, they all returned to their correct grid positions, the red light came on, engine notes screamed and then it was green for go – at which point Jarier's Ligier barely moved due to a sudden transmission failure! The other 25 cars, though, got away very cleanly indeed with Patrese's Brabham, benefiting slightly from being on the higher side of the gently sloping Brabham Straight, just beating de Angelis's Lotus into Paddock Bend to take the lead. Directly behind them, Mansell was darting all over the track in a vain attempt to find an opening, taking the outside line for Paddock, where he only just held off Piquet trying a run down the inside, and then flicking over to the right-hand side of the track to challenge his team-mate going up the hill to Druids. However, de Angelis was obviously in no mood to concede another place and promptly claimed the line, forcing Mansell to back off and Piquet to lock up his brakes. This, in turn, enabled Cheever to capitalize on another excellent start by driving around the outside of the Brabham at the hairpin only to find himself being quickly repassed on the downhill run

to Graham Hill Bend. To add to what was an already exciting start, Piquet then tried to go through on the inside of Mansell at Surtees and again going into Westfield Bend but, on both occasions, the Englishman fended off his attacker and went on to complete the opening lap still holding down third place. Even so, he had already lost well over a second on the two leading cars of Patrese and de Angelis and, moreover, was having a problem with his Pirelli tyres not warming up evenly, which was causing his Lotus to slide about rather a lot. Piquet, of course, could sense this only too well and, approaching Hawthorn Bend on the second lap, made a bold run up on the outside of the track before finally making it past the black and gold car. At Dingle Dell Corner Cheever also forged on ahead and by the time that Mansell had reached the same spot next time round he was down in seventh position behind Prost and Arnoux. After that, though, he managed to hold on without losing any more places and rather more interest became centered on Prost as he closed right up to Cheever and set about overtaking him, eventually succeeding by diving down on the inside of his team-mate going into Paddock Bend on lap 9. By then Piquet had long since settled down to the task of reeling in the two leaders but, with Patrese driving as hard as he knew how to keep de Angelis at bay, it was turning out to be no easy proposition. Then came lap 11. Having already tried on at least a couple of occasions to draw alongside the leading Brabham, de Angelis now made a determined run down the inside approaching Surtees and attempted to nip through under braking. Once again, though, Patrese firmly closed the door on him only this time there was a collision, the left rear wheel of the Brabham collecting the right front wheel of the Lotus. In the next instant both cars were spinning off onto the grass. Despite the commotion, the two drivers succeeded in keeping their engines running but, by the time that they had recovered, Piquet had sailed past into the lead and, whereas Patrese was away again in second place just before Prost arrived, de Angelis slipped to sixth spot due to taking considerably longer to regain the track. Unfortunately that was not all, as after just two more laps a hitherto highly successful weekend for de Angelis ended in the pits. His engine had expired – possibly as a result of having over-revved it whilst on the grass. So the order now became Piquet - Patrese - Prost - Cheever - Arnoux - Mansell with Tambay, Winkelhock, de Cesaris, Warwick and the two McLaren-TAGs of Lauda and Watson all running virtually nose to tail behind the surviving Lotus, and Rosberg hanging on really well to them in the leading normally-aspirated car.

At the start of lap 16 the situation from the point of view of the World Championship, in

The start of the race with Riccardo Patrese (Brabham) about to draw alongside pole-sitter Elio de Angelis (Lotus) and take an early lead. *(Autosport)*

Assistance comes to René Arnoux after spinning his Ferrari at Surtees on the 20th lap, an incident that considerably reduced his World Championship hopes. *(L.A.T. Photographic)*

particular, became really exciting for Prost scythed past on the inside of Patrese approaching Paddock Bend and was left with a clear run at Piquet. The gap between the two leading cars at this point was a shade over 10 seconds, but after initially coming down by a few tenths it began to grow again indicating that Piquet had everything nicely under control. Meanwhile Patrese, troubled by a small handling imbalance caused by the rear axle of his Brabham being slightly bent in the incident with de Angelis, was soon coming under the close scrutiny of Cheever who, in turn, had Arnoux moving right in on his tail. However, as the three of them went into Surtees in tight formation on lap 20 the French Ferrari driver made an expensive error of judgement, spun through 180 degrees and came to rest with the underside of his 126C3 stuck on the high kerb on the outside of the corner. He at least managed to keep the engine running but by the time that he had summoned some nearby marshals to push him back on to the track most of the field had gone by. Indeed, fifth position had become 19th! As anticipated, though, Arnoux quickly set about regaining lost places, taking a mere three laps to go by Sullivan, Alboreto and Johansson in quick succession and three more to catch and pass Surer's Arrows – just as the TAG-Porsche engine in Lauda's McLaren suddenly blew up and ended the Austrian's race in the pits. Rather surprisingly this was still only the third retirement, although minutes later there was another and a somewhat spectacular one at that owing to an oil line coming adrift on Sullivan's Tyrrell as the American approached Paddock Bend going into lap 28. Not only did this allow oil to trickle on to the car's hot exhaust pipes, accompanied by dense plumes of grey smoke, but it also allowed some of it to find its way on to the left rear tyre. Consequently, as Sullivan turned into the downhill right-hander he

unavoidably spun off on to the grass. That, however, was not quite the end of the saga for after making a brilliant recovery his engine compartment became engulfed in flames as the oil ignited and he eventually pulled off behind the paddock where some marshals immediately set to work with their fire extinguishers. By now, with the situation up amongst the leaders staying largely unchanged apart from Mansell joining Patrese and Cheever in their scrap for third place and Tambay and de Cesaris showing every sign of soon following suit, Watson also had a problem. For several laps, in fact, part of the right-hand side support for the McLaren's massive rear aerofoil had been breaking away from its mounting and this was now allowing a section of the aerofoil to sag perilously close to the right rear tyre. As a result the team decided to take the precautionary measure of bringing forward the Ulsterman's planned pit stop, and signalled him to come in at the end of lap 33. Then, after all four wheels had been changed, fuel added and the offending section of the rear aerofoil torn away, Watson was sent back out into the fray with every intention of stopping again once a complete new rear aerofoil assembly had been made ready for him. Unfortunately, though, the opportunity of returning to the pits never arose. Just over three laps later part of the original component broke away completely and led to what was Watson's 150th Grand Prix ending with his McLaren skating off the track at Westfield Bend, careering through the catchfences and on into the tyre wall where it finally came to rest with quite extensive damage, particularly around the left front corner. The incident, from which Watson escaped injury, also very nearly had disastrous consequences for the closely-following Johansson due to the detached part of the McLaren's rear aerofoil narrowly missing his head as it flew through the air. Even then it

still left the Swede driving with a smashed windscreen for the remainder of the race. That's how close it had been!

At half-distance (38 laps) Piquet was still going unchallenged out in front but now the routine pit stops were getting under way. Cheever and Baldi, in fact, had already just made theirs and over the next few minutes the rush was really on with one driver stopping after another. For the vast majority of them everything went much according to plan, although Patrese was held up for more than 25 seconds at the end of lap 39 owing to trouble in replacing one of his Brabham's rear wheels. This, in turn, dropped him right back from the third place that he had previously been busily defending, to tenth. Piquet, too, was not much better off when he became the last driver, apart from Palmer, to stop at the end of lap 44 for once again the Brabham mechanics, usually the slickest in the business, ran into a problem. This time the wheel-nut gun being used on the left rear wheel refused to function properly. Unlike his team-mate, though, Piquet eventually rejoined the race without losing his position and, despite being delayed for 19.6 seconds, still led the race by the comfortable margin of just over 10 seconds from Prost, who was back in second place once more following his pit stop (13.9 seconds) three laps earlier. A further 20 seconds in arrears, Tambay had come through to third place and Mansell, by reason of having enjoyed the quickest stop of all (9.6 seconds) was only another couple of seconds away in fourth place, directly in front of Cheever. However, the American now had an unusual problem to contend with and one that at the end of lap 45 brought him back into the pits. The right-hand side of his visor had come adrift! Moreover, by the time that the Renault mechanics had carried out makeshift repairs using sticky tape de Cesaris, Warwick, Giacomelli, Patrese, Winkelhock, Arnoux, Surer, Alboreto and Boutsen had all been able to take advantage of his predicament, and when Cheever finally charged back out on to the circuit he was way down in 14th place, over a lap behind. Rosberg would also have moved on ahead of him but only a lap earlier the outgoing World Champion had coasted to rest out on the circuit with an engine failure and become the seventh retirement, Baldi having gone out a few minutes beforehand with an inoperative clutch.

With Piquet carrying on from where he had left off immediately prior to his pit stop by continuing to dominate the race, the only real interest now revolved around Mansell (completely happy with his fresh set of Pirelli tyres) trying to come to terms with Tambay's Ferrari, and also around Warwick as he gradually started closing up to de Cesaris's fifth-placed Alfa Romeo. So far as the British Toleman driver was concerned, however, any realistic chance of making further progress effectively vanished on lap 56 when the on-board fire extinguisher in his car suddenly began showering him with foam. Furthermore, this went on for well over a lap, badly restricting his vision as well as virtually freezing his right hand and thigh. Nevertheless, Warwick pressed on regardless of the obvious discomfort, and whilst the problem caused him to drop well back from de Cesaris he at least managed to hold on to his sixth place. Mansell, meanwhile, still had his sights firmly fixed on the the scarlet Ferrari ahead of him and at the start of lap 66 was finally rewarded for his perseverance when he was able to make a successful bid for third place by charging down on the inside of Tambay approaching Paddock Bend. Initially, it appeared that the Frenchman would try to retaliate, especially after locking up his right front wheel going into Druids,

but in reality his rear brakes were fast disappearing and just two laps later the same thing happened again. Sadly, on this occasion, he was unable to prevent the Ferrari from sliding straight off the track at the hairpin and gently striking the tyre wall, thus ending his race along with any lingering hopes of winning the 1983 World Championship. After that the Grand Prix of Europe ran free of any further incident, and at the end of the 76 laps Piquet crossed the line a comfortable winner for the second race in succession to move up into second place in the Championship table, just 2 points behind Prost who duly followed him home 6.571 seconds later. Third, of course, was Mansell and delighted to be in the points again even though he was a bit disappointed with how his first set of tyres had behaved. Then, at varying intervals behind him, came de Cesaris and the two

Toleman TG183Bs of Warwick and Giacomelli, also in the points, followed by Patrese, the last driver to complete the full race distance. Although Surer and Alboreto had both joined the retirement list with engine failures during the latter half of the race, that still left another nine finishers right back to Ghinzani, who was too far behind to be classified after a succession of lengthy pit stops with gear selector and throttle support bracket problems. Included amongst them were Palmer, who had done everything that could be expected of him in his first Grand Prix, and a very disgruntled Arnoux, who had been obliged to make a second tyre stop on lap 52 on his way to a disappointing ninth place: in the vain hope that he might have been able to salvage some Championship points he had earlier been given softer tyres only to have blistered them within 14 laps!

Results				
1	N. Piquet (Brabham-BMW)	1 hr 36 min 45.865 sec (198.214 kph/ 123.165 mph)		
2	A. Prost (Renault)	1 hr 36 min 52.436 sec		
3	N. Mansell (Lotus-Renault)	1 hr 37 min 16.180 sec		
4	A. de Cesaris (Alfa Romeo)	1 hr 37 min 20.261 sec		
5	D. Warwick (Toleman-Hart)	1 hr 37 min 30.780 sec		
6	B. Giacomelli (Toleman-Hart)	1 hr 37 min 38.055 sec		
7	R. Patrese (Brabham-BMW)	1 hr 37 min 58.549 sec		
8	M. Winkelhock (ATS-BMW)	1 lap behind		
9	R. Arnoux (Ferrari)	1 lap behind		
10	E. Cheever (Renault)	1 lap behind		
11	T. Boutsen (Arrows-Ford)	1 lap behind		
12	R. Guerrero (Theodore-Ford)	1 lap behind		
13	J. Palmer (Williams-Ford)	2 laps behind		
14	S. Johansson (Spirit-Honda)	2 laps behind		
15	R. Boesel (Ligier-Ford)	3 laps behind		

Also running at finish: P. Ghinzani (Osella-Alfa Romeo) 13 laps behind

Fastest lap: N. Mansell (Lotus-Renault) on lap 70 in 1 min 14.342 sec (203.683 kph/ 126.563 mph)

Retirements
J.P. Jarier (Ligier-Ford) transmission on lap 1, E. de Angelis (Lotus-Renault) engine on lap 13, N. Lauda (McLaren-TAG) engine on lap 26, D. Sullivan (Tyrrell-Ford) oil pipe on lap 28, J. Watson (McLaren-TAG) accident on lap 37, M. Baldi (Alfa Romeo) clutch on lap 40, K. Rosberg (Williams-Ford) engine on lap 44, M. Surer (Arrows-Ford) engine on lap 51, M. Alboreto (Tyrrell-Ford) engine on lap 65, P. Tambay (Ferrari) accident on lap 68.

XXIXth South African Grand Prix

Kyalami: October 15
Weather: Hot
Distance: 77 laps of 4.104 km
circuit = 316.01 km (196.36 miles)

For the final Grand Prix of 1983 it was off to South Africa and to Kyalami, the superb 4.104 km circuit situated 6,000 feet up in the Transvaal. Originally, of course, the race had been scheduled for the beginning of the season, but the introduction of the new rules following the ban on skirts and under-car aerodynamics had indirectly led to it being moved to the other end of the calendar. At the time the race organizers had not exactly been over-enthusiastic about the idea of having to go the best part of two years without a Grand Prix but, in common with the Southern Sun Hotel Group, the race sponsors, they had subsequently seen events make the wait well worthwhile. Now, with both World Championships to be decided, the race could be guaranteed to attract maximum spectator and media support. To recap, the position at the top of the Drivers' table was now Prost-57 points, Piquet-55 points, Arnoux-49 points, which meant that all three

men effectively had to aim for victory for any one of them to be sure of carrying off the coveted title, while in the Constructors' table Ferrari had amassed 89 points compared to the 78 points of Renault, the only remaining contender who could overhaul the Italian team. In fact, in many respects the situation was not unlike that of the previous two years inasmuch as the title chase had gone all the way to the last race, although this year it was at least going to be decided at a real drivers' circuit rather than within the confines of an uninspiring Las Vegas hotel car parking lot. Entry-wise, the numbers had been reduced to 26 by the withdrawals of two of the regular teams: Spirit had pulled out to concentrate on preparing for 1984 following a decision made by Honda to stop supplying them with their V6 turbo-charged engines, and Theodore had not considered the long trip viable, especially as Kyalami's high altitude would almost certainly result in the normally-

aspirated cars being even more off the pace than usual. Otherwise, the line-up was as normal except that McLaren had the benefit of a spare MP4/1E for the first time, Renault had come equipped with a total of four RE40s as well as a batch of engines capable of running with higher turbo boost pressure during practice and, most significant of all, Williams had now joined the ranks of the turbo runners by being ready to race a pair of their new Honda-powered FWO9s.

On the day following the extremely successful and enjoyable European Grand Prix at Brands Hatch, news had filtered through from the Ferrari headquarters at Maranello that Patrick Tambay was being released for 1984 to be replaced by the Italian Tyrrell driver, Michele Alboreto. For some, the fact that Alboreto would be joining the team had come as no big surprise as there had been strong rumours that Enzo Ferrari had already approached him earlier in the year, possibly in the hope of seeing another Italian World Champion in one of his cars. However, given Ferrari's well-known reluctance to employ Italian drivers in the past it had been by no means certain that anything would come of it, and even then it had been considered that Arnoux would be the more likely of the two current drivers to be elbowed out in any reshuffle. As it was the general feeling was that Tambay's impending departure had been perpetuated by team manager Marco Piccinini and because of Arnoux, after a rather disappointing start to the season, having eclipsed his team-mate somewhat in recent months in terms of achieving results. Whatever, Tambay had taken the news philosophically and, instead of reacting negatively as preparations began for what would now be his last drive for the Italian team, responded in the best fashion possible by setting himself up as the man to beat right from the moment that he took to the track. This was actually on the Monday of race week, the first of two consecutive days of unofficial testing. More importantly, though, he continued in the same forceful

manner throughout the opening qualifying session on Thursday afternoon. During the untimed session in the morning he had only covered a handful of laps or so before returning to the pits with a badly misfiring engine caused by a suspected sticking exhaust valve. But now, with a fresh V6 unit installed in his car, Tambay began to fly again, recording a time of 1 min 07.631 sec on his first set of Goodyear qualifying tyres and an even better 1 min 06.841 sec on his second set. Only Piquet, whose Michelin-shod Brabham-BMW had also been sidelined in the morning, because of an engine failure, offered any real challenge and, indeed, he eventually pipped the Frenchman by going around in 1 min 06.792 sec. Not to be outdone, Tambay then had the best four tyres from his two used sets slapped on to his 126C3, had water poured over them and proceeded to regain the provisional pole by going out in the dying minutes of the hour-long session and squeezing in one more timed flying lap – 1 min 06.554 sec!

Whilst his team-mate was busy stealing the headlines, Arnoux ran into an unexpected problem. He had already driven Mauro Forghieri (Ferrari's chief engineer) close to distraction during the test sessions earlier in the week by failing to provide any real feedback in an engine development programme that included trying different turbo-charger installations, but now there was even more cause for dismay: there was a distinct possibility that he might have to miss the race! Unfortunately, before using up his quota of tyres, his Ferrari had come to rest out on the circuit at Leeukop because of an electrical failure. Then, after having summoned some marshals to push the car away from what was considered to be a dangerous position, Arnoux had somehow managed to catch his right foot under one of its rear wheels. The only good thing about it was that once he had limped back to the pits subsequent medical examination revealed no broken bones but, even so, with severe bruising and swelling his immediate prospects were looking decidedly shaky. Prior to this he had lapped in 1 min 07.222 sec and although it was probably the last thing on his mind this placed him fourth on the time-sheets, one spot lower than Prost (1 min 07.186 sec) and immediately ahead of the very impressive-looking new Williams-Honda of Rosberg (1 min 07.256 sec). In fact, the British team had every reason to be more than happy with how things were progressing for whilst Laffite had been obliged to complete his qualifying run in Rosberg's car following problems with a sticking waste-gate valve, and both drivers were complaining of a touch too much understeer, he, too, was well up the order, actually seventh fastest behind Winkelhock. Meanwhile, after their excellent practice performances at Brands Hatch, the Lotus duo had been in

trouble with engines that refused to run properly. Of the two, Mansell had been particularly bothered by a sudden drop of turbo boost pressure and had even resorted to the team's spare car, only to find that running with a persistent misfire. Patrese, who like his team leader had lost an engine in the morning, had also had his efforts frustrated by a turbo-charger failure, as had de Cesaris, while Cheever, trying one of his team's new high-boost engines but finding it refusing to pull at peak revs despite a turbo change between sessions, was yet another to have wound up somewhat disappointed with his lap times. Nevertheless, as if to underline yet again the vast power differential all of them had still lapped considerably faster than the nine normally-aspirated runners in the field with even Alboreto, easily the quickest non-turbo driver, over 1½ seconds behind the slowest turbo-charged car, this actually being Mansell's Lotus.

Throughout Thursday conditions had been very warm indeed, and on Friday it was even hotter, which led to the majority of drivers being unable to improve on their lap times once it came round to the final qualifying session. Tambay, though, was not in the least bit worried about that. After turning in one good lap of 1 min 07.029 sec on his first set of tyres he returned to the pits and casually sat in his Ferrari waiting to counter any threat to his pole position. But just like de Angelis, who had done the same thing on the second day at Brands Hatch, he needn't have bothered as despite Piquet and Patrese, in particular, giving it all they had got his Thursday time proved beyond reach. Consequently, the Frenchman never did use his second set of tyres and later took great delight in donating the prize of $3,000 awarded for winning the top spot to his loyal mechanics, who were leaving no-one in any doubts as to their views about their driver being ousted from the team. Piquet, meanwhile, at least went away with the satisfaction of having achieved the afternoon's fastest time of 1 min 06.821 sec, despite indulging in a harmless spin in the midst of his fruitless efforts to steal away the pole, and team-mate Patrese recovered from his problems of the previous day and the loss of another engine during the morning untimed session with a quite spectacular performance that moved him up from 12th place on the time-sheets to an eventual fine third spot on the grid at 1 min 07.001 sec. Even more heroic were the efforts made by Arnoux. Notwithstanding the fact that he was still in considerable pain and discomfort from his foot injury he not only cast aside the fears about him being unable to drive any more over the weekend but he also produced a fractionally quicker time than the day before of 1 min 07.105 sec. This, in turn, enabled him to leap-frog over Prost and left the Championship leader (hampered by oversteer this time out, along with team-mate Cheever, owing to a bad choice of qualifying tyres) faced with the prospect of starting the race from the third row of the grid alongside Rosberg.

Of the remaining few drivers to pick up on their lap times, only Mansell and de Cesaris made any significant headway as regards their ultimate grid positions. Mansell, enjoying a much better day altogether, improved by almost 2 seconds to 1 min 07.643 sec and from 17th to seventh place on the grid, while de Cesaris found well over a second in spite of looking to be on the brink of disaster as he hurled his Alfa Romeo around the circuit and jumped up six places to ninth, behind a consistent Winkelhock. This, of course, also meant that some of the others lost out somewhat. Among them were Laffite, now complaining of erratic handling; de Angelis, who paid the price for opting to use different qualifying tyres from his team-mate as well as suffering a slight loss of turbo boost pressure; Warwick, obviously none the worse for a heavy shunt at Clubhouse during Tuesday's test session but whose engine was also a bit short on power; Cheever and both McLaren drivers, Watson undergoing a most frustrating afternoon. On his first set of tyres he had to back off due to coming up behind Rosberg and Winkelhock involved in an enthusiastic wheel-banging match after the outgoing World Champion had inadvertently baulked the German ATS driver through Sunset Bend. Then, before he had chance to settle down on his second set of tyres, Watson found the TAG-Porsche engine in his MP4/1E developing a chronic misfire and was soon consigned to the pits. The end result was that the Ulsterman was a disappointing 15th on the grid with only Giacomelli and Baldi of the turbo runners winding up behind him. After that, and now separated from their more powerful rivals by an even bigger gap of 2½ seconds, there were just the nine normally-aspirated runners with Alboreto, despite a down-on-power engine prompting him to complete practice in his team-mate's car, once again the fastest, albeit a couple of tenths slower than the first day. Fabi and Ghinzani, though, had both failed to lap below or equal to 110% of the average of the fastest three times set by Tambay, Piquet and Patrese. Consequently, both were officially regarded as non-qualifiers. However, the other team managers later signed a statement to the effect that they had no objections to the rule being waived and eventually both drivers were invited to line up at the back of the grid behind Acheson, who had at last qualified for his first Grand Prix even though a crown-wheel and pinion failure had ended his practice in the morning.

Clear blue skies and hot sunshine were still very much in evidence on Saturday and this was something that the Goodyear runners,

Ferrari in particular, could well have done without: such conditions would almost certainly favour the Michelin (and Pirelli) radial tyres. The morning warm-up session only served to confirm the suspicions for the first five names to appear on the time-sheets were Lauda (causing everyone to sit up and take note), Patrese, Piquet, Prost and de Cesaris, with Tambay only sixth fastest and Arnoux an even more depressing tenth. Meanwhile, Rosberg caused a bit of a flap in the Williams camp by returning to the pits after only a few minutes with the Honda V6 engine in the back of his FWO9 having blown up and Winkelhock had a big moment at Crowthorne when a broken rear suspension link sent his ATS flying off the track. The McLaren team, too, were rather perplexed to find a replacement engine fitted to Watson's MP4/1E overnight giving problems and eventually set about changing various electrical components to try to effect a cure. Otherwise, most of the pre-race drama was confined to a few rather ugly scenes in the pit lane when the officials took steps to eject just about everyone apart from team managers and mechanics. The idea behind it was to minimize the possibility of an accident during the tyre/refuelling stops in what were obviously going to take place in comparatively cramped surroundings, but the action, which should have been taken sooner, was rather heavy-handed and met with a predictable response. Nevertheless, calm was eventually restored, the pit lane was cleared as required and some two hours later preparations were nicely in hand for the start of the race with the 26 starters leaving the pits for the warm-up lap, Rosberg's Williams now running again with a fresh engine and Winkelhock's ATS having been bolted back together. Much to his dismay, though, Watson immediately discovered that his engine was running as badly as ever and so, at the end of the lap, he drove back into the pits before setting off once more in the team's spare chassis. Even then there were still more problems to come. As the field was subsequently signalled off on the pace lap the engine in the spare McLaren was reluctant to start, which led to Watson being last away and then, somewhat to everyone's amazement, making the same mistake that Winkelhock had made in Holland: he caught the others up and proceeded to take up his original grid position!

Piquet had deliberately come to the grid with an even lighter fuel load than normal with every intention of making an early pit stop in the hope that in the meantime he could make a break and perhaps cause Prost and Arnoux to overstress their engines. It was a ploy that immediately showed signs of working, for at the green Piquet must have left Tambay watching in total disbelief at the manner in which he scorched off the line and shot into an undisputed lead. Furthermore, he proceeded to pull away at an almost

insolent rate, opening out a full 2-second advantage by the end of just the first lap. Tambay, meanwhile, had also lost out to Patrese on the run down to Crowthorne and very nearly to de Cesaris, who had come storming through from the fifth row of the grid to fourth place in the race. Prost was fifth, but within moments he was following de Cesaris past Tambay down the main straight as they went into lap 2. Then it was Rosberg from Arnoux, de Angelis, Winkelhock, Lauda, Warwick, Laffite and the rest right back to Ghinzani, who was already in trouble with the Alfa Romeo V12 engine in his Osella, and about to retire. Laffite didn't last long either, for as he was approaching Crowthorne for the second time Cheever went charging down the inside in most unruly fashion, forced the Frenchman over to the outside of the track to avoid their wheels from becoming interlocked and ultimately caused him to spin off into the catch-fences. Understandably, Laffite was absolutely furious that his first race in the new Williams-Honda should end under such circumstances. Cheever, on the other hand, simply drove on and before the lap was out had moved up two more places, to tenth, by finding a way past Warwick's Toleman and overtaking Winkelhock's ATS when the German suddenly slowed prior to pulling off the track, his BMW engine having expired. At this point, though, rather more importance was attached to the progress of Cheever's team leader for, with Piquet continuing to extend his lead, it was patently clear that Prost had to do something and be quick about it. He was certainly trying hard enough. But de Cesaris was proving to be a hard nut to crack and it was not until the ninth lap that Prost could finally outwit the Italian, by which time Piquet was around 10 seconds away with Patrese, of course, still between them. In the meantime, Lauda had just come through to fifth place by beating Tambay's Ferrari into Crowthorne after having earlier gone past de Angelis, Arnoux and Rosberg in quick succession, and at the end of this same lap Arnoux went trickling into the pits, his already slim World Championship hopes in tatters. Within just a few minutes of the start he had been troubled by a slowly deflating left front tyre but now his engine had blown out most of its water and it was all over for him. Since being passed by Lauda, de Angelis had also pulled into the pits where the Lotus mechanics were still trying in vain to cure a chronic engine misfire, while Baldi, following an encouraging start, had suffered a similar fate to Arnoux and stopped out on the circuit on the sixth lap.

With Piquet still sprinting away into the middle distance and Prost making no appreciable headway in overhauling Patrese, largely because the Renault's throttle response was deteriorating, more and more attention now became fixed on Lauda. This was par-

Aided by an even lighter fuel load than usual, Nelson Piquet arrives at Crowthorne Corner for the first time already well in the lead from team-mate Riccardo Patrese and the rest of the field. *(Autocar & Motor)*

ticularly true once he had caught and passed de Cesaris going into Crowthorne on lap 12, for in no time at all after that the Austrian was moving up to challange Prost. Indeed, it took him just six more laps to make the possibility of a Frenchman winning the World Championship for the first time look even more remote by almost effortlessly going through into third place, again on the approach to Crowthorne. Not finished yet, Lauda then immediately knuckled down to the task of reeling in Patrese's Brabham and before long was looking all set for even better things. However, whilst he made comparatively light work of catching the blue and white car, it became increasingly obvious that Patrese had the edge on straight-line speed, and by an amount sufficient to compensate for the McLaren's apparent superiority through the corners. Consequently, the situation developed into an exciting cat-and-mouse affair that went on right through until the end of lap 33 when Patrese received a welcome respite by Lauda veering off into the pits to make his scheduled tyre/refuelling stop. Unfortunately, there then followed a problem in removing the McLaren's right rear wheel, which led to Lauda losing over 23 seconds and dropping from a fighting third place to seventh behind Prost, de Cesaris, Tambay and Cheever. It would have been ninth but Rosberg now also made his pit stop (another comparatively long one due to the Williams FWO9 not being designed with refuelling in mind), while Warwick, who had repassed Cheever earlier in the race, had already stopped at the end of lap 31 and was

currently lying eighth. Apart from that there had been relatively few changes taking place. Mansell, though, had been forced to undergo a lengthy pit stop after 13 laps because of a broken gear linkage bracket, seven laps later Boesel had similarly lost a lot of time for attention to a sticking throttle, and three more drivers had dropped out of the race altogether. First Watson had been shown the black flag on lap 18 prior to being disqualified for his transgression on the pace lap. Then, more recently, Fabi had retired the surviving Osella because of an engine failure, and de Angelis had finally given up the unequal struggle in his misfiring Lotus 94T, which even a second visit to the pits for a new spark box had done nothing to alleviate. Meanwhile, the moment that could well have provided the turning point in the race had come at the end of lap 28 – Piquet's pit stop. The effect, though, had been negligible for the Brabham mechanics had taken just under 12 seconds to change all four wheels and top up the fuel load and this had enabled their driver to charge back out into the fray without losing his lead. At the time his advantage had shrunk to little more than 3 seconds but since then he had pulled away once more and now obviously had both the race and the World Championship crown well within his grasp.

At the end of lap 35 Prost turned off into the pits for what, initially, appeared to be no more than his routine stop. However, within moments of the Renault mechanics stepping into action Prost was unfastening his belts, climbing out of his car and walking away

convinced that it was pointless continuing because of a dramatic loss of turbo boost pressure. Naturally, this was a quite incredible development and not only meant that the French team could now kiss goodbye to their chances of preventing Ferrari from winning the Constructors' Championship for the second year running but also that Prost could now virtually forget about his dreams of winning the Drivers' title. Nevertheless, it was not quite all over for him as Piquet still had to finish the race in the top four, and with another 42 laps to go it was not inconceivable that he, too, could run into a problem. This was obviously something that had crossed Piquet's mind as well. He had already had harder tyres fitted during his pit stop and before long was responding to pit signals advising him of Prost's retirement by winding down the turbo boost pressure in his Brabham to protect his engine. Even then he was still left with an advantage of over half a minute once Patrese had rounded off the remaining tyre/fuel stops at the end of lap 46 and rejoined the fray without losing his second place. Meanwhile, Lauda had come through to third spot once more and de Cesaris was now fourth ahead of Tambay, Warwick, Rosberg (lapped), Cheever and Alboreto in the leading normally-aspirated car. Interestingly enough, though, Tambay had only minutes earlier just failed to make it out of the pits in time to prevent de Cesaris from beating him into Crowthorne, which suggested that there could well be a good scrap in the offing. Unfortunately, it was not to be. Ever since the early stages of the race Tambay had been troubled by increasing throttle lag, quite apart from being short of traction due to necessarily running on comparatively hard Goodyears to cope with the extremely hot track conditions. And now, to make matters worse for him, the Ferrari's turbo boost pressure was dropping quite dramatically and eventually, on lap 57, the resultant loss of power became so acute that he was left with no alternative other than to park out on the circuit. So, for Tambay, a race that he would dearly loved to have won (to prove conclusively just what a mistake Ferrari had made in elbowing him out of their plans for 1984) ended in disappointment.

By lap 60, with Giacomelli now also out due to suffering an extremely smoky (and fiery) turbo-charger failure and Alboreto's last race with Tyrrell before joining Ferrari about to end with a blown-up engine, speculation was mounting that Piquet was in some sort of trouble. He had slowed to such an extent that Patrese was now able to take over the lead. In reality, though, Piquet had simply decided that winning the World Championship was far more important than winning the race and was not in the least bit bothered to see his team-mate go by, preferring, instead, to continue cruising round for a finish. Indeed, only nine more laps passed

One of the highlights of the race, the superb performance of Niki Lauda in the TAG-Porsche-powered McLaren MP4/1E. *(Autocar & Motor)*

before he also allowed Lauda to move on ahead of him, at which point there seemed to be a distinct possibility that the former double World Champion could yet win the race. Either way there certainly seemed to be an exciting climax in store, for Lauda had already brought the gap to Patrese down to less than 5 seconds despite having lost some 13 seconds more than the Italian in the pits. However, after reducing the gap still further, Lauda began to drop away a little and on lap 72 saw a hard afternoon's work come to nought when an electrical failure suddenly caused his McLaren to roll to a silent halt out on the circuit. Obviously, this was a bitter disappointment to him, especially being within sight of the finish, but at least he was able to walk away in the knowledge that the McLaren-TAG package was now a potential race winner. In the meantime, of course,

Lauda's departure left Patrese under no pressure whatsoever, not even when de Cesaris caught and passed the exceptionally well-disciplined Piquet on lap 75 to move up into a fine second place. Consequently, he was able to stroke his way home to a comfortable victory, the second of his career, and round off what had otherwise been a dreadful season for him in the best possible manner. Naturally, though, most of the celebrations in the Brabham camp were reserved for Piquet, who received a rapturous reception from his team as he crossed the line in third place to become the 1983 World Champion. It was, of course, his second such success in three years but on this occasion he was making history by being the first driver to win motor sport's highest accolade in a turbo-charged car.

Behind these first three everyone else still

there at the finish was at least a lap in arrears. Nevertheless, Warwick was well pleased to bring his Toleman home in the points for the fourth race on the trot, and considerable significance was placed on Rosberg finishing fifth in the new Williams FWO9. In fact, the Williams team were almost beside themselves with joy at such an impressive debut by their Honda-powered car. The only sign of a problem had been the engine running too hot, which Rosberg had overcome by periodically easing off to allow it to cool down again. This, in turn, had given Cheever the opportunity to go past him on a couple of occasions during the latter part of the race, but each time Rosberg had subsequently been able to retaliate, the last such moment having come with just under three laps to go. As a result Cheever, later to complain that his engine had been well down on power, had to make do with an eventual sixth place ahead of the six surviving normally-aspirated runners and Mansell's badly delayed Lotus 94T.

Results

1	R. Patrese (Brabham-BMW)	1 hr 33 min 25.708 sec (202.939 kph/ 126.100 mph)	
2	A. de Cesaris (Alfa Romeo)	1 hr 33 min 35.027 sec	
3	N. Piquet (Brabham-BMW)	1 hr 33 min 47.677 sec	
4	D. Warwick (Toleman-Hart)	1 lap behind	
5	K. Rosberg (Williams-Honda)	1 lap behind	
6	E. Cheever (Renault)	1 lap behind	
7	D. Sullivan (Tyrrell-Ford)	2 laps behind	
8	M. Surer (Arrows-Ford)	2 laps behind	
9	T. Boutsen (Arrows-Ford)	3 laps behind	
10	J.P. Jarier (Ligier-Ford)	4 laps behind	
*11	N. Lauda (McLaren-TAG)	6 laps behind	
12	K. Acheson (March-Ford)	6 laps behind	

Also running at finish: N. Mansell (Lotus-Renault) 9 laps behind, R. Boesel (Ligier-Ford) 11 laps behind

*Not running at finish

Fastest lap: N. Piquet (Brabham-BMW) on lap 6 in 1 min 09.948 sec (211.219 kph/131.245 mph)

Retirements

P. Ghinzani (Osella-Alfa Romeo) engine on lap 2, J. Laffite (Williams-Honda) accident on lap 2, M. Winkelhock (ATS-BMW) engine on lap 2, M. Baldi (Alfa Romeo) engine on lap 6, R. Arnoux (Ferrari) engine on lap 10, J. Watson (McLaren-TAG) disqualified on lap 19, E. de Angelis (Lotus-Renault) engine on lap 21, C. Fabi (Osella-Alfa Romeo) engine on lap 29, A. Prost (Renault) turbo-charger on lap 36, P. Tambay (Ferrari) turbo-charger on lap 57, B. Giacomelli (Toleman-Hart) turbo-charger on lap 57, M. Alboreto (Tyrrell-Ford) engine on lap 61.

World Champion for the second time in three years – Nelson Piquet, who is shown above driving his Brabham BT52B to victory in the European Grand Prix at a sunny Brands Hatch. *(Phipps Photographic)*

René Arnoux and Patrick Tambay, who between them ensured that Ferrari retained the Constructors' Championship. *(Autosport)*

1983 Points Tables

Driver	Nationality	Car	Mar 13 Brazilian (Rio de Janeiro)	Mar 27 USA (West) (Long Beach)	Apr 17 French (Paul Ricard)	May 1 San Marino (Imola)	May 15 Monaco (Monte Carlo)	May 22 Belgian (Spa-Francorchamps)	Jun 5 USA (Detroit)	Jun 12 Canadian (Montreal)	Jul 16 British (Silverstone)	Aug 7 German (Hockenheim)	Aug 14 Austrian (Österreichring)	Aug 28 Dutch (Zandvoort)	Sep 11 Italian (Monza)	Sep 25 European (Brands Hatch)	Oct 15 S. African (Kyalami)	Total points
N. Piquet	BR	Brabham-BMW	9	–	6	–	6	3	3	–	6	–	4	–	9	9	4	59
A. Prost	F	Renault	–	–	9	6	4	9	–	2	9	3	9	–	–	6	–	57
R. Arnoux	F	Ferrari	–	4	–	4	–	–	–	9	2	9	6	9	6	–	–	49
P. Tambay	F	Ferrari	2	–	3	9	3	6	–	4	4	–	–	6	3	–	–	40
K. Rosberg	SF	Williams-Ford / Williams-Honda	–	–	2	3	9	2	6	3	–	–	–	–	–	–	2	27
J. Watson	GB	McLaren-Ford / McLaren-TAG	–	9	–	2	–	–	4	1	–	2	–	4	–	–	–	22
E. Cheever	USA	Renault	–	–	4	–	–	4	–	6	–	–	3	–	4	–	1	22
A. de Cesaris	I	Alfa Romeo	–	–	–	–	–	–	–	–	–	6	–	–	–	3	6	15
R. Patrese	I	Brabham-BMW	–	–	–	–	–	–	–	–	–	4	–	–	–	–	9	13
N. Lauda	A	McLaren-Ford / McLaren-TAG	4	6	–	–	–	–	–	–	1	–	1	–	–	–	–	12
J. Laffite	F	Williams-Ford / Williams-Honda	3	3	1	–	–	1	2	–	1	–	–	–	–	–	–	11
M. Alboreto	I	Tyrrell-Ford	–	–	–	–	–	–	9	–	–	–	–	–	1	–	–	10
N. Mansell	GB	Lotus-Ford / Lotus-Renault	–	–	–	–	–	–	1	–	3	–	2	–	–	4	–	10
D. Warwick	GB	Toleman-Hart	–	–	–	–	–	–	–	–	–	–	–	3	1	2	3	9
M. Surer	CH	Arrows-Ford	1	2	–	1	–	–	–	–	–	–	–	–	–	–	–	4
M. Baldi	I	Alfa Romeo	–	–	–	–	1	–	–	–	–	–	–	2	–	–	–	3
D. Sullivan	USA	Tyrrell-Ford	–	–	–	–	2	–	–	–	–	–	–	–	–	–	–	2
E. de Angelis	I	Lotus-Ford / Lotus-Renault	–	–	–	–	–	–	–	–	–	–	–	–	2	–	–	2
J. Cecotto	YV	Theodore-Ford	–	1	–	–	–	–	–	–	–	–	–	–	–	–	–	1
B. Giacomelli	I	Toleman-Hart	–	–	–	–	–	–	–	–	–	–	–	–	–	1	–	1

N.B. Brazilian GP – K. Rosberg finished 2nd but not awarded points because of push-start.

Constructors

Constructor	Mar 13	Mar 27	Apr 17	May 1	May 15	May 22	Jun 5	Jun 12	Jul 16	Aug 7	Aug 14	Aug 28	Sep 11	Sep 25	Oct 15	Total
Ferrari	2	4	3	13	3	6	–	13	6	9	6	15	9	–	–	89
Renault	–	–	13	6	4	13	–	8	9	3	12	–	4	6	1	79
Brabham-BMW	9	–	6	–	6	3	3	–	6	4	4	–	9	9	13	72
Williams-Ford	3	3	3	3	9	3	8	3	–	1	–	–	–	–	–	36
McLaren-Ford	4	15	–	2	–	–	4	1	1	2	1	4	–	–	–	34
Alfa Romeo	–	–	–	–	1	–	–	–	–	6	–	2	–	3	6	18
Tyrrell-Ford	–	–	–	–	2	–	9	–	–	–	–	–	1	–	–	12
Lotus-Renault	–	–	–	–	–	–	–	–	3	–	2	–	2	4	–	11
Toleman-Hart	–	–	–	–	–	–	–	–	–	–	–	3	1	3	3	10
Arrows-Ford	1	2	–	1	–	–	–	–	–	–	–	–	–	–	–	4
Williams-Honda	–	–	–	–	–	–	–	–	–	–	–	–	–	–	2	2
Theodore-Ford	–	1	–	–	–	–	–	–	–	–	–	–	–	–	–	1
Lotus-Ford	–	–	–	–	–	–	1	–	–	–	–	–	–	–	–	1

Cancellations: Swiss GP (July 10), USA (New York) GP (Sept 25), USA (Las Vegas) GP (Oct 9).

1984 McLaren supremacy

Twelve months earlier preparations for the season ahead had seen the spotlight fall firmly on the chassis designers following the decision by FISA to slap a ban on aerodynamic skirts and to insist upon a full flat bottom on the car between the rear tangent of the front wheels and the front tangent of the rear wheels. This year, however, it fell firmly on the engine designers as at the same time that the various changes were announced for 1983 new rules had also been laid down for 1984 whereby the maximum fuel tank capacity was to be reduced from 250 to 220 litres and a ban imposed on in-race refuelling. Consequently, there was now a vital need to ensure that engines, besides being competitive, were fuel-efficient and to the extent of being able to cope with a full Grand Prix distance on no more than the new limit. In other words, the emphasis was now on obtaining a crucially fine balance between power and economy. This, in turn, created an engineering problem that demanded commitment, investment, inspiration and perspiration to unlock, and one that led to fuel management becoming a prime area of development whether controlled electronically, electro-mechanically or purely mechanically. Nor was the problem confined simply to making 220 litres of fuel last out. On the contrary. The economy factor was also to have a profound effect as regards cooling the turbos and reducing the engines' thermodynamic loads as hitherto, with fuel in virtually unlimited supply, this could be achieved by running a little rich. Now, of course, that was out of the question. As a result, and bearing in mind the importance of running a turbo-charged engine as near as possible to optimum working temperatures in the interests of better reliability and saving horse-power, the teams were obliged to place increasing emphasis on more efficient inter-coolers and radiators as an alternative means of improving engine cooling, even though it frequently meant a compromise as regards chassis installation. One of the few exceptions was McLaren, who had incorporated large radiators and achieved the essential requirement of a good air-flow from virtually the beginning of the TAG-Porsche engine project. Drivers, too, would now have their race performances governed by the rate of fuel consumption and, to assist in this respect, the teams were to devise sophisticated fuel-flow meters linked to a new gauge in the cockpits of their cars to indicate the amount of fuel being consumed. The general idea then was that during the course of a race, drivers would be advised of the amount of fuel that should have gone unused at various stages by means of pit signals so that after comparing the figures with the digital read-outs in their cockpits they would know whether or not they were using too much fuel and could respond to the situation by adjusting the turbo boost pressure as required. One or two teams, notably Renault and Williams, were also to adopt a one-way radio system (controlled by the driver) to achieve the same purpose, something that had the added advantage of enabling the driver to give advance notification to his pit of any unexpected problems that might arise, such as a punctured tyre, thereby saving valuable time.

Apart from the introduction of the new fuel limit, which many seasoned observers were to feel reduced Grand Prix racing to little more than an economy run, another important factor shaping the forthcoming season concerned tyres. First of all, over the weekend of the 1983 European Grand Prix at Brands Hatch in September, Michelin had confirmed that it would be supplying only Brabham, Renault and McLaren in 1984. This, of course, meant that Euroracing Alfa Romeo, Osella and Ligier all had to look elsewhere for tyres, although whereas the first two subsequently came to arrangements with Goodyear and Pirelli respectively, Ligier were later successful in persuading Michelin to include them in their 1984 programme after all. Secondly, and of even greater significance, Goodyear decided to change from bias-ply tyre construction to wholly radial ply in order to maintain better tyre profiles and thereby flat-bottom car ride heights, the very reason, in fact, why Brabham had switched from Goodyear to Michelin at the end of 1982.

Although the monitoring of fuel consumption necessarily became top priority over the winter months, this in no way detracted from the enormous amount of other development work and testing that went on. Ferrari, winners of the Constructors' Championship for the second year running in 1983, were no exception in this respect, as apart from designing and building a brand new car, the 126C4, a considerable amount of work was also carried out on the 120-degree, V6 engine. This included the introduction of a redesigned cylinder block and heads with the aim of improving torque and response, a smaller and lower

René Arnoux putting the Ferrari 126C4 through its paces. *(Dave Webb)*

crankcase, and a new Marelli/Weber electronic engine management system. At the same time the transverse gearbox also underwent a redesign and, like the revised engine, which was capable of producing around 680 bhp at 11,500 rpm, was lightened and mounted lower to give the entire car a lower centre of gravity. So far as the new chassis was concerned, it was based around a Kevlar and carbon-fibre composite monocoque almost identical to that of the 126C3 and, once again, was bonded together, complete with the magnesium bulkheads, to form a single structure with the nose cone, cockpit surround and fuel cell (smaller and lower than the C3) all integral. Consequently, its overall appearance was also similar to the C3 except at the rear, which was both lower and much tidier due to the revised engine/gearbox installation, together with a new cooling system, and also the introduction of shorter and slightly flatter side-pods. To drive his new cars, the Commendatore had decided even before the end of the 1983 season to retain the services of René Arnoux, but to release Patrick Tambay in favour of the Italian Tyrrell driver Michele Alboreto, who were now both going to be paid for the privilege by Marlboro, a situation that led to small Marlboro decals appearing on the bodywork of the scarlet cars.

Ferrari might well have won the Constructors' Cham-

The Parmalat Brabham BT53 of reigning World Champion Nelson Piquet pictured during practice for the British Grand Prix at Brands Hatch, by which time the original design had been uprated to 'B' specification. *(Dave Webb)*

pionship again in 1983, but the team to have finished the season as pace-setters had undeniably been Brabham with the strikingly elegant BT52/52B series of cars that had carried Nelson Piquet to his second World Championship title. In fact, the late season charge had caused a certain amount of controversy: it had led to accusations being brandished by Renault, in particular, that the specially brewed fuel used by the team – produced by BASF Chemicals in Germany – had exceeded the statutory 102 octane limit. However, BMW maintained that its fuel rating was acceptable within the rules and this was subsequently confirmed by FISA, who added that there was a 0.9 tolerance. As a result nothing further came of the matter. In the meantime, Brabham designer Gordon Murray used the winter months to progressively modify the team's existing cars in detail, first to 'C' specification and later to 'D' specification, until eventually finalizing the design for a brand new car. This was the BT53, which was based around a slightly revised monocoque of folded aluminium outer tub skin with moulded carbon-fibre composite inner-cum-tank top and fully machined solid aluminium bulkheads, and one that necessarily incorporated a larger fuel cell – of 220 litres capacity as distinct from the 191-litre 'pit stop' fuel cell of the BT52. Appearance-wise, the new car was very similar to its predecessor, although amongst the more noticeable changes were the introduction of newly-styled side-pods, slightly altered aerodynamics, that included a new rear undertray, and subtle differences to the suspension geometry, the suspension itself still being by inboard-mounted coil-spring/damper units all round activated by push-rods. The engine, too, was still the same four cylinder BMW M12/13 unit which, following continuous development work carried out at the German firm's factory in Munich, was now capable of producing a reputed 850 bhp at 11,000 rpm. Not surprisingly, Nelson Piquet was once again to remain as team leader, but his former number two, Riccardo Patrese, had decided that there was insufficient financial incentive to stay on for another year. Consequently, a replacement driver had to be found and, because the team's main sponsor – now just Parmalat owing to Fila having withdrawn their support after only one year – insisted that it should be an Italian, the final choice was Teodorico Fabi, who had previously driven for Toleman in 1982. It wasn't quite as simple as that, though, for he was already under contract to the Forsythe Indy car team in the United States. This, in turn, led to a somewhat unique arrangement whereby in the event of a clash of dates between a Grand Prix and an Indy car race Fabi's younger brother, Corrado, who had won the 1982 European Formula 2 championship, would act as his deputy in the second Brabham.

In direct contrast to Brabham, Renault-ELF had ended the 1983 season on an extremely disappointing note. They had just missed out on the Constructors' Championship and Prost, riding high at the top of the Drivers' table for much of the year, had been pipped to the post by Nelson Piquet in the final race after sagging turbo boost pressure had led to his retirement. Moreover, the repercussions of what was seen as a bitter defeat were enormous. Only a few days later a high-level management meeting had taken place and Prost, who had clearly made known his views on the matter and more or less demanded a major restructuring of the team, was subsequently told that his services were no longer required! After just one season with the French team, Eddie Cheever was also told that he had no role to play in its future plans either and, instead, two new drivers were signed up, the first being Patrick Tambay following his release by Ferrari and the second eventually being Derek Warwick, who was lured away from Toleman. Various other changes were made as well, including an internal re-organization whereby arrangements were made to set up a completely separate chassis department in new premises at Evry, leaving the existing factory at Viry-Châtillon to serve entirely as an engine shop under the technical direction of Bernard Dudot. In addition, a brand new car (the RE50) was evolved and, after thoughts had been given to designing and building a new four-cylinder engine, a revised version of the team's 90-degree, V6 unit produced. Dubbed the EF4, this featured a new, all-aluminium alloy cylinder block as standard and revised cylinder heads, weighed in at 12 kilogrammes lighter and was capable of producing up to 750 bhp at 11,500 rpm. Because of certain reservations about the KKK turbocharger units being too small, Renault also decided to switch to new and larger American Garrett AiResearch counterparts for 1984, a decision that was further influenced by the fact that Garrett was a bigger concern than the German company and had the facilities to develop turbo-chargers to exact requirements. Meanwhile, the new car was built around a carbon-fibre composite honeycomb monocoque manufactured by the French aerospace firm Hurel-Dubois, the same firm that had produced the RE40 monocoque. It immediately differed, however, by being a single-piece affair that effectively doubled as the bodywork in similar style to the Ferrari 126C3/C4 and the ATS D6. The side-pods, too, were much shorter than those of the RE40 and, at the rear, Michel Tetu designed the bodywork to taper inwards along similar lines to that of the 1983 McLarens. The suspension was by tubular double wishbones and pull-rods activating inboard-mounted coil-spring/damper units all round, and the overall result was an extremely purposeful-looking car that was both smaller and neater than the RE40.

In addition to running their own cars, of course, Renault-ELF had started making their V6 engines available to John Player Team Lotus in 1983, and this was a policy that was to be extended still further in 1984 to encompass the Ligier team. So far as Lotus were concerned, the most significant change made for the new season ahead involved tyres, as after a somewhat disappointing year with Pirelli, Peter Warr was able to termin-

Britain's Derek Warwick, now driving for Renault, behind the wheel of the RE50 at Monaco. *(Autosport)*

ate the existing contract with the Italian company and conclude a new deal with Goodyear. Apart from that, the only other major change – Elio de Angelis and Nigel Mansell were both retained as drivers – was the arrival of a brand new car, the 95T, which was a logical development of the hastily-built 94T designed by Gerard Ducarouge and introduced at the 1983 British Grand Prix. Again the work of Ducarouge, this featured a larger, 220-litre, fuel cell, pull-rod rather than rocker-arm front suspension, shorter side-pods and improved aerodynamics, and was based around a carbon-fibre/Kevlar composite monocoque similar to that of its predecessor. At Ligier, on the other hand, the winter months brought all sorts of changes, something that was badly needed after the failure to score a single World Championship point in 1983. For a start the fact that Guy Ligier had finally concluded a deal with Renault to use their V6 engines, after having come so close to it twelve months earlier, meant that the French team was about to field a turbo-charged car for the very first time. There were also two new drivers signed up,

John Player Special Team Lotus manager Peter Warr (left) and designer Gerard Ducarouge with the Renault V6 turbo-charged type 95T. *(Autocar & Motor)*

Andrea de Cesaris and François Hesnault (a French Formula 3 ace), to replace Jean-Pierre Jarier and Raul Boesel, two new and additional sponsorship ties forged with Antar Petroleum (a subsidiary of ELF) and the Loto

Francois Hesnault in action in the Renault V6 turbo-charged Ligier Loto JS23. *(Phipps Photographic)*

The Euroracing Alfa Romeo 184T in its, new for 1984, Benetton livery. *(Dave Webb)*

national lottery, and a brand new car designed specifically by Michel Beaujon and Claude Galopin to accommodate the Renault EF4 V6 engine as distinct from the previously used Ford-Cosworth V8 unit. Designated the JS23, this also broke new ground so far as Ligier was concerned as instead of being based around an aluminium honeycomb monocoque, employed in the team's previous cars, it was based around an increasingly fashionable single-piece carbon-fibre composite monocoque, which effectively doubled as the bodywork and was very similar to that of the Ferrari 126C3. Unlike its immediate predecessor, the JS23 also had medium-length side-pods, tapered-in rear bodywork similar to the 1983 McLarens and a suspension system consisting of upper and lower wishbones and pull-rods activating inboard-mounted coil-spring/damper units all round, the oleo-pneumatic Citroen-based suspension that had appeared on the JS21 having been put to one side.

The three other teams already firmly established as turbo runners – Euroracing Alfa Romeo, Toleman and ATS – also came up with brand new cars for 1984. Of these, however, Toleman and ATS both began the new season with existing chassis that were essentially unchanged and only Euroracing Alfa Romeo actually had a new car ready to race. This was the 184T, which was designed by Luigi Marmiroli and based around a distinctively slim and rounded, British-built, carbon-fibre composite monocoque that, once again, followed the increasingly popular trend of effectively doubling as the bodywork. It had medium-length as distinct from the full-length side-pods of the 183T to house the water radiators, a push-rod front and pull-rod rear suspension, a totally new Euroracing-built 5-speed gearbox and was fitted with a Ferrari-like rear aerofoil. Because of the decision by Michelin to limit the supply of tyres in 1984, the 184T was Goodyear-shod, was powered by the now familiar (and fuel thirsty) Alfa Romeo twin turbo-charged V8 engine (now capable of producing a claimed 670 bhp at 11,800 rpm following continuous development work) and

appeared in a completely new, predominantly light green livery with Benetton lettering, the very successful Italian knitwear firm having taken over from Marlboro as the team's major sponsor. For 1984 Euroracing also had two new drivers as Andrea de Cesaris had defected to Ligier and was replaced by Riccardo Patrese, while Renault refugee Eddie Cheever was signed up by Gianpaulo Pavanello in favour of retaining Mauro Baldi, a move that was almost certainly responsible in part, at least, in attracting new sponsorship from Benetton due to its numerous marketing outlets in the United States.

Although ATS had completed their new car by the end of the winter, it wasn't considered to be raceworthy for the opening event in Brazil and, instead, had its debut deferred until the South African Grand Prix in April. Designed by Gustav Brunner, who had by then left the team and joined Euroracing, the D7, as this latest ATS

The ATS D7. *(Phipps Photographic)*

was designated, was very much a logical development of the D6 in its late-1983 specification. In fact, the only major difference between the two cars was the carbon-fibre composite monocoque which, whilst still being a one-piece affair with the upper section at the front doubling as the bodywork, was somewhat lower and narrower. Once again BMW had agreed to make their four-cylinder M12/13 turbo-charged engines available – presumably on the understanding that Manfred Winkelhock would continue as the driver (the main reason for coming to the arrangement in the first place) – but, for the second year running, Gunther Schmidt had been obliged to look elsewhere for tyres and had now concluded a deal with Pirelli.

Toleman were even later than ATS in introducing their new 1984 car as it took until the French Grand Prix in May, by which time the British team had ended its 3-year association in Formula 1 with Pirelli and switched to Michelin for the supply of tyres. Prior to that, other changes had taken place within the team as well and included Peter Gethin being appointed as team manager, a change of sponsor and the signing up of two new drivers to replace Derek Warwick, following his departure to Renault, and Bruno Giacomelli, who had not been offered a new contract. At one point there had also seemed a distinct possibility of agreement being reached with BMW for the supply of the German firm's four-cylinder M12/13 turbo-charged engines in 1984, but nothing had come of it, not so far as Toleman were concerned, at least. Instead, the arrangement continued with Brian Hart for the use of his Holset turbo-charged 415T engine which, following yet more development work over the winter, was now capable of producing around 600 bhp at 10,750 rpm. In the meantime, while Rory Byrne and his design team were completing work on the new 1984 car, essentially unchanged versions of the TG183B were brought into use at the start of the season, as already mentioned. However, one immediate difference, apart

from the fact that they were now being driven by a complete newcomer to Formula 1, Brazilian and 1983 Marlboro British Formula 3 champion Ayrton Senna, and also by former Theodore driver Johnny Cecotto, was their colour: they were now painted red, blue and white due partly to Cecotto bringing with him sponsorship from the Italian coffee importers Segafredo and partly because of the loss of support – yet again – from Candy. This then remained the situation for the first four races until finally the all-new Michelin-shod TG184 emerged, three examples being built ready for use at Dijon. Although based around a very similar carbon-fibre composite monocoque to that of the TG183B, this new car was totally different in general concept and aerodynamic package and was the result of considerable wind-tunnel work, which had led to some 25% additional downforce being achieved without any adverse effect on straight-line speed. Certainly one of the most noticeable aspects compared to its predecessor was the adoption of a much more conventional nose section made possible by transferring the water and oil radiators to the right-hand of two medium-length side-pods, the left-hand side-pod being used to house the single inter-cooler for the Holset turbo-charger unit. The new car also had a four-inch longer wheelbase, but a similar push-rod front and pull-rod rear suspension system was retained, as was the team's distinctive double rear aerofoil arrangement, albeit in slightly modified form with a much cleaner profile.

Two other well-established teams to have joined the ranks of turbo runners in 1983, albeit very late in the season, were, of course, McLaren International and Williams Grand Prix Engineering, the first being McLaren with their TAG-Porsche-powered MP4/1E, which had made its debut at the Dutch Grand Prix in August. At the

The Toleman TG184, carrying a new colour scheme in 1984. *(Dave Webb)*

1984

Alain Prost, new to the Marlboro McLaren team in 1984, captured at speed in what was quickly to become the car of the year, the TAG-Porsche-powered MP4/2. *(Dave Webb)*

time this had been very much an 'interim' chassis and had been built only after pressure from Niki Lauda through Marlboro to have the new TAG-Porsche engine tested under race conditions to iron out any teething problems that might arise before it came to the new season. In the event, Lauda's actions had been proved right for there certainly had been teething problems, and the experience gained because of them had proved invaluable. Meanwhile, by the season's end John Barnard had already set about designing a totally new, tailor-made, turbo-charged chassis, work that was governed by the TAG-Porsche V6 being shorter than the Ford-Cosworth V8 and also by the introduction of the 220-litre fuel limit. The result was the MP4/2, which was based around a moulded carbon-fibre/honeycomb composite monocoque similar to those of the Ford-Cosworth-powered McLarens previously designed by Barnard, but differing considerably in detail – to the point where it had been necessary for the team to retrieve the complex tub tooling from the Hercules Corporation in the United States (where the McLaren monocoques were moulded) and to return it after it had been part revised, part replaced and remachined! Among the revisions incorporated in the new tub sections were a lower, longer fuel cell behind the cockpit and the lower sides around the bottom wishbone rear pick-up points being flared out to enhance the flow of air into the side-pods, which were shorter than on the MP4/1E, but still long (and large) relative to those of other cars. As before, each of the side-pods contained the Behr inter-coolers, oil and water radiators, but now dual-purpose radiator cores lay raked steeply forward in them – each core's left side cooling the water and their right cooling the oil – in place of the previous arrangement whereby two separate cores had been employed with oil ahead of water. Each pod also

tapered inwards ahead of the rear wheels in similar fashion to the team's 1983 cars so as to encourage air to flow between the rear wheels and bodywork and thus create down-force on part of the top surface of the flat undertray in the vicinity of the rear suspension. However, the body waist was further forward than on the MP4/1E and this had meant turning the KKK turbo-charger units around at a sharper angle. Numerous other detail changes had also been incorporated into the design of the new car, particularly in the field of aerodynamics, and these extended to the rear suspension where the mounts for the coil-spring/damper units had been moved further forward (as permitted by the shorter V6 engine) and the rocker arms raked back from inboard, thereby allowing an even slimmer rear bodyline. Throughout the winter months, while the new car was being completed, the TAG-Porsche engine underwent a lot of further development as well, with particular emphasis on improving power (subsequently quoted at around 750 bhp at 11,500 rpm), fuel consumption and reducing throttle lag, much of the work being carried out in close co-operation between Porsche and Bosch. The 1984-spec engine was also lighter due, in part, to the adoption of titanium main crankcase studs and a lightweight cast-magnesium inlet manifold, which replaced the somewhat hefty 'bolt-together', machined-section type previously used for shape experimentation. In the meantime, besides building the new car, McLaren International now had a new driver (to partner Niki Lauda) as for the second year running John Watson had delayed signing a fresh contract with the team – in the hope of obtaining a bigger retainer – and had been replaced by Alain Prost, following the Frenchman's sudden departure from Renault. Furthermore, although the Ulsterman had subsequently entered into negotiations with other teams, particularly Lotus, nothing had ulti- mately come of them and, instead, he found himself unemployed after a Grand Prix career that had spanned eleven seasons and included no less than 151 appearances.

Whereas John Barnard had designed an 'interim' chassis to serve as the first turbo-charged McLaren, Wil- liams' Patrick Head had produced a tailor-made turbo- charged chassis at the outset following the deal struck up between Frank Williams and the Honda Motor Company to run the Japanese firm's V6 engine. This, of course, was the FW09 that had made its debut in the 1983 end-of- season South African Grand Prix at Kyalami. Conse- quently, the Williams team began the new year essentially from where it had left off, especially as Keijo (Keke) Rosberg and Jacques Laffite both stayed on as drivers. Nevertheless, after carrying out an intensive programme of testing and development with the new car over the winter, a number of detail changes were made to the original design and these included the introduction of a new, pull-rod, rear suspension and a revised version of the team's own modified Hewland gearbox. Alterations were also made to the cooling arrangements for the Honda RA163-E engine which, similarly, received a lot of atten- tion and was now fitted with twin Japanese IHI turbo- charger units. In addition, like so many other designers, Patrick Head was looking into the possibility of 'waisting- in' the rear bodywork in similar style to the McLarens to

The 'B' version of the Williams FW09 being driven by Jacques Laffite in Holland. *(Phipps Photographic)*

achieve extra downforce around the back of the car, something that ideally called for a rocker-arm operated rear suspension, which the new gearbox casing could not accept. This, in turn, resulted in the team's earlier gearbox and FW08-like wider track, rocker-arm rear suspension being re-introduced soon after the start of the season and to the cars gradually being developed into a definitive 'B' specification just prior to the British Grand Prix in July. In this form the cars, besides reappearing with McLaren-like reprofiled side-pods, which accommodated repositioned radiators and inter-coolers, had a five-inch longer wheel- base made possible by a larger oil tank casting being

Although Honda discontinued their supply of engines to the team at the end of 1983, Spirit persevered in 1984 using Brian Hart's 4-cylinder engines installed in an uprated 101B chassis, shown above in the hands of Mauro Baldi. *(Phipps Photographic)*

located between the engine and the gearbox, a new exhaust system and yet more slight alterations to the rear suspension.

Originally, it will be recalled, Honda had made their return to the Grand Prix arena in 1983 with their V6 turbo-charged engine installed in the back of a car that brought a completely new name into the sport – Spirit. Sadly, though, for this little team run by former March Formula 2 manager John Wickham and the ex-McLaren designer Gordon Coppuck the Japanese firm had announced in October (1983) that in future it would be concentrating all of its efforts on Williams. As a result Spirit Racing had to look elsewhere for an engine supplier and eventually came to an arrangement with Brian Hart for the use of his Holset turbo-charged 415T units. Out of necessity, Gordon Coppuck then designed a completely new rear end for the team's 101 chassis that had appeared briefly during practice for the 1983 European Grand Prix at Brands Hatch. This included bringing into use a new magnesium casting with supporting A-frames to carry the engine, which was not suitable to serve as a fully-stressed member, and also a new oil tank/bell-housing. The rear suspension, too, was replaced by a new system, although one that still employed rocker arms to activate inboard- mounted coil-spring/damper units. At one point there was considerable speculation that former double World Cham- pion Emerson Fittipaldi would be driving the car in 1984 (now Pirelli-shod and dubbed the 101B), but despite testing it at Rio de Janeiro during the winter he subse- quently decided to join a new Indy car team in the United States. Instead, after the team's existing driver, Stefan Johansson, failed to attract sufficient sponsorship, it was handled, initially, by Euroracing Alfa Romeo refugee, Mauro Baldi, with backing from Topolino, Italy's equiva- lent to Walt Disney.

With a turbo-charged engine having become virtually essential for achieving competitive speeds, the other teams (all of whom had continued relying on normally-

The Hart-powered Skoal Bandit RAM 02. *(L.A.T. Photographic)*

aspirated engines throughout 1983) were now attempting to jump on the band-wagon. The only exception was Theodore, which had folded as a Grand Prix team soon after the end of the season due to Theodore Yip deciding that in the unlikely event of a turbo-charged engine materializing it was pointless continuing. Instead, both he and Mo Nunn, who had pulled out of the partnership even before the end of the season, switched their attentions to North American CART racing, while designer Nigel Bennett had already moved over to Lola by then to help design a new Indy car. Meanwhile, of the remainder, John MacDonald's RAM outfit joined Toleman and Spirit inasmuch as it became a customer for Brian Hart's four-cylinder 415T engines, which were installed in brand new, though fairly conventional, Dave Kelly-designed RAM 02s (entered for Jonathan Palmer and Philippe Alliot and finished off in the green and yellow colours of the team's new main sponsor, Skoal Bandit); Osella reached agreement with Alfa Romeo for the supply of their V8 turbo-

The Alfa Romeo-powered Kelémata Osella FA1F. *(L.A.T. Photographic)*

charged engines and began the season with a singleton entry for Piercarlo Ghinzani using a Pirelli-shod, Kelémata-sponsored car built up around an ex-Euroracing Alfa Romeo 183T monocoque until introducing their purpose-built, albeit similar, FA1F at the Belgian Grand Prix; and Arrows, through Jack Oliver, succeeded in negotiating a deal with BMW for the use of the German firm's M12/13 turbo-charged engines, for which Dave Wass produced a totally new car, the A7, based around a similar aluminium honeycomb monocoque to that of the A6, but with a carbon-fibre inner moulding. However, because this latter arrangement did not reach fruition until the Belgian Grand Prix – and then only in part due to a limited supply of BMW engines – Arrows began the new season with essentially unaltered versions of their existing Ford-Cosworth-powered car. These were entered for the team's retained drivers, Marc Surer and Thierry Boutsen, and painted in a new cream and brown livery following a much-needed sponsorship tie-up with Barclay cigarettes and Nordica ski boots. Last, but by no means least, Tyrrell had been hoping, like Toleman, to do a deal with BMW for 1984 only to have found themselves subsequently losing out to Arrows. As a result it was simply a case of plugging on with the normally-aspirated Ford-Cosworth DFY engines and with slightly modified versions of the 012 that had first appeared during practice for the 1983 Austrian Grand Prix. In the meantime, the team was obliged to start afresh with two new drivers as, apart from Michele Alboreto moving over to Ferrari, Danny Sullivan decided to return to the United States to take part in the North American CART Championship. The outcome was the arrival of two young newcomers to Formula 1, English Formula 3 ace Martin Brundle and German World Endurance Championship driver Stefan Bellof, the latter bringing with him much-needed sponsorship – following Lucien Benetton's decision to shift his support to Euroracing Alfa Romeo – which had been arranged by his manager, Willi

The BMW-powered Barclay/Nordica Arrows A7. *(Phipps Photographic)*

Maurer, through a Monaco-based agency. Unfortunately, though, after some quite encouraging results and modest success in obtaining additional sponsorship, 1984 rapidly turned into a year that in the eyes of Ken Tyrrell was best forgotten. This followed the introduction, at the beginning of the new year, of a water-injection system on his cars in which water was pumped from a rubber bag tank to a spraying mechanism over the air-intake trumpets to cool the fuel-injection process. The ultimate aim was that of improving engine reliability, but during post-race scrutineering at the Detroit Grand Prix impurities were to be found in the water and also a large quantity of miniscule lead balls lying loosely at the bottom of the rubber bag tank, which was fitted inside the monocoque. The upshot of it was that Tyrrell was ultimately to find his team being excluded from the 1984 World Championship.

The ill-fated Tyrrell team was left to persevere with normally-aspirated engines, using the Ford-Cosworth-powered 012. *(Phipps Photographic)*

1984

XIII° Grande Prêmio do Brasil

Rio de Janeiro: March 25
Weather: Hot
Distance: 61 laps of 5.031 km circuit = 306.89 km (190.69 miles)

Once again the close season had seemed an eternity but now, after more than five months since the last Grand Prix of 1983, the long wait was almost over. It was late March and time for the teams to head for Brazil and start preparing themselves for the opening round of the 1984 World Championship at the Autodromo Internacional do Rio de Janeiro. Throughout the winter months the amount of development work and testing carried out had been absolutely colossal and had resulted in no less than eight of the teams (Ferrari, Brabham, Renault, McLaren, Euroracing Alfa Romeo, Lotus, Ligier and RAM) being in a position to field completely new cars. The remaining seven teams, too, were all well equipped with extensively modified cars, some rebuilt but the majority built up from scratch. Indeed, with so much new machinery, combined with some different engine installations, a number of new or revised sponsorship deals and wholesale changes on the driver front, the overall scene had virtually been transformed and suggested that there was an even better season of Grand Prix racing in store than that of the previous year. To add to what was an already exciting prospect, there was also a completely unknown factor to consider – fuel. Not only were refuelling stops now a thing of the past but the maximum fuel tank capacity of each car had been reduced from 250 litres to 220 litres in accordance with the rule changes announced on 3 November 1982. Consequently, it remained to be seen just how everyone would cope with this situation for whilst fuel consumption had been carefully monitored during testing there was still no way of realizing the full impact on competitiveness until it came to the actual race. This, in turn, meant that performance pointers during the test sessions didn't necessarily count for much, and there was a similar feeling about qualifying: it was no longer any use having a car on pole position if it ran out of fuel before the end of the race!

If nobody was taking test performances too seriously one aspect that had not gone unnoticed was the progress made by Goodyear with their radial tyre development. On the few occasions that such tyres had appeared from Akron during 1983 the results had been less than encouraging. However, over the winter the situation had improved to such an extent that the American company's racing department had now apparently abandoned any further development programme on its range of cross-plies in favour of shifting the emphasis on radials so as to maintain better tyre profiles and to keep in touch with

Michelin and Pirelli. The new Lotus 95Ts, in particular, had really shone on the new range of Goodyear radials during the test sessions with de Angelis and Mansell more often than not setting the pace. Furthermore, this was a pattern that was to continue once it came round to the first qualifying session on Friday afternoon. During the morning untimed session de Angelis, whose 95T was fitted with new and very large Garrett turbo-charger units that had been designed specifically for qualifying, had complained of high engine temperatures, while Mansell had been bothered by a series of niggling problems that included an electrical short-circuit from the battery underneath his seat. But now, with the Italian having had a revised undertray and bodywork recently developed from wind-tunnel tests replaced by an earlier set-up and his team-mate enjoying better fortune, the pair of black and gold cars were right to the forefront once again. In fact, by the time that they had each gone through their two sets of marked tyres Mansell and de Angelis had done more than enough to occupy first and second places on the time-sheets at 1 min 29.364 sec and 1 min 29.625 sec respectively, the Englishman adamant that he could have gone even quicker but for a busy moment through one of the left-handers after moving off line to overtake Ghinzani's slower-moving Osella. Close behind this happy duo, Prost achieved a very satisfying third fastest time of 1 min 29.823 sec, especially as he was driving a brand new McLaren MP4/2 chassis that had apparently not even turned a wheel prior to the start of the weekend, and Lauda was little more than a tenth of a second slower in the original MP4/2, although separated from his new team-mate by Alboreto's extremely well-driven Ferrari 126C4. Arnoux would almost certainly have been up amongst the early pace-setters as well but his Ferrari, fitted with a Lucas fuel-injection system as opposed to a modified Marelli/Weber system in Alboreto's sister car, was plagued by a persistent fuel pressure problem. As a result the Frenchman never really got into his stride and did well even to wind up seventh fastest between the two Renault RE50s of Tambay and Warwick, both drivers rather perplexed at finding their cars not handling nearly so well as in the winter test sessions at this circuit. Without doubt, though, the biggest disappointment was the reigning World Champion's performance, even allowing for the fact that he had lost a fair amount of time with minor engine problems in the morning. But, somehow, Piquet just couldn't seem to get his act together in the new Brabham

BT53 and at one point almost ran out of road through one of the faster turns on his way to setting a comparatively lowly tenth fastest time of 1 min 31.068 sec – almost 2 seconds off the pace!

After another busy 90 minutes of untimed practice on Saturday morning, which saw the majority of teams running their cars in race trim and meticulously checking fuel consumption figures, preparations were soon in hand for the start of the second and final hour of qualifying. These included the Lotus mechanics replacing the revised undertray and bodywork on Mansell's 95T by the earlier set-up due to their English driver having begun to experience a problem with high engine temperatures, just like de Angelis on the previous morning, and the Renault team also doing a U-turn by altering the aerodynamics on their RE50s to a similar, high downforce, configuration used in winter testing as a means of trying to eradicate continuing handling problems. Over at Brabham, meanwhile, Piquet was planning to use the spare BT53, which had been specially set up for qualifying to save the Brazilian's race chassis. However, this last move proved to be futile for within minutes of the car leaving the pits shortly after the start of final qualifying its BMW engine failed, therefore leaving Piquet with no alternative other than to fall back on his race chassis after all. Just to add to growing concern in the Brabham pit Fabi (T.), who had already suffered a frustrating first day with throttle linkage and gearbox problems, also returned to the pits quite early on to report that he had spun off at the end of the back straight, an incident that meant the Italian sitting things out until the damage, mainly superficial, had been repaired. One driver for whom things seemed to be coming good at long last, on the other hand, was Warwick. Apart from suffering the handling imbalance with his Renault, he had spent much of the morning dashing in and out of the pits with something apparently amiss with the car's water-injection system only for the source of the problem to have finally been traced to nothing worse than a faulty warning light switch. But now, with that no longer to worry about and the Renault's handling becoming somewhat more manageable, Warwick was really beginning to show his mettle and actually topped the time-sheets for a while with a new fastest lap of 1 min 29.025 sec – and this was in spite of a big sideways moment at the first right-hander beyond the pits! In the final reckoning, though, de Angelis restored the status quo for Lotus with an even quicker, pole-winning, time of 1 min 28.392 sec, while Alboreto also went on to beat the new Renault recruit to earn a thoroughly well-deserved second place on the grid at 1 min 28.898 sec. Meanwhile, Mansell's hopes of defending the overnight pole were spoiled by an incident involving Prost when the new McLaren driver apparently decided to retaliate for being inadvertently baulked by the Lotus a little earlier whilst going for a quick time. Whatever, when Mansell came up behind him whilst in the midst of a quick lap himself, Prost moved out to overtake the Ligier JS23 of de Cesaris at the same instant that the Englishman was about to go past both of them. Consequently, with his path suddenly becoming blocked, Mansell had to slam on the brakes and, almost before realizing it, was spinning off the track, the Lotus damaging its undertray into the bargain. Furthermore, it ultimately resulted in Mansell being one of only a handful of drivers not to improve on their Friday times and caused him to slip back to fifth spot on the grid

where he would line up between the two McLaren-TAGs of the rather 'unfriendly' Prost and Lauda.

Behind Lauda, no-one had broken the 1 min 30 sec barrier with Piquet having come nearest at 1 min 30.149 sec to hoist himself up to a still rather disappointing seventh place on the grid for his home Grand Prix. He was followed by a rather unimpressive Tambay, Rosberg, who had clawed his way up to an eventual ninth spot after fighting vicious understeer throughout the two days (the new pull-rod rear suspension systems on the Honda-powered Williams FWO9s seemed to be working too well compared to the front ends and were giving too much grip), and a very dejected Arnoux, the French Ferrari driver blaming the traffic and a late turbo-charger failure for his lack of progress. The two Euroracing Alfa Romeo 184Ts of Patrese and Cheever were next after both drivers had been hampered by a string of engine and turbo-charger failures, particularly on Friday, while Laffite, having spent much of practice in the spare Williams due to the Honda engine in his proposed race chassis refusing to pull cleanly, rounded off the front half of the grid by being at least a full second quicker than any of the others. Nevertheless, Brundle had gone exceptionally well on his first official outing in the normally-aspirated, Ford-Cosworth DFY-powered Tyrrell 012 and another new boy, Senna, had certainly not disgraced himself in the Toleman-Hart, especially when taking into account that both he and team-mate Cecotto had found themselves on the receiving end of a faulty batch of Pirelli qualifying tyres. Hesnault, despite the Ligier JS23s proving to be quite a handful, and Bellof, too, had both shown plenty of promise on their first public appearances in a Formula 1 car, but Alliot had never really had much chance due to his new RAM-Hart being plagued by near-continuous fuel vaporization problems. Palmer, taking part in only his second Grand Prix meeting, had been experiencing much the same trouble with the earlier and heavier RAM 01 that he was driving and was actually at the bottom of the time-sheets with 27th fastest time of 1 min 37.919 sec. As a result, he was the only non-qualifier but was still destined to have a role to play on race day as later came word that Winkelhock was being excluded from the meeting due to an infringement of the rules: towards the end of qualifying the German's ATS had come to rest near the entrance to the pit lane apparently out of fuel and two of the team's mechanics had then ignored a warning from a race steward that they were not allowed to push the car into the pits. This, of course, was correct according to Article 10 of the Standard Regulations for the Formula 1 World Championship, which also stated that the car should be weighed under such circumstances, and any

possibility of the Stewards confining their action to a reprimand at a subsequent meeting had been lost by team owner Gunther Schmidt's apparent unrepentant and abrupt attitude.

Conditions throughout practice had been hot and dry and it was much the same on race day, although the heat was certainly not stifling by South American standards. The 30 minute warm-up session, which began at the early hour of 9.30 a.m. (four hours before the scheduled starting time for the race in accordance with another rule change for 1984), was highlighted by the speed of the two McLaren MP4/2s for Lauda was comfortably fastest ahead of team-mate Prost, suggesting that the Marlboro-sponsored team had arrived at a very good race set-up. Other than that the main talking points as preparations continued for the 62-lap race concerned the minimum weight limit and the fuel limitations. So far as the weight limit was concerned some of the teams were relying on large water tanks to bring their cars up to the required 540 kg under the pretext of being necessary for water-injection systems and/or brake-cooling purposes. Then, because pit stops for fresh tyres were still very much on the agenda, these same teams were proposing to top up their cars' water supply at the same time that the tyres were being replaced which, in turn, suggested that for some while before the pit stops the cars would be running under weight. The situation regarding fuel, on the other hand, was even more complex. As a means of exceeding the 220-litre limit, several teams had brought along purpose-built refrigeration plants in which to hyper-cool their fuel, thereby increasing its density and causing it to contract (at the rate of approximately 1% per 10 degrees Centigrade reduction in temperature) and so occupy smaller volume – before being added to the 220-litre tanks just prior to the start of the race! Pressurized tank filling was another means being tried to achieve a similar effect, and whilst there was nothing actually illegal about these methods they were certainly not within the spirit of the rules nor, indeed, was the business of trying to circumvent the minimum weight limit.

Unfortunately, the first attempt to start the race, already delayed slightly by a power failure at the circuit, had to be aborted because of de Cesaris being unable to select any gears in his Ligier at the end of the parade lap, the Italian frantically waving his arms in the air to attract the starter's attention. This, of course, meant that the race distance would be reduced by one lap but, in the time that it took to wheel away the stricken car and for the starting procedure to be set in motion all over again with a second parade lap, over 20 minutes went by. Consequently, there was mounting anxiety about fuel vaporization, notwithstanding the fact

1984

Alain Prost, who scored a rather unexpected victory in the brand new McLaren MP4/2, shown here leading a group of mid-field runners whilst lying in tenth place on the opening lap. *(L.A.T. Photographic)*

that many cars had silver foil and the like draped over their fuel tanks during the lull in order to reduce the risk, as had been the case following the original warm-up lap. Even then, the second attempt to start the Brazilian Grand Prix was not over-successful for when the green light eventually flashed on, Piquet and Cecotto both stalled their engines, causing a considerable amount of confusion as drivers further down the grid, darted towards the centre of the track to avoid them. More by luck than judgement, it appeared, there were no collisions and the two stationary cars were subsequently push-started into the fray, where they were left bringing up the rear along with the Ligier of de Cesaris, who joined the race from the pit lane in his team's spare car. Alboreto, meanwhile, made a superb start in his first race with Ferrari and snapped into an immediate lead, but the pole-sitter, de Angelis, was rather hesitant in the run up to the first right-hander due to the Renault engine in his Lotus 95T refusing to rev cleanly. This, in turn, also enabled Warwick and Mansell to rush on ahead of him and before the end of the opening lap the Italian was down in fifth place behind a hard-charging Lauda. Tambay was sixth but Prost had made a dreadful start due to allowing his revs to drop away too much as he dropped the clutch, and was down in tenth place behind Arnoux, Rosberg and Cheever.

For a driver not exactly familiar with leading a Grand Prix Alboreto was looking serenely confident out in front and before long was gradually dropping Warwick, in spite of the Renault driver obviously doing his best to keep up. Very quickly, though, it was the two red and white McLarens that were the cars to watch. Once he had made comparatively light work of overtaking Mansell on the second lap Lauda was almost imme-

diately gaining on Warwick, while Prost was steadily working his way to the front of a really absorbing battle going on for the other leading positions. These were being fought over by de Angelis (still troubled by his engine not running very cleanly), Tambay, Arnoux, Rosberg, Cheever, Fabi and Patrese, with all eight, including Prost, running virtually nose to tail. At the same time Piquet was giving the large and enthusiastic Brazilian crowd plenty to cheer about by consistently picking off tail-enders following his delayed start. In fact, by lap 6 the local hero was already up amongst the mid-field runners and about to take over 15th place at the expense of the other Brazilian in the race, Senna. He, unlike Piquet, was progressing backwards due to falling turbo boost pressure and, unfortunately, on lap 9 this was to result in the retirement list being opened. By then Piquet was up into 14th place between Bellof and Laffite, Prost had just moved into a points position due to following Tambay and Arnoux past de Angelis prior to getting the better of the French Ferrari driver and, of even greater significance, Lauda was right up with Warwick. Furthermore, the Austrian was now looking for a way past the Renault and finally pounced on the tenth lap by pulling out from behind Warwick along the fast back straight and then going through on the inside under braking for the left-hander that followed. But there was a bit more to it than that. On his way past, Lauda actually brought his right rear wheel into contact with the Renault's left front wheel owing to hitting a bump on the track, which threw his McLaren fractionally off line. Nevertheless, both drivers continued apparently none the worse for the incident except for Warwick, of course, now being down in third place.

Towards the end of lap 12, and enjoying a

reasonably comfortable 6-second cushion over Lauda, Alboreto suddenly spun away the lead at the last right-hander before the pits. At first it appeared to be the result of a mistake in the cockpit but, after regaining the track in third place, Alboreto spun again at the very next corner and went on to complete the 13th lap by touring into the pits to report that his front brakes were suddenly playing up. Sure enough a bolt had worked loose on the right front caliper – allowing the fluid to seep away – and although Alboreto subsequently rejoined the race not realizing the full extent of the problem, one more lap was enough to convince him that it was pointless continuing. Only moments earlier Bellof and Baldi had also pulled out of the contest, with a broken throttle cable and a distributor malfunction respectively, while not long afterwards Laffite's race was ended by an acute loss of power caused by an electrical failure on one bank of cylinders of his Honda engine. For the McLaren team, on the other hand, the situation was looking better by the minute, for apart from Lauda having automatically assumed the lead and already pulled away from Warwick, Prost had displaced Tambay on the 13th lap and now, on lap 16, was in the throes of doing the same to Mansell. Indeed, after just eight more laps Lauda and Prost were lying first and second, just over 10 seconds apart, with Warwick now also having fallen victim to his predecessor at Renault. At this point Mansell was still pounding along in a pretty solid-looking fourth place, a further 12 seconds adrift, but of rather more relevance to the partisan crowd was the progress of Piquet, who had continued his climb up through the field and was currently lying ninth behind Tambay, Arnoux, de Angelis and Rosberg.

Just before half-distance the scheduled pit stops for fresh tyres and, in some instances, 'weight-gaining' water began with Tambay setting the ball rolling at the end of lap 26. After locking up his brakes and quite literally sliding into the Renault pit apron he eventually rejoined the race in tenth place between Cheever and Patrese. But when Warwick pulled in three laps later it was a different story for the Englishman subsequently succeeded in getting out on to the track once more with his third place still intact, due partly to Mansell following him into the pits and slipping to eighth spot behind Piquet. Over the next few laps other drivers also went through their pit stop routine but the McLaren duo stayed out until the end of lap 38. Then Lauda and Prost suddenly both appeared in the pit lane together! Initially, it seemed that there had been a major breakdown in communications but, in fact, Lauda had already slowed right up, even to the point of allowing de Angelis to unlap himself, and was coasting in to retire with what later transpired to be a faulty electrical connection to the McLaren's wiring loom. To make matters worse for the team Prost, who was merely in for tyres, was held up for over 25 seconds owing to a problem tightening up his car's left rear wheel nut and when he did finally set off once more Warwick had not only become the new race leader but was almost half a minute clear. Furthermore only five other drivers, Tambay, Rosberg, Brundle (yet to make his pit stop), de Angelis and Cheever, were now on the same lap: prior to Lauda's retirement the battery on Arnoux's Ferrari had ceased to function properly and caused his engine to cut out on lap 31, accompanied by a brief fire around the back of the car, Piquet had suffered an engine failure almost immediately following his pit stop at the end of lap 32 and Mansell had just spun off into the catch-fences at the end of the back straight in the midst of trying to stave off the Renault of a fast-recovering Tambay. Lower down the order, too, the field had thinned right out as, since Laffite's departure back on the 16th lap, Cecotto had suffered a similar loss of turbo boost pressure to that of his team-mate earlier in the race, Alliot had had the battery fall off his RAM, Hesnault's Ligier had

blown up its Renault engine, Ghinzani had gone out with a broken gearbox in the sole Osella and Fabi had retired the second Brabham-BMW with a seized turbo-charger unit only seconds before his team-leader's demise. By lap 43 Patrese (broken gearbox) and de Cesaris (broken gear linkage – again!) had also dropped out of the fray, reducing the field to just ten cars with nearly a third of the race distance still to go.

As the 50-lap mark approached Warwick looked to be assured of winning his first Grand Prix for the gap between himself and Prost was still around half a minute, even though the Frenchman was chasing hard and had already set what was to be the fastest lap of the race. However, just when he thought that he was more or less home and dry Warwick noticed that the Renault's left front suspension was beginning to sway slightly, particularly under braking and acceleration. Normally, of course, this would have brought him into the pits but with just over ten laps remaining and that first Grand Prix victory there for the taking Warwick made the understandable decision of staying out in the hope that the car would hold together. Sadly, it was to be a forlorn hope. As he

braked for the hairpin leading on to the back straight on lap 51 the upper wishbone in the Renault's left front suspension suddenly snapped, almost certainly the long-term effect of the wheel-bumping incident with Lauda. That then immediately sent the car gently spinning off the track and although Warwick recovered he could do no more than tour round to the pits to retire, allowing Prost to take over an unexpected lead. Now almost a full minute behind the McLaren, Tambay similarly moved up into second place, but his Renault was destined not to finish the race either. Already a problem with the fuel metering unit was taking the edge off his engine and allowing a hard-charging Rosberg to gobble him up. Then, just over two laps after being passed by the Finn on lap 57, and less than two laps from home, the Renault engine cut out completely due to a lack of fuel. Eight cars left! And that's how it finished, with Prost romping home to a comfortable, if somewhat fortuitous victory, followed by Rosberg (he was more than happy to finish second after struggling with understeer throughout the race) and de Angelis. A lap down, Cheever brought his Alfa Romeo home in fourth place, complaining bitterly about the fuel limitations turning the race into an economy run (he was by no means alone in this respect), while Brundle, tight up behind the American, was a superb fifth on his Grand Prix debut ahead of Tambay, who was classified in sixth place, Boutsen, Surer and, finally, Palmer.

Incredibly, for the third year running the race ended on an acrimonious note. On this occasion it arose as a result of Jack Oliver lodging a protest against Brundle's fifth place on the grounds that his Tyrrell had taken on fuel as well as water and fresh tyres during its pit stop. However, after the car had been checked to see if there was any means in which fuel and water could be added simultaneously through the same intake the protest was rejected, so Brundle held on to his well-deserved fifth place – only to fall victim to the Tyrrell affair later in the year!

Derek Warwick, whose first drive for Renault was ended prematurely by a front suspension failure. *(L.A.T. Photographic)*

<table>
<tr><td colspan="3">Results</td></tr>
<tr><td>1</td><td>A. Prost
(McLaren-TAG)</td><td>1 hr 42 min
34.492 sec
(179.511 kph/
111.543 mph)</td></tr>
<tr><td>2</td><td>K. Rosberg
(Williams-Honda)</td><td>1 hr 43 min
15.006 sec</td></tr>
<tr><td>3</td><td>E. de Angelis
(Lotus-Renault)</td><td>1 hr 43 min
33.620 sec</td></tr>
<tr><td>4</td><td>E. Cheever
(Alfa Romeo)</td><td>1 lap behind</td></tr>
<tr><td>*</td><td>M. Brundle
(Tyrrell-Ford)</td><td>1 lap behind</td></tr>
<tr><td>**5</td><td>P. Tambay
(Renault)</td><td>2 laps behind</td></tr>
<tr><td>6</td><td>T. Boutsen
(Arrows-Ford)</td><td>2 laps behind</td></tr>
<tr><td>7</td><td>M. Surer
(Arrows-Ford)</td><td>2 laps behind</td></tr>
<tr><td>8</td><td>J. Palmer
(RAM-Hart)</td><td>3 laps behind</td></tr>
</table>

* Excluded

** Not running at finish.

Fastest lap: A. Prost (McLaren-TAG) on lap 42 in 1 min 36.499 sec (187.686 kph/116.623 mph)

Retirements

A. Senna (Toleman-Hart) turbo-charger on lap 9, S. Bellof (Tyrrell-Ford) throttle cable on lap 12, M. Baldi (Spirit-Hart) distributor on lap 13, M. Alboreto (Ferrari) front brake caliper on caliper on lap 15, J. Laffite (Williams-Honda) electrics on lap 16, J. Cecotto (Toleman-Hart) turbo-charger on lap 19, P. Alliot (RAM-Hart) battery on lap 25, F. Hesnault (Ligier-Renault) engine on lap 26, P. Ghinzani (Osella-Alfa Romeo) gearbox on lap 29, R. Arnoux (Ferrari) battery on lap 31, T. Fabi (Brabham-BMW) turbo-charger on lap 33, N. Piquet (Brabham-BMW) engine on lap 33, N. Mansell (Lotus-Renault) accident on lap 36, N. Lauda (McLaren-TAG) electrics on lap 39, R. Patrese (Alfa Romeo) gearbox on lap 42, A. de Cesaris (Ligier-Renault) gearbox on lap 43, D. Warwick (Renault) front suspension on lap 52.

1984

XXXth South African Grand Prix

Kyalami : April 7
Weather: Hot
Distance: 75 laps of 4.104 km circuit =
307.78 km (191.25 miles)

Back in the winter the prospects of the South African Grand Prix going ahead had not looked at all promising. FISA had been demanding improvements to the circuit, in particular the widening of the pit lane and the realignment of the dauntingly fast Crowthorne Corner, and a change in local tax law had forced the race sponsors, the Southern Sun Hotel Group, to pull out. However, following representations from the organizers to the effect that there was insufficient time to build a new pits complex, and taking into account that refuelling stops were no longer applicable, FISA had subsequently compromised and put aside the requirement until the 1985 race. Similarly, it had accepted that Crowthorne Corner could remain unchanged provided that the run-off area was extended and the barriers also moved back at one or two of the other more vulnerable parts of the circuit. Of course, there still remained the question of sponsorship but this, too, was finally overcome by a deal being struck with the South African importers for National Panasonic, and so at the end of the day the race was on.

As usual in South Africa, the race itself was taking place on a Saturday, which meant that practice started on Thursday – and only 11 days after the Brazilian Grand Prix! The result, with the cars and equipment having been air-freighted direct from Rio de Janeiro, was a line-up that was virtually identical to that of the season opener. In fact, the only differences, apart from the odd modification here and there, were that ATS were proposing to use their new D7 rather than the older D6 model, and McLaren had built up a third MP4/2, which had been flown out from base to serve as a communal spare for Lauda and Prost. Among the few modifications to have been carried out, meanwhile, were the Lotus 95Ts being equipped with larger water radiators, Arnoux's Ferrari 126C4 now being fitted with a similar Marelli/Weber fuel-injection system to that of Alboreto's sister car, the Spirit 101B reappearing with a new central pillar rear aerofoil and the Williams FW09s being tried with revised differential units. This last move had been made in a further attempt to eliminate the understeer characteristics of the green and white cars. In Rio their front wings had been set at a steeper angle for the actual race and this had certainly eased the problem a bit but it was hoped that the change of differential, designed by Patrick Head, to allow the rear of the cars to slide around more freely, would cure it completely. However, whilst Laffite seemed reasonably satisfied with the revised set-up Rosberg, who

freely admitted that he was unable to cope with understeer so well as his team-mate, preferring, instead, to have a touch too much oversteer, was still not too impressed. Nevertheless, the former World Champion certainly didn't let it show in his driving. On the contrary, following a frustrating morning due to his proposed race chassis becoming stranded out on the circuit with a broken fuel pump drive-belt, he started to fly in the afternoon's first hour of qualifying and went on to record an unbeaten 1 min 05.127 sec. Laffite, on the other hand, was a full 2 seconds slower, but this was understandable to a point after a seemingly incurable engine misfire had left him with little alternative other than to use the team's spare car for his qualifying runs. Even the Frenchman, though, ended the day higher up the time-sheets than either of the two Ferrari drivers. For no obvious reason the 126C4s were suddenly lacking grip and any attempt to overcome the problem by running more wing was having a noticeably adverse effect on straightline speed. The Euroracing Alfa Romeo 184Ts of Patrese and Cheever, already handicapped by using what were now small turbo-charger units relative to those of other cars, were similarly afflicted, and for different reasons there were plenty of long faces in the McLaren pit. Here the main problem was that of trying to encourage the TAG-Porsche engines to run cleanly for between 7,000 and 8,000 rpm there was a persistent misfire, added to which they were refusing to pick up properly out of slow corners. The only logical explanation seemed to be the onboard computers failing to take into account the differences in altitude between Kyalami and Rio but, whatever, it led to Lauda and Prost being able to muster only seventh and ninth fastest times of 1 min 06.238 sec and 1 min 06.576 sec respectively, to wind up on either side of the Lotus 95T of de Angelis (1 min 06.305 sec). In complete contrast, the Brabham team seemed to be in much better shape than in Rio, where the rather poor practice performance of Piquet had been put down to lack of testing at the Brazilian circuit. Not only were the BT53s proving to be the fastest cars through the speed trap, at around the 190 mph-mark, but the World Champion's lap times were only a shade slower than those of the impressive Rosberg, his best coming out at 1 min 05.280 sec. Despite having a turbo-charger let go early in the afternoon, Fabi (T.) put himself well up in the reckoning, too: after being allowed out in the spare Brabham, the Italian went on to set fifth fastest time of 1 min 05.923 sec, narrowly beating Warwick

(1 min 06.056 sec) and finishing up immediately behind Tambay (1 min 05.588 sec) and Mansell (1 min 05.792 sec).

Conditions on Friday were a little hotter than those of the previous day and at the end of the morning untimed session the majority of the drivers were convinced that the track was marginally slower. However, it was certainly not reflected in the lap times once it came to the final hour of qualifying for only five drivers (Fabi, Warwick, Cheever, Winkelhock and Brundle) ultimately failed to register any improvement. Furthermore, Piquet, who had suffered an oil pump failure during the morning, but had been intending to use the spare Brabham BT53 for qualifying in any case as this was fitted with a larger KKK turbo-charger unit than his race car, put in a quite astounding performance of

Starting Grid	
N. Piquet Brabham-BMW (1 min 04.871 sec)	K. Rosberg Williams-Honda (1 min 05.058 sec)
N. Mansell Lotus-Renault (1 min 05.125 sec)	P. Tambay Renault (1 min 05.339 sec)
A. Prost McLaren-TAG (1 min 05.354 sec)	T. Fabi Brabham-BMW (1 min 05.923 sec)
E. de Angelis Lotus-Renault (1 min 05.953 sec)	N. Lauda McLaren-TAG (1 min 06.043 sec)
D. Warwick Renault (1 min 06.056 sec)	M. Alboreto Ferrari (1 min 06.323 sec)
J. Laffite Williams-Honda (1 min 06.762 sec)	M. Winkelhock ATS-BMW (1 min 06.974 sec)
A. Senna Toleman-Hart (1 min 06.981 sec)	A. de Cesaris Ligier-Renault (1 min 07.245 sec)
R. Arnoux Ferrari (1 min 07.345 sec)	E. Cheever Alfa Romeo (1 min 07.704 sec)
F. Hesnault Ligier-Renault (1 min 07.787 sec)	R. Patrese Alfa Romeo (1 min 08.042 sec)
J. Cecotto Toleman-Hart (1 min 08.298 sec)	M. Baldi Spirit-Hart (1 min 09.923 sec)
J. Palmer RAM-Hart (1 min 10.383 sec)	P. Alliot RAM-Hart (1 min 10.619 sec)
M. Surer Arrows-Ford (1 min 11.808 sec)	S. Bellof Tyrrell-Ford (1 min 12.022 sec)
M. Brundle Tyrrell-Ford (1 min 12.233 sec)	T. Boutsen Arrows-Ford (1 min 12.274 sec)

Non-starter:
P. Ghinzani (Osella-Alfa Romeo) 1 min 09.609 sec.

on-the-limit driving, and went on to better Tambay's pole-winning time for the 1983 race – set less than 6 months earlier – by almost 2 seconds, at 1 min 04.871 sec. In the meantime, Thursday's pace-setter was spending most of the session on race rubber in order to make up lost time caused by his Williams having become stranded out on the circuit with a broken fuel pump drive-belt for the second morning on the trot. But when the news of Piquet's new lap time filtered through Rosberg immediately changed tactics, switched to his single set of qualifiers and held everyone spellbound as he made a determined bid to retrieve the pole. He almost succeeded, despite a busy moment overtaking a slower car through the Jukskei Sweep, but after arriving at Clubhouse Bend a fraction too quickly and running wide the Finn failed in his ambition by just under two-tenths of a second. Nevertheless, his time of 1 min 05.058 sec did at least keep him on the front row of the grid as, almost unnoticed in the wonderfully tense atmosphere Mansell, enjoying the benefit of the new and larger Garrett turbo-charger units throughout practice, also put in a super-quick lap of 1 min 05.125 sec, which would otherwise have been second fastest time overall. Instead, the Englishman had to settle for third spot on the grid immediately ahead of a pretty consistent Tambay (1 min 05.339 sec), using the spare Renault for his qualifying runs, and also Prost, who improved by well over a second on the first day, to 1 min 05.354 sec, after pinning his hopes on the new, so-called spare McLaren MP4/2. This, fitted with smaller turbo-charger units, was giving better throttle response as Prost had already discovered during Thursday's untimed session until the car had been sidelined with broken gear linkage and slight fire damage due to a turbo-charger heat-shield catching alight. Lauda, on the other hand, was in much the same trouble as before with his car and was left down in eighth place on the grid. Here he was sandwiched between de Angelis, another to have made little progress in spite of having had the KKK turbo-charger units on his Lotus 95T replaced by the larger Garretts overnight, and Warwick, whose afternoon had been ruined by a whole series of problems that included an engine that refused to rev properly as well as fading turbo boost pressure. Over at Ferrari, meanwhile, the situation was as fraught as ever. Even Alboreto, who was once again the quicker of the two drivers, had qualified in only tenth spot on the grid, while a very disgruntled Arnoux was a further five places away, the Frenchman's humour not having been helped by a moment's inattention earlier in the day when he had inadvertently triggered off the onboard fire extinguisher in his car and coasted to rest with dead electrics. There was no respite for the Eurorac-

ing team either. Both Alfa Romeo 184Ts had been desperately short of straightline speed again, in addition to which Patrese's efforts had been further hampered by a persistent engine misfire due to a leaking turbo-charger. The end result was that Cheever was one place lower down the grid than Arnoux, while his Italian team-mate was another two places adrift behind Hesnault in the slower of the two Renault-powered Ligier JS23s. After that there was just Cecotto, confined to the spare Toleman following a heavy shunt at the exit from Barbeque Bend on Thursday morning, Ghinzani's Osella, Baldi's Spirit, which had shown a healthy appetite for distributor rotor arms besides having stopped with broken throttle linkage at one point, the two RAM-Hart cars of Palmer and Alliot and the four normally-aspirated runners who, as anticipated given the circuit's altitude, were hopelessly outclassed. Even they, though, had all ended the first day in better shape than the RAM duo. Palmer's car had been sidelined by a broken crankshaft in the morning and then, after plans had been made for the Englishman to share his team-mate's car for the first qualifying session due to the lack of a spare chassis, Alliot had become stranded out on the circuit on his very first lap with no fuel pressure. Consequently, neither driver had been able to set a lap time, and to make matters worse the Frenchman had been fined $2000 for an earlier incident in which he had also stopped out on the circuit with an engine problem and prevented some marshals from pushing his car out of what was considered to be a dangerous position until practice had been halted. Up to that point he had kept his foot on the brake pedal!

The hot weather continued into Saturday, but a very disappointing aspect for the organizers was the size of the crowd, only 30,000 or so spectators eventually making their way to the circuit. For the teams the first real business of the day, as always, was the customary half-hour warm-up, but after little more than 15 minutes this was brought to an abrupt halt due to Ghinzani inexplicably losing control of his Osella through the ultra-fast Jukskei Sweep, careering off into the catch-fences and on into the earth bank beyond. However, this was no ordinary accident. Far from it. The impact with the bank was so great that the whole rear assembly of the Osella was torn right off from the rear bulkhead of the carbon-fibre monocoque, the fuel lines were split and a fire rapidly took hold. The rest of the car, meanwhile, somersaulted and came to rest a little further along the side of the track. Fortunately, it landed the right way up or else the consequences would have been unthinkable, for in no time at all the trail of fuel leading to the main fuel cell was catching alight. But, as it was, some quick-thinking marshals released Ghinzani from his cockpit with commend-

able promptitude and along with some of the drivers, who pulled up at the scene to assist in the rescue operations, carried him well away from what was soon a blazing inferno. He was then rushed off to hospital from where word was later received that there were no broken bones and that, instead, his injuries were confined to burns around his left hand – he had removed his glove to unfasten his safety harness – his neck and his forehead. It had been a miraculous escape! In the meantime, the warm-up session was eventually allowed to run its normal course, once the remains of the Osella had been hauled back to the pits and the catch-fences repaired, and finally ended with a somewhat relieved Lauda recording second fastest time to split the two Brabham-BMWs of Piquet and Fabi. Relieved, because until the accident his McLaren, fitted with similar (smaller) turbo-charger units to those of the team's spare car overnight, had been running with a chronic misfire, but the delay had enabled his mechanics to cure the problem by changing various electrical components.

With Ghinzani obviously a non-starter, all of the drivers who had qualified behind him were moved up a place on the grid, and Boutsen, the odd man out in failing to qualify, was invited to join in at the back. Consequently, a full complement of 26 cars subsequently lined up on the dummy grid for the 76-lap race. But then, as the final countdown began the engine in Prost's McLaren refused to start owing to what was believed to be a seized mechanical fuel pump drive. Whatever, it led to the MP4/2 being pushed off the grid and to Prost running into the pits, leaping into the spare McLaren as soon as a few hurried cockpit adjustments had been made for him (the car had originally been set up for Lauda) and chasing after the others who, by that stage, were well on their way to completing the parade lap. This, however, was entirely against the rules, even though an official had waved Prost out on to the track. So, as he came into view of the pits just over a minute later, the Frenchman was signalled back into the pit lane and, in the meantime, Derek Ongaro aborted the start: quite apart from Prost's misdemeanour, Patrese now had his hands in the air to signify that he had stalled his engine! As a result, once some order of semblance had been established, the starting procedure began all over again with another 5-minute countdown, and after that the 30th South African Grand Prix, now reduced to 75 laps to allow for the extra parade lap, finally got under way. Even then it was still a rather untidy start due to Piquet almost stalling his engine, and Mansell, who drove out around the Brabham, finding his Renault engine reluctant to pick up properly after changing up into second gear. Fortunately, the width of the track proved more than adequate to cope with what could have been a tricky   231 situation and all 26 starters were soon safely on their way towards Crowthorne Corner with Piquet recovering exceptionally well to slot into second place as they arrived at the braking area. Rosberg, meanwhile, had charged off into an undisputed lead only to realize all too soon that it was unlikely to last for long: some adjustments made to his car after the warm-up session were already turning out to be a step in the wrong direction – the understeer was worse and there was a distinct lack of grip. Sure enough, as the leaders crossed the line to complete the opening lap Piquet was already pulling out from behind the Williams and then breezed past almost as if it wasn't there. Next time round Fabi did exactly the same thing at precisely the same spot, and by the end of lap 4 Rosberg had not only lost yet another place to Lauda but was now coming under threat from the two Renaults of Warwick and Tambay. Only a little further back, de Angelis was running strongly in seventh place but his team-mate, having lost out badly because of his engine's hesitation at the start, was still trying to recover from 12th spot behind Alboreto, Laffite, Winkelhock and Patrese. Prost, of course, was in an even worse position due to having started from the pit lane. However, he had already scythed past the tail-end of the field and had just come through to 16th place at the expense of Cheever, who was about to become the first retirement with a holed water radiator caused by a balance weight flying off one of the Alfa's front wheels.

By lap 9 Piquet was fast disappearing into the middle distance, but Lauda had caught Fabi and now took a run at him on the long drag down to Crowthorne Corner. Given the speed of the Brabham this was by no means easy, but Lauda succeeded in sneaking ahead and held on to his new position by gently weaving in the middle of the track until arriving at the braking area for the right-hander. Thereafter he almost immediately began to draw away, and at the end of the following lap was left with even more breathing space when Fabi suddenly veered off into the pits for fresh tyres – already! Both Brabhams, in fact, had come to the grid on a rather marginal choice of Michelins which, as Piquet was also beginning to find out to his cost, were obviously failing to cope with the tremendously fast pace combined with the heavy fuel loads at this early stage of the race. Lauda, on the other hand, was in no such trouble, due as much as anything to his McLaren enjoying a better handling balance, with the result that within just nine more laps he had been able to wipe out the deficit to the leader and was making serious moves to find a way past. It was now only a question of time and Piquet, being only too aware of that as his tyres grew worse, ultimately responded by obligingly raising a hand as he came round to complete lap 21 to signal to Lauda that he,

too, was going into the pits. However, unlike his team-mate, who had dropped right away to a poor mid-field position and since retired with a broken turbo-charger in any case, Piquet had opened up such an advantage earlier in the race that he was subsequently able to rejoin in amongst a whole group of cars stacked up behind Rosberg's Williams. These included the Renault of an increasingly frustrated Warwick, which was all over the green and white car through the corners but lacked the necessary punch to get by on the straight. In complete contrast, this was to be no problem at all for Piquet. With the superior horse-power of his BMW engine, he first flew past de Angelis, Tambay and Warwick on successive laps and then treated Rosberg with the same disregard as that soon after the start to move up into second place. At that point it still seemed possible that Lauda might have a fight on his hands later in the race only for the Brabham's turbo boost pressure to start dropping away and force Piquet to join his team-mate in retirement at the pits after just four more laps. Although it was of no relevance so far as the leading positions were concerned three other drivers had also been forced to drop out of the contest by now. These were Palmer, who had already been running short of gears when his engine had cut out due to some obscure electrical fault on lap 23, team-mate Alliot, who had retired the other RAM two laps later with the Hart engine having pumped out most of its water, and Cecotto, who had just had a busy moment bringing his Toleman to rest on the approach to Crowthorne Corner after a rear tyre had delaminated and damaged the rear suspension. Senna, too, had run into a problem earlier in the race. The upper bodywork of his car's nose cone had come adrift, but the new Toleman recruit had managed to adjust his driving to cope with the change of handling characteristics and was still plugging on gamely in 14th place.

With Piquet out, Lauda was left leading the race by a massive margin of well over half a minute from Rosberg, who now had none other than Prost biting at his heels. Almost unnoticed, due to so much attention having stayed firmly fixed on the leaders, the French McLaren driver had continued carving his way up through the field as if there was no tomorrow. However, at the end of lap 31 it was time for Prost to make his scheduled tyre stop, along with Tambay, and in the ensuing delay Warwick, de Angelis, Alboreto, Laffite, Arnoux and Mansell were all able to move on ahead of him once more. Consequently, when Prost rejoined the race, directly in front of Tambay, he was down in ninth place. Even so, he soon settled back into his rhythm. He repassed Mansell (hoping to go the distance on one set of tyres) on lap 37, automatically moved up three more places when Rosberg, Warwick and de

Angelis made their tyre stops in quick succession, gained another when Arnoux was forced to retire on lap 41, owing to a malfunction with his Ferrari's electronic fuel-injection system, and then barged past Alboreto and Laffite (two other drivers planning to go through non-stop) on successive laps to move up into a superb second place on lap 43. That, of course, meant it was now a McLaren 1–2 for although Lauda had also stopped for tyres, at the end of lap 34, the Austrian had been able to rejoin the race still holding a comfortable lead. Rosberg, on the other hand, was now in only eighth place, behind the two Renaults, owing to a rather poor pit stop in which he had almost stalled his engine as he was about to set off once more. De Angelis, too, had disappeared from the leader-board. Within just one lap of his tyre stop, the Italian had been forced to return to the pits with deranged throttle linkage and with flames licking around the undertray of his Lotus 95T. Furthermore, the delay whilst repairs were being carried out cost him well over three laps and when de Angelis finally took off again he was left bringing up the rear along with Winkelhock, who had begun a series of pit stops with a misfiring engine at around the time of Piquet's departure. Later the German would retire when the BMW engine in his new ATS D7 dropped a valve but, in the meantime, there were a number of other changes. On lap 46 Tambay, already plagued by an intermittent engine misfire ever since the start, had to stop for another set of Michelins and dropped to eighth place between Rosberg and Senna (lapped); minutes later Brundle tore off the nose cone of his Tyrrell against Hesnault's Ligier while trying to squeeze through on the inside of the Frenchman at Leeukop Bend and had to bring forward his pit stop for tyres and weight-gaining water; this was followed almost immediately by Mansell touring into the pits to retire his Lotus 95T with a lack of turbo boost pressure caused by a cracked turbo inlet tract and also by Rosberg rolling to a halt out on the circuit with a broken drive-shaft joint. A superb scrap that had developed between Alboreto and Warwick for fourth place didn't last much longer either, as on lap 56 the Englishman was seen heading for the pits with a punctured right rear tyre and subsequently slipped to sixth place behind team-mate Tambay.

On lap 61, with Lauda and Prost out on their own and even further apart, the rout continued when Laffite's good drive in third place was ended abruptly at The Esses by his Williams gently skating off the track minus its right rear wheel. The wheel retaining nut had come undone! At almost precisely the same moment Bellof similarly stirred up the dust down at Crowthorne Corner when he suffered a brake failure. Fortunately, despite travelling at high speed, the young German

Niki Lauda well on the way to scoring a most resounding victory, the 20th of his career. *(L.A.T. Photographic)*

The victorious McLaren duo stand aside as Derek Warwick gets down to the business of spraying the champagne after the race. *(L.A.T. Photographic)*

managed to bring his Tyrrell to rest without hitting anything by making full use of the extended run-off area. Even after that, though, there was still more drama to come. First Tambay, who caught and repassed Alboreto on lap 62 prior to setting what was to be the fastest lap of the race, suddenly had

his Renault splutter to a halt through lack of fuel for the second time in a fortnight. That was on lap 67. Then, only four laps later and having been repassed by Warwick again, even though the Englishman no longer had the use of his clutch, Alboreto suffered a similar problem to that of Arnoux earlier in

the race and he, too, coasted to rest. All the while Lauda was romping home to a most resounding victory and after reeling off the last few remaining laps crossed the line for the final time having lapped everyone bar his own team-mate who, nonetheless, was more than a minute in arrears at the finish. Behind Warwick, taking a well-deserved third place for perseverance alone, the high rate of attrition helped Patrese to bring the first Goodyear-shod car home in fourth place and, for similar reasons, de Cesaris and an exhausted Senna unexpectedly found themselves in the points by finishing fifth and sixth ahead of the other six survivors.

Lauda's 20th Grand Prix victory had been a long time coming – he had last won at Brands Hatch in 1982 – but he had certainly achieved it in style. Even being presented with the Rand Grand Prix trophy after the race (somewhat to their embarrassment the organizers couldn't find the correct one in time for the presentation!) failed to hide his joy. After all, the 9 points were far more important.

Results			
1	N. Lauda (McLaren-TAG)	1 hr 29 min 23.430 sec (206.587 kph/ 128.367 mph)	
2	A. Prost (McLaren-TAG)	1 hr 30 min 29.380 sec	
3	D. Warwick (Renault)	1 lap behind	
4	R. Patrese (Alfa Romeo)	2 laps behind	
5	A. de Cesaris (Ligier-Renault)	2 laps behind	
6	A. Senna (Toleman-Hart)	3 laps behind	
7	E. de Angelis (Lotus-Renault)	4 laps behind	
8	M. Baldi (Spirit-Hart)	4 laps behind	
9	M. Surer (Arrows-Ford)	4 laps behind	
10	F. Hesnault (Ligier-Renault)	4 laps behind	
*	M. Brundle (Tyrrell-Ford)	4 laps behind	
**11	M. Alboreto (Ferrari)	5 laps behind	
12	T. Boutsen (Arrows-Ford)	5 laps behind	

* Excluded

** Not running at finish.

Fastest lap: P. Tambay (Renault) on lap 65 in 1 min 08.877 sec (214.492 kph/133.279 mph)

Retirements

E. Cheever (Alfa Romeo) radiator on lap 5, T. Fabi (Brabham-BMW) turbo-charger on lap 19, J. Palmer (RAM-Hart) electrics on lap 23, P. Alliot (RAM-Hart) engine on lap 25, J. Cecotto (Toleman-Hart) rear suspension on łap 27, N. Piquet (Brabham-BMW) turbo-charger on lap 30, R. Arnoux (Ferrari) fuel-injection on lap 41, N. Mansell (Lotus-Renault) turbo-charger on lap 52, K. Rosberg (Williams-Honda) drive-shaft on lap 52, M. Winkelhock (ATS-BMW) engine on lap 54, S. Bellof (Tyrrell-Ford) brakes on lap 60, J. Laffite (Williams-Honda) lost wheel on lap 61, P. Tambay (Renault) fuel metering unit on lap 67.

N.B. T. Boutsen was actually 4 laps behind and should have been classfied 9th but the error was not officially corrected.

1984

XLII Grote Prijs van Belgie

Zolder: April 29
Weather: Sunny and breezy
Distance: 70 laps of 4.262 km circuit =
298.34 km (185.38 miles)

Many people had been hoping that this year's Belgian Grand Prix would take place on the beautiful and historic Circuit Nationale de Spa-Francorchamps, as in 1983, but it was not to be. Instead, national politics demanded that the race should take place on Flemish territory once more, which meant a return to the rather dreary confines of Zolder. It was here, of course, that two years earlier the much-lamented Gilles Villeneuve had lost his life and, as if anyone needed reminding of the fact, the organizers had erected a tall monument to his memory,

complete with one of the French-Canadian's helmets and a symbolic prancing horse. In itself the idea was plausible, but the monument was unnecessarily large and was sited in which had to be the most inappropriate place imaginable – in the pit lane and adjacent to the Ferrari pit!

In spite of this poignant reminder of events past, and an almost universal dislike of the venue, at least the weather was doing its best to brighten things up when the opening session of practice started on Friday morning. The skies were clear and the circuit was bathed in warm sunshine with just enough of a breeze to make conditions ideal. Entry-wise, there was a surprising number of new cars on hand, especially when bearing in mind the superb array of new machinery already seen in Brazil and South Africa. In all there were actually nine of them, one apiece from Ferrari (Alboreto), Renault (Tambay), Euroracing Alfa Romeo (Cheever), Ligier (de Cesaris), RAM (Palmer) and Spirit (Baldi), which had all been built to the same basic design as each of the teams' existing 1984 cars, another from Osella, the FA1F, to replace the chassis written off by Ghinzani in South Africa and two from Arrows, which were totally new, these being a pair of Dave Wass-designed, BMW-powered A7s. Ideally Jack Oliver and Alan Rees would liked to have seen both Marc Surer and Thierry Boutsen in their team's first turbo-charged cars, but as the supply of BMW engines was severely limited at this early stage of the new Anglo-German partnership it had been decided to continue campaigning a Ford-Cosworth-powered A6 alongside the new BMW-powered A7 for the time being. The idea then was that the two drivers should swap cars on a race-to-race basis with Boutsen chosen to set the ball rolling so far as the new turbo-charged project was concerned owing to this being his home Grand Prix. Compared to the line-up for the South African Grand Prix there were also a number of other changes on the mechanical front. Among them were the Ferrari 126C4s reappearing with Lucas mechanical fuel-injection systems following the problems experienced with the newer Marelli/Weber electronic systems in the previous race (the new chassis also had a modified exhaust system to the turbines as a means of trying to improve engine response still further); the Ligier JS23s running with revised front and rear suspension in an attempt to improve their handling; the ATS D7 having revised rear bodywork to improve the flow of air to the rear aerofoil as well as a spacer inserted between its engine and gearbox to

give a fractionally longer wheelbase along with subtle suspension alterations designed to eliminate an oversteer problem; the two McLaren MP4/2s of Lauda and Prost each being equipped with a newly-designed rear aerofoil; and the Williams FW09s being fitted with yet another type of differential unit, in addition to which the spare Williams had new, home-made, water-to-air inter-coolers and a new pit-to-car radio system similar to that already being employed by Renault. Over at Spirit, meanwhile, both the original 101B and the new car were painted white instead of in the team's previous red colour scheme in anticipation of a new sponsorship deal that had failed to materialize and, similarly, Bellof's Tyrrell had changed to a predominantly black colour scheme following a somewhat more successful venture by the German in obtaining the backing of the Maredo chain of steak-houses.

Throughout the morning the main priority was that of setting up cars for the first hour of qualifying and a particularly noticeable aspect was the progress that had obviously been made by the brake specialist firms. In the past the stop-go nature of this tight and very demanding little circuit had caused all sorts of problems with braking systems but, on this occasion at least, there was no serious trouble at all in this respect. Given the number of laps that some drivers were covering, there were also comparatively few other major problems, although Palmer had trouble with the gearbox in the new RAM 02 before being sidelined by a broken turbo, Baldi had the engine let go in the older of the two Spirit 101Bs and Lauda lost a considerable amount of time owing to having to abandon his McLaren out on the circuit after a fuel leak led to its rear bodywork briefly catching fire. These incidents, in turn, resulted in Baldi having to switch to the new Spirit 101B for qualifying and Lauda to the spare McLaren. Even then the Austrian still had to wait around until Prost used up his quota of tyres so that he could borrow his team-mate's new rear aerofoil, there being none other of the same type available. In the meantime, a leaking constant velocity joint seal followed by a similar problem with the gearbox input shaft bearing also forced de Angelis into the spare Lotus 95T, and before qualifying had been in progress very long a whole spate of engine problems suddenly started cropping up. Already the two Williams drivers had been bothered by a plethora of minor problems in the morning but now, before either of them really had much of an opportunity to set about recording some respectable lap times, the situation rapidly deteriorated with both of their cars suffering piston failures. Then, to cap it all, the spare Williams that Rosberg subsequently took over underwent a similar fate. In the Brabham camp, too, it was much the same story with Piquet and Fabi both being on the receiving end of blown-up BMW engines, while over at Toleman Senna became redundant when the Hart engine in his TG183B quietly expired because of an electrical failure. Other drivers were now having their share of trouble as well. Arnoux and Alboreto were finding it virtually impossible to encourage the Goodyear qualifying tyres on their Ferraris to warm up evenly, Tambay was having his progress in the new Renault hampered by a stiff gear-change, de Cesaris stopped early with a blown turbo in his new Ligier and then Hesnault put his Ligier out of commission by demolishing its two right-hand corners against the barriers after running out of road at the fast right-hander behind the paddock. Even Warwick, who was vying with Prost for the provisional pole, was not exactly having things all his own way due to some new, experimental, ventilated carbon-fibre brake discs and Renault-made calipers fitted to his RE50 causing the car to weave rather alarmingly under braking. Nevertheless, after swapping from a set of race tyres to a single set of qualifiers and then back again, Warwick overcame the problem admirably in a last-minute do-or-die effort that produced a lap in 1 min 16.311 sec to settle the issue, Prost having achieved a personal best of 1 min 16.587 sec. Earlier, prior to the engine failing in the spare Brabham that he was using (his 'qualifying special'), Piquet had gone around in what was to be third fastest time of 1 min 16.604 sec and both Mansell (having to use KKK turbo-charger units once again due to a lack of Garretts) and de Angelis were well up the order with fourth and 1 min 17.705 sec respectively. Then came Arnoux, who had at least managed to came Arnoux, who had at least managed to achieve one reasonable lap in 1 min 18.017 sec to narrowly pip Winkelhock and Patrese. Alboreto, on the other hand, had come out only tenth fastest between de Cesaris and Cheever, while Rosberg was an even more lowly 12th immediately ahead of two other extremely unhappy drivers, Tambay and Lauda.

By Saturday morning everything seemed to be back under control. Engines had been replaced where necessary, Hesnault's Ligier had been repaired, the Renault team had discarded the carbon-fibre brakes on Warwick's RE50 and Williams had reprogrammed the fuel-injection systems of their FW09s after discovering that the cause of the succession of piston failures had almost certainly been too lean a mixture to take into account the use of lighter density, higher octane, Mobil petrol. However, once practice resumed there were soon more problems arising with one of the main casualties being Lauda – again! First he spent well over half an hour in the pits before his mechanics could trace an electrical fault on his McLaren to the ignition coil. That fixed, he took to the track once more only for a

gearbox pinion to seize and then, after switching to the spare McLaren, it was not long before he was back in the pits a third time, the problem now being a sticking fuel pressure relief valve. Furthermore, it took such a time to replace the gearbox in his race chassis that Lauda only managed to take part in the last 15 minutes or so of the all-important final qualifying session. Consequently, he did well even to improve to 1 min 18.071 sec, albeit still only fast enough for an extremely disappointing 14th place on the grid at the end of the day. In the meantime, Brabham were still in dire trouble with their BMW engines failing with alarming regularity due to a detonation problem. Indeed, final qualifying was a complete disaster for the team: Fabi's car developed a chronic misfire whilst the Italian was out on his first set of tyres and Piquet, on only his first timed lap of the afternoon in his 'qualifying special', suffered one of the biggest blow-ups seen for a long time, a con-rod punching a fist-sized hole in the side of the BMW block! The outcome of this was that Fabi, unable to progress beyond 1 min 18.848 sec, finished up a very lowly 18th on the grid, while Piquet, deciding that there was no point in going out again in his race car, saw his Friday time gradually being beaten by one driver after another until he was ultimately left down in ninth spot directly in front of Mansell, who lost out badly in the traffic. Prost, troubled by a malfunction with the Bosch Motronic engine management system on his McLaren, which was allowing the engine to persist in momentarily cutting out (and causing him to spin, harmlessly, on no less than three occasions!), was another of the few drivers not to improve on his Friday time. As a result he, too, found himself sliding down the order – to an eventual eighth place on the grid – while Warwick, consigned to the spare Renault as his regular car had already been set aside for the race, had his chances of defending the overnight pole spoiled by an engine that was slightly less responsive than that of the first day, by intermittent clutch slip and, finally, by a broken exhaust. Instead, despite making a worthwhile improvement to 1 min 15.611 sec, the Englishman now had to make do with fourth place on the grid immediately ahead of de Angelis (1 min 15.979 sec), Winkelhock (1 min 16.130 sec) and Patrese (1 min 16.431 sec) thanks to an exciting tussle that developed for pole position between Rosberg, Arnoux and Alboreto. Here, with the Honda engine in Rosberg's Williams now proving to be reliable and the Goodyear qualifying tyres fitted to the Ferraris suddenly working really well in what were slightly warmer conditions than the previous day, all three were responding in the best possible manner by setting a succession of new fastest laps. Moreover, this went on right through until the dying minutes of

qualifying when Alboreto, having just had more turbo boost pressure wound on, finally clinched the coveted spot by the fairly convincing margin of over half a second with a lap in 1 min 14.846 sec (204.996 kph), Arnoux coming closest to this at 1 min 15.398 sec to make it an all-Ferrari front row. Even so, Rosberg was only a further 0.016 sec away and, rather significantly, was the best part of 3 seconds quicker than team-mate Laffite, who was left languishing in 15th place on the grid after a most disappointing performance. Tambay's was not much better either for he was only three places higher than his compatriot, winding up between Cheever's Alfa Romeo and the Ligier-Renault of de Cesaris, which had suffered another turbo-charger failure. After that, though, the rest of the order was more or less much as anticipated with the possible exception of Senna, who had been troubled by a slight engine misfire on his way to qualifying in 19th spot, and also Hesnault, who was down amongst the three normally-aspirated runners in the field after an early turbo-charger failure had put paid to all hopes of improving on his Friday time. Nevertheless, Boutsen had been making steady progress in the new BMW-powered Arrows A7, especially when taking into account that it was running with only a modest amount of boost pressure to reduce the risk of any major engine disasters, and Ghinzani, with his left hand not yet fully healed from the burns received in Kyalami, had done extremely well to qualify in 20th spot. Considerably less impressive were Baldi's Spirit and the two ill-handling RAM 02s of Palmer and Alliot, which were the slowest cars of all. This, in turn, had resulted in the Frenchman ultimately being the odd man out in failing to qualify for the race after his hopes had effectively been dashed by an engine failure late in the morning untimed session followed by a turbo-charger failure on his first timed lap of the afternoon whilst behind the wheel of Palmer's car.

Following the succession of engine disasters during practice, the BMW personnel were of the opinion that a bad consignment of fuel was the most likely cause of the Brabham team's troubles. So, as a means of trying to rectify the situation, arrangements were made for a fresh supply of fuel to be brought up from Munich overnight and on the following morning everyone in the Brabham pit was keeping their fingers tightly crossed that all would now be well. Certainly, if the 30 minute mid-morning warm-up session was anything to go by, it seemed like the correct answer had been found, for Piquet and Fabi both enjoyed trouble-free runs at long last. In fact, apart from the Hart engine in Cecotto's Toleman cutting out for some rather obscure reason and Winkelhock suffering a turbo-charger failure with his ATS D7 before going out in the spare D6 and setting a time beaten only by Alboreto, there were no other problems of any consequence. Instead, as they all went away to prepare for the 70-lap race, there was, in the main, just the usual vexed question of tyre choice to worry about. This included the Goodyear runners trying to make up their minds whether to use a new type of rear tyre that had arrived from Akron since the previous day and also many of the teams pondering over the possibility of dispensing with a planned pit stop during the race.

By 2.30 p.m. final decisions had been taken, the 26 starters had all formed on the dummy grid after the warm-up lap, some having squeezed in an extra lap by using the pit lane, and now they were away on the parade lap, led by Alboreto's Ferrari. This was the first time that the Italian had been on pole position for a Grand Prix and he was not about to squander it. On the contrary. Once he had brought them all back to their grid positions, and the lights had changed from red to green, Alboreto simply rocketed off the line and arrived at the first left-hander a full car length clear of Warwick, who was leading the pursuit from a slightly hesitant Arnoux. Most of the others, meanwhile, were darting this way and that to avoid Rosberg's Williams, which was barely moving due to a sudden drop of revs from its Honda engine. Fortunately, despite some near-misses as drivers weaved past on either side of the stricken car, there were no untoward incidents with the result that within a matter of seconds they were all setting off after the leaders, Rosberg eventually included. Almost immediately, though, Mansell was in trouble with a slipping clutch and so, to an even greater extent, was Cecotto. Indeed, as the field came round to complete the opening lap the Venezuelan was in the throes of being elbowed back to last place from where he was soon destined to end his race by crawling into the pits to

become the first retirement. Alboreto, on the other hand, was absolutely flying along and had already started the second lap even further ahead of Warwick, who appeared to be having his work cut out to keep Arnoux at bay. Winkelhock, after a very good start, was in fourth place and then it was de Angelis from Patrese, Prost, Cheever, Piquet, Tambay, de Cesaris, Lauda and the rest, including Mansell and Rosberg, who were lying only 16th and 20th respectively.

Although Warwick now began to shake off the close attentions of Arnoux, there seemed to be nothing at all that he could do about coming to terms with Alboreto. Instead the Italian, running a slightly different type of tyre from that of his team-mate, continued to extend his lead by around half a second per lap and looked to have everything well under control, even at this early stage of the race. Winkelhock, meanwhile, was doing an excellent job of holding down fourth place in the ATS D7 but de Angelis, who received a brief respite on the third lap when Patrese's Alfa Romeo stopped with ignition failure, soon had the daunting sight of Prost's McLaren looming in his mirrors. On this occasion, however, it was to be of little consequence. Almost as soon as de Angelis had been forced to give way to the Championship leader on the fifth lap, Prost was coasting to rest out on the circuit with a dead engine caused by a broken distributor component. Furthermore, by the time that he had pulled off the track some oil had also started leaking on to the McLaren's hot exhaust pipes and, in dealing with the minor conflagration that resulted, some rather over-enthusiastic marshals succeeded in covering virtually the entire car with fire extinguisher foam. In the meantime, of course, de Angelis automatically moved back up into fifth place only for the situation to change yet again on lap 8 when Piquet, having earlier made light work of dispensing with Cheever, caught and

passed him. All the while a lot of changes were also taking place further down the order. Rosberg, in particular, was really stirring things up as he endeavoured to recover from the problem at the start. Already he had scythed through the lower half of the field and, by lap 10, was up into tenth place between Lauda and de Cesaris, who had only just swapped places themselves. In complete contrast, Mansell was making no impression at all owing to the trouble with his clutch, and was finding it difficult even to stay ahead of the two well-driven Tyrrells of Bellof and Brundle. Moreover, by lap 14 he had decided that enough was enough and ended the lap by pulling off into the pits to give up the unequal struggle. This was then followed, in quick succession, by Ghinzani having a most encouraging run in the new Osella brought to an abrupt halt when something broke in its transmission; by Hesnault withdrawing his Ligier with soaring water temperatures caused by a leaking radiator; and by Laffite concluding an extremely uninspiring weekend by spinning off into the sand at the second chicane for reasons that were associated with the fact that his Honda engine had been momentarily cutting out ever since the start. Shortly afterwards a disappointing debut for the new Arrows A7 also ended when Boutsen went into the pits – for a second time – with a bad engine misfire, the source of the trouble later being traced to a loose electrical connection to the alternator which, in turn, had allowed the battery to go flat. None of these incidents, though, were affecting the position at the front of the race where Alboreto was now almost exactly 10 seconds clear of Warwick, who was content to consolidate second place for the time being, at least, especially as he was hoping to last the distance on one set of tyres. A further 8 seconds adrift, Arnoux was at long last showing signs of dropping Winkelhock, Piquet was making steady progress in fifth place as he drew away from de Angelis and Cheever, despite being concerned about rising engine temperatures, and Rosberg had just come through to eighth spot by forging past Lauda and Tambay on successive laps.

As the race progressed drivers were becoming increasingly concerned about the state of the track for there was now an accumulation of sticky gravel building up just off the racing line at one corner in particular, suggesting that the surface was disintegrating. However, this was to do nothing to prevent Rosberg from continuing his impressive climb through the field as he demonstrated only too well by catching Cheever on lap 22 and finding a way past him almost immediately. Piquet, too, responded in the same positive manner by relieving Winkelhock of his fourth position on lap 23 and then overtaking Arnoux in a rather audacious manoeuvre on a fast right-hander half way

Michele Alboreto led from the start and became the first Italian to win a Grand Prix for Ferrari since 1966. *(Autosport)*

round lap 25 to move up into third spot. At that point Arnoux then made for the pits for fresh tyres – the same type already being used by his team-mate – but, after an untypically long stop by Ferrari standards of almost 20 seconds, the Frenchman was left in a pretty demoralizing 13th position. Even then it would have been worse except that Tambay, who had rather surprisingly slipped behind Lauda, Fabi and de Cesaris in quick succession soon after being passed by Rosberg, had also stopped for fresh tyres by now and was in an even more lowly 16th place. In the meantime, Rosberg was still on the up and up. Since going past Cheever he had already added de Angelis and Winkelhock to his list and by lap 34 was taking over a quite incredible second place, going by Piquet on lap 32, when the reigning World Champion made a rare mistake at the hairpin and momentarily left the track, before automatically moving on ahead of Warwick when the Englishman totally unexpectedly pitted for fresh tyres. Winkelhock also stopped at the end of the same lap but, whereas Warwick was away again in a still very respectable third place, the German was held up almost half a minute in a chaotic pit stop, which put him well over a lap in arrears. Furthermore, his problems didn't end there, as on lap 40 a broken exhaust pipe snagged an electrical lead on his ATS and brought the car to a silent halt out on the circuit. By this time Cheever, who had finally outwitted de Angelis back on the 24th lap, had dropped out of the contest as well owing to his Alfa Romeo having blown up its engine and so, too, had Lauda, the Austrian having switched off rather hurriedly on lap 36 (less than six laps after his tyre stop) when he felt his engine start to tighten. Most significant of all Alboreto, despite worn rear tyres having contributed to a huge moment at the first left-hander beyond the pits only a minute or so earlier, which had seen his Ferrari momentarily sliding right off the track, had just been in and out of the pits for fresh tyres without losing the lead.

On lap 43 came another flurry of drama

and excitement, both in the pits as Rosberg became the last of the front-runners to stop for tyres (Piquet and de Angelis were both planning to go through non-stop) and out on the circuit at the Bianchibocht. Here, first Fabi inadvertently made contact with one of the rear wheels of Palmer's RAM as he attempted to lap the Englishman and went sliding off into the barriers. Then, only seconds later, de Cesaris went off at almost exactly the same spot when something broke in the rear suspension of his Ligier. Rosberg's tyre stop, meanwhile, took a relatively long 15 seconds or so and by the time that he had charged back out into the fray second place had become sixth. Now, instead, it was Warwick who was lying second once more, almost half a minute behind the leading Ferrari, with Piquet third ahead of de Angelis and a fast-rising Bellof (yet to stop). In fact, the young German was becoming the source of acute embarrassment to the Lotus driver ahead of him as he piled on the pressure. Even when he experienced somewhat greater difficulty in lapping Surer's Arrows shortly afterwards, eventually going past in a somewhat desperate move at the first left-hander, which saw the Swiss nearly run out of road as the Tyrrell barged through on the inside, it made little difference for in no time at all Bellof was menacing de Angelis as much as ever. To add to the excitement Rosberg and Arnoux (lapping much quicker on their new tyres) were soon up with them as well, and on lap 55 the tension became almost unbearable with cars seemingly all over the track: Arnoux slammed past Rosberg, Belloff and de Angelis one after the other, while Rosberg followed that up by pulling out from behind Bellof's Tyrrell along the pit straight before jinking over to the left-hand side of the track in front of him and then squeezing through on the inside of de Angelis under braking for the first left-hander going into lap 56, this providing the spectators with a moment to savour. Despite trying harder than ever, though, Bellof just could not find a way round de Angelis and, in any case, at the end of lap 61 it was time for

the Tyrrell to stop off at the pits for weight-gaining water but not, interestingly enough, new tyres. This may or may not have had something to do with his team-mate's experience ten laps earlier. Whatever, within seconds of rejoining the race from his pit stop at the end of lap 51, Brundle had gone gently skating off the track on three wheels and a brake disc – an incorrectly seated wheel nut had allowed his Tyrrell's left front wheel to come adrift!

An already incident-packed Belgian Grand Prix continued to provide drama aplenty right up until the finish. By now Arnoux (currently the fastest man out on the circuit) had already caught and passed Piquet, but on lap 65, with Rosberg having just followed suit, the French Ferrari driver suddenly overdid things in his efforts to try to reel in Warwick's Renault and spun wildly at the Kanaalbocht. Fortunately, after receiving the assistance of some marshals, he was able to rejoin the race, albeit with Rosberg and Piquet both in front of him once more. However, whilst Alboreto was stroking home to a beautifully-driven victory – the first by an Italian in a Ferrari since the late Ludovico Scarfiotti at Monza in 1966 – and Warwick was heading for his best-ever Grand Prix result in a comfortable second place, Piquet suffered a spectacular engine failure just over three laps from home, which sent his Brabham careering off into the barriers, and then, on the very last lap, Rosberg had the misfortune of running out of fuel. Consequently, despite the spin, Arnoux was able to go on and take third place after all. Nevertheless, Rosberg at least took some reward for his heroic drive by being classified fourth due to being the last driver not to have been lapped by the victorious Alboreto. Meanwhile, with Baldi having been yet another late casualty owing to a shock-absorber mounting breaking on his Spirit, the only others still there at the finish were de Angelis, Bellof, Senna, the distinctly off-form Tambay (his race had not been helped by the loss of second gear), Surer and Palmer.

Results

1	M. Alboreto (Ferrari)	1 hr 36 min 32.048 sec (185.430 kph/ 115.221 mph)
2	D. Warwick (Renault)	1 hr 37 min 14.434 sec
3	R. Arnoux (Ferrari)	1 hr 37 min 41.851 sec
**4	K. Rosberg (Williams-Honda)	1 lap behind
5	E. de Angelis (Lotus-Renault)	1 lap behind
*	S. Bellof (Tyrrell-Ford)	1 lap behind
6	A. Senna (Toleman-Hart)	2 laps behind
7	P. Tambay (Renault)	2 laps behind
8	M. Surer (Arrows-Ford)	2 laps behind
**9	N. Piquet (Brabham-BMW)	4 laps behind
10	J. Palmer (RAM-Hart)	6 laps behind

* Excluded

** Not running at finish.

Fastest lap: R. Arnoux (Ferrari) on lap 64 in 1 min 19.294 sec (193.497 kph/120.233 mph)

Retirements

J. Cecotto (Toleman-Hart) clutch on lap 3, R. Patrese (Alfa Romeo) ignition on lap 3, A. Prost (McLaren-TAG) distributor on lap 6, N. Mansell (Lotus-Renault) clutch on lap 15, P. Ghinzani (Osella-Alfa Romeo) transmission on lap 15, F. Hesnault (Ligier-Renault) water radiator on lap 16, T. Boutsen (Arrows-BMW) electrics on lap 16, J. Laffite (Williams-Honda) spun off on lap 16, E. Cheever (Alfa Romeo) engine on lap 29, N. Lauda (McLaren-TAG) engine on lap 36, M. Winkelhock (ATS-BMW) electrics on lap 40, T. Fabi (Brabham-BMW) accident on lap 43, A. de Cesaris (Ligier-Renault) rear suspension on lap 43, M. Brundle (Tyrrell-Ford) lost wheel on lap 52, M. Baldi (Spirit-Hart) shock-absorber mounting on lap 54.

1984

IV° Gran Premio di San Marino

Imola: May 6
Weather: Mainly overcast but dry
Distance: 60 laps of 5.040 km circuit =
302.40 km (187.90 miles)

Michele Alboreto's overwhelming victory in the Belgian Grand Prix had done much to boost morale in the Ferrari camp and had been very well timed, coming only a week before the Italian team would be competing on home soil in the San Marino Grand Prix at Imola. For this next round of the 1984 World Championship, and because of the close proximity of the dates of the two races, most of the teams arrived at the circuit direct from Zolder (Ferrari was one of the few exceptions) with the result that the entry was essentially unchanged. As expected, though, Arrows had reversed the roles of their drivers by entering Surer in the new BMW-powered A7 and Boutsen in the older Ford-Cosworth-powered A6, and Osella, in addition to their regular entry for Piercarlo Ghinzani, had refurbished one of their 1983 FA1Es – fitted with a normally-aspirated V12 Alfa Romeo engine – and entered it for the Austrian Formula 2 driver, Jo Gartner. Other than that the only differences in the line-up were that Ferrari had brought along all four of their 126C4s so that Alboreto and Arnoux both had the luxury of having a spare chassis, and some of the cars had undergone a few subtle alterations to suit the circuit. These included the Tyrrell 012s reappearing with smaller, centre-pillar, rear aerofoils in the interests of achieving maximum straight-line speed.

Practice began 30 minutes late on Friday morning owing to a bout of brinkmanship with the 'medical' helicopter. However, apart from some of the large number of spectators present showing signs of becoming impatient, no-one was unduly bothered as in stark contrast to the superb weather of the previous weekend the skies were grey and overcast and the circuit was still wet from overnight rain. For Toleman it was of even less consequence due to a message having earlier come through from the team's headquarters in England stating that no attempt should be made to take part in the proceedings pending further instructions. Subsequently, rumours began circulating to the effect that there was a difference of opinion between the team's management and Pirelli over some money due from the latter in respect of winter tyre testing but, whatever, practice eventually started with the Toleman pit the scene of complete inactivity. Elsewhere, though, it was soon down to business as usual or, at least, as near as possible in the adverse conditions, not improved by more intermittent rain falling throughout most of the morning, allowing drivers little opportunity of learning much. Some also had to contend with various mechanical problems,

and among the early casualties were Cheever's Alfa Romeo, which suffered a turbo-charger failure after only one lap, and both McLarens. First Prost pulled into the pits complaining that his engine was refusing to run cleanly and subsequently took over the spare McLaren. Then, not long afterwards, Lauda stopped with rising engine temperatures caused by a broken water pump. Furthermore, this last incident left the Austrian with no alternative than to become a reluctant spectator for well over half an hour until his team-mate had finished with the spare car, by which time the 90-minute session was fast drawing to a close. As a result, Lauda could only squeeze in a few laps but, thanks to making the most of the rain having finally stopped and a dry line beginning to emerge, he at least took some consolation by ultimately recording third fastest time behind the two evenly-matched Renaults of Tambay and Warwick.

Almost as soon as everyone (except the Toleman team!) had gone away to start preparing for the more important opening hour of qualifying the rain returned with a vengeance, and although it had more or less stopped again when the official timekeepers took up duty at 1.30 p.m. the track was wetter than ever. Consequently, the overall scene was largely one of gloom and despondency and particularly so far as the many thousands of bedraggled spectators were concerned for their beloved Ferraris were right off the pace. To make matters worse for them only 15 minutes or so went by before Alboreto pulled off the track with a dead engine and began walking back into the pits. Much to his chagrin he had run out of fuel! Just prior to this, Warwick had struck rather more serious trouble in the form of a turbo-charger failure. But, unlike Alboreto, who was left with no alternative other than to resort to his spare Ferrari, the Englishman had been able to drive back to the pits and was later able to continue using the same car, the Renault mechanics, much to their credit, replacing the broken component in under 20 minutes. In the meantime, Tambay was carrying on from where he had left off in the morning by turning in the fastest times and, with just a quarter of an hour remaining, looked to have the provisional pole sewn up. However, by this stage the conditions were taking a turn for the better, enabling drivers to discard their wet-weather covers for slick tyres, and in no time at all the Frenchman suddenly found himself being eased out of the limelight by the McLaren MP4/2s of Lauda (back in his regular car) and Prost. Then Piquet, using his Brabham 'qualifying

special', changed the situation again by setting yet another new fastest time as the racing line became drier, and so it went on with more drivers getting in on the act and making it virtually impossible to keep abreast of developments. At the same time, of course, with the order constantly changing, it became really exciting and even the 'Tifosi' took a moment to savour when Arnoux took his turn to head the time-sheets. Much to their obvious disappointment, though, it was short-lived. Worse, when the field was eventually flagged off the Frenchman's best time of 1 min 38.389 sec had been beaten by no less than nine drivers – Piquet, who had ultimately clinched the provisional pole with a lap in 1 min

35.493 sec, Prost (1 min 35.687 sec), Tambay (1 min 36.250 sec), de Cesaris (1 min 36.613 sec), Warwick (1 min 36.706 sec), Rosberg (1 min 37.024 sec), Fabi (1 min 37.594 sec), Lauda (1 min 38.021 sec, before having lost the use of fifth gear) and even Mansell (1 min 38.363 sec), whose qualifying run had been ended prematurely by Gartner inadvertently moving over on him through one of the right-handers and breaking the left front suspension of his Lotus into the bargain. Alboreto's afternoon, meanwhile, had gone from bad to worse, for no sooner had he begun settling down in his spare Ferrari than the car's fuel-injection pump had failed and brought him to rest out on the circuit once again, the result of which left the Belgian Grand Prix winner in only 24th place on the time-sheets. Cheever, too, had had his efforts marred by another turbo-charger failure, while others out of luck had included Winkelhock and Hesnault, also because of broken turbo-charger units, and the two RAM drivers, who had suffered a plethora of problems with their Hart engines.

Whilst it was still far from clear what exactly was going on behind the scenes, Toleman were back in business on Saturday morning with Senna and Cecotto both joining the other 26 drivers for the second untimed session of practice. Unfortunately, though, the weather was now even worse than the day before and so far as making any worthwhile progress was concerned it was next to impossible owing to light rain persisting throughout the entire 90 minutes. In fact, when it was all over most observers were convinced that the grid order would be decided on Friday's times but then, as 1 p.m. approached, the rain finally stopped and slowly but surely the track began to dry out. This, in turn, led to the first part of the final qualifying session being unusually quiet owing to a large number of the drivers being content to bide their time in the pits in the hope that the improvement would continue. However, not everyone was prepared to risk it, especially as there were still ominous-looking clouds hovering overhead, and among those to go out comparatively early was Cheever. At the time it seemed to be a wise move for in spite of the track still being very damp the American, now showing a preference for the spare Alfa Romeo, put on a very impressive display and returned to the pits at the end of his run with a new fastest time of 1 min 34.455 sec to his credit – just as spots of rain fell! In the event, it didn't develop into anything and, instead, the track continued to dry, but with no way of knowing what would happen next other drivers gradually took the view that it was time to get stuck in. The result, another succession of fastest laps just like the previous afternoon, for as the track became drier so the pace increased. Not only that, it turned the battle for grid positions into nothing short of

a lottery, the final outcome being largely dependent on who was prepared to risk waiting behind in the pits the longest. This was particularly true of pole position as after Prost (twice), Alboreto and Rosberg had all joined Cheever in heading the time-sheets at one point or another it was a very cool Piquet who once again ultimately came out on top – by holding back on his second set of tyres until virtually the last moment and then tearing around in the spare Brabham BT53 in just 1 min 28.517 sec (204.977kph). Meanwhile Prost, after having switched his attentions to the spare McLaren, had at least done enough by lapping in 1 min 28.628 sec to take the other front row spot, and Rosberg was not too upset to find himself in third place at 1 min 29.418 sec, especially as his Williams had been understeering and its Honda engine had momentarily cut out at one stage. Cheever, on the other hand, had dropped away to only eighth spot, in spite of having slashed almost 4 seconds off his earlier time, and was also behind Warwick (1 min 29.682 sec), Lauda (1 min 30.325 sec), Arnoux (1 min 30.411 sec), who had ended his practice in a cloud of smoke from a late and spectacular engine failure, and Winkelhock (1 min 30.723 sec). Alboreto? Probably the least said the better as through a combination of having been over-cautious about the weather and having run out of fuel – again! – after just one lap on his single set of qualifiers, the crowd's hero had been elbowed down to an extremely disappointing 13th place. This was not the only unusual aspect of the final grid order either: Tambay had qualified in only 14th spot thanks to a turbo-charger failure whilst out on his first set of tyres in the spare Renault that he had been obliged to use because of his regular car having already been put to one side for the race; Mansell was a further four places adrift following another eventful afternoon in which he had spun wildly at Rivazza after being forced on to the grass there to avoid being carved up by Alliot's RAM (later he had been stranded out on the circuit with a dead engine); and neither Ghinzani nor Senna were even included in the line-up. Instead, both had failed to qualify for the race owing to having been sidelined by ignition and fuel pressure problems respectively while the track had still been damp.

On Sunday morning there was a welcome change in the weather, for at long last the skies had cleared and it was gloriously sunny. However, whilst this undoubtedly contributed to a large crowd making its way to the Autodromo from an early hour, it also led to a complete rethink on setting up cars and, consequently, to the pre-race warm-up session being even more important than usual. During the 30 minutes Prost, having decided to race the 'spare' McLaren, caused no great surprise by turning in the quickest time, but

up there in second and third places on the time-sheets at the end of it all were none other than the Ferrari 126C4s of Arnoux and Alboreto, which came as a real tonic, both to the team and to the 'Tifosi'. Meanwhile, over at Renault an overheating problem (traced to the car's radiator shield not having been removed beforehand!) had already led to Tambay's RE50 being wheeled away for an unscheduled engine change and, because of similar trouble with Mansell's Lotus 95T, only caused by the car's water radiators apparently not being large enough to cope with the higher ambient temperature, Lotus ultimately decided that their English driver should race the spare 95T. Even this, though, was not the end of the pre-race drama: some three hours later, with the sky now becoming increasingly cloudy, Rosberg's Williams developed a serious water leak whilst the Finn was taking part in a so-called parade of the leading six drivers in the World Championship table (a new public relations exercise instigated by FISA for 1984), which led to the spare FW09 being hurriedly brought into service. Then, as the 26 starters were taking part in the warm-up lap (or laps!) shortly afterwards, prior to lining up on the dummy grid, de Cesaris quickly discovered that the Renault engine in his Ligier was misfiring badly and drove straight back into the pits. Furthermore, before the engine could be encouraged to run on all six cylinders the pit exit was officially closed, so the Italian had to face up to the prospects of waiting behind in the pit lane until the rest of the field had completed the pace lap and been given the green light.

At the green it was much like Zolder all over again for whilst Piquet made a clean start from pole position and Prost made an even better one to outdrag the Brabham to the first left-hander, Rosberg barely moved due to the Honda engine in his Williams almost cutting out once more. To make matters worse, Lauda also had a problem. He couldn't get his McLaren into first gear and although most of the drivers lower down the order, apart from Palmer, who was stationary with a stalled engine, managed to avoid one another in the ensuing confusion, Hesnault's Ligier finished up at the side of the track with deranged left front suspension after being struck by Laffite's Williams. In the meantime, Rosberg and Lauda both finally got under way, Palmer was push-started into the race and de Cesaris charged out of the pit lane, but within a matter of seconds there was another collision. This time it was at Tosa where Tambay, after a good start, tried to run up on the inside of Cheever under braking only to find the American closing the door on him and the right front wheel and suspension of his Renault being knocked out of shape, along with the car's nose cone. As a result he, too, had to retire, while Cheever was left crawling

Alain Prost leads an already depleted field around on the opening lap. *(Autosport)*

round to the pits with a flat left rear tyre. Then, as if there had not already been enough excitement for one lap, Rosberg indulged in a spectacular, though harmless, spin owing to his engine still misbehaving and eventually crossed the line for the first time in a pretty hopeless-looking 19th place. Moreover, any hopes of seeing a repeat performance of his superb drive a week earlier were shattered almost immediately. Mid-way round the third lap the Honda engine cut out completely because of an electrical failure and the Finn was left with no alternative other than to park out on the circuit at Rivazza – at almost precisely the same moment that Mansell was abandoning his Lotus in the sand at the Acque Minerali! A front brake failure had caused the Englishman to spin off. While all this was happening Prost was not only maintaining the lead but rapidly pulling away from Piquet, who had Warwick's Renault hard on his heels. Fourth, after a small gap, was Arnoux, then came Alboreto (already up into fifth place!), Winkelhock, Patrese, de Angelis, Lauda (already staging a recovery following his problem at the start), Fabi, an impressive-looking Brundle and the others currently being led by the two Arrows of Boutsen and Surer.

Prost, running on a comparatively soft combination of Michelin tyres, was now consistently lapping more than a second quicker than Piquet with the result that the McLaren soon disappeared into the middle distance. Even so, the fastest man on the track at this early stage of the race was turning out to be Lauda, in the other McLaren. Obviously intent on continuing to make up lost ground,

he was absolutely flying and by lap 11 had made such good progress that he had not only gone by de Angelis, Patrese and Winkelhock in quick succession, but had also closed right up to the two Ferraris, which were still circulating virtually nose to tail in fourth and fifth places. For the Italian spectators, of course, this was a most unwelcome sight and whilst there seemed to be a glimmer of hope when Alboreto staved off a strong challenge from the McLaren driver on the approach to Tosa on the following lap, by tightly hugging the racing line, it quickly faded. Instead, Lauda immediately renewed his attack by getting the power on that little bit earlier as the two cars exited the uphill left-hander, drawing alongside the Ferrari under acceleration and then finally winning the dispute on the way into the double left-hander that followed. Thereafter, Lauda lost even less time in dealing with Arnoux and was soon posing a real threat to Warwick's third place. However, before anything really came of that a puff of blue smoke suddenly appeared from the back of the red and white car as it went into Tosa on lap 16 and only a moment or so later it was seen coasting to rest at the side of the track. A piston had failed, so an extremely good drive from the Austrian was over with nothing to show for it. Just a few minutes earlier Laffite had also disappeared from lower down the order with the same complaint and prior to that Patrese had stopped for similar reasons to those of Rosberg. Consequently, with the race barely at quarter-distance, the field was now down to 19 runners and even some of those were having problems. For a start Winkelhock was in trouble with fading

brakes and was about to be overtaken by Fabi, who had soon followed Lauda past de Angelis and Patrese (before his retirement) earlier in the race. Piquet, meanwhile, had lost the use of his clutch and Warwick was already becoming so concerned at the rate at which his Renault was gulping up its fuel that he was now driving to a self-imposed rev limit.

On lap 23 it was the turn of Prost to have a problem when a faulty master cylinder caused a front brake to momentarily lock on as he was approaching the downhill Rivazza. Fortunately, in spite of spinning through 360-degrees, the Frenchman succeeded in keeping his engine running and subsequently carried on as if nothing had happened still in a commanding lead, only now over Warwick who, regardless of driving to conserve fuel, had finally overtaken Piquet on the previous lap. Alboreto, too, had just moved up into fourth place owing to Arnoux having stopped off at the pits a few minutes earlier for fresh tyres, but it was of little comfort to him as he was now yet another running into a problem – fluctuating turbo boost pressure. In fact, at the end of lap 24 this brought the Belgian Grand Prix winner into the pits and there his race ended, the source of the trouble being traced to a split in the Ferrari's new exhaust system, first seen at Zolder, allowing the exhaust gases to escape before reaching one of the turbines. Not surprisingly the reaction of the crowd was spontaneous. Silence! Nevertheless, at least the other Ferrari was still there and, moreover, going really well after its tyre stop with Arnoux already catching Fabi's Brabham, the only other car to have gone by while he

Andrea de Cesaris drove impressively in the Renault-powered Ligier JS23 and, despite starting from the pit lane, looked well set to take third place until running out of fuel just under two laps from home. Here he leads Marc Surer's Arrows and Stefan Bellof's Tyrrell comparatively early in the race whilst lying 11th. (L.A.T. Photographic)

enough, on lap 40, Warwick had to undergo the humiliating experience of watching the Ferrari go flying past him. Naturally, Arnoux then immediately pulled away and nine laps later was just about up with Piquet when the Brabham suddenly began belching out dense smoke. Its turbo-charger waste-gate had failed, allowing the Ferrari driver to take over second place – much to the approval of the crowd – and leaving the reigning World Champion to trickle into the pits to face up to the harsh reality of still having a blank score-sheet in 1984. There would still be no Championship points for his team either. Incredibly, no sooner had Piquet stepped out of his car than along came Fabi in exactly the same trouble! Although it was of little consolation, this suggested that there was something basically wrong with the KKK turbo-charger units or, at least, so far as the four BMW-powered cars were concerned, as only a few minutes earlier Surer's first race in the new Arrows A7 had also ended under identical circumstances. What made matters worse was that the BMW engines had otherwise been reliable all weekend after the succession of breakages at Zolder had finally been traced to a duff batch of big end bolts – and now this!

There were now just ten laps remaining, but while Prost reeled them off with consummate ease to record his second victory of the season, and Arnoux duly followed him home in a distant second place, the situation throughout the rest of the already badly depleted field altered dramatically. For a start third place changed hands twice. First de Cesaris, doing an excellent job at keeping de Angelis at bay, led his compatriot past Warwick's Renault, which was now suffering from a lack of fourth gear in addition to the fuel consumption problem. Then, with less than two laps to go, the Ligier suddenly ran out of fuel. Consequently, it was de Angelis who finally took third spot, but only just, as on the final lap his Lotus stopped out on the circuit for the same reason. In fact, if Warwick had had any means of knowing this, had unlapped himself (he was directly behind Prost's McLaren for the final four laps) and his fuel had lasted out for another lap it would have been a different story again. As it was the Englishman had to settle for an eventual fourth place. Meanwhile Cheever, who had driven really hard ever since the first lap incident with Tambay and steadily worked his way up into sixth place, became yet another driver to run out of fuel within sight of the finish; Brundle's storming drive in the Ford-Cosworth-powered Tyrrell, which had been temporarily halted by a problem in lapping Palmer's RAM for the second time and also by a pit stop on lap 47 to take on ballast, was similarly ill-rewarded by a fuel pick-up problem stranding him out on the circuit just over four laps from home; and three of the tail-enders all retired in

had been in the pits. Further back, de Angelis was now up into sixth place, although that didn't last for long as at the end of lap 27 he became the next visitor to the pits for fresh rubber and, in the ensuing delay, dropped behind a fast-rising de Cesaris, the impressive Brundle, Winkelhock (now falling away dramatically and soon to retire with a broken turbo-charger waste-gate) and Surer. After thirty laps, exactly half-distance, Prost became another of what were to be comparatively few drivers to stop for fresh tyres, but he had already built up such an advantage that he subsequently emerged from the pits

still very much a clear leader. In fact, the main point of interest now, certainly so far as the crowd was concerned, was the progress of the surviving Ferrari, especially when Arnoux repassed Fabi on lap 31 and began reeling in a highly frustrated Warwick. Frustrated, because after just five laps of running in second place he had had to slacken his pace still further owing to his fuel situation, allowing Piquet to move on ahead of him once more, and was now merely driving round in the hope of making it to the finish. It was, therefore, simply a question of waiting for the inevitable to happen and sure rapid succession. Gartner, who had at least kept out of everyone's way which was something more than could be said of him during practice, had the V12 Alfa Romeo engine in his Osella blow up and both Cecotto and Alliot suffered late turbo-charger failures.

As a result, after Warwick, the only others still running at the finish were Bellof, Boutsen, Baldi and Palmer.

Results		
1	A. Prost (McLaren-TAG)	1 hr 36 min 53.679 sec (187.254 kph/ 116.354 mph)
2	R. Arnoux (Ferrari)	1 hr 37 min 07.095 sec
**3	E. de Angelis (Lotus-Renault)	1 lap behind
4	D. Warwick (Renault)	1 lap behind
*	S. Bellof (Tyrrell-Ford)	1 lap behind
5	T. Boutsen (Arrows-Ford)	1 lap behind
**6	A. de Cesaris (Ligier-Renault)	2 laps behind
**7	E. Cheever (Alfa Romeo)	2 laps behind
8	M. Baldi (Spirit-Hart)	2 laps behind
9	J. Palmer (RAM-Hart)	3 laps behind
**	*M. Brundle (Tyrrell-Ford)	6 laps behind

* Excluded

** Not running at finish.

Fastest lap: N. Piquet (Brabham-BMW) on lap 48 in 1 min 33.275 sec (194.521 kph/ 120.869 mph)

Retirements
F. Hesnault (Ligier-Renault) accident on lap 1, P. Tambay (Renault) accident on lap 1, N. Mansell (Lotus-Renault) spun off on lap 3, K. Rosberg (Williams-Honda) electrics on lap 3, R. Patrese (Alfa Romeo) electrics on lap 7, J. Laffite (Williams-Honda) engine on lap 12, N. Lauda (McLaren-TAG) engine on lap 16, M. Alboreto (Ferrari) exhaust on lap 24, M. Winkelhock (ATS-BMW) turbo-charger on lap 32, M. Surer (Arrows-BMW) turbo-charger on lap 41, J. Gartner (Osella-Alfa Romeo) engine on lap 47, N. Piquet (Brabham-BMW) turbo-charger on lap 49, T. Fabi (Brabham-BMW) turbo-charger on lap 49, J. Cecotto (Toleman-Hart) turbo-charger on lap 53, P. Alliot (RAM-Hart) turbo-charger on lap 54.

LXXe Grand Prix de France

Dijon-Prenois: May 20
Weather: Overcast but dry
Distance: 79 laps of 3.887 km circuit = 307.07 km (190.80 miles)

Immediately following the San Marino Grand Prix it was learned that Toleman and Pirelli had agreed to end their 3-year association in Formula 1 and that the British Team would be using Michelin radial tyres for the remainder of the season. Apparently negotiations between Alex Hawkridge and the French tyre firm had been going on for several weeks and the reason for Toleman missing the first day of practice at Imola had been a ploy to highlight what were considered to be financial irregularities with Pirelli as a rather badly-handled means of dissolving the partnership. Either way the transition had now been made and, in fact, just one day later Toleman had gone to the little Dijon-Prenois circuit in Eastern France, the venue of this year's French Grand Prix, and begun a testing programme on the French rubber. Moreover, they had carried out the tests using the first two examples of their new 1984 car, the TG184, and been sufficiently encouraged by the results to rely on the new chassis for the forthcoming race, Senna being entered in TG184/2 and Cecotto in TG184/3, which was completed in the meantime. This apart, the line-up for the French round of the Championship was pretty familiar, although Lotus arrived with a brand new 95T, their fourth such chassis, which was being set aside as a spare car at this stage, Tyrrell similarly brought along a new 012, also their fourth, for the use of Bellof, and ongoing development work had resulted in a number of existing cars receiving further various modifications. Of particular significance in this latter respect, following a recent statement issued by Gerard Larrousse to the effect that Renault

might be temporarily withdrawing from Grand Prix racing later in the season if they were unable to overcome their fuel consumption problem within the next couple of months, was the appearance of a small, additional, heat exchanger on Warwick's RE50. Working from an air-to-air rather than the more familiar air-to-water inter-cooler, this had been designed to re-heat chilled fuel before it was injected into the engine on the basis that an engine consumed more cold fuel than it would if the fuel was at ambient temperature. Lotus, whilst retaining air-to-water inter-coolers, were also trying a similar system for the same reasons. Meanwhile, among the other cars to have been modified by varying degrees were two of the four Ferrari 126C4s, the team's proposed race cars, which reappeared with revised front and rear suspension (both also had the latest exhaust system notwithstanding Alboreto's problem at Imola); the Euroracing Alfa Romeo 184Ts, which had now been given marginally longer side-pods to house larger radiators; the pair of BMW-powered Arrows A7s (delegated to Boutsen this weekend), which had new rear suspension geometry; and the Williams FW09s, which were being tried with a new front wing and revised front suspension geometry in yet another bid to rid them of their continuing understeer problem.

After several days of near-continuous rain in the locality, Friday morning was clear and bright thereby enabling practice to get off to a nice smooth start. For some it stayed that way or, at least, relatively speaking as throughout most of the 90 minutes of testing drivers were working away at trying to find a

combination of tyres, wing angles, suspension settings and the like that they could cope with round as much as the little circuit as possible. As usual at this particular venue it was the downhill left-hander at the start of the 'new' loop that was causing the biggest problem, for here cars were invariably entering it in a state of understeer and then quickly switching to oversteer on the way out. There were exceptions, of course, and amongst them were the well-balanced Lotus 95Ts of de Angelis and Mansell, being tried with a revised rear aerofoil arrangement, and also the McLaren MP4/2s of Lauda and Prost which, in turn, was being reflected in their lap times. For others, meanwhile, there seemed to be nothing but trouble. Engines were refusing to run cleanly, one or two were blowing up, there were complaints of poor handling or lack of traction or even both and so on with the result that at times there appeared to be more activity going on in the pits than out on the actual track. Cecotto was particularly unfortunate as his new Toleman was in trouble with a fuel pressure problem that even a new fuel pump failed to cure and then, after subsequently switching to the team's spare chassis (the prototype TG184), he found that to be suffering in exactly the same manner. However, before the morning was out Alliot was even less happy due to having spun off and put his RAM out of action for the rest of the day with two of its corners knocked out of shape. He would be sharing Palmer's car for the first qualifying session! Other names on the early casualty list also included Warwick, who had to fall back on the spare Renault owing to the engine in his race car breaking after only three laps, Piquet, who was plagued by a persistent misfire before his Brabham was eventually wheeled away for an engine change, and even Lauda, when the TAG-Porsche engine in his McLaren suddenly blew up without warning.

For the afternoon's hour of qualifying Lauda and Warwick were both preparing to use their respective teams' spare cars, but for entirely different reasons. In Lauda's case it was simply due to his own car still being out of commission. Warwick, on the other hand, had spent so much time sorting the spare Renault in the morning that he had taken the view that his interests would be best served by sticking to it, even though the engine in his race car had now been replaced and the cockpit settings in the spare were not exactly ideal for him. Otherwise, apart from the unfortunate Alliot's situation, all was more or less back to normal once again with the result that before long everything was soon in full swing. Well, not quite, for as usual

now some drivers were intent on holding back on their two sets of marked tyres longer than others, which led to the early stages of the session being comparatively quiet. Even so, it was no less interesting and a pleasant surprise was to see Winkelhock's name appear at the top of the time-sheets during the opening minutes, his ATS D7, no longer fitted with the large caliper brakes that had been giving problems recently, running really well. As anticipated, though, this situation didn't last for long and, indeed, by mid-session de Cesaris, Tambay and Mansell (despite a problem with a jammed turbo waste-gate) had all gradually stepped up the pace. Then Piquet poked his nose into the limelight as well only to find himself being displaced by a very on-form de Angelis who, having already turned in fastest time in the morning, suddenly lapped half a second clear of the field by putting in a real flier at 1 min 02.336 sec. After that the Italian returned to the pits and coolly played the waiting game until Tambay upset things yet again by going out on his second set of tyres and whistling round in 1 min 02.200 sec (224.971 kph) – immediately prior to a turbo-charger letting go and causing the back of his Renault to briefly catch fire! Naturally, this really put the cat amongst the pigeons but, in spite of some brave efforts as the minutes ticked away to 2 p.m., not least from de Angelis, whose 'fast' lap was spoiled due to coming upon Alboreto's slower-moving Ferrari at a crucial point, the time went unbeaten. Consequently, when Tambay eventually walked into the pits (he had been obliged to abandon his Renault out on the circuit) the Frenchman was greeted with the good news that he had won the provisional pole. A somewhat disillusioned de Angelis, meanwhile, at least saw his earlier time stand good for second place on the time-sheets and Piquet was not too disappointed to wind up in third place, his best lap having come out at 1 min 02.806 sec. In contrast Mansell, another to have lost the benefit of his second set of tyres due to being caught up in traffic (at one point almost causing him to spin off!), had been elbowed back to sixth spot in the final reckoning by Rosberg and Prost, even though the French McLaren driver had blown up his engine shortly after leaving the pits for his second run. Winkelhock, after losing an engine second time out, and de Cesaris had slipped back as well and were left in eighth and ninth places behind Warwick, who had failed to make the hoped-for impression in the spare Renault. Nevertheless, all of them were still ahead of the likes of Lauda, who had lost another engine in the latter stages of qualifying, the two Ferrari drivers, who were complaining of understeer and lack of grip, and also Patrese and Cheever in their Euroracing Alfa Romeo 184Ts, both of which had been handling rather poorly before being sidelined by a

broken turbo-charger and engine respectively. Among the others, Senna had planted the first of the new Tolemans half-way up the list of times, directly ahead of Hesnault's particularly well-driven Ligier and the Arrows A7 of Boutsen, but Fabi, confined to little more than a brief outing in Piquet's car in the closing minutes following an early turbo-charger failure, had been able to make no real impression at all. Neither had Ghinzani, whose lone Osella was right at the bottom of the time-sheets following problems with its V8 Alfa Romeo engine.

Little did anyone realize at the time, but that was it so far as any more serious practice was concerned due to torrential rain setting in and continuing throughout the following day until just before the end of the final qualifying session, by which time it was too late to make much difference. Nevertheless, every single driver ventured out on wet-weather tyres at some time during the course of the morning and the vast majority carried on in the afternoon, for quite apart from anything else there was no guarantee that it wouldn't be a wet race. Of course, the overall scene was more akin to power-boat racing and the lap times seemed ridiculous when compared to the first day, being around 20 seconds slower. Be that as it may, there was still a lot of hard and fast driving going on given the conditions, and the two Lotus drivers, in particular, looked most impressive. Indeed, it came as no surprise at all to find them in first and second places on the time-sheets at the end of the day with Mansell having stopped the clocks at 1 min 20.061 sec on his best run and de Angelis (fastest in the morning) having achieved a personal best of 1 min 20.859 sec. Then, wait for it, third fastest was none other than Hesnault. But he, too, had excelled on the soaking wet track and put up a truly magnificent performance in his Ligier to narrowly pip team-mate de Cesaris and also Arnoux and Alboreto in their Ferraris. The irony of it all was that the Frenchman wouldn't even be taking part in the race. Instead, because the fire extinguisher bottle in his team-mate's car had been found to be empty during post-practice scrutineering on the previous afternoon and de Cesaris had had his lap times scrubbed, Hesnault now found himself being asked (or, more likely being told!) to stand down so that the Italian could be allowed to start from 26th and last place on the grid.

Overnight the weather turned a full circle and on Sunday morning it was clear and bright once more, although with a forecast of rain returning during the afternoon there was a certain degree of uneasiness apparent. Anyhow, for the time being all was well with the world and when, at 10.30 a.m., the circuit was opened for the half-hour warm-up session the response was predictable: one mad rush as drivers sought to make the most of the opportunity of being able to try their cars on dry settings again at long last. During the previous evening McLaren had taken delivery of two brand new TAG-Porsche engines, which had been specially built with larger tolerances and lower compression in the hope of preventing a recurrence of the problems experienced on Friday. Even so there was still cause for concern for whilst Prost went on to narrowly pip Lauda for third fastest time, behind Arnoux and Tambay, he later returned to the pits complaining of a high-speed misfire. However, the Frenchman realized only too well that this was something that he would have to live with unless his mechanics could find a cure before the start of the race owing to the spare McLaren obviously being fitted with the earlier type of engine. Meanwhile, some of the other drivers had run into far worse trouble, including de Angelis and Mansell, whose Lotus 95Ts had developed serious engine maladies, Cheever, whose Alfa Romeo had stopped with a broken turbocharger unit, and Alliot, who was convinced that he had heard peculiar noises coming from the Hart engine in his repaired RAM. As a result, final preparations for the race entailed quite a lot of unscheduled work, but by 2 p.m. everything had just about been sorted out and all 26 drivers were preparing to leave the pits prior to forming on the dummy grid, Mansell and Alliot having had fresh engines installed in their cars, while de Angelis had been assigned to the new, spare Lotus 95T. And the weather? Sure enough, the clouds were back but the rain appeared to be holding off.

As usual, the final countdown seemed to last an eternity, but eventually engines were being fired up and then the field was away on the pace lap led, for the first time since joining Renault, by Tambay. On the way round Alliot did his best to provide the spectators with a little extra entertainment by indulging in a quick spin, otherwise it was all very orderly and within a couple of minutes the 26 cars were correctly lined up in their grid positions once more ready to face the starting lights. Needless to say, the large crowd present was hoping to see Tambay turn his pole position into a home victory and the Frenchman, no doubt, felt the same way. At the red light, however, he had an immediate problem: his Renault was creeping forward due to its clutch beginning to overheat. Fortunately, amidst fears that he might well wind up with a stalled engine, Tambay found the green light coming on just in the nick of time, so a possible disaster was averted. Nevertheless, it still resulted in what appeared to be a rather poor start so far as he was concerned for as the pack rushed away Tambay found himself becoming engulfed by Piquet (he had also crept forward on the line until checking himself by momentarily applying the brakes) moving up on his right and by

de Angelis and Rosberg on his left. Indeed, for a moment it looked certain that de Angelis would take the lead as he began to nose ahead, only for Tambay to gain the upper hand on the approach to the first right-hander. Here he first of all succeeded in squeezing out Piquet, actually making light contact with the Brabham, and then, by tightly hugging the inside lane through the corner, forced the Italian Lotus driver to eventually back off. Meanwhile, Piquet, thrown slightly off-guard by Tambay's rather forceful manner, not only had to give best to Rosberg – he had been practising standing starts during the closing minutes of Friday's qualifying session and certainly got it right this time – but also to Mansell, who was charging through from sixth place on the grid. Lower down the order, Laffite was another to have got away exceptionally well, but after moving up from 12th place to sixth he was forced to lift off to avoid Winkelhock's ATS, which suddenly hesitated in front of him, and saw his efforts come to nought. In the meantime, Tambay was already starting to assert himself and went on to complete the opening lap four or five car lengths clear of de Angelis, who was still in second place. Mansell was third after having driven round on the outside of Rosberg's

Williams through the long first right-hander, but Piquet was now about to be elbowed back to sixth place by Warwick, the Englishman pulling out from behind the Brabham along the main straight and going neatly past it on the approach to the first turn. Right behind them, Prost was lying seventh, then it was Alboreto from Winkelhock and Lauda, also soon to swop places, Senna, Arnoux, Boutsen, Patrese, Cheever and Fabi before the somewhat unfortunate Laffite, who was now down in 17th place ahead of the rest.

During the early stages of the race the three leading Renault-powered cars looked pretty evenly matched. Tambay was not pulling away to any great extent and de Angelis, despite being unhappy with the settings of the spare Lotus, was successfully resisting a strong challenge from Mansell until the Birmingham lad began to drop back a bit – with a blister already appearing on his left rear tyre! Meanwhile Rosberg, whose Williams was refusing to handle properly either with or without the revised front suspension (this had been replaced by an earlier set-up following more complaints of understeer during the first day's practice), was soon sliding out of contention. First Warwick, who had been bothered by an acute lack of grip in the morning warm-up session, sailed past him at

Derek Warwick comes under pressure from Nelson Piquet and eventual winner Niki Lauda during the early stages of the French Grand Prix which, this year, returned to Dijon. *(Autosport)*

the start of the third lap. Then, on the following lap, the Finn lost three more places in quick succession to Piquet, Prost and also Lauda, who had already moved on ahead of Alboreto since dealing with Winkelhock. In fact, the McLarens were quickly turning out to be the cars to watch for on lap 5 Prost was at it again, this time pulling out from behind Piquet's Brabham along the main straight and storming past it on the approach to the first right-hander. Not satisfied with that, he then took only one more lap to dish out the same treatment to Warwick and before long was closing to within striking distance of Mansell's third-placed Lotus. Lauda, too, was soon moving up to challenge Piquet, although this resolved itself in a totally unexpected manner on lap 12 when the reigning World Champion suddenly slowed and went touring into the pits trailing plumes of smoke, subsequently accompanied by flames licking around the Brabham's left-hand sidepod. Another turbo-charger failure! By now Alliot had also disappeared, the fresh Hart engine in his RAM having cut out back on the fifth lap, and so, too, had both Winkelhock, with clutch trouble, and Bellof, who had just pulled off the track incorrectly thinking that his engine was about to blow up when, in fact, it was merely that the rev-limiter had cut in whilst his Tyrrell had been running in Laffite's slip-stream along the main straight. In the meantime, Rosberg had lost yet another place to Arnoux, while Alboreto had dropped well back, to ninth position (it had been tenth until Piquet's demise), following a quick spin and was now looking in danger of being over-hauled by a fast-rising Fabi.

By lap 20 Patrese was another to have retired, his Alfa Romeo having stopped a few minutes earlier with a blown-up engine, but more to the point Prost had carved his way past the two black and gold Lotus 95Ts of Mansell and de Angelis and now had Tambay's Renault firmly in his sights. To make matters even more interesting they were starting to lap back-markers although, if anything, this initially worked in Tambay's favour and enabled him to pull away again slightly. Nevertheless Prost, who lost a bit of ground lapping Palmer's RAM, quickly recovered, and before long was looking all set to pounce at any moment. For several laps, though, he had been bothered by a small front end vibration and on lap 28 it was almost certainly this that led to the McLaren's left front wheel retaining nut working loose. Whatever, as Prost was negotiating the fast uphill right-hander leading on to the main straight he noticed the left front wheel begin to wobble and was powerless to prevent his car from sliding very wide indeed, its two nearside wheels even momentarily running over the dirt at the side of the track. Fortunately the wheel stayed put and the Frenchman managed to keep

things going before immediately turning off into the pits. Once there, all four wheels were changed but Prost, after being a little too eager with the clutch, lost even more time than necessary, and when he did eventually set off found himself rejoining the race in a miserable 11th place, almost a lap down. Tambay, on the other hand, now had a bit more breathing space, although he could ill afford to relax, for by this stage Lauda had not only flown past Warwick, Mansell and de Angelis in the space of just six laps but had moved up to within 2 seconds of him. Indeed, before long it became another Renault versus McLaren affair and this went on right through until lap 41 when Tambay, growing increasingly concerned about the state of his brakes and his Michelin tyres, finally made a mistake going into the left-hander at the exit from the 'new' loop. Quite simply he turned in a shade too early, got a bit sideways and drifted wide on to the outside kerbing, which was all that was needed for Lauda to nip by on the inside and into the lead. Thereafter Tambay resigned himself to second place and, in any case, stayed out for only three more laps before stopping off at the pits for fresh tyres. Meanwhile, throughout this absorbing little scrap at the front of the race the other leading positions had been undergoing a complete reshuffle due to Mansell, Arnoux, Warwick and de Angelis each having taken turns to make their tyre stops. In fact, at one point this had enabled Rosberg (yet to stop) to climb as high as third place, but since then he had already been repassed by Mansell and Warwick and was now about to be swallowed up by a fast-recovering Prost, de Angelis and Arnoux. Further back Fabi, another still on his original tyres, was currently lying ninth (he had briefly held sixth spot during the pit stop roulette) and Laffite, whose engine had been misfiring earlier in the race until eventually clearing itself, had come through to tenth place, although apart from being a lap down, he, too, had yet to take on fresh rubber. After that there were just eight other cars still running as a rather disappointing performance from Alboreto had ended on lap 34 with a blown-up engine and both Senna and Cecotto had gone out with broken turbo-chargers in the space of 13 laps following an otherwise reasonably encouraging debut from their new Tolemans.

Although Tambay rejoined the race from his tyre stop without losing second place, Lauda was able to pull out a lead of more than half a minute in the meantime and so was now completely out on his own. Moreover, the gap continued to steadily increase until the end of lap 54 when Lauda finally took his turn to go into the pits. At this point it seemed almost certain that he would still emerge as race-leader, but it was not to be. Instead, after the McLaren pit crew had taken the best part of an agonisingly long 18

seconds to change all four wheels, Lauda found himself behind Tambay once more and to the tune of almost exactly 10 seconds. Naturally the Renault pit was overjoyed yet, at the same time, had reason for concern as Warwick had suddenly gone missing. In fact, their English driver, who had been going better than ever on his fresh tyres and started to become embroiled in an exciting scrap with Mansell, had momentarily locked a wheel whilst attempting to follow his compatriot through on the inside of Surer's Arrows at the left-hander where Tambay had earlier run wide, struck the cream and brown car, quite literally flown over the top of it and finished up in the catch-fences. That was not the end of the saga either. Warwick was sat there motionless with his head slumped forward for several seconds and then, after regaining consciousness, was unable to move his legs due to a right front suspension arm having pushed its way into the Renault's footwell. However, much to everyone's relief he was eventually freed by some marshals, and subsequent medical examination revealed nothing worse than a badly bruised leg. In the meantime, Surer had been obliged to abandon his Arrows at the side of the track and now Cheever was out of the race as well, the American having spun off into the catch-fences at the fast uphill right-hander before the main straight – less than a lap after undergoing a lengthy pit stop to replace a lost rear aerofoil! Mansell, on the other hand, was still lapping as regular as ever in third place, and at the end of lap 57 could even afford to relax when Prost, looking all set to pose a threat before much longer, suddenly swung off into the pit lane. Incredible as it seemed, the McLaren's left front wheel was working loose again or, at least, that's how it felt to Prost. Actually it was a loose disc mounting that was the source of the trouble, but by the time that his mechanics had discovered this, tightened it up and the Frenchman had taken to the track once more over a minute had lapsed and fourth place had become tenth.

By lap 62 Lauda had got back on terms with Tambay, waited until they had both lapped Baldi's Spirit – destined to soon blow up its Hart engine – for the umpteenth time and then breezed past the Renault along the main straight. After that it was all over as Tambay, not prepared to turn up his turbo boost pressure any further for fear of running out of fuel and still troubled by a soft brake pedal, more or less settled for second place. Consequently, Lauda was able to drive on to a reasonably comfortable, though nonetheless hard-driven, victory, his second of the season and his 21st in total. His team-mate, meanwhile, spent the last 21 laps of the race treating the appreciative spectators to a superb display of skill and bravery in a determined bid to get back into the points. Sadly, though, his efforts were to go unrewarded and, instead, Prost just failed in his quest by winding up in seventh place – a mere 3 seconds or so behind Rosberg's evil-handling Williams. Other than that the closing stages of the race had produced little change, which meant that Mansell scored his first points of the season by finishing in third place after an impressive afternoon's work (this was even more commendable when it was learned that he had been bottling up the fact that his mother had died of cancer only

three days earlier) and that Arnoux and de Angelis were the other point scorers, despite both complaining that their cars had been suffering from lack of grip. Further back, in ninth place between Laffite and de Cesaris, Fabi had at least provided a crumb of comfort for the Brabham team by actually giving a BT53 its first race finish and much the same applied to Boutsen with the BMW-powered Arrows A7 – although only just. As the Belgian came up to the line in 11th place the

cream and brown car suffered a massive turbo-charger failure! Also still there at the end were Brundle, who had mis-read a pit signal intended for Mansell earlier in the afternoon and made an unscheduled pit stop in his Tyrrell (running with sponsorship from the DeLonghi portable heater specialists for the second race on the trot), Ghinzani and Palmer, the latter having had a physically exhausting drive in his RAM contending with vicious understeer.

Results

1	N. Lauda (McLaren-TAG)	1 hr 31 min 11.951 sec (202.023 kph/ 125.531 mph)
2	P. Tambay (Renault)	1 hr 31 min 19.105 sec
3	N. Mansell (Lotus-Renault)	1 hr 31 min 35.920 sec
4	R. Arnoux (Ferrari)	1 hr 31 min 55.657 sec
5	E. de Angelis (Lotus-Renault)	1 hr 32 min 18.076 sec
6	K. Rosberg (Williams-Honda)	1 lap behind
7	A. Prost (McLaren-TAG)	1 lap behind
8	J. Laffite (Williams-Honda)	1 lap behind
9	T. Fabi (Brabham-BMW)	1 lap behind
10	A. de Cesaris (Ligier-Renault)	2 laps behind
11	T. Boutsen (Arrows-BMW)	2 laps behind
*	M. Brundle (Tyrrell-Ford)	3 laps behind
12	P. Ghinzani (Osella-Alfa Romeo)	5 laps behind
13	J. Palmer (RAM-Hart)	7 laps behind

* Excluded

Fastest lap: A. Prost (McLaren-TAG) on lap 59 in 1 min 05.257 sec (214.432 kph/ 133.242 mph)

Retirements

P. Alliot (RAM-Hart) electrics on lap 5, M. Winkelhock (ATS-BMW) clutch on lap 6, S. Bellof (Tyrrell-Ford) suspect engine on lap 12, N. Piquet (Brabham-BMW) turbo-charger on lap 12, R. Patrese (Alfa Romeo) engine on lap 16, J. Cecotto (Toleman-Hart) turbo-charger on lap 23, M. Alboreto (Ferrari) engine on lap 34, A. Senna (Toleman-Hart) turbo-charger on lap 36, E. Cheever (Alfa Romeo) spun off on lap 52, M. Surer (Arrows-Ford) accident on lap 52, D. Warwick (Renault) accident on lap 54, M. Baldi (Spirit-Hart) engine on lap 62.

XLII\u1d49 Grand Prix de Monaco

Monte Carlo: June 3
Weather: Very wet
Distance: 31 laps of 3.312 km circuit = 102.67 km (63.80 miles)

The magic of Monaco! Well, there nearly wasn't any this year or, at least, not so far as a World Championship event taking place in the Principality was concerned owing to what FISA considered had been a breach of the Concorde Agreement by the Automobile Club de Monaco in not assigning its television rights to the FIA. Instead, the ACM had entered into an agreement with the American ABC network to cover all Monaco Grands Prix up until 1987 with a further option available until 1991. However, at a meeting of the FISA Executive Committee held at Estoril in mid-March it had been decided to inflict 'a reprimand on the ACM' and to keep the race on the 1984 World Championship calendar 'on condition that the ACM pays FISA its 1983 television fee'. At the same time it had also decided that after this year's race to henceforth exclude the event from the FIA World Championship with the proviso that the ACM could 'only put forward its candidature on the conditions of having regularized its situation in compliance with the Concorde Agreement, and in respect of the FIA General Assembly decisions'. So, amidst a considerable amount of political turmoil which had led to several weeks of speculation as to whether or not there would be a Monaco Grand Prix in 1984 and, if so, whether it

would carry World Championship status, one of the most popular races of them all was definitely on – for one more year, at least!

Since 1981 the organisers at Monaco had reduced the number of drivers taking part in official practice to 26 by holding an early morning pre-qualifying session on the first day. This year, however, they had abandoned the idea on the grounds that with 27 entries one extra car wasn't going to make that much difference. Of course, not everyone agreed with this line of thinking and there was no denying that it did seem to make a mockery of the fact that the organizers were maintaining their policy of being alone in restricting the size of the starting grid to 20 cars once again. However, whilst feelings were running a bit high on the matter, there were no official protests, so at 10 o'clock on Thursday morning everybody started out on an equal footing and in every sense of the word due to the lack of any pre-race testing on this famous old street circuit. Entry-wise, there were no significant changes from Dijon except that because Teo Fabi had gone off to North America to fulfil his commitments with the Forsythe Indy car team his younger brother, Corrado, was acting as stand-in for the first time at Brabham. Nevertheless, Ferrari, Renault and Osella had each brought along a new car to

their current designs for Alboreto, Warwick and, as a spare chassis, for Ghinzani, and Brundle's Tyrrell, whilst still carrying DeLonghi lettering, had changed from dark blue to maroon and gold to mark the arrival of sponsorship from Yardley: the one-time sponsors of BRM and McLaren were using the opportunity to promote their recently introduced 'Yardley Gold for Men' range of products. The new Toleman TG184s of Senna and Cecotto were also running with additional sponsorship since France, following revived support (again!) from the Candy domestic appliances firm, but here the main interest revolved around the team's spare car as this had been fitted with the latest version of Brian Hart's four cylinder engine, complete with a newly-developed electronic engine management system.

Apart from Tambay clipping the back of Boutsen's Arrows and damaging a front suspension pick-up point badly enough to force him into the spare Renault for the rest of the day, the untimed session produced little in the way of serious trouble. Consequently, the vast majority of drivers were able to go through the routine of sorting cars and trying different tyres largely unhindered, and they seemed to be making reasonably good progress going by the unofficial lap times. Already, though, the amount of traffic was becoming the source of increasing irritation and during the first hour of qualifying in the afternoon this became even more apparent owing to a combination of the short life of the qualifying tyres and the business of find-

Starting Grid

A. Prost
McLaren-TAG
(1 min 22.661 sec)

N. Mansell
Lotus-Renault
(1 min 22.752 sec)

R. Arnoux
Ferrari
(1 min 22.935 sec)

M. Alboreto
Ferrari
(1 min 22.937 sec)

D. Warwick
Renault
(1 min 23.237 sec)

P. Tambay
Renault
(1 min 23.414 sec)

A. de Cesaris
Ligier-Renault
(1 min 23.578 sec)

N. Lauda
McLaren-TAG
(1 min 23.886 sec)

N. Piquet
Brabham-BMW
(1 min 23.918 sec)

K. Rosberg
Williams-Honda
(1 min 24.151 sec)

E. de Angelis
Lotus-Renault
(1 min 24.426 sec)

M. Winkelhock
ATS-BMW
(1 min 24.473 sec)

A. Senna
Toleman-Hart
(1 min 25.009 sec)

R. Patrese
Alfa Romeo
(1 min 25.101 sec)

C. Fabi
Brabham-BMW
(1 min 25.290 sec)

J. Laffite
Williams-Honda
(1 min 25.719 sec)

F. Hesnault
Ligier-Renault
(1 min 25.815 sec)

J. Cecotto
Toleman-Hart
(1 min 25.872 sec)

P. Ghinzani
Osella-Alfa Romeo
(1 min 25.877 sec)

S. Bellof
Tyrrell-Ford
(1 min 26.117 sec)

Did not qualify:
M. Surer (Arrows-Ford) 1 min 26.273 sec
M. Brundle (Tyrrell-Ford) 1 min 26.373 sec
E. Cheever (Alfa Romeo) 1 min 26.471 sec
T. Boutsen (Arrows-BMW) 1 min 26.514 sec
J. Palmer (RAM-Hart) 1 min 27.458 sec
M. Baldi (Spirit-Hart) 1 min 28.360 sec
P. Alliot (RAM-Hart) 1 min 29.576 sec.

ing a clear lap turning out to be next to impossible. The Goodyear runners were finding it particularly frustrating as their qualifying tyres were proving to be effective for barely one lap – the Michelins were lasting about three – with the result that there were, at best, just two chances of achieving a quick lap. At least, that's how it was for most of them. However, Alboreto had opted for a hard left rear tyre on his Ferrari when making his selection of tyres which, in turn, led to him being able to cover more laps and thereby increase his chances of finding a gap in the traffic. And it worked a treat for not only did the Italian go on to post the fastest time among the Goodyear-shod brigade but he also wound up on the provisional pole with a time of 1 min 23.581 sec. As if to highlight just what a difference it made, Mansell, who had turned in the morning's fastest time, was well over a second slower after going through his two

sets of tyres that much quicker and being held up by slower cars on both occasions. In fact, the Englishman was now only eighth fastest as his best time of 1 min 24.927 sec was also beaten by six other drivers. These were Warwick, who recovered remarkably well from a morning spoiled by terminal understeer (this had apparently been eradicated by a change of suspension settings between sessions) and a broken third gear whilst out on his first set of tyres to clock second fastest time of 1 min 23.726 sec after the Renault's gearbox had been stripped down and repaired, Prost (1 min 23.944 sec), Piquet (1 min 24.139 sec – despite complaining of poor engine pick-up out of the many slow turns), Lauda (1 min 24.508 sec), Arnoux (1 min 24.661 sec) and Tambay (1 min 24.828 sec). At the end of the afternoon some of the other drivers were also lower down the order than anticipated, among them de Angelis (only ninth fastest at 1 min 25.602 sec) and also Rosberg, who was another two places away behind the Ligier of de Cesaris after his efforts had been further hampered by an acute lack of grip. Without doubt, though, the two most unfortunate drivers were Corrado Fabi and Manfred Winkelhock, who finished up in the last two places on the time-sheets. The young Italian's problem had been an engine that persisted in misfiring until cutting out completely and stranding him out on the circuit, while the German ATS driver had first been forced to abandon his D7 with a broken turbo-charger and then, after reverting to the spare D6, had crashed heavily at Casino Square due, apparently, to the car grounding on its skid-plates and causing him to lose control of it. Whatever, the impact with the guard-rail had demolished the rear end of the car, littering the track with debris moments before Warwick had arrived on the scene (he had only just about made it through unscathed!) and, Winkelhock had emerged from the wreckage with a suspected torn muscle in his shoulder.

Following the established time-table in Monaco, Friday was given over to participants of the various supporting events scheduled to take place over the weekend, including the prestigious Formula 3 race, so it was not until Saturday that attention became fixed on preparations for the Grand Prix once more. Since his accident on Thursday afternoon Winkelhock had received treatment from Willi Dungl and, contrary to expectations, was now ready to start all over again. Elsewhere, too, everything was according to plan and before long the second untimed session was in full swing with drivers busily preparing themselves and their cars for the all-important final hour of qualifying. Once more the most common complaint was the traffic but, in spite of this, they all just about managed to keep out of one another's way except Mansell and Arnoux, who had a

slight coming-together, fortunately with no serious consequences. Later Mansell also glanced the barriers at the harbour chicane with his two nearside wheels, but again with little damage ensuing, although when Baldi had a similar moment in the vicinity of the swimming pool the Italian was not so fortunate as the impact with the guard-rail tore away a rear wishbone mounting from the gearbox bellhousing/oil tank of his Spirit. This, in turn, led to an oil leak and to Winkelhock half-spinning on some of the oil in front of the pits. In the meantime, Fabi spent nearly half the session in the pits waiting around for a broken carbon-fibre air-box to be replaced on his Brabham and a turbo-charger failure resulted in Prost having to switch to the spare McLaren, otherwise most drivers had a relatively trouble-free outing.

For the vital afternoon session the Goodyear runners followed the lead set by Alboreto on Thursday by opting for a hard left rear tyre when selecting their two sets of qualifying rubber. However, so far as Mansell was concerned it proved to be a virtual waste of time, as within a few minutes of leaving the pits he was forced to abandon the spare Lotus 95T that he was driving by the entrance to the tunnel with a dead engine – and on it was the hard left rear tyre! Consequently, he had to walk in and prepare to take over his proposed race chassis (this had earlier been specifically put to one side for the race) knowing full well that with just four soft tyres remaining he almost certainly had just one lap in which to register any further improvement. Much the same also applied to Alboreto when a slight mistake on the entry to Ste. Devote led to the Italian having to abandon his Ferrari with bent front suspension after glancing the barriers there. Unlike Mansell, though, Alboreto did at least have the consolation of returning to the pits in the knowledge that he had just recorded a new fastest time of 1 min 22.937 sec. Even so, it didn't last long as shortly afterwards Prost, still using the spare McLaren and finding that all-important gap in the traffic, stopped the clocks at an even quicker 1 min 22.661 sec. Furthermore, when Alboreto eventually took to the track in his spare Ferrari he was unable to respond due to being baulked by slower cars. As a result pole position slipped from his grasp, and not only that but Mansell, who recovered brilliantly from his early problem with a scintillating display of on-the-limit driving, and team-mate Arnoux added to the Italian's obvious disappointment by elbowing him back to fourth place on the grid with times of 1 min 22.752 sec and 1 min 22.935 sec (a mere 0.002 sec quicker!) respectively. After that everybody else was on the wrong side of the 1 min 23 sec barrier with Warwick next along at 1 min 23.237 sec, a time achieved near the end of what had been an eventful afternoon for the

1984

Englishman as he had spun at La Rascasse and brushed the guard-rail twice in the vicinity of the swimming pool. Then came Tambay with the other Renault, de Cesaris, who had survived a brief argument with Patrese over the same piece of road at one point, Lauda, Piquet (still unhappy with the response from his BMW engine) and, finally, Rosberg to round off the front half of the grid, the Finn having done well even to have made it. First he had suffered a spectacular turbo-charger failure whilst out in his proposed race car and then, almost immediately after taking over the spare Williams, the Honda engine in that had cut out. Among the rest, meanwhile, de Angelis had also been obliged to switch chassis due to a turbo-charger failure (fortunately the Lotus team had brought along four cars) on his way to qualifying in a relatively poor eleventh place on the grid; Winkelhock had done extremely well to hoist himself from the bottom of the time-sheets on Thursday to an eventual twelfth spot, especially as he was still far from 100% fit; Senna, after having made only a brief appearance in the spare Toleman with the new electronic engine management system on Thursday, had moved up to 13th; and Fabi, following a trouble-free outing at long last, had finally got himself into the race. So, too, had Cecotto (he had ended the first day in 21st place), but less successful were Baldi, the RAM duo, Palmer and Alliot, and a particularly unhappy Cheever, whose hopes had been dashed by a distinct lack of power from his V8 Alfa Romeo engine throughout both days. They, in turn, were joined as non-qualifiers by three other drivers to have all been bumped off the grid since Thursday. These were Surer, who had only just missed out in the final reckoning, team-mate Boutsen, whose progress during the afternoon

had been hampered by engine problems with both of the BMW-powered Arrows A7s, and Brundle, whose gallant efforts had been abruptly terminated by a huge accident at Tabac in which his Tyrrell had charged the barriers (almost head-on) and gone skating along the track on its side minus the two right-hand wheels. In fact the young Englishman, who had arrived at the left-hander too quickly, was extremely fortunate to have walked away from the scene suffering from nothing worse than mild concussion and minor cuts and bruises. It was also a tribute to the Tyrrell team (and Courtaulds) that their carbon-fibre/aluminium honeycomb monocoque had withstood the impact as well as it did.

Throughout practice Monte Carlo had just about been at its best weather-wise, but on race day completely the opposite was true. The nearby mountain tops were totally enshrouded by mist, the skies were grey and the rain was absolutely bucketing down. Needless to say this made the track conditions atrocious and of particular concern to the drivers during the half-hour warm-up session (in which Alboreto slightly damaged the back of his Ferrari after being just one of several drivers to spin) was the tunnel section. By all accounts it was just like a skid pad owing to water thrown off the cars mixing with the accumulation of oil and rubber. Indeed, this ultimately led to the start of the race being delayed as with conditions showing no sign of any improvement representations were eventually made to the organizers to douse the tunnel section so as to make it as wet as the rest of the track and to try to wash away the grease. As a result a water-tanker was called in and it was not until almost 3.45 p.m. that the 20 starters were finally unleashed.

At the green Prost and Mansell more or

less took off in unison, once their rear wheels had gained some traction on the soaking wet surface, and were safely away in first and second places. But behind them the worst fears were confirmed when Warwick, following an excellent start and already nosing ahead of Arnoux's Ferrari, was suddenly punted into the tyre barrier at Ste. Devote by the Frenchman due, apparently, to his right front wheel sliding off the bevelled kerbing. That, not surprisingly, then triggered off a chain reaction. Tambay, next along after having surged past Alboreto's Ferrari on the outside and with nowhere else to go, slid straight into the side of his team-mate's car, de Angelis and Patrese had to stand on their brakes and subsequently pulled up behind the two stationary Renaults with just inches to spare and Hesnault made contact with the back of his team-mate's Ligier as they funnelled for the gap on the right-hand side of the track. Somehow, though, the rest made it through unscathed and eventually they were joined by de Angelis and Patrese. The pair of Renaults, on the other hand, were out on the spot with a surprising amount of damage given the comparatively low impact speeds. On Warwick's car the front end of the carbon-fibre monocoque had been torn away: on Tambay's car the left front suspension was smashed and, furthermore, a suspension arm had pushed its way into the footwell, breaking the fibula in the Frenchman's left leg. Warwick had hurt his left leg as well but whereas he was able to hobble away on his own, Tambay had to be lifted out of his car and carried off for obviously needed medical treatment. The accident, of course, also meant that the field was already down to 18 cars, but barely 2 minutes later it had been depleted still further by de Cesaris driving straight into the pits to retire his damaged Ligier and by Cecotto stopping at Ste. Devote, damp electrics having caused the Hart engine in his Toleman to cut out. Up front, meanwhile, Prost and Mansell were out on their own with the English Lotus driver hanging on to the McLaren really well, especially when taking into account that he was almost being blinded by the spray. Then, after a gap of some 3 seconds, Arnoux was in third place and Alboreto was fourth before another large gap to Lauda, Rosberg, Winkelhock, Laffite and Senna. Next came Fabi with Bellof (already up to 11th!) in his wheel-tracks followed by the others, including Piquet, who had got off to a very slow start, and Hesnault, who was carrying on without a nose cone.

Enjoying the enormous advantage of a clear track in front of him, and driving in his usual smooth style, Prost went on to dominate the early stages of the race yet, at the same time, Mansell seemed able to match him move for move, never being more than a second or so away. Meanwhile, Lauda (fastest in the late morning warm-up session)

The remains of Martin Brundle's Tyrrell after the spectacular accident during Saturday afternoon's qualifying session. *(Autosport)*

quickly homed in on the two Ferraris before overtaking Alboreto on the inside approaching the old Station Hairpin on the fourth lap and Arnoux in another audacious manoeuvre on the rise to the Casino a couple of laps later, to move up into third place. Two other drivers making exceptionally good progress were new boys Senna and Bellof. In fact, it was hard to believe that this was their first Monaco Grand Prix, especially given the appalling conditions. But here they were driving like seasoned veterans and putting on a wonderful display of car control which, by the end of the ninth lap, had carried them up to sixth and eighth places respectively. Admittedly they had just been helped on their way by Alboreto spinning and stalling his engine at Ste. Devote, even so it was still mighty impressive and there was obviously more to come, for Senna was now giving chase to Rosberg's misfiring Williams, while Bellof was rapidly gaining on Winkelhock's ATS. At this point attention was also becoming focused more and more on Mansell as he had closed right up to Prost's McLaren and was beginning to look a real threat to the race-leader. As if to add spice to the situation Prost now found himself with the additional task of having to lap Alboreto's Ferrari, which had been push-started back into the fray just before he had arrived at Ste. Devote on the tenth lap. However, whilst the Ferrari driver may, unwittingly, have helped Mansell's cause before being lapped, the real crunch came just beyond Portier on lap 11 when Prost clipped a marshal in the throes of helping to push Fabi's Brabham to safety, the young Italian having just spun through 180-degrees and stalled his already misfiring engine. Thankfully, the marshal was more shocked than injured, but the momentary confusion gave Mansell just the opportunity he needed to emerge from the tunnel leading a Grand Prix for the first time in his career. To the obvious delight of the British spectators dotted around the bedraggled crowd, the Englishman then quickly drew away with Prost in no position to do much about it as even before losing the lead he had started to experience a slight problem with uneven brakes. The unfortunate thing about it was that Mansell possibly drove on harder than really necessary. Whatever, on lap 16, as he was about to crest the hill leading into Casino Square, he made the mistake of putting a rear wheel on to the white carriageway markings. In the dry it wouldn't have mattered one iota, but in the wet it was just like hitting a sheet of ice and in the next instant the back of the Lotus had walloped the guard-rail, even though Mansell did his utmost to correct the slide. Not surprisingly, the impact damaged the right rear suspension but, in spite of this and the rear aerofoil being badly twisted, Mansell seemed determined to carry on and it was not until

spinning round at the Mirabeau – moments after Prost had slipped through on the inside to re-take the lead – that he finally called it a day, his moment of glory over. While this was happening there was also drama at La Rascasse due to Piquet, after doing little more than driving round near the back of the field, allowing his Brabham to get away from him and stalling the engine. As a result he, too, was now out of the race, as was Hesnault, who had retired under similar circumstances a few minutes earlier.

With Mansell out, the McLarens were left in first and second places almost exactly half a minute apart and ordinarily would probably have walked away with the race. However, by now the remarkable Senna had not only dealt with Rosberg and Arnoux (his Ferrari was another car to have developed an audible misfire) but had also moved up to within striking distance of Lauda – and this was in spite of an anxious moment back on the 11th lap in which he had gone kerb-hopping at the harbour chicane and put a slight kink in the Toleman's right front suspension! Furthermore, he was not about to show the former double World Champion any mercy as he emphatically demonstrated at the end of lap 18 by pulling out from behind him as they exited La Rascasse, notwithstanding the thick blanket of spray, and bravely charging through on the outside on the approach to Ste. Devote. Bellof, too, was still on the up and up: he had been pressing Winkelhock so hard in the diabolical conditions, which were obviously negating any power advantage, that his compatriot had eventually waved him past. Since then he had also latched on to Rosberg's Williams and on lap 21 came another moment to savour when the young German closed right up to the Finn through the tunnel section and nailed him on the entry to the harbour chicane to take over a superb fifth place.

Thereafter Bellof immediately gave chase to Arnoux's spluttering Ferrari, but before anything came of that there was a real surprise in store when, on lap 24, the usually so-precise Lauda, himself coming under increasing pressure from Arnoux, suddenly ended his race by spinning through a full 360-degrees at Casino Square and stalling his engine. Immediately prior to this he had been experiencing similar problems with his brakes to those of his team-mate, but whilst a locking rear brake had almost certainly contributed to the incident a somewhat modest Lauda subsequently put it down to nothing more than 'driver error'. Either way he was now a spectator and so, too, was Winkelhock, who had just slid off into the barriers at the harbour chicane after trying unsuccessfully to emulate Bellof in overtaking Rosberg's Williams.

Instead of the weather improving, the rain now came on harder than ever, yet nothing seemed to stem the progress of Senna, who was eating into Prost's advantage at the quite phenomenal rate of three or four seconds per lap. It was just the same with Bellof for he was lapping every bit as fast and even quicker once he had disposed of Arnoux by diving down on the inside of the Frenchman's Ferrari at the Mirabeau on lap 27. At the same time, however, Jacky Ickx, in his capacity as Clerk of the Course, was fast coming to the conclusion that the worsening conditions were making it too dangerous to allow the race to continue. Moreover, rather than discuss the matter with the FISA officials present, the Belgian eventually decided that enough was enough and acted on instinct just after Prost, pointing to the front of his car (not, as some people thought, to have the race stopped but to indicate to the McLaren pit that his front brakes were vibrating badly), had gone through to complete his 31st lap. Consequently, as he came

Ayrton Senna rushes through the tunnel on his way to a superb second place in a rain-shortened Monaco Grand Prix. *(Autosport)*

round to complete the next lap, and with his lead having shrunk dramatically to little more than 3 seconds, Prost was greeted by black flags and by a red flag accompanied by a chequered flag at the start/finish line. He then correctly pulled up on the line in accordance with the rules, knowing full well that in the unlikely event of a re-start he had won the race. Senna, on the other hand, kept his right foot hard down on the Toleman's accelerator, actually overtook Prost as he drew to a halt and was convinced that he, himself, was the race winner, even to the point of waving to the crowd on his slowing-down lap. Only afterwards was he told the bad news that the rules demanded that the results would be based on the positions after 31 laps, at which point his jubilation turned to fury. As if to add insult to injury, the Brazilian also learned that he would not even be scoring six points, let alone nine, as again the rules dictated that where a race was stopped before 75% of the full race distance had been covered only half points could be awarded. In the meantime, Bellof had finished in a magnificent third place – his heroic

drive was to go even less rewarded due to the Tyrrell affair that was soon to rear its ugly head – and Arnoux had soldiered on in fourth place with his badly misfiring Ferrari to wind up ahead of the only other finishers, Rosberg, de Angelis, Alboreto, Ghinzani and, finally, Laffite, who had been delayed by an early pit stop for fresh tyres following a suspected puncture.

The decision taken by Ickx in having the race stopped, together with the lack of any attempts by the organizers even to consider a re-start as required under the rules where less than 75% of the full race distance is covered, led to much discussion, both immediately afterwards and for several weeks to follow. That was not all either as Jean-Marie Balestre subsequently publicly criticized the Automobile Club de Monaco and, in particular, Ickx for stopping the race – to which the Belgian responded by suggesting that he would be considering legal action against the FISA president for his comments and others made concerning, mainly, his appointment as Race Director – and two official complaints were submitted to FISA. One was

lodged by the International Stewards of the Meeting to the effect that the red flag and the chequered flag should not have been shown concurrently and that faults were committed by the Clerk of the Course and the organizers during the race and scrutineering; the other was lodged by the President of the Brazilian Automobile Confederation to the effect that the race had been stopped without justification on the grounds that the weather conditions were the same as when the race started and that the purpose was to ensure that a Frenchman (Prost) won the race before being overtaken by a Brazilian (Senna). This, in turn, led to the matter being referred to the FISA Executive Committee, and at a meeting held at Paris in mid-July Jacky Ickx was fined $6,000 and had his FISA Clerk of the Course Super Licence suspended for failing to consult the Stewards of the Meeting and not respecting Articles 141 and 142 of the Sporting Code, Article 1 of the F1 World Championship General Prescriptions and Article 19 of the F1 Standard Regulations.

Results			
1	A. Prost	1 hr 01 min	
	(McLaren-TAG)	07.740 sec	
		(100.775 kph/	
		62.619 mph)	
2	A. Senna	1 hr 01 min	
	(Toleman-Hart)	15.186 sec	
*	S. Bellof	1 hr 01 min	
	(Tyrrell-Ford)	28.881 sec	
3	R. Arnoux	1 hr 01 min	
	(Ferrari)	36.817 sec	
4	K. Rosberg	1 hr 01 min	
	(Williams-Honda)	42.986 sec	

5	E. de Angelis	1 hr 01 min
	(Lotus-Renault)	52.179 sec
6	M. Alboreto	1 lap behind
	(Ferrari)	
7	P. Ghinzani	1 lap behind
	(Osella-Alfa Romeo)	
8	J. Laffite	1 lap behind
	(Williams-Honda)	

* Excluded

Fastest lap: A. Senna (Toleman-Hart) on lap 24 in 1 min 54.334 sec (104.283 kph/64.798 mph)

Retirements

D. Warwick (Renault) accident on lap 1. P. Tambay (Renault) accident on lap 1, A. de Cesaris (Ligier-Renault) accident damage on lap 1, J. Cecotto (Toleman-Hart) electrics on lap 2, C. Fabi (Brabham-BMW) spun and stalled on lap 10, F. Hesnault (Ligier-Renault) spun and stalled on lap 13, N. Piquet (Brabham-BMW) spun and stalled on lap 15, N. Mansell (Lotus-Renault) accident on lap 16, M. Winkelhock (ATS-BMW) accident on lap 23, N. Lauda (McLaren-TAG) spun and stalled on lap 24, R. Patrese (Alfa Romeo) electrics on lap 25.

XXIIIrd Canadian Grand Prix

Montreal: June 17
Weather: Hot
Distance: 70 laps of 4.410 km circuit = 308.70 km (191.82 miles)

As if to underline yet again the hurly-burly of the Grand Prix world, in little more than a week the teams had returned to base from Monaco, several had taken part in two days of pre-race testing at Brands Hatch for the forthcoming British Grand Prix, cars and equipment had been crated up for air-freighting and they had all made their way across the Atlantic. Furthermore, they were now about to embark on a gruelling tour of North America that was to encompass three races spread over just four weekends! The first of these was the Labatt-sponsored Canadian Grand Prix which, once again, was taking place at the 4.41 kilometre Circuit Gilles Villeneuve on the man-made Ile Notre Dame in the St. Lawrence Seaway. For Renault, more so than most, preparations for this next round on the Championship trail

had been very much a case of blood, sweat and toil, as following the disastrous first corner incident at Monaco they had been left with just one RE50 intact. Consequently, a complete reorganization had been needed, and to overcome their difficulties they had had to rebuild the chassis damaged by Warwick at Dijon as well as complete work on a brand new chassis, RE50/7, for Tambay, both, rather significantly, incorporating stronger front bulkheads. Tyrrell, too, had been obliged to take stock of their situation following Brundle's spectacular practice shunt at the Principality. In this instance the original 012 had been refurbished to act as a spare car and Brundle, still being sponsored by Yardley Gold and still feeling a bit bruised and battered, had been entered in what had previously been the spare 012.

There was also a slight rearrangement of cars at Ferrari as another new 126C4 had been built and assigned to Alboreto, while Arnoux was down to drive what had been the new car for the Italian at Monaco. Otherwise, though, it was mainly a case of the same drivers in the same cars, except that Mauro Baldi and Jonathan Palmer were both absent due to participating in the Le Mans 24-hour race. In their places were Dutchman Huub Rothengatter, a complete newcomer to Formula 1, and New Zealander Mike Thackwell, who had made history at this particular circuit four years earlier by being the youngest man ever to take part in a Grand Prix.

After the rain-soaked Monaco Grand Prix it was a welcome relief to see clear blue skies once more at the start of practice on Friday morning and this, together with the obvious lack of any pre-race testing at the circuit, meant that there was soon a lot of activity. For Tambay it was a moment of reckoning because, in spite of having received physio-

N. Piquet
Brabham-BMW
(1 min 25.442 sec)

A. Prost
McLaren-TAG
(1 min 26.198 sec)

E. de Angelis
Lotus-Renault
(1 min 26.306 sec)

D. Warwick
Renault
(1 min 26.420 sec)

R. Arnoux
Ferrari
(1 min 26.549 sec)

M. Alboreto
Ferrari
(1 min 26.764 sec)

N. Mansell
Lotus-Renault
(1 min 27.246 sec)

N. Lauda
McLaren-TAG
(1 min 27.392 sec)

A. Senna
Toleman-Hart
(1 min 27.448 sec)

A. de Cesaris
Ligier-Renault
(1 min 27.922 sec)

E. Cheever
Alfa Romeo
(1 min 28.032 sec)

M. Winkelhock
ATS-BMW
(1 min 28.909 sec)

F. Hesnault
Ligier-Renault
(1 min 29.187 sec)

R. Patrese
Alfa Romeo
(1 min 29.205 sec)

K. Rosberg
Williams-Honda
(1 min 29.284 sec)

C. Fabi
Brabham-BMW
(1 min 29.764 sec)

J. Laffite
Williams-Honda
(1 min 29.915 sec)

T. Boutsen
Arrows-BMW
(1 min 30.073 sec)

P. Ghinzani
Osella-Alfa Romeo
(1 min 30.918 sec)

J. Cecotto
Toleman-Hart
(1 min 31.459 sec)

M. Brundle
Tyrrell-Ford
(1 min 31.785 sec)

S. Bellof
Tyrrell-Ford
(1 min 31.797 sec)

M. Surer
Arrows-Ford
(1 min 32.756 sec)

H. Rothengatter
Spirit-Hart
(1 min 32.920 sec)

M. Thackwell
RAM-Hart
(1 min 33.750 sec)

P. Alliot
RAM-Hart
(1 min 35.286 sec)

Withdrawn:
P. Tambay (Renault) No time.

therapy every day since breaking the fibula in his left leg, there were considerable doubts about whether or not he would be able to take part in the race. Unfortunately, these quickly turned to reality. Just three or four laps were enough to convince him that working the clutch pedal, combined with having to contend with the inevitable cockpit vibrations, were simply more than he could withstand, so he reluctantly resigned himself to becoming a spectator for the weekend. His team-mate, meanwhile, was soon in trouble for rather different reasons, barely 5 minutes going by before Warwick was coasting into the pits with a broken engine. That, though, proved to be just the beginning of a thoroughly frustrating morning for the Englishman as, incredibly, he went on to suffer similar failures with both the spare Renault,

when its oil pump broke, and with Tambay's car, when a water pipe became detached, thereby losing most of the opportunity of being able to learn anything. Indeed, what with this, and the now confirmed fact that Tambay would not be racing, the Renault pit was the scene of growing gloom and despondency. Nevertheless, whilst there was no denying that the French equipe was having the worst of it there were also early problems cropping up in other quarters. Among them were Winkelhock being made redundant due to a transmission failure stranding his ATS D7 out on the circuit after less than a handful of laps (the German team no longer had a spare car as a result of their driver's practice accident at Monaco); Arnoux having to walk in and take over his spare Ferrari after a fuel pump failure had led to his proposed race chassis rolling to a halt; and both Senna and Cecotto being forced to abandon their Tolemans with engine problems caused by what was later believed to have been a duff batch of valve gear components. Even Mansell, who ultimately recorded the fastest unofficial time in his familiar black and gold Lotus 95T, didn't exactly get off scot-free as his run ended with a broken gearbox pinion. At the time it didn't appear to be of any particular significance but, apart from keeping the Lotus mechanics busy changing the gearbox, the engine later proved reluctant to start and led to Mansell being unable to take part in the afternoon's opening hour of qualifying until there was little more than 20 minutes of it remaining. Ordinarily that probably wouldn't have mattered too much, but when Mansell did eventually return to the track it coincided with de Cesaris suffering a major engine failure in his Ligier and liberally coating the circuit with oil. Consequently, there was no realistic hope of Mansell reinstating himself as the man to beat, and in the end he did extremely well even to set what was to be fifth fastest time of 1 min 28.277 sec to finish up immediately ahead of Lauda (1 min 28.548 sec) and Alboreto (1 min 28.604 sec), especially as his engine blew up during his second run. Instead, it was now Prost who had taken up the role of pace-setter or, at least, once he had recovered from a spin at the hairpin leading round to the pits whilst out on his first set of qualifiers. It had been caused by too much masking tape on the brake ducts allowing the McLaren's carbon-fibre brakes to overheat but Prost, obviously none the worse for the incident, had then gone out on his second set of tyres and whistled around in 1 min 26.477 sec – a good 2 seconds inside Arnoux's pole-winning time for the 1983 race! Well over half a second slower at 1 min 27.139 sec, de Angelis had nonetheless set second fastest time after being at the top of the time-sheets during the early part of the afternoon (the oil from de Cesaris's Ligier had killed off any chance of responding to

Prost), while Piquet (1 min 27.154 sec – before a drive-shaft snapped on his Brabham 'qualifying special') and Arnoux (1 min 27.917 sec) were the others to have beaten Mansell. In the meantime, Warwick and Winkelhock had never really recovered from the time lost in the morning and were left way down the order in only 13th and 19th places respectively, both drivers (Warwick back in his proposed race car with a fresh engine) complaining of diabolical handling. Not that this was any surprise in Winkelhock's case, in particular, owing to Gunther Schmidt's refusal to change the settings of his car from those used in the Monaco Grand Prix – and that, of course, had taken place in the wet! The German's efforts had also not been helped by becoming stranded out on the circuit again, this time with a blown-up engine.

On Saturday the weather was warmer than the first day, but it was still very pleasant and certainly not hot enough to have any adverse effect on lap times. During the morning untimed session Winkelhock, who had finally persuaded Gunther Schmidt that the settings needed altering on his ATS, ran into clutch trouble and continued his habit of returning to the pits on foot, and Patrese didn't exactly improve his chances by indulging in an off-course excursion at the chicane, the ensuing damage being sufficient to bring out the spare Alfa Romeo for the rest of the day. Senna was another obliged to take over his team's spare car (this was now running with mechanical fuel-injection once more after being tried with Brian Hart's newly-developed electronic engine management system on the previous day) when his Toleman stopped just beyond the pit lane exit with a dead engine, while team-mate Cecotto's progress was hampered by fluctuating fuel pressure. So far as the others were concerned, however, the business of chassis tuning and trying out different tyres went on largely unimpeded, except that Mansell had to bow out early when the replacement engine in his Lotus 95T suddenly let go towards the end of the morning. Unfortunately for him, that then led to similar repercussions to those of the previous afternoon. First of all he had to sit out the first half of final qualifying until his mechanics had completed work on installing another fresh Renault V6 engine. Then, lo and behold, just as he was about to set off the track became coated in oil all over again. On this occasion the culprit was Prost or, at least, the TAG-Porsche engine in his McLaren, which had blown up in a big way just after the Frenchman had done a lap in 1 min 26.198 sec. Moreover, such had been the rate of progress made by some of the other drivers beforehand that even a subsequent improvement of more than a second on his Friday time, to 1 min 27.246 sec, was not enough to enable Mansell to defend his grid position. Instead, after losing yet another engine whilst out on his second set of qualifiers, he had to settle for an eventual seventh spot. By contrast, the oil was of no concern at all to Piquet as he had already staked a claim to pole position with a stunning performance on his first flying lap of the afternoon. This had produced a new fastest time of 1 min 25.442 sec (185.810 kph) and whilst the reigning World Champion felt that he could have gone even quicker had he warmed up his second set of tyres properly it was of no consequence. The oil from Prost's McLaren made sure of that for it affected everyone and, indeed, turned the final battle for grid positions into something of a lottery as Lauda, for one, had found out to his cost. By running on race rubber during the early part of the afternoon and not using his single set of qualifiers until it was effectively too late, the Austrian (concentrating on the spare McLaren this time out) had been unable to progress beyond 1 min 27.392 sec, a time good enough for only eighth place on the grid. Even Prost, himself, had been hampered by the oil for when he had gone out later in Lauda's proposed race car the Frenchman had failed to make any further impression. Nevertheless, he at least had the consolation of still being on the front row of the grid by reason of his earlier time as the best anyone else had managed was 1 min 26.306 sec, which had been recorded by de Angelis. Meanwhile Warwick, after finding a change of settings had eliminated most of the handling problems experienced throughout Friday, had moved up from 13th position to fourth on the grid with a vastly improved time of 1 min 26.420 sec and also well placed were Arnoux (1 min 26.549 sec) and Alboreto (1 min 26.764 sec), fifth and sixth respectively. However, whereas the Ferrari duo had enjoyed a relatively trouble-free practice, apart from Alboreto becoming involved in a heated argument with a journalist on the previous day over some article that had appeared in an Italian magazine (this had ended with Alboreto being punched in the face!), Warwick's problems had continued with the engine in the new Renault suffering from pre-ignition – just after he had completed his quick lap – and his own car subsequently stopping with a broken turbo-charger unit.

As for the rest, headed by Senna who had qualified the spare Toleman in a well-earned ninth spot, the biggest disappointment was to find Rosberg languishing in the lower half of the grid, actually in only 15th place. But like his team-mate, who was a further two places away behind Fabi's Brabham, the Finn had been finding his Williams FW09 a real handful with the familiar complaint of understeer compounded by a tendency for the chassis to bottom out through the right-hander immediately beyond the pits. Rosberg had also been caught out in similar fashion to Lauda

inasmuch as he had been on race rubber during the quickest part of the afternoon. Winkelhock, on the other hand, had finally had things go right for a change and had responded by clipping over 3 seconds off his previous best time to move up to a somewhat more respectable 12th on the grid. Here he was in amongst the two Ligiers of de Cesaris and Hesnault and also the two Euroracing Alfa Romeos of Cheever and a rather unhappy Patrese, who was one of just two drivers not to have made any improvement following turbo-charger problems in the spare 184T. The other was Alliot, who was left right at the back of the grid in his evil-handling RAM directly behind his new, temporary, team-mate, Thackwell, and new-boy Rothengatter, whose first experience at the wheel of a Formula 1 car had been punctuated by gearbox trouble on both days.

Race day produced more superb weather, but there was little opportunity for the Lotus mechanics, in particular, to enjoy the bright sunshine as during the half-hour warm-up session both of their drivers pulled up with engine failures following more pre-ignition problems. And, because of the mandatory interval of 3½ hours required between the end of free practice and the start of the race (1 p.m.), this was all before 9.30 a.m.! Over at Renault, meanwhile, Warwick was also unhappy with the V6 engine in his RE50, complaining that it was down on power, and in the Ferrari pit Arnoux, after pipping team-mate Alboreto for fastest time, completed his run by commenting that he had gradually been losing turbo boost pressure. Nevertheless, by 1 p.m. everything had more or less been put right again, except that de Angelis was having to pin his hopes on the spare Lotus 95T (lack of time precluded more than one engine change), pre-race formalities had been completed and all 26 starters were away on the final warm-up lap, led by Piquet's Brabham.

The start turned out to be the tidiest seen all season to date with everyone getting away really well, none better than Prost who drew alongside Piquet's Brabham, nosed ahead and then snatched the lead on the way into the first right-hander. At that point there was every suggestion that a repeat of Imola was in store but, after leading down to the hairpin at the far side of the circuit, Prost quickly realized that he was in trouble. The TAG-Porsche engine in his McLaren just wouldn't pick up properly with the result that he more or less had to sit there and watch Piquet go surging past him as they accelerated away from the tight turn. Directly behind them, de Angelis had slotted into an initial third place, but that didn't last very long either. At the last hairpin leading round to the pits he was outbraked by Alboreto, and then Arnoux also rushed on ahead of him, so at the end of the opening lap it was Brabham-McLaren-Ferrari-Ferrari-Lotus. Warwick had the lone

Renault in sixth place and then it was Mansell from Lauda, Senna, de Cesaris, Cheever, Winkelhock, Patrese, Rosberg and the rest right back to the two RAM-Hart cars of Alliot and Thackwell, which were bringing up the rear.

Keen to conserve his tyres and brakes, and being only too aware that the fuel limitations were a bit marginal for this rather tight, acrobatic circuit, Piquet drove just hard enough to maintain the lead over the next dozen or so laps without attempting to build up any significant advantage. Consequently Prost, in spite of his problem, was able to contain the Brabham and, at times, even closed up fractionally, especially when he had to respond to mounting pressure from the two, very competitive-looking Ferraris. De Angelis, on the other hand, was soon losing all contact with the leading quartet and before the end of the fifth lap was having to give best to none other than Lauda, who had already seen off Mansell on the second lap and Warwick two laps later. Thereafter the Italian Lotus driver, being forced to contend with an engine reluctant to deliver full power, was kept busy trying to fend off Warwick's Renault, but Lauda was soon in free air and setting about closing the gap to the leaders. It was a path that was to be considerably eased by both Ferrari drivers unexpectedly running into problems. First of all, on the 11th lap, Alboreto suddenly pulled off to the side of the track with a dead engine caused by a broken fuel pump drive and then, after just over three more laps, Arnoux obligingly turned off into the pits screaming for fresh tyres. Quite obviously an earlier choice of soft, 'C' compound Goodyears all round had not proved equal to the punishment dished out by the Frenchman in his efforts to catch Prost's McLaren. Meanwhile, Lauda went through into third place, Warwick moved up into fourth after having finally outwitted de Angelis a couple of laps earlier – he had drawn alongside the Lotus across the start/finish line and then driven round the outside of it through the first right-hander, notwithstanding the fact that his Renault wasn't handling too well – and Senna, who had followed Lauda past Mansell back on the second lap, took over sixth spot just as Arnoux was leaving the pits. By now, various changes had also taken place lower down the order. Hesnault had ended his eighth lap by crawling into the pits with his Ligier suffering from an acute loss of turbo boost pressure and only minutes later Ghinzani's Osella had rolled to a halt with a broken drive-shaft. However, this was only part of the story as there were some really good scraps going on throughout almost the entire field with one of the best involving no less than five drivers – de Cesaris, Cheever, Winkelhock, Bellof and Laffite. Even so it was Rosberg, currently in the throes of setting about Mansell's eighth-placed Lotus, who was giving the many thousands of spectators the best value for their money for he was hurling his unwieldy Williams around the track as if there was no tomorrow and conducting a series of the most desperate-looking overtaking manoeuvres imaginable. Yet, at the same time, it was nothing short of brilliance, and completely belied the fact that he was driving on the hard 'A' compound Goodyear tyres.

From around the 20-lap mark Piquet ran into quite heavy traffic as he came up to lap more and more backmarkers. In the main, though, this worked to his advantage and for the first time in the race the gap between himself and Prost started to increase noticeably until, after 30 laps, it was as much as 5 seconds. However, once Prost had followed him past Patrese and Brundle, having a real set-to over 18th place, and also another great scrap going on between Fabi, Boutsen and Cecotto, the gap began to come down again and just to make things even more interesting Lauda was rapidly gaining on both of them. This was in spite of the fact that the Austrian was experiencing increasing difficulty in selecting fourth gear. Further back, Arnoux had also been making good progress since his early tyre stop, having quickly repassed Senna and, more recently, both de Angelis and Warwick by diving through on the inside of them at the second hairpin. On lap 39, however, the Frenchman very nearly ended his race by a moment's inattention whilst lapping Patrese's Alfa Romeo. As it was he survived the incident, which saw him virtually drive over the green and black car's left front wheel, but that certainly didn't apply to his unsuspecting victim – a furious Patrese skated off into the barriers with broken suspension! That actually brought the retirement tally up to seven as on lap 33 Rosberg, after having moved up two more places at the expense of Mansell and a tiring Senna, had seen his gallant efforts come to nought due to an apparent electrical failure, and immediately prior to this team-mate Laffite and young Thackwell had both gone out with broken turbo-chargers. Boutsen wasn't around for much longer either before the BMW engine in his Arrows blew up, neither was Fabi, when a turbo-charger failure produced worried-looking faces in the Brabham pit, nor de Cesaris, who had used up his brakes. In the meantime, the three leading cars were moving ever closer to one another, while just ahead of them on the road Mansell, having long since repassed Senna, was trying his utmost to find a way past de Angelis. Team-mates? Well, there certainly wasn't any obvious indication of it, apart from the similarity of their cars. Instead, it was turning out to be a real cut-and-thrust affair with the Italian using just about every trick in the book to stay ahead, even though it was patently clear that he was in the slower car. Eventually, on lap

42, Mansell had quite literally to force his way past at the first hairpin, by which time Piquet was preparing to lap the pair of them. Now this was really interesting for if Piquet was held up at all Prost, who was less than 2 seconds behind him, would close right up and so, too, would Lauda, the hard-charging Austrian having just moved in on his team-mate's tail. In the event Piquet flew past both of the black and gold cars within the space of a lap almost as if they weren't there and even began to extend his lead again. Lauda, meanwhile, waited only until lap 44 before neatly overtaking Prost – without encountering any of the problems that Mansell had just experienced from his team-mate – but then came near-disaster. As he was about to lap de Angelis on the following lap the Italian suddenly got a bit sideways on the approach to one of the right-handers leading down to the first hairpin, took to the grassy infield and regained the track at the exit from the corner just in time to almost collect the McLaren sideways on. Fortunately, Lauda had the situation weighed up. He flicked his car over to the outside of the track, momentarily put all four of his wheels into the dirt as a last resort to avoid being hit and controlled the inevitable slide beautifully to carry on in one piece. Nevertheless, apart from almost allowing Prost to snatch back second place, the loss of momentum cost Lauda at least a couple of seconds and enabled Piquet to complete the lap over 7 seconds clear, his lead, consequently, now even more secure.

After 50 laps Piquet was still the best part of 6 seconds ahead, stepping up the pace in response to pit signals advising him of Lauda's progress and looking to be very much in control of the situation. Prost, on the other hand, was now dropping away with an engine that besides not picking up properly out of the slower corners was becoming reluctant to pull at peak revs. Even so, there

was little danger of the Frenchman losing third place as apart from being almost a lap behind, Arnoux was running into trouble as well. His Ferrari was gradually losing turbo boost pressure owing to a cracked exhaust. In fact, he was now in the throes of being bundled out of fourth place by Warwick although, as it happened, this was to be of no consequence. Five laps later the Renault, proving to be more and more of a handful, was in the pits with what Warwick suspected was a slow puncture. There, all four wheels were changed, but when the Englishman charged back out into the fray he quickly discovered that the problem was as bad as ever and responded by immediately returning to the pits. On this occasion it was discovered that the Renault, which had been bouncing around rather a lot, especially as the fuel load lightened, had broken part of its aerodynamic undertray and, although Warwick was subsequently sent on his way again, one more lap was enough to convince him that the car had become undriveable. Just prior to this another spirited drive from Bellof had also come to an end due to his Tyrrell stopping out on the circuit with a broken drive-shaft, while Arnoux had been obliged to suffer the humiliation of watching Mansell, de Angelis and Cheever taking turns to elbow his ailing Ferrari down to seventh place. By now, though, Mansell had become yet another of the walking wounded – with gearbox trouble. He had already lost the use of second gear, now it was becoming increasingly difficult to select third. Consequently, his lap times, too, were growing longer and on lap 62 Mansell found himself in much the same situation as Arnoux when first de Angelis flew past him and then Cheever. At this point there seemed to be a good chance of the American finishing in fourth place going by the manner in which his Alfa Romeo was performing. But, with

Reliability at last as Nelson Piquet heads for his first victory (and Championship points) of the year. Here he leads the two Marlboro McLaren MP4/2s of Alain Prost and Niki Lauda, Ayrton Senna (Toleman) and Eddie Cheever (Euroracing Alfa Romeo) both having just been lapped. *(Autosport)*

just over six laps remaining, the V8 engine in the green and black car suddenly started spluttering and then cut out completely. Much to his vexation, Cheever had run out of fuel! All the while Piquet was driving on to a well-judged victory and never allowing Lauda to get near him, a situation that continued right up until the last couple of laps when he eased right off and yet still crossed the line 2.612 seconds to the good. Almost a lap behind at the finish, Prost, nonetheless, succeeded in holding on to a reasonably comfortable third place in his down-on-power McLaren and de Angelis brought his similarly-afflicted Lotus home in fourth spot, but Mansell was pipped to the

post on the very last lap by Arnoux – just before the Ferrari ran out of fuel! After that came a totally exhausted Senna followed by Winkelhock (he had driven most of the way without a clutch and, latterly, with no fifth gear), Cecotto, Brundle, Alliot and lastly, because Surer had gone out with a blown-up engine in the closing stages, Rothengatter. The Dutchman, however, was too far behind to be classified on his Grand Prix debut after a race spoiled by gearbox problems similar to those that he had experienced during practice.

For the Brabham team there was at last something to celebrate following a quite appalling run of unreliability that had now

apparently been stemmed by a combination of improved quality control of various components back at the BMW factory and Gordon Murray introducing an extra oil cooler into the nose section of the BT53s. This, after all, was not only Piquet's first win of the season but also his first actual race finish since South Africa, 1983. And there was even more to it than that. It had been a triumph of mind over matter for whilst the new oil cooler might well have played an important role as regards improved reliability it had sent so much heat through into the cockpit that the pedals had got hot enough to burn the sole of Piquet's right foot!

Results					
1	N. Piquet (Brabham-BMW)	1 hr 46 min 23.748 sec (174.085 kph/ 108.171 mph)	9	J. Cecotto (Toleman-Hart)	2 laps behind
2	N. Lauda (McLaren-TAG)	1 hr 46 min 26.360 sec	*	M. Brundle (Tyrrell-Ford)	2 laps behind
3	A. Prost (McLaren-TAG)	1 hr 47 min 51.780 sec	10	P. Alliot (RAM-Hart)	5 laps behind
4	E. de Angelis (Lotus-Renault)	1 lap behind	**11	E. Cheever (Alfa Romeo)	7 laps behind
5	R. Arnoux (Ferrari)	2 laps behind			
6	N. Mansell (Lotus-Renault)	2 laps behind			
7	A. Senna (Toleman-Hart)	2 laps behind			
8	M. Winkelhock (ATS-BMW)	2 laps behind			

Also running at finish: H. Rothengatter (Spirit-Hart) 14 laps behind

* Excluded

** Not running at finish

Fastest lap: N. Piquet (Brabham-BMW) on lap 55 in 1 min 28.763 sec (178.858 kph/ 111.137 mph)

Retirements
F. Hesnault (Ligier-Renault) turbo-charger on lap 8, M. Alboreto (Ferrari) fuel pump drive on lap 11, P. Ghinzani (Osella-Alfa Romeo) drive-shaft on lap 12, M. Thackwell (RAM-Hart) turbo-charger on lap 30, J. Laffite (Williams-Honda) turbo-charger on lap 32, K. Rosberg (Williams-Honda) electrics on lap 33, R. Patrese (Alfa Romeo) accident on lap 38, T. Boutsen (Arrows-BMW) engine on lap 39, C. Fabi (Brabham-BMW) turbo-charger on lap 40, A. de Cesaris (Ligier-Renault) brakes on lap 41, S. Bellof (Tyrrell-Ford) drive-shaft on lap 53, D. Warwick (Renault) loose undertray on lap 58, M. Surer (Arrows-Ford) engine on lap 60.

IIIrd United States (Detroit) Grand Prix

Detroit: June 24
Weather: Warm and sunny
Distance: 63 laps of 4.0233 km circuit = 253.47 km (157.50 miles)

The 500-odd mile trek from Montreal to Detroit, combined with the fact that there were just four clear days between packing up from one race and starting practice for the next, meant that the teams had a pretty hectic schedule and certainly little opportunity to work on their cars. Consequently, the entry for what was already the third event through the streets of the heartland of the United States automobile industry was just about identical to that of the Canadian Grand Prix. Indeed, the only obvious changes on the technical front, apart from the newer of the two BMW-powered Arrows A7s having had a 4″ spacer inserted between its engine and gearbox to provide a longer wheelbase, were to be found at Ferrari, where Arnoux and Alboreto's race cars had both been fitted with revised electronic Marelli/Weber fuel-injection systems; at Williams, where revised, FW08-type, front uprights had been brought into use as a further means of trying to sort the handling of the FW09s; and at Spirit, where the newer

of the 101Bs had been suitably modified around the rear by Gordon Coppuck so as to accommodate a Ford-Cosworth DFV engine. This was because of a shortage of Hart turbo-charged engines within the team. On the driver front, too, it was much the same story, the only differences here being brought about by Teo Fabi returning to drive the second Brabham owing to being free of any CART commitments over the weekend, and by Jonathan Palmer taking up his place at RAM once more following his trip to Le Mans. Interestingly enough, though, the Spirit was down to be driven by Huub Rothengatter for the second weekend running owing, apparently, to Mauro Baldi experiencing problems over sponsorship money. Whatever, this certainly didn't apply to the Dutchman as apart from enjoying the benefit of a contract with Marlboro he also had the financial backing of a group of businessmen from his native Holland.

Practice, and qualifying in particular, turned out to be a very disjointed affair

owing to numerous drivers making contact with the unforgiving walls, and the organizers' insistence in repeatedly hanging out the black flags so that damaged cars could be retrieved. In many instances the response from the organizers was understandable to a point because stranded cars effectively meant a partially blocked track. Yet, at the same time, it was felt that they frequently over-reacted and should simply have made arrangements for the offending cars to be pushed to safety, allowing practice to go uninterrupted, rather than continually assigning tow-trucks to take them back to the pits. Either way, there was no doubt that if the organizers had taken a leaf out of the book of their counterparts at Monaco, for example, by employing an adequate number of cranes to haul away stricken cars, it would have saved a lot of unnecessary irritation, besides preventing each day's programme from falling badly into arrears. The opening qualifying session on Friday afternoon highlighted this latter aspect only too well. First it was late in starting following interruptions in the morning caused by de Cesaris and Warwick both clobbering walls in separate incidents, the Renault, rather worryingly, winding up with a front suspension arm pushed into its footwell in like manner to that seen at Dijon and Monaco, which gave Warwick more leg bruises. Then, when qualifying did eventually get under way, it went on for well over twice as long as it should have done owing to yet more lengthy interruptions. On this occasion the main hold-ups were caused by Fabi making an unsuccessful attempt to overtake Surer's Arrows, which saw the Italian plough into the side of the Ford-Cosworth-powered car and shove his unsuspecting victim (on only his first qualifying lap!) into the wall, besides damaging the front suspension of his own car, and by Senna and Cecotto both losing control of their Tolemans at different times.

Meanwhile, even some of those drivers succeeding in keeping their cars in one piece were not exactly having an easy time as the track surface was not only dirty but bumpier than even the previous year following a hard winter. However, none of this seemed to be of the slightest concern to Mansell, in particular. Instead, apart from a minor incident in the morning, which had sent his Lotus hobbling into the pits with a broken right rear wheel, the Englishman was taking to the tight confines like the proverbial duck, and turning out to be consistently the fastest man out on the circuit. Furthermore, this was a pattern that continued right through until the field was finally flagged off for the day, by which time he had made the most of some new, flatter-profile, rear tyres produced by Goodyear and stopped the clocks at an unbeaten 1 min 45.130 sec. Only Lauda, driving in his usual smooth style, had provided any really serious opposition by lapping just over a tenth slower at 1 min 45.238 sec. But sadly, so far as the Austrian was concerned, it was an effort that counted for nothing. In post-practice scrutineering the rear aerofoil of his McLaren was found to exceed the maximum permitted width limit due to what his team believed had been caused by heat distortion of the bonding material used for the side-plates and, in consequence, Lauda had his lap times scrubbed – even though the infringement was little more than a millimetre! This, of course, also meant that everybody else moved up a place on the time-sheets and left Piquet in the runner-up spot with what had been third fastest time of 1 min 45.407 sec. After that the only other driver to have lapped even to within a second of Mansell was Prost at 1 min 45.717 sec. Nevertheless, one of the most pleasing aspects was to see Tambay having come out best of the rest after a quite remarkable performance that had given no indication at all that his left leg was still rather weak or, indeed, the fact that he had been hampered by a broken fourth gear. Moreover, the Frenchman was now convinced that he would be able to cope with the race and left Mario Andretti, who had been called in by Renault as a possible stand-in over the weekend, quite happy to spend the time spectating and helping his two sons prepare for their involvement in a couple of the supporting races. Meanwhile Warwick, now confined to the spare Renault following his accident in the morning, had not been able to make anywhere near the hoped-for impression after suffering two turbo-charger failures. In fact, his best time of 1 min 47.341 sec was almost a full second slower than that of his team-mate's and placed him only tenth in the revised standings behind Arnoux, de Cesaris (using the spare Ligier for similar reasons), Senna, Winkelhock and de Angelis, the Italian Lotus driver having been another to have switched to his team's

spare car due to a down-on-power engine.

Mansell was again the pace-setter during Saturday morning's untimed session when it became abundantly clear that the track, thanks to more and more rubber going down, had become considerably quicker. The Englishman, himself, proved that by clipping the best part of a massive 4 seconds off his previous best time and going around the 2.5-mile circuit, unofficially, in 1 min 41.338 sec. However, during the one that really mattered, the final 'hour' of qualifying, he failed to hold on to that seemingly elusive first-ever pole position for reasons that were not helped by picking up too much traffic whilst out on his first set of tyres. He still managed to register what, up to that point, was fastest time of 1 min 42.172 sec, but over the next few minutes this was bettered by two other drivers. First Piquet reeled off two super-quick laps in his Brabham 'qualifying special', the second coming out at a quite remarkable 1 min 40.980 sec in spite of his BMW engine lapsing on to three cylinders along the river front. Then Prost, who had switched to the spare McLaren during the morning after being somewhat perplexed at discovering that his regular car (still fitted with the Montreal engine, but since equipped with fresh turbo-charger units) was still suffering from poor throttle response, went out and turned in a new second fastest time of 1 min 41.640 sec. Furthermore, any hopes that Mansell had of retrieving the pole were scuppered, when he later went out on his second set of tyres, by Bellof overstepping the mark once too often in his Tyrrrell, slamming backwards into the wall almost directly in front of him and bringing out the inevitable black flags yet again. This, though, was an incident that also affected a good number of the other drivers for when qualifying eventually resumed, following a near-20 minute delay, it was discovered that the Tyrrell had deposited so much oil that the track had become too slippery for any more really quick laps. Consequently, the session more or less fizzled out with little in the way of further excitement, leaving Piquet firmly ensconced on pole position for the second race on the trot and Prost and a slightly disappointed Mansell in second and third places on the grid respectively. Meanwhile, Alboreto had done enough during the early part of the afternoon to clinch fourth spot with a vastly improved time of 1 min 42.246 sec in his Ferrari, and under similar circumstances de Angelis, despite brushing the wall slightly at one point, had wound up just one place lower at 1 min 42.434 sec. Warwick, too, had fought his way up to a somewhat more respectable sixth starting position, in spite of suffering another turbo-charger failure in the spare Renault, but Tambay, after feeling in worse physical shape than the previous day and also losing a turbo-charger on his Renault, had failed to keep abreast with the much faster conditions and had slipped away to an eventual ninth place on the grid. Here, he was separated from his team-mate by Senna, whose badly damaged Toleman had been repaired overnight (along with Cecotto's sister car) and been fitted with the Hart 415T development engine incorporating the new electronic engine management system, and by Cheever in what had proved to be the only reliable Euroracing Alfa Romeo of the afternoon: Patrese's proposed race chassis had been running with a persistent misfire until stopping out on the circuit with a broken fuel pump and then the Italian had experienced more engine problems with the team's spare car. As a result it was hardly surprising that Patrese had failed to improve on his Friday time (the only driver not to have done so), but at least he had made the cut unlike Rothengatter, whose hopes of qualifying the hastily-converted Spirit had not exactly been enhanced by overheating problems.

Patrese, winding up in only 25th place on the grid, was not the only surprising aspect of the final order. On the contrary, Lauda, effectively having had to start all over again, had qualified in a somewhat disappointing tenth place following problems with traffic on both of his runs; a disgruntled Arnoux, who had lost an engine in the morning, was an even more lowly 15th after first of all having spun at the chicane by the entrance to the open-air pits and then having been one of the unfortunates to suffer because of the oil from Bellof's Tyrrell; and the Williams duo were way down in 19th (Laffite) and 21st (Rosberg) positions, the revised FW09s having been an absolutely appalling handful over the bumps. For rather less obvious reasons, apart from the fact that he was freely admitting that the business of hopping between Grand Prix and Indy car racing was turning out to be a mistake, Fabi also had the second Brabham much lower down the grid than expected, actually in only 23rd place. On a somewhat happier note, however, Brundle had done remarkably well in his Tyrrell and could now look forward to starting a Grand Prix from the front half of the grid for the very first time. He had qualified a most creditable 11th, immediately ahead of de Cesaris, who had been obliged to use the spare Ligier for the second afternoon running following another wall-banging incident in the morning (he had also ended up with the spare Ligier against the wall right at the end of the afternoon!) and Boutsen, who had somehow got the Arrows A7 into the front half of the grid for the first time despite a whole catalogue of mechanical problems with both chassis throughout the two days.

On Saturday evening quite a vicious storm developed with heavy rain – even hail – accompanied by thunder and lightening, but by the following morning all was well with the weather again. The skies had cleared and conditions were warm and sunny. For the teams it was another comparatively early start as the Grand Prix was scheduled for 1.15 p.m., which meant that the warm-up session began at 9.15 a.m. During this 30 minute thrash the drivers quickly discovered that the rain had effectively washed the track and left the surface even more abrasive than at the start of practice. Nevertheless, bearing in mind that the cars were now in race trim, the lap times were still relatively quick and it was interesting to note that the best of 1 min 47.668 sec, recorded by Arnoux, was identical to the fastest lap set in the 1983 race by John Watson at the wheel of a Ford-Cosworth-powered McLaren MP4/1C. Alboreto was not that much slower in the other Ferrari either, although between him and his team-mate was none other than Bellof, notwithstanding the fact that the spare Tyrrell that the German had been obliged to take over following his accident of the previous afternoon stopped out on the circuit with ignition problems before it was all over. Meanwhile, Laffite switched to Rosberg's original race car (the Finn had elected to use the spare Williams for the race) for a few laps because of clutch trouble, high water temperatures produced worried-looking faces in the Euroracing Alfa Romeo pit and the Lotus 95T of de Angelis developed a chronic misfire. Furthermore, subsequent attempts to cure this latter problem by changing the turbo-charger and fuel metering units failed miserably as when the Italian later joined Prost (proposing to race

The tower blocks dominate the skyline in Detroit as Alain Prost streaks away into the lead at the original start to the race. Nelson Piquet's Brabham, on the other hand, is out of control after being struck by Nigel Mansell's Lotus (to the left of the picture) and as a result of the chain of events that followed the race had eventually to be stopped and re-started. *(Phipps Photographic)*

the spare McLaren), Lauda, Arnoux, Warwick (still confined to the spare Renault) and Rosberg in the pre-race parade involving the six leading drivers in the World Championship table the misfire was still there. Consequently, it was no surprise when the grid formed to see de Angelis in the spare Lotus 95T for the second race running.

Right on time Piquet led the field around on the final warm-up lap, they all safely returned to their starting positions, the red light went on, engine notes rose and then it was green for go – and chaos! It began with Mansell, later to be accused of taking off a fraction too early, optimistically aiming his Lotus for the gap between the two front row cars and promptly finding himself being squeezed out. With nowhere to go, he then struck the left rear wheel of Prost's McLaren with his right front wheel and bounced off into the side of Piquet's slightly hesitant Brabham. Somehow, Prost managed to gather it up, as did Mansell eventually, and charged off into the lead. However, Piquet, after his right front wheel had become momentarily interlocked with the left front wheel of the Lotus, lost control of his Brabham, went sliding off to the outside of the track and spun – just in time to T-bone Alboreto's Ferrari! At first it appeared that the Italian might have got away with it, despite making contact with the wall, but, in fact, the radiator in the Ferrari's left-hand side-pod had been holed and at the first right-hander (Turn 2) Alboreto spun on his own water before pulling over to the side of the track and switching off. Meanwhile, there was even more drama taking place behind him. For a start the Brabham's right rear wheel, which had been torn away along with the rear aerofoil, shot up into the air and came crashing down on the left front suspension of Senna's Toleman, something that must have given the young Brazilian the fright of his life. Then, at almost precisely the same moment, Surer came charging through from near the back of the grid, found his path blocked and unavoidably drove straight into the Brabham's left front wheel, jarring Piquet's neck quite badly in the process. This, in turn, left two badly damaged cars partially blocking the track, not to mention a considerable amount of debris lying around, so the organizers responded by taking the only realistic option open to them: they made immediate arrangements to stop the race. There then followed a clearing-up exercise that went on for almost exactly half an hour until, eventually, preparations were in hand for the re-start with the commencement of another 5-minute countdown. By that stage Brabham, Ferrari and Toleman (disappointed that the opportunity of giving the Hart development engine its first race had been lost) had all wheeled out their spare cars for Piquet, Alboreto and Senna respectively, but

the Arrows team could no longer offer a car to Surer as quite simply there was no spare A6 available. As a result the unfortunate Swiss had now become a spectator.

Much to everyone's relief, the second start proved to be a clean and tidy affair and saw Piquet, with no sign of any hesitation whatsoever on this occasion, accelerate away into an undisputed lead from Prost and Mansell. This was still the order at the end of the opening lap with Alboreto chasing hard in fourth place followed by Cheever, Warwick, de Angelis, Lauda, Tambay, Senna, Brundle, Boutsen, Arnoux, Bellof and the others all strung out behind except for Winkelhock and de Cesaris. Already the German had been obliged to park his ATS out on the circuit with a smouldering BMW engine, while the Ligier team leader was heading for the pits with a dented wheel rim, subsequently rejoining the fray at the back of the field. On the second lap it was much the same, but next time round Palmer's race came to an abrupt halt when his RAM slid off into the wall following a suspected rear tyre failure, and Arnoux completed the lap by touring into the pits. The Frenchman, in the midst of trying to make up for his poor starting position, had simply overdone things, spun, also hit the wall and was now forced to retire his Ferrari with a damaged nose cone and bent front suspension. Even before he was out of the car, though, there was yet more drama unfolding. This time it was caused by Ghinzani, after an excellent start, arguing over the same piece of road with Hesnault and the pair of them slithering into a run-off area. And, once again, it was to have dire consequences. The Ligier stayed put and the Osella made it no further than the pits, so with barely 5 minutes gone the field had already dwindled to 20 cars. Out in front, meanwhile, Piquet appeared to be employing much the same tactics as in Montreal by driving just hard enough on a full tank of petrol to maintain the lead without opening up any appreciable advantage. Consequently, at this stage, Prost was still a close second, but over the new few minutes the McLaren driver started losing grip from his rear tyres and steadily dropped back into the clutches of Mansell, a situation that existed until the tenth lap when he finally had to concede to mounting pressure from the Englishman on the approach to one of the left-handers. By then Piquet was more than 5 seconds up the road and looked to have the race really under control. In the meantime, Warwick had come through to fourth place at the expense of Cheever and Alboreto (about to swop places themselves), Lauda, who had earlier overtaken de Angelis, had just been repassed by the Italian and was now a long way back owing to experiencing similar tyre problems to those of his team-mate and, behind Tambay, an almighty scrap had developed between Senna, Boutsen, Bellof and Brundle. They were really going at it and with such ferocity that even the perpetually

hard-charging Rosberg, who was gaining on them, was impressed.

During the course of the next three or four laps Mansell fought like a tiger to get on terms with the leader and closed up at the rate of over a second per lap until he was almost to within striking distance of the blue and white car. However, Piquet continued to do just enough to hold sway, and towards the end of lap 17 could even afford to relax again when Mansell slowed dramatically on his way into the Atwater tunnel. It was gearbox trouble. Second gear had gone, and although he eventually slammed the Lotus in third Mansell realized only too well that he now faced an uphill task even to hold on to second place let alone do anything about Piquet. Even so, Prost was no longer a threat as since being elbowed out of second place his tyres had deteriorated to such an extent that he had dropped right away and was now about to go into the pits to change to a set of harder Michelins. The Renault duo, too, had run into the same trouble. In fact, Warwick had already stopped for fresh rubber at the end of lap 14 and Tambay, having just indulged in a quick spin, was currently in the throes of following suit. Lauda would be next, but the surprising thing about it was that Piquet, who had started out on a similar combination of the comparatively soft Michelins, was enjoying perfect grip in his Brabham and experiencing no problems at all with the abrasive track surface.

On lap 22 came the start of another spate of retirements when Senna, coming under increasing pressure from Rosberg (he had now scrambled past the two Tyrrells), suddenly slid off into the tyre barrier at Turn 1. This was then followed only moments later by Cheever pulling out of an excellent third place with an acute loss of turbo boost pressure caused by a cracked inter-cooler on his Alfa Romeo and by his team-mate, who had earlier been seen limping into the pits with a punctured right rear tyre, spinning and deciding that the other Benetton-sponsored car had become undriveable. That was by no means the end of the rot either. At the end of his 24th lap Cecotto went into the pits to complain that he was having to make clutchless gear changes (he completely overlooked the fact that if he stopped there was no way in which the Toleman would start again without a clutch!), and within just four more laps three other drivers had departed the scene. These were de Cesaris, out with suspension damage after trailing round at the back of the field, Boutsen, who was sidelined by an engine failure whilst lying fifth, and Mansell, whose hopes of holding down second place ended in the pits with his gearbox showing every sign of breaking up completely. Naturally, quite apart from thinning out the field, these incidents were changing the order considerably and now, with half-distance approaching, it was

1984

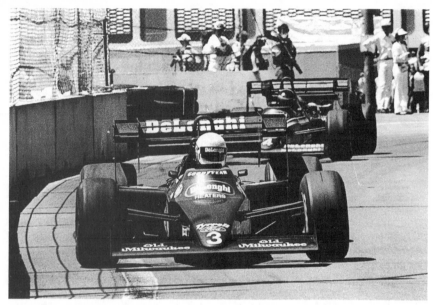

Martin Brundle and Stefan Bellof both performed admirably in their Tyrrells and ran in close formation for several laps. Unfortunately, though, Bellof (car No. 4) failed to finish due to clipping the chicane before the pits and Brundle, who wound up a close second to Nelson Piquet, was subsequently disqualified, an event that heralded the beginning of a major controversy. *(L.A.T. Photographic)*

Alboreto up into second place, a good 15 seconds behind Piquet, with de Angelis a close third. Then, after another fairly long gap, Rosberg, Brundle and Bellof were running in virtual nose-to-tail formation followed by Warwick (recovering well from his tyre stop), Prost, Fabi, Laffite, Lauda, Tambay and Alliot (lapped). No-one else was left – but there were soon to be even fewer of them! Indeed, the first indication of that came on lap 34 when Bellof's Tyrrell suddenly shuddered to a halt in front of the pits due to the young German allowing his enthusiasm to get the better of him and clobbering the wall at the exit from the chicane with his left rear wheel. This was followed, at the end of the same lap, by Tambay disappearing into the pits with a rapidly disintegrating gearbox and only a minute or so later by Lauda going in to retire his McLaren with a badly misfiring engine after a change of plugs on the previous lap had failed to make the problem go away. And, just for good measure, Alliot joined the rock-ape brigade, which left his RAM with both of its two near-side corners in tatters. In the meantime, Brundle had made a pit stop for weight-gaining water in his red Tyrrell (running with additional sponsorship from Old Milwaukee Beer for race day only) and Warwick, currently the fastest man out on the circuit, had just overhauled Rosberg and de Angelis on successive laps to take over third spot. However, incredible as it seemed, no sooner had Warwick settled down to the task of trying to catch Alboreto's Ferrari than his gearbox started playing up. First of all fifth gear broke, which enabled de Angelis and Rosberg to repass him on lap 37, and from there

on things went from bad to worse until on lap 41 the Renault driver suddenly pulled off to the side of the track with no gears left at all. As a result Brundle, who was already making up lost ground after his pit stop, and who had only minutes earlier charged past none other than Prost, automatically moved back up into fifth place and the Frenchman took over sixth spot – only for a slowly deflating right rear tyre, which had already caused a quick spin, to bring about an enforced stop for yet more Michelins at the end of the very next lap. This, in turn, allowed Fabi and Laffite to go by and left Prost in the most unusual situation of bringing up the rear, in eighth place.

After 50 laps of this so-called race, in which accidents and mechanical failures had played the major role in determining positions, Piquet's lead had suddenly increased to over half a minute due to Alboreto having just joined the long list of retirements with a blown-up engine. Rosberg, too, had stopped out on the circuit on the previous lap with a seized turbo-charger so, apart from the fact that the field had dwindled to a mere six cars, Brundle had now been promoted to a quite incredible third place. Furthermore, he was soon making inroads on the second-placed Lotus of de Angelis, which was not altogether surprising for the Italian had now run into similar gearbox problems to those of Mansell earlier in the race inasmuch as he was now having to drive without second gear. Even the Tyrrell was not exactly enjoying a trouble-free run as a little earlier an exhaust pipe had broken and this was making its engine sound decidedly flat. If this was having any effect on the car's performance,

however, it certainly wasn't showing. On the contrary. By lap 56 Brundle had not only made up the 10 seconds or so on the Lotus but was flying past on the outside of it on the approach to the chicane. At this point Piquet, still around 20 seconds clear, had already wound down the boost and on lap 60 even allowed Prost to unlap himself. Brundle, on the other hand, was keeping his head down and, after a brief interruption to his pursuit caused by a loose fluid reservoir cap finding its way into the Tyrrell's footwell area, produced an unexpectedly exciting climax to the race by closing up to the Brabham at the rate of almost 5 seconds per lap. In fact, by the start of the 63rd and last lap there were barely 4 seconds between the two cars, and still the gap continued to come down. In reality, though, it was not quite what it appeared to be: Piquet was simply playing it cool – very cool – and, despite Brundle moving up to within a second of him as they entered the Atwater tunnel for the final time, the reigning World Champion went on to chalk up his second victory on successive weekends just a few car lengths clear. Over half a minute later de Angelis brought his ailing Lotus home in third place and then, well spaced out behind, came Fabi (in the points for the first time), Prost and, the only other remaining survivor, Laffite, who had been repassed by his compatriot in the McLaren almost immediately following the second tyre stop.

Shortly after the victory celebrations came word that during post-race scrutineering officials of the SCCA (the national club organizing the Detroit Grand Prix) had discovered impurities in the water used for the water-injection system on Brundle's Tyrrell. At the same time it was learned that they had also discovered a large quantity of miniscule lead balls lying loosely in the bottom of the rubber bag (fitted inside the monocoque) containing the water, water which was then pumped to a spraying mechanism over the engine air-intake trumpets to cool the fuel-injection process and fulfil the ultimate aim of improving engine reliability. It was, of course, this same rubber bag (water tank) that had been topped up during Brundle's pit stop.

The immediate outcome was that the results of the race were regarded as being only provisional and samples of the contents of both the Tyrrell's water and petrol tanks were given to the Clerk of the Course (Burdie Martin), SCCA's chief scrutineer (John Timanus), FISA representatives and to the Tyrrell team. This, however, proved to be just the starting point of a major controversy for whilst Tyrrell didn't even bother to keep their samples, believing the water to be no more than ordinary tap water, FISA sent its samples to the MB Analy-Co laboratory in Nanterre, France and both Martin and Timanus sent theirs to the Southwest Research Institute in San Antonio, Texas for analyses. As a result of these tests Ken Tyrrell was then summoned to attend a meeting of the FISA Executive Committee in Paris on July 18 to answer charges that he had refuelled his car during the race! Both the French analyses and those carried out by the Southwest Research Institute had revealed the presence of hydrocarbons in the water and, at the meeting, Ken Tyrrell was told that the first sample of water checked in the United States had contained 27.5% Aromatics.

When he heard this, Ken Tyrrell, who had not previously been given any written report of the findings, was apparently completely dumbfounded and found himself in no position to offer any defence. It appears that the Executive Committee then confirmed their view that the hydrocarbons found to be present in the water were power-boosting additives and that the water-injection system was all part of the Tyrrell's fuel system. Whatever, in application of Article 152 of the International Sporting Code, it subsequently voted in favour of dishing out the most draconian punishment imaginable: it banned the Tyrrell team from the remainder of the 1984 World Championship with immediate effect (besides cancelling its 13 points

previously scored) for the reasons set out below, which were made available in the form of a Press Release:

The Tyrrell team: after having heard Mr Ken Tyrrell, given the analyses which resulted from the samples taken from Tyrrell No. 3 at the Detroit Grand Prix, given the witnesses heard, and from deep-seated convictions, for violation of the following articles of the F1 Technical Regulations:

Art. 6-14: any refuelling during the race is forbidden.
Art. 14.1.2: fuel not complying with the regulation.
Art. 6.9: fuel lines must have safety breakaway valves.
Art. 6.11: fuel lines must be capable of supporting a given pressure and temperature.
Art. 4.2: ballast may be used provided that it is secured in such a way that tools are necessary to remove it. It must be possible to affix seals to it.

The Tyrrell team entered for the FIA Formula One Championship is excluded from this Championship, and as a result its entry is cancelled. This decision takes immediate effect. The appeal before the FIA Court of Appeal does not suspend this desision.

So far as the reference to ballast was concerned, this was in connection with the use of lead balls. Ken Tyrrell had contended that as tools were required to remove the tank in which they were carried he had complied with the regulations, but the FISA Executive Committee had obviously decided otherwise. Furthermore, it had expressed the opinion that the system used was such that ballast could be added during a pit stop and outside the control of the officials without it being possible to affix seals.

Although it was almost insignificant by comparison, the Detroit Grand Prix was also to leave a sour taste in Nigel Mansell's mouth. At the same meeting of the FISA Executive Committee (the same one that also voted a $6,000 fine on Jacky Ickx for his actions at the Monaco Grand Prix) he was to be severely reprimanded for 'dangerous driving and overtaking at the start of the Detroit Grand Prix' and fined $6,000. At the time he was also given a 'deferred licence suspension for the whole of the current season applicable for a fault of the same nature', although at a subsequent sitting of the FIA International Court of Appeal at the end of August the deferred licence suspension was to be lifted.

Results

1	N. Piquet	1 hr 55 min	
	(Brabham-BMW)	41.842 sec	
		(131.449 kph/	
		81.679 mph)	
*	M. Brundle	1 hr 55 min	
	(Tyrrell-Ford)	42.679 sec	
2	E. de Angelis	1 hr 56 min	
	(Lotus-Renault)	14.480 sec	
3	T. Fabi	1 hr 57 min	
	(Brabham-BMW)	08.370 sec	
4	A. Prost	1 hr 57 min	
	(McLaren-TAG)	37.100 sec	
5	J. Laffite	1 lap behind	
	(Williams-Honda)		

* Excluded.

Fastest lap: D. Warwick (Renault) on lap 32 in 1 min 46.221 sec (136.358 kph/84.729 mph)

Retirements
Original race: M. Surer (Arrows-Ford) accident on lap 1.

Re-started race: M. Winkelhock (ATS-BMW) engine on lap 1, J. Palmer (RAM-Hart) accident on lap 3, R. Arnoux (Ferrari) accident damage on lap 3, F. Hesnault (Ligier-Renault) accident on lap 4, P. Ghinzani (Osella-Alfa Romeo) accident damage on lap 4, R. Patrese (Alfa Romeo) handling on lap 21, A. Senna (Toleman-Hart) accident on lap 22, E. Cheever (Alfa Romeo) inter-cooler on lap 22, J. Cecotto (Toleman-Hart) clutch on lap 24, A. de Cesaris (Ligier-Renault) suspension damage on lap 25, N. Mansell (Lotus-Renault) gearbox on lap 28, T. Boutsen (Arrows-BMW) engine on lap 28, S. Bellof (Tyrrell-Ford) accident on lap 34, P. Tambay (Renault) gearbox on lap 34, N. Lauda (McLaren-TAG) engine on lap 34, P. Alliot (RAM-Hart) accident on lap 34, D. Warwick (Renault) gearbox on lap 41, K. Rosberg (Williams-Honda) turbo-charger on lap 48, M. Alboreto (Ferrari) engine on lap 50.

Ist United States (Dallas) Grand Prix

Dallas: July 8
Weather: Very hot
Duration: 2 hours (67 laps of 3.901 km circuit
= 261.37 km (162.41 miles)

For the third and final stop on this whirlwind tour of North America the Grand Prix 'circus' made its way to a completely new venue – the Texas State Fair Park, situated on the southern outskirts of the oil-rich city of Dallas. The idea of holding a Formula 1 race here had first been mooted by local businessmen Don Walker and Larry Waldrop (the Can-Am sponsors of Michael Roe and Price Cobb), whose intention it was to promote Dallas as a 'world class city'. They, together with race director and former driver Carroll Shelby, had then succeeded in per-

suading the State Park officials to sanction a road circuit within the precincts of the fairground and, after much hard work, had gradually seen their idea turn into reality with the official blessing of both FOCA and FISA. So far as the actual track was concerned, for which a certain amount of credit was due to Chris Pook (the initiator of the Long Beach Grand Prix, who had been employed as a circuit consultant during the early stages of the project), it was based on the usual principles associated with American street circuits, being a fairly tight and

twisty affair lined mainly by a combination of concrete walls and eight feet high debris fencing. Consequently, appearance-wise it was not exactly awe-inspiring yet, at the same time, the layout (anti-clockwise) was quite interesting and included two hairpin bends, one at the far side of the circuit alongside the Music Hall and the other near the Livestock Pavilion and just before the entrance to the pits. The rest of it was made up of 14 other turns of varying degrees of severity interspersed by what were almost without exception short straights, all of which added up to a total distance of 2.424 miles (3.901 kilometres) and anticipated lap speeds of somewhere in the region of 90 mph.

Originally there was to have been an hour-long session of unofficial practice at 9 o'clock

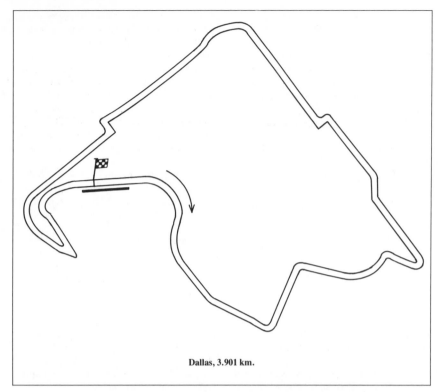

Dallas, 3.901 km.

on Thursday morning to allow the drivers an opportunity to become acclimatized to the new surroundings. However, at the appointed hour engines were silent and about the only noises to be heard were emanating from a somewhat heated argument between Bernie Ecclestone and the organizers over circuit credentials for team personnel. Even lawyers and insurance men became involved, but eventually some form of compromise was reached whereby the same system used at other circuits was agreed upon (as required by Bernie Ecclestone), and the drivers finally got their hour of practice. Unfortunately, though, this did nothing to improve the already strained atmosphere, as at a brief Press Conference held after its conclusion most of the drivers present were full of criticism. There were complaints that the track was extremely bumpy, notwithstanding the fact that some 2½ million dollars had been spent on resurfacing work; complaints that there were insufficient or inadequate run-off areas; complaints that the walls were so close that it was virtually impossible to see around corners; complaints that the organization was not up to scratch (there were no cranes to remove stranded and damaged cars), and so on, with the result that one way and another it was not turning out to be a very auspicious start to the weekend. It also seemed to underline yet again the questionable decision made by FISA in no longer requiring some form of an inaugural race to take place on a new circuit prior to giving the go-ahead for a World Championship event. Nevertheless, there was no dissention from the drivers as

such and at 10 a.m. on the following day all 27 of them entered for the race were ready and waiting for the start of official practice, the line-up unchanged from Detroit except that Corrado Fabi was once again deputizing for his elder brother in the second Brabham.

Usually, of course, the opening session of practice is a period used by drivers to fine-tune their cars and to try to arrive at the best possible compromise as regards tyres, wing angles, suspension settings and the like to enable them to cope with as much as a given circuit as possible. The trouble here, though, was that the bumpy track surface, combined with a steadily rising ambient temperature that changed conditions almost by the minute, made it more or less a futile exercise. There were soon problems emerging for the tyre people as well. All three companies found out to their dismay that even soft race tyres were lasting only a handful of laps or so, while their selection of qualifying rubber (based on guesswork due to the lack of pre-race testing at this venue) was turning out to be a complete joke, going 'off' within half a lap at the most. On a positive note, however, it appeared that the Michelin-shod McLaren MP4/2s were well suited to the trying conditions with both Lauda and Prost setting themselves up as the early pacesetters. Indeed, the former double World Champion ultimately went on to narrowly pip his team-mate for the morning's fastest time by producing a lap in 1 min 36.317 sec (90.600 mph), although shortly after achieving it he also blotted his copybook by clipping the wall and knocking the McLaren's left-hand suspension out of shape, both at

the front and at the rear. Numerous other drivers had their moments as well during the course of the morning but, apart from the odd damaged wheel rim or such like, most of them got away with it. In fact, about the only other exceptions were Rothengatter, who was forced to abandon his Spirit (fitted with a four-cylinder Hart engine once more) out on the circuit with its left rear corner all but torn away, and de Angelis, who bent the rear suspension of his Lotus 95T.

By the start of the first qualifying session the heat had become almost unbearable, with the ambient temperature now over 100°F (38°C) and the track temperature considerably higher. The immediate effect, quite apart from making the job of the drivers even harder, was that instead of the

Starting Grid	
	N. Mansell
	Lotus-Renault
	(1 min 37.041 sec)
E. de Angelis	
Lotus-Renault	D. Warwick
(1 min 37.635 sec)	Renault
	(1 min 37.708 sec)
R. Arnoux	
Ferrari	N. Lauda
(1 min 37.785 sec)	McLaren-TAG
	(1 min 37.987 sec)
A. Senna	
Toleman-Hart	A. Prost
(1 min 38.256 sec)	McLaren-TAG
	(1 min 38.544 sec)
K. Rosberg	
Williams-Honda	M. Alboreto
(1 min 38.767 sec)	Ferrari
	(1 min 38.793 sec)
P. Tambay	
Renault	C. Fabi
(1 min 38.907 sec)	Brabham-BMW
	(1 min 38.960 sec)
N. Piquet	
Brabham-BMW	M. Winkelhock
(1 min 39.439 sec)	ATS-BMW
	(1 min 39.860 sec)
E. Cheever	
Alfa Romeo	J. Cecotto
(1 min 39.911 sec)	Toleman-Hart
	(1 min 40.027 sec)
A. de Cesaris	
Ligier-Renault	S. Bellof
(1 min 40.095 sec)	Tyrrell-Ford
	(1 min 40.336 sec)
P. Ghinzani	
Osella-Alfa Romeo	F. Hesnault
(1 min 41.176 sec)	Ligier-Renault
	(1 min 41.303 sec)
T. Boutsen	
Arrows-BMW	R. Patrese
(1 min 41.318 sec)	Alfa Romeo
	(1 min 41.328 sec)
M. Surer	
Arrows-BMW	H. Rothengatter
(1 min 42.592 sec)	Spirit-Hart
	(1 min 43.084 sec)
J. Laffite	
Williams-Honda	
(1 min 43.304 sec)	
J. Palmer	
RAM-Hart	
(1 min 44.676 sec)	

Non-starters:
P. Alliot (RAM-Hart) 1 min 43.222 sec
M. Brundle (Tyrrell-Ford) 2 min 31.960 sec.

track being quicker now that more and more rubber was going down, it was slower. More worrying still, it was starting to show signs of breaking up in places, most noticeably at the right/left sequence by the Cotton Bowl stadium just beyond the pits. The continuing change in conditions also started to swing the pendulum in favour of the Goodyear runners, although before this became apparent the circuit claimed its first really serious casualty when Brundle, after going out early and whilst on only his first flying lap of the afternoon, suddenly hit the wall on the left-hand side at Turn 8 due to a suspected deflating tyre. The Tyrrell then cannoned off into the wall on the other side of the track and finally came to rest with its front end badly crumpled. At first, the sight of the young Englishman levering himself out of the cockpit and perching on the roll-over bar suggested that he, at least, was perfectly alright. Sadly, though, this was not the case at all: he had broken the fibula in his left leg and sustained other fractures to both of his feet, injuries that were to prevent him from driving again for several weeks. In the meantime, qualifying was held up for almost half an hour while Brundle was being taken to the medical centre (prior to being transferred to the nearby Baylor Hospital) and the track was being cleared but, eventually, the early battle for grid positions began again in earnest. And it was now that Goodyear appeared to have the upper hand with Mansell playing the prime role in the changing fortunes. Using soft race tyres (the qualifying rubber had, by now, been put away), he completely cast aside his inhibitions about the circuit and by sheer grit and determination went on to lap well over half a second clear of the field, his best effort ultimately coming out at 1 min 37.041 sec (89.925 mph). Although he was even less happy than his team-mate about the working environment, de Angelis also put the other Lotus 95T well to the forefront with second fastest time of 1 min 37.635 sec, while Arnoux rounded off the top three places on the time-sheets for Goodyear with a lap in 1 min 37.785 sec. This was in spite of his Ferrari 126C4 behaving pretty abysmally over the bumps as well as losing time in the pits having a damaged rear aerofoil replaced and the car's rear bodywork checked over following a brief argument with the wall at one point. Meanwhile, Lauda lapped quickly enough to at least keep himself at the head of the Michelin contingent. But again – rather surprisingly – he finished up against the wall, this time behind the wheel of the spare McLaren, of course, and at the first right-hander beyond the pits where he tore away the car's right rear corner. Fortunately, unlike Brundle, he subsequently walked away from the scene unharmed and with what was to be fourth fastest time of 1 min 37.987 sec to his credit. Prost, on the other hand, was more than half a second slower at the end of the afternoon and was also beaten by an impressive Senna, making the most of the Hart development engine installed in his Toleman, and by Warwick. Not that this was in any way particularly surprising. On the contrary. The Championship leader's first run had been interrupted by a deflating tyre and his second by the appearance of yellow flags due to Alliot losing control of his RAM and reducing the Skoal Bandit-sponsored car to little more than a pile of wreckage. Alboreto was another to have been affected by this incident, which went some way to explaining why he was almost exactly a second slower than Arnoux and only ninth in the standings between Rosberg and a slightly off-form Tambay. Nevertheless, at the end of the day it was Alliot, himself, who was worst affected as, with no hope of his car being repaired in time for the race, and because his team had no spare chassis available, the Frenchman was left facing up to the reality of being a non-starter.

Since the beginning of the weekend Brabham had been running their BT53s with an even larger front-mounted oil cooler than that seen at Montreal and Detroit, and with revised front bodywork, obviously to allow for the anticipated higher ambient temperatures. The extra weight, though, had upset the aerodynamic balance of the cars, causing excessive understeer and keeping Piquet out of the limelight. In fact, after losing time in the morning because of fuel pump failure on a new BT53 that had been flown out to replace the chassis damaged in the start-line shunt at Detroit, he had lapped even slower than his considerably less experienced team-mate and wound up only 12th fastest. Consequently, on Saturday it was no real surprise to see that his team had converted their cars back to the previous set-up, but with an additional oil cooler now located in the left-hand side-pods. Even so, it was to make no difference so far as Piquet's grid position was concerned. After tweaking the suspension of both his new race car and the spare Brabham against the wall in the morning untimed session, the reigning World Champion failed to register any improvement over his Friday time on the steadily deteriorating track surface during the afternoon, despite coming out third fastest on this occasion. Indeed, because of the state of the track, this second day was to count virtually for nothing as only three drivers actually picked up on their lap times. One of them was Warwick, who created by far the greatest impression with a truly magnificent effort early in the afternoon that sent him soaring to the top of the time-sheets at 1 min 37.708 sec and up into third place on the grid at the expense of Arnoux, Lauda and Senna. Other than that the first 19 places on the grid went totally unaffected, as the two remaining drivers to find a bit more speed, Boutsen and Surer, were still left languishing in only 20th and

22nd places respectively, both incidentally, now driving (somewhat unreliable) BMW-powered Arrows A7s. Among the others, Mansell and de Angelis (he had damaged the rear suspension of his Lotus 95T again during the morning) didn't even bother to take part in final qualifying, preferring, instead, to conserve their cars for the race. The Toleman team, too, made a similar decision, although this was almost certainly influenced by the fact that Cecotto had damaged his proposed race car beyond immediate repair earlier in the day with the result that there were now only two serviceable TG184s left. Hesnault, who had bent the front suspension of his Ligier during the previous afternoon, was not allowed out either, presumably because his team was down to just two cars following Detroit. So, all in all, the final hour of qualifying was a rather low-key affair, not helped by Lauda and Prost both packing up early after failing to break the 1 min 40 sec barrier on their first sets of tyres, Palmer becoming stranded out on the circuit when the Hart engine in his RAM cut out through some obscure electrical fault and Cheever spending most of the session stood around in the pits waiting for a blown-up engine to be replaced in his Alfa Romeo. However, in addition to Warwick's superb showing, at least Rosberg did his best to give the spectators something to watch by performing his usual heroics in the Williams. Unfortunately, though, the Finn eventually overstepped the mark once too often, hit the wall, pulled a right front suspension pick-up point away from the monocoque and left his mechanics with the task of rebuilding the car around the monocoque of the spare Williams before the race. Immediately prior to that he had gone around in what was to be the afternoon's second fastest time of 1 min 39.438 sec which, if nothing else, underlined just how hard he had been trying. Laffite, on the other hand, was almost 7 seconds slower in the second Williams this time out and having an extremely disappointing weekend, qualifying in only 24th and penultimate position on the grid.

In order to avoid the worst of the heat from a Texas summer sun the Grand Prix was due to start at the very early hour of 11 a.m. on Sunday, with the 30 minute warm-up session planned for 7 a.m. This, of course, meant awaking almost literally at the crack of dawn although, as it happened, everyone might just as well have stayed in bed a little longer due to the warm-up first of all being postponed for a couple of hours and then eventually being scrubbed. Indeed, it seemed as if Laffite had the right idea: he arrived at the circuit in his pyjamas! Naturally, this was the Frenchman simply displaying a sense of humour and was something that was badly needed to help lift some of the gloom and despondency that was rapidly creeping in. The problem? A 50-lap Can-Am race held after the end of practice on the previous afternoon had left the track surface in an absolutely appalling state and, thanks to a bad batch of normally quick-drying cement, overnight repair work had achieved virtually nothing. Already there had been talk of Lauda and Prost both being in favour of a drivers' boycott and from now up until about 30 minutes before the scheduled starting time it was almost anybody's guess as to what exactly was going to happen. In the meantime, the resurfacing contractors were called back in to make another attempt at patching up the track using more quick-drying cement, some of the drivers returned to their hotels for a while – including Rosberg, who was particularly scathing with his views on the matter – and all kinds of proposals emerged from seemingly never-ending debates. These included postponing the race until the following day, cancelling it altogether and shortening the race distance over and above an earlier decision to cut it back from 78 laps to 68 laps, which had been done merely with the aim of avoiding the imposition of the regulatory two-hour limit. Eventually, though, rather more positive signs began to emerge. The contractors completed their work with somewhat more successful results and, after carrying out a track inspection with official starter Derek Ongaro, Lauda expressed the opinion that a final decision should be taken on the completion of ten exploratory laps. This seemed fine in principle but Bernie Ecclestone, by now fretting over television schedules, was not at all keen on the idea and promptly decided to assert his authority by declaring that there would be three warm-up laps, at the end of which the cars were immediately to form on the dummy grid and to await the normal final count-down. Not surprisingly, the announcement was greeted by the drivers with mixed feelings. But, after taking everything into account, not least a 90,000-strong crowd that included a number of celebrities such as most of the cast from the popular television series named after the nearby city, former drivers and even former United States President, Jimmy Carter, and his wife, all of the drivers duly complied and just ten minutes later than planned they were being sent away on the parade lap by Larry Hagman ('J.R.') waving a green flag. So, at last, there really was a race in prospect, although for Arnoux there was also an immediate problem: he was left behind on the dummy grid with an engine that was proving reluctant to start. Eventually, the Ferrari had to be push-started away leaving the unlucky Frenchman with the frustrating business of having to catch up with the other 24 starters and line up at the back of the grid, his brave efforts throughout practice counting for nothing.

Having taken his long-awaited first pole position, Mansell made a near-perfect start,

staved off a brief challenge from his team-mate on the way into the first right-hander and from there went on to complete a tense opening lap already several car lengths clear. Directly behind the pair of black and gold Lotuses, Warwick had shot straight into third place and Senna, after capitalizing on the vacant grid position in front of him where Arnoux's Ferrari should have been, was fourth ahead of Lauda, Rosberg and Prost. Then it was Alboreto from Tambay and Cheever with Piquet leading the rest apart from Hesnault, who had already spun into the wall, and Cecotto, who was limping round to the pits with a punctured front tyre after making contact with the Ligier. At this point Senna, darting this way and that behind Warwick's Renault, looked to be in a very strong position indeed and was almost certainly behind the wheel of one of the best-handling cars in the race. However, half-way round the second lap the young Brazilian effectively threw away his chances of a good result by shaving the wall at the apex of the right-hander before the first hairpin, for besides causing a quick spin this also sent him into the pits to have a damaged right rear wheel replaced. Furthermore, on the tenth lap, he was to make the same mistake, which put him right out of contention, but, in the meantime, Mansell was driving flawlessly and setting a surprisingly fast pace. De Angelis, who was finding his efforts being hampered by an engine that was refusing to run cleanly, certainly wasn't keeping up and by the end of the fourth lap had been forced to give way to sustained pressure from Warwick, before conceding another place to Lauda three laps later. By then even Mansell's position was looking rather less secure for Warwick was gaining on his compatriot hand over fist and had already wiped out most of the near-4 second advantage that he had earlier accrued. Indeed, within another lap or so the two leading cars were running nose to tail and it was patently clear that the Renault had the edge over the Lotus. Be that as it may, Mansell was not about to surrender the lead without a fight and continued to hold sway by tightly hugging the racing line all around the circuit. Early on lap 11, though, Warwick decided to go for it. He drew alongside the black and gold car approaching one of the tight right-handers and nosed ahead under braking only to drift wide on to the 'marbles', because his brakes momentarily snatched, and finished up sliding off into a tyre barrier, the impact putting Warwick out of the race and robbing him of a possible victory. So now Lauda moved up into second place, but only very briefly as on the following lap de Angelis, his engine having gradually cleared itself, repassed the Austrian and left him at the mercy of Rosberg and Prost, who were tightly bunched up behind and just a short distance ahead of Tambay.

Further back, meanwhile, Alboreto had dropped away for no obvious reason apart from a distinct lack of enthusiasm for the whole affair, and Cheever had been another to have joined the early casualty list by damaging the rear suspension of his Alfa Romeo against the wall. Bellof, too, had just retired the only Tyrrell (and Ford-Cosworth-powered car) in the race, actually a brand new chassis, under similar circumstances, but one driver making noticeably good progress was Arnoux. He was almost literally hurling his Ferrari around the circuit and had already carved his way up into a strong mid-field position, despite having experienced a lot of trouble finding a way past Boutsen's Arrows a few minutes earlier.

By the end of lap 16 the field had become further depleted by Patrese and de Cesaris both being caught out on a track surface that was deteriorating all over again (they had hit the wall in separate incidents with fairly predictable consequences) and also by a somewhat relieved Rothengatter abandoning the Spirit with apparent fuel-feed problems. Relieved, because ever since the opening laps petrol had been seeping into the Spirit's cockpit and made life decidedly uncomfortable for the Dutchman. At the front of the race, meanwhile, things were shaping up nicely again. De Angelis had latched on to his team-mate's tail and now Rosberg, after having overtaken Lauda a couple of laps earlier, and enjoying better grip than he had anticipated in the rebuilt Williams, was looking all set to make it an exciting three-cornered contest for the lead. Sure enough, within a few more minutes the 1982 World Champion was right up with the two black and gold cars, and a slight mistake from de Angelis as he tried in vain to outwit Mansell in a somewhat desperate manoeuvre on lap 19 was all it needed for Rosberg to go charging through into second place. Once there, he then immediately began to set about the leader but, despite the enormous pressure, Mansell continued to defend his position admirably, and four laps later even made a bit of breathing space for himself by picking a clever moment to lap Surer's Arrows – just before one of the tight turns. Nevertheless, it was only to be a brief respite as Rosberg soon followed him past the Swiss, as did a recovering de Angelis, Prost and Lauda, the McLaren duo having swopped places back on the 17th lap. In fact, before long Mansell had quite a queue forming behind him and up until lap 26 there was a distinct possibility that Tambay would soon be part of it in the sole surviving Renault. At that point, however, the Frenchman became just another name on the growing retirement list by making contact with the wall and skating to rest with his right rear wheel missing. Only a minute or so later Cecotto disappeared from near the back of the field through making a similar mistake and then, on lap 28, even the usually so-precise Prost brushed the wall with his right rear wheel. Fortunately for him the impact was insufficient to do any damage and, as if to prove the point, he proceeded to scramble past de Angelis on lap 30 to take over third spot. All the while Rosberg was trying harder than ever to find a way past Mansell, but the Englishman was obviously unimpressed by the Williams darting and weaving all over the track behind him and was blocking every move. After the race this would produce what most observers felt were unnecessarily harsh comments from the Finn, which he chose, rather untactfully, to make in public. For the time being, though, Mansell continued to defend his slender advantage (as he was perfectly entitled to do), and it was not until lap 36 that Rosberg, after previously swapping places with Prost on two occasions in almost as many minutes, finally snatched the lead. Even then it was pretty desperate stuff as Mansell immediately tried to retaliate, and it was only through a fist-shaking Rosberg employing blocking tactics of his own that he succeeded in staying ahead. Thereafter, Mansell quickly began to fade with front tyres that were steadily losing their grip. First of all he dropped behind Prost, de Angelis and Lauda within the space of a lap and then, after lightly brushing the wall with a front wheel, pulled into the pits for fresh rubber. This, in turn, cost him two more places to the hard-charging Arnoux, still on the up and up, and Piquet, whose hopes of achieving a hat-trick of victories in North America were being thwarted by a race-long problem with a slightly sticking throttle.

By lap 40 Rosberg had pulled out a 5 second advantage, but any thoughts that he might now run away with the race were soon quelled by Prost starting to reassert himself and closing up at the rate of around a second per lap. As the gap continued to come down de Angelis slipped from third place to fifth in the space of just five laps after being overhauled by Lauda and the seemingly unstoppable Arnoux, while Piquet disappeared from the lap charts altogether by going off into a tyre barrier when his throttle stuck at an awkward moment as he was about to negotiate the last right-hander before the pits. Over the next two or three minutes Palmer and Senna also departed the fray from the back of the field with an electrical failure and a broken drive-shaft respectively, although this went largely unnoticed as in the meantime Prost not only caught Rosberg but went sailing past him to become the third different race leader. This was on lap 49, and for the next seven laps it really did look to be all over bar the shouting with the McLaren steadily pulling away and Rosberg in no position to do much about it due to his tyres now lacking grip. But then, on lap 57, surprise of surprises – Prost hit the wall again! On this occasion it was with the McLaren's

Keke Rosberg's Williams heads for victory towards the end of a dramatic and surprisingly close-fought inaugural Dallas Grand Prix. *(L.A.T. Photographic)*

right front wheel and at the apex of the right-hander before the first hairpin where the track was just about at its worst. And, on this occasion, the result was rather more terminal as the impact damaged the wheel rim and Prost was forced to park the McLaren with a flat tyre, allowing a somewhat disbelieving Rosberg to assume the lead once more. Just three laps prior to this, and after displaying rather more enthusiasm following a relatively early tyre stop, Alboreto had hit the wall as well and torn a wheel off his Ferrari whilst lying sixth. Consequently he, too, was now out of the contest, as were Boutsen, with a broken engine, and Surer, who had been yet another to have knocked off a wheel against the unyielding wall. Somewhat contrary to expectations, Lauda wasn't destined to be around at the finish either. He had already been caught and passed by Arnoux but, with Prost out,

still looked all set to take third place only to throw it away on lap 61 by damaging his McLaren's right rear suspension too badly to continue, again through striking the wall at the apex of the right-hander before the first hairpin. Meanwhile Rosberg, wearing a chilled skull cap, was keeping everything nicely under control in the Williams and was now looking more and more assured of victory. Sure enough, at the end of 67 laps (one shorter than planned due to the two-hour mark coming up first) the Finn was happily acknowledging the chequered flag to win a dramatic and surprisingly close-fought inaugural Dallas Grand Prix as well as giving Honda their first Grand Prix success since 1967. Over 20 seconds later, Arnoux followed him across the line in a most creditable second place after starting from the back of the grid, remember, and de Angelis, lapped in the dying minutes, rounded off a consis-

Despite starting from the back of the grid, because of the engine in his Ferrari proving reluctant to fire up prior to the parade lap, René Arnoux fought his way through the field splendidly to take a most creditable second place. *(L.A.T. Photographic)*

tent drive by bringing his Lotus 95T home in third spot, a long way clear of Laffite in the second Williams. Mansell, on the other hand, had brushed the wall again in the closing stages and, instead of completing the race, coasted to rest just beyond the exit of the last corner with a broken gearbox. But, rather than calling it a day, the Englishman leapt out of his cockpit and began pushing his car towards the line amidst hearty applause from the crowd, even though this was something entirely against the rules. In any event the effort needed proved to be just too much for him: after a few yards Mansell collapsed and had subsequently to be taken away to the medical centre to undergo treatment for heat exhaustion. This, in turn, enabled Ghinzani to snatch fifth place and left Mansell being classified an eventual sixth ahead of the only remaining finishers, Fabi and Winkelhock, who, whilst being out of the points, at least had the satisfaction of having kept their cars in one piece unlike some of their more esteemed colleagues.

Results

1	K. Rosberg (Williams-Honda)	2 hr 01 min 22.617 sec (129.203 kph/ 80.283 mph)
2	R. Arnoux (Ferrari)	2 hr 01 min 45.081 sec
3	E. de Angelis (Lotus-Renault)	1 lap behind
4	J.Laffite (Williams-Honda)	2 laps behind
5	P. Ghinzani (Osella-Alfa Romeo)	2 laps behind
*6	N. Mansell (Lotus-Renault)	3 laps behind
7	C. Fabi (Brabham-BMW)	3 laps behind
8	M. Winkelhock (ATS-BMW)	3 laps behind

* Not running at finish.

Fastest lap: N. Lauda (McLaren-TAG) on lap 22 in 1 min 45.353 sec (133.302 kph/82.830 mph)

Retirements
F. Hesnault (Ligier-Renault) accident on lap 1, E. Cheever (Alfa Romeo) accident on lap 9, S. Bellof (Tyrrell-Ford) accident on lap 10, D. Warwick (Renault) accident on lap 11, R. Patrese (Alfa Romeo) accident on lap 13, A. de Cesaris (Ligier-Renault) accident on lap 16, H. Rothengatter (Spirit-Hart) fuel leak on lap 16, P. Tambay (Renault) accident on lap 26, J. Cecotto (Toleman-Hart) accident on lap 26, N. Piquet (Brabham-BMW) accident on lap 46, J. Palmer (RAM-Hart) electrics on lap 47, A. Senna (Toleman-Hart) drive-shaft on lap 48, M. Alboreto (Ferrari) accident on lap 55, M. Surer (Arrows-BMW) accident on lap 55, T. Boutsen (Arrows-BMW) engine on lap 56, A. Prost (McLaren-TAG) accident on lap 57, N. Lauda (McLaren-TAG) accident on lap 61.

XXXVIIth British Grand Prix

Brands Hatch: July 22
Weather: Warm and sunny
Distance: 71 laps of 4.2061 km circuit = 298.64 km (185.57 miles)

Just two days before the start of official practice for the John Player Special British Grand Prix at Brands Hatch the FISA Executive Committee had held a meeting in Paris and, as previously mentioned, amongst its decisions was that of excluding the Tyrrell team from further participation in the 1984 World Championship. However, besides immediately submitting an appeal, Ken Tyrrell had successfully applied, at considerable cost, for a London High Court injunction against the RAC Motor Sports Association (the organizer of the British Grand Prix) and FISA to allow him to run his cars at Brands Hatch. In the meantime, he had already secured the services of former Spirit driver Stefan Johansson to deputize for the injured Martin Brundle and, on a somewhat happier note (especially as DeLonghi had responded to the news of the team's ban by immediately withdrawing its support), had attracted new sponsorship from Systime. The only unfortunate part about it was that this new association had been formed around Brundle with the aim of having an all-British effort but, despite the Englishman's accident, the computer company was abiding by its original commitment.

Apart from the enforced change at Tyrrell, the driver line-up differed from that at Dallas only by Teo Fabi returning to drive the second Brabham on a 'permanent' basis (he had now secured a release from his CART contract with Forsythe Racing) and by Jo Gartner being entered to drive alongside Piercarlo Ghinzani in a second Osella. The young Austrian had, of course, already made one previous appearance for the little Italian team at Imola driving a 1983 chassis fitted with a normally-aspirated V12 Alfa Romeo engine but, on this occasion, he was being entrusted with a brand new FA1F, complete with a V8 turbo-charged Alfa Romeo engine. As if to underline yet again the amount of work going on behind the scenes, most of the other teams were also preparing to field new or modified cars, including Renault who, besides introducing new rear under-bodies, had produced a new RE50 for Warwick with a stiffer and stronger monocoque than its immediate predecessors. There was also a new Toleman TG184 for Cecotto, a new ATS D7 to provide Winkelhock with the luxury of a spare chassis for the first time since Monaco and a new RAM 02 for Alliot, which featured revised suspension geometry to provide for greater camber change, as did Palmer's older car, and had been built to replace the chassis badly damaged by the Frenchman during practice at Dallas. Meanwhile, among the teams continuing to rely entirely on existing cars Euroracing Alfa Romeo were experimenting with a new electronic fuel-injection system, oddly enough utilizing a mechanical fuel pump, and Arrows, in addition to revising the rear suspension of one of their A7s (Boutsen's car), had altered the rear bodywork on both with the aim of improving the flow of air over the rear aerofoils as well as encouraging the cars to bring their rear tyres up to working temperature more effectively. Without doubt, though, the most significant changes of all had been made by the Brabham, Williams and Ferrari teams. Brabham had updated their BT53s to 'B' specification to denote a whole host of detail refinements that included slightly restyled bodywork, revised rear suspension geometry, subtle aerodynamic changes and the adoption of taller side-pods to house more steeply angled water radiators and inter-coolers; Williams had similarly converted their FW09s to 'B' specification, in which the cars appeared with a five-inch longer wheelbase made possible by a larger oil tank casting being located between the engine and the gearbox, with reprofiled side-pods that tapered inwards at the rear in similar fashion to the McLaren MP4/2s and accommodated repositioned water radiators and inter-coolers, with a new exhaust system and with slight alterations to the rear suspension; finally Ferrari had modified two of their four 126C4s, mainly by mounting the water radiators and inter-coolers at a different angle in what were much larger side-pods and by making minor aerodynamic changes. So, all in all, there was a very impressive array of machinery on hand for a race that was about to offer a refreshing contrast to the comparatively slow and tight confines of Detroit and Dallas.

Although the skies were overcast, conditions were dry and reasonably warm on Friday morning and there was no reason to doubt that the weekend's activities were going to get off to a good start. Certainly, when it came round to 10 o'clock, there was no lack of enthusiasm apparent from the drivers, many of whom were ready and waiting to go straight out. However, it appeared that Cecotto, who had never driven a racing car around the Kent circuit before, was a little too enthusiastic and possibly went too quickly on cold tyres or, at least, failed to take into account the somewhat dusty and slippery track conditions. Whatever, on only his third lap the Venezuelan suddenly lost control of his new Toleman on the way through Westfield Bend and was unable to prevent it from careering off the track and charging, head on, into the guard-rail on the left-hand side at Dingle Dell. With hindsight,

Starting Grid

	N. Piquet (1)
	Brabham-BMW
A. Prost (2)	(1 min 10.869 sec)
McLaren-TAG	
(1 min 11.076 sec)	N. Lauda (3)
	McLaren-TAG
E. de Angelis (5)	(1 min 11.344 sec)
Lotus-Renault	
(1 min 11.573 sec)	K. Rosberg (–)
	Williams-Honda
D. Warwick (4)	(1 min 11.603 sec)
Renault	
(1 min 11.703 sec)	A. Senna (6)
	Toleman-Hart
N. Mansell (9)	(1 min 11.890 sec)
Lotus-Renault	
(1 min 12.435 sec)	M. Alboreto (7)
	Ferrari
P. Tambay (8)	(1 min 13.122 sec)
Renault	
(1 min 13.138 sec)	M. Winkelhock (–)
	ATS-BMW
T. Boutsen (10)	(1 min 13.374 sec)
Arrows-BMW	
(1 min 13.528 sec)	R. Arnoux (12)
	Ferrari
T. Fabi (–)	(1 min 13.934 sec)
Brabham-BMW	
(1 min 14.040 sec)	M. Surer (14)
	Arrows-BMW
J. Laffite (13)	(1 min 14.336 sec)
Williams-Honda	
(1 min 14.568 sec)	R. Patrese (15)
	Alfa Romeo
E. Cheever (–)	(1 min 14.568 sec)
Alfa Romeo	
(1 min 14.609 sec)	A. de Cesaris (11)
	Ligier-Renault
F. Hesnault (18)	(1 min 15.112 sec)
Ligier-Renault	
(1 min 15.837 sec)	P. Ghinzani (16)
	Osella-Alfa Romeo
H. Rothengatter (19)	(1 min 16.466 sec)
Spirit-Hart	
(1 min 16.759 sec)	J. Palmer (–)
	RAM-Hart
P. Alliot (–)	(1 min 17.265 sec)
RAM-Hart	
(1 min 17.517 sec)	S. Johansson (–)
	Tyrrell-Ford
S. Bellof (17)	(1 min 17.777 sec)
Tyrrell-Ford	
(1 min 17.893 sec)	J. Gartner (–)
	Osella-Alfa Romeo
	(1 min 18.121 sec)

Non-starters:
J. Cecotto (Toleman-Hart) No time
N.B. Numbers in brackets denote grid positions for restart.

Cecotto was perhaps fortunate even to survive the shunt for the impact was so great that not only did it smash the front of the Toleman but it also demolished a large section of the barriers. Even so, he was still in a bad way with two severely broken ankles and a damaged right knee cap and, after eventually being cut free from the wreckage, had to be rushed off by helicopter to Sidcup hospital to undergo an emergency operation. Furthermore, the injuries were such that, sadly, they were to bring about a premature end to his Grand Prix career. In the meantime, practice was interrupted while the rescue and repair crews dealt with the accident and it was not until after 11.30 a.m. that this opening untimed session, now reduced to just one hour, could continue. When it did finally resume it was left to Senna to make the morning's other headlines by overcoming his obvious concern for his team-mate and achieving the fastest lap (1 min 12.633 sec), the first time that he, or Toleman, had ever headed a Grand Prix practice session.

After playing second fiddle to the Brazilian in the morning, Prost and Lauda took over the reins during the first qualifying session which, out of necessity, had to be put back from 1 p.m. to 2 p.m. Driving their essentially unchanged McLaren MP4/2s, both were almost immediately setting new standards and, by the time that he had used up his two sets of marked tyres, Lauda appeared to have the provisional pole sewn up with a lap in 1 min 11.598 sec – already almost exactly half a second faster than the pole-winning time set by de Angelis for the European Grand Prix held at this same circuit the previous September! At that point, though, Prost had still to complete his second run and in the dying minutes went on to upstage his team-mate with an even quicker time of 1 min 11.494 sec leaving Lauda, who thought that he had found a near-perfect lap, somewhat bemused. It also cost the Austrian 100 bottles of champagne, the prize for being the overnight pole-sitter! Meanwhile, as if to prove that his earlier performance had been no flash in the pan, Senna was still mighty impressive in the Toleman and would almost certainly have been third fastest had it not been for being baulked whilst out on his second set of tyres. As it was he still came out a very respectable fourth in the standings at 1 min 11.890 sec and was just over a tenth of a second slower than de Angelis (1 min 11.734 sec) in the quicker of the two Lotus 95Ts, Mansell winding up sixth fastest in the other black and gold car and well over a full second slower following problems with an engine that refused to rev properly. In fact, the only remaining driver really anywhere near on the pace was Warwick, and that was thanks only to a late charge just before the field was flagged off, which netted fifth fastest time of 1 min 12.278 sec. Prior to that both he and his somewhat slower team-mate

had spent half the session waiting around for broken turbo-charger units to be replaced on their Renaults, and this followed a morning that had seemingly been wasted carrying out inconclusive tests with some new experimental carbon-fibre brake discs. Nevertheless, if the French team was struggling a bit that was nothing compared to the situation in the Brabham camp where Piquet and Fabi were finding the revamped BT53s to be a major disappointment. The main problem was lack of grip, caused partly by the blue and white cars proving reluctant to warm up their Michelin tyres properly, and resulted in Piquet, who pulled off the track at the bottom of Hailwood Hill with an engine failure in the closing minutes, finishing up a most disappointing 12th on the time-sheets with Fabi ten places lower. The Goodyear-shod Ferraris were also somewhat off the pace for similar reasons, although, in addition, Arnoux and Alboreto (he was another to suffer an engine failure during the course of the afternoon) were both complaining of lack of straight-line speed. Apart from that, there were few surprises at the end of the day as most people were more or less in their usual places, including Rosberg, who was ninth fastest and rather disenchanted to find his modified Williams, after performing reasonably well during recent testing at the Osterreichring, plagued by understeer once more. Nor was his mood improved by a pipe coming adrift between the car's turbo-charger and inter-cooler right at the end of the session and bringing him to rest at Graham Hill Bend.

By the following morning Brabham's Gordon Murray had taken a step backwards and arranged to have two of the BT53Bs converted back to their previous configuration. The difference was quite incredible for Piquet, driving the team's spare chassis, rapidly improved from being little more than an also-ran to become the man to beat. First he completed the untimed session with comfortably the fastest lap of 1 min 11.572 sec under his belt, despite sliding off the track at one point and damaging the car's undertray. Then, whilst out on his first set of qualifiers soon after the start of the all-important final hour of qualifying, and with the 'B'-type rear suspension geometry and aerodynamics making a reappearance on the spare Brabham, he whistled around in the now very warm and sunny conditions in a staggering 1 min 10.869 sec (213.615 kph/132.734 mph). Thereafter, the Brazilian calmly returned to the pits, had his second set of tyres slapped on and played the waiting game, watching the opposition. What he saw was impressive for the overall pace was on the up and up yet, at the same time, it was not quick enough to cause him any alarm. Nevertheless, towards the end of the session Piquet decided to play it safe by taking to the track once more just in case someone made a last-ditch attempt to wrestle away the pole. In the event he might just as well have stayed put for his earlier time went unchallenged. Not that this was altogether surprising as quite apart from anything else de Cesaris, who had already made himself a bit unpopular by spinning at Westfield Bend during the first part of the afternoon and scattering dirt on to the track, had just laid an oil slick half way round the circuit following a major engine failure. Consequently, any more really quick laps were out of the question as several drivers, who had held back on their second sets of tyres, found out to their dismay. Prior to that Prost had already gone around in 1 min 11.076 sec to pose the most serious threat to the reigning World Champion, and Lauda had improved to 1 min 11.344 sec. So, with second and third places on the grid respectively, the McLaren team was still in a very strong position. De Angelis, meanwhile, had kept Lotus hopes alive by whittling his times down to 1 min 11.573 sec to claim fourth spot on the grid and Rosberg, after switching to the spare Williams and finding it a little more responsive in the handling department than his proposed race chassis, had improved to 1 min 11.603 sec to line up fifth. Senna, on the other hand, had dropped away somewhat after a frustrating day in which he had returned to the pits with flames licking around the back of both his own car and the spare Toleman during the morning following turbo-charger failures, and had then been badly baulked on his two qualifying runs. In fact, he was one of the very few drivers not to improve on their Friday times and he had to make do with an eventual seventh spot on the grid, sandwiched between Britain's two main hopes for the race, Warwick and Mansell. They, too, had suffered their fair share of problems: Warwick, who had survived a gentle off-course excursion into the catch-fences at Hawthorn Bend mid-way through the untimed session, had seen his best lap (1 min 11.703 sec) spoiled by a slower car before being plagued by a sticking throttle (for the second afternoon running) that, eventually, had led to another trip across the grass, while Mansell's hopes of progressing beyond 1 min 12.435 sec had been dashed by a broken gearbox.

Once again the Ferraris, both the older-spec and revised 126C4s, had proved rather disappointing. Even Alboreto, consistently the quicker of the two drivers, had qualified in only ninth place, while Arnoux was four places lower on the grid behind Tambay, Winkelhock and Boutsen in the first of the two Arrows A7s, the Belgian having recovered well from lost time caused by turbo-charger failures in each of Friday's sessions. Further down the order Fabi, like his team-mate, had obviously benefited from the changes made at Brabham, climbing from 22nd fastest at the end of the first day to

an eventual 14th on the grid, and Surer had also found a lot more speed in the second Arrows to move up to 15th spot. By contrast a very unhappy Laffite had been another of the very few drivers not to have improved due to a combination of suffering an acute loss of turbo boost pressure during his initial run and then not being able to get out again, in Rosberg's car, until after the oil from de Cesaris' Ligier had gone down. Indeed, the Frenchman was right at the bottom of the afternoon's time-sheets, but 16th fastest overall. After that the rest of the grid consisted of the evenly-matched Euroracing Alfa Romeos of Patrese and Cheever, both drivers handicapped by having only relatively modest amounts of turbo boost pressure at their disposal, the two rather poor-handling Ligiers of de Cesaris and Hesnault, Ghinzani's Osella, the three remaining Hart-engined and not exactly over-reliable cars of Rothengatter, Palmer and Alliot and, finally, the only two Ford-Cosworth-powered cars in the field, the Tyrrells of Johansson and Bellof. That left just Gartner, who was seemingly destined to be a spectator on race day after his efforts to qualify had not been improved by the loss of his lap times during the first part of the afternoon – an intermediate spot check had revealed the rear aerofoil of his Osella to have been a millimetre too high. However, after practice, and in view of the uncertainties over the Tyrrell affair (the subject of two post-practice Press Conferences) Enzo Osella put forward a request to the Stewards of the Meeting for the size of the grid to be increased to 27 cars and this was subsequently granted after he had obtained written agreement from all of the other teams. Consequently, the young Austrian could now look forward to taking part in his second Grand Prix after all.

Considerable pre-race publicity had obviously paid dividends, for spectator attendance during practice had been high, and on race day it was absolutely colossal with around 100,000 people pouring into the circuit from every conceivable direction. For a large proportion of them, who had arrived early, the Grand Prix was several hours away but, with the weather gradually developing into a gloriously warm and sunny summer's day and an action-packed supporting programme to savour, that included a most impressive lunch-time air and track display, the time passed quickly enough. In addition, of course, there was the customary warm-up session for the Formula 1 cars, which took place between 10.45 a.m. and 11.15 a.m. and saw the TAG-Porsche-powered McLaren MP4/2s of Prost and Lauda lap well over a second clear of the field. However, whilst they both enjoyed a trouble-free outing, Piquet had to contend with a leaking intercooler on his way to setting fifth fastest time, behind the Renaults of Tambay and War-

wick, and among others to run into problems were both Lotus drivers, with misfiring engines, and also Rosberg, who had to abandon the spare Williams that he was planning to race due to lack of fuel pressure. As usual, though, the mechanics proved equal to the task of sorting everything out and when, at 2.15 p.m., the pit lane was officially opened all 27 starters were soon taking to the track once more and making their way round to the dummy grid to await the final countdown for the 75-lap race. This, as always, seemed to last an eternity, but eventually, with 2.45 p.m. approaching, engines were being fired up again and then they were away on the final warm-up lap led by Piquet.

By now the adrenalin was really flowing and a couple of minutes later came the moment that everyone was awaiting, the start. And a good one it was, too, with the entire field getting away really well, Piquet leading into Paddock Bend from Prost, de Angelis, Lauda, Warwick and Mansell. A few seconds later that was still the order as the leaders streamed out of Druids and roared down the hill into Graham Hill Bend, but amongst the tail-enders there was trouble brewing. It all began with Patrese allowing the back of his Alfa Romeo to get away from him under braking for the left-hander and sliding sideways directly in front of his team-mate after apparently attempting to nip through on the inside of Laffite's Williams. Somewhat ironically the Italian got away with it but, after Cheever and Johansson (he had made an excellent start) had responded by immediately standing on their brakes, Alliot failed to spot what was happening in time and ran straight into the back of the Swede's Tyrrell. Furthermore, he then proceeded to give the spectators an extended air display by flying right over the top of the predominantly blue car before crashing down on to the rear of Cheever's Alfa and finally skating to rest on the grassy infield, mercifully unharmed. Meanwhile, as if that wasn't drama enough, the general confusion also led to Gartner losing control of his Osella and slamming into the tyre wall on the right-hand side of the track, again without coming to any personal grief. Even so, there was quite obviously no way in which either the RAM or the Osella could continue, and although Cheever and Johansson both managed to make it round to the pits the rear end damage to their cars was such that they, too, were forced to retire. In the meantime, the rest of the field was already well into the second lap with Piquet maintaining his lead over Prost, but with Lauda now up into third place, de Angelis down in fifth spot between Warwick and Rosberg, and Mansell, suffering from unexpected understeer, an unhappy tenth behind Alboreto, Senna and Tambay. On the third lap it was much the same except that Lauda was now rapidly pulling away from Warwick and doing his best to get on terms with the two leading cars. Indeed, within another lap it had become essentially a three-car race and this is how it continued with Piquet just about holding his own against Prost, and with Lauda steadily catching them both until, after another two or three laps, they were all circulating in virtual nose to tail formation. By that stage, though, Piquet knew only too well that he had been over-optimistic when making his tyre choice. Quite simply his soft Michelins were not only blistering already but were also losing their grip, thus making the business of trying to keep Prost at bay all the more difficult. Even the crowd was starting to sense that the two McLarens were handling better than the Brabham, and whilst Piquet had the slight edge on straight-line speed it was not enough to make up the difference. Consequently, as Piquet's tyres continued to deteriorate, so Prost began making serious moves to take over the lead until finally, at the start of the 12th lap, he neatly darted through on the inside of the Brabham under braking for Paddock Bend. This, in turn, caused a somewhat startled Piquet to run fractionally wide and, almost before realizing it, he found himself being nailed by Lauda on the approach to Druids. At that point the Brazilian then decided that the time had come to take on harder tyres. However, before he actually got to the pits Palmer's RAM suddenly suffered a steering failure at Clearways, veered straight off into the tyre wall on the outside of Clark Curve and then bounced backwards across the grass to finish up perilously close to the edge of the track with its left front corner torn off. A small fire also developed around the car's left-hand sidepod, but by then the Englishman was already out of the cockpit with nothing worse than a sore neck and, in any event, some marshals were soon on the scene with extinguishers.

Nevertheless, with the RAM stranded in such a vulnerable position the officials wasted little time in displaying the red flag at the start/finish line – just after Prost and Lauda had gone through to start the 13th lap – and brought the race to a grinding halt.

For Piquet this couldn't have happened at a better time if it had been planned: the rules not only dictated that the British Grand Prix would now be a two-part affair but also that because the red flag had been shown at the end of the 12th lap the order at the end of the first part of the race would be that at the end of the 11th – the last lap on which he had led the race! Consequently, when the grid reformed and another 20 minute count-down began for the second part of the race (60 laps), following a delay of around half an hour while the circuit was being cleared of derelict cars, Piquet was on pole position once more. Then it was Prost in second spot, Lauda third and so on right back to Rothengatter, who was in 19th and last place. Missing, besides Palmer and the four first lap casualties, were Winkelhock, who had spun and stalled at Surtees on the ninth lap (he was not allowed to take the restart due to having officially retired) and also Rosberg and Fabi, both of whom had gone into the pits before the red flag. Rosberg's initial problem had been another pipe coming adrift between his car's turbocharger and inter-cooler, as had happened in practice, but then the engine had gone rough and precluded any possibility of taking the restart, while Fabi had retired the second Brabham with some obscure electrical fault.

When, at approximately 4 p.m., the race was finally set in motion once more an angry Prost (he, and de Angelis, had been particularly incensed about the stoppage and implied that someone was being charitable to Piquet!) made rather better use of being on

the higher side of the gently sloping Brabham Straight on this occasion and tore off into an immediate lead. Like the original start, the rest of the field also got away cleanly and this time they all went on to complete the 'opening lap' intact with Prost, still in front, being hotly pursued by Piquet and Lauda. Warwick was fourth, just ahead of team-mate Tambay and de Angelis, but Mansell, who had been lying seventh, had already lost two places to Alboreto and Senna and was finding the earlier understeer problem persisting. In addition, a slight engine misfire that had also been apparent during the first part of the race was still there, and within another lap the unfortunate Englishman had slipped away to the 12th spot behind de Cesaris, Boutsen and Arnoux. Initially it appeared that Alboreto might well be another on the downward slide for he had just been bundled out of seventh place by Senna and, on the third lap, found himself being outwitted by de Cesaris. However, after that the Ferrari driver held his ground and before long was doing his utmost to repass his compatriot, especially when Arnoux moved up to join him once he had disposed of Boutsen on the sixth lap. Up front, meanwhile, the three leading cars were soon into a race of their own in much the same fashion as earlier in the afternoon except that Piquet, of course, was now the meat in a McLaren sandwich. Furthermore, this situation went on lap after lap and after a while became rather tedious in many respects for it was patently clear that Prost, gradually edging away, was well in control of things, while Lauda never seemed able to get quite close enough to Piquet to mount a really serious challenge. Only at the start of lap 29 (lap 18 of the restarted race) was the sequence broken when Lauda finally launched an all-out attack on the Brabham going up Hailwood Hill and successfully scrambled past it under braking for Druids. At that point there was every hope of a stirring battle developing between the two McLaren drivers later in the race but, sadly, it was not to be. First of all Prost, already over 5 seconds clear by now, responded to pit signals advising him of his team-mate's progress by putting on a spurt and then, early on lap 38, the hopes vanished completely when the Championship leader suddenly slowed dramatically, was passed by Lauda and Piquet in quick succession and completed the lap by touring into the pits. A pinion bearing had failed in the McLaren's gearbox – Prost was out of the race! By then Warwick had long since settled into a lonely fourth place, so now automatically took over third spot, but Tambay had only just rejoined the race a few minutes earlier following a tyre stop and slipped behind a duelling de Angelis and Senna. Prior to that Bellof and Surer had also been into the pits for fresh rubber, Rothengatter had lost sev-

The battle for supremacy at Brands Hatch as Alain Prost hangs on to a tenuous lead over Nelson Piquet and team-mate Niki Lauda during the early stages of the re-started race. *(Autosport)*

eral laps having a damaged nose cone replaced on his Spirit following a slight argument with the back of Hesnault's Ligier and there had been three other retirements. Laffite had gone out with overheating problems caused by a broken water pump, Mansell's unhappy weekend had been made complete by a broken gearbox and Boutsen, another to have made an early tyre stop, had parked his Arrows out on the circuit owing to an electrical failure killing its BMW engine. As a result there were now only 15 cars still running and mainly well spread out at that. Indeed, the only real entertainment for the crowd, apart from the continuing de Angelis-Senna duel, was a prolonged battle, now for seventh place, going on between de Cesaris and the two Ferrari drivers, both, incidentally, in the revised 126C4s. Arguably, de Cesaris was being downright obstructive and, arguably, he had no right to be driving in the manner that he was. But either way, he was certainly being successful in defending his position, even if it was causing several heart-stopping moments and increasing anger in the cockpit of car number 28, which had just slid wide enough at Paddock Bend for Alboreto to take up the cudgels once more after earlier dropping behind his team-mate.

By lap 44 (lap 33 of the restarted race), with Hesnault shortly destined to become the next retirement with a broken engine, Piquet was starting to show every sign of getting back on terms with Lauda, who was now coming up to lap the de Cesaris – Alboreto – Arnoux entourage. This, in turn, suggested that there might well be a fight to the finish after all but, again, nothing much was to come of it. For a start Lauda made comparatively light work of picking his way through the traffic ahead of him, despite a worrying moment approaching Druids on lap 46 when he was confronted by de Cesaris and Alboreto nearly – very nearly – tripping over one another as the Ferrari driver finally forced his way through on the inside of the Ligier under braking. Then, once he had done likewise, Piquet soon discovered that he could make no, or very little, further impression on the McLaren, the gap remaining at an almost constant 2 seconds for the next dozen or so laps. Moreover, at that point the Brabham's turbo boost pressure began to gradually drop away until, with just over five laps remaining, it disappeared completely and left Piquet in the unhappy position of having to sit and watch one car after another go surging past him as he crawled round for a finish. Consequently, Lauda was able to drive on to what, ultimately, was a most comfortable (and popular) victory, his winning margin, on aggregate times, being 42.123 seconds over Warwick, who gave the British fans plenty to cheer about with a fine second place, even if it was at the expense of the reigning World Champion. Meanwhile, so far as the other finishers were concerned, Piquet was by no means alone in being responsible for changing the order in the closing stages of the race. Only a few laps earlier Arnoux had made contact with the Ligier of de Cesaris at Druids and left the Italian limping round with slightly damaged rear suspension following a quick spin; de Angelis had finally been forced to concede to sustained pressure from Senna at Paddock Bend on lap 66 and only just made it home, in fourth place, owing to running into similar turbo boost pressure problems to those of Piquet in the last couple of laps; Patrese had stopped just beyond the start/finish line with the end in sight, the reason being almost certainly lack of fuel; and Tambay had to forego a finish in the points by pulling off the track at Surtees on his very last lap with the engine compartment of his Renault on fire, the result of an oil leak. So, all in all, it was quite a dramatic conclusion to an otherwise mainly uninspiring race from which two of the only three really serious contenders had nothing to show for their afternoon's work. The other, of course, was Lauda, who had scored just the sort of result that was needed to keep him in touch with his team-mate at the top of the Championship table, for the gap was now down to a mere 1½ points. Although it appeared to be of rather less interest to him, Lauda had also just set a new record by becoming the top points scorer of all time with an accumulated total of 367½ points compared to the previous record of 360 points held by Jackie Stewart.

Results		
1	N. Lauda (McLaren-TAG)	1 hr 29 min 28.532 sec (200.212 kph/ 124.406 mph)
2	D. Warwick (Renault)	1 hr 30 min 10.655 sec
3	A. Senna (Toleman-Hart)	1 hr 30 min 31.860 sec
4	E. de Angelis (Lotus-Renault)	1 lap behind
5	M. Alboreto (Ferrari)	1 lap behind
6	R. Arnoux (Ferrari)	1 lap behind
7	N. Piquet (Brabham-BMW)	1 lap behind
**8	P. Tambay (Renault)	2 laps behind
9	P. Ghinzani (Osella-Alfa Romeo)	3 laps behind
10	A. de Cesaris (Ligier-Renault)	3 laps behind
*	S. Bellof (Tyrrell-Ford)	3 laps behind
11	M. Surer (Arrows-BMW)	4 laps behind
**12	R. Patrese (Alfa Romeo)	5 laps behind

Also running at finish: H. Rothengatter (Spirit-Hart) 9 laps behind

* Excluded

** Not running at finish

Fastest lap: N. Lauda (McLaren-TAG) on lap 57 in 1 min 13.191 sec (208.837 kph/ 128.523 mph)

Retirements

J. Gartner (Osella-Alfa Romeo) accident on lap 1, P. Alliot (RAM-Hart) accident on lap 1, E. Cheever (Alfa Romeo) accident damage on lap 1, S. Johansson (Tyrrell-Ford) accident damage on lap 1, K. Rosberg (Williams-Honda) engine on lap 6, M. Winkelhock (ATS-BMW) spun and stalled on lap 9, T. Fabi (Brabham-BMW) electrics on lap 10, J. Palmer (RAM-Hart) accident on lap 11, J. Laffite (Williams-Honda) water pump on lap 15, N. Mansell (Lotus-Renault) gearbox on lap 25, T. Boutsen (Arrows-BMW) electrics on lap 25, A. Prost (McLaren-TAG) gearbox on lap 38, F. Hesnault (Ligier-Renault) engine on lap 44.

(Results given are the aggregate for the two-part race.)

XLVI Grosser Preis von Deutschland

Hockenheim: August 5
Weather: Overcast but dry
Distance: 44 laps of 6.797 km circuit = 299.07 km (185.83 miles)

The Tyrrell affair had continued capturing most of the headlines even after the British Grand Prix and since then the situation had taken a turn for the better or, at least, for the time being. Essentially, after drumming up the support of the other competing teams, Ken Tyrrell had filed a fairly lengthy petition with the FISA Executive Committee requesting that his team be allowed to participate in all races up until the date of his appeal hearing, and this had received a favourable response. At the same time, however, the ban had been lifted on the basis that his team would be competing 'outside the World Championship' and, as such, would be ineligible for Championship points. Even so, Tyrrell was only too relieved to be allowed to continue racing and arrived at the Hockenheim-Ring, the venue for the next round on the Championship trail, with renewed optimism, notwithstanding the fact that both of his regular drivers were unavailable. Martin Brundle was still on the casualty list, while Stefan Bellof was away in Canada fulfilling a commitment under his Porsche World Endurance Championship contract. As a result it had been necessary to seek out the services of yet another fresh driver for this particular race and, on this occasion, the choice turned out to be the new 1984 European Formula 2 champion, Mike Thackwell. He, of course, had last stood in for Jonathan Palmer at the Canadian Grand Prix when the Englishman had temporarily vacated his RAM seat to take part in the Le Mans 24-hour race.

Practice for what was now the eighth successive German Grand Prix to be held at Hockenheim began under clear blue skies and bright sunshine on Friday morning with the main priority for the drivers, as always,

---

Starting Grid

A. Prost
McLaren-TAG
(1 min 47.012 sec)

D. Warwick
Renault
(1 min 48.382 sec)

N. Piquet
Brabham-BMW
(1 min 48.584 sec)

N. Lauda
McLaren-TAG
(1 min 48.912 sec)

A. Senna
Toleman-Hart
(1 min 49.395 sec)

A. de Cesaris
Ligier-Renault
(1 min 50.117 sec)

M. Winkelhock
ATS-BMW
(1 min 50.686 sec)

T. Boutsen
Arrows-BMW
(1 min 51.551 sec)

F. Hesnault
Ligier-Renault
(1 min 51.872 sec)

K. Rosberg
Williams-Honda
(1 min 52.003 sec)

P. Ghinzani
Osella-Alfa Romeo
(1 min 54.546 sec)

J. Gartner
Osella-Alfa Romeo
(1 min 55.594 sec)

J. Palmer
RAM-Hart
(1 min 56.797 sec)

E. de Angelis
Lotus-Renault
(1 min 47.065 sec)

P. Tambay
Renault
(1 min 48.425 sec)

M. Alboreto
Ferrari
(1 min 48.847 sec)

T. Fabi
Brabham-BMW
(1 min 49.302 sec)

R. Arnoux
Ferrari
(1 min 49.857 sec)

J. Laffite
Williams-Honda
(1 min 50.511 sec)

M. Surer
Arrows-BMW
(1 min 51.475 sec)

N. Mansell
Lotus-Renault
(1 min 51.715 sec)

E. Cheever
Alfa Romeo
(1 min 51.950 sec)

R. Patrese
Alfa Romeo
(1 min 52.769 sec)

P. Alliot
RAM-Hart
(1 min 55.505 sec)

H. Rothengatter
Spirit-Hart
(1 min 56.112 sec)

S. Johansson
Tyrrell-Ford
(1 min 59.461 sec)

Did not qualify:
M. Thackwell (Tyrrell-Ford)
1 min 59.516 sec.

---

being that of adapting their cars to the circuit before the opening hour of qualifying. This meant trying different tyres, going through the rigours of delicate chassis tuning and, at this particular circuit, paying special regard to wing angles with the aim of arriving at the best possible compromise in terms of generating sufficient downforce to cope with the three chicanes and the twisty stadium section, without sacrificing too much outright speed for the fast straights. That, at least, was the general idea, but so far as the recently renamed John Player Special Team Lotus was concerned it didn't quite work out like that, and for Mansell in particular. Instead, the Englishman ran into immediate problems with a bolt coming adrift inside a freshly built gearbox containing some new Italian-made gears, and then, to cap it all, his engine expired as the result of an electrical failure, stranding him out on the circuit after only a couple of laps. Ordinarily he could almost certainly have taken over his team's spare car once he had made his way back to the pits, but any chance of that had already been scuppered by de Angelis. The Italian had suffered an early piston failure! Consequently Mansell was forced to sit things out, but apart from this stroke of bad luck in the Lotus camp most people went on to complete the 90 minute untimed session largely unhindered, and ultimately finished up reasonably satisfied with their progress. In the Ferrari pit, though, Mauro Forghieri was being driven close to distraction due to the lack of any useful feed-back being provided by Arnoux or Alboreto following some back-to-back tests with the quartet of 126C4s on hand. All four of them now had the larger side-pods and revised cooling arrangements first seen at Brands Hatch but, in addition, two had been given reprofiled under-bodies and also revised rear suspension systems in which the pull-rod activated coil-spring/damper units had given away to a (narrower track) push-rod arrangement. However, neither driver, it seemed, could make up his mind as to whether or not it was an improvement, and the mood wasn't exactly enhanced when they both subsequently announced that they would be concentrating their efforts on the two cars with the older-type rear suspension for the rest of the weekend.

After being sidelined for most of the morning, Mansell was to enjoy little better fortune in the afternoon qualifying session. For a start the gearbox was still not right, despite attempts having been made to repair it during the interval, and now, in addition, he found himself running into fuel pump and turbo-charger problems. Eventually the fuel pump trouble was traced to a blocked bleed hole in the filter causing air bubbles to remain in the system, but by that time it was too late to help Mansell's qualifying efforts and in the final reckoning he did well even to squeeze in a lap of 1 min 52.958 sec, 16th

fastest. Nevertheless, he was not the only one to hit serious trouble this time out, as it developed into a particularly frustrating afternoon for Rosberg and Tambay. Indeed, for the Finn it was more than that: it was a disaster. His first qualifying run was effectively ruined owing to being badly held up by Patrese, his second ended soon after leaving the pits when a brand new Williams FW09B that he was driving suffered a turbo-charger failure and then, before he could try to hoist himself off the bottom of the time-sheets in the spare Williams, the field was being flagged off for the day. Tambay's problems, on the other hand, arose from not one but two engine failures, the first occurring on his opening lap of the afternoon and whilst out in a brand new Renault RE50 that had been built to the same, stronger, specification as the car prepared for his team-mate immediately prior to the British Grand Prix. However, it was when the spare Renault suffered a similar fate some time afterwards that it became really significant, for not only did this result in the Frenchman having to wait around in the hope of taking over Warwick's car to set a time, but it also left the track coated with oil through the twisty stadium section, thus putting paid to any more really quick times. Even Tambay found that out, for when he was subsequently allowed a turn behind the wheel of Warwick's car the best that he could manage was a lap in 1 min 51.414 sec which, besides being almost 3 seconds slower than that achieved by his team-mate earlier in the afternoon, left him only tenth fastest. In fact, by lapping in 1 min 48.576 sec, Warwick had put himself right in amongst the pace-setters and finished up in a fine second place on the time-sheets between Piquet (1 min 48.698 sec) and an impressive de Angelis, who had won the provisional pole convincingly at 1 min 48.033 sec and brought some much-needed cheer to the Lotus pit. Meanwhile Lauda, quickest in the morning, was still well in the picture with fourth fastest time of 1 min 48.912 sec, but after that only three other drivers had managed even to break the 1 min 50 sec barrier. These were the ever-improving Senna (the sole Toleman representative this weekend), who had made good use of a new TG184 featuring a Ferrari-type rear wing in place of the more familiar double rear aerofoil arrangement and lapped in 1 min 49.395 sec, Prost, who had got down to 1 min 49.439 sec, after being obliged to sit out the early stages of qualifying whilst a turbo-charger unit was replaced on his McLaren, and Alboreto, who had taken the quicker of the two Ferraris around in 1 min 49.782 sec.

Overnight the weather underwent a complete transformation and led to the second untimed session on Saturday morning taking place in conditions that were thoroughly wet and miserable. However, almost as soon as it

269

was over, with everyone, by and large, having contented themselves with no more than a few exploratory laps on wet-weather tyres, the sun reappeared, and by 1 p.m., the start of final qualifying, much of the track had already become reasonably dry. Rather than rush straight out, though, the majority of the drivers, particularly those to have recorded reasonable times on Friday, were quite happy to bide their time in the pits and let the warm sunshine continue to do its good work of drying the track properly. As a result, the first 20 minutes or so proved to be a relatively quiet period highlighted only by a typically enthusiastic performance from Rosberg as he endeavoured to make up for the disappointing first day. Using race rubber, he quite literally flung his Williams through the twisty stadium section in a series of glorious power slides and eventually completed his opening run with a lap of 1 min 52.003 sec to his credit, fast enough to have put him half way up Friday's time-sheets. After that other drivers gradually started joining in until, shortly past 1.30 p.m., it became absolutely hectic. Sadly, though, Rosberg was destined to make no further progress, for when he later went out on his only set of qualifiers the gremlins struck again in the form of an electrical failure – just as he was about to complete his first flying lap! In the meantime, the battle for the leading grid positions was growing more intense by the minute with de Angelis and Prost, in particular, setting a furious pace. Piquet, Warwick and Tambay (fastest in the wet) were right up in the thick of it as well, but Lauda appeared to be struggling a bit due to an engine that besides smoking rather a lot was losing power. Moreover, just prior to completing his initial run, the Austrian suddenly spun off on to the grass at the last right-hander leading round to the pits straight, after apparently trying a fraction too hard, and damaged the McLaren's nose cone. He then switched his attention to the team's spare car, but still failed to improve on his Friday time and ultimately slipped from a provisional fourth place on the grid to seventh. By contrast, his team-mate was making noticeably good progress and in the closing minutes put in a real flier at 1 min 47.012 sec (228.658 kph). That, not surprisingly, settled it so far as pole position was concerned, although had it not been for coming upon Fabi's slower-moving Brabham on the approach to one of the chicanes de Angelis might well have rewritten the script. As it was the Italian, easily the quickest Goodyear runner, just failed in his quest to win back the top spot by being clocked at 1 min 47.065 sec moments before the field was flagged off. Despite both being more than a full second slower at 1 min 48.382 sec and 1 min 48.425 respectively, Warwick and Tambay were next up in their Renaults and they, in turn, were immediately ahead of an angry Piquet, whose best

lap of 1 min 48.584 sec had been spoiled by Patrese and Mansell almost tripping over one another at the Sachskurve right in front of him. At the time Mansell had also been on his best lap (1 min 51.715 sec), had dived through on the inside of the Italian under braking but had then slid wide and been repassed, an incident that together with the previous day's troubles went a long way to explaining why the Englishman was left languishing in only 16th place on the grid. Even so, it was still three places higher than the unfortunate Rosberg. Meanwhile, Alboreto had recovered well enough from an early electrical problem that had forced him into his spare Ferrari with the revised rear suspension to claim sixth spot on the grid at 1 min 48.847 sec, but Arnoux, complaining of lack of straight-line speed, had failed to make the same impression as his team-mate. Instead, he had lapped over a second slower and was down in tenth spot behind Lauda, Fabi, who had been making steady progress in the second Brabham, and Senna, whose hopes of capitalizing on Friday's impressive performance had been dashed by a high-speed misfire. After that the rest of the grid had a pretty familiar look about it (apart from Mansell and Rosberg being so far down the order) and least surprising of all was the fact that only one of the hopelessly outpaced, Ford-Cosworth-powered, Tyrrells had made the cut, Johansson having pipped young Thackwell for 26th and last place on the grid by less than a tenth of a second.

More rain set in on Saturday night but, thankfully, on Sunday morning it dispersed even more quickly than the previous day and enabled the warm-up session to take place on a dry track, albeit under overcast skies. For

the McLaren team, in particular, this proved to be quite a fraught 30 minutes. Prost was soon back in the pits complaining that his engine wasn't running properly, while Lauda arrived in the pit lane with his engine almost literally screaming its head off – the throttle mechanism had stuck and the ignition switch had broken! Other drivers also ran into unexpected problems, including Warwick, whose clutch started playing up, but the only real disaster befell the little Spirit team when Rothengatter's 101B suffered a major engine failure, which stranded the Dutchman out on the circuit. Nevertheless, in the three hours that followed before the pit lane was officially opened, and the count-down began for the start of the race, everything was sorted out (this included preparing the spare Spirit 101B for Rothengatter) and shortly past 2 p.m. all 26 starters were setting off on the warm-up lap seemingly in good shape. Despite a change of fuel pump, however, Prost's McLaren was still not behaving itself, so the Frenchman responded by driving straight back into the pits, transferred to the spare McLaren, that had already been prepared for him in case of such an eventuality, and left his original car to be wheeled away with a suspected broken fuel pump drive. After that, he then set off on another warm-up lap and eventually joined the others waiting on the dummy grid prior to leading them round on the parade lap.

At the green Prost got off to a rather mediocre start from his pole position on the outside of the track and was emphatically beaten into the first right-hander by the black and gold Lotus 95T of de Angelis. Warwick almost made it past him as well by attempting to follow the Italian through on the

Early pace-setter Elio de Angelis keeps a wary eye on Alain Prost's McLaren and Nelson Piquet's Brabham as he leads the field out of the stadium at the start of the third lap. *(Autosport)*

inside, but Prost had the better line, swooped across the front of the Renault and was in second place as the field disappeared into the forest. This was still the situation a minute or so later when they arrived at the fast right-hander off the return straight and made their way through the twisty stadium section before setting off on the second lap, although Warwick had since been forced to give way to Piquet and was currently lying fourth. Next came a rather perplexed Tambay (he had been fastest in the morning warm-up but for no obvious reason his engine was no longer delivering full power), followed by Senna, Alboreto, Lauda, Fabi, de Cesaris, Arnoux and the rest except for Surer, who was not even in sight. Then, when the Swiss did eventually appear in the stadium, he went crawling into the pits with his BMW engine being starved of fuel due to a fault with its injection system, and was obliged to become the first retirement. Unfortunately, it was also to be a rather short race for Senna. After breezing past Tambay on the second lap, only three more laps passed before a support stay suddenly broke on the new Toleman's rear wing. That, in turn, led to the entire rear wing tilting over backwards and to the red, white and blue car being pitched into a series of lurid spins until, finally, it slammed backwards into the guardrail on the left-hand side of the track. At the time Senna had been flat out in fifth gear along the ultra fast section of track leading towards the Ostkurve but amazingly, in spite of the enormity of the accident, he subsequently walked away from the scene perfectly alright, apart from being quite obviously very disappointed. Meanwhile, the leaders were still running in the same order and, with the exception of Warwick, who was being left behind somewhat in fourth place, were staying close enough to one another to make things decidedly interesting, especially as it entailed three different chassis powered by three different engines. Further back, too, there was a lot of close racing going on but, above all else, it was the progress being made by Rosberg that had the spectators on the edge of their seats, for the Finn was making a complete mockery of his lowly grid position and charging up through the field in leaps and bounds. In fact, with Senna out, he was now up into a quite incredible seventh place and already giving chase to Lauda and Fabi, who had earlier picked off Alboreto's Ferrari, which was misfiring rather badly, as well as Tambay's down-on-power Renault.

After seven laps, with Rosberg now ahead of Fabi and still going like the clappers, the situation up front was even more tense as de Angelis, Prost and Piquet were closer than ever and a change was beginning to look imminent. Sure enough, on the following lap it came, although in a manner least expected: the Renault engine in the leading Lotus

suddenly blew up in just about the biggest possible way imaginable. As a result the unfortunate de Angelis was left touring into the pits to post his first retirement of 1984. But, instead of a McLaren completing the lap in the lead, it was a Brabham due to Prost having lost sufficient momentum in lifting off to avoid the stricken Lotus as to allow Piquet the opportunity of sneaking on ahead of him. In the meantime, of course, Warwick automatically moved up into a relatively distant third place only to find himself falling prey to Lauda and the seemingly unstoppable Rosberg next time round, thus the order after nine laps was Piquet-Prost-Lauda-Rosberg-Warwick-Fabi, with Tambay plugging on gamely in seventh place ahead of the others. However, the retirements now started coming thick and fast and led to the race losing even more of its intensity. They began again with Boutsen withdrawing the second Arrows from mid-field with its BMW engine suffering from lack of oil pressure. This was then followed, in quick succession, by Alliot disappearing from the back of the field with a badly overheating engine that an early pit stop had done nothing to alleviate; by Laffite being forced to bow out of a promising eighth place because of a piston failure; and, most significant of all, by Rosberg having his brilliant drive curtailed by an electrical fault that sent his Williams coasting to rest in the stadium on the 11th lap. Palmer wasn't around much longer either, a broken turbine blade causing an acute loss of turbo boost pressure, while over the next few minutes Gartner suffered a fiery turbo-charger failure; Alboreto called it a day with his misfiring Ferrari after an abortive pit stop a few laps earlier; Ghinzani's Osella stopped out on the circuit with some obscure electrical problem; and then Patrese pulled into the pits with a broken gearbox. The upshot of all this mechanical mayhem was that after little more than half an hour's racing only 14 cars were left, and most of them well spaced out at that. Nevertheless, there still seemed to be a reasonable chance of the Brabham/McLaren battle going all the way to the flag, for whilst Piquet had crept away a little from Prost the gap was no more than around 5 seconds and Lauda was not that much further behind his team-mate in third place. Moreover, by the 20th lap the gaps had even come down a fraction, which only served to heighten the tension. Alas, it was to be short-lived. Unbeknown to the spectators Piquet was beginning to lose gears – a pinion bearing had broken in his gearbox – and by lap 22 the situation was becoming so hopeless that the Brabham slowed sufficiently to enable Prost to surge past into the lead. Before they had reached the stadium again Lauda had also moved up into second place, and one more lap was enough to convince Piquet that it was pointless continuing. Obviously this was a bitter blow, both from the

point of view of the race and Piquet's hopes of retaining the World Championship crown, but for all that the Brazilian went on to display a remarkably good sense of humour by pointing to his tyres on arriving at the pits and encouraging the Brabham mechanics to go through their well-drilled wheel-changing routine. Only after all four wheels had been changed did he switch off the engine and step out of the car, at which point the joke became apparent and did much to hide the disappointment felt by the entire team.

Although Piquet was out, there was still hope for Brabham salvaging something as Fabi was driving really well in the second blue and white car, and currently causing more than a passing degree of concern to the now third-placed Warwick. Indeed, this was one of the few points of interest left in the race, barring the possibility of Lauda becoming embroiled in a duel with his team-mate for the lead. After less than another five laps, however, there was more bad news when the Italian, who had been bothered by a slight engine misfire ever since the start, slowed dramatically and became yet another name on the retirement list, his Brabham now having lost virtually all of its turbo boost pressure. Twelve cars left! Soon it was ten. Only a minute or so later the V8 engine in Cheever's rather sluggish Alfa Romeo cried 'enough', and then, after 31 laps, Winkelhock sounded the final death-knell for Munich by retiring the last remaining BMW-powered car from near the back of the field with a broken turbo-charger unit. Fortunately, with the track already looking deserted at times, the German was to be the last of the afternoon's casualties, although by now a lot of the spectators had become so bored with what they were seeing that it didn't seem to matter any more. As it was Lauda had more or less settled for second place after finding his team-mate responding to everything that he could throw at him, including fastest lap; Warwick was now on his own in third place; and about the only hint of any actual racing going on, apart from the two Ligier drivers passing and repassing each other at fairly frequent intervals as they fought among themselves for what had become seventh place, was between Tambay and Mansell. For a while, at least, this did attract a bit of interest as it was turning out to be a real old cat-and-mouse affair that had already been going on for several laps, the Englishman having steadily risen from 16th place on the grid to fifth place in the race. Essentially Tambay, whose tyres were in better shape, was quicker through the twisty stadium section and through the chicanes, whereas Mansell clearly had the upper hand in straight-line speed. On lap 34, though, Mansell finally put an end to that as well by powering past the Renault along the fast return straight and immediately pulling away to consolidate his new position. Thereafter, the only other change to occur came in the closing stages when de Cesaris overtook his team-mate for the last time, and for most people it was a relief when the chequered flag was hung out at the end of the 44 laps to bring the high-speed procession to a conclusion. At the finish Prost and Lauda crossed the line a whisker over 3 seconds apart (after the Frenchman had eased off during the last couple of laps) and whilst it had been a rather dreary German Grand Prix it was certainly a resounding 1–2 victory for the McLaren team and one that gave every bit as much pleasure to the Porsche engineers from Stuttgart. After all, their TAG-financed engine had just trounced the opposition – and on home soil at that! With Warwick finishing in third place, albeit more than half a minute in arrears, it was also a happy day for Michelin, who had now swept the board with a 1–2–3 for the second race on the trot. As for the rest, Mansell duly brought the first Goodyear-shod car home in fourth spot ahead of Tambay, Arnoux (lapped) salvaged a point for sixth place in his Ferrari, in spite of a tyre stop shortly past half-distance, and de Cesaris, Hesnault (he coasted over the line out of fuel!), Johansson and Rothengatter completed the short list of finishers.

Smiles all round after the race as Alain Prost celebrates yet another McLaren victory in the company of team-mate Niki Lauda and Derek Warwick, who finished third in his Renault. (*Autosport*)

Results

1	A. Prost (McLaren-TAG)	1 hr 24 min 43.210 sec (211.803 kph/ 131.608 mph)
2	N. Lauda (McLaren-TAG)	1 hr 24 min 46.359 sec
3	D. Warwick (Renault)	1 hr 25 min 19.633 sec
4	N. Mansell (Lotus-Renault)	1 hr 25 min 34.873 sec
5	P. Tambay (Renault)	1 hr 25 min 55.159 sec
6	R. Arnoux (Ferrari)	1 lap behind
7	A. de Cesaris (Ligier-Renault)	1 lap behind
8	F. Hesnault (Ligier-Renault)	1 lap behind
*	S. Johansson (Tyrrell-Ford)	2 laps behind
9	H. Rothengatter (Spirit-Hart)	4 laps behind

* Excluded

Fastest lap: A. Prost (McLaren-TAG) on lap 31 in 1 min 53.538 sec (215.515 kph/ 133.915 mph)

Retirements

M. Surer (Arrows-BMW) fuel-injection on lap 2, A. Senna (Toleman-Hart) accident on lap 5, P. Alliot (RAM-Hart) overheating on lap 8; E. de Angelis (Lotus-Renault) engine on lap 9, T. Boutsen (Arrows-BMW) oil pressure on lap 9, J. Laffite (Williams-Honda) engine on lap 11, K. Rosberg (Williams-Honda) electrics on lap 11, J. Palmer (RAM-Hart) turbo-charger on lap 12, J. Gartner (Osella-Alfa Romeo) turbo-charger on lap 14, M. Alboreto (Ferrari) electrics on lap 14, P. Ghinzani (Osella-Alfa Romeo) electrics on lap 15, R. Patrese (Alfa Romeo) gearbox on lap 17, N. Piquet (Brabham-BMW) gearbox on lap 24, T. Fabi (Brabham-BMW) turbo-charger on lap 29, E. Cheever (Alfa Romeo) engine on lap 30, M. Winkelhock (ATS-BMW) turbo-charger on lap 32.

XXII Grosser Preis von Österreich

Österreichring: August 19
Weather: Warm and sunny
Distance: 51 laps of 5.9424 km circuit = 303.06 km (188.31 miles)

McLaren International had gone away from Hockenheim looking unbeatable in the Constructors' Championship for they had boosted their points tally to well over double that of even their closest rivals – 82½ points compared to the 35½ points of Ferrari and Lotus. The Drivers' title, too, was rapidly developing into a two-horse race between Prost (43½ points) and Lauda (39 points), their strongest challenger, if not in terms of actual results, being Piquet, who was now trailing badly with only 18 points and lying a rather disappointing seventh in the table behind de Angelis (26½ points), Arnoux (24½ points), Warwick (23 points) and Rosberg (20 points). In fact, the red and white Marlboro-sponsored cars from Woking with their TAG-Porsche engines were beginning to completely dominate the Grand Prix scene and the outcome of the first day's practice for the Austrian Grand Prix at the magnificent Österreichring only served to ram home the point; on top of the time-sheets at the end of the opening hour of qualifying were the names of the drivers of cars 7 and 8. Not only that, but they were there by a pretty convincing margin and Prost, in particular, as he had lapped the 5.9424 kilometre circuit over half a second faster than even his team-mate at a quite staggering average speed of 154.192 mph (248.149 kph), his time being 1 min 26.203 sec. Lauda's best time, on the other hand, was 1 min 26.715 sec but, in some ways, this was even more commendable for he had achieved it on a lap (his last flying lap of the afternoon) in which he had been forced to put two wheels on to the dirt just beyond the Boschkurve in order to avoid Warwick's Renault. At the time the Englishman had been cruising in the middle of the track wiping his visor and had failed to spot the red and white McLaren rushing up behind him but, fortunately, it had led to no serious consequences. Neither were there any hard feelings between the two drivers about the incident, although it had, once again, highlighted the problem of the short life qualifying tyres causing drivers to take unnecessary risks by not being able to afford to lift off, an aspect particularly apparent at this fast circuit where the soft rubber was lasting barely a lap at best.

Whilst the McLaren duo had every reason to feel well satisfied with their efforts at the end of the first day's practice, a good number of the other drivers had been struggling against all manner of problems. Engines had been blowing up or not running properly, turbo-chargers had been failing, gearboxes had been breaking, cars hadn't been handling properly, and so on. In addition, the morning untimed session had been charac-

terized by an unusually high number of spins. Most of them had arisen as a direct result of over-enthusiasm in the cockpit, although when Bellof's Tyrrell had gone off into a tyre barrier it had almost certainly been caused by the young German, back from a successful trip to Canada, spinning on his own oil following a major engine failure. Yet another of the more serious incidents involved Fabi, who had spun at the fast downhill Jochen Rindt Kurve and slammed, backwards, into the guard-rail, demolishing the two right-hand corners of his Brabham. However, like Bellof, who had subsequently taken over the spare Tyrrell, he had at least escaped personal injury, and the same had also applied to de Angelis after spinning wildly towards the end of the morning and treating the spectators to a particularly fine exhibition of how to go corn cutting in a Formula 1 car. Entertaining to watch, perhaps, but so far as the Italian Lotus driver was concerned it had not been at all funny as he had already been obliged to abandon his proposed race chassis owing to suffering an early piston failure. Be that as it may, once the spare Lotus 95T had been retrieved and thoroughly cleaned of its wheat harvest, de Angelis had staged a good recovery in the afternoon and lapped quickly enough at 1 min 27.531 sec to claim fourth place on the time-sheets. Here, he was directly behind Piquet who, true to form, had provided the main opposition to the McLarens by lapping in 1 min 26.928 sec prior to handing his 'qualifying special' over to Fabi, in order that his team-mate could set a time. Meanwhile, Tambay and Warwick had both overcome an understeer problem with their Renaults well enough to post fifth and sixth fastest times of 1 min 27.748 sec and 1 min 27.928 sec respectively. Mansell, having run only a relatively modest amount of turbo boost pressure in the interests of trying to avoid a repetition of his team-mate's early problem, was next up at 1 min 28.430 sec and then, completing the top ten, came Rosberg (1 min 28.760 sec), Laffite (1 min 29.228 sec) and Senna (1 min 29.463 sec). This was in spite of the Williams FW09Bs still understeering rather a lot and the young Brazilian having switched to the spare Toleman because it had a better engine than that installed in his proposed race chassis only to have found it suffering from inferior handling. The Ferraris? Probably the least said the better. Amidst various experiments going on with different exhaust systems, rear suspension configurations, wheelbase dimensions and aerodynamics, Alboreto (using a car with the older-type rear suspension, but with a revised gearbox casting to provide a slightly longer wheelbase) had come out only 11th fastest, while Arnoux (with a brand new 126C4 at his disposal) had been an even more disappointing 14th. Both men complained of indifferent straight-line speed and lack of

grip from their Goodyear tyres. Other than that, about the only real surprise was to see Winkelhock way down in 21st place, although the German had had a most unhappy day with persistent gearbox and fuel pressure problems in the newer of the two ATS D7s. Ordinarily he would almost certainly have switched his attentions to the older car, but Gunther Schmidt had now recruited leading European Formula 3 Championship contender Gerhard Berger into his team, so there was no longer a spare chassis available. Only after the Austrian new-boy had completed his qualifying runs (and set 18th fastest time) had Winkelhock had a serious crack at qualifying, but the lack of practice had obviously taken its toll.

After a dampish start, the weather on Friday had steadily improved and the next day was even better, just about perfect, in fact, not least for the many spectators to have already set up camp at the circuit for the weekend. During the morning the second untimed session appeared to go off reasonably well for most people but, once again, there was some trouble, and this was partly responsible for Ghinzani and Berger both ultimately having to sit out the final hour of qualifying. In essence, the little Osella team was suffering such a spate of engine failures that only Gartner's FA1F was still usable in the afternoon, while at ATS, more gearbox and fuel pressure problems resulted in Winkelhock commandeering his new team-mate's D7. At the start of final qualifying Rothengatter, who had yet to set a time due to the Hart engine in his Spirit having blown up on his first lap of the previous afternoon, was also unable to go out. Instead, the Dutchman was left waiting around for yet another broken engine to be replaced – by a fresh unit loaned by John MacDonald's RAM outfit! Mansell, too, found himself being delayed for similar reasons, but Tambay, another to have lost an engine in the morning, and Boutsen, who had crashed heavily at the Hella-Licht Schikane, had both been able to switch to their respective teams' spare cars.

Initially Prost and Lauda were quite happy to remain in the pits keeping an eye on the times being recorded by the opposition through a TV monitor, but when Piquet's name flashed up on the screen with a time of 1 min 26.490 sec to his credit, after going out relatively early, both of them were soon stirred into action. Unlike the previous afternoon, however, little seemed to go right for them. Whilst they were out on their first sets of tyres Prost had his engine let go, and Lauda, besides having to contend with slightly sticking throttle linkage, found his car oversteering too much following adjustments made to stiffen the front roll-bar. Then, by the time that Prost had transferred to the spare McLaren and Lauda's problems had been looked at, the track conditions had deteriorated somewhat due to oil being deposited by de Cesaris' Ligier, which had blown up its Renault engine for the second afternoon running, and also by the spare Renault suffering a similar fate after Gerard Larrousse had insisted on winding on more turbo boost pressure for Tambay's second qualifying run. The outcome was that neither Prost, who was also hampered by traffic on his final run, nor Lauda improved on their Friday times and, instead of a McLaren being on pole position at the end of the afternoon, it was a Brabham, Piquet having gone out on his second set of tyres – before the oil – and recorded a new fastest time of 1 min 26.173 sec (154.256 mph/248.252 kph). Moreover, whereas Prost was still on the front row of the grid thanks to his efforts of the previous afternoon, Lauda had now been relegated to fourth spot by de Angelis, who had put up a particularly brave performance during the closing minutes of qualifying and set the afternoon's second fastest time of 1 min 26.318 sec. This was in spite of the oil and a problem with his Goodyear qualifying tyres going off before the end of the lap. Earlier, Tambay had almost beaten Lauda's Friday time as well, and went away convinced that had his engine withstood the increased turbo boost pressure he might well have wound up on the pole. As it was, the Frenchman's time of 1 min 26.748 sec from his first run still left him handily placed in fifth spot on the grid and alongside team-mate Warwick, who had enjoyed a fairly uneventful practice on his way to setting sixth fastest time overall of 1 min 27.123 sec.

Apart from Fabi having progressed to 1 min 27.201 sec in his repaired Brabham to claim seventh place on the grid, and Mansell having achieved a lap in 1 min 27.558 sec for eighth spot (amidst experiencing tyre problems similar to those of his team-mate) the rest had all been 3 seconds or more off the pace. Among them, of course, were both Williams drivers, who had failed to pick up on their lap times following problems with sagging turbo boost pressure (Rosberg) and fluctuating fuel pressure (Laffite); Senna, whose attempts to move up the grid had been thwarted by a down-on-power engine; and the two Ferrari drivers, who had remained completely out of the picture. Indeed, it was hard to believe that only 12 months earlier it had been an all-Ferrari front row. Yet, here they were now in only 12th and 15th positions on the grid, and in amongst the likes of Winkelhock's ATS and also the two Euroracing Alfa Romeos of Patrese and Cheever which, despite being fitted with the older mechanical fuel-injection systems once again, had been aflicted by seemingly never-ending engine (and other) problems throughout the two days. Meanwhile, down amongst the tail-enders, both Osella drivers had qualified quite comfortably after a troubled couple of days, as had the RAM

duo, also under somewhat difficult circumstances. But, once again, the Ford-Cosworth-powered Tyrrells had been hopelessly outpaced. Nevertheless, right up until the closing minutes of qualifying it had looked fairly certain that Johansson, consistently quicker than Bellof, would be in the race, only for the delayed Rothengatter to have charged out on to the circuit just in time to bump the Swede off the grid. Needless to say, this had given rise to mixed emotions. In the Spirit camp the scene had been one of immense joy and satisfaction, whereas at Tyrrell it had been one of gloom and despondency, a situation not improved by the fact that earlier in the afternoon Bellof's car had been weighed at random – and come out 3 kilogrammes below the minimum weight limit! Furthermore, the lack of any Tyrrells on the starting grid meant that not a single car in the race would be powered by the ultra-successful Ford-Cosworth V8 engine, the first such occurrence since its arrival at Zandvoort in 1967. At the same time, of course, the Austrian Grand Prix would now not only be the 400th World Championship event (a fact that went largely unrecognized) but also the first-ever in which the entire field consisted of 1.5-litre turbo-charged cars, so it was almost like the dawning of a new era.

The possibility of Lauda scoring a home victory (something that he had never previously done), combined with the presence of two other Austrian drivers in the starting field and the current healthy state of Grand Prix racing, had already generated a considerable amount of spectator interest during practice. On race day, however, it was enormous with estimates putting the size of the crowd at around the 90,000-mark, the vast majority arriving early enough for the warm-up session at 10.30 a.m. For most of the drivers this last opportunity of preparing for the race appeared to go off quite well, although Piquet was troubled by a spongy brake pedal and Prost, after pipping team-mate Lauda for fastest time, returned to the pits with the replacement engine in his McLaren overheating badly enough as to warrant work commencing on installing another fresh V6 unit. There were also more problems in the Euroracing Alfa Romeo pit caused by Cheever's 184T suffering a turbocharger failure, but without doubt the most unfortunate driver of all was Winkelhock as a broken gearbox ultimately led to the German becoming a non-starter: after the gearbox had been replaced the gear-selection mechanism would not operate and by then there was insufficient time left to carry out any more remedial work.

The start of the 52-lap race turned out to be a very confused affair. De Angelis and Rothengatter both raised their arms at virtually the last moment – after the red light – to indicate that they were not ready because of being unable to select a gear and because of a

stalled engine respectively; then, when Derek Ongaro pressed the button to abort the start, an electrical malfunction somewhere in the system led to the green light momentarily appearing before the yellow flashing lights, by which time most of the field was already on the move. Fortunately, in spite of one or two anxious moments as drivers lower down the grid weaved past the stationary Lotus or, as in the case of Tambay and Laffite, were obliged to stop behind it until the Italian finally found a gear, there were no untoward incidents. Nevertheless, it was quite clear that the race would have to be restarted, so out went the black flags, together with a red flag at the start/finish line, to bring everything to a halt. There then followed a delay of almost exactly half an hour while the grid reformed and another count-down took place, but eventually all was ready and on went the starting lights once again for what would now be a 51-lap race. And, as had happened at the original start, it was Prost who surged off into the lead, only on this occasion Piquet came straight back at his arch-rival by giving everyone a clear demonstration of the superior power of his BMW engine and drawing alongside the McLaren on the approach to the Hella-Licht Schikane before squeezing past on the inside under braking. Directly behind him, Tambay, having opted to race the spare Renault, got away extremely well to take up third spot ahead of de Angelis, Warwick and Lauda, while further back a somewhat over-enthusiastic Gartner gained a few places in rather less conventional style by first of all side-swiping Berger's ATS, causing his compatriot a lurid moment, and then by running into the back of Ghinzani's Osella at the chicane: this, in turn, resulted in his team-mate taking an unscheduled trip across the grass. Fabi, on the other hand, was last away due to stalling his engine just as the green light had appeared.

During the initial stages of the race the leadership issue quickly developed into a straight fight between Piquet and Prost, the pair of them dropping Tambay's third-placed Renault at the rate of around half a second per lap and leaving the others even further behind. However, after only five laps even Prost's hopes of staying with the fleeing Brabham received a setback due to his gearbox starting to play up. The problem was mainly that of fourth gear jumping out of engagement with alarming regularity and one that left the World Championship leader in the difficult position of having to hold his car in gear through most of the corners. In the meantime, Warwick had taken only until the Jochen Rindt Kurve on the opening lap to find a way past de Angelis and, of even greater significance, Lauda had since made amends for a relatively sluggish start by overtaking them both to move up into fourth place. Moreover, he was now hard on the heels of Tambay's Renault, and on lap 9 continued his progress towards the front of the race by neatly slipping through on the inside of the Frenchman at the exit from the Boschkurve. Thereafter, Lauda immediately set his sights on the two leading cars, but Tambay, by now realizing only too well that he had started out on an over-optimistic choice of Michelins, completed the following lap by diving into the pits for fresh (and harder) rubber, dropping away to tenth place in the process. By that stage Warwick was running into similar tyre problems in the other Renault. In fact, the Englishman had just been repassed by de Angelis, who had only minutes earlier come out on top of a spirited duel with Senna for what had been seventh place. Meanwhile, the little Osella team was already packing up for the day, as Ghinzani had completed a mere four laps before going out with a broken gearbox, while Gartner's first home Grand Prix had ended just over two laps later with a blown-up engine. It was also to be a rather brief affair for the Williams team. After twelve laps Laffite was pulling off into the pits with an expensive-looking engine failure, and this was followed shortly afterwards by Rosberg simply giving up on the grounds that his car was 'undriveable', an earlier change of tyres and adjustments to the front wing having apparently done nothing to eradicate acute understeer. Rothengatter, too, was effectively out of the running for although he had been allowed to take the re-start after spinning off during the opening lap of the original race, the Spirit's exhaust system had been damaged and the resultant loss of power had brought about an early pit stop for repairs – a task that was still in progress and destined to take well over half an hour!

With 20 laps completed Piquet appeared to be still well in command of the race. Nevertheless, it was by no means turning out to be easy for him as Prost, giving no indication whatsoever of the fact that he was having to drive with only one hand on his steering wheel more often than not, was keeping the pressure on all the way, added to which Lauda was now only a further 3 seconds adrift in the other McLaren. Further back, de Angelis had settled into a lonely fourth place but Warwick, who had earlier withstood considerable pressure from Senna until stopping for fresh tyres at the end of lap 16, had since pulled off the track because of a major engine failure. Consequently, it was now the young Brazilian who was in fifth spot, with Mansell next followed by a fast-recovering Tambay, Alboreto, Fabi (he was doing an excellent job of climbing through the field after his delayed start) and, completing the top ten, Patrese in the sole surviving Alfa Romeo, Cheever having just added his name to the growing casualty list with a broken engine. Only minutes earlier de Cesaris had also disappeared from lower

down the field due to fuel-metering unit problems, and on lap 28 de Angelis went out in even more dramatic fashion when the Renault engine in his Lotus blew up in a similar manner to that at Hockenheim. However, on this occasion there was rather more to it than that. After once again choosing to tour round to the pits rather than park out on the circuit, regardless of smoke and flames at the rear of his car, the Italian succeeded in liberally coating the track surface with oil and nowhere more apparent than at the Jochen Rindt Kurve. Furthermore, as the leaders arrived at the downhill right-hander on the following lap the marshals there were still in the throes of putting out the oil flags and, whereas Piquet succeeded in checking the inevitable slide, Prost, now tight up behind the Brabham and with one hand holding his car in fourth gear, had little chance of doing anything about it. Instead, he spun off to the outside of the track and eventually came to a stop facing the barriers with a stalled engine, his race over and a possible victory lost. Meanwhile, Lauda, having just had ample warning of the oil, successfully negotiated the corner without any fuss or bother and found himself left with a clear run at the leader, a whisker under 3 seconds ahead of him. Of course, the retirements of de Angelis and Prost in such quick succession also promoted Senna to a distant third, while Tambay, who had caught and repassed Mansell just before all the drama, was now up into fourth place.

Much to the obvious delight of the crowd, Lauda took only a couple of laps to move in on Piquet's tail and was soon looking all set to take over the lead at any moment. However, Piquet appeared to have other ideas about that and proceeded to steadfastly defend his position, even though his rear tyres were now well past their best. As this enthralling tussle between two double World Champions continued, Mansell pulled off the track following the failure of another Renault engine, and then Senna, who had

just been overhauled by Tambay, bowed out at the pits with the Hart engine in his Toleman having lost power and showing signs of seizing. So, in a race of changing fortunes, Fabi and Patrese unexpectedly found themselves in the top six, while only Piquet, Lauda, Tambay and Alboreto were left still on the same lap. Nevertheless, with Lauda now all but climbing over the back of the blue and white car ahead of him at times, there was certainly nothing lacking in the way of excitement, and right through until the start of lap 40 it was anyone's guess as to how the matter would finally be resolved. Then came the answer: amidst a certain amount of confusion arising from an unsuccessful attempt to lap Alboreto's Ferrari going into the Hella-Licht Schikane, Piquet slid badly off line at the exit and presented Lauda with just the opportunity he needed to take a run at him and snatch the inside line for the gentle left-hander that followed. Realizing only too well that he was in no position to launch a counter-attack due to the worn state of his rear tyres, Piquet then immediately eased right off to concentrate on finishing second with the result that it looked to be all over. Barely two laps later, though, that idea suddenly went out the window when Lauda heard a loud bang behind his head, raised an arm and slowed sufficiently for Alboreto, whom he had just lapped, to repass him and for Fabi to also unlap himself a few seconds later. At first the lack of any drive to his wheels convinced the Austrian that his McLaren had broken its differential, but after fishing for gears he discovered that it was fourth gear that had gone, so he pressed on in the hope of being able to nurse the car home by choosing the right moments to change from third gear to fifth. Naturally, on a circuit where fourth gear was of paramount importance, his lap times immediately grew longer – by around 4 seconds – but, by keeping calm and giving no indication that anything was amiss, Lauda led everyone to believe that he was merely reeling off the few

Niki Lauda laps the Ferrari of Michele Alboreto on his way to achieving a long-awaited victory on home soil – despite losing the use of fourth gear shortly after this photograph was taken. *(Autosport)*

remaining laps at his own pace. Consequently, Piquet made no attempt to speed up, or to consider the possibility of stopping for fresh tyres in order to put in a late spurt. Instead, the race ran out with Lauda limping home to that first elusive victory on home soil just over 23 seconds to the good, a result that also knocked team-mate Prost off the top of the Championship table for the first time all season. Meanwhile, because a fine drive from Tambay had been ended by yet

another Renault engine blowing up with just over eight laps to go, Alboreto at least gave the Ferrari team a crumb of comfort by finishing third, and Fabi's perseverance was rewarded with fourth spot. After that the rest, all at least a lap behind, should have been led home by Patrese's Alfa Romeo. But the V8 engine's fuel consumption had decided otherwise on the penultimate lap and left the unfortunate Italian being classified tenth behind the two Arrows A7s of

Boutsen and Surer, which crossed the line virtually together, Arnoux's disappointingly-driven Ferrari, Hesnault's Ligier and also Palmer's RAM, which had actually overtaken Lauda's McLaren during the latter stages of the race. Also still there at the finish were Alliot, Berger (after a difficult debut caused by gearbox problems most of the way) and Rothengatter, although the Dutchman was much too far behind to be classified due to the lengthy pit stop.

Results

1	N. Lauda (McLaren-TAG)	1 hr 21 min 12.851 sec (223.883 kph/ 139.114 mph)	
2	N. Piquet (Brabham-BMW)	1 hr 21 min 36.376 sec	
3	M. Alboreto (Ferrari)	1 hr 22 min 01.849 sec	
4	T. Fabi (Brabham-BMW)	1 hr 22 min 09.163 sec	
5	T. Boutsen (Arrows-BMW)	1 lap behind	
6	M. Surer (Arrows-BMW)	1 lap behind	
7	R. Arnoux (Ferrari)	1 lap behind	
8	F. Hesnault (Ligier-Renault)	2 laps behind	
9	J. Palmer (RAM-Hart)	2 laps behind	
*10	R. Patrese (Alfa Romeo)	3 laps behind	
11	P. Alliot (RAM-Hart)	3 laps behind	
12	G. Berger (ATS-BMW)	3 laps behind	

Also running at finish: H. Rothengatter (Spirit-Hart) 28 laps behind

* Not running at finish.

Fastest lap: N. Lauda (McLaren-TAG) on lap 23 in 1 min 32.882 sec (230.305 kph/ 143.105 mph)

Retirements

P. Ghinzani (Osella-Alfa Romeo) gearbox on lap 5, J. Gartner (Osella-Alfa Romeo) engine on lap 7, J. Laffite (Williams-Honda) engine on lap 13, K. Rosberg (Williams-Honda) handling on lap 16, A. de Cesaris (Ligier-Renault) fuel-metering unit on lap 16, D. Warwick (Renault) engine on lap 18, E. Cheever (Alfa Romeo) engine on lap 19, E. de Angelis (Lotus-Renault) engine on lap 29, A. Prost (McLaren-TAG) spun off on lap 29, N. Mansell (Lotus-Renault) engine on lap 33, A. Senna (Toleman-Hart) oil pressure on lap 36, P. Tambay (Renault) engine on lap 43.

XXXII Grote Prijs van Nederland

Zandvoort: August 26
Weather: Warm and sunny
Distance: 71 laps of 4.252 km circuit = 301.89 km (187.59 miles)

With this year's Dutch round of the Championship being held on the weekend immediately following the Austrian Grand Prix there was little opportunity for anyone to do much other than load up transporters and set off on the long trek across Europe from the Österreichring to the coastal resort of Zandvoort, unload, set up camp again and prepare the cars for the start of practice on Friday morning. Fortunately the weather was fine and everybody seemed to be in reasonable good order when testing got under way at 10 a.m., so there was soon plenty of activity. It was, of course, the Dutch Grand Prix weekend 12 months earlier that had marked the first public appearance of the Porsche-designed, TAG-financed V6 turbo-charged engine installed in the back of Niki Lauda's McLaren MP4/1E, and little could anyone have realized at the time just what a pronounced effect its arrival would have on the Grand Prix scene. Now, a year later, the German engine had not only powered the superb McLaren MP4/2 chassis to victory in eight of the season's twelve races to date but it had also played a major role in more or less already assuring the Woking-based team of carrying off the 1984 Constructors' Championship. Indeed, it was a quite remarkable success story and one that looked all set to continue, the first signs of

that coming when Prost went out and set the early pace with a best (unofficial) time of 1 min 15.865 sec, a mere tenth of a second slower than the fastest time recorded by Rosberg during recent pre-race testing at the circuit. Lauda, amidst hopping from his race car to the spare McLaren to make back-to-back comparisons with different suspension and turbo-charger set-ups, was also right to the forefront and ended the morning third fastest behind the most consistent challenger to the Marlboro-sponsored cars, Piquet. He, too, tried out both his race car and his team's spare chassis, but was forced to abandon the latter out on the circuit after a few laps because of an electrical problem. Meanwhile, the only Dutchman in the field, Rothengatter, made the early headlines for rather less desirable reasons, by understeering off the track at the 'Bos Uit' during the closing stages of the session and putting one of the two Spirit 101Bs out of action for the rest of the weekend with substantial rear end damage. This apart, there were few serious problems, although amongst those who may well have thought otherwise at the end of the morning were Laffite and Hesnault, following turbo-charger trouble, de Cesaris, after the Renault engine in his Ligier had overheated and forced him into his team's spare car, and Alliot, whose RAM

also needed a fresh engine after 'some strange noises had started coming from behind my ears'.

During the afternoon's hour of qualifying Prost was unable to defend his position at the top of the time-sheets, despite going out on his first set of tyres and lapping almost a full second quicker than in the morning at 1 min 14.946 sec. Instead, after the Frenchman's engine began losing power because of a leaking inter-cooler, preventing any further improvement, the battle for the provisional pole developed into a straight fight between Piquet (using his race car due to the spare Brabham – his 'qualifying special' – still being sidelined) and de Angelis, which concluded with the reigning World Champion narrowly coming out on top. Nevertheless, it could quite easily have gone the other way. Indeed, de Angelis was convinced that had it not been for rather oily track conditions during a late counter-attack on his second set of tyres to try to beat Piquet's best time of 1 min 13.872 sec, he could almost certainly have lapped quicker than the 1 min 14.027 sec that he ultimately achieved. Early in the session Rosberg, whose worse-than-usual understeer problems in the last race had subsequently been attributed to a slowly deflating front tyre, had looked like being another contender for the provisional pole. However, after completing his first run with what had been fastest time of 1 min 15.137 sec to his credit at that point, the Finn's hopes of staying up there had been dashed by an extremely smoky turbo-charger failure at the start of his second run. As it was he still wound up much higher in the order than of late, actually fourth fastest between Prost and Warwick, the English Renault driver having overcome considerable personal discomfort in the form of a tummy upset well enough to post fifth fastest time of 1 min 15.184 sec. In the meantime, apart from Lauda having squeezed in a lap of 1 min 15.556 sec towards the end of an afternoon spoiled by a faulty rev-limiter, which had been cutting in too early, the rest were all at least 2 seconds off Piquet's time. Even so, a rather pleasant change in view of the recent downward trend in Maranello fortunes was to see the Ferrari drivers occupying the next two places on the time-

sheets, even if it was partly as a result of drivers such as the likes of Mansell, Senna and Tambay having been badly affected by varying degrees of engine problems. Be that as it may, Arnoux, driving an early 126C4 with yet another revised rear suspension set-up employing new tubular wishbones and push-rods, had lapped in 1 min 16.121 sec – prior to a turbo-charger failure forcing him into his spare, short wheelbase, car – while Alboreto had gone around in 1 min 16.248 sec.

The weather was again fine on Saturday and, although a few mechanical problems cropped up during the second untimed session of practice in the morning (these included the Hart engine failing in Senna's Toleman, the fuel-injection system playing up on Rosberg's Williams and a steering rack working loose on de Angelis' Lotus, which very nearly sent the Italian hurtling off the track), everyone seemed to be in pretty good shape for the start of final qualifying at 1 p.m. Unlike the previous afternoon Piquet was now preparing to use the spare Brabham, but after going out on his first set of tyres he returned to the pits complaining that the engine wasn't delivering full power, and decided to switch his attentions to his proposed race car once more. This was in spite of the fact that he had just gone around in 1 min 13.953 sec – only marginally slower than his previous best – and was still the only driver below the 1 min 14 sec barrier. For quite some while it looked as if it was going to stay that way, too, as the next best times were all coming out at around the mid-1 min 14 sec bracket. But then the situation was suddenly changed by Prost, after making no more than a slight improvement to 1 min 14.832 sec on his first run, going out again, ensuring that his tyres were up to optimum working temperature, finding that vital clear lap and responding magnificently to stop the clocks at a new fastest time of 1 min 13.567 sec (208.071 kph/129.289 mph). That, not surprisingly, really put the cat amongst the pigeons, and with just under 10 minutes of the session remaining, attention became firmly fixed on Piquet as he went out for his second run. However, the question of whether or not he could have retrieved the pole was to go unanswered. Instead, early on his flying lap the Brabham's nose section bottomed out on the way through the fast right-handed Gerlachbocht and in the next instant Piquet had spun off the track, knocking the car's right front suspension slightly out of shape, and come to rest with a stalled engine. So, after the disappointment of the previous afternoon, it was Prost who ultimately took the coveted spot, and in the final reckoning Piquet only just retained a front row position on the grid; de Angelis, holding back even longer on his second set of tyres and obviously none the worse for his fright in the morning, subsequently failed to beat the

Brazilian's Friday time by a mere hundredth of a second – 1 min 13.883 sec! Meanwhile, their respective team-mates had all been unable to make any noticeable impression for various reasons. A slightly irate Lauda, after being badly held up by slower cars on both of his qualifying runs, had been restricted to a best lap of 1 min 14.866 sec and was left in sixth place on the grid; Fabi, who had already suffered similar problems with the traffic during the previous afternoon and run into turbo-charger trouble this time out, was languishing in only tenth place; and Mansell, having set fastest time in the morning, had found the fresh Renault engine installed in his Lotus overnight suddenly developing a pick-up problem just when it mattered most, and had wound up in a very disappointing 12th place. It had also been an afternoon of mixed fortunes for the Ferrari team. Alboreto, having followed his team-mate's example by switching to the latest rear suspension set-up, had just about kept abreast with the progress being made by other drivers around him to clinch ninth place on the grid, whereas Arnoux had slipped right away to 15th spot owing to efforts to improve on his Friday time having been thwarted by a faulty heat exchanger. By contrast the Renault duo, Tambay showing a preference to the spare RE50 again, as in Austria, had turned in very evenly-matched times of 1 min 14.405 sec (Warwick) and 1 min 14.566 sec (Tambay) to line up in fourth and fifth places on the grid, and similarly Rosberg and Laffite had lapped closely enough to one another at 1 min 15.117 sec and 1 min 15.231 sec to make it an all-Williams fourth row.

With the exception of Boutsen giving Arrows their best grid position of the season so far by qualifying in 11th spot, in spite of having been forced to bow out early because of a major turbo-charger failure (his slower team-mate had already commandeered the spare A7 by that stage owing to a seemingly incurable engine misfire), the rest of the line-up was, in the main, pretty familiar looking. Nevertheless, there were a few other anomalies. These included Senna having only just squeezed into the top half of the grid amidst complaints that his Toleman had proved reluctant to warm up its Michelin qualifying tyres properly, and also Winkelhock (the sole ATS representative this weekend) having failed to do even that after being hampered by fuel-feed problems on the first day and fluctuating turbo boost pressure on the second. The two Euroracing Alfa Romeo 184Ts were a long way down the order as well, but this was hardly surprising either as the Benetton-sponsored team's efforts to improve the throttle response of their cars by modifying the piping for the turbo-charger units had been repaid by a string of turbo failures throughout the two days, Cheever having pulled up twice for this

1984

reason during the first afternoon. Ordinarily, there would have been every reason for Rothengatter to have gone away even more disappointed, as for the second day running problems with understeer and low turbo boost pressure had left him in 27th and last place on the time-sheets, with the result that strictly he had failed to qualify for the race. However, because the Tyrrells, which had made the grid in 24th (Bellof) and 25th (Johansson) places respectively, were no longer officially recognized by FISA under the terms imposed in permitting the British team to continue participating in World Championship events pending the outcome of the appeal hearing, the Dutchman was automatically allowed in.

Much to everyone's satisfaction, race day produced more fine weather and this obviously played its part in attracting a very large crowd to the circuit, even if there was in all probability yet another demonstration of McLaren superiority in the offing. As usual in Holland, local noise restrictions on Sunday mornings meant delaying the warm-up session until mid-day but, unfortunately, just before the action was about to start there was a nasty accident in the paddock caused by part of a walkway giving access to the pits balcony collapsing. This, in turn, led to proceedings being delayed for a further 40 minutes while several of quite a large number of people to receive injuries, including Arrows boss Jack Oliver and his son, were given medical treatment and, in a few instances, even taken off to hospital. Eventually, though, the drivers got their final 30 minutes of free practice. That is, all but for Ghinzani, who had to remain behind in the pits because of a fuel pump failure on his Osella, and as largely anticipated the McLaren duo turned in the fastest times. Nevertheless, it was not all plain sailing as Lauda, the slower of the two, pulled off into the pits early to complain of fluctuating turbo boost pressure, and subsequently he had to have his car wheeled away for a fresh turbo-charger unit to be fitted. Alliot, meanwhile, had a steering arm break on his RAM, which sent him spinning wildly along the track at the Panoramabocht, and problems with his brakes caused Laffite a couple of similar moments. Otherwise, it was all pretty orderly, although Warwick and Tambay both completed their runs somewhat dismayed to have found their Renaults suddenly lacking grip for no accountable reason, and Rosberg was left in much the same frame of mind about the handling of his Williams on full tanks. However, it was the off-track activities, rather than the warm-up session, that really captured the pre-race headlines when, shortly afterwards, the team manager of John Player Special Team Lotus (Peter Warr) took great delight in announcing at a press conference that Senna had signed a contract to drive for his team in the 1985 and

1986 seasons. There had, in fact, been rumours over recent weeks that the talented Brazilian might well be on the move at the end of the season yet, at the same time, it was known that he was under a 3-year contract with Toleman. Consequently, the news still came as something as a shock to most people, and it was this that obviously accounted for a rather strained atmosphere that had been apparent in the Toleman pit ever since the start of the weekend.

Because of the delayed warm-up session there was a much shorter gap than usual before the start of the race (scheduled for 3 p.m.) and, indeed, little more than an hour later the first cars were leaving the pits again and being driven round to the dummy grid. For quite some time, though, Lauda was unable to join them. Instead, having had that fresh turbo-charger unit installed in his car, he now had to wait around for the McLaren mechanics to change a water radiator that had sprung a leak as his engine was being warmed up. There was also a late problem for Surer, who appeared in the pit lane at the end of his warm-up lap with his Arrows looking the worse for wear after a sticking throttle had caused a trip into the sand. As a result the Swiss had to be hurriedly ushered into the spare Arrows but, like Lauda, he eventually joined the others waiting on the grid for the final count-down to draw to a conclusion without any further fuss or drama. Thereafter everything ran smoothly, and the start, preceded by Prost leading the field around on the final warm-up lap, turned out to be one of the best seen for a long time with very nearly all of the 27 cars getting away really well, one of the few exceptions being Lauda's McLaren, which hesitated rather badly. Initially, it looked like Prost would be first to arrive at Tarzan only for Piquet, once again, to demonstrate the superior power of his BMW engine by drawing alongside the McLaren from the outside of the track before neatly nipping through into the lead under braking. At the same time Tambay managed to beat both teammate Warwick and de Angelis into third place, and there was so much jostling going on behind that it was difficult to imagine how they could all possibly make it through the tight 180-degree turn intact. But make it through they did, and it was not until the downhill hairpin behind the pits that there was any trouble when Winkelhock spun, stalled his engine and subsequently had to be push-started back into the fray after the rest had gone by. Further around the lap there was also a bit of commotion caused by de Cesaris and Cheever bringing their cars into contact with one another. However, apart from the two of them losing places as they briefly took to the grass verge, there were no casualties, and from then on the opening lap ran out devoid of any further drama, with Piquet a clear leader from Prost.

After another small gap Tambay was still lying third ahead of de Angelis, but Warwick, finding his Renault down on turbo boost pressure, had slipped behind Rosberg and was now being hotly pursued by Laffite, Alboreto and a fast-recovering Lauda, who had already regained a couple of lost places since the start at the expense of Fabi and Boutsen.

At the end of the second lap the gaps between the three leading cars had grown noticeably bigger, and before long Piquet was showing every sign of running away with the race, the Brazilian lapping fairly consistently around half a second quicker than even Prost. As this continued an aggressive-looking Rosberg fought his way past de Angelis and Tambay in quick succession to move up into third place early on the fifth lap, and Lauda flew right back into contention with a series of superb outbraking manoeuvres at Tarzan that carried him past one car after another. In fact, after little more than eight laps the new Championship leader had made such good progress that he had not only come through to fourth place but was also well within striking distance of Rosberg's Williams. Moreover, there was not much that the Finn could do to try to stem the advance of the McLaren. Instead, quite apart from anything else, a decision by the Honda engineers to enrich the fuel mixture for their engines – in an attempt to prevent a recent spate of problems with piston failures from continuing – was having such an adverse affect on Rosberg's fuel consumption readings that he had already been obliged to respond to the situation by winding down the boost somewhat. Consequently, Lauda was able to close up very quickly indeed and going into Tarzan (again!) on lap 11 made to go through on the inside of the Williams under braking. On this occasion, however, Rosberg successfully staved off the challenge and it was not until arriving at the same spot on the following lap that Lauda finally made it through, by which time an even more significant development had occurred: Piquet, hitherto enjoying a 4-second cushion over Prost, had pulled off the track with no oil pressure as the result of a leaking oil pipe! So, in the space of under a minute, the McLarens had moved up from second and fourth places to first and second, a whisker under 9 seconds apart. Meanwhile, aside from everyone else automatically moving up a place at the expense of the unfortunate Piquet, the situation with the other leading positions was going largely unchanged as Tambay was still successfully keeping de Angelis at bay, and close behind them Warwick was similarly just about holding his own against Laffite's Williams. Lower down the order, though, Alboreto had gone into the pits after only seven laps to retire his Ferrari with an engine failure, while shortly afterwards Ghinzani had disappeared from near the back of the field following more fuel pump trouble with his Osella. Even so, there were still several good scraps in progress throughout most of the field, one of which involved Fabi and Senna disputing what had now become eighth place in front of Arnoux's short-on-grip Ferrari, Boutsen's Arrows and Mansell's Lotus.

With a clear track ahead of him, Lauda now settled down to the business of trying to catch his team-mate and over the next ten laps or so steadily reduced the deficit to less than 3 seconds. To some extent his efforts were aided by Prost easing off slightly in response to pit signals showing an ever-increasing advantage over Rosberg, not realizing that the Finn was no longer leading the pursuit. Only when he could see Lauda looming in his mirrors did Prost cotton on to what was really happening, at which point he immediately stepped up the pace once more. But there was another factor to take into account – tyres. Prost had opted for the relatively hard Michelin 10s all round, whereas Lauda had chosen a mixture of the 10s on the left and the softer 05s on the right with the aim of trying to steal a slight advantage. And, at this stage, it looked as if what was undeniably something of a gamble was about to pay off, for in spite of the increased pace the gap between the two red and white cars continued to come down until, after 25 laps, they were barely a second apart. Thereafter, though, the gap began to steady and then Prost, benefiting from one or two good breaks whilst lapping slower cars, even began to creep away with the result that for the time being, at least, prospects of seeing a change of leadership slowly subsided. In the meantime, Rosberg was continuing to do an excellent job of holding down third place from Tambay, notwithstanding his fuel consumption problem, and de Angelis, who had survived a trip over the kerbing a little earlier whilst attempting to lap Winkelhock's ATS, was still pounding along in fifth spot only a further couple of seconds away. However, the remaining positions had undergone a complete reshuffle as all sorts of things had been happening. Certainly one of the most significant changes had come about on lap 24 when Laffite, having only minutes beforehand overtaken Warwick's Renault, had suddenly suffered a major engine failure at Scheivlak. Not only had this put paid to one of the best drives seen from the Frenchman for quite some time, but it had also had dire consequences for Warwick and Winkelhock, both of whom had spun on the oil deposited by the Williams-Honda and gone off backwards into a tyre barrier with stalled engines. Only four laps earlier Senna had similarly disappeared from ninth place due to the Hart engine blowing up in his Toleman, Surer had previously gone out with wheel bearing trouble and, on lap 22, Fabi had lost several places by first of all indulging in a quick spin

at Tarzan after locking up his rear brakes and then by stopping for fresh tyres. The upshot of all of this drama and excitement was that Arnoux had been able to move up into a distant sixth place without actually overtaking anybody, only for Mansell to have speeded up somewhat following a comparatively leisurely start and gone surging past Boutsen's Arrows and the Ferrari within the space of just three laps. In fact, with half-distance approaching, the Englishman was now rapidly catching team-mate de Angelis who, in turn, was starting to show signs of coming back at Tambay after losing time with a spin on the oil dropped by Laffite's Williams.

At the mid-way point, with de Cesaris now another out of the contest because of a blown-up engine, the two Mclarens were well over half a minute clear of the field, and the only remaining question seemed to be which would be first across the line at the end of the 71 laps, for even now they were little more than 4 seconds apart. One thing was sure, Lauda certainly wasn't giving up the pursuit of his team-mate as he clearly demonstrated on lap 37 by setting what was to be his fastest time of the afternoon – 1 min 20.470 sec. Unfortunately, though, not long afterwards Lauda began to realize that his tyre gamble wasn't going to pay off. Suddenly he was losing grip and this, combined with being delayed whilst lapping a group of slower cars, led to a change of tactics whereby the Austrian decided to concentrate on a finish, even if it was second place. Meanwhile, the situation with the other leading positions was growing more interesting by the minute, notwithstanding the fact that Tambay (and Boutsen) had been obliged to stop for a change of tyres at the end of lap 37. As things stood Rosberg was steadily being reeled in by the two black and gold Lotus

95Ts of de Angelis and Mansell, which were now virtually together, while further back Arnoux, who had already just suffered the ignominy of being lapped and was not exactly having his progress helped by a worsening engine misfire, was coming under mounting pressure from Fabi and Tambay, both of whom were going really well on their fresh rubber. In fact, on lap 47 the French Ferrari driver was unable to prevent either of them from going past him and then, just four laps later, Tambay overtook Fabi – only to slow and be repassed by the Italian shortly afterwards when fifth gear suddenly broke on the Renault! Most of this, however, went largely unnoticed as in the meantime de Angelis and Mansell closed right up to Rosberg to form a tight-running trio. To add to the excitement Prost was rapidly coming up to lap them, and going into Tarzan on lap 51 came the start of a very busy few minutes indeed when Mansell took a look up the inside of his team-mate. On this occasion he was forced to back off, but next time round de Angelis was so busy trying, unsuccessfully, to find a way through on the inside of Rosberg's Williams that the Englishman seized the initiative and took a run round the outside of him. A couple of corners later Prost also made it past the Italian and then, on the approach to Tarzan on the following lap, came an even more tense moment when Mansell dived through on the inside of Rosberg under braking, the Lotus visibly snaking and looking to be on the brink of going out of control. Nevertheless, Mansell got his third place and once Prost had lapped both of them shortly afterwards things began to quieten down again somewhat with de Angelis, running into problems with fading brakes and worn tyres, seemingly stuck behind the Williams.

For Prost (and Lauda for that matter) the

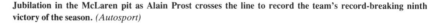

Jubilation in the McLaren pit as Alain Prost crosses the line to record the team's record-breaking ninth victory of the season. *(Autosport)*

closing stages of the race were merely a formality, the Frenchman easing off sufficiently to enable Mansell to unlap himself on lap 64, and yet still running out a comfortable winner by a margin of 10.283 seconds over his team-mate at the end of an afternoon that to all intents and purposes had been dominated by the Marlboro-sponsored cars. It was a result that also confirmed McLaren International as winners of the 1984 Constructors' Championship (with three races still to go!) and one that put the team in the World Championship record books for the highest number of Grand Prix victories in a season – nine, compared to the previous best of eight achieved by Lotus in 1978. Meanwhile Mansell, by taking a well-deserved third place, at least had the satisfaction of beating his team-mate on a day in which his future at Team Lotus looked to be in jeopardy, but Rosberg, despite doing his best to conserve fuel, had gone into the pits with dry tanks just two laps from home. Consequently, the unfortunate Finn had nothing to show for his efforts and, instead, de Angelis had been able to finish fourth, and Fabi and Tambay fifth and sixth respectively. After that only Hesnault's Ligier, the two Tyrrells, the two RAMs and Gartner's Osella (all at least two laps down) had gone on to complete the race owing to a string of late retirements. Cheever, after a hard drive following the first lap incident with de Cesaris, had joined Rosberg in running out of fuel with the end in sight, Patrese had earlier suffered an engine failure in the other Alfa Romeo, and Rothengatter's Spirit had stopped with a broken throttle cable. In addition, Boutsen had been involved in an alarming incident with Arnoux in which the Frenchman, directly in front of him, had suddenly turned off into the pits for fresh tyres at the end of his 59th lap without giving any sort of warning and caused their two cars to make contact. At the time Arnoux had continued on his way into the pits with nothing to show for his misdemeanour, and had even gone on to set the fastest lap of the afternoon only for his Ferrari to have ground to a halt shortly afterwards with dead electrics. Boutsen, on the other hand, had been extremely fortunate to have come out of it unharmed for his Arrows, flat out in fifth gear, had rode up over the Ferrari's left rear wheel, become airborne and then gone crashing down on to the track with its right front suspension badly deranged. Somehow, though, the Belgian had been able to maintain sufficient control over his car to bring it safely to rest further along the track, so what could well have been a very nasty episode to mar an otherwise fine afternoon of racing had been avoided.

Results

1	A. Prost (McLaren-TAG)	1 hr 37 min 21.468 sec (186.050 kph/ 115.606 mph)	*	S. Bellof (Tyrrell-Ford)	2 laps behind	
2	N. Lauda (McLaren-TAG)	1 hr 37 min 31.751 sec	**8	K. Rosberg (Williams-Honda)	3 laps behind	
3	N. Mansell (Lotus-Renault)	1 hr 38 min 41.012 sec	9	J. Palmer (RAM-Hart)	4 laps behind	
4	E. de Angelis (Lotus-Renault)	1 lap behind	10	P. Alliot (RAM-Hart)	4 laps behind	
5	T. Fabi (Brabham-BMW)	1 lap behind	**11	R. Arnoux (Ferrari)	5 laps behind	
6	P. Tambay (Renault)	1 lap behind	12	J. Gartner (Osella-Alfa Romeo)	5 laps behind	
7	F. Hesnault (Ligier-Renault)	2 laps behind	**13	E. Cheever (Alfa Romeo)	6 laps behind	
*	S. Johansson (Tyrrell-Ford)	2 laps behind				

* Excluded
**Not running at finish.

Fastest lap: R. Arnoux (Ferrari) on lap 64 in 1 min 19.465 sec (192.628 kph/ 119.693 mph)

Retirements

M. Alboreto (Ferrari) engine on lap 8, P. Ghinzani (Osella-Alfa Romeo) fuel pump on lap 9, N. Piquet (Brabham-BMW) oil pipe on lap 11, M. Surer (Arrows-BMW) wheel bearing on lap 18, A. Senna (Toleman-Hart) engine on lap 20, M. Winkelhock (ATS-BMW) spun off on lap 23, J. Laffite (Williams-Honda) engine on lap 24, D. Warwick (Renault) spun off on lap 24, A. de Cesaris (Ligier-Renault) engine on lap 32, R. Patrese (Alfa Romeo) engine on lap 52, H. Rothengatter (Spirit-Hart) throttle cable on lap 54, T. Boutsen (Arrows-BMW) accident on lap 60.

LV° Gran Premio d'Italia

Monza: September 9
Weather: Warm and sunny
Distance: 51 laps of 5.800 km
circuit = 295.80 km (183.80 miles)

During the week immediately following the Dutch Grand Prix the FIA International Court of Appeal had convened in Paris, primarily to hear the appeal lodged by Ken Tyrrell against the decision made at the FISA Executive Committee meeting back in July to exclude his team from the 1984 World Championship. Since that meeting Tyrrell had contacted the Southwest Research Institute in San Antonio and discovered that the analyses of the water samples had been conducted on the hydrocarbon content only and that the figure of 27.5% quoted for Aromatics was, in fact, the percentage found in the hydrocarbons rather than in the water sample as a whole. Furthermore, following a request made by Tyrrell through SCCA's John Timanus, a further test had since been carried out and this had revealed the hydro-carbon content of the water to be just 1%. At around the same time Tyrrell had also contacted the MB Analy-Co laboratory in Nanterre, which had conducted the analyses on behalf of FISA, and been told that the tests revealed an even smaller hydrocarbon content. However, the Appeal Court, rather than acknowledging that a mistake had been made in the interpretation of the original reports, merely revised the charge to 'the presence of hydrocarbons in the liquid contained in the water tank supplying the engine injection system, which is forbidden by Art. 6, paras 9, 11 and 14 and by Art. 14 of the Technical Regulations of the World Formula One Championship'. Somewhat incredulously for an Appeal Court, it also introduced a third and completely new charge that 'holes existing in the flat bottom of the Tyrrell car was an infraction under Art. 3.3' (. . . 'all these parts must produce a uniform, solid, hard, rigid, impervious surface, under all circumstances'). These were, in fact, two small holes situated on the underside of the Tyrrell's flat-bottomed monocoque which, according to Ken Tyrrell, were used solely as an escape route for air in the water tank displaced by water added during pit stops. Interestingly enough, he had already been informed (for the first time!) that these holes were in contravention of the regulations over the weekend of the British Grand Prix and had responded by sealing them off and introducing an alternative means of disposing of the air.

After a prolonged hearing, that extended over two days and included all sorts of suggestions being made, such as that Ken Tyrrell had used fuel additives during the first part of the race, had flushed them out with water during the pit stop and then been caught with traces of the illegal substance in the tank afterwards, and also that he had

N. Piquet
Brabham-BMW
(1 min 26.584 sec)

A. Prost
McLaren-TAG
(1 min 26.671 sec)

E. de Angelis
Lotus-Renault
(1 min 27.538 sec)

N. Lauda
McLaren-TAG
(1 min 28.533 sec)

T. Fabi
Brabham-BMW
(1 min 28.587 sec)

K. Rosberg
Williams-Honda
(1 min 28.818 sec)

N. Mansell
Lotus-Renault
(1 min 28.969 sec)

P. Tambay
Renault
(1 min 29.253 sec)

R. Patrese
Alfa Romeo
(1 min 29.382 sec)

E. Cheever
Alfa Romeo
(1 min 29.797 sec)

M. Alboreto
Ferrari
(1 min 29.810 sec)

D. Warwick
Renault
(1 min 30.113 sec)

J. Laffite
Williams-Honda
(1 min 30.578 sec)

R. Arnoux
Ferrari
(1 min 30.695 sec)

M. Surer
Arrows-BMW
(1 min 31.108 sec)

A. de Cesaris
Ligier-Renault
(1 min 31.198 sec)

S. Johansson
Toleman-Hart
(1 min 31.203 sec)

F. Hesnault
Ligier-Renault
(1 min 31.274 sec)

T. Boutsen
Arrows-BMW
(1 min 31.342 sec)

G. Berger
ATS-BMW
(1 min 31.549 sec)

*M. Winkelhock
ATS-BMW
(1 min 32.866 sec)

P. Ghinzani
Osella-Alfa Romeo
(1 min 33.456 sec)

P. Alliot
RAM-Hart
(1 min 34.120 sec)

J. Gartner
Osella-Alfa Romeo
(1 min 34.472 sec)

H. Rothengatter
Spirit-Hart
(1 min 34.719 sec)

J. Palmer
RAM-Hart
(1 min 35.412 sec)

*Non-starter:
M. Winkelhock (ATS-BMW) 1 min 32.866 sec

Did not qualify:
P. Martini (Toleman-Hart) 1 min 35.840 sec.

been running his cars below the minimum weight limit for a large proportion of the race prior to adding the lead balls (as well as water) at the time of the pit stop, the Court rejected the appeal. It also confirmed the outrageously harsh and unprecedented penalty imposed by the FISA Executive Committee in excluding the Tyrrell team from the 1984 World Championship and from taking any further part in it. Amongst its findings, which were included in a lengthy judgement were:

1. 'It is sufficient for the tribunal to note that the presence of traces, however infinitesimal, of hydrocarbons which should not have been there, were found in the water.'
2. The lead balls used for ballast (defined as 'unsecured mobile ballast' by reason of the fluidity of the lead balls): 'contravened the regulations, notably because of the impossibility for the stewards to fix seals on the ballast and to affirm that the ballast remained permanently fixed throughout the duration of the event.' Also, 'in the absence of the guarantees required by Art. 4.2 of the Technical Regulations ("ballast may be used provided that it is secured in such a way that tools are necessary to remove it. It must be possible to fix seals to it.") the infraction is found to have been committed in a particularly serious fashion because of the impossibility of ensuring that the weight of the car really was that minimum weight throughout the event.'
3. 'Contrary to this mandatory regulation (Art. 3.3) holes were pierced in the flat bottom of the car for, according to Tyrrell, the evacuation of air or excess liquid in order to facilitate the replenishment of the tank in an extremely short time, although that evacuation could have been done without difficulty at another position.'

In other words the Court effectively dismissed every aspect put forward by Ken Tyrrell in support of his appeal. This included statements indicating that he had no idea how or why hydrocarbons came to be present in the Tyrrell's water except for the contamination possibly being caused by such items as the water-injection pipe, the flexible synthetic material in the wall of the water tank, the pump or the fuel churn used to transport the water to the pits; statements insisting that his cars had never dropped below 540 kg during a race and that lead ballast had not been added during pit stops; and evidence given on his behalf by Patrick Head (supported by an affidavit from John Barnard) to the effect that the two small holes situated on the underside of the Tyrrell's flat-bottomed monocoque could have had absolutely no discernible effect upon the car's aerodynamics.

Needless to say the consequences of what many observers felt was a sentence way above the normal course of justice were enormous. For a start exclusion from the 1984 World Championship and the loss of Championship points scored earlier in the year meant that Ken Tyrrell would lose his FOCA travel concessions in 1985, reputed to be worth around one million dollars alone. There were substantial legal fees, a claim of over £½ million in damages from Stefan Bellof's manager, Willi Maurer, who had arranged sponsorship through his Monaco-based agency for the young German, and a whole host of other aspects, quite apart from the fact that Ken Tyrrell would now be looked upon as a cheat and might well experience difficulty in attracting future potential sponsors. At the time the Surrey timber merchant was convinced that he could well have been 'stitched up' by someone, and this was something that seemed quite feasible. He had, after all, been involved in various protests against other teams, particularly concerning the use of turbo-charged engines, and, more recently, had been the sole objector to a FOCA proposal to have the 220-litre fuel limit retained in 1985, when it was due to be reduced to 195 litres. Either way, it was interesting to reflect that only days after the FISA Executive Committee's decision to exclude Tyrrell, an announcement had come from FISA stating that 'from 1 January 1985 and until 31 December 1988, the total maximum fuel storage capacity of the car must not exceed 220 litres'!

Not surprisingly, the outcome of the appeal hearing was a major topic of conversation as the teams arrived at Monza for the Italian Grand Prix weekend. But it was not the only one as the statement made by Peter Warr at Zandvoort that Ayrton Senna had signed a contract to drive for John Player Special Team Lotus in 1985 and 1986 had produced almost inevitable repercussions. In fact, Senna's current team, Toleman Group Motorsport, had responded in three ways. First, they had issued their own statement later that same afternoon reaffirming that Senna was still in the midst of a 3-year contract with them, and generally setting out their views on the matter, adding that action would be taken for damages against Senna and others (the contract did include a 'buy-out' clause but, at the same time, specified that the driver was not to enter into any negotiation with any party regarding sponsorship of the driver or the team, or future prospects whilst the contract was still in force). Second, and this was the source of the real talking point, they had subsequently decided to exercise their contractual rights by suspending Senna until further notice, a decision influenced by the manner in which the negotiations had been carried out rather than the fact that Senna wanted a move and, in particular, because of Alex Hawkridge taking exception to a badly worded remark included in Peter Warr's statement which said, somewhat arrogantly, that 'He [Senna] will, of course, continue to drive for Toleman for the rest of the season.' Third, they had secured the services of Stefan Johansson to drive for them for the remainder of the season. For this particular race, Toleman had also renewed an association with the Italian domestic appliances firm Candy whereby a second car was being entered (for the first time since Johnny Cecotto's nasty accident at Brands Hatch) for the 1983 European Formula 3 champion, Italian Pierluigi Martini.

When practice began on Friday morning in cool, but dry, conditions the enforced absence of the Tyrrell team and the revised driver line-up at Toleman represented only some of the differences to that of the entry at Zandvoort. On the driver front another change had been brought about by Gunther Schmidt installing Gerhard Berger in the newer of the two ATS D7s to drive alongside Manfred Winkelhock, as in Austria. There were also some interesting developments on the technical front. Primarily these involved Lotus trying out a new and more robust gearbox in the 95T of de Angelis, and the Ferrari and the Euroracing Alfa Romeo teams both running extensively modified cars featuring reprofiled side-pods that tapered inwards at the rear in similar fashion to the McLaren MP4/2 (and the Williams FW09B) and repositioned water and oil radiators. However, so far as Ferrari was concerned it soon became clear that the alterations, which had led to the cars being dubbed the 126C4/M2s, were unlikely to have any significant effect on the team's recent dismal performances. Neither Arnoux nor Alboreto made any noticeable impression at all during the 90 minute test session, especially compared to the likes of Piquet and the McLaren duo. In fairness, though, the Frenchman had nothing but trouble. First he was obliged to switch to his older-spec spare car following an early turbo-charger failure and then, not long after that, broken transmission led to him being strapped into Alboreto's older-spec spare car. Nevertheless, Arnoux was by no means alone in having problems. Engines certainly caused a lot of trouble, several of which proved reluctant to run properly, mainly because of electrical or fuel-injection faults, while others, such as those in Rosberg's Williams, Ghinzani's Osella and Palmer's RAM, gave out completely. In addition, no less than three drivers put their cars out of commission for the rest of the day with varying degrees of front-end damage after making contact with the barriers at different times. These were Winkelhock, who went off at the Ascari chicane when the right rear suspension of his ATS broke under braking, Gartner, who went off at almost exactly the same spot when the throttle jammed open in his Osella, and Boutsen, whose Arrows (a brand new chassis) suffered a rear brake failure on the approach to the Parabolica due to the turbo waste-gate working loose and melting a brake pipe. Consequently, the morning ended with a lot of work needed in some quarters – and this was all before the start of qualifying!

When the opening timed session did begin 1½ hours later conditions had changed somewhat due to a brief shower of rain falling during the interval. It had not made the track wet enough to send everyone scurrying for wet-weather tyres yet, at the same time, there was sufficient dampness around to convince most drivers that it was worth waiting behind in the pits for a while in the hope that things would improve. As a result the first part of qualifying was a relatively quiet affair, but gradually a dry line began to emerge and during the final 20 minutes or so, despite a number of damp patches remaining where trees lined the circuit, the overall situation was transformed. So, too, were the lap times, which started coming down in leaps and bounds until the leading lights were hovering around the 1 min 30 sec mark. Indeed, before long a few of them were lapping below it, including Piquet, who had already achieved that distinction in the morning and looked like coming out fastest again. But then, soon after the Brazilian set off on his second run, his Brabham 'qualifying special' suffered a major engine failure, and although he later made a marginal improvement to 1 min 28.709 sec, after switching to his proposed race chassis, it was not enough to hold sway. De Angelis, the sole remaining driver in with a mathematical chance, at least, of pipping Lauda or Prost for the Championship crown, saw to that by putting in a real flier during the closing minutes of the session and recording a new unofficial lap record time of 1 min 28.014 sec – all but seven-tenths quicker! Meanwhile, the ever-improving Fabi did an excellent job in the second Brabham, setting third fastest time of 1 min 29.383 sec, and Alboreto gave the unusually quiet hordes of Ferrari supporters at the circuit a glimmer of hope by narrowly pipping Prost for fourth place on the time-sheets, 1 min 29.810 sec compared to the Frenchman's 1 min 29.854 sec. This was in spite of having to rely on Arnoux's spare car after abandoning both his own 126C4/M2 and spare 126C4 because of a lack of turbo boost pressure and a gearbox problem respectively. After that the rest all finished up on the wrong side of the 1 min 30 sec barrier and the vast majority by quite a considerable margin thanks, in part, to a number of them also having had problems. Rosberg certainly had a bad day, suffering another engine failure in his Williams and finding the team's spare car running with a persistent misfire, all of which went a long way to explaining why he had come out only 20th fastest. Palmer, too, had lost another engine in his RAM, as had Alliot this time out, while among others to have had their efforts compromised were Cheever, because of a turbo-charger failure, Winkelhock, who had run into almost immediate gearbox trouble after being allowed out late in Berger's car, and a very unhappy Tambay. First of all the Frenchman had spun wildly at the Curva Grande and had been forced to abandon his car with a stalled engine – nothing worse – and then, after walking back to the pits and taking over the spare Renault, he had been sidelined again shortly afterwards by a broken turbo-charger. His team-mate, openly disenchanted with the circuit, in particular what he considered to be the extremely tedious business of having to negotiate three chicanes on every lap, had also spun at one point in the other Renault. However, Warwick had been able to gather it up and subsequently gone on to set quite a reasonable time of 1 min 30.113 sec, sixth fastest and immediately ahead of Lauda (1 min 30.142 sec), who'd had a busy moment himself on one lap avoiding Mansell's stationary Lotus: the Birmingham lad had stopped out on the circuit with dry tanks!

The weather was still looking a bit unsettled on Saturday morning, but at least the track was dry when the second session of untimed practice started at 10 a.m. Overnight the damaged cars of Boutsen, Gartner and Winkelhock had all been put back together, engines had been replaced where necessary and various other essential repair work completed, so everything was back to normal. However, hopes of it staying that way were dashed almost immediately by Winkelhock, who had yet to qualify for the race, being forced to become a frustrated spectator once more after discovering something badly amiss with the gearbox in his repaired ATS. Later, Arnoux also had a gearbox problem develop in his Ferrari 126C4/M2, while Surer, Palmer (again!) and Prost all had their progress interrupted by another bout of engine failures. Nevertheless, the most worrying moment of the morning, particularly for the McLaren team, came when Lauda pulled up at his pit screaming in agony. He had subsequently to be helped out of his car before being sent off to receive treatment from his trainer and mentor, Willi Dungl. It transpired that whilst negotiating one of the chicanes the Austrian had somehow jarred his back and slipped a disc, which immediately gave rise to doubts about his ability to take any further part in the weekend's proceedings.

By 1 p.m., with Lauda still in a lot of pain, but seemingly determined not to miss out on final qualifying, the possibility of rain had passed over completely and it was turning out to be a very pleasant day. Consequently, bearing in mind that Friday's qualifying session had taken place on a partly damp track, it was quite obvious that the next hour was going to be even more important than usual. This, in turn, gave rise to a certain degree of urgency and nowhere more so than in the Brabham camp where Piquet went straight out with the aim of trying to avoid the worst of the traffic. It was a ploy that was to pay off handsomely, as after completing his 'warm-up lap' the Brazilian got just the chance he needed, put his head down and proceeded to fly around the 5.8 km circuit in a quite staggering 1 min 26.584 sec. Apart from

1984

being a massive 2 seconds quicker than his best time from Friday, this represented an average speed of 149.845 mph (241.153 kph) and included the Brabham being clocked across the start/finish line at almost 195 mph! If it had been a Ferrari the spectators would have gone wild with excitement but, as it was, there was barely a murmur from them. Nevertheless, it certainly woke up everyone in the pits, as in no time at all quite a number of the other front-runners had changed their original plans and were taking to the track earlier than expected, just as Piquet had done. Unfortunately, though, what promised to be a really exciting afternoon failed to materialize. For a start, by the time that the drivers had all gone through their first sets of tyres, only Prost, using the spare McLaren following the engine failure in the morning, had put up any realistic challenge to Piquet by lapping in 1 min 26.671 sec (just under a tenth slower). Then, instead of becoming quicker, the track became fractionally slower owing to small accumulations of oil building up and resulted in neither of these first two times being beaten, which meant that Piquet, who actually put in two subsequent appearances after his second run had been ruined by a turbo-charger failure, was on the pole for the seventh time in 1984. Meanwhile de Angelis, the overnight pole-sitter, had certainly not disgraced himself by setting the afternoon's third fastest time of 1 min 27.538 sec, even if it was the best part of a second off the pace, and a very brave performance from Lauda, that had produced an improvement of over 1½ seconds to 1 min 28.533 sec, was rewarded with fourth place on the grid. Next was Fabi on 1 min 28.587 sec, in spite of the BMW engine in his Brabham having been reluctant to pull at peak revs. Then came Rosberg (1 min 28.818 sec), following an altogether happier day, Mansell (1 min 28.969 sec – achieved on a lap in which his engine had momentarily cut out on a couple of occasions!), Tambay (1 min 29.253 sec), notwithstanding two turbo-charger failures during the course of the afternoon, and finally, completing the first ten places on the grid, Patrese (1 min 29.382 sec) and Cheever (1 min 29.797 sec) in their revised Alfa Romeo 184Ts. This was a really encouraging sign for the Euroracing team, although ever since the start of the weekend both drivers had been openly delighted with the performance of their cars. They had not only been handling better, but also giving improved throttle response and more straight-line speed thanks to the new rear bodywork allowing them to be run with less wing, and the turbo-charger units now receiving more clean air. To add to the team's obvious delight, they had also upstaged the Ferraris on home soil. Alboreto, who had had to abandon his 126C4/M2 because of an engine failure and switch to his older-spec 126C4, had slipped

away to 11th place on the grid after being among a handful of drivers not to register any improvement, while Arnoux, late in going out because of the gearbox problem, and then troubled by lack of grip, had wound up in an even more lowly 14th spot behind Warwick (another not to have improved following engine problems in both his proposed race car and the spare Renault) and a rather uninspired Laffite. Among the others, all at least 4½ seconds slower than Piquet, a disappointed Surer had dropped away from ninth place on Friday to an eventual 15th on the grid after the fresh BMW engine in his Arrows had refused to pick up properly out of the corners and prevented any further improvement (he was still four places higher than his seemingly off-form team-mate) and Johansson, who had had a promising first day with his new team, had slipped back to 17th spot between the Ligier duo: his hopes of making any further progress had been dashed by acute oversteer caused by what was later found to be a broken engine mounting. After that the rest of the grid was made up by the two ATS D7s of Berger and a somewhat relieved Winkelhock, who had only qualified in the closing stages of the afternoon due to delays in repairing his gearbox, the two Osellas, the two RAMs and Rothengatter's Spirit. That left just new-boy Martini as the sole non-qualifier after his chances of making the cut in the second Toleman had not exactly been improved by transmission failure on Friday afternoon and a broken turbo-charger this time out.

Trouble was rife even before the start of the race on Sunday, as during the late morning warm-up session both the two McLarens and the two Williams suffered engine ailments, Piquet's Brabham had its turbo-charger break and Warwick's Renault ran with a persistent misfire. In addition the Ferrari team, following its worst practice performance at Monza for years, was so concerned by its drivers' complaints of transmission vibrations and lack of straight-line speed that the 126C4/M2s were put away in favour of the older-spec 126C4s, and similarly, at Toleman, more handling problems led to Johansson taking over the spare TG184: it was only after he had later requested that the engine from his original race chassis be transferred to the spare car that the broken engine mounting, previously mentioned, was discovered. Then, some three hours later as preparations were in hand for the start, and with the cars of Lauda and Rosberg fitted with fresh engines (Prost, Laffite and Warwick had also switched to their teams' spare chassis), there was more unwanted drama. This time it involved Winkelhock being able to select only two gears, fourth and fifth, in his ATS, and also Surer finding that the BMW engine in his Arrows had suddenly gone off-song, a problem that subsequently led to the Swiss having to start

the race from the pit lane. Winkelhock, on the other hand, pulled up at the back of the grid at the end of the parade lap and abandoned his car in disgust to become a non-starter for the second time in three outings. Consequently, only 24 starters ultimately lined up in their grid positions, but without more ado the 55th Italian Grand Prix was set in motion in front of what, at best, could be described as a modest crowd by Monza standards and under clear blue skies. At the front Piquet made only a mediocre start, as did Prost, but de Angelis took off like a scalded cat, squeezed between the Brabham and the McLaren and went nosing into the lead. In next to no time, though, Piquet was taking full advantage of the quite incredible power of his BMW engine to restore the status quo and, after drawing alongside the black and gold Lotus, succeeded in just beating it into the Goodyear chicane. After that he simply walked the rest of the opening lap to open out an advantage of well over a second, whereas de Angelis first dipped out to Prost at the Parabolica and then found a very quick-off-the-mark Tambay out-accelerating him past the pits. Behind them, Fabi was looking good in fifth place, and Lauda, who had received more treatment on his back from Willi Dungl overnight and was driving with extra support around the cockpit seat to ease the discomfort (this had ended considerable speculation as to whether or not he would be able to race), was holding down sixth spot ahead of Mansell. Then came Patrese, Cheever, Rosberg, Alboreto, Warwick, de Cesaris, Arnoux and the rest, including Johansson, who was going like the clappers and already up into 17th place after almost stalling his engine on the line and being last away – apart from the delayed Surer.

On the second lap Piquet ran extremely wide on the way out of the first of the two Lesmo bends, skipped up over the kerbing and had a very busy moment indeed keeping his Brabham pointing in the right direction. Somehow he succeeded, but the loss of momentum allowed Prost and Tambay to close right up to him, and with it came the makings of an exciting leadership tussle. Alas, it was a situation that was to be short-lived. No sooner had Prost crossed the start/finish line at the end of the third lap than ominous-looking blue smoke starting pouring out from the back of the McLaren and moments later he was pulling off on to the grass just beyond the Goodyear chicane with a comprehensively blown-up engine. Naturally this was a bitter blow to the Frenchman's World Championship hopes, but there was certainly no sympathy from the spectators, who chose to express themselves by jeering and, in a few instances, by even throwing stones at him as he stepped out of the stricken red and white car. The incident also did nothing to improve Tambay's immediate

283

chances, as apart from being held up a bit through the chicane, he became so plastered in oil that he was obliged to remove the tear-off strip on his visor, in order that he could see where he was going. This, in turn, enabled Piquet to pull out an advantage of a couple of seconds or so and for Fabi to close up to him in the second Brabham, the Italian having overtaken de Angelis early on the third lap. Since then Lauda, in spite of taking things relatively easy at this early stage of the race, had also passed the Lotus, so was now up into fourth place, while further back Alboreto was keeping the partisan crowd well contented by making steady progress in his Ferrari. In fact, he had already picked off Rosberg's Williams as well as the two Euro-racing Alfa Romeos of Cheever and Patrese, and was currently setting about Mansell's sixth-placed Lotus. Arnoux, on the other hand, seemed to be getting nowhere in the second Ferrari, and on lap 6, with Patrese now well down the order following a brief off-course excursion, even less so for he was pulling off the track with a broken gearbox. Predictably, this was accompanied by groans from the spectators, but almost immediately these changed to loud cheers when Alboreto, by now having got the better of Mansell, went surging ahead of de Angelis past the pits to move up into fifth place, some 5 seconds behind Lauda. A lap later, more joy – Alboreto was fourth: Fabi, pushing Tambay really hard for second place, had over-done things at the second chicane and spun through 360-degrees. Fortunately, he had avoided the barriers and succeeded in keeping his engine running, but by the time that the Brabham was properly on its way again third place had become eighth and it was only just ahead of Rosberg's Williams and Mansell's Lotus, which had started losing places hand over fist. Nevertheless, the Italian applied himself to the job of making up lost ground admirably and proceeded to repass Warwick, Cheever, de Angelis and Alboreto on successive laps prior to giving chase to Lauda's McLaren. While this was happening there was also a string of retirements. First Alliot stopped out on the circuit with a dead engine caused by some obscure electrical fault and this was followed, in quick succession, by de Cesaris rather thoughtlessly touring round to the pits rather than pulling off the track when the Renault engine blew up in his Ligier; by Hesnault apparently spinning off on his team-mate's oil and being forced to abandon his Ligier with a stalled engine; and by the Honda engines in both of the Williams expiring within the space of just a couple of minutes.

After twelve laps, Piquet, far from running away with the race, was still only around 2 seconds clear of Tambay's Renault. In fact, if anything, the gap was starting to come down slightly, and over the next couple of laps this was something that became even more

apparent. What was not apparent to the outside world at this stage, however, was that Piquet's engine was running hot as the result of its coolant escaping through a split water radiator, a problem possibly caused by that early kerb-hopping incident. Only on lap 15, as the Brabham arrived at the Ascari chicane, was there a clue that all was not well when a puff of smoke suddenly appeared from the back of the blue and white car. Moreover, there were soon clouds of the stuff and from then on things rapidly went from bad to worse for the Brazilian until, just over a lap later, and with Tambay now the new race leader, he went touring into the pits to clock up yet another retirement in 1984. Almost unnoticed in this somewhat dramatic turn of events, Mansell had spun off at the second chicane and become hopelessly stuck in a sandy run-off area, while de Angelis, who had not exactly been finding life comfortable through having pulled a shoulder muscle during the morning warm-up session, had only just preceded Piquet into the pits with the loss of second and fourth gears: the new gearbox had failed to live up to expectations. Consequently, in common with Ligier and Williams, it was now all over for the Lotus team, but that was certainly not true for Brabham as Fabi was pressing on as hard as ever. Indeed, he had now caught Lauda's McLaren and, on lap 17, lost little time in blasting past the Championship leader to move up into a superb second place, some 7 seconds behind the leading Renault. Further back, meanwhile, Alboreto was still pounding along in what had now become a rather lonely fourth place, but Cheever was coming under increasing pressure from Warwick who, in turn, could see Johansson's Toleman looming ever larger in his mirrors, the Swede having continued climbing through the field

in leaps and bounds.

By the end of lap 19 Warwick had finally made it past Cheever and before long Johansson was threatening to do the same. Instead of succeeding, though, the Swede found himself being caught up in what was to be a prolonged cat-and-mouse affair, his Toleman proving to be a better proposition than the Alfa Romeo under braking and traction at the three chicanes yet losing out slightly on sheer horsepower along the straights. As this rather intriguing situation continued, with Johansson all but climbing over the back of the green and black car at times, so another developed, as by lap 25 Fabi had closed to within striking distance of Tambay's Renault, and Lauda was also right up there to make it a close-running trio. Over the laps that followed, however, Tambay seemed well able to cope with the enormous pressure, and successfully staved off each and every challenge from Fabi, while Lauda seemed quite content just to sit and watch – and wait. In all, this went on for well over 20 minutes. But then Lauda, thinking about the extra Championship points at stake, began to assert himself, and as he followed Fabi past the pits to start the 40th lap he went darting this way and that behind him to try to find a way through before the Goodyear chicane. On this occasion Fabi succeeded in defending his position, only for Lauda to take another run at him as they exited the Ascari chicane later on the same lap, and then finally he broke the deadlock by neatly nipping through on the inside just before the Parabolica. Thereafter, Lauda immediately set about closing the small gap to Tambay and, on lap 42, left no-one in any doubt that he meant business by setting what was to be the afternoon's fastest lap, 1 min 31.912 sec. Furthermore, the Frenchman

After leading much of the way, Patrick Tambay had his hopes of even finishing the race dashed by a broken throttle cable only seven laps from home. Here he has just been overhauled by the McLaren of Niki Lauda, who went on to score the 24th victory of his career and to stretch his lead at the top of the Championship table to 10½ points. (*Autosport*)

was in no position to respond as for about ten laps now he had been having to contend with a slightly sticking throttle, which was gradually growing worse and causing him to exert more and more pressure on the accelerator pedal. Lauda, of course, had no way of knowing this, but when the Renault hesitated momentarily as it accelerated away from the second chicane on the following lap that was all it needed for him to seize upon the opportunity to snatch the lead, leaving Tambay to persevere as best he could in second place. Even that, though, didn't last long for as he came to accelerate away from the Parabolica next time round the throttle cable suddenly snapped and led to him coasting to rest directly in front of the Renault pit before stepping forlornly out of his car. Although it was unlikely to be of any consolation to him, only a minute earlier Fabi had also pulled up in front of the pits with the BMW engine in his Brabham having seized due to a broken oil pipe having allowed all of its lubricant to seep away. So that, too, had been a sad end to an equally impressive performance. By now Warwick had become yet another retirement in the second Renault, the Englishman having pulled off the track on lap 32 with a loss of oil pressure,

while earlier Palmer had quietly bowed out in the pits with the Hart engine in his RAM on the verge of seizing. Consequently, the field was thinning fast, and by the time that Surer had gone into the pits at the end of his 44th lap to retire his Arrows with engine trouble only ten cars were left. None of this, however, was of the slightest concern to the crowd or the fact that Johansson, who had finally succeeded in scrambling past Cheever's Alfa Romeo on lap 42, had just dropped behind the American once more following a quick pit stop: the Toleman had developed a rear end vibration caused by what had been diagnosed to be a failing wheel bearing. Instead, the spectators were beside themselves with joy as Alboreto was now in a totally unexpected second place, albeit a distant one, as well as being the only driver, apart from Cheever, still on the same lap as the new leader.

As Lauda proceeded to leisurely reel off the last seven laps the race continued to provide unexpected drama. Already Johansson was driving noticeably slower since his pit stop as he endeavoured to nurse his Toleman home, and he was rapidly being caught by Patrese and Ghinzani. But on lap 46 Cheever, looking all set to finish in third

place, stopped altogether through running out of fuel just like a fortnight earlier at Zandvoort. Then, within minutes of following Patrese (now third) past the ailing Toleman, and with only two laps to go, Ghinzani found himself in exactly the same predicament. Nor was that quite the end of it. On the final lap the Alfa Romeo engine in the other Osella also started spluttering out of fuel and it was only through switching on the electric starting pump that Gartner eventually made it across the line to finish in fifth place ahead of Berger, who had driven most of the way with no fourth gear, Rothengatter and a delayed Boutsen, the Belgian having made two pit stops because of engine problems. In the meantime, Alboreto had just received a rapturous reception after crossing the line in second place, and there was even applause for Lauda from the partisan crowd for achieving what on paper, at least, had ultimately been a most comfortable victory, the 24th of his career. Even more important, it was also his fifth win of the season, to put him level with Prost once more, and one that stretched his lead at the top of the Championship table to 10½ points. And now there were just two races remaining!

Results

1	N. Lauda (McLaren-TAG)	1 hr 20 min 29.065 sec (220.514 kph/ 137.021 mph)
2	M. Alboreto (Ferrari)	1 hr 20 min 53.314 sec
3	R. Patrese (Alfa Romeo)	1 lap behind
4	S. Johansson (Toleman-Hart)	2 laps behind
5	J. Gartner (Osella-Alfa Romeo)	2 laps behind
6	G. Berger (ATS-BMW)	2 laps behind
*7	P. Ghinzani (Osella-Alfa Romeo)	3 laps behind
8	H. Rothengatter (Spirit-Hart)	3 laps behind
*9	E. Cheever (Alfa Romeo)	6 laps behind
10	T. Boutsen (Arrows-BMW)	6 laps behind

*Not running at finish.

Fastest lap: N. Lauda (McLaren-TAG) on lap 42 in 1 min 31.912 sec (227.173 kph/ 141.158 mph)

Retirements

A. Prost (McLaren-TAG) engine on lap 4, R. Arnoux (Ferrari) gearbox on lap 6, P. Alliot (RAM-Hart) electrics on lap 7, A. de Cesaris (Ligier-Renault) engine on lap 8, F. Hesnault (Ligier-Renault) spun and stalled on lap 8, K. Rosberg (Williams-Honda) engine on lap 9, J. Laffite (Williams-Honda) engine on lap 11, N. Mansell (Lotus-Renault) spun off on lap 14, E. de Angelis (Lotus-Renault) gearbox on lap 15, N. Piquet (Brabham-BMW) engine on lap 16, J. Palmer (RAM-Hart) engine on lap 21, D. Warwick (Renault) oil pressure on lap 32, T. Fabi (Brabham-BMW) oil pipe on lap 44, P. Tambay (Renault) throttle cable on lap 44, M. Surer (Arrows-BMW) engine on lap 44.

N.B. Although J. Gartner and G. Berger finished in 5th and 6th places respectively no points were awarded as Osella and ATS had entered only one car each for the 1984 World Championship.

XXXVI Grosser Preis von Europa

New Nürburgring: October 7
Weather: Sunny and breezy
Distance: 67 laps of 4.542 km circuit = 304.31 km (189.09 miles)

For the second year running the proposed New York Grand Prix, originally scheduled for September 23, had failed to get off the ground. As a result, after the Italian Grand Prix at Monza there was an unusually long interval of four weeks between races, the next not being until October 7. This was the European Grand Prix, a title that had been resurrected in 1983 for a second World Championship event to be held in Great Britain as a replacement for that year's ill-fated New York Grand Prix and one, that this year, was being used again for a second

such event in Germany. On this occasion, though, the circumstances were rather different. It had not been arranged to take the place of a cancelled race, but had been included on the Grand Prix calendar in anticipation of the completion of a brand new circuit in the Eifel mountains to replace the Nürburgring, which had fallen into disuse as a Formula 1 track after Niki Lauda's accident there in 1976. Not surprisingly, the thought of Grand Prix racing returning to this region after such a long gap had, initially, generated considerable interest and more than a little

excitement. But the multi-million Deutschmark circuit that materialized (it had been officially opened in May and was named the New Nürburgring) had already proved to be a major disappointment to a lot of people. The general facilities were alright. In fact, they were first class and included provision for somewhere in the region of 175,000 spectators with maximum safety and comfort, an ultra smooth track surface, wide run-off areas, a spacious pits/paddock complex and more than ample service roads for rescue vehicles. The track layout, on the other hand, fell well short of expectations, for instead of the circuit builders making use of the natural contours that hitherto existed on the land, they had spent huge sums of money on earth-moving operations and produced a

1984

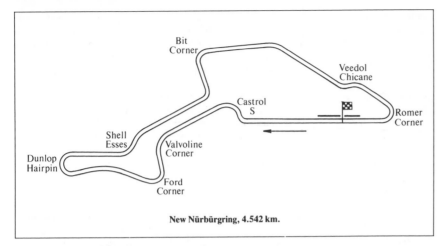

New Nürburgring, 4.542 km.

series of undemanding constant-radius corners. Consequently, rather than being a scaled-down version of the nearby famous North Circuit, with its spectacular swoops and climbs, the end-product was a commendably safe yet bland and featureless autodrome, which several drivers (past as well as present) felt was utterly boring.

Although this was going to be the first Grand Prix to take place on the new 4.542 km circuit, a few of the Formula 1 drivers had already raced here in a World Endurance Championship event back in July. In addition, several more had taken part in three days of testing at the track in mid-September, so by the time that it came round to the start of official practice on Friday morning most of the drivers were already reasonably familiar with the surroundings. Consequently, with conditions dry and fairly bright, the majority of them were able to go straight out and quickly settle down to the usual business of sorting cars for the first hour of qualifying without having the extra task of learning their way round. As always this meant juggling with variables where necessary, trying out different tyres, and so on. But, because the lack of any long straights meant a lot of stopping and starting, brakes were also a vital factor and resulted in the teams paying a considerable amount of attention to cooling and heat dissipation. Entry-wise there were few changes from that at Monza, which was of no real surprise at this advanced stage of the season. Nevertheless, on the driver front sponsorship considerations had led to Mauro Baldi returning to drive the Spirit in place of Huub Rothengatter; Toleman had decided that Ayrton Senna had been punished enough for his breach of contract and invited him back to partner Stefan Johansson, who had now signed a 2-year contract with the team; and, conversely, Gunther Schmidt had fired Manfred Winkelhock for apparently making derogatory comments about his team over recent weeks with the result that there was only one ATS entry this weekend, for Austrian Gerhard Berger. Meanwhile, on the technical

front Brabham and Williams had each produced a new chassis to their 1984 designs for Nelson Piquet and Jacques Laffite respectively, and amongst existing chassis to have undergone modifications was one of the Ligier JS23s, which was now in 'B' specification and featured McLaren-type rear bodywork and revised pull-rod suspension all round. One of the Osella FA1Fs, Ghinzani's car, was yet another to have recently received the 'McLaren rear bodywork treatment', Spirit had lengthened the wheelbase of one of their 101Bs by some four inches as well as having carried out subtle aerodynamic changes and fitted a different water radiator, and Toleman, besides running their TG184s with larger Holset turbo-charger units and trying out a revised electronic fuel-injection system for the Hart engine in Senna's car, had reverted back to the double rear aerofoil arrangement as it was felt that this was a better proposition at what was a medium-speed circuit, average lap speeds being around 200 kph. Otherwise all was much as normal except that Ferrari had brought along only 3 cars, all to the new M2 specification seen in practice at Monza but not raced, and Renault were experimenting with a new electronic fuel-injection system on Warwick's RE50. That, at least, was the French team's idea, but unfortunately the engine was proving reluctant to deliver full power and this eventually led to Warwick taking over the spare RE50. During the morning other drivers also swapped chassis for one reason or another. These included Lauda, who set off in the spare McLaren only to find something obviously amiss with its electronic fuel-injection; Senna, who had a wire break in the electronic control box of his Toleman; and Berger, who overdid things, careered off into the unforgiving guard-rail and put his ATS out of commission for the rest of the weekend. Even then neither Lauda nor Senna were able to spend much time out on the track, as within a couple of laps the engine in the spare Toleman cut out due to an apparent electrical fault, while the McLaren (the Austrian's

proposed race chassis) had a gearbox oil seal fail, allowing oil to seep on to its clutch. Johansson also became sidelined when his Toleman stopped with a broken rotor arm and there were a few other problems, mainly with engines not running properly, but by and large most drivers went on to complete the untimed session seemingly in good shape.

By 1 p.m. the skies had clouded over and there was sufficient moisture in the air to suggest that rain was imminent. Sure enough, within just a few minutes of qualifying getting under way it began to drizzle, which resulted in only those drivers going straight out having the benefit of a dry track. Among them was Piquet, who immediately set himself up as the man to beat by lapping in 1 min 18.871 sec, more than half a second quicker than the fastest time of 1 min

19.41 sec recorded by de Angelis during the recent test sessions at the circuit. Meanwhile Prost, after having pipped the outgoing World Champion for fastest time in the morning, was kept waiting behind in the pits while the McLaren mechanics completed work on changing the fuel pump and turbo-charger units on his car. As a result he was one of a number of drivers not to take to the track until it was effectively too late, another being Fabi who was having a down-on-power engine replaced in his Brabham. In fact, some weren't even bothering to venture out at all, preferring, instead, to stay put in the hope that the rain might stop. Eventually it did, and gradually a dry line began to emerge, but by that time there were only 10 minutes or so of the session remaining. This, in turn, produced a problem in itself for now, of course, more or less everyone charged out, leading to the track becoming somewhat overcrowded. Consequently, the chances of finding a clear lap became next to impossible and turned the entire business of qualifying into little more than a lottery. Nevertheless, some drivers succeeded in finding a gap in the traffic better than others, and amongst those to do so were Prost and Tambay, who both set very impressive times on the still damp track of 1 min 19.175 sec and 1 min 19.499 sec respectively to wind up second and third to Piquet. Apart from them nobody succeeded in breaking the 1 min 20 sec barrier, but a typically spirited effort from Rosberg in his understeering Williams netted fourth fastest time of 1 min 20.652 sec – achieved on a lap in which his engine developed a serious misfire as he accelerated away from the last corner – and the two Ferrari drivers were both encouragingly well up the order with the next best times of 1 min 20.910 sec (Alboreto) and 1 min 21.180 sec (Arnoux). This was in spite of the fact that the 126C4/M2s were also under-steering rather a lot.

Meanwhile, Warwick's attempts to progress beyond 1 min 21.571 sec for seventh place on the time-sheets were thwarted by the spare Renault that he was still using jumping out of third gear (he also indulged in a quick spin on one lap whilst moving off line for his team-mate) and, similarly, fluctuating turbo boost pressure prevented Fabi from bettering 1 min 22.206 sec, which left the Italian Brabham driver tenth fastest behind Mansell (1 min 21.710 sec) and Patrese (1 min 21.937 sec). Even they, though, were much better placed than some of the other notables at the end of the afternoon. Senna had come out a rather disappointing 12th fastest behind Boutsen, Lauda was three places lower behind Cheever and Laffite (he had been hampered by low turbo boost pressure) after the fuel-injection system in the spare McLaren had continued playing up and de Angelis was way down in 23rd place following a string of turbo-charger failures.

The first had occurred right at the beginning of the session whilst out in the spare Lotus, a second had occurred almost as soon as he had switched to his proposed race chassis and then, after having hopped back into the spare car (since fitted with a fresh turbo-charger unit) the same thing happened again, all of which had prevented even one decent flying lap. Johansson, too, had suffered a particularly frustrating hour as the engine in the spare Toleman, to which he had been consigned, had initially been extremely reluctant to start and had then refused to run cleanly. In fact, the Swede had managed just one timed lap and that had taken an absolutely hopeless 1 min 41.178 sec, which left him in 26th and last place on the time-sheets.

Saturday was an absolute disaster with rain followed by more rain throughout both the second untimed session of practice in the morning and the final hour of qualifying in the afternoon. In spite of the dreadful conditions all of the drivers ventured out on wet-weather tyres at some time or another during the day and, as always, some were more enthusiastic than others. Obviously, there was no hope of anyone improving on their Friday qualifying time but, if nothing else, it was a useful exercise in the event of a wet race as Lauda and Prost, in particular, testified by both putting in quite prolonged appearances on the soaking wet track. After his troubled afternoon on Friday it was in many ways ironic that de Angelis should set the fastest time, 1 min 39.762 sec, although even this was more than 20 seconds slower than what had now become Piquet's pole-winning time. Lauda, too, made a complete mockery of having to start the race from 15th position on the grid by setting second fastest time of 1 min 40.392 sec, while team-mate Prost, one of a number of drivers to take to the grass during the course of the day, Mansell, Cheever, Patrese and Alboreto also excelled in the wet by recording the other leading times, all lapping inside the 1 min 42 sec bracket – and at average speeds of around 100 mph!

Contrary to expectations, the weather had relented by Sunday morning, but even though the skies had cleared to give way to bright and sunny conditions it was still not very warm owing to the presence of quite a stiff breeze. With the start of the race scheduled for 2.30 p.m., the warm-up session took place between 10.30 a.m. and 11.00 a.m. and produced a complete contrast of fortunes so far as the McLaren duo was concerned. While Lauda confidently set the fastest time Prost, who had really to win the race to keep his Championship hopes alive, had the misfortune to collide with a stationary VW Passat 'safety car' after putting a wheel over the kerbing at the last corner before the pits and spinning across the grass. Quite why the car came to be parked beside a tyre barrier rather than behind it was a mystery but,

whatever, the impact severely dented its bodywork and broke the left rear wheel of the McLaren. Subsequent examination of the MP4/2 also suggested that the rear suspension might have suffered and so, as a precautionary measure, Prost's mechanics set about replacing some of the components, added to which they knuckled down to the task of installing a fresh TAG-Porsche engine owing to the fact that the unit fitted overnight had been showing signs of over-heating. Over at Renault, meanwhile, Tambay was all smiles after setting second fastest time in his repaired RE50 (he had torn away the right rear corner of the car against the barriers during the previous morning whilst trying out some carbon-fibre brakes), but Warwick had discovered that the engine in his race chassis was still refusing to pull properly. As a result the Englishman decided to opt for the team's spare car with the normal fuel-injection system, even though its handling characteristics were less to his liking. Johansson, too, ultimately chose to rely on the spare Toleman after comparing it with his own car, but otherwise as the time of the race approached everything appeared to be running much according to plan. A rather disappointing aspect, however, was the size of the crowd as the huge concrete grand-stands, far from being crammed to capacity, were more than half-empty with the attendance figure only around the 60,000-mark.

By 2.30 p.m. the 26 starters had left the pits, they had all completed their warm-up lap (or two, or even three, laps in many instances), the final count-down had taken place and Piquet was leading them round to their grid positions once more at the end of the parade lap. There was then a brief pause once they had all correctly lined up, the starting lights came on and moments later the first Grand Prix at the New Nürburgring was under way. At that point Piquet, who was out to win on BMW's home soil, was expected to surge forward into an immediate lead but, instead, the Brabham hesitated slightly and it was Prost's McLaren that was first to show. Tambay also outgunned the pole-sitter and, moreover, almost succeeded in snatching the lead himself at the first corner until being forced to give way to Prost at virtually the last moment. As it was, he was still able to slot neatly into second place and found himself directly in front of Piquet and team-mate Warwick, another to have made an exceptionally good start. Rosberg, on the other hand, was already down in mid-field by the time that he arrived at the first corner owing to a problem with the Honda engine in his Williams refusing to pick up cleanly. That, though, was of little significance compared to what happened next, for as the Finn turned into the right-left ess-bend so Senna, somewhat restricted due to Cheever's Alfa Romeo being immediately to his right, suddenly ran into the back of

The chaotic start of the European Grand Prix at the New Nurburgring, which eliminated the cars of Ayrton Senna, Keke Rosberg, Gerhard Berger, Marc Surer and Piercarlo Ghinzani. (*Autosport*)

him. The Toleman then rode up over the Williams' right rear wheel, leaving black tyre marks on its bodywork perilously close to Rosberg's head, and spun round on to the grass before coming to rest with extensive rear-end damage. Rosberg's Williams also finished up on the grass with broken right rear suspension, and in the ensuing confusion Berger spun backwards into Surer's Arrows, while Ghinzani became involved in yet another collision with Fabi's Brabham. The upshot was that Senna, Rosberg, Berger, Surer and Ghinzani all subsequently abandoned their cars, and Fabi, who had apparently come out of it with nothing worse than a stalled engine, later rejoined the race after being towed (illegally!) back on to the track by a rescue vehicle. Meanwhile the leaders, blissfully unaware of the mayhem that had just occurred, were soon coming round to complete the first lap with Prost already a full second clear of Tambay, who was still being pursued by Piquet and Warwick. A short distance behind them, Alboreto had settled into fifth place ahead of team-mate Arnoux, then came Patrese, an unscathed Cheever, Lauda (already up into ninth spot), Boutsen and the rest of the survivors being led by de Angelis, the Italian having made up even more places than Lauda. So, too, for that matter had Johansson as he had come through from last pla' on the grid to 14th in the race. By contrast Laffite, following even more trouble than Rosberg in getting his Williams off the line, and Mansell, who had also made a poor start and been further delayed by an unscheduled trip across the grass at the first corner, were bringing up the rear, apart from Fabi.

With Prost continuing to edge away from

Tambay at the rate of around half a second per lap, and Piquet (running only a modest amount of turbo boost pressure in the interests of engine reliability) doing no more than just about keeping up with the Renault in third place, most of the attention during the early stages of the race became fixed on Lauda as he steadily worked his way up into contention. However, once the Championship leader had disposed of the two Alfa Romeos on successive laps and then picked off Arnoux's Ferrari on the fifth lap he became bogged down behind Warwick and Alboreto, busily disputing fourth place. Furthermore, this was a situation that went on and on with the first sign of a change not coming until the start of lap 18 when Alboreto made a bold run down the outside of the Renault with the intention of nipping through under braking at the first corner. Even then nothing came of it as Warwick kept the door firmly shut, and it was just the same a few moments later when Lauda tried a similar manoeuvre on Alboreto at the next left-hander. Nor was there much else happening to keep the crowd amused, although de Angelis, after having overtaken Boutsen on the second lap, had since come out on top of a spirited scrap with the Alfa Romeo duo and, more recently, had barged past Arnoux's Ferrari to take up station in a relatively distant seventh place. Mansell and Laffite, too, had both been making steady progress since the opening lap and were now up into 11th and 13th places respectively, but Johansson's early promise had dissipated due to a faulty water pump causing a loss of coolant and an associated overheating problem that was now about to end his race in the pits. Boutsen, meanwhile, had just rejoined the race following an early tyre stop and

from a reasonably strong mid-field position had dropped right down amongst the tailenders.

By lap 22 the Warwick-Alboreto-Lauda train was coming up to lap Gartner and Baldi, which suggested that this may well present one or other of them with an opportunity of breaking the deadlock. It did to a point, although not quite in the manner expected. Instead, after Warwick had passed the Spirit on the entry to the fast ess-bend behind the pits, Lauda tried to follow Alboreto through on the inside of the white car under braking for the final hairpin, realized at virtually the last moment that he wasn't going to make it, stood on his brakes and suddenly spun through 360-degrees amidst a huge cloud of tyre smoke. Although the McLaren finished up on the grass, Lauda at least succeeded in keeping the engine running and subsequently took off once more still in sixth place, albeit now a long way behind Warwick and Alboreto and with his already slim chances of ever catching his team-mate effectively over. Furthermore, the incident not only flat-spotted his tyres, causing a chassis vibration, but also enabled de Angelis to close right up to him. The Italian, however, wasn't destined to be around much longer as within less than four more laps he was pulling off the track with a repeat of Friday afternoon's problems – another broken turbo-charger! In any event, by that stage Lauda had already started pulling away from the black and gold car and was pressing on as hard as ever in an endeavour to make up for the loss of time. Even this, though, failed to put any real life into what was turning out to be a very processional affair being dominated by Prost. In fact, apart from Mansell overhauling the two

Alfa Romeos and also Arnoux's Ferrari, which was misfiring slightly, the only changes of any significance at all to occur over the next dozen or so laps came about as a result of the retirements of Laffite (turbo-charger failure), Palmer (engine trouble), Cheever (loss of fuel pressure) and Alliot (turbo-charger failure).

After 40 laps Prost had increased his lead to more than 20 seconds and was still driving absolutely flawlessly in a car that was performing perfectly in every sense of the word, despite the problems earlier in the day. Tambay, too, was looking just as impressive in his Renault, even if he was unable to live with his compatriot. Unfortunately, though, he was now beginning to suffer the first effects of an electrical problem that was causing his engine to lose its edge. Essentially, the symptoms were a misfire through the left-hand turns, and over the next three laps this slowed him sufficiently for Piquet to wipe out a deficit of some 5 seconds that had accrued between them and go sailing past into second place. On the very next lap Warwick and Alboreto also moved on ahead of him and, with the problem growing worse, Tambay soon made up his mind to head for the pits in the hope that something could be done about it. However, in spite of a lengthy stop while the Renault's spark box was changed, the misfire was as bad as ever when Tambay eventually rejoined the race and just two more laps were enough to convince him that it was pointless continuing. To make matters worse for the French equipe, Warwick also began to slow slightly in the meantime, was finally forced to concede to Alboreto on lap 49 and then started dropping back into the clutches of Lauda, who had just gone around in a new fastest time of 1 min 23.729 sec regardless of his flat-spotted Michelins. Indeed, by the time that an extremely disappointed Mansell was abandoning his Lotus in the vicinity of the last hairpin on lap 52 with its Renault engine having blown up in a big way, robbing him of an otherwise certain points finish (he had been lying sixth), Lauda had closed right up

to Warwick and was already looking for a way past. Even so, for a while Warwick seemed well able to cope with the mounting pressure and this, together with the fact that Alboreto was rapidly closing to within striking distance of Piquet, produced some much-needed excitement in an otherwise uninspiring race. By lap 55, though, the Renault's left-hand exhaust system had broken, not only making its V6 engine sound very rough but also causing a drop in turbo boost pressure, and as Warwick arrived at the last hairpin he was almost literally powerless to prevent Lauda from nipping through on the inside. Thereafter, the Englishman steadily dropped away from the McLaren until a little over six laps later his engine finally cried 'enough!' and sent him coasting to rest out on the circuit – at almost precisely the same moment that the question of Fabi being disqualified for the tow on the opening lap became academic due to the Italian stopping with a broken gearbox.

For Prost the closing stages of the 67-lap race couldn't have been easier, but whilst he was cruising home to a resounding sixth victory of the season Piquet couldn't afford to relax for a moment due to Alboreto hounding him all the way round the circuit. To indicate just how hard they were going at it, on lap 62 Piquet set a new fastest time of 1 min 23.146 sec and so, too, did Alboreto – right down to the same third decimal place! Nevertheless, up until the final lap Piquet seemed to have just that little bit extra in hand to hold sway. Then, suddenly, it all changed. Coming round on the return leg of the circuit behind the pits, the BMW engine in the Brabham began spluttering out of fuel and in the next instant Alboreto had shot past into second place. But, incredible as it seemed, only moments later on the way out of the last hairpin the Ferrari started suffering from exactly the same symptoms and finished up by coasting over the line just over a second clear of the Brabham, which Piquet succeeded in bringing home third by jabbing the steering wheel from side to side to encourage the fuel system to pick up the last

few drops of petrol. Both drivers then pulled up by the exit from the pit lane, stepped out of their cars and greeted one another by shrugging shoulders and bursting into smiles. Meanwhile, behind all of this last-minute drama and excitement, Lauda arrived in fourth place some 18 seconds later to claim three extremely valuable Championship points, and after a similar gap Arnoux brought the second Ferrari home to a somewhat fortuitous fifth place ahead of Patrese (lapped), de Cesaris, Baldi and Hesnault, another to have coasted over the line out of fuel. Gartner, on the other hand, had been somewhat less fortunate as his Osella had run out of fuel on its 61st lap and Boutsen, too, had suffered the misfortune of his Arrows-BMW stopping with an electrical failure on its very last lap.

Whilst the race had been something of a disappointment in many respects it had certainly produced the right sort of result to keep the Championship title chase alive, for Prost had now clipped his team-mate's lead to just 4½ points. That, at least, was the situation as everyone packed up for the day, but during the following week FISA announced that because of the exclusion of Tyrrell from the 1984 World Championship it had decided to revise the results of earlier races in the season as if the British team had never taken part. So far as Lauda was concerned, this was largely irrelevant as he had either always finished ahead of the Tyrrells or retired. Prost, on the other hand, now found his fifth place at Detroit (where Brundle had finished second) automatically becoming fourth and, consequently, on the receiving end of a bonus Championship point, which reduced the deficit over Lauda still further – to a mere 3½ points! A number of the other drivers also benefited, although this was of no significance at all from the point of view of affecting the outcome of the World Championship, as even de Angelis, who actually gained 2½ points in third place in the table, was still a massive 34 points adrift of Lauda's tally.

Results

1	A. Prost (McLaren-TAG)	1 hr 35 min 13.284 sec (191.751 kph/ 119.148 mph)
2	M. Alboreto (Ferrari)	1 hr 35 min 37.195 sec
3	N. Piquet (Brabham-BMW)	1 hr 35 min 38.206 sec
4	N. Lauda (McLaren-TAG)	1 hr 35 min 56.370 sec
5	R. Arnoux (Ferrari)	1 hr 36 min 14.714 sec
6	R. Patrese (Alfa Romeo)	1 lap behind
7	A. de Cesaris (Ligier-Renault)	2 laps behind
8	M. Baldi (Spirit-Hart)	2 laps behind
*9	T. Boutsen (Arrows-BMW)	3 laps behind
10	F. Hesnault (Ligier-Renault)	3 laps behind
*11	D. Warwick (Renault)	6 laps behind

*Not running at finish.

Fastest lap: N. Piquet (Brabham-BMW) and M. Alboreto (Ferrari) on lap 62 in 1 min 23.146 sec (196.656 kph/122.196 mph)

Retirements
A. Senna (Toleman-Hart) accident on lap 1, K. Rosberg (Williams-Honda) accident on lap 1, G. Berger (ATS-BMW) accident on lap 1, M. Surer (Arrows-BMW) accident on lap 1, P. Ghinzani (Osella-Alfa Romeo) accident on lap 1, S. Johansson (Toleman-Hart) water pump on lap 18, E. de Angelis (Lotus-Renault) turbo-charger on lap 26, J. Laffite (Williams-Honda) turbo-charger on lap 28, J. Palmer (RAM-Hart) engine on lap 36, P. Alliot (RAM-Hart) turbo-charger on lap 38, E. Cheever (Alfa Romeo) fuel pressure on lap 38, P. Tambay (Renault) electrics on lap 48, N. Mansell (Lotus-Renault) engine on lap 52, T. Fabi (Brabham-BMW) gearbox on lap 58, J. Gartner (Osella-Alfa Romeo) out of fuel on lap 61.

1984

X Grande Premio de Portugal

Estoril: October 21
Weather: Warm and sunny
Distance: 70 laps of 4.350 km circuit =
304.50 km (189.21 miles)

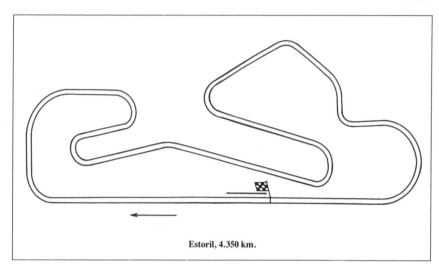

Estoril, 4.350 km.

the rest of the family under what were obviously extremely sad circumstances. On learning of the news, Bernie Ecclestone had first tried, unsuccessfully, to contact Stefan Bellof to act as a stand-in over the weekend, and although he had later had somewhat better luck with Manfred Winkelhock, the German had not yet arrived due to his flight departure from Frankfurt airport having been delayed by bad weather. In complete contrast to the British team, Renault had three drivers in action, as in addition to the usual entries for Patrick Tambay and Derek Warwick, they were giving their young test-driver Philippe Streiff the opportunity to make his Grand Prix debut. And, at the end of the hour-long session, it was one of the

Starting Grid	
	N. Piquet Brabham-BMW (1 min 21.703 sec)
A. Prost McLaren-TAG (1 min 21.774 sec)	
	A. Senna Toleman-Hart (1 min 21.936 sec)
K. Rosberg Williams-Honda (1 min 22.049 sec)	
	E. de Angelis Lotus-Renault (1 min 22.291 sec)
N. Mansell Lotus-Renault (1 min 22.319 sec)	
	P. Tambay Renault (1 min 22.583 sec)
M. Alboreto Ferrari (1 min 22.686 sec)	
	D. Warwick Renault (1 min 22.801 sec)
S. Johansson Toleman-Hart (1 min 22.942 sec)	
	N. Lauda McLaren-TAG (1 min 23.183 sec)
R. Patrese Alfa Romeo (1 min 24.048 sec)	
	P. Streiff Renault (1 min 24.089 sec)
E. Cheever Alfa Romeo (1 min 24.235 sec)	
	J. Laffite Williams-Honda (1 min 24.437 sec)
M. Surer Arrows-BMW (1 min 24.688 sec)	
	R. Arnoux Ferrari (1 min 24.848 sec)
T. Boutsen Arrows-BMW (1 min 25.115 sec)	
	M. Winkelhock Brabham-BMW (1 min 25.289 sec)
A. de Cesaris Ligier-Renault (1 min 26.082 sec)	
	F. Hesnault Ligier-Renault (1 min 26.701 sec)
P. Ghinzani Osella-Alfa Romeo (1 min 26.840 sec)	
	G. Berger ATS-BMW (1 min 28.106 sec)
J. Gartner Osella-Alfa Romeo (1 min 28.229 sec)	
	M. Baldi Spirit-Hart (1 min 29.001 sec)
J. Palmer RAM-Hart (1 min 29.397 sec)	
	P. Alliot RAM-Hart (1 min 30.406 sec)

Originally, when it had been confirmed at the end of February that the New York Grand Prix wasn't going to take place, the news had been accompanied by a statement to the effect that the Spanish Grand Prix was being revived as a replacement and being held on a new street circuit at Fuengirola, near Marbella, on October 21. However, within a matter of weeks that, too, had been called off (apparently because of lack of finance) and, instead, FISA had accepted, subject to circuit approval, an application from the Portuguese ASN to hold a Grand Prix at the Estoril autodrome near Lisbon. To most people this last move had come as a major surprise for, although the circuit had been built in the early '70s and had been used for just about every racing category apart from Formula 1, it had fallen largely into disuse over recent years. It was also a known fact that both the general facilities and the track surface were in very poor condition. Nevertheless, amidst considerable doubts that the race would ever get off the ground, the organizing club had responded in a most positive manner and, working in close liason with FISA's Circuit Inspector Derek Ongaro and also FOCA supremo Bernie Ecclestone, had embarked on a major redevelopment programme to bring the track up to the required standard for a full-blooded Grand Prix, the first in Portugal since 1960. A major problem had been the time factor and, indeed, even as the teams arrived at the winding and undulating track, which was set on a hillside above the coastal resort bearing the same name, the finishing touches were still being carried out. By and large, though, everything was ready and a most encouraging aspect, particularly for the organizers, who were already blessed by the fact that their race had now become the World Cham-

pionship decider, was the initial reactions of the drivers at the end of a special two-hour unofficial test session on Thursday afternoon. Almost to a man, there was nothing but praise for the little 4.350 kilometre circuit with the only hint of any criticism, apart from comments about the track surface being a little bumpy in places, being over the lack of any run-off areas at a couple of the faster corners.

In many respects it was just as well that the drivers were given a preliminary opportunity to learn their way round the circuit, as conditions were absolutely atrocious for the start of official practice on the following morning due to torrential rain having set in overnight. In fact, because it was still pouring at 10 o'clock and parts of the track were flooded, the untimed session had to be re-scheduled for just one hour starting at mid-day, by which time the rain had finally stopped and a mopping-up exercise had been carried out. Even then wet-weather tyres were very much the order of the day, and whereas the fastest lap of the previous afternoon had come out at 1 min 26.696 sec (Prost), anything approaching 1 min 40 sec was now, initially, considered to be quite impressive. Not surprisingly, the extremely slippery surface was also causing a lot of problems but, fortunately, among those to have their 'moments' only Patrese actually made contact with the barriers after sliding off the track just beyond the first right-hander past the pits, his Alfa Romeo sustaining sufficient front-end damage as to bring the spare 184T into service for the rest of the afternoon. Over at Brabham, meanwhile, only Piquet was out practising, as word had come through during the previous evening that Teo Fabi's father had died suddenly and the Italian was now on his way home to join yellow, white and black cars that headed the unofficial time-sheets, with Warwick having made the most of a slowly drying line (this had encouraged some of the braver drivers to change to slick tyres) and nipped around in 1 min 36.544 sec immediately prior to the field being flagged off.

Because of the delayed start to the day's programme the opening hour of qualifying eventually got under way at 2.30 p.m. and on a track that was now only moderately damp except for one particular stretch between the first and second right-handers, where there appeared to be a major drainage problem. Unfortunately, though, almost as soon as the first group of drivers ventured out – the majority on slick tyres – the rain came on again. Even worse, after barely five minutes Berger brought everything to a grinding halt by suddenly losing control of his ATS and demolishing a section of guard-rail, the impact also causing extensive damage to the D7's two right-hand corners. There then followed a long delay while the German car was retrieved and the barriers were reinstated, although even when qualifying was allowed to resume it was still not very satisfactory due to the track being wetter than ever. Nevertheless, there was one driver not in the least bit concerned about the situation. That was Johansson, who had rushed out at the beginning of the session and produced a most creditable lap in 1 min 28.891 sec. In fact, until well past 3.30 p.m. the Swede was perched firmly at the top of the time-sheets with the only sub-1 min 30 sec lap, and an even stranger sight was that of the two Osella drivers, Ghinzani and Gartner, lying in second and third places respectively after they, too, had got stuck in at the outset. However, during the final ten minutes or so, with the rain having long since passed over once more and a keen wind already having a marked effect on drying the track, a rather more familiar pattern began to take shape owing to the likes of Prost, Lauda and Piquet steadily moving up into contention. As this continued, Streiff emulated Patrese and Berger by glancing the barriers, his Renault winding up almost in the middle of the track with a stalled engine and minus a wheel, and then Laffite did exactly the same thing at almost the same spot, actually making contract with his compatriot's car. Rosberg, meanwhile, was in trouble with turbochargers failing in both his proposed race chassis and the spare Williams, and for similar reasons Warwick had been forced into the spare Renault only to stop again with a damaged nose cone due to being yet another to be caught out on the slippery track surface. Piquet was also obliged to sit out the last few minutes owing to an engine failure, but by that time the two Championship protagonists, Prost and Lauda, were riding high at the top of the time-sheets at 1 min 28.276 sec and 1 min 28.837 sec respectively.

That, at least, was the situation right up until the dying moments of the session when de Angelis was suddenly clocked at 1 min 28.428 sec to split the McLaren duo. This, in turn, elbowed Johansson back to an eventual fourth place after failing to improve on his earlier time, but he was certainly still in amongst the elite, as the only other driver to have produced a sub-1 min 30 sec lap was Tambay. In spite of having to put up with petrol seeping into the cockpit of his Renault, he had lapped in 1 min 29.409 sec to finish up immediately ahead of Senna (1 min 30.077 sec), Piquet (1 min 30.889 sec) and Alboreto (1 min 31.192 sec). Ghinzani, on the other hand, had slipped away to ninth spot in the last few hectic minutes, and Gartner to 14th, although both were still considerably higher up the list than such notables as Warwick, Arnoux, Patrese and Laffite.

By Saturday morning the weather had finally cleared up and it was both warm and dry with even patches of much-welcomed blue sky overhead. Consequently, when it came round to 10 a.m. the drivers (Winkelhock now included) were able to go out and settle down to some serious testing at long last without having constantly to stop for adjustments or different tyres as had been the case throughout much of the previous day, due to the ever-changing conditions. It also became evident that the final hour of qualifying was going to be even more vital than usual, for the overall pace was altogether quicker right from the outset with laps in the 1 min 25 sec bracket or thereabouts soon commonplace. Indeed, as the morning wore on so the times continued coming down, although some people started getting left behind somewhat through running into various problems. De Angelis was certainly in trouble, for whilst attempting to nip through on the inside of Streiff's repaired Renault at one of the left-handers quite early on, the French new-boy inadvertently moved over on him and in the ensuing collision the Lotus had its right front lower suspension pick-up points torn away from the monocoque. The Renault, on the other hand, came out of it with nothing worse than a bent wheel rim and punctured left rear tyre, although once the two drivers had crawled round to the pits Streiff also found himself on the receiving end of a few harsh words! Like de Angelis, Rosberg and Tambay were later obliged to switch to their teams' spare cars because of a seriously overheating engine and an electrical problem respectively, while amongst others to have their progress adversely affected were Cheever, whose Alfa Romeo ran with a persistent misfire, and, most significant of all, Lauda. Whereas Prost was making his usual good impression, the Austrian seemed to be forever dashing in and out of the pits with a whole series of minor ailments and was never able to get into

any sort of rhythm. Moreover, he was forced to sit out most of the final half-hour with dead electrics caused by what was eventually traced to a faulty ignition switch. As a result he missed the opportunity to try out some qualifying tyres and was right out of the picture as regards lap times, whereas his team-mate ultimately came out second fastest to Senna's Toleman, the young Brazilian taking full advantage of the latest-spec Hart 415T engine with its electronic fuel injection as well as a superbly handling chassis (fitted with a more conventional rear aerofoil once again) and setting the standard by lapping in a whisker under 1 min 22 sec.

As largely anticipated, the final hour of qualifying produced virtually non-stop drama and excitement, even though to all intents and purposes it was dominated by Piquet. Using his Brabham 'qualifying special', the Brazilian was in absolutely scintillating form and, after setting the ball rolling in only the first few minutes of the session by reeling off the fastest lap seen up until that point, 1 min 21.790 sec, he later achieved an even quicker time of 1 min 21.703 sec (191.670 kph) on his second set of tyres to clinch a quite incredible ninth pole position of the season. It looked all so easy, although in actual fact Prost only just failed in his quest to take the coveted spot for himself through steadily whittling down his times to 1 min 21.774 sec, while the impressive Senna, on his way to giving Toleman their best-ever starting position, finished up little more than a couple of tenths slower at 1 min 21.936 sec. These three apart, no-one broke the 1 min 22 sec barrier, but there were still plenty of other heroic performances and none more so than that produced by Rosberg. With barely 15 minutes of qualifying remaining he was still to go out having been kept waiting behind in the pits while his mechanics completed the task of replacing the Honda engine in his Williams. Then, when he did finally take to the track, the car suddenly jumped out of top gear just after he had crossed the start/finish line to begin his first flying lap, and two corners later he was pulling off, the replacement engine having blown up amidst a cloud of smoke. Instead of panicking, however, Rosberg responded by calmly walking back to the pits, stepping aboard the spare Williams, which had already been wheeled out for him, and taking off just in time to complete one flying lap. It turned out to be the most memorable of the afternoon as in a brilliant demonstration of mind over matter the Finn, perhaps more than slightly niggled, scorched around in 1 min 22.049 sec. Even more remarkable was the fact that had he not had the misfortune to come upon Winkelhock's slow-moving Brabham at the last corner, forcing him to run wide, he might well have snatched the pole. As it was this one single lap hoisted him from 27th and last place on

1984

the time-sheets to a quite amazing fourth spot and put him at the head of no less than six other drivers to have lapped in the 1 min 22 sec bracket. These were the Lotus duo, de Angelis (using the spare 95T) and Mansell, who were destined to line up on the third row of the grid, Tambay (he had also had to rely on his team's spare car), Alboreto, Warwick and, finally, Johansson, who had set his best time only after juggling round his tyres and putting in a third appearance following problems with the traffic – in particular Arnoux's Ferrari and Streiff's Renault. Lauda, meanwhile, had seen his day turn from bad to worse. First of all he had slid up an escape road after missing his braking point for one of the uphill right-handers, flat-spotting his tyres into the bargain. Then, after setting off on his second set of qualifiers, he had discovered all too soon that his engine was losing revs and, instead of winding up at, or near, the front of the grid, was left facing the prospect of starting the race from only 11th spot, his best time having come out at 1 min 23.183 sec. Laffite, Arnoux and Winkelhock also finished up lower down the grid than had been anticipated, the last two after being hampered by leaking inter-coolers. Otherwise, it was all pretty much as usual, and although Alliot had technically failed to qualify due to having come out 27th fastest following Rosberg's late spurt, the Frenchman was later given special dispensation to join the back of the grid owing to the late substitution of Fabi by Winkelhock in the second Brabham.

The weather on race day was absolutely glorious, although it appeared to be of no great consequence to the local populace that a World Championship title was about to be decided judging by the number of spectators that arrived at the autodrome. There were little more than 40,000 of them, which was rather disappointing. Be that as it may, the warm-up session set the scene nicely with the McLaren duo setting first and second fastest times, Lauda beating his team-mate by almost half a second. Once again, though, little seemed to be going right for the Austrian, as after being delayed by a problem with a jammed wheel nut, his engine was showing signs of losing water when it was all over and had, subsequently, to be replaced. The engine in Streiff's Renault, which had blown up and stranded the young Frenchman out on the circuit, also needed changing, as did the 4-cylinder Hart unit in Senna's Toleman, while others to have run into trouble included Boutsen and de Cesaris, with broken turbo-chargers, and also de Angelis, with a leaking inter-cooler. Consequently, there was a fair amount of work in progress as the day's supporting programme kept the rather sparse crowd entertained, but everything was completed in good time, and by 2.30 p.m. all was ready for the start of the final Grand Prix of the season, with the 27 starters lined up in their grid positions waiting for the starting lights to come on.

At the green Piquet's Brabham hesitated slightly just as it had done in Germany a fortnight earlier, but whilst Prost succeeded in beating the Brazilian off the line and moving across in front of him there was nothing at all that he could do about Rosberg, who went charging down the outside of the track and smartly into the lead on the approach to the first right-hander. Mansell, too, had got off the mark exceptionally well from the third row of the grid and was able to follow the Williams through into second place, which left the slightly bewildered Frenchman in third spot, directly in front of Piquet. This, of course, was totally unexpected and there was an even bigger surprise in store half a minute later when the pole-sitter made a rare mistake on his way through one of the uphill right-handers, spun and only managed to sort himself out after the rest of the field had gone by. Rosberg, meanwhile, was really putting the hammer down and had his Williams quite literally sliding through some of the corners. And it was certainly having the desired effect, for as the green and white car flashed across the start/finish line at the end of the opening lap it was already more than a full second clear. By contrast, Mansell had Prost breathing right down his neck and a slight error from the Englishman early on the following lap, in which he allowed his Lotus to run fractionally wide through one of the left-handers, was all that was needed to change things round. Thereafter, Prost quickly homed in on the leader, but finding a way past proved

A quick-off-the-mark Keke Rosberg leads the field into the first right-hander. *(Autosport)*

to be a somewhat tougher proposition altogether owing to the Finn still giving it all he had got. In addition, Prost realized only too well that he had to play it safe, something that he clearly demonstrated at the start of the eighth lap by aborting an attempt to go through on the inside of the Williams under braking for the first right-hander past the pits. Next time round, though, he was just that little bit closer as the two cars came on to the main straight and on this occasion executed a similar manoeuvre absolutely perfectly to finally move ahead. In the meantime, behind a closely-following Mansell, the other leading positions were still the same as at the end of the opening lap, with Senna maintaining a strong fourth place ahead of Alboreto and de Angelis. However Tambay, who had completed the first lap in seventh place, was finding a freshly-installed V6 engine (with electronic fuel-injection) in his Renault down on power, and had since slipped behind team-mate Warwick, Johansson and Lauda: the Austrian had made an extremely cautious start and had, initially, been lying as low as 13th! Further down the order still, Piquet was beginning to slowly make amends for his mistake and was now coming up behind Streiff's Renault, which was currently running in 19th place, and the only retirement so far had been Alliot with a blown-up engine.

With a clear track ahead of him, Prost quickly began to stamp his authority on the race and was soon building up a healthy advantage in the knowledge that he now had the World Championship title within his grasp – provided that his team-mate finished no higher than third. Rosberg, on the other hand, was almost immediately coming under attack from Mansell, who pulled over to the inside of the track along the main straight going into lap 10 and tried to squeeze through under braking for the first right-hander. On this occasion it proved to be a rather over-ambitious move and even resulted in the two cars lightly rubbing wheels as Rosberg firmly closed the door on his assailant. Two laps later, however, Mansell was at it again at the same spot and this time, after starting his run a fraction earlier, was somewhat more successful in getting past the Williams, which then gradually fell back into the clutches of Senna's Toleman until being relegated to fourth place on lap 19. At that stage Alboreto was still pounding along in fifth spot, but de Angelis, not at all happy with his engine or his rather conservative choice of tyres, had just lost two places in quick succession to Johansson and Lauda. Earlier, on lap 10, he had also been overtaken by Warwick only for the Englishman, suffering from a slight brake imbalance, to have spun shortly afterwards and been forced into the pits for fresh rubber due to flat-spotting his tyres. At the same time this had caused Warwick to drop right away to

19th place, although he had since repassed Arnoux (having a most uninspiring race) and Streiff, and was currently chasing hard after Piquet's steadily-rising Brabham. So far as the rest of the field was concerned, meanwhile, few changes were taking place and even now there had still been only two retirements, the other being Surer's Arrows, which had stopped out on the circuit back on the ninth lap with dead electrics. However Palmer, who had already been into the pits to have a minor problem rectified with the front suspension of his RAM, was destined soon to add his name to the casualty list with a seized gearbox, while Laffite was about to drop to the back of the field having been forced to make what was to be the first of two pit stops for loose rear bodywork to be refastened on his Williams.

Although Prost looked to have everything firmly under control out in front, Mansell was certainly staying close enough to keep him on his toes. In fact, at the end of the 24th lap the two leading cars crossed the line barely 5 seconds apart after the Frenchman had just experienced more than a little difficulty in lapping a very unhelpful Arnoux. Apart from Mansell, though, no-one else was really in it any longer as even Senna was around half a minute away in third place, while Rosberg, who now had Alboreto, Johansson and Lauda queuing up behind him, was even further adrift. Furthermore, the World Championship looked to be all but settled as Lauda had what now appeared to be an impossible task on his hands even to achieve that vital second place. To make matters worse for him, he was finding his engine under-performing slightly through what later transpired to be a damaged turbo-charger unit, and it was mainly for this reason that he had been stuck behind Johansson's Toleman for such a long spell. Nevertheless, realizing only too well that time was beginning to run out for him, Lauda decided to throw caution to the wind at around this point by winding on more turbo boost pressure and going on the offensive. Then, on lap 27, he was finally presented with just the sort of opportunity that he needed. Johansson, who had been driving beautifully, suddenly missed a gear change as he accelerated away from one of the right-handers on the far side of the circuit and slowed just enough for Lauda to be able to drive out around him before the left-hander that followed. That was not all either, for as the Austrian swooped across the bows of the Toleman he clipped its right-hand nose fin with his left rear wheel and two laps later Johansson was obliged to stop off at the pits for a fresh nose cone, the ensuing delay dropping him almost to the back of the field. The McLaren, on the other hand, came out of the incident unscathed and within less than a lap of overtaking the Swede, Lauda had gained another place by nipping through

on the inside of Alboreto's Ferrari at the end of the main straight. He then followed that up by first of all surging past Rosberg's Williams on lap 31, again by pulling over to the inside of the track just past the pits, before taking only two more laps to carry out a similar manoeuvre on Senna. So, in the space of less than ten minutes, Lauda had moved up from seventh place to third, although he was still faced with an awful lot of work to do if he was to catch Mansell for the Englishman was currently 35 seconds up the road with just over 37 laps of the 70-lap race remaining. By now a number of changes had also occurred lower down the order. For a start Boutsen and Hesnault had become the latest retirements with a broken drive-shaft and dead electrics respectively, while Cheever, who had been running in a pretty consistent tenth place, had just rejoined the race at the back of the field following a lengthy pit stop having a gear-selector problem rectified. In addition, Streiff had previously indulged in a time-consuming spin due to locking up his rear brakes and, on lap 27, Warwick had done exactly the same thing (again!) whilst attempting to scramble past Piquet, who had since been obliged to stop for a fresh set of Michelins following his own error on the opening lap. As a result both Piquet and Warwick were now well over a lap behind and in only 12th and 14th places respectively, with no-one to blame but themselves.

After 40 laps, with Rosberg having just had his spirited drive ended by a blown-up engine, Prost had once again pulled away from Mansell and to the tune of 16 seconds by, as much as anything, making better progress through the traffic. Without doubt, though, the main point of interest now was Lauda's progress in third place, for the Austrian was really charging and closing the gap between himself and Mansell at the rate of more than a second per lap. However, just when things were starting to look promising for him, Lauda had the misfortune to run up against a group of backmarkers fighting amongst themselves and, in getting past them, lost almost as much time as he had made up. Indeed, as the 50-lap mark approached Mansell was over half a minute ahead once more and it looked to be all over. But then, on lap 51, the situation changed dramatically – Mansell suddenly spun! It was caused by a brake failure and resulted in Lauda, amidst setting what was to be the afternoon's fastest lap, being able to close to within a few seconds of the Lotus before it was on its way again. Furthermore, the lack of brakes meant that Mansell was now in a hopeless position and on the following lap, moments after being overhauled by the McLaren, he spun a second time prior to touring into the pits to call it a day, a sad end to a hard drive. Almost unnoticed by this totally unexpected twist to the race, War-

1984

happened: Lauda, of course, was now in that vital second place and, barring mechanical failure, well on the way to clinching his third World Championship title. There was absolutely nothing that Prost could do about it either. Instead, he had to contend with the bitterly frustrating position of leading the race by almost 50 seconds knowing full well that unless his team-mate did strike trouble his ambition to become the first French World Champion was to go unfulfilled for yet another year – all because of a mere half-point!

The final 18 laps were to make no difference. Prost, obviously extremely disappointed with how things had turned out, duly went on to score a magnificent seventh victory of the season, thereby equalling the record set by the late Jim Clark in 1963 as well as giving the Marlboro McLaren team a quite remarkable twelfth win in sixteen races, while Lauda had no trouble at all in following him across the line in second place. In fact, because his team-mate had eased right off in the latter stages, the new World Champion had been able to reduce the gap between the two red and white cars to less than 14 seconds at the finish. After that nothing else seemed to matter very much. Nevertheless, Senna came home in a fine third place in his last race for Toleman, Alboreto was a very close fourth in spite of a spin shortly past half-distance whilst attempting to outbrake the Brazilian, and de Angelis was fifth, the last driver to complete the full distance after Prost had allowed both him and Alboreto to unlap themselves. Meanwhile, for the second race running Gartner had run out of fuel with the end in sight, and team-mate Ghinzani had suffered a late engine failure, but that still left a total of 16 finishers, including Piquet, who had pipped Tambay for sixth place in the closing minutes – because the Renault pit had failed to realize that the outgoing World Champion had earlier overtaken Patrese's eighth-placed Alfa Romeo and given no warning to their driver!

Alain Prost drives serenely on to his seventh victory of the season – equalling the record set by the late Jim Clark in 1963 – but it was still not enough to win the World Championship title. *(Autosport)*

wick's unhappy afternoon was also brought to a conclusion at about the same time, his Renault stopping out on the circuit with a broken gearbox, while only minutes earlier

Streiff's debut in the third Renault had been ended by a fractured drive-shaft joint. These two incidents, though, were of little significance, especially compared to what had just

Results		
1	A. Prost (McLaren-TAG)	1 hr 41 min 11.753 sec (180.540 kph/ 112.182 mph)
2	N. Lauda (McLaren-TAG)	1 hr 41 min 25.178 sec
3	A. Senna (Toleman-Hart)	1 hr 41 min 31.795 sec
4	M. Alboreto (Ferrari)	1 hr 41 min 32.070 sec
5	E. de Angelis (Lotus-Renault)	1 hr 42 min 43.922 sec
6	N. Piquet (Brabham-BMW)	1 lap behind
7	P. Tambay (Renault)	1 lap behind
8	R. Patrese (Alfa Romeo)	1 lap behind
9	R. Arnoux (Ferrari)	1 lap behind
10	M. Winkelhock (Brabham-BMW)	1 lap behind
11	S. Johansson (Toleman-Hart)	1 lap behind
12	A. de Cesaris (Ligier-Renault)	1 lap behind
13	G. Berger (ATS-BMW)	2 laps behind
14	J. Laffite (Williams-Honda)	3 laps behind
15	M. Baldi (Spirit-Hart)	4 laps behind
*16	J. Gartner (Osella-Alfa Romeo)	5 laps behind
17	E. Cheever (Alfa Romeo)	6 laps behind

*Not running at finish.

Fastest lap: N. Lauda (McLaren-TAG) on lap 51 in 1 min 22.996 sec (188.683 kph/ 117.242 mph)

Retirements
P. Alliot (RAM-Hart) engine on lap 3, M. Surer (Arrows-BMW) electrics on lap 9, J. Palmer (RAM-Hart) gearbox on lap 20, T. Boutsen (Arrows-BMW) drive-shaft on lap 25, F. Hesnault (Ligier-Renault) electrics on lap 32, K. Rosberg (Williams-Honda) engine on lap 40, P. Streiff (Renault) drive-shaft on lap 49, D. Warwick (Renault) gearbox on lap 52, N. Mansell (Lotus-Renault) brakes on lap 53, P. Ghinzani (Osella-Alfa Romeo) engine on lap 61.

1984 Points Tables

Driver	Nationality	Car	Mar 25 Brazilian (Rio de Janeiro)	Apr 7 S. African (Kyalami)	Apr 29 Belgian (Zolder)	May 6 San Marino (Imola)	May 20 French (Dijon-Prenois)	Jun 3 Monaco (Monte Carlo)	Jun 17 Canadian (Montreal)	Jun 24 USA (Detroit)	Jul 8 USA (Dallas)	Jul 22 British (Brands Hatch)	Aug 5 German (Hockenheim)	Aug 19 Austrian (Österreichring)	Aug 26 Dutch (Zandvoort)	Sep 9 Italian (Monza)	Oct 7 European (New Nürburgring)	Oct 21 Portuguese (Estoril)	Total points
N. Lauda	A	McLaren-TAG	–	9	–	–	9	–	6	–	–	9	6	9	6	9	3	6	72
A. Prost	F	McLaren-TAG	9	6	–	9	–	4½	4	3	–	–	9	–	9	–	9	9	71½
E. de Angelis	I	Lotus-Renault	4	–	2	4	2	1	3	6	4	3	–	–	3	–	–	2	34
M. Alboreto	I	Ferrari	–	–	9	–	–	½	–	–	–	2	–	4	–	6	6	3	30½
N. Piquet	BR	Brabham-BMW	–	–	–	–	–	–	9	9	–	–	–	6	–	–	4	1	29
R. Arnoux	F	Ferrari	–	–	4	6	3	2	2	–	6	1	1	–	–	–	2	–	27
D. Warwick	GB	Renault	–	4	6	3	–	–	–	–	–	6	4	–	–	–	–	–	23
K. Rosberg	SF	Williams-Honda	6	–	3	–	1	1½	–	–	9	–	–	–	–	–	–	–	20½
N. Mansell	GB	Lotus-Renault	–	–	–	–	4	–	1	–	1	–	3	–	4	–	–	–	13
A. Senna	BR	Toleman-Hart	–	1	1	–	–	3	–	–	–	4	–	–	–	–	–	4	13
P. Tambay	F	Renault	2	–	–	–	6	–	–	–	–	–	2	–	1	–	–	–	11
T. Fabi	I	Brabham-BMW	–	–	–	–	–	–	–	–	4	–	–	3	2	–	–	–	9
R. Patrese	I	Alfa Romeo	–	3	–	–	–	–	–	–	–	–	–	–	–	4	1	–	8
J. Laffite	F	Williams-Honda	–	–	–	–	–	–	–	2	3	–	–	–	–	–	–	–	5
T. Boutsen	B	Arrows-Ford / Arrows-BMW	1	–	–	2	–	–	–	–	–	–	–	2	–	–	–	–	5
E. Cheever	USA	Alfa Romeo	3	–	–	–	–	–	–	–	–	–	–	–	–	–	–	–	3
S. Johansson	S	Tyrrell-Ford / Toleman-Hart	–	–	–	–	–	–	–	–	–	–	–	–	–	3	–	–	3
A. de Cesaris	I	Ligier-Renault	–	2	–	1	–	–	–	–	–	–	–	–	–	–	–	–	3
P. Ghinzani	I	Osella-Alfa Romeo	–	–	–	–	–	–	–	–	2	–	–	–	–	–	–	–	2
M. Surer	CH	Arrows-Ford / Arrows-BMW	–	–	–	–	–	–	–	–	–	–	–	1	–	–	–	–	1

Constructors

	Mar 25	Apr 7	Apr 29	May 6	May 20	Jun 3	Jun 17	Jun 24	Jul 8	Jul 22	Aug 5	Aug 19	Aug 26	Sep 9	Oct 7	Oct 21	Total
McLaren-TAG	9	15	–	9	9	4½	10	3	–	9	15	9	15	9	12	15	143½
Ferrari	–	–	13	6	3	2½	2	–	6	3	1	4	–	6	8	3	57½
Lotus-Renault	4	–	2	4	6	1	4	6	5	3	3	–	7	–	–	2	47
Brabham-BMW	–	–	–	–	–	–	9	13	–	–	–	9	2	–	4	1	38
Renault	2	4	6	3	6	–	–	–	–	6	6	–	1	–	–	–	34
Williams-Honda	6	–	3	–	1	1½	–	2	12	–	–	–	–	–	–	–	25½
Toleman-Hart	–	1	1	–	–	3	–	–	–	4	–	–	–	3	–	4	16
Alfa Romeo	3	3	–	–	–	–	–	–	–	–	–	–	–	4	1	–	11
Arrows-BMW	–	–	–	–	–	–	–	–	–	–	–	3	–	–	–	–	3
Arrows-Ford	1	–	–	2	–	–	–	–	–	–	–	–	–	–	–	–	3
Ligier-Renault	–	2	–	1	–	–	–	–	–	–	–	–	–	–	–	–	3
Osella-Alfa Romeo	–	–	–	–	–	–	–	2	–	–	–	–	–	–	–	–	2

Italian GP: No points awarded for 5th and 6th places as Osella and ATS had entered only one car each for the World Championship.

Half points only awarded in Monaco GP as race stopped before 75% complete.

Cancellations: USA (New York) GP (September 23), Spanish GP (October 21).

1984

The story of 1984, new World Champion Niki Lauda, Alain Prost and the Marlboro McLaren MP4/2. *(Autosport)*

Appendices

Appendix I: Driver's Individual Results 1981 to 1984

Driver	Nationality	Period	Races	Pole positions	Fastest laps	Wins	Points	Notes
ALBORETO, Michele*	I	1981–1984	55	1	1	3	65½	
ANDRETTI, Mario	USA	1981–1982	18	1	0	0	7	
		(1968–1972						
		(1974–1980	110	17	10	12	173)	
de ANGELIS, Elio*	I	1981–1984	60	2	0	1	73	
		(1979–1980	28	0	0	0	16)	
ARNOUX, René*	F	1981–1984	61	13	6	5	115	
		(1978–1980	34	5	6	2	46)	
BALDI, Mauro*	I	1982–1984	33	0	0	0	5	
BELLOF, Stefan*	D	1984	11	0	0	0	0	
BORGUDD, Slim	S	1981–1982	10	0	0	0	1	

Michele Alboreto (*Champion*)

Elio de Angelis (*Phipps Photographic*)

René Arnoux (*Champion*)

Appendices

Driver	Nationality	Period	Races	Pole positions	Fastest laps	Wins	Points	Notes
BOUTSEN, Thierry*	B	1983–1984	25	0	0	0	5	
BRUNDLE, Martin*	GB	1984	7	0	0	0	0	
CECOTTO, Johnny	YV	1983–1984	18	0	0	0	1	
de CESARIS, Andrea*	I	1981–1984	60	1	1	0	24	
		(1980	2	0	0	0	0)	
CHEEVER, Eddie*	USA	1981–1984	58	0	0	0	50	
		(1978, 1980	11	0	0	0	0)	
DALY, Derek	GB	1981–1982	23	0	0	0	8	
		(1978–1980	26	0	0	0	7)	
FABI, Teodorico*	I	1982, 1984	19	0	0	0	9	
GHINZANI, Piercarlo*	I	1981 1983–1984	22	0	0	0	2	
GIACOMELLI, Bruno	I	1981–1983	45	0	0	0	10	
		(1977–1980	24	1	0	0	4)	
JABOUILLE, Jean-Pierre	F	1981	3	0	0	0	0	
		(1975 1977–1980	46	6	0	2	21)	
JARIER, Jean-Pierre	F	1981–1983	37	0	0	0	3	
		(1971 1973–1980	97	3	3	0	28½)	

Alan Jones *(Champion)*

Jacques Laffite *(Champion)*

Niki Lauda *(Phipps Photographic)*

298

Appendices

Driver	Nationality	Period	Races	Pole positions	Fastest laps	Wins	Points	Notes
JOHANSSON, Stefan*	S	1983–1984	12	0	0	0	3	
JONES, Alan*	AUS	1981, 1983 (1975–1980	16 81	0 6	5 8	2 10	46 156) (149)	
LAFFITE, Jacques*	F	1981–1984 (1974–1980	59 93	1 6	1 4	2 4	65 133)	
LAUDA, Niki*	A	1982–1984 (1971–1979	44 113	0 24	7 16	7 17	114 292½)	World Champion in 1984 driving for McLaren
MANSELL, Nigel*	GB	1981–1984 (1980	57 2	1 0	1 0	0 0	38 0)	
MASS, Jochen	D	1982 (1973–1980	9 96	0 0	0 2	0 1	0 71)	
PATRESE, Riccardo*	I	1981–1984 (1977–1980	61 51	2 0	3 0	2 0	52 21)	
PIQUET, Nelson*	BR	1981–1984 (1978–1980	60 34	15 2	9 2	9 3	158 57)	World Champion in 1981 and 1983 driving for Brabham
PIRONI, Didier	F	1981–1982 (1978–1980	25 45	2 2	3 2	2 1	48 53)	Killed in a power-boat race off the Isle of Wight in 1987

Riccardo Patrese *(Champion)*   **Nelson Piquet** *(Phipps Photographic)*   **Didier Pironi** *(Champion)*

Appendices

Driver	Nationality	Period	Races	Pole positions	Fastest laps	Wins	Points	Notes
PROST, Alain*	F	1981–1984 (1980	62 11	13 0	11 0	16 0	205½ 5)	
REBAQUE, Hector	MEX	1981 (1977–1980	14 27	0 0	0 0	0 0	11 2)	
REUTEMANN, Carlos	RA	1981–1982 (1972–1980	17 129	2 4	2 4	2 10	55 255) (243)	
ROSBERG, Keijo (Keke)*	SF	1981–1984 (1978–1980	55 27	2 0	0 0	3 0	91½ 6)	World Champion in 1982 driving for Williams
SALAZAR, Eliseo	RCH	1981–1983	24	0	0	0	3	

Alain Prost (*Champion*)

Carlos Reutemann (*Champion*)

Keke Rosberg (*Champion*)

Patrick Tambay (*Champion*)

Gilles Villeneuve (*Champion*)

John Watson (*Champion*)

Driver	Nationality	Period	Races	Pole positions	Fastest laps	Wins	Points	Notes
SENNA, Ayrton*	BR	1984	14	0	1	0	13	
SERRA, Francesco (Chico)	BR	1981–1983	18	0	0	0	1	
SULLIVAN, Danny	USA	1983	15	0	0	0	2	
SURER, Marc*	CH	1981–1984	55	0	1	0	12	
		(1979–1980	10	0	0	0	0)	
TAMBAY, Patrick*	F	1981–1984	50	5	2	2	77	
		(1977–1979	35	0	0	0	13)	
VILLENEUVE, Gilles	CDN	1981–1982	19	1	1	2	31	Killed during practice for
		(1977–1980	48	1	7	4	76)	1982 Belgian Grand Prix
							(70)	
WARWICK, Derek*	GB	1981–1984	42	0	2	0	32	
WATSON, John*	GB	1981–1983	44	0	3	4	88	
		(1973–1980	107	2	2	1	81)	
WINKELHOCK, Manfred*	D	1982–1984	39	0	0	0	2	

*Denotes drivers who continued to participate in World Championship events after 1984.
Details shown in brackets are for those drivers who also participated in World Championship events prior to 1981.

Notes on Appendix 1
Fastest laps – The credit of fastest lap has been shared on one occasion as shown below and this is not included in the table:
      1984 European Grand Prix: M. Alboreto and N. Piquet.
      The credit of fastest lap in the 1982 British Grand Prix was made to B. Henton who has yet to score a Championship point.

Points –   The figures shown in brackets are the actual totals retained after restrictions were made for a total of best results during a season.
      Stefan Bellof and Martin Brundle scored 5 points and 8 points respectively in 1984, but these were subsequently disallowed following the exclusion of the Tyrrell team from the 1984 World Championship.

Appendix II: Manufacturers' World Championship Race Wins 1981 to 1984

Car/ Manufacturer	Engine (where different)		Wins	Period (during which cars raced)
Ferrari*	–		10	1981–1984
			(79	1950–1980)
Lotus*	Ford-Cosworth	1)	1	1981–1984
	Renault	0)		
			71	1958–1980)
McLaren*	Ford-Cosworth	6)	18	1981–1984
	TAG-Porsche	12)		
			(24	1966–1980)
Brabham*	Ford-Cosworth	4)	11	1981–1984
	BMW	7)		
			(23	1962–1980)

Appendices

Tyrrell*	Ford-Cosworth		2	1981–1984
			(21	1970–1980)
Williams*	Ford-Cosworth	6)	7	1981–1984
	Honda	1)		
			(11	1972–1976, 1978–1980)
Renault*	–		11	1981–1984
			(4	1977–1980)
Ligier*	Matra	2)		
	Ford-Cosworth	0)	2	1981–1984
	Renault	0)		
			(6	1976–1980)

*Denotes cars which continued to participate in World Championship events after 1984.
Details shown in brackets are for those cars which also participated in World Championship events prior to 1981.

Appendix III: Grand Prix Formulae from 1947 to 1984 (Formula One)

1947–1951	Maximum engine capacities of 4500cc unsupercharged and 1500cc supercharged. No weight or fuel restrictions.
1952–1953	The preceding Formula did, in fact, exist until the end of 1953, but all World Championship Grands Prix were held to Formula 2 rules: maximum engine capacities of 2000cc unsupercharged and 500cc supercharged.
1954–1960	Maximum engine capacities of 2500cc unsupercharged and 750cc supercharged. No weight or fuel restrictions except that with effect from 1958 alcohol-based fuel 'brews' were banned and aviation fuel of 100/130 octane became compulsory. (These regulations did not apply to the Indianapolis 500-mile race, which was a round of the World Championship from 1950 to 1960 inclusive).
1961–1965	Minimum engine capacities of 1301cc and maximum of 1500cc unsupercharged. No supercharged alternative permissible.

Commercial fuel as specified by the FIA compulsory.

Minimum weight (defined as the weight of the car without the addition of ballast and in full running order, complete with all lubricants and coolants, but without fuel) 450 kg. It was specified, however, that it was permissible to complete the weight of the car through one or several ballasts incorporated to the materials of the car, provided that solid and unitary blocks were used, and that they were fixed by means of a tool and offered the opportunity of being sealed on, should the scrutineers have deemed it necessary: the ballast prohibited was that of a removable type.

An automatic starter with an electrical or other source of energy had to be carried on the car and be capable of being operated by the driver when seated behind the steering wheel.

As a fire precaution the car had to be equipped with a general electric circuit-breaker, either operating automatically or at the disposal of the driver.

The driver's seat had to be constructed in such a manner that the driver could occupy or vacate it without having to open a door or move a panel.

Attachments for a seat-belt had to be fitted, the wearing of which was optional.

A roll-over (crash) bar was compulsory but was not allowed to over-hang the driver's head. It had to exceed in height the driver's head, and in width the driver's shoulders, when he was sitting behind the steering wheel.

All wheels had to be exposed and with the bodywork unable to cover them in any plane, even when they were on full lock.

A dual-braking system operated by the same pedal was compulsory and was defined as follows:
The pedal was normally to control the four wheels. In case of a leakage at any point of the brake system pipes or of any kind of failure in the brake transmission system, the pedal was still to control at least the two front wheels (later amended to any two wheels of one same axle).

Fuel tanks had to comply with the following requirements:
1. the filling port(s) and their caps were not to protrude beyond the coachwork material.
2. the opening was to have a sufficient diameter to permit the air to escape at the time of quick refuelling (i.e. when being done under pressure) and, if necessary, the breather pipe connecting the tank to the atmosphere had to be such as to avoid any liquid leakage during the running.

No replenishment of lubricants was allowed during a race, and the filling ports of the oil tanks and radiators had to make provision for the possibility of affixing seals: the leads sealing the filling port(s) of the oil tank(s) could not be removed at any time during a race, although those sealing the filling port(s) of the radiator(s), which had to be in place at the start of a race, could be removed during any pit stop. By 1965 it was also a requirement that any drain or overflow pipe for oil was to be arranged so that any overflow was directed into a catch-tank of a size adequate to prevent any spillage on to the track.

1966–1984 Maximum engine capacities of 3000cc unsupercharged and 1500cc supercharged. Other regulations originally much the same as for 1961–1965 except that the initial minimum weight was set at 500 kg and there was provision made for the use of rotary piston engines covered by the NSU-Wankel patents and also for the use of turbine engines, subject to a defined equivalency formula. Since 1966, however, numerous alterations/additions were made to the regulations from time to time, the most significant being as follows:
1969 – With effect from January 1 the fitting of a general electric circuit-breaker, indicated by a blue triangle and a spark emblem, became mandatory and had to be within easy reach from both inside the car and outside.

With effect from March 1 a much larger and stronger roll-over (crash) bar had to be fitted, made of a specified material and in a specified manner, which included incorporating tubes and braces that had a minimum diameter of 3.5 cm and a wall thickness of at least 2 mm. It had to have a minimum height of 36 inches (92 cm) measured along the line of the driver's spine from the metal seat to the top of the roll-bar, a minimum width of 38 cm measured inside the roll-bar between the two vertical side pillars and be measured at 60 cm above the metal seat on the perpendicular to the line of the driver's spine. In addition, the top of the roll-bar had to be at least 5 cm above the driver's helmet when he was sitting in the normal driving position and, taking the weight of the car in starting order (i.e. with the driver aboard and with full tanks), the roll-bar had to be able to withstand three simultaneously applied loads of 1.5G lateral, 5.5G fore and aft and 7.5G vertical, the induced loads being carried over into the primary structure.

Cables, lines and electrical equipment (unless they complied with the requirements of the aircraft industry as regards their location, material and connections) now had to be placed or fitted in such a way that any leakage could not result in an accumulation of liquid, entry of liquid into the cockpit or contact between liquid and any electrical line or equipment, and had to be fully enclosed in a cover of a liquid-tight and fire-proof material where they passed through or were fitted in the cockpit.

Tank fillers and caps, apart from not being allowed to protrude beyond the bodywork, now had to have the caps designed in such a manner as to ensure an efficient locking action, which reduced the risk of an accidental opening following a crash impact or incomplete locking after refuelling, and the fillers now had to be placed away from points vulnerable in the case of an accident: similarly the air vents had to be located at least 25 cm to the rear of the cockpit.

From the same date cars also had to be fitted with two fire-extinguishing systems, which could be fed by a single 5 kg bottle. One had to be a manual system operated by the driver from his driving position, the outlets being directed towards the engine induction and the injection pump: the other, which had to discharge into the cockpit, also had to be a manual system operated by the driver from his driving position but was one that could, additionally, be operated by another person outside the car. The trigger device had

Appendices

to be indicated by a red-painted circle with the letter 'E'. (To accommodate this extra equipment, the minimum weight limit was increased by 10 kg and also by a further 10 kg to allow for the redefined roll-over bar).

After the Spanish Grand Prix on May 4 aerofoils were first of all banned and then new regulations introduced, which took effect from the Dutch Grand Prix on June 21. These stipulated that with the exception of the roll-over bar, no part of the bodywork could exceed in height a horizontal plane 80 cm above the lowest point of the entirely sprung structure of the car. Behind the front wheels the bodywork could not exceed a maximum width of 110 cm (subject to a proviso for the mounting of lateral fuel tanks), while the maximum width of the bodywork ahead of the front wheels was restricted to 150 cm, although any part of the bodywork ahead of the front wheels exceeding 110 cm was not allowed to extend above the height of the front wheel rims. At the same time it was made clear that all external parts of the car which extended above the highest point of either the front or rear wheels (with tyres), apart from units connected with the functioning of the engine or transmission and the roll-over bar, were considered as the bodywork, i.e. aerofoils. Furthermore, any specific part of the car which had an aerodynamic influence on the stability of the car had to be mounted on the entirely sprung part of the car and be firmly fixed whilst the car was in motion. In addition, neither the roll-over bar, nor any of the units associated with the functioning of the engine or transmission were allowed to have an aerodynamic effect by creating a vertical thrust, and all external projections swinging in a horizontal plane had to have a minimum radius of 1.5 cm, while the leading edge of the front aerofoil was not allowed to be sharp.

1970 – With effect from January 1 'rubber bag' fuel tanks, complying with USAC specifications or any other set of specifications approved by the FIA became mandatory, the aim being to reduce the danger of tank rupture. Essentially, it had to consist of a flexible bladder constructed in nylon or dracon woven fabric impregnated and coated with a nitrile type of fuel resistant elastomer, and be enclosed in a container of 20-gauge (0.5 mm) steel, 1½ mm aluminium or equivalent thickness fibreglass or plastic.
(As a consequence of the introduction of this requirement the minimum weight limit was increased by 10 kg, thereby bringing the total figure up to 530 kg).

1972 – With effect from January 1 the bodywork opening giving access to the cockpit had to have a minimum length of 60 cm and a minimum width of 45 cm maintained over 30 cm from the most rearward point of the seat-backrest towards the front. Furthermore, the cockpit had to be such that the driver could get in or out within a maximum time of 5 seconds.

A maximum of twelve cylinders was placed on engines with reciprocating pistons.

The 'rubber bag' fuel tanks introduced in 1970 now had to be fitted with safety foam complying with the American military specifications Mil – B.83054 – (Baffle material) and the only fuel tanks to be used were to comply with the FIA/Spec/FT3 specifications whereby the flexible tank skin had to be manufactured from a woven fabric in polyamide, polyester or equivalent impregnated and coated with a fuel resistant elastomer, and be capable of maintaining specified minimal physical properties throughout, including seams, joints and fittings. It also became a requirement that all fuel cells be replaced within a maximum period of 5 years from the fabrication date indicated on the cell.
(As an alternative to the use of safety foam, manufacturers could insert a supplementary internal bag, made of a supple synthetic material, inside the rubber bag tanks to contain the fuel. In this instance the space between the inner bag and the elastomer outer bag had to be pressurized with an inert gas. Such a system did away with the need for air vents, besides avoiding any mixtures of air and fuel inside the tank). The part of the structure surrounding the fuel tank, which was in direct contact with the external air-stream, had now to include an aluminium-magnesium sheet alloy of at least 1.5 mm thickness (or other authorized material) with a minimum tensile strength of 14 tons per square inch and a minimum elongation of 5%.

It was now permissible to increase the overall width of the car to 130 cm provided that the extra 10 cm on each side formed a 'deformable structure' containing no fuel or fuel lines, electrical power sources or lines, but any aerodynamic device situated behind the front wheels had to remain within 55 cm on either side of the car's centre-line.

Cars now had to be equipped with a 'six-point' safety harness consisting of two shoulder straps, one abdominal strap and two crutch straps and this had to be worn by the driver (the wearing of seat-belts had already become compulsory with effect from April 1 1971). Cars also had to be fitted with a rearward facing red warning light of at least 15 watts, mounted as high as possible on the centre line of the car and be clearly visible from the rear: it had to be switched on by order of the clerk of the course.

Other additional safety measures introduced at this same time, which also saw the minimum weight limit increased to 550 kg, included:

1. A requirement for at least one-half of the fire extinguisher capacity (2.5 kg) to be placed forward of the engine but rearward of the foremost pick-up points of the front suspension.
2. The compulsory fitting of a headrest capable of restraining 17 kg under a rearward acceleration of 5G and with such dimensions as to prevent a driver's head from becoming trapped between the roll-over bar and the headrest itself.
3. Banning the use of magnesium sheet unless its thickness exceeded 3 mm.
4. Forbidding the chromium plating of steel suspension members of over 45 tons per square inch tensile strength.
5. A requirement for the battery to be capable of starting the engine at least twice. It was permitted, however, to start the engine in the pits or on the dummy grid with an external power source provided that the starter socket was installed at the rear of the car, faced rearwards and, if any male sockets were used, they were recessed and provided with a cover.

With effect from July 1 provision had to be made for a clearly indicated external emergency handle, which could be actuated, without difficulty, by circuit rescue personnel, even at a distance with a hook. It had simultaneously to trigger the on-board fire-extinguisher, cut out the engine and isolate the battery.

1973 – With effect from January 1 the overall maximum width of the bodywork behind the front wheels to the leading edge of the rear wheels was increased to 140 cm, although with the remainder of the rules concerning overall body dimensions remaining unchanged the maximum width of the rear aerofoil was still restricted to 110 cm. No oil, fuel or electrical lines could be situated beyond 60 cm on either side of the car's centre-line and they were not permitted to run adjacent to the main fuel cells or within the crushable structure (see below).

The total capacity of the fuel tanks was restricted to 250 litres, of which not more than 80 litres could be contained in any one tank, and the minimum weight limit was increased to 575 kg to accommodate the protection of fuel tanks by a crushable structure (see below).

With effect from the first Grand Prix in Europe (the Spanish Grand Prix – April 29) the entire fuel tank area of the car in direct contact with the open air-stream had to incorporate a crushable structure as follows:

1. The crushable structure had to be a sandwich construction based on fire resistant core of minimum crushing strength of 25 pounds per square inch (water pipes were allowed to pass through the core). The sandwich construction had to include two sheets of 1.5 mm thickness, one of which had to be aluminium sheet having a tensile strength of 14 tons per square inch and minimum elongation of 5%.
2. The minimum thickness of the sandwich construction had to be 10 mm. At the same time, however, the fore and aft fuel tank area had to provide for a crushable structure of at least 100 mm thickness at the structure's thickest point (the position of this widest point was at the constructor's discretion) over a length of at least 35 cm, after which it could be gradually reduced to 10 mm.

In addition, all fuel tanks now had to be situated within the main structure of the car (those beyond 30 cm either side of the car's centre line had to be non self-sealing rubber bladders) and be fitted with self-sealing break-away couplings in compliance with the requirements of the aircraft industry, as regards their location and material, to prevent spillage in the event of an accident; although because of supply problems at the time, this latter requirement was waived until a date to be determined with 6 months notice. It was also stipulated that whilst a collector tank of one gallon capacity (maximum) could be placed outside the main chassis, it had to be surrounded by a crushable structure conforming to the specifications set out above of at least 10 mm thickness, be of the current 'rubber bag' type and connected to the engine by means of a self-sealing break-away coupling, again of the aviation type. The fuel system, itself, had to be arranged so that no part of it was the first object to be struck in an accident.

1974 – With effect from January 1 all oil storage tanks, located outside the main structure of the car, had to be surrounded by 10 mm thick crushable structure and could not be sited behind the gearbox or final-drive casing.

The entire fire-extinguishing system of cars now had to be located within the main structure.

Appendices

Overall body dimensions: nothing above the rear wheels was allowed to protrude more than one metre behind the rear axle line i.e. the rear aerofoil overhang was restricted to one metre.

1975 – With effect from January 1 all electrical wiring had to be enclosed in fire-proof material.

At the same time it became compulsory for a driver's life-support system to be provided, consisting of a medical air bottle connected to the driver's helmet by a fire-proof pipe. It was also recommended that drivers should have in their suit a small knife capable of cutting the safety harness straps.

1976 – With effect from May 1 the total rear overhang beyond the centre line of the rear wheels was reduced from one metre to 80 cm, while the total front overhang was restricted to 120 cm.

The maximum width of the front and rear wheels (with tyres) was set at 21 inches, and the diameter of the rear wheel (measured between two vertical planes) could not exceed 13 inches: there was no restriction as regards the diameter of the front wheel.

The overall width of the car was restricted to 215 cm.

The maximum height of an engine air-box was set at 85 cm, measured from the lowest point of the entirely sprung structure of the car, although its air-intake orifice could not exceed a height of 80 cm, the existing limit for bodywork.

Oil pipes and oil coolers now had to be protected by a 10 mm thick crushable structure, and no part of the car containing oil could be sited behind the rearmost casing (gearbox or differential).

In the cockpit area there was now a requirement for a 'substantial structure' to extend in front of the pedals, subsequently defined as a structure capable of withstanding a 25G deceleration without causing the pedals to move backwards by more than 150 mm with the car on full tanks and containing the driver. In addition, a 'substantial structure' such as a forward roll-over bar was now required near the dashboard in such a manner that a straight line drawn to its highest point from the top of the main roll-over bar would pass above the driver's helmet when he was sitting behind the steering wheel: it was subsequently stipulated that this had to consist of a tube with a minimum diameter of 35 mm and a minimum thickness of 2 mm, conforming with the SAE 4130 or SAE 4125 specifications, or in a substantial structure capable of withstanding the same loads as the main roll-over bar.

1977 – With effect from January 1 the maximum height of an engine air-box was set at 95 cm, although its air-intake orifice, or any part of a car's bodywork with the exception of the roll-over bar, could not exceed a height of 90 cm, both measurements taken from a horizontal plane above the ground with the driver aboard the car.

1978 and 1979 – During 1978 a waiver was granted to permit the maximum amount of fuel (250 litres) to be carried in one single tank between the cockpit and the engine, and by 1979 a number of other detail changes had been made to the existing Technical Regulations, which were now set out much more comprehensively. Among the revised requirements were the following:
1. No part of the car (including the engine air-box) could be higher than 90 cm from the ground with the car in normal racing trim with the driver aboard seated normally, and any part of any roll-over structure exceeding that figure could not be shaped to have a significant aerodynamic influence on the performance of the car.
2. No part of the car containing oil could be more than 70 cm from the longitudinal centre-line of the car.
3. Containers used for refuelling purposes during a race had to have a leak-proof coupling which connected it to the tank filler on the car, and the air vent of the container had to be fitted with a non-return valve.
4. All cars now had to have at least two roll-over structures (see 1976 above), the design concept of which was free, including the provision of forward-facing stays even if these infringed the dimensions required for the cockpit access – provided that the driver could still vacate the cockpit within a maximum time of 5 seconds. The first had to be in front of the steering wheel and at least as high as the top of the steering wheel rim but not more than 25 cm forward of it: the second had to be at least 50 cm behind the first and high enough so that a straight line drawn to its highest point from the top of the first structure would pass above the driver's helmet when he was sitting normally in the car with the safety harness fastened. Furthermore, if this second roll-over structure was not located behind the driver there had to be a structure behind him, which was high enough so that a straight line drawn to

its highest point from the top of either structure in front of him would meet the same requirement. All roll-over structures also had to be capable of withstanding three loads applied simultaneously to the top of the structure, now based on the racing weight of the car, these being 1.5 (times the racing weight of the car) laterally, 5.5 longitudinally and 7.5 vertically.

Behind the driver there now also had to be a structure which was wider than and extended above his shoulders when he was seated normally in the car with his safety harness fastened, capable of withstanding a sustained lateral load applied to its top of 1.5 times the racing weight of the car, as well as a headrest which did not deflect more than 5 cm rearwards when a rearward force of 85 kg was applied. As before, this latter item had to be of such design as to prevent the driver's head from becoming trapped between the roll-over structure and the headrest itself.

In the footwell area the 'substantial structure' to protect the driver's feet was now required to withstand a compression load of 25 times the racing weight of the car applied to the front of the car without allowing the pedals to move rearwards more than 15 cm when the car was at racing weight.

1980 – With effect from January 1 new regulations became compulsory concerning piping and fuel tanks, cables and electrical equipment – although some were not new at all! These stipulated that the total capacity of the fuel tanks was not to exceed 250 litres, all fuel tanks had to be situated within the main structure of the car and, except for a collector tank not exceeding 5 litres capacity, had to be rubber bladders conforming to or exceeding the FIA/Spec/FT3 specifications and made by manufacturers recognized by the FIA. They had to have a printed code indicating the name of the manufacturer, the specification to which the tank had been manufactured and the date of manufacture, and the rubber bladders could not be used more than 5 years after the date of manufacture.

In addition, all fuel fittings (including air vents, inlets, outlets, tank fillers, inter-tank connectors and access openings) had to be metal fittings bonded into the fuel tank, and all connections between any fuel tanks and the chassis (including tank fillers, air vents, access openings, inlets and outlets) had to be frangible – this was defined as meaning that should the fuel tank move relative to the chassis during an accident the connection between the fuel tank and the chassis would fail at a load which was less than 50% of the load required to pull the bonded metal fitting out of the tank.

All fuel lines between any fuel tank and the engine had to have a self-sealing breakaway valve and this, similarly, had to separate at less than 50% the load required to fail the fuel line or to pull the fuel line fitting out of the fuel tank.

1981 – The controversy and acrimony resulting from the decision by FISA to ban sliding aerodynamic skirts led to the formulating and concluding of the 'Concorde Agreement', which took effect immediately prior to the weekend of the United States (West) Grand Prix at Long Beach commencing on March 13. Among the more significant alterations/additions made to the existing Technical Regulations were the following:
1. The minimum weight limit was set at 585 kg.
2. The provisions previously in existence for the use of Wankel, Diesel, two-stroke and turbine engines were deleted.
3. A ban was placed on sliding aerodynamic skirts, accompanied by the wording: 'Any device bridging the space between the bodywork and the ground is prohibited. Under no circumstances shall any suspended part of the car be less than 6 cm from the ground, with the car in its normal racing trim and the driver on board. Apart from the wheels, no part of the car shall systematically and permanently touch the ground, at any moment, when the car is in motion. No entirely sprung part of the car shall touch the ground when two tyres situated on the same side are deflated. If corrections of suspension height can be made with the car in motion, the conditions defined above must be respected with the adjustment at the lowest static position usable in racing'.
4. The maximum tyre width (subsequently defined as the complete wheel width) was set at 18 inches and its maximum diameter at 26 inches, the rim being free. Initially these measurements were to be taken with the wheels removed from the car, but this was subsequently altered whereby the measurements were to be taken horizontally at axle height.
5. The chassis now had to include an impact absorbing structure (which could be attached) ahead of the driver's feet. This had to be an extension of all the skins of the main chassis construction to a point at least 30 cm ahead of the soles of the driver's feet when normally resting on the pedals in the inoperative position. At this point (30 cm ahead of the driver's feet) it had to have a cross section of at least 200 square centimetres.

Appendices

The material and thickness had to be the same as the corresponding skins of the main chassis structure, and the cross section of the material had to be at least 3 square centimetres in non-stabilized material and 1.5 square centimetres in stabilized material. Holes or cut-outs had to be strongly reinforced to maintain the cross section of any wall of this base over more than 50%. It was further stipulated that this structure could not be an integral part of the chassis, but had to be solidly fixed to it.

The chassis also had to incorporate at least one transversal hoop at the roll-bar level, one at the steering wheel level, and one in the area of the pedal box to protect the pedals.

1982 – With effect from January 1 the minimum weight limit was reduced to 580 kg, and the rules concerning the requirement for the chassis to include an impact absorbing structure were replaced by a new requirement (subsequently deferred until March) whereby cars now had to incorporate a driver survival cell. This had to consist of two continuous box members (one on either side of the driver), which extended from behind the driver to a point 30 cm in front of the soles of his feet with him seated normally, and with his feet on the pedals in the inoperative position, and conformed to the following:

1. Throughout its length the structural material in the cross section of each box member had to have a minimum area of 10 square centimetres, a minimum tensile strength of 31 kg per square mm and a minimum panel thickness of 1 mm on unstabilized skins or 5 square cm area and 0.5 mm thickness on stabilized skins.
2. Throughout its length from behind the driver to the soles of his feet each box had to have a minimum cross sectional area of 150 square cm: forward of this the boxes could taper to a minimum cross section of 100 square cm and the structural material could have a minimum cross section of 5 square cm for unstabilized skins or 2.5 square cm for stabilized skins.
3. All holes and cut-outs in the boxes had to be strongly reinforced and all material sections through such holes had still to comply with a minimum area requirement of 10 square cm for unstabilized skins or 5 square cm for stabilized skins.
4. The internal cross sectional area of the cockpit from the soles of the driver's feet to behind his seat could nowhere be less than 700 square cm, and the minimum width over the whole length of the cockpit had to be 25 cm.
5. The minimum height of each box between the front and rear roll-over structures had to be 30 cm.

At the same time new rules came into effect concerning side panels. These now had to be at least 20 cm high, as well as being of a length at least 60% of that of the wheelbase, and had to be situated between the front and rear wheels a minimum of 55 cm from the car's longitudinal axis. Moreover, they had to be made from a minimum 10 mm thick composite material with a honeycomb core in metal or Nomex with expanded foam giving adequate resistance to compression, and covered externally in aluminium alloy, plastic or carbon-fibre (or in similar material offering the same degree of efficiency) of at least 0.5 mm thickness. The panels, themselves, had to be linked transversely to the tub by a series of structural struts ensuring the absorption of a lateral impact, although it was permissible for the radiators to perform this latter role.

One other major change concerned the use of aerodynamic skirts as these were now officially 'tolerated' once more, although they had to be fixed, not sliding, and the word 'skirt' was tactfully avoided. Instead, the official wording was that 'to the bottom of the two mandatory side panels may be attached a single piece of solid material of rectangular section'. This had to have a maximum height of 60 mm and a maximum uniform thickness of between 5/6 mm. In addition, it was permissible to attach a single rubbing strip, although this, too, had to consist of a solid material (which could not produce dangerous fragments of debris on the track), fit within a rectangle of 30 × 15 mm and be rigidly secured to the 'single piece of solid material of rectangular section'.

1983 – With effect from January 1 numerous modifications to the regulations came into force following growing concern for the safety (and well-being) of the drivers and the spectators, arising largely from the vastly-increased cornering speeds of the cars and their rock-hard suspensions. These were as follows:

1. Introducing a full flat bottom on the car between the rear tangent of the front wheels and the front tangent of the rear wheels whereby all sprung parts of the car visible from directly beneath the car had to lie on one plane within a tolerance of plus or minus 5 mm and produce a uniform, solid, hard, rigid (no degree of freedom in relation to the body/chassis unit), impervious surface under all circumstances. The periphery of the surface formed by the sprung parts of the car could be curved upwards with a maximum radius of 5 cm.
2. Banning aerodynamic skirts and, indeed, any device or construction designed to bridge the gap

between the bodywork (the sprung part of the car) and the ground, accompanied by a stipulation that no part having an aerodynamic influence and no part of the bodywork could under any circumstance be located below the geometrical plane generated by the plane surface provided for by 1. above.

3. Increasing the height of the rear wing by 10 cm to increase the rear visibility of the driver by stipulating that no part of the car could now be higher than 100 cm from the ground with the car in normal racing trim with the driver aboard seated normally. The only exception was the roll-over structures, although any part of these higher than 100 cm from the ground could not be shaped to have a significant aerodynamic influence on the performance of the car.

4. Reducing the width of the rear wing (or any bodywork behind the centre-line of the rear wheels) from 110 cm to 100 cm and its overhang (or any part of the car behind the centre-line of the rearmost driving wheels) from 80 cm to 60 cm.

5. Increasing the frontal protection of the driver's feet by stipulating that each box member forming the survival cell now had to extend from a point behind the driver to a point 50 cm (previously 30 cm) in front of the soles of his feet with the driver seated normally and with his feet on the pedals in the inoperative position. The foremost 40 cm of each box member, however, did not need to be an integral part of the chassis, although it did have to be solidly fixed to it.

6. Improving the fuel tank protection and the side panels of the car: fuel could not be stored at more than 40 cm from the longitudinal axis of the car or in the longitudinal box members forming the survival cell, while the side panels now had to be the outermost extremities of the bodywork and be fixed in such a manner as not to move relative to the main structure of the car.

7. Improving the rear red warning light by increasing the power from 15 to 25 watts.

8. Introducing a new system of checking the weight of the cars during practice, at the entrance to the pits, and after the race.

9. Introducing a new definition of the weight of the car (the minimum weight was now regarded as the weight of the car with the petrol on board, in order to simplify checks).

10. Reducing the minimum weight limit to 540 kg.

11. Banning the use of four-wheel-drive cars.

12. Banning the use of cars with more than four wheels.

13. Placing an obligation on a competitor to prove the eligibility of his car(s) to the scrutineers.

1984 – With effect from January 1 the maximum fuel capacity was reduced from 250 to 220 litres and in-race refuelling was no longer permitted.

Appendix IV: Grand Prix Race Distances/Duration from 1950 to 1984

1950–1953	300 km or 3 hours (minimum)
1954–1957	500 km or 3 hours (minimum)
1958–1965	Between 300 km and 500 km or 2 hours (minimum)
1966–1970	Between 300 km and 400 km
1971–1972	Between 250 km and 325 km
1973–1976	200 miles (321.87 km) or 2 hours (whichever is the shorter)
1977–1980	Between 250 km and 200 miles (321.87 km) or 2 hours maximum
1981–1983	Between 250 km and 320 km or 2 hours maximum
1984	Between 300 km (including the official warm-up – 'pace' or 'parade' – lap), and 320 km or 2 hours maximum

(These regulations have not always been strictly adhered to.)

Appendix V: International Abbreviations

A	Austria	**BR**	Brazil
AND	Andorra	**CDN**	Canada
AUS	Australia	**CH**	Switzerland
B	Belgium	**COL**	Colombia
BOL	Bolivia	**CS**	Czechoslovakia

Appendices

D	Germany	NZ	New Zealand
DK	Denmark	P	Portugal
E	Spain	RA	Argentina
F	France	RCH	Chile
GB	Great Britain	RSM	San Marino
I	Italy	RSR	Rhodesia
IRL	Ireland	S	Sweden
J	Japan	SF	Finland
MA	Morocco	U	Uraguay
MC	Monaco	USA	United States of America
MEX	Mexico	YV	Venezuela
NL	Netherlands	ZA	South Africa

Appendix VI: Distance/Speed Conversions

1 mile:	1.60934 km
1 km:	0.62137 mile

$$1 \text{ kph} = \text{mph} \times 1.60934$$
$$1 \text{ mph} = \text{kph} \times 0.62137$$

Appendix VII: Flag Signals

National Flag: The national flag was traditionally used to start all races though nowadays it is more common to use red and green 'traffic lights'.

Red Flag: The red flag can only be used under the instruction of the Clerk of the Course, and is a signal for drivers to stop racing immediately, proceed slowly to the pits or the dummy grid and be prepared to stop if necessary. In such an event a black flag is normally also shown at each marshal's post around the circuit. The red flag can also be used to signal the end of practice sessions.

Yellow Flag: A yellow flag is shown to indicate an obstruction on the course. Drivers seeing it must slow down, not attempt to overtake another competitor and be prepared to stop if necessary until passing a green flag. It is normally held stationary, but waved at the marshal's post immediately preceding the obstruction.

Yellow Flag with vertical red stripes: A yellow and red flag held stationary indicates that the track surface has become slippery, usually because of oil. In the event of the oil slick (or conditions) appearing particularly hazardous the flag is waved.

Green Flag: The green flag signifies the disappearance of a danger previously notified. It can also be used to signal the start of practice sessions or the start of a warm-up lap.

Blue Flag: A blue flag held stationary warns a driver he is being closely followed. Waved, it means the driver behind is trying to overtake.

White Flag: When a white flag is shown it appears simultaneously at various points around the circuit to signify that a service vehicle, or a slow-moving competing car, is on the track.

Black and White diagonal Flag: This flag is used as a warning to the driver of a car (the competition number of which is shown) that he is displaying unsportsmanlike behaviour and may be subsequently shown the black flag if it continues.

Black Flag: A black flag, accompanied by the competition number of the car concerned, is an order for the driver to slow and call at his pit at the end of the lap.

Black Flag with Orange Disc: Accompanied by the competition number of the car concerned, a black flag with an orange disc is a warning to the driver that his car is in trouble (mechanical fault, fire, etc.) and that he must stop at his pit on the next lap.

Chequered Flag: The black and white chequered flag signifies the end of a race. It is brought down as the winning car crosses the finishing line.

Mike Lang

Above all else, Mike Lang is a motor racing enthusiast: his dedication to the sport can be measured by the time, and effort, needed to produce a reference work of this calibre. A former civil servant by profession, Mike has spent literally hundreds of hours of his spare time compiling this premier record of Formula One Grand Prix racing which, combined with the three volumes already published, forms a definitive 35-year history of the World Championship since its inception in 1950.

In 1971, Mike became personally involved in motor racing when he completed a course at the Motor Racing Stables, Brands Hatch, and subsequently drove in the occasional Formula Ford race. However, like so many other young aspirants, lack of financial resources meant failure to

fulfil an ambition to progress to Formula 3.

It was in 1972 that the idea of *Grand Prix!* first came to light. Prior to this Mike had already collated a mass of Grand Prix facts and figures so he decided to incorporate these in a book that concentrated essentially on the World Championship. Naturally, the research necessary to write a race-by-race account, together with appropriate technical data, was enormous, but the results of his efforts have been rewarded with the publication of *Grand Prix!* Volumes 1 to 4.

Mike lives in Devon with his two teenage sons, Roger and Peter, and young daughter, Christina, and in addition to his obvious interest in Grand Prix racing, enjoys horse riding and walking on Dartmoor, motorcycling, tennis and swimming.

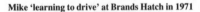

Mike 'learning to drive' at Brands Hatch in 1971